BUSINESS AND ECONOMICS PUBLICATIONS

WILLIAM HOMER SPENCER, *Editor*

Hobart W. Williams Distinguished Service
Professor of Government and Business
The School of Business
The University of Chicago

SOCIAL CONTROL OF BUSINESS

The quality of the materials used in the manufacture of this book is governed by continued postwar shortages.

SOCIAL CONTROL

OF

BUSINESS

BY

JOHN M. CLARK

Professor of Economics, Columbia University

SECOND EDITION
FOURTH IMPRESSION

McGRAW-HILL BOOK COMPANY, INC.

NEW YORK AND LONDON

1939

COPYRIGHT, 1926, BY THE
UNIVERSITY OF CHICAGO

COPYRIGHT, 1939, BY THE
McGRAW-HILL BOOK COMPANY, INC.

PRINTED IN THE UNITED STATES OF AMERICA

TO MY WIFE

EDITOR'S FOREWORD

This is no ordinary textbook. It is a penetrating interpretation of modern business as a social institution. It is doubtful whether in the literature on business it is possible to find anywhere within reasonable compass so thoroughgoing, so stimulating, and so objective an analysis of the fundamental issue: Can we control business or must it control us?

This edition of Professor Clark's *Social Control of Business*, while carrying forward the fundamental analysis of the original edition, has been revised throughout and brought completely up to date. It is so modern in its interpretation that it carries comment on the recent decision of the Supreme Court of the United States in the Fansteel case. This edition, however, is something more than a mere revision of the earlier one. Professor Clark has added new chapters in which he discusses the activities of the government and the problems of business during the critical years since 1930. The chapters dealing with Business Cycle and Depressions, Depression and Emergency Control: The "New Deal," and Economic Planning contain a concise, thorough, fair, and objective evaluation of the experimentation in which the government has engaged in the past decade.

This book is recommended as indispensable reading for the business executive who is apprehensive about the future of private business. Here he will find a completely dispassionate analysis of the reasons why the system of free enterprise has failed to function more effectively under modern conditions, the attempts of the government to preserve a system of free enterprise, and the limitations and weaknesses of the government's efforts. He will also find a most illuminating discussion of the fundamental issue whether democratic control of business can succeed under modern conditions. For similar reasons this book is just as strongly recommended for the general reader, the labor leader, and the legislator.

Professor Clark's treatise originally appeared as a title in the Materials for the Study of Business, published by the University of Chicago Press. In the Editor's Preface to that edition it was stated that "the present volume in the series is designed to give the student an understanding of the issues involved in the social control of business activity from the impartial standpoint of economic science. It thus presents one aspect of the social environment of the business executive." This volume, as now revised, even more effectively than as originally presented, will serve the purpose set forth. Every student of business as a social institution should have acquaintance with its point of view and analysis.

This title admirably carries forward the objective set forth at the inauguration of the present series of Business and Economics Publications that "the great need at the present time is for treatises presenting clear, direct, and analytical treatment of modern business and economics in the light of current developments."

WILLIAM H. SPENCER.

CHICAGO, ILL.,
April, 1939.

PREFACE TO THE SECOND EDITION

During the thirteen years which have passed since this book was written, social control of business has not merely expanded vastly, but has entered upon a new era. Government has assumed responsibility for dealing with the problems of depression and unemployment, and these problems dominate the present scene. It is not a matter of incidental abuses, but of an economic system failing in its main task, of energizing production. It calls, not for piecemeal reforms, but for comprehensive treatment of an organic malady, ramifying throughout the economic system. Public utilities and trusts, selected in 1925 as a representative sample of the field of control, can no longer serve this purpose. The main effort in the present revision has been to summarize the most important aspects of this newly dominant problem, in its setting as a part of our general scheme of control, and illuminated by comparisons with radically different schemes.

The three parts of the original volume are preserved, and to them is added a fourth part, dealing with the new era. This includes three long new chapters—on depressions, the "New Deal," and economic planning—and four others, based on chapters in the original volume, three of which have been almost completely rewritten. The former Chapter xxviii is now Chapter xxix, with only moderate changes. The present Chapter xxx is based on old Chapter iv, and the present Chapter xxxi on former Chapter xv, but both have been rewritten. The final chapter, picturing an imaginary democratic dictator, came near being abandoned, but a brief fresh treatment was finally retained, with mention of such matter from the earlier version as might still be pertinent. In all, the new material may amount to one-fourth the bulk of the older volume.

The result is merely one approach to an overwhelming array of problems. It is presented, not as embodying final solutions, but in the hope that it may have some orienting value to a generation facing a difficult and dangerous era of transition.

J. M. CLARK.

WESTPORT, CONN.,
April, 1939.

PREFACE TO THE FIRST EDITION

This volume is an experiment in the interpretation of one of the most all-embracing aspects of economic life, about which present-day thought and action are more and more centering. Through all the special departments which crowd our curricula and through all the numberless "problems" in which students and men of affairs are alike engaged, this common question runs. It is at bottom the problem of adjusting conflicting interests and claims of "rights" and harnessing selfish interests to that mutual service which the division of labor has made one of the most fundamental and most commonplace features of industry.

Individualism and socialism are alternative schemes for accomplishing this one end. Trusts and public utilities are simply industries to which different schemes of control appear appropriate. Common law, statute law, and codes of economic ethics are complementary parts of the whole process. To present this process in its unity, as well as in its variety, is an end well worth striving for, whatever the difficulties of the task.

To the common-sense mind individualism appears as the absence of control, and control as the antithesis of individualism. This is, of course, simply the result of the fact that, when things are too familiar to raise problems, we cease to be conscious of them at all. One of the difficult tasks, then, is to exhibit individualism as itself a system of control, and to analyze the institutions of control on which it rests. Legal rights of person and property are at the basis of it, supplemented by the informal controls of morals and public opinion and the many-sided institution of competition.

It is also essential to distinguish pure individualism as a principle from actual individualistic systems of social organization, which always contain a generous mixture of other principles. Many persons think of business as if the pure individualistic principle explained the whole of this very mixed institution, and as a result they conceive it as solely a matter of private rights, rather than essentially an affair of community interest, in which individualism is tolerated only so far as it serves the common interest better, on the whole, than any other system. The principle of free exchange offers expression to certain needs, and oppor-

xi

tunity to certain interests to organize themselves into a sort of partial community. But this partial community of free exchange never includes all the interests that make up a complete community; and a complete community, capable of sustaining life, can never be made up of the transactions of free exchange alone. The community of free exchange cannot maintain itself except in the enveloping medium of a broader community life, which furnishes the conditions on which free exchange depends and stands ready to do the innumerable things it leaves undone and to care for the interests which it neglects.

The first half of the present book, including Parts I and II, deals with this general problem. It illustrates the effects of systems of control by the method of comparison: comparing the present with the past and with proposed alternative systems; comparing also the theoretical conditions of perfect individualism with the actual conditions, and from the discrepancies deriving a reasoned statement of the grounds for further state or community action. Five chapters in all, including the later chapter on valuation of public utilities, are devoted to legal institutions, and two to codes of economic ethics. This first portion of the book is, in a sense, a search for principles of control: the principles which are actively at work in the problems of "applied economics," where it seems evident that most of the ideas and forces being applied are not those found in the principles of free exchange.

The second half of the volume concentrates on a related group of definite and tangible problems: those of price control, public utilities, and trusts, introduced by a survey of the underlying conditions furnishing the framework of these problems. It has seemed better to devote enough space to this one group of problems to afford at least an adequate introduction to the character of the issues involved, rather than to attempt the hopeless task of covering the entire field of economic life in the same way. This group of problems is to be viewed as a large and significant sample of the whole, illustrating some of the more obvious issues. The final chapter makes some slight amends to the neglected portions of the field.

For classroom purposes, and to secure a rounded treatment, the present volume might be used in connection with such a book as Hamilton's *Current Economic Problems*. It might serve as an introduction to whatever advanced courses in special problems the student might take, or it might follow such courses, as a means of linking together the separate bodies of material. Among the works referred to in the bibliographical lists, certain ones appear repeatedly, the purpose being to indicate a compact core of supplementary readings which may be made easily accessible, as well as a wider list of special references on special topics.

Grateful acknowledgments are due Professor L. C. Marshall, who read a large part of the manuscript and made many valuable suggestions. Professor Jay F. Christ has given assistance with the legal chapters, and Professors Freund and C. W. Wright have commented on portions of the manuscript, as has also Professor K. N. Llewellyn of the Columbia University School of Law. But especial acknowledgment is due one who has borne the trials of an author's wife with fortitude and has followed the slow progress of the work with unfailing sympathy.

J. M. CLARK.

CHICAGO, 1925.

CONTENTS

PART IV. THE NEW ERA: DEPRESSION AND COMPREHENSIVE CONTROL

PART I

UNDERLYING CONCEPTIONS AND CONDITIONS

CHAPTER I

INTRODUCTION AND FUNDAMENTAL CONCEPTIONS

1. THE MODERN ECONOMIC REVOLUTION

We are living in the midst of a revolution—a revolution which is transforming the character of business, the economic life and economic relations of every citizen, and the powers and responsibilities of the community toward business and of business toward the community. Most people would prefer to call it an evolution, but it is such a rapid evolution that it will look like a revolution to our grandchildren, much as the movement we call the "Industrial Revolution" does to us from a distance of a hundred years. This earlier movement began with the textile inventions of 1764–1792 (some were made as early as 1730), gained full force from the steam engine, the steamship, and the railroad, and its full effects are still in process of materializing.

In fact, our present economic revolution, dating from about fifty to sixty-five years ago, and this earlier industrial revolution of, let us say, 1764–1830, are but two phases of one greater revolution, which consists of the development of science and its application to economic life. This has been definitely under way for more than the hundred and seventy-five years which roughly mark the mechanical era. Galileo, Copernicus, and Newton were forerunners, and Columbus a pioneer, in the practical application of science. Darwin was its most characteristic prophet in the nineteenth century, and its economic destiny has been shaped by men like Arkwright, Cartwright, Watt, Fulton, Stephenson, Morse, Edison, Marconi, and Steinmetz, flanked by others of the type of Carnegie, Rockefeller, and Henry Ford. These great names, however, may exaggerate the personal element in the process. The number of inventions made almost simultaneously by different inventors suggests that they came when the time was ripe and the necessary preliminary steps had been made. And some great corporate dynasties have shown vitality and growth without any one overshadowing personality.

3

As for our present-day phase of this revolutionary movement, in most countries it has not been violent and bloody, though everywhere there have been some violent conflicts. Civilization should be able to avoid the danger of bloody social warfare, granted wisdom, patience, and a willingness to work together even where that calls for facing new issues and making new adjustments of rights and privileges. But if these adjustments are cramped by selfishness, fear, and mutual distrust, the situation may easily end in a terrible catastrophe.

In a general way, everyone realizes that private business is no longer private, as this phrase was used a hundred years ago. The managers of large businesses in particular are subject to so many kinds of inquiry, control, and interference that they often feel that their power to manage their businesses has virtually disappeared. Most of these changes have taken place since, say, 1873 and have been going on at an accelerating pace. These sixty-five years have seen the growth of effective control of railroads and of public utilities; while electricity and the telephone have developed, first, into recognized public utilities and, second, into businesses which transcend state boundaries and thus become essentially national problems. Irrigation, land reclamation, and flood prevention also belong properly in the class of interstate public interests, while radio and aerial navigation have but recently been added to the list. The trust movement and anti-trust laws, conservation, the Federal Reserve system, vast developments in labor legislation, social insurance, minimum-wage laws and the compulsory arbitration of industrial disputes, pure-food laws and the growing control of public health, prohibition, control over markets and marketing, enlarged control over immigration and international trade, city planning and zoning, and municipal control of municipal growth in general, all have come about within this period. On the frontier are health insurance, the control of the business cycle and of unemployment, and the insertion of social control within the structure of industry itself, through the "democratization of business." Back of these stand the stabilization of the dollar and all the questions raised by birth control and the movement toward eugenics, while the control of large fortunes and of the unequal distribution of wealth is an ancient and ever new question which is becoming more and more acute as the masses gain a growing sense of their political power.

This many-sided movement toward control cannot be disregarded. Even those who are honestly opposed to it are bound to realize that they cannot simply forbid this tide to rise. It may be guided and directed, its movements made more informed and enlightened, but it cannot be stopped, and no one group can dictate its course. It is the inevitable result of many causes, centering, however, in three things. One is organized large-scale production, another is the growth of democracy, and the third is the growth of science and the changing attitude of the human mind itself toward the world at large and toward human organization in particular, especially the scientific attitude toward social institutions which has been developing slowly throughout the past hundred and fifty years.

This attitude regards institutions as means to ends, but not as sheer bits of social machinery to be tinkered with and altered wholly at the will of the tinkerer. They are themselves in a very real sense living things, evolving according to their own laws, and these laws the human understanding has not yet mastered. Yet their course is subject to some degree of direction, and man is continually calling on them to justify themselves by their results, and trying to improve them where they do not seem to meet this test.

Another cause of change is the growth of democracy; but the most far-reaching forces arise from the changing character of business itself. They are merely the culmination of the forces set in motion when men learned to spin many threads at once on one frame, to drive the whole with steam power, to market the product at great distances by rail, and to back up the ingenuity of the mechanic with the researches of the scientist.

But before we go far in the study of this great movement of control, it will be worth our while to ask the meaning of our title. What is "control"? What is "social control"? And what is "business" or, more broadly speaking, economic activity?

2. WHAT IS "CONTROL"?

"Control" means, primarily, coercion: orders backed by irresistible power. In a sense, no coercion is truly irresistible, or almost none. One can always break the law if one will take the consequences—and sometimes the penalty is less than the profits of the offense. But the earmark of coercive control is penalties, imposed by a power which can, if it will, make them heavier than anyone but the most desperate would deliberately incur.

But there are other and less obvious ways of exercising control. In a broad sense, you can control me if you can make me do what you want, no matter what motive you use. However, if you want me to buy your cabbages and use a "good bargain" as your only argument, no one would say you "controlled" me: control and voluntary bargaining are not the same thing. But if you have cornered the market in cabbages, then you begin to have power over me; though if you had cornered bread, your power would be far greater.

Before you gained your corner, your price had to conform more or less to the market, that is, to what your competitors were charging. And if I refused your offer I could accept someone else's. But now you can control your price, and if I refuse your offer I must do without a commodity to which I have become accustomed as a part of a well-ordered existence, or even a necessity of life. Thus there can be control under the form of free contract, if there is a monopoly.

Can there be such private control under competition? A laborer must work for some employer or other, and if he has a family and no savings he may not be easily able to go to his employer's competitors and find out what they are offering. Even under competition, some control may be exercised if the individual cannot easily take advantage of the competition by canvassing the market.

Suppose a laborer canvasses the field and finds no one offering a satisfactory living wage for his grade of work. He is "compelled" to accept less; but whence comes the compulsion? Does it come from the employer who last discharged him, or from an informal control of the market by the employers in general, or from the customs and habits of business, or from the "impersonal and immutable laws" of supply and demand? If he is actually getting the benefit of active competition, he will have chances to get approximately as much as some typical employer can afford to pay him, so that if he is still underpaid it is due to the forces of supply and demand, and not to deliberate oppression. But this occurs chiefly at times of business depression, which is coming to be regarded as a remediable disease of industry, so that society has some responsibility for the compulsions of supply and demand, to the extent that it has power to alleviate them. And this impersonal machinery of private industry evidently has penalties at its disposal which often carry more material hardship than a jail sentence. Yet a jail sentence is coercion such as only the state can employ, while the loss of one's job is merely an incident of "free bargaining." The difference clearly lies, not in the weight of the penalty, but in the fact that putting a man in jail is a positive act, and leaving him to walk the streets looking for work is a negative act for which no one feels fully responsible. It is a mere failure to cooperate in a purely voluntary arrangement for mutual gain.

Originally, this voluntary system of employment tempted some from their feudal status by offering them decidedly larger rewards, while others simply lost their feudal status (at the time of the "enclosures") and were forced to find some new way of making a living.

At the present time, the worker has no feudal status to fall back on, so that he is wholly dependent on the continued cooperation of employers. But it is the cooperation of *employers in general* on which he depends: no single employer is held responsible for the coercive pressure which the fear of unemployment exercises—not yet, that is, though the germs of such an obligation are becoming visible.

A monopolist, on the other hand, can exercise a compulsion which is clearly arbitrary and not the mere reflection of natural and inevitable scarcities. And wherever this happens, the state steps in to assert its right to supervise the compelling if compelling must occur. Out-and-out discretionary coercion is supposed to be reserved to the sovereign power, and its exercise by irresponsible private persons is not tolerated.

One possible meaning of control is to cause someone to do something apart from his voluntarily deciding to do it. He may consent to something and then find himself committed to consequences which he was not wise enough to foresee. Or he may be governed by the suggestive force of custom, example, or importunity. The most pervasive forces of control are of this intangible sort, just as the most omnipresent penalties are those of opinion. The contempt of one's class is often a stronger force than many a legal punishment. In former times the church had power over the penalties of which men stood most in awe—largely because they were material penalties, either in this world or the next. At present, the power of the church is moral rather than material, and it is often less compelling than the opinion of one's business group. After all, it is easier nowadays to change one's church than one's business.

One very important thing about control is that it is possible to control absolutely the way particular things shall be done without exercising more than an optional control over the people who are doing them. The running of factories is controlled by safety-appliance laws and a deal of other legislation, but no person is subject to those laws except as he (shall we say "voluntarily"?) undertakes to run a factory. But all alike must obey the command "Thou shalt not steal."

3. WHAT IS "SOCIAL CONTROL"?

"Social control," as we shall conceive it, is control exercised by or in behalf of the entity we call "society." It might also be conceived simply as control *of* society, but this conception we shall pass by as not useful for our purposes. We shall also pass by the conception of society embodied in the dogmas of the totalitarian state and view it after the more democratic conception of an aggregate of individuals, interests, and groups which, however organically bound together, are still distinguishable. Ideally, it should include all the interests affected by its economic system. From this standpoint even the nation is not the whole of society. Some of its interests conflict with those of other nations, and our economic society has a way of disregarding national boundaries when it is allowed. The International Labor Office is only one recognition of the fact that our modern economic society is international. For most purposes, however, the nation is an adequately comprehensive group; its most definite and powerful agency is government; and in this country the municipal, state, and federal governments between them exercise the formal legal power of control in economic life. In internal matters the question whether governmental control is truly social is mainly a question whether the government is truly representative of the various interests and groups in the nation. But social control is wider than this, as we have already seen. One's newspaper, one's trade union, one's neighbors, one's church, all exercise some measure of social control.

Within the nation are groups with differing interests and growingly divergent standards, and control by such groups may be distinguished as group control. Where it involves no important conflicts of interests and standards between different groups, it may be regarded as a part of the whole system of social control. The trade union keeps its members in line during a strike; and this may be called "group control" rather than social control, since it is part of a conflict of interest with other groups and represents the interest of only one side. In a strict sense, it is no more and no less social than a nation passing a protective tariff against other nations or a "pressure group" forcing measures of selfish interest through a national congress. There is, however, a real difference of degree, since the nation can adopt a group attitude which disregards the interests of other nations and still get along somehow, while if the trade-union interest were equally unchecked and supreme, it could disrupt our whole economy. Perhaps the main point is that all the controls we have are imperfectly comprehensive or imperfectly representative, or both, and therefore are imperfectly social.

Some groups are more inclusive than others, and the more inclusive the group is, the better socialized is the control which it exercises. One of the difficulties of control lies in the fact that the groups whose voice speaks loudest to a given individual are precisely those smallest groups which are farthest from expressing the interest of the whole community. Trade unions can control their members fairly effectively in matters they have at heart, but what they have most at heart is getting as much as possible out of the employer. There is need of social control of this standard by a group including laborer, employer, consumer, and public,

INTRODUCTION AND FUNDAMENTAL CONCEPTIONS

but this group is too heterogeneous to act with the easy effectiveness of smaller groups. Many a man genuinely wants to be moral as his associates see morality and goes on doing as they do, only to suffer a painful shock when the standard of his associates suddenly has the light of a broader community standard turned upon it. Too often this test reveals merely organized group selfishness. Something of this sort happened when Charles E. Hughes made his famous investigation of the abuses of insurance in New York.

But when the state acts, is the whole community of its citizens acting? By no means, not even in the kind of state we call democratic. The state is an abstraction. When it acts, it is always some individual official who is really acting—a person with friendships and prejudices, one who is very likely to be more interested in the welfare of the family to whom he goes home at the end of the working day than in the convictions of the persons responsible for the passage of the laws he is carrying out. He is an agent, executing the orders of his superior, with whom he may or may not be in full sympathy. His superior has another superior over him, and so on, up to the head of a department, who has to interpret and enforce laws passed by Congress, with which he may or may not be in full sympathy. And Congress may have been doing the will of a "pressure group" with or without "log rolling." There is a certain margin of discretion within which the immediate official makes the law. Within that margin, for all practical purposes, he is the state.[1]

Another significant feature of the half-social character of actual state control is illustrated by the absorption into the English common law of the "law merchant," which represented the custom of the trading community, developed by them to meet their class needs and enforced by special courts for traders as a class. The law of partnerships and that of negotiable instruments are derived from this source. This law did not touch agriculture—that was governed by the manorial system—or industry, which was in the hands of the craft guilds. It did not deal with the great conflicts between class and class, but with the relations of traders with traders; it was primarily a law of contractual relations between equals whose central occupation was bargaining. This class developed the system of free contract into a well-differentiated and adaptable organism while the relation of landlord to tenant and of apprentice to master were still in the stage of control by feudal custom. This furnishes an interesting instance of "class" control. It has not the sinister quality which the term suggests, because it is con-

[1] This point is well brought out by Commons, *Legal Foundations of Capitalism*, pp. 122–123, 149.

fined to dealings between members of the class itself, in which the interests of other classes are not obviously involved.

But it is a different story when the idea of contract between equals is extended to "industrial relations" or to other relations between members of different classes. For here not only is the bargain no longer between equals, but the two parties perform functions which differ more widely than anything found in the dealings of the world of traders. As a result, it becomes far more difficult so to order the system of contract that it will satisfy both sides of its fairness. The situation lacks the saving grace of reversibility, which causes the man who suffers from a given rule today to realize that he may benefit by the operation of the same rule tomorrow. And if the contending parties harmonize their interests at the expense of the public, that also is a form of class tyranny and not to be borne in a self-governing community. The method of allowing a class to build up its own instrument of control is still more unthinkable in the case of trust control or tariff legislation, where the essential question is one of conflicting interests between the class in question and the public.

Statutes in America are voted for by the majority of two legislative houses and signed by the chief executive. Yet it commonly happens that not one person who votes for a law gets exactly the law he wants. Partial concessions are made to the conflicting ideas of different members or the conflicting interests of their constituents. To secure support for a measure his constituents want, their representative may vote for others which are at their expense, with no guarantee that the whole is in the social interest. Back of the legislative process lies the agitation responsible for the framing and introduction of the law. Here a few always take the initiative and bear the brunt. Others lend support of a more mildly active sort; others merely acquiesce. Without attempting to trace all the steps in this process, we may say that a law is always the active work of a minority, with the cooperation of a majority of a supposedly representative body who may be barely willing to vote for it. And after it is on the statute books, it requires some support and cooperation to enforce it. Unless the majority of the citizens will voluntarily obey it because it is the law, it will soon become a dead letter. The law must be upheld in this passive way by a much larger majority than it requires to place it on the statute books in the first place, if it is to be a real success in a democratic country, where the ideal of the "consent of the governed" serves to temper the rule of the majority by the concession of some rights to minorities.[1]

[1] If society is willing to coerce minorities, it can do so, even where the minority feels morally justified in resisting, but only at a heavy expense. Autocratic governments can coerce majorities in the same way, at a corresponding cost.

Society's enforcing power is limited. If all who are not in favor of measures resist them and compel society to use its force upon them or see its laws disobeyed, it can make but few rules effective. Such a state will not get beyond the defensive stage of control, in which all its forces are needed to hold it together and preserve the most elementary necessities of safety and order. If a state is to have enough power left to care for welfare in a positive way, it must have a citizenship most of whom are willing to obey even those laws they do not favor—"self-government works best with those who have learned to self-govern."

This is true, even on the assumption that the agent of government is really trying to enforce the law, but this is not to be too easily taken for granted. He is not an automaton but a human being, and social control as he exercises it depends on the question Who controls him? How are the state and its officers socially controlled? There is no organized group behind them representing the whole community; if there were, it would itself be the state, and it is precisely because there is no such group that the state is necessary. What lies back of the state is a medley of groups with conflicting economic interests or points of view, and the fusing of these in a social decision is largely the task of the machinery of the state itself.

Greater unanimity and submissiveness can be secured by controlling education, news, propaganda, and all embodiments of thought as completely as the totalitarian states have learned to control them. But for the type of state we are considering, this would represent a surrender of its most basic values.

4. WHAT IS "BUSINESS"?

Before we begin to study control, we certainly need to know what it is we are controlling. And while everyone knows what "business" is, not everyone keeps clearly in mind those features which are important from the standpoint of social policy. Business is bargaining; buying and selling, and producing goods and services for sale. Business is the struggle for wealth. Business is the system of social cooperation by mutual exchange. And—since part of a definition consists in knowing what a thing is not—business is not charity or benevolence, though motives of various generous sorts enter in to shape the essential character of the institution. It is not play but work; a means to an end rather than an end in itself, though, like any worth-while activity, it has a way of becoming an end in itself and of enlisting people's interest in "the game" as such. It is not warfare and it is not anarchy, for not everything is fair in business, and the rules to which it is subject have at least an orderly intent.

Like any game subject to rules, business is a thing of double purpose: the purpose of the rules and that of the contestant under them. The purpose of the contestant is a simple one—to win. He is not responsible for the rules, but he must adapt his play to them. According to his lights, he may aim to win in harmony with the spirit of the rules, or according to the letter, which he may stretch as far as possible. He may aim to stop just short of things for which he would be penalized if the umpire saw them, or he may aim to violate the rules as much as he can when the umpire does not see him. All these classes of tactics are found both on the football field and in the struggles of business. As for the purpose of the rules themselves, they generally aim, first, to codify and standardize something which has grown up spontaneously. This very process of codification is a cause of changes in the game, as players devise new plays which are calculated to gain the maximum advantage which the rules permit. These changed methods of play provoke new rules, aiming to meet new situations or to prevent new methods of play as far as they are found undesirable. This leads to a more conscious effort to control the sport, striving to make it a good test of strength, skill, and coordination, to keep it reasonably safe, and incidentally to make it enjoyable for the spectators. This whole process is exhibited no less in business than in American Rugby football.

For this reason, when we speak of the "social control of business," we must take some pains to avoid the implication that business exists first and is then controlled. Control is rather an integral part of business, without which it could not be business at all. The one implies the other, and the two have grown together. But it is worth while distinguishing three levels of control: the informal kind which economic groups developed out of their own needs and customs, the kind which courts can develop in the course of settling disputed cases as they arise, and the kind resulting from legislation which changes the rules for the future, with the definite purpose of bringing about some new result which the legislators foresee and desire. When people speak of the social control of business, "business" usually means the system as it develops under the first two classes of control, which are taken for granted; and "control" refers to control of the last class only. But one cannot look at legislative control intelligently unless one starts with at least a fair understanding of the character and tendencies, virtues and limitations, of the more stable substratum of law which furnishes the point of departure for legislation. Indeed, it does far more than this, for it pervades legislation itself, via the process of interpretation, and shows a considerable capacity to resist attempts to change it by the legislative route. This underlying system of control maintains what we call "individualism"; and the essential meaning of business, from our present standpoint, is private gain getting subject to at least the individualistic variety of restraints. Of course, no mere definition can possibly convey the full significance of such a vast institution. That will appear somewhat more fully when we come to discuss the public and private aspects of business, the services it renders to the community, and the things it does to people without their foreknowledge or consent.[1]

5. THE MEANING OF "INDIVIDUALISM"

The chief of these restraints can be summed up under the protection of the rights of personal security, personal liberty, and private property, working hand in hand with the maintaining of a system of inheritance and the enforcing of contracts, and the systems of bankruptcy and poor relief. To these has been added, relatively recently, a legally established institution in the shape of the business corporation, whereby an associated organization acquires by legislative grant some of the privileges of real persons. The persons composing it thus gain privileges they would not otherwise possess; they can "sell out" without interrupting the continuity of the organization, and their personal liability is limited, with some exceptions, to the assets of the corporation as such. This is not an individualistic institution, as the term was understood by the individualists of one hundred to one hundred and fifty years ago, but it has become incorporated into the twentieth century meaning of the term and has produced far-reaching changes in the character of business.

Can we describe this whole system of control by any simple formula? Not in all its ramifications, certainly, but it has a few prevailing characteristics.

(1) In the first place, it prefers to tell people what they shall not do rather than to dictate what they shall do, and the larger part of the duties it imposes are of this negative kind; not all, however—witness the care of children and the enforcing of contracts.

(2) Another characteristic is that it prefers to impose duties which are more or less self-enforcing, in the sense that good and moral people will perform them voluntarily, and others will have the general moral sense of the community against them if they refuse. This means that the chief conception of protecting rights is to prevent wrongs, that is, things which are held to be wrong by the existing moral sense of the community.

[1] See esp. Chap. iii, below, and Chap. xxx, Sec. 2.

Other rules may be self-enforcing largely because they represent the customary way of doing things. Custom has a tendency to become law, and it is the kind of law which requires the least enforcement. Sometimes new inventions are grafted on a stem of custom and derive force from it; for instance, traffic rules. There is a long-standing custom of turning to the right in some countries, or to the left in others, and as long as some rule is followed by all, no one cares which it is. Some sort of reliable behavior is an absolute necessity. In recent years the growth of motor traffic has called for more and more complex rules which cannot be based on custom, but the custom of following the accepted system, whatever it may be, makes it easier to enforce the new rules.

(3) Thus control under individualism tends to follow precedent; and where it has to deal with new kinds of cases, it does its best to settle them on principles similar to those which have governed in previous cases. Settling things by precedent is economical and relatively safe. One knows that the thing has been done before without fatal consequences and argues that it can be done again, whereas one can never be quite sure what will be the outcome of an absolutely new experiment. Furthermore, when things are settled in this way, people know what to expect, most business transactions being based on a general idea that things will go on as they have gone on in the past, and that people will construe their obligations in the customary way.[1] Where the underlying conditions change radically, it becomes impossible to follow customs in this complete fashion, and any attempt to do so produces many injustices. This simply means that self-enforcing control cannot take care of all the needs of a rapidly changing society.

(4) Individualistic control also involves telling people what they shall do, to a limited extent. It goes into the realm of positive duties where necessary. However, it tries to confine these positive duties to those which are (a) "natural," in some such fashion as the care of children by their parents is natural, and thus fairly adequately enforced by the ordinary rules of morality; (b) duties to which the individual himself has consented and for which he has received compensation which he voluntarily accepted, namely, the duty of fulfilling contracts. (c) Other positive duties the state commonly finds it easier to assume itself than to try to impose on private individuals, although some of them may be left to be enforced by public opinion, religion, and morals.

To sum up: under individualism the state does as little as it can in the way of coercive control, but it always has to do a great deal. The

[1] Cf. Hoyt, "The Economic Function of the Common Law," *Jour. Polit. Econ.*, XXVI (1918), 168–199.

ideal of the "pure" individualist is a state which does nothing but protect property and enforce contracts, but there has never been any such state and never can be, for reasons which will become amply evident as this study proceeds.[1]

6. COMMON ELEMENTS OF THE TASK OF CONTROL

Covering as many different fields as it does, the task of control is not one task but many, yet there are certain common features which must always be taken into account. The first is the need of defining an objective with as much precision as possible. In attempting to do this we are engaging in a search for conditions which are just, wholesome, and generally satisfactory. Nothing short of this can give permanent contentment. But frequently the clash of interests is so insistent and the danger of an open break so serious that long-run considerations are lost sight of and the aim becomes simply to patch up some settlement in which the contending parties will acquiesce, something which will permit the day's work to go on. This is the true objective of arbitrators of labor disputes in more cases than they would enjoy admitting.

In such cases it is not wise for the community to attempt to fix all the specific terms of the settlement. Its chief objective is to see that there are proper channels by which the interested parties may express their needs and desires and work out an adjustment of their conflicts. It is not legislation that is needed but economic constitution making.

A second task of control is to decide on the kind of pressure to be employed. Shall it be positive or negative, a command or a prohibition? Shall it be formal or informal, regulated or spontaneous, etc.? In order to answer these questions satisfactorily, three other things must be taken into account: the nature of the ultimate source of control, the character of the resistances to be overcome, and the amount of independent discretion which can safely be intrusted to the individuals who act as the transmitting mechanism. It makes a vast difference what a movement has behind it. It makes a difference whether there is a well-formed body of public opinion which knows what it wants, or whether this remains to be built up by the active minority. It makes a difference whether there is a white-hot moral earnestness, a cool intellectual judgment, an exasperated feeling of class hostility, a canny sense of class interests, or sheer apathy. Something very similar is true of the resistances to be overcome, as far as they consist of human feelings. Other resistances are of a more objective sort, including the momentum of things established and their "natural laws," as far as they may have natural laws which furnish obstacles to any desired

[1] See esp. Chaps. ii, iii, vi, vii, below.

change. A course must somehow be steered between the mistake of attempting the impossible and the worse mistake of assuming too easily that whatever is, is an unchangeable law of nature.

As for the discretion accorded what we have called the "transmitting mechanism," this raises the whole question of the place of expert guidance in a democracy. Can scientific standards be worked out in which the average man can safely trust even though he cannot understand them? This is one of the most far-reaching and difficult questions which present-day social policy is forced to meet.

7. WHAT IS A GOOD SYSTEM OF CONTROL?

A good system of control must meet a number of tests, some of them quite difficult. (1) It must be democratic. This means that it must be exercised in the interests of the governed as they see their interests (not as some benevolent overlord might see them). (2) It should know what it wants. This sounds obvious and simple; but after what has been said as to how society acts, one can see that it presents some difficulties. (3) It must be powerful—powerful enough to make an unwilling minority obey the will of the majority. Incidentally, this means that it must be searching enough to detect evasions, and prompt enough to forestall violations so far as possible. (4) It must be efficient, and at the same time it must not destroy the efficiency of the thing it is regulating. (5) It must "economize coercion." (6) It must utilize all the strongest and most persistent motives of human nature, both generous and selfish: hope of reward, fear of punishment, and those loyalties, persuasions, and suggestions which have nothing directly to do with rewards or punishments, but which rest upon the deeper fact that the individual is essentially a part of the community. (7) The duties imposed must be simple enough to be understood; and this means, among other things, that social control must follow precedent a great deal of the time. (8) Control must be guided by experience or be wisely experimental. (9) It must be adaptable. (10) It must be farseeing. It must look beyond the immediate effect of doing a given thing to the further results of leading people to expect it in the future. It is possible to reward unselfish devotion once, but can it be made a habit? There is a story of an Irishman who was sent on an errand. When he returned the change, he was told, "Keep it for your honesty." Next time no change was forthcoming, and his employer asked him what he had done with it. "Kept it for me honesty," replied Pat. Beyond the rather short-range foresight suggested by this anecdote, there is the true gift of prophecy needed to foresee the ultimate effects of policies on men and on society. (11) And, lastly, social control must be capable of progressively raising the level of mankind. In a democracy, where the mass of mankind does the ultimate controlling, this amounts to saying that social control must contrive, somehow, to rise higher than its source. This miracle is possible in the social world, thanks to the occasional power of enlightened leadership, but nothing can make it easy.

Can any system meet all these requirements? They include many a pair of contradictory elements, between which compromise is likely to be both difficult and unsatisfactory, while complete reconciliation seems utterly out of the question. How reconcile liberty with coordination? Modern specialized and integrated industry demands a thorough and efficiently standardized coordination which is threatening the liberty of the common workers to a really serious extent. And how reconcile the liberty of the manager with that of the managed, in any system which requires management? Or how expect to reconcile our modern democracy with real leadership, when one sees how insistently representatives of the people are required to represent the class prejudices of their constituents and are martyred if they fail to conform?

Or how reconcile stability with endless change, the method of trial and error with the demand for a course which is consciously directed toward some known goal, and the shortsightedness of popular policies with the need of building for posterity? Or how reconcile the fundamental requisite, that there shall be but one power which can coerce, with the patent facts of an economy in which there are many minorities each of which has some essential process at its mercy and can use it to coerce the rest? How keep our supreme coercive power organized in geographical units, as seems inevitable, and yet recognize the growing pressure toward organization for control on lines of economic interests? Or how resolve the direct contradictions between the conflicting claims of these economic groups, not only as to their shares in the national dividend, but also as to matters of power and jurisdiction? For instance, is shop discipline an exclusive right of the employer, or should the workers have a share in it and, if so, within what limits? Truly these are matters which cannot be settled by cold logic alone or after the fashion of a mechanic. For he does not have to reckon with the feelings of his material or its sense of injustice when he sets some parts to do duty in spots where the stress is hard or the wearing friction heavy, while other parts are purely ornamental.

8. THE IMPORTANCE OF CONTROL

The importance of control need hardly be stressed, since without some coordinating system we could not produce or consume or live at all. And we are becoming acclimated, by slow degrees, to the idea that, if the system of control becomes too thoroughly obsolete, the whole social fabric may be shattered by a revolution. More concretely, we are often told that the world possesses productive power enough to enrich the lives of all with leisure and comforts, if not luxuries, and that it is only our stupid system of social organization, or disorganization, which prevents our brains, work, and equipment, between them, from abolishing poverty and making the whole world reasonably well off. Yet the system we have is most often defended on the ground that any available substitute would be even more wasteful and less efficient.

Certain it is that we have, for example, medical knowledge sufficient to stamp out many of mankind's great plagues, if the doctors could only control the behavior of the population or otherwise get their knowledge put into effect. And it is just as clear that we have physical capacity and technical ability to produce more than we do, even allowing for the fact that in many cases the limiting factor would be, not the capacity to manufacture, but the power of the earth to yield increased raw produce. One of the things that keeps us short of our ultimate capacity is a failure of social coordination—the failure to coordinate supply and demand or demand and need. In the main, no one is normally to blame for this condition, but to cure it is to release enormous powers of production which are now imprisoned and make a greater contribution to human welfare than any conceivable technical invention could possibly do. At present, the greatest field open to invention for bettering the lot of mankind is the field of improvements in our system of social control.

9. THE DIFFICULT TASK OF THE CITIZEN

Can we measure up to this opportunity and this need? It is only human to hold that anything that must be done can be done; men would not be where they are if they had not this confidence and the power, at least at times, to make it good. But even such faith must take account of the unpromising material it has to work with, if it is to have its feet on the ground. And the material often appears hopelessly discouraging.

Here, for instance, is the ultimate seat of control: a voter, electing an official who will pass on many public issues, some of which the voter has heard of, but of most of which he is totally ignorant. The office in question is the sixteenth on the ballot, and the voter, who has given more than the average amount of thought to this office, chose his man because the conservative newspaper of the city was against him. The voter knows that this paper is chiefly devoted to the financial interests of its owners and, from distrusting what it advocates, he has come to taking for granted that it is always on the wrong side. In this case the official he has voted for is honestly opposed to the exploiting of the public—by the large financial interests—and believes in giving the smaller fellows their turn. Which is likely to cost the voter more heavily? Where the larger interests are content with a 20 per cent inflation of the valuation of a public-utility property, raising rates to the consumer perhaps four cents in every dollar, those with smaller capital must steal more crudely in order to make away with a satisfactory aggregate of plunder, especially if their tenure of office is likely to be short. They may sell the city paving of low quality or useless equipment for the schools, at twice or three times their cost. So the voter, trying to oppose the large exploiter, opens the doors to a horde of smaller looters and does not even make serious inroads upon the power of the large interests, for their valuation is protected by commissions and courts and is beyond the reach of demagogues.

Poor voter! Poor bewildered, misguided, ineffective sovereign! If he cannot prevent his city administration from robbing him, how can he ever hope to elect officials who will carry out far-reaching projects of social betterment calling for energy, prophetic foresight, and that self-sacrificing kind of devotion which is willing to take the risks of social experimentation, for the benefit of posterity? And yet somehow, sometimes, some of these projects are realized.

REFERENCES FOR FURTHER READING

BEARD, *The Economic Basis of Politics*, Chap. 1.

CARVER, *Essays in Social Justice*, Chap. ii.

COMMONS, *Legal Foundations of Capitalism*, Chap. ii, Sec. 3; Chap. iii.

COOLEY, *Social Process*, Chaps. ii, iii.

DOUGLAS, HITCHCOCK, AND ATKINS, *The Worker in Modern Economic Society*, Chap. xxvi.

HANDLER, M., *Cases and Materials on Trade Regulation*, Chap. i.

HOBSON, J. A., *Work and Wealth*, Chap. vi.

LIPPMANN, WALTER, *The Good Society*, pp. 3–7, 22–29, 241–312, 1937.

MARSHALL, L. C., *Business Administration*, Chap. i.

———, *Readings in Industrial Society*, Chap. xv b.

MOSCA, G., *The Ruling Class* (trans. by A. Livingston), 1939.

ROSS, *Social Control*, Chap. i.

SHAW, A. W., *An Approach to Business Problems*, Chap. xiv.

SLICHTER, S. H., *Modern Economic Society*, Chaps. i, iii, 1928.

SMITH, J. RUSSELL, *Elements of Industrial Management*, Chap. xxv.

SWENSON, *National Government and Business*, Introduction.

TAWNEY, *The Acquisitive Society*, Introduction.

TAYLOR, H., *Contemporary Problems in the United States*, Vol. II, Chap. i, 1934.

VEBLEN, *Theory of Business Enterprise*, Chaps. ii–iv.

CHAPTER II

THE DEVELOPMENT OF CONTROL

Introduction, 20—The primitive clan, 20—The military-aristocratic slave state, 21—The medieval rural economy, 22—The town economy, 23—The "just price" and the condemnation of usury, 23—The early national system, or mercantilism, 25—The historical meaning of individualism, 27—Transition and piecemeal control, 29—The new era, 30.

1. INTRODUCTION

Our task is to understand this intricate network of control in which we all live our economic lives. We must understand it, first, in order to thread our own way as individuals through its highways and bypaths, but we also need a deeper understanding in order to play our part as members of a self-governing community in guiding its development into wise channels and preserving as much liberty as possible, without being afraid to impose as much control as is necessary. And this is a kind of understanding which we cannot gain unless we have some idea of the past out of which this present system of control has come. A complete understanding of the past would leave us no time to wrestle with the present, but we may, in a brief space, be able to get some light which will help us in the perplexing task of separating the permanent from the temporary, the "natural" and inevitable from the accidental, and the genuine requirements of human living-together from the impertinent devisings of professional politicians. We shall see how the forms of control adapt themselves to the range and complexity of the human contacts and conflicts with which they deal, and to a great variety of other conditions. Geographical area, war and peace, religion and science, technical methods of production, and the racial and class composition of the people, as well as the level and distribution of intelligence—all have their effect on this great development.

2. THE PRIMITIVE CLAN

The primitive human clan was an enlarged family, bound together by real or imaginary ties of blood, and its system of control was correspondingly close and complete. Backed by the priesthood and enforced by superstitious fear and awe, it prescribed many observances and taboos, regulating life in great detail. Among interesting germs of private property are customs of taboo whereby one member of a tribe can leave articles with some mark of his own upon them, and the others will respect the mark as a notice to leave the goods untouched. The fundamental "means of production" were the gifts of nature, not yet so scarce as to raise serious questions of ownership. While customs varied widely, there was some collectivism in primitive institutions, and hunting, house building, and similar activities were frequently carried on in common. There was also exchange on a noncontractual basis: reciprocal services relying on custom or pride and prestige to ensure adequate fulfilment.

3. THE MILITARY-ARISTOCRATIC SLAVE STATE

The bounds of the social group are extended by conquest beyond the recognized kinship of race, and there develops the impersonal relation of ruler and ruled as exploiter and exploited. Here obedience rests on force rather than on custom, and commands need no longer be in harmony with the subject's customary feelings of what is right and rule him through his own sense of fitness, as was the case with the rule of tribal custom. By this time private property has taken on a very definite form; there are courts to settle disputes and definite penalties for offenses against the property rights of others. The slave is ruled by compulsion, while the other citizens, who respect the master's rights, are ruled by a system of government which has taken on a definitely political character.

The greatest usefulness of the slave is to cultivate the soil, which also becomes private property, and the community becomes a group of more or less self-sufficing estates, each of which has within itself considerable division of labor among the slaves. In such a state, private property in all movables is well established, and also free exchange to a limited extent. But it is still of secondary importance as a method of economic production, most of the things people want being produced directly on the slave estates.

The Roman Empire extended this military-predatory system of control until it embraced the entire known world, virtually enslaving whole peoples to the Roman nation collectively; to the extent that the magnificence of Rome and in later times even its necessary subsistence were largely supported by direct tribute from the conquered peoples. This system of control did not endure, and probably could not endure permanently, on account of inherent weaknesses. It is hard to maintain a system of predatory and parasitic tribute-taking on a world scale by an entire community of absentee exploiters.

Yet, despite fatal weaknesses, the Romans were great in those arts of control which form the art of government, and their principles of law constitute their chief gift to the civilizations which have followed them. Under the Roman Empire there was a great increase in economic relations between persons of different laws and customs, and the Roman courts, in settling the disputes arising out of such relations, gradually built up a body of "law of the peoples" (*jus gentium*) which ultimately became more individualistic than the separate customs out of which it grew. The Code of Justinian, the ultimate embodiment of Roman law, marks a large step in the growth of individualism.

Perhaps this is truly natural, where economic relations have to be established over great areas and between people of widely different cultures and institutions. They can meet on this basis if on no other. It enables them to cooperate, up to a certain point, without becoming responsible for each other in any permanent and organic way, as the members of a close-knit community are. Thus there is built up a community of cooperation by free exchange which can be extended indefinitely for the very reason that it does not assume the full quota of responsibilities which go to make up a complete social unit. It is a partial community, not a complete one.

4. THE MEDIEVAL RURAL ECONOMY

During the Middle Ages, control was of several kinds. There was the arbitrary power of feudal overlords, and there was custom, which set limits on the lords' powers. There was also the church, which, besides governing all men's conduct by its general precepts and its power over penances here and the remission of eternal penalties hereafter, came also to be the actual owner of a large portion of the land of Europe and the developer and exploiter of important industrial processes. Then there were the guilds and the municipal governments, which were sometimes almost indistinguishable from them. Ultimately, the monarch developed substantial economic power and ushered in the modern system of economic nationalism.

The typical medieval cultivator of the soil, serf or villein, was born into a fixed status and was governed by it. It included a system of customary obligations which carried with them customary rights and customary immunities. He was allotted his strips of land in the tilled fields, which he might cultivate in the time that was his own, though where the "three-field system" was in force, it virtually dictated his methods of cultivation. He owed dues in kind and in service, and custom was his chief protector against unlimited extortion. There was little chance for economic freedom to arise; that was cradled and gained its first growth among the craftsmen and traders of the towns.

5. THE TOWN ECONOMY

The chief organ of control in the towns was the guild merchant and later the craft guild. These bodies limited their own membership and set standards of workman-like proficiency and quality of wares. They also enforced the contracts of their members. The would-be master in a craft guild must first pass through the stages of apprentice and journeyman, pay the fees of mastership, and produce a "master-piece" which would pass the scrutiny of the other masters and would prove his fitness to practice the craft. These regulations did not eliminate competition, but they determined its level and limited its scope. If a man won through to the rank of mastership, he could marry with the assurance that there was a place for him in the economic order and a chance to make a living suitable to his station in life. Meanwhile, as an apprentice, he was a member of his master's household and in contact with the problems both of the work and of the guild system of control.

To the town came the countrymen of the district to sell their products in its market, and these markets were also regulated with a view to eliminating speculation, middlemen, and corners. The laws against "regrating, forestalling, and engrossing" have this as their dominant purpose, and in them we have the origin of the settled hostility which our English law displays toward combination and monopoly. Thus there were laws, of town origin, aiming to enforce competition in the things the townsmen bought, while the guild regulations limited and controlled competition in the things they sold—an evidence that human nature was not totally different then from what it is now. As for distant trade, the foreign trader was subject to special restrictions, exhibiting a spirit like that of later protective-tariff systems.

6. THE "JUST PRICE" AND THE CONDEMNATION OF USURY

The Middle Ages were as far as possible from accepting the idea that the seller of goods is justified in getting as high a price as he can find a buyer to pay. The church insisted upon the doctrine of the "just price," and prices were actually regulated by the authority both of the municipal governments and of the sovereign. But it requires some discrimination to estimate justly the true character and effect of these regulations. We must distinguish at least three types of goods and three corresponding systems of prices. The just price was commonly thought of as that price which would give the producer a just living, one suitable to his station in life. This idea is clearly applicable to the products of local handicraft industry, making goods to order for sale within the community, but not so clearly or so easily to certain other types of prices. Goods coming from distant countries where the producers had widely different standards of living could hardly be expected to sell on this principle. The buyers were not responsible for the standard of living of Indian pepper growers or weavers of textiles, while the trader's calling was so speculative that his margin could hardly be fixed on any stable basis; he needed a liberal allowance to make up for his many perils and heavy losses.

Agricultural produce is still another problem. Unlike the craftsman, who works when he has a buyer, the peasant raises his crop first and then markets it, with the result that if the market will not take it at a price which pays the farmer a fair living, he cannot withhold his product. Such goods must almost inevitably sell at prices governed by the relation between supply and demand, and there is little evidence that the systems of control in the Middle Ages were strong enough to overcome this economic force. Prices of bread were sometimes regulated on a sliding scale, varying with the price of wheat, and in other cases committees of men expert in the particular commodity determined what would be a fair price for a given market period, taking into account supply and demand.

This might seem to amount to nothing at all, but in reality it undoubtedly accomplished a great deal in protecting buyers from sellers who might take advantage of their ignorance or haste and charge them far more than the market rate which supply and demand would naturally fix. The fact that people might still secure "good bargains" was recognized in another way, for some of the guilds had rules requiring a member who got materials cheaply to share his bargain with his fellow-guildsmen. There might be a great deal to be said for some of the results of such a rule, for competition in getting a better bargain in the market is not the same thing as competition in efficient use of materials or in quality of workmanship and may ultimately prove to be of no industrial service whatever. The difficulty lies in eliminating it without crippling the machinery by which prices change in response to economic law; but of that we shall inquire in its proper place. If a modern trade association enforced such a rule, it would probably be prosecuted for restraint of trade.

This doctrine of the fair price was, in part, the expression of the idea of value as something absolute, implying that if one party to an exchange gained, the other necessarily lost. Thus prices must correspond to the "true values" of the goods, else people are continually being robbed in trade. It remained for modern writers to show that each party may receive something worth more to him than what he gives in exchange, so that exchange may be a gain to both parties, without much regard to the precise rate of exchange at which the transaction is made. Whereupon enthusiasts hailed this as proof that every ostensibly free exchange is necessarily a mutual gain, under any and all conditions, and carried the principle beyond all reason. But that also is another story.

7. THE EARLY NATIONAL SYSTEM, OR MERCANTILISM

There are several reasons why this system deserves more than passing mention. One is that it is the system out of which our modern "individualism" directly sprang. And its abuses and excesses are directly responsible for the *laissez faire* or "let-alone" theory of economic control, for this theory arose as a direct and conscious revolt against the mercantile system. Furthermore, mercantilism is anything but obsolete. As the aftermath of the World War it is now more virulent and destructive then ever before.

As European civilization outgrew the loose organization of feudalism, the national state took its place. These states were militant autocracies, chronically at war and jealous of the population, wealth, and trade of their rivals. The king had replaced the feudal levies by a paid standing army which was under his undivided control, not, like the feudal forces, owing a prior and stronger allegiance to some powerful vassal. But the standing army required vastly more actual money than the feudal system of dues and services in kind; more, in fact, than feudal Europe possessed. America, newly discovered, supplied the deficiency and poured a flood of precious metals into Europe, largely via Spain, from which it spread through the course of trade to the other commercial countries, while Spain grew rich and the other countries eyed her enviously and did their best to turn as much as possible of the specie in their own direction. They took for granted without argument that a large supply of money is a good thing for a nation, which they thought of as getting rich in the same way in which an individual does, by selling more than he buys and building up a surplus of money income. They failed to follow out this analogy to its last step and to give expression to the fact that the individual gets no good out of this surplus except by turning it into something other than money.

Mercantilism has sometimes been described as if it meant nothing but this struggle to get money into the country, but this is altogether too narrow a view. Monetary policy was only a part of a much more comprehensive system of control, designed to further the ends of rival militaristic powers, as seen by those of the upper classes who were most actively interested in such matters.[1] These ends were neither democratic nor humanitarian. They viewed the masses as means to be utilized in the pursuit of national greatness and typically thought that they should be kept poor in order that they might work hard, for the benefit of the gentry.[2] They wanted to concentrate as much population and wealth as possible within their national boundaries, which could be done by building up manufactures which would use the raw produce of a larger area, and secure all the resulting profits. In order to have control of areas from which to get their raw supplies and for which they were incidentally to do all the manufacturing, they built up colonial empires which were expected to play the part of handmaidens to the power and prosperity of the mother country. It was against this plan of exploitation, moderate though it was in their case, that the American colonies revolted in 1776.

Where an occupation had a direct military or naval value, it was especially encouraged, often by direct bounties. Thus the colonists received bounties on masts from the forests of Maine and on other naval stores. By the Navigation Acts, initiated by Cromwell, British trade was virtually confined to British vessels, and the commercial leadership of Holland, based on free trade, was destroyed. Restrictive duties were laid on the importation of manufactured products, while their exportation was encouraged in every way. Further than this, desirable trades were often encouraged by importing skilled workers, setting standards of workmanship, and in many other ways. In general, the presumption of this school of control was that any especially useful branch of production should, as a matter of course, receive artificial support, and the most useful branches were thought to be foreign trade, shipping, and manufactures. Agriculture and domestic trade suffered relative neglect, though in England agriculture was protected by the "Corn Laws."

The mercantilist ideas were not so very different from those of the medieval towns, and there were many advantages in applying them on a national scale. To the extent that this resulted in removing the local customs barriers and the guild privileges, now grown monopolistic, it meant a very important increase in freedom of trade. Many of these obsolete restrictions survived, however, especially in France, where the abuses of the Bourbon monarchy were rapidly bringing on the Revolution. And meanwhile, another revolution was preparing—a technical

[1] See Schmoller, *Mercantilism*, for a development of this view.
[2] See Furniss, *The Position of the Laborer in a System of Nationalism.*

revolution which was to burst all bonds of guild control and make England the foremost manufacturing nation of the world, irrespective of protective systems. This, then, was the scheme of thought and practice out of which our system of individualism developed.

8. THE HISTORICAL MEANING OF INDIVIDUALISM

Historically, individualism was a reaction against the excessive and perverted restraints of the mercantile system. It has often been set forth as a statement of eternal and universal truth by those who were in the midst of the movement and could not see it in its historical perspective. Some believed that a benevolent Creator had so ordered the world that the natural impulses of men worked together for the good of the whole; and yet few of them carried this belief to its logical conclusion, which would mean rejecting all government. The government to which they were accustomed appeared to them as natural, except for the restrictions of mercantilism.

To the founders and fathers of individualism, liberty had a very specific meaning: it meant freedom from the shackles of mercantilism. It meant that individuals should work in what places and at what trades they chose, free of guild control; that enterprise should determine for itself what branches of production to develop, choosing those in which the greatest value could be produced at the lowest cost, with no weighting of the scales by bounties or duties; and that the control of quality and workmanship should be left to the consumer, instead of to the guild or the officers of the king. The control from which they wanted to be free was control in the immediate interests of classes seeking special privileges (traders or manufacturers), supported by unsound ideas of the superior value to the nation of these branches of production, and viewing trade as a game in which the nations were necessarily grabbing from each other—a game in which it was impossible for all to win.

The state should not undertake to dictate, direct, or influence (as by protective tariffs) what should be produced or how much, of what quality, or by what methods. That was to be left to the demand in a free market and the responses of free-choosing producers to that demand. Freedom in these basic matters was the main concern of early individualism, and about other matters it had less, or nothing, to say.

Such a realistic individualist as Adam Smith did not claim perfection for the system of free exchange but was continually falling back on comparative statements, contending that, while scarcities of food would occur, the world could feed itself if it could mobilize its supplies, and that actual famine was due to mistaken restrictions on trade.[1] Or he thought of commercial employments as making for independence and security because he saw so much more striking insecurity among the domestic servants of the rich aristocrats.[2] Even the most ardent apostles of liberty approved of some measures of control. Some admitted the desirability of limiting rates of interests; others approved of factory acts. Adam Smith justified some sorts of control on the ground that defense is more important than opulence; while the laws in the interest of labor he said were always just, since they must be passed by a Parliament whose chief advisers were always the employers of labor. One might conclude that the truth of individualism consisted, at bottom, in the errors of eighteenth century mercantilism.

To some extent, however, any system of control is probably exposed to the same weaknesses which made the world so ready to welcome individualism in 1776. The machinery of government cannot be trusted to pick out unerringly the true needs of the community as a whole, and it is always exposed to being captured and perverted to the uses of class privilege, though the class in power may change and the character of the privilege may be totally revolutionized. And it is inherently hard to frame regulations without hampering some perfectly legitimate and useful kinds of private dealing or encountering unexpected and insuperable obstacles. To the extent that these difficulties beset control today, the gospel of individualism still has force, as it had in the eighteenth century. We must distinguish, however, control of the basic factors of supply and demand, mentioned above, from control of more incidental matters such as safety appliances and hours and conditions of labor. In the latter field the difficulties are far less, and even in the former field, if modern types of control are more truly directed to the public interest and avoid crude misdirections of productive effort, the whole case may need to be reheard.

Individualistic business itself was in its infancy when its philosophy was capturing the imagination of the civilized world. In 1776, the year the American colonies formally withdrew from Great Britain's mercantilistic-colonial empire and Adam Smith's *Wealth of Nations* was published, Watt's steam engine was not yet perfected. There was no large-scale industry as we now know it. Adam Smith did not believe that corporations were qualified to succeed in most lines of business, and even John Stuart Mill, writing in the middle of the nineteenth century, did not apply his individualism to corporations.[3] And this on

---

[1] See *The Wealth of Nations* (Bax ed.), Vol. II, p. 30.
[2] See his *Lectures on Police, Revenue and Arms*, p. 155
[3] John Stuart Mill, *Principles of Political Economy*, Book V, Chap. xi, Sec. 11.

the threshold of the movement which was to make the corporation the dominant form of business organization! Trade unions were conspiracies at law, and collective bargaining was unknown, to say nothing of the sympathetic strike, compulsory insurance for industrial accidents, or railroad rebates.

From this analysis one thing should be sufficiently clear. If we are to keep an individualistic philosophy in the twentieth century, we must build it new, in the light of present-day forms of industry and present-day pressures of democracy. What the present-day individualist has to defend is not individualism as Smith saw it, but a system of vast impersonal organizations in constant danger of being paralyzed by a deadlock of the interests involved. It is as far as possible from the simple one-man business system which Adam Smith defended so successfully. The control which the present-day individualist resists is not the present-day equivalent of mercantilism—the "individualists" generally favor the protective tariff—but democratic and humanitarian control in the interest of just the classes which mercantilism neglected. It is largely an extension of precisely the kind of control which Adam Smith said was always justified. Even the governments which do the controlling are vastly different from that of eighteenth century England.

It is not a question whether our great-grandfathers were right or wrong; the thing they defended no longer exists. Individualism and control are both new, and the case for both needs to be completely restated. Now that we have come to realize this, we can see that it is a condition which has been developing, unrealized, for generations.

9. TRANSITION AND PIECEMEAL CONTROL

The nineteenth century was a period of rapid transition which was, as far as systems of control were concerned, largely unconscious. We thought of it as quantitative advance in want-gratification going on in a substantially fixed institutional framework. This was fixed because in democracy and individualism we possessed the final, correct principles, needing only piecemeal rectification here and there. These piecemeal rectifications expanded rapidly, but without unsettling the basic philosophy in the minds of the majority. Socialism arose, but it was a minority aberration.

One phase of control began with the factory acts. another (in this country) with the attempt to control trusts, railroads, and public utilities. The first did not unsettle our basic principles because it dealt with adjustments regarded as incidental and did not interfere with the central matters of supply, demand, and price. The second did not subvert individualistic principles because, while it did deal with supply, demand, and price, it was following, rather than departing from, the competitive-individualistic standard. In the case of trusts it attempted to restore competition, and in the case of railroads and public utilities it attempted to restore an approximation to the competitive standard of fair price. Both were efforts to bring the system back to the individualistic model. Other types of control arose, such as conservation and pure-food laws, but they were each viewed as a special and exceptional case. Depressions were unfortunate accidents or results of some sort of misguided excesses in business. As to the socialists, who explained them as inherent results of the business system, economists were content to point out fallacies in their theories. Depressions and other evils, pointing toward the need of more far-reaching types of control, could not permanently be ignored; though in this country effective recognition might have been staved off a long while but for the World War. The World War definitely brought this period to an end.

10. THE NEW ERA

From 1914 to 1918 the economic resources of the combatant nations were marshalled by their governments as never before. Supplies, means of transport, and capital funds were rationed, prices fixed, wages adjusted, and organization of labor and of business fostered and utilized. After the war, European countries, driven partly by crippling postwar maladjustments, entered upon an intensified supermercantilism. With the postwar paper currencies, a balance of foreign trade became a vital national necessity and was sought by limiting the amount of imports through quotas, more absolutely than tariffs could limit them. With the growing threat of another war, national self-sufficiency came to seem to some nations a necessity at almost any economic sacrifice.

Russia became communistic, and the threat of communism in Italy contributed to the rise of Mussolini's fascist dictatorship, with an interesting theory of a "corporative state" organized around economic groups instead of territorially—a theory which has not yet been fully achieved in practice. Germany set up a socialistic republic without an economic revolution, but the ill-fated Treaty of Versailles ultimately bore its natural fruit in a militant resurgence of German nationalism, producing the Hitler dictatorship with its dogma of the totalitarian state, in which all member interests are submerged, and with its virtually absolute control of all phases of national life: economic, social, intellectual, and religious.

In this country, wartime controls were rapidly dissolved; the country rebounded quickly from the depression of 1920–1921 and returned to a conservative "normalcy," which soon passed into the "new era" of supposedly depression-proof prosperity. This was thought to be guaranteed, be it noted, by the Federal Reserve System: a new agency of banking control established in 1913 as a result of the crisis of 1907.

After the prosperity turned into unprecedented economic paralysis, we found we were indeed in a new era, but not of depression-proof prosperity. It is a new era in which we face the grim menace of long and disastrous depression; and most of our policies of social control center for the first time around this fact. For the first time, the failure of private business to produce steadily and to afford adequate employment has been made by the government a matter of primary public concern and responsibility. This is the central job of business, and official recognition of its inadequacy is a new thing in our system. Attempts to remedy this go to the heart of the system of private enterprise and grapple with the central questions of supply, demand, and price, not in special cases and guided by competitive norms, but throughout the business system and seeking results different from those which any actual competitive system would produce.

If our ideal of steady and full operation of industry is in any sense a competitive norm, it is the norm of an ideal competitive system which is now recognized as not only nonexistent but inherently and fundamentally impossible under modern industrial conditions. For these reasons the present stage of control marks a new era.

REFERENCES FOR FURTHER READING

"The Attas: A Jungle Labor Union," *Atlantic Monthly*, July, 1921.
AYRES, C. E., *The Problem of Economic Order*, 1938.
BEARD, *The Economic Basis of Politics*, Chap. ii.
BUCHER, *Industrial Evolution*, Chap. iii.
CUNNINGHAM, *Growth of English Industry and Commerce*, Book III, Chaps. iii, iv; Book IV, Chaps. i, ii; Secs. 82–84, 267–272.
DAY, CLIVE, *History of Commerce*, Chaps. vi, xviii.
DOUGLAS, HITCHCOCK, and ATKINS, *The Worker in Modern Economic Society*, Chap. iv.
FABRE, J. H., *Social Life in the Insect World*.
———, *The Wonders of Instinct*.
FURNISS, *The Position of the Laborer in a System of Nationalism*.
HAMILTON, W. H., *Current Economic Problems*, 3d ed., Chap. ii, Chap. vi D.
HANDLER, M., *Cases and Materials on Trade Regulation*, Chap. ii.
LAWLEY, F. E., *The Growth of Collective Economy*, 1938.
LUBBOCK, SIR J., *Ants, Bees and Wasps*, Chap. 1, pp. 18–29; Chaps. ii, iv–vi, xi.
MARSHALL, L. C., *Readings in Industrial Society*, Chap. ii, e, Selections 390–398.
MODLIN and DE VYER, *Development of Economic Society*, esp. Chaps. ix, xiv, xxii.
SCHMOLLER, GUSTAV, *Mercantilism*.
SUMNER, WILLIAM G., *Protectionism*, Chap. i, Secs. a, b.
VEBLEN, *Theory of Business Enterprise*, chap. x.

CHAPTER III

BUSINESS: PRIVATE RIGHT OR PUBLIC INTEREST?

1. INTRODUCTION

We have just seen that at the time when the theory and philosophy of individualism became supreme in the realm of educated public opinion, individualism as a working system of economic organization did not exist, in any complete sense, and that so far as it did exist, it was a very different thing from the large-scale pseudo-individualism of today. *Complete individualism never has existed.* The great countries of Europe remained protectionist with the exception of England, and even in England, long before the mercantile restrictions were abolished, other regulations of a different complexion were being introduced. The first Factory Acts were on the statute books in 1802, and the more important factory legislation dates from 1833, while the "Corn Laws," or protective tariffs on grains, did not disappear until 1849.[1] Thus complete *laissez faire* was and remains an abstraction not to be found existing anywhere in the world of business and political reality. It is an aspiration unfulfilled and unfulfillable; a principle which is allowed to govern some of the relations of economic life, but never all; a system of control fairly adequate for some purposes, but never all-sufficient.

2. OPPOSING VIEWS OF THE NATURE OF PRIVATE BUSINESS

Of this system of control the most violently opposing views prevail, resting upon equally opposing views of the fundamental nature of business. Some look on it as nothing more or less than the exercise of the eternal "natural rights" of individuals. And while it is developed into marvelous and elaborate forms, these should not, according to this view, obscure the simple and elemental character of the basis of it all.

---

[1] The act of 1842, the first under Sir Robert Peel, moderated the duties, and the act of 1846 provided that in three years' time they should cease entirely. The work of the "Manchester School" and the Anti-corn-law League, under the leadership of Cobden and Bright, was largely responsible for this result and furnishes a fine example of the voluntary organization which often lies behind legislation.

With most thinkers of today, however, the phrase "natural rights" stands discredited.

Most modern thinkers judge a system by its results, approving or condemning it according as it does or does not meet the essential needs of humanity in a satisfactory way, or as well as they can be met in a world of imperfect individuals, born to toil and hardship. Among those who adopt this standard and regard industry as a community service, many, nevertheless, believe firmly that individualism meets the test better than any other possible system and organizes production so as to render the greatest possible service. Others believe that it can be kept as a central principle and subjected to control in cases where it works badly. But the volume of these special cases has swollen so inordinately in the last fifty years that one wit has defined a liberal as "one who believes that this is the best of all possible worlds, and that almost everything in it is an unfortunate exception."

Still others, looking on the course of past history with its endless change and its spirals which never return quite upon themselves, conceive that, whatever the existing order, it must be temporary, moving toward a future which cannot be predicted, save that it is bound to be different from the present. To these the present system, with its magnification of individualism, is neither sound nor unsound; it has played its part, fulfilling certain human desires and defeating or cramping others, and the forces within it are transforming it into something based upon it and yet different. From this standpoint, measures of control are neither attempts to discover and establish the ultimate right system, the goal to which all human progress hitherto has been tending, nor are they attempts to cure permanently the evils of industrialism or establish a fixed and stable balance of power between opposing principles. They are merely the next step in this unpredictable evolution.

It is important to keep the backbone of the existing order, not because we are sure it will be permanently needed, any more than we are sure it will be utterly discarded in a thousand years, but because we are sure that too violent and destructive a break will mean untold suffering to ourselves, our children, and possibly our children's children. And as it seems doubtful whether such sufferings will bring the world materially farther or faster on its way to its "far-off, divine event," whatever that may be, it hardly seems worth while to incur them; all the more so because suffering is not, in itself and always, a civilizing influence. It is quite as likely to be debasing and brutalizing. And so these evolutionists join the liberals in their reforms, but with a bolder sweep of the imagination, regarding such measures as experiments which may develop new organs of social life, possessed of vitality sufficient to carry them on to an end different from what anyone now can see or intend.

And, finally, there are those who feel the present system to be so intolerably bad, or who visualize so clearly the form of the better order which is to take its place, that the only form of social control in which they have any interest is an immediate and complete revolution. To them, the business of production is so thoroughly and completely a public function, and the pretense of private enterprise to perform that function such a ghastly mockery, that no compromise is endurable. And the attempts at control are equally empty mockeries, for how are we to control something which is stronger and more vital in its nefarious life processes than the agencies on which we must rely to control it—something which reaches back and corrupts the fountains of control themselves? It even manufactures public opinion, taking control of control at its source, if it cannot manage to divert or capture or stultify it at some one of the many delicate stages of transmission. When a powerful beast cannot be domesticated but remains savage and dangerous, the only thing to do is to put an end to it.

Taking for granted that the fundamental interest in production is to serve the needs of the community, opinions as to the public nature of business seem to fall into three broad classes. There are those who hold that the forces of control which are an essential part of individualism take adequate care of this public interest, so that all that is left may fairly be regarded as the private affair of the business man and his customers or his laborers as the case may be. Next come those who hold that business is a private affair which occasionally becomes public, and third come those who count all business as wholly a public function.

There is another way of describing the general cleavage of opinion with which we are dealing. One group, a growing one, says quite simply and directly that the essential nature of private business is to pursue private gain and not humanitarian service or even efficient production. Any elements of efficient service which find their way into business are perversions of its true profit-seeking nature and are there in spite of it rather than because of it. The institution is fundamentally wrong, and we shall never have real social efficiency until we get rid of it and put production under the control of people who are primarily interested in producing, and producing efficiently, and to whom this is not a mere incidental concession which it seems wise or necessary to make in order to hold the market or to avoid undue political interference. Still more people hold exactly the opposite view, that the essential nature of business is to promote productive efficiency, and that undue profits, scamped quality, or other predatory symptoms are exceptions to its true nature. The institution is sound; the abuses are such excrescences as come upon any structure of orderly cooperation and are due to the ever present faults of human nature, not to the social structure in which it works.

This is a most interesting contradiction, since both sides are aware of triumphs of productive efficiency, and both are aware of serious wastes and disgraceful abuses. They seem to differ chiefly as to which kind of thing represents the natural and essential tendencies of business and which is incidental and exceptional.

It is like discussing the essential character of a caged tiger in a menagerie. Is it to amuse the multitude or to rend them? To amuse them, perhaps, as long as the bars hold! Or which is the essential character of a spring flood: to furnish a store of power to run industries during the dry months of the summer, or to wreck homes and drown the inhabitants? Assuredly it is a force of destruction, save for the size of the reservoirs and the strength of the dams. They harness some of it—not all—to useful purposes. So with business. Its very nature is twofold; it is harnessed self-interest, and the key to the clash of opinion about it, which we have just outlined, lies in the fact that one side is looking at the self-interest, the other at the harness. It is the inherent nature of self-interest to break the harness if it can, and it is the inherent nature of the harness to make the efforts of self-interest drag the burdens of production, willingly or not. And any substitute way of getting things done would have self-interest, in some form, to control and would need to use some kind of harness, somewhat different from the harness in which present-day business travels, but made up of roughly corresponding elements. The question which side is nearest right and which most seriously wrong depends chiefly on the further question How well does the harness hold? In a still more practical sense, it depends on the question How well does the harness we now use hold, compared to other possible types of harness?

3. THE INDIVIDUALISTIC THEORY

What is the nature of this harness which converts what would otherwise be sheer anarchy or predatory warfare into a moderately orderly business procedure, with that modicum of serviceability to the public which even the radical critic admits the system contains? Its outstanding features are maintaining and protecting rights of persons and property, enforcing contracts, and preserving competition. All is based on a foundation of equality of opportunity. The underlying theory of rights of person and property is the theory of a mutual limitation of liberty: no one may use his liberty of property or person to injure another.

At this point one seems to hear an echo from *Pinafore:* "What, never?" "Well, hardly ever." People can legally do things which reduce the value of other people's property, or which make their personal liberty less useful and effective, or which actually reduce its cash value to them. Not all interests are legally protected against being injured by other people—only "rights." And what are rights? Legally, they are those interests which society chooses to protect.[1] Which reduces our proposition to a very simple form: those injuries are forbidden which the law forbids; those interests are protected which the law protects. It is earnestly to be hoped that the law is wise in deciding which interests to protect and always protects any interest unless by doing so some greater interest would be balked of fulfillment. For without such wisdom the formula loses all its supposed meaning. And for such wisdom there is no simple formula.

If we are to understand our system of control, we must find out in more detail in what the rights, actually protected under individualism, consist. They include, in general, equal opportunity for all to play the game and to have access to the cards and the counters, and they include freedom from out-and-out coercion. On this basis free exchange is built up. This fundamental act of exchange is conceived after the following fashion: Two people meet. They have no positive obligations toward one another of an economic sort, and no power over one another; no duties and no fears; they are independent entities, and if they pass each other by, neither is the worse. However, in this case they choose not to pass each other by, but to parley and agree to an arrangement whereby each induces the other to do something for him by agreeing to do something in return. Neither one can bind himself to do anything which would injure others—injure the rights of others, that is—and therefore the two parties concerned are furthering their own private ends at no one's expense, and the transaction is strictly their own private affair and none of the public's concern. Any public interference is of the nature of paternalism and tyranny, an unjustifiable infringement upon the natural liberties of free citizens in an individualistic society. Even if one party loses in the transaction, that is his mistake, against which society has no business to protect him, and it is no one else's injury. Out of such elemental unit transactions

[1] This refers to what may be called "substantive rights" rather than "procedural rights" or measures by means of which interests are protected. The legal meaning of rights will be gone into more fully in a subsequent chapter.

is business built. They become differentiated from their hypothetical origin in a simple barter of surplus products between self-sufficing producers, into the transactions of buyer and seller, borrower and lender, employer and employee, principal and agent, lessor and lessee, mortgagor and mortgagee, and the special immunities and complexities of the negotiable instrument and the limited-liability corporation. But the general blanket conception of voluntary arrangements for mutual advantage covers them all in the mind of the thoroughgoing individualist.

— In such direct transactions the parties are the best judges of their own interests. And if they are not perfect judges, at least they can further their own interests more effectively in such a relatively simple and direct fashion than they could if acting through some complicated delegated agency, such as the state. Voting for what one wants with goods, services, and dollars is, wherever it can be done, more effective than voting with ballots.

Of course, in an economy based on the division of labor, people are not self-sufficing, and if other people will not exchange with them, they cannot live at all. They must either own productive resources and be able to buy the instruments and materials they need to use, as far as they cannot produce them themselves, or they must find a buyer for their labor and then find dealers who will sell them all the goods they need at prices their wages will cover. Everyone is dependent on relations which no one is obliged to establish with him and on services which no one has a positive duty to render. To this fact of dependence the individualistic philosophy makes one great concession: there must be no monopoly. The reason why no particular person need be under obligation to serve me is that, if one refuses or asks unreasonable terms, I can turn to another, and if he also is unreasonable, I can find still others, with the further condition in the background that anyone at all who is able and desirous to serve me is free to do so, whether he is in the business at the moment or not. Competition extends, not merely to those in the trade, but to all those who might like to enter it; it is a part of their individualistic freedom.

It is only the force of competition which makes it safe to leave the rendering of essential economic services on a purely voluntary basis, the supposition being that in a free market someone will always be found willing to render them on reasonable terms. Certain businesses are classed as "public utilities" or "businesses affected with a public interest," and these have a positive duty to serve all comers on terms which involve, for the out-and-out public utilities, public control of rates and earnings. Where this positive duty is set up, the business will be found to be not naturally competitive, or else it is one in which the public cannot get the full benefit of such competition as exists.[1]

Under competition, demand is an effective governor of production, and the competitive meeting of supply and demand is the core of that "economic law" we are so often counseled not to violate. This law bestows profits where supply is short of demand, stimulating businesses to expand production in order to gain more profits from a larger output; it inflicts losses where supply exceeds demand, thus urging contraction; and where supply meets demand, it gives each business and each contributing factor the rewards necessary to maintain that supply and no more. Competition eliminates the least efficient organizers of production and tends to concentrate business in the hands of those who give the consumer the greatest satisfaction, or the greatest attractions, for his money. And as far as competition does its part in standardizing the price of labor, the result is that cheap production cannot be had by underpaying the workers but must depend on superior organization, so as to produce a given result with a minimum expenditure of actual labor power and materials. What we actually have is, of course, admittedly only an approximation to this happy state.

The essential nature of competition, then, is rivalry in efficient service to the consuming public, including the laborers in their capacity as consumers. This does not deny the patent fact that the interest of the business man is to get as much as possible and give as little as possible in exchange, nor that this interest of his is directly opposed to the interrests of everyone with whom he deals. If business men in a given trade acted as a group, following their group interest, they could exploit consumers and laborers alike; but the whole theory of competition is to prevent them from following their group interest, pitting them each against all the others in a contest for the favor of the classes they would otherwise be exploiting.

This is, frankly, a very difficult status to maintain, especially as competition is itself a voluntary activity. But it has a strong basis both in custom and in individual psychology, not to mention a very impressive record of works. Hence it is begging the question to assert dogmatically that the essential nature of business is to exploit; the case for individualism begins where this statement leaves off, and the adversary must overthrow this case before his sweeping condemnation is entitled to serious consideration. The essential nature of *competition* is

---

[1] Cf. what was said of economic compulsion in relation to competition (Chap. 1, Sec. 2) above. Cf. also Tugwell, *The Economic Nature of Public Interest*, 1922. Here the main thesis is that public interest rests upon conditions which subject customers to some disadvantage but is not limited to absolute monopoly.

to harness the predatory interest, perverting it, if you will, to a rivalry in attracting voluntary patronage by methods which necessarily center largely in service.

In such a system, when it is working ideally, the individual might properly be held responsible for finding his own place and controlling his own fortunes. Granted a fair start in life, competition insures that equal opportunity will continue, and that everyone will have open to him chances to make his services as valuable as the state of the industrial arts permits, and to collect approximately the full economic value of his services. If an able-bodied person does not find a satisfactory position, that is his own fault and he should suffer; his prosperity or poverty depends on his own efforts. This not only is just but also affords the most effective stimulus to make everyone do his utmost and makes for a self-reliant people and an efficient community.

Great business depressions may be admittedly hard to square with this theory. Here the individualist is likely to accept these catastrophes as natural, and to fall back on the view that they would be less serious, and recovery prompter and more complete, if business were left alone or at most made more competitive, usually with emphasis on competition of labor in the fixing of wages. The depth and duration of the last great depression are likely to be ascribed, in part at least, to the well-meant but mistaken efforts of government to intervene.

Rewards are unequal in accordance with the unequal value of services; and this fact is at the bottom of one condition often criticized, namely, the fact that, while rewards are supposed to compensate the sacrifices of production, some of the heaviest human sacrifices receive relatively low compensation. Yet, after all, it is logical that the poor should incur the greater sacrifices of production, just as they suffer the greatest privations in consumption. That is what being poor means: having less enjoyments and exemptions in all the departments of life where money counts.

Thus lies the general outline of the case for regarding competitive business under individualism as primarily a private affair. Government may step in to regulate the natural monopolies, to maintain competition in general, to prevent internal abuses in corporations, to improve the quality of the market as a meeting place of supply and demand, to safeguard educational and other opportunities, and to provide some sort of harbor of last resort for the inevitable mass of human derelicts. In short, control should aim chiefly at liberating economic forces, not at restraining or diverting them; at maintaining the "natural" economic laws rather than at overthrowing them. Perfect competition is the economic ideal, and the goal of control should be to bring the actual world as close as possible to this model, wherever for any reason it departs from it or fails to run true to type.

4. THE OTHER SIDE OF THE CASE

And what is to be said on the other side? In the face of the case which has been built up, it will not do merely to enter a blanket reversal of the individualist thesis and claim that exploitation is the rule and that such modicum of efficient service as persists represents a more or less haphazard exception, in which the institution is not running true to form. But if we give a thoroughgoing critic a chance to say his say, he will do much more than this. He will cite a sickening mass of abuses, and he will organize them into an attack upon the very foundations on which the individualistic case is built. Let us try to present his point of view, fairly and forcibly, without bias or extenuation.

First and foremost, business depressions are a natural product of the business system, not removable by any conceivable efforts merely directed to increasing competition. This creates a tremendous public interest in industry, whether or not we have yet learned how to take care of it successfully. We shall not stop trying so long as the conditions are as unsatisfactory as at present.

As to the groundwork of the system of which depressions are the unpalatable fruit, what are the "rights" of persons and property, on the protection and exercise of which the whole system rests? On this point the individualistic argument was noticeably wabbly, and with good cause. People love to talk as if protecting rights were nothing but preventing wrongs, but they are merely deceiving themselves with the double meanings of words. In fact, many of the legal rights are themselves but the perpetuation and sanctification of moral and social wrongs. They cover, for instance, the loot gained in the past by such wrongs as unfair competition and monopoly, corrupt acquisition of public resources, the looting of corporate funds by their guardians and trustees, laborers contracting under the duress of economic compulsion, human lives sacrificed to material commodities and to the increase of employers' profits, children deprived of a fair start in life, and the crowning wrong of the inheritance of the swollen fortunes gained by all the other wrongs, whereby a favored few acquire the hereditary overlordship of great economic principalities, in a country where hereditary overlordships are supposed to be things of the past.

The fundamental rights of persons in our system are supposed to be natural and inalienable, yet, inconsistently enough, the entire fabric is built upon an almost unlimited right to alienate all one's other rights, and a liberty to alienate everything that makes liberty worth having, everything in which the real and valuable content of liberty consists. A man may alienate his health through patent medicines or through working at an unhealthy trade or merely through unduly long hours or low wages. And what is more, he may be alienating, for his children, the opportunity of a fair start in life. But laws setting limits on his power to alienate these things have sometimes been held unconstitutional. Minor gaps in the system of property and personal rights enable industries to escape payment of many of their real costs, with the result that a financial profit is no guaranty of a balance of economic usefulness to the community. An industry may escape with an unpaid responsibility for a smoke nuisance, a deterioration of neighborhood land values, unemployment, poor relief, or the peril of a social revolution. Thus the system of private industry is perverted at the source, in the system of rights on which its entire social meaning depends.

As for the idea of equality of opportunity, and the conception of exchange as a mutual gain, affecting third parties not at all, enough has been said already to show that these are polite fictions. Opportunity is not equal as between the child of successful parents and the child of the slum; and the business system is responsible for making the inequality as great as it is. While genius can make its way through anything, the majority of the incomes above $5,000 are not received by geniuses. A moderately intelligent man with "advantages" will easily rise above this line, while without them he would fall below it. There are inequalities of opportunity among businesses also, but they are chiefly due to imperfect competition and can best be treated under that head. "Unfair competition" often means that a would-be competitor is not given an equal opportunity to render service. And the abuses of individualism are not confined to the immediate contracting parties but ramify out to the farthest corners of the industrial system: witness the contagious character of panics and industrial depressions, not to mention lesser instances.

And what comfort is to be derived from the thought that demand is the governor of production, when demand is the plaything of the arts of advertising hypnotism? Or when the customer does not know what he is getting on account of adulterations which are virtually compulsory on the producer because of the pressure of competition? Or when demand is turned into channels of utter waste by the rivalry in display which industrialism does its best to cultivate, and warped by such extremes of inequality in purchasing power that it no longer has more than a remote connection with human needs? Industrialism has itself ruined the validity of demand as an index of community efficiency. And this "demand" which is so sanctioned in common argument is not the demand for human conditions of work or for reasonable relations between man and man or between class and class, but almost solely the demand for consumable goods and services. It is ready to sacrifice life to meat and body to raiment and does so daily—one man's life to another man's meat and one man's body to the raiment of another man's wife. Not that meat and raiment are unimportant, even as prerequisites to the "higher" things, but that the individualistic economy tends to give them a disproportionate value and to make them masters of human lives, instead of servants only. The market is well organized to give effect to desires for these things, if one can pay the price, but very poorly organized to give effect to any desire the workers may have for that kind of work and working conditions and that quality of human relations in their work which are necessary to make them adequate human beings and good members of society. Whatever effective demand there is for such values comes chiefly through other channels than the price bargains of individual with individual.

As for our supposed law that prices tend to be fixed at a level at which supply and demand will be equal, what is it but a form of words? What shreds of real meaning can it have in a community where the incessant question is: What percentage of our supply of productive power is standing idle, and what part of our supply of labor is unemployed because the demand for it does not exist? Or where the producer fixes his price first and, if his goods remain unsold, withholds further production rather than lower the price to a level that will move the entire product? The whole equation of supply and demand reduces itself to an impossible travesty when builders are out of work and cannot buy shoes because there are too many buildings for the demand, shoemakers cannot buy clothes because the demand for shoes is not up to the supply, and clothing workers cannot rent large enough living quarters because there is an oversupply of clothing. As a group they suffer for lack of all these things because too many of them have been produced. What really exists is a shortage of goods to meet the aggregate needs of those who are willing and able to produce other needed goods in exchange; but through a cumulative series of misfits, all that the business eye can see is an excess of supply over "demand." Some things the law of supply and demand goes far to explain; but the business cycle is a standing proof of its failure to explain some of the most critical factors in the relation of production to consumption. And it is evident that demand is a very imperfect index of need.

And what of competition? Industry has undoubtedly passed through a stage in which this force was dominant, but the economic revolution of the last fifty years has brought with it such a growth of combination that those who still think of our society as a "competitive system" are placed decidedly on the defensive. Railroads, public utilities, and a growing mass of public services are already noncompetitive, industry has its "trusts," banking its Federal Reserve system, and labor's bargains are made between national or regional unions and bodies of employers who associate for the purpose, with frequent resort to judicial processes, privately or publicly set up. These judicial protections are very necessary, because the new "competitive" bargaining process involves long stoppages of production, waiting for the forces of "supply and demand," or their modern equivalent, to have their effect and to settle the disputes. And the public has a vital interest in preventing these stoppages, especially as modern industry is so interdependent that the whole machine feels the results of a break at almost any point in the chain of operations.

Actual competition works in some cases more severely than the theoretical ideal and in some cases less so. In agriculture it is generally more severe than elsewhere, constituting a real and serious handicap. This has been lessened in some branches by cooperative marketing organizations; elsewhere it has led, under the "New Deal," to publicly controlled systems of limiting acreage and raising prices, openly defended as a means of offsetting the farmer's handicap as compared to industry. In industry and trade, hybrid conditions between monopoly and "pure competition" frequently prevail, together with trade associations with their more or less friendly gettings-together and their codes of fair dealing and understandings as to "sound business practice," which try to steer on the safe side of the law against combinations, while still mitigating the dangers of business for the business man. These various conditions lead to relative stability in some prices, while others fluctuate markedly. Competition has by no means disappeared, but there are few types of transactions in which complete and wholehearted competition of the theoretical sort rules on both sides. The theory of simple competition no longer explains the typical operations of industry.

As for the competitive scheme of prices and other incentives to production, there is no sufficient reason to suppose that they represent the exact rewards necessary to call forth just the quotas of productive efforts and resources that are needed to make just the supplies of goods that are worth making. What seems clear is that, under competition, businesses pay all they can afford in order to get valuable services and resources away from other businesses and charge prices which cover the cost of getting customers away from their competitors. But to say that this is what society must needs pay to bring these things into use at all, that is sheer guesswork, with the probabilities all against its being generally true. The salary of a member of the Cabinet is not enough to command the services of an outstanding man for an indefinite time, but this is chiefly because private business offers so much more. If business paid no more than the public service, outstanding men would not on that account let their abilities lie idle. High-grade talent would still be forthcoming, and it would be easier for the government to get its fair share. Private business tends to offer those at the top more than they need to stimulate them to their best efforts; so much, in fact, that they can afford to retire early and rear their sons to idleness. And it tends to pay those at the bottom less than they need to maintain their working efficiency.

As for interest, it is a debated question whether a reduction in the rate of interest would materially reduce the volume of savings, and a further question whether any such reduction of savings would deprive society of any effective social productive power it would otherwise enjoy, or whether it would merely reduce the waste of surplus capacity which afflicts most industries. Be that as it may, while the business system of incentives undoubtedly calls forth large amounts of efforts and resources which would not come without some incentive, nevertheless it seems to be decidedly wasteful about it. And the public has a vital interest in keeping this waste down to a minimum.

Then there are the human wrecks that the business machine leaves by the wayside, and for whom no one seems to be responsible. "Their own fault," says the extreme individualist. They are the failures, the inefficient or improvident, or the victims of others' improvidence. Perhaps the father should have insured his life before he went into the mine, though miners' wages are not large enough or steady enough to furnish any reliable surplus above immediate physical necessities. Many of these drifters are mentally subnormal. Many of them are sick physically; others are sick mentally and morally of contagions that breed in the darker byways of industrialism. And many of them are not sick at all, though deplorably lacking in the "economic virtues" of the individualist's ideal; they have simply accepted the philosophy of casual labor, which is the kind of labor which the business system offers them and which many of them must take, if they are to take anything at all. It is not the best philosophy—for one who can achieve a more solid position than that of the casual laborer. But the employer who offers casual work should be the last to condemn the philosophy that goes with it. And for that matter what right have any of us to do so, we who ride on the railroads the casual laborer built and are fed with the wheat he harvested?

In order to assert the responsibility of industry for such things, there is no need of denying the responsibility of the individual. The onus is so clearly joint. If either the individual or the industry were different, the result would presumably be different. It is enough here to show that there is a responsibility traceable to industry, to which the individualistic theory is totally blind. It does not ask what the full costs of employment were to the employee or how much of his life went into his employer's service, but only what compensation he agreed to accept.

And so we could go on indefinitely, but there is no need. The case is strong enough and to spare already. For we are not trying now to decide whether private business is utterly bad and communism the only true program, but merely whether business is essentially a thing of private concern only, or whether it is through and through a matter of public interest. We have been looking for the social stake in private business, and we have found it. The individualistic system of checks and balances, by which it seeks to harness private greed, clearly leaves many and important public interests unprotected or unaccounted for. The effect which business has upon these interests cannot be treated as a matter of purely private concern. To do so would mean ignoring the greatest dangers which threaten our social structure. Without a wise handling of these issues, industrialism may easily collapse.

5. AN APPRAISAL

In attempting to appraise these conflicting views, the most general statement that can be made appears to be that each side is for the most part right in so far as it is pointing out the imperfections of the other's case. The effects of business transactions are not limited to the parties directly engaged in them; and therefore they cannot properly be regarded as simply an exercise by those parties of their "natural rights." They can be justified only in so far as they form a part of the most just, workable, and effective system humanly available for organizing the work of creating wealth and distributing it.

At almost every point the business system lacks some of the conditions necessary to the satisfactory performance of its functions, even if we set a standard far short of theoretical perfection. Judged by this standard, a variety of public interests exist throughout the structure of industry. But when we look at the corresponding imperfections of our systems of control, we must recognize that many of these public interests are matters which we are not prepared to make immediately effective. They remain matters of public interest and will remain so, as long as our system of control appears susceptible of improvement;

but it is not the part of wisdom to attempt to deal with them immaturely and hastily. The general case, then, must be decided in favor of the advocates of public interest, with the large and important reservation that this does not justify any and all extensions of public control over any and all imperfect aspects of private business.

In addition to the arguments already brought out, there is a matter of fundamental concepts which deserves some serious attention. The definition of production adopted by traditional economics has been an unduly narrow one, lending itself to the view that production can safely be treated as a private affair, whereas a more adequate definition would include aspects of which this is obviously not true, or at least not to be taken for granted. Production has been defined as the making of goods (or utilities) to gratify existing wants. Viewed thus, it appears as something constructive, always adding to the total social dividend, neutral as between different wants or different persons, involving in itself no conflicts of interest and not responsible for unequal opportunity, unjust distribution, waste, or parasitism. Demand is there, and the natural resources are there with which to satisfy it, though in limited amount. Production uses the materials to satisfy the demands in proportion to their urgency, and if some do not get enough, that is due to causes for which production itself is not responsible. It is chiefly because there is not enough to go around. But production does its best to remedy this, since under competition the producer cannot gain by reducing or withholding his services, as he could under monopoly, but can only increase his own income by increasing the sum total of goods and resulting gratifications for the consumers. Actually, this conception presents only one aspect of production, and it is the one aspect of which these things could be said, and then only on condition that the other aspects are properly taken care of. What are these other aspects?

Production actually involves not only the making of goods to gratify existing wants, but also the creation and guidance of demand, the whole process of bargaining and negotiation by which the terms of division are settled, and the underlying function of defining and enforcing rights of person and property, which determines to just what extent business can be parasitic and still remain legal. And in a more fundamental way still, the individual is so molded in body, mind, and character by his economic activities and relations, stimuli and disabilities, freedoms and servitudes, that industry can truly be said to make the men and women who work in it no less truly than the commodities it turns out for the market. These human effects of industry are, in the long run, its most important products, and yet, as we have seen, the demand for this class of product is very inadequately expressed in the bargainings of the industrial market. These different aspects of industry are, moreover, not separate things but interdependent. Industry as a molder of character cannot be adequately studied apart from the question whether the quota of material goods it furnishes spells privation, comfort, or luxury. And its success as an instrument for turning out goods is conditioned at every point by its effect on the workers, as well as by all the other features which have been suggested in this list of essential characteristics.

Now either these other features all involve a contest over the division of the existing stock of wealth, or the control over it, wherein one gains to just the extent that someone else loses; or else they undertake to rule men's wants instead of merely serving them; or both, as in the struggle of competing advertisers for the consumer's dollar. Such processes cannot be justified except by determining whether the ultimate outcome is just and good or not. And since the industrial process of production stands ready to serve the winner of these struggles, whoever he may be, therefore, to just the extent that the outcome of the struggles proves to be unjust, production itself, neutral though it tries to be, "takes sides" and is perverted thereby.

A legal system which cannot maintain a fair degree of order is so obviously crippling to economic production that we take for granted a minimum of order as an absolute necessity and are ready to tolerate a system full of misfits and anachronisms as vastly more productive than none at all. But that is only a beginning, and must not blind us to the fact that the further improvement of the system can bring further vast increases in its economic effectiveness. Again, the concentration of effort on mere negotiation is so wasteful that, in order to bring the work of merchandising to even its present stage of effectiveness, it was absolutely necessary to do away with the old-fashioned personal dickering which still prevails in nonindustrial countries and substitute something approaching a "one-price system," which eliminates at a stroke the most clearly unproductive part of this whole process of negotiation and makes large-scale and efficient selling at least possible. But that, again, is only a beginning, and the market is still full of bargainings which serve to bring gain to some at the expense of others without making any contribution to the great general function which bargaining subserves; and these bargainings command high premiums.

And this function, the organizing of supply to meet and serve demand, is wasteful and far short of its possible effectiveness for lack of the best collective devices for bringing supply and demand together, including machinery for information, communication, and fair competition. Its effectiveness is conditioned by these things and in turn conditions the material output of goods, for a maladjustment of demand and supply means idle factories, and an efficient factory with plant and labor idle is not so good as an inefficient one at work. And so it goes. The reader's own experience will supply him with abundant illustrations of the interdependence of all these aspects of production, each conditioning the effectiveness of the others.

To just the extent that the advertiser of patent medicines prevails over the dignified professional silence of the responsible and competent medical practitioner, so far perfectly innocent chemical elements are perverted to the ruination of the constitutions of people whose chief offense is that they feel that they cannot afford the doctor, and choose the less expensive substitute. To just the extent that the system of inheritance needlessly perpetuates and increases our too great inequality of wealth, so far it causes perfectly innocent labor to take perfectly harmless building materials, capable of providing separate four-room apartments for a dozen or twenty families who now are forced to "double up" in that scanty accommodation; and out of these materials to build instead a third or fourth country estate for a family which will make little use of it because their others are already more than ample for even their most overgrown desires. If the particular materials are not literally diverted, there will be a series of shiftings, coming to the same result in the end. Thus the neutral and inherently serviceable work of physical production is stultified and perverted by failures of justice in the complementary parts of the great joint process. It does not stand alone.

What of the individual who is the center of this whole system, both as active force and as ultimate beneficiary? Modern intelligence tests cast serious doubts on his competence and reveal unmistakably the presence of large percentages of various grades of deficiency and arrested mental development among the supposedly normal population, those who must bear the responsibility for their own support and commonly for that of their families. So much can be said, even without taking at their face value the particular tests and ratings now in vogue. And normal individuals are helpless before the great upheavals of modern industry. For many such individuals, the task of maintaining a livelihood is beyond their powers.

But the most powerful individuals in modern industry are corporations: not persons at all, except by legal courtesy, but huge associations. They act, of course, through real persons who are their agents, officials, or employees. Presumably a corporation follows its own interests precisely as a single individual would do, but why? If individuals are by nature so devoted to their personal interests that they cannot be trusted to manage their affairs as a collective enterprise (as individualism assumes, and with considerable reason), why will not the agents, officials, and employees follow their personal interests at the expense of the corporation? The answer is that they frequently do, and that the maintenance of integrity in our corporate business organizations is one of the fields of public interest and action in modern industry. To this extent all corporate industry is "affected with a public interest."

And, lastly, the individual is not quite so independent in his liberty to bargain or not to bargain as the individualist theory supposes. If every person had a tolerable living assured, whether or not he accepted a given offer or entered into a given bargain, then it would be hard indeed to exploit him under the guise of free exchange. But we members of modern society are born under compulsion to exchange if we are to live. We cannot maintain ourselves in isolation. Even the dweller in the Canadian wilderness sells furs, buys guns and traps, and awaits the coming of the yearly "flour brigade." The resource we have to fall back on if we refuse one person's offer is some other person's offer, and the practical worth of this resource depends on competition. But even where competition exists, it is not always easy for a given individual to take advantage of it. Knowledge of the competitive offers does not come of itself, and an employee may well be slow to seek a new job if that means moving his family to a new home and sacrificing any seniority he may have gained with his present employer. The typical individualist likes to see workers own their own homes, but the system also requires them to better their positions by using the leverage of competition between employers; and the two do not always go together.

So labor bargains collectively, and here a new public interest arises, for labor can be monopolistic as well as employers, and the new test of bargaining strength is likely to mean a long stoppage of an industry on which the public depends. This is one of the new forms of public interest in industry, and one of the most perplexing.

6. CONCLUSION

But we must not try to anticipate all the problems with which this book is to deal. It is sufficiently clear that industry is essentially a matter of public concern, and that the stake which the public has in its processes is not adequately protected by the safeguards which individualism affords. Thus society has ample ground for interfering, wherever it sees its interests clearly and can devise appropriate and effective means to safeguard or to promote them. This last proviso represents perhaps the chief limit on the proper field of public action. Many common interests are left at the mercy of individualism in sheer default of any clear social judgment or effective social policy. Society does not know what it wants or cannot devise means that will secure it.

With respect to our greatest present evil—depression—there is no doubt as to what we want. We want reasonably steady and full operation of industry, with jobs for all who deserve them. The difficulty is that we do not know how to get this without abolishing the system of private business altogether. In the face of such a dilemma the usual course in the past has been to let individualism hold the field, this being the line of least resistance and justified as being the lesser evil and the safer line of policy. In 1933, however, this course came to seem no longer safe, and the emergency too urgent to wait for prolonged expert inquiry, useful as that often is. In this hard case, the government adopted a frankly experimental policy, recognizing the likelihood of some mistakes. In meeting this most baffling problem, some experimentation appears unavoidable, preferably guided by as much expert inquiry as conditions permit. This course may now be the lesser danger; but nothing can make it wholly safe. Such "experiments" are not like those of science, and the results often remain highly controversial. For the needed measure of light, we must probably look to a course of social research and social education which may be a matter of generations.

REFERENCES FOR FURTHER READING

CLARK, J. B., *Essentials of Economic Theory*, Chap. xxx.
CLAY, HENRY, *Economics for the General Reader*, Chap. xxii.
COOLEY, *Social Process*, Chaps. xvi, xxvi–xxviii.
FEDERATED ENGINEERING SOCIETIES, *Waste in Industry*.
HAMILTON, W. H., *Current Economic Problems* (3d ed.), Chap. i *E*, Chap. iv *A*, *B*.
HOBSON, JOHN A., *Work and Wealth*, Chaps. v, vii–ix.
KELLEY, FLORENCE, *Modern Industry*.
MARSHALL, L. C., *Readings in Industrial Society*, Chaps. i *c*, iv *c*.
SKELTON, *Socialism*, Chaps. ii, iii.
SUMNER, WILLIAM G., *Protectionism*, Secs. 44, 123–127.
———, *The Challenge of Facts*, "Reply to a Socialist."
TAWNEY, *The Acquisitive Society*, Chaps. iii–v, ix.

CHAPTER IV

PURPOSES OF SOCIAL CONTROL

1. PURPOSES EXPRESSED IN ACTUAL MEASURES

It is characteristic of modern social control of business, in a country of prevailingly democratic and humanitarian character, that it is directed to a rather disconnected series of purposes, rather than governed by an integrated and coherent picture of an ideal economic society. In this it is different from the policies of dictatorships and thoroughgoing militaristic states generally. They know what they want and set out to get it. It is otherwise with the democratic state of individualistic traditions. In the main, it does not know what it wants, except to give its millions of citizens a chance to get whatever they may severally want, without in general attempting to dictate what that shall be. Control is likely to become a piecemeal matter, dealing with one particular felt evil after another, and directed toward alleviating a succession of specific sore spots. The result is a joint product of the pressure of particular group or class interests and the general underlying ideals or attitudes of the community, with the community attitudes commonly playing a passive or permissive rôle, umpiring between the various interests and deciding which shall have their way. One underlying predisposition or purpose, if one may call it that, has been to interfere with free exchange as little as felt needs would permit. This predisposition, needless to say, is weakening.

The more obvious general purposes of control under different systems have been briefly indicated in the discussion of the development of control. Many particular purposes appear clearly on the face of specific policies. The chief original purpose of the protective tariff was to stimulate the growth of manufactures which would ultimately be able to stand on their own feet; now it has become a permanent measure of defense for existing industries against foreign competition. The purpose of public-utilities commissions is to protect the public interests—mainly those of consumers—in cases of "natural monopoly."

51

Policy toward trusts aims to maintain free and fair competition, where-ever possible. The concept of monopoly in the field of labor is less clear, and the public purpose with respect to it more ambiguous. In the early days of the factory system, trade unions were banned as conspiracies; now the right of labor to organize and bargain collectively through representatives of its own choosing is being actively protected by the National Labor Relations Board under the Wagner Act. This change registers both an increase in the political power of labor and a feeling on the part of the disinterested or humane public that labor suffers undue disadvantage in bargaining with employers, and that the state should exert some influence to redress the balance. Only such a feeling could justify an act which is in its terms one-sided in favor of labor. The same combination of factors presumably explains why labor practices are permitted, the formal counterpart of which, on the part of business, would bring prompt prosecution under the anti-trust laws. There is a feeling that formal legal equality means unequal economic power, and that this needs some compensating offset.

Other measures evidence a desire for safe work places, safe and sanitary homes, compensation for industrial accidents, the abolition of child labor, a limit on injuriously long hours of labor, and a minimum standard of wages, intended to raise wages at the bottom fringe, where they are inhumanly low; and with regard also to the ability of the industry to pay the wages fixed.

Pure food and drug acts protect consumers' interests by prohibiting some peculiarly harmful goods and requiring informative labeling on others, while greater accuracy in advertising is also being sought. Conservation policies seek to protect future generations from being impoverished by wasteful use of natural resources in the present. Soil conservation, most recently added to the list, has long been an urgent need. Purposes of banking control have developed in a significant way. Starting with the aim of preserving the redeemability of notes issued by individual banks, it went on to protecting general banking solvency, first via individual banks and then, as the need developed, to the meeting of financial crises and the prevention of banking panics through collective organization (the Federal Reserve System). This instrument soon acquired the more far-reaching purpose of controlling or mitigating booms and depressions in industry at large. Policies adopted by Herbert Hoover as Secretary of Commerce under President Coolidge looked toward reducing wastes in industry and succeeded in promoting some voluntary standardization of industrial products.

One purpose which overshadows the economies of some countries has never made much impression on ours, namely, economic preparedness for war. For this we may thank the accidents of geography, our relatively high degree of natural self-sufficiency, and the wealth which permits us easily to afford the luxury of a navy stronger than that of any probable enemy. Considerations of military strategy have not, so far as the general observer can judge, entered into the location of railways and industries. There is some advocacy of nationalizing the munitions industries, not as a measure of preparedness, but for the purpose of removing a private economic interest which stands to profit by war. This opposition includes the sale of munitions to other warring countries. The War Department has its plans for economic mobilization in case of war, governed largely by the defects of our impromptu mobilization of 1917; but these hardly enter into the general national consciousness. As far as war enters into our scheme of national purposes, the dominant motive is the wish to avoid it.

If these heterogeneous purposes can be summed up in any general ideal of a goal of policy, it would seem to be that of an economic system adapted to serving the interests and the most definitely felt needs of the masses of the people, and one in which free exchange is so directed as to be capable of serving these interests and needs reasonably well, as far as they may be felt and expressed. But there has been no very definite integrated picture of the nature of a "good life" for the masses, which the economic system should promote. In that respect, our system has been that of a nation which does not, as a nation, know what it wants. And this is a very natural characteristic of systems dominated by democratic principles.

2. THE PRESENT CRISIS

This indefiniteness of our economic objectives was radically changed by the crisis which culminated in 1933. This crisis contributed certain very definite and dominant purposes, by depriving us of something of which we thought we were assured, namely, full operation of industry, a large national dividend, and an adequate supply of jobs. Since then, as a nation, we have known what we wanted: we wanted these things of which we had been deprived; or, failing that, we wanted the jobless assured of an income as of right, without the stigma of charity. We also wanted first aid applied to definitely sick industries. Far-reaching ideals of a good life can wait until our lack of these essential features of it has become less urgent. And preferences as to the type of political and economic organization are likely to give way somewhat to the search for a system which will at least hold together and work.

We want democracy, and we hold that decentralized power is at least an important adjunct of it. Yet since the adoption of the Federal

Constitution we have been moving toward greater centralization, under pressure of the things government has had to do. And it is clear that decentralized democracy, even to the extent that we had it in 1929, cannot easily be adapted to deal with the present dominant problem. With reference to depressions, it is peculiarly true that the nation is one economic unit. Some hold that under this same pressure we are rapidly moving toward dictatorship; and some claim that the present problem calls for such a basic overhauling of our economic system as requires time to show substantial results and cannot be successfully carried out by any administration which must satisfy its constituents at the next biennial election or be turned out of power. These are serious questions; and no easy answer can be given; but the coming generation must at least work out some sort of adjustment.

In the meantime, it will still be well to pay some attention to the underlying values which are destined to be affected by the current struggle, even though we may not be free to shape our course toward them as single-mindedly as we should like.

3. IMPLICATIONS OF DEMOCRACY

The term "democracy" will be used here, as it is being generally used nowadays, to signify rule by popular will, rather than any one specific form in which this rule may be organized. It is threatened now from two sides: by radicals who feel that a dictatorship by an organized proletarian minority is the only way to bring about the revolution that is needed to organize a society that will give the good things of life to the masses; and by conservatives who feel that organized repression is the only way to maintain an ordered society in the face of destructive discontent. Both rest on the idea that the masses are not competent to formulate and pursue their own ideals and aspirations.

Is this true? The first requirement of successful democracy is a competent and responsible people. Can this requirement be met? Is it possible to give everyone the education which is necessary to meet the terribly exacting demands of real democratic organization in the modern Great Society? Would such education prove an unattainable ideal, and would the realized results merely be to create demands for more of the good things of life than industry can supply and doom the masses to destructive discontent? Can industry do no better for the masses than to offer them some modernized equivalent of the Roman "bread and circuses"? If so, we may expect a corresponding outcome, a downfall paralleling that of the Roman Empire.

The masses can organize and they can achieve, slowly and painfully, to be sure, whatever education they demand. The only immovable limit will be the capacity of their minds to absorb the results of education and experience. Would that scientists could prove to us whether we are or are not breeding out the types most capable of education and filling up the ranks with types whose innate mental capacity is not equal to the needs of modern democracy! At present that is a matter of conjecture, and scientists are disputing what the innate qualities are. No race can succeed in the struggle for civilization whose institutions promote a kind of breeding selection which multiplies the really inferior biological types at the expense of the superior; this is the unforgivable biological sin. And as fast as we discover demonstrably inferior biological types, we shall have to face the thorny question of controlling their propagation. But until the evidence is clear, we had best pin our faith to education in the broadest sense and of the broadest kind.

This means self-education more than instruction and includes all the factors of environment which may serve to develop intelligence. And a good education need not spoil men for being good laborers, though it may spoil them for the rôle of acquiescent members of a submerged class. The feeling of incongruity between manual labor and education is largely a legacy from the aristocratic background of our traditional higher education. No one is proposing to send all laborers through the present type of college, or to teach them the accomplishments of the idle rich. But a knowledge, for example, of history, economics, and politics is needed by all. It should, of course, be fundamentally the same for all—not one economics for one class and another for other classes. That way lies the disruption of society. And this requirement may be difficult to fulfill until we have a society which treats the various classes even-handedly enough so that a really impartial economics or history can gain general acceptance. If this is possible, it should make people better cooperators and hence better workmen, able to take a more constructive and responsible part in the evolution of industry. And this is the key to the reality of democracy.

What, then, does democracy mean, especially in the social and economic realms? It is made up of self-government, equal opportunity, absence of privilege, and the ranking of men according to personal desert or personal achievement; but these ideas themselves need a deal of defining. Furthermore, democracy reaches into many fields—political, economic, social, and intellectual—and has various aspects within each of these fields. By examining some of these aspects we may be led to a clearer judgment as to what things are essential.

What, for instance, does self-government mean in industry? Presumably it should mean that the "boss" should be elected, but how and by whom? In a sense, if he is to succeed, he must be elected by his customers to serve them, his first start in business amounting to no more than nomination. Should such election be by the customers or by the workers, and should either group control what corresponds to the nominating machinery? The answer may depend on what we regard as the more important product of industry, goods or men. Giving control to the customer is clearly the thing if goods are the most vital product. But suppose men are; suppose quality of activity means more than quantity of product. Then the answer is not so clear, for letting the workman choose his boss may be the very poorest way to insure that his job shall be what he needs for his fullest development. The average worker is not ready for such heavy responsibility and would abuse it, as witness the fact that schemes of "producers' cooperation" have very seldom succeeded. Experiments persist, however, and men do learn by them, so that there may sometime be a different story to tell.

Another phase of self-government is the vote, not on men, but on measures: a direct voice in what is to be done. Without discussing all the phases of this or all the difficulties in the way, it seems clear that some measure of this kind of self-government is becoming a necessary thing in modern industry. In simpler conditions, personal contact with the right kind of boss was enough to fill the need, but in large-scale industry it must be planned and provided for in the constitution of the shop. Should labor be admitted to the financial councils and have a voice on questions of production, buying and selling policy, or merely on matters of shop conditions, employment policy, etc.? Only experiment will tell, but there are obvious gains in having labor a participant in the broadest questions of economic policy, if it can be done successfully. Organized labor has, in many quarters, so much strength that the results cannot be good without corresponding responsibilities.

Another fundamental of democracy is the absence of social barriers or castes. People must be free to rise (or sink) from one class to another, preferably according to their deserts, and in any case according to their personal performance. Furthermore, members of different classes must be able, somehow, to mingle on a common footing, not in an artificial attempt to ignore real differences, but on a natural basis of genuine partnership in the community. There must be at least fairly equal opportunity to win whatever prizes the system has to offer, but this alone might prove to be utterly meaningless if, for instance, there were twenty persons almost equally deserving of prizes and only two prizes to be distributed. In other words, to make this substance rather than shadow, there must be some fair relation between the prizes and the relative deserts of those who win them or lose them. This applies not merely to the number of the prizes, blanks, and penalties, but to their size as well. One of the most obvious violations of this standard occurs when an industrial depression decrees that a certain percentage of the employees in a given shop are to be laid off. Even if the least efficient are picked, there is no ground for saying that their inefficiency was just serious enough to deserve precisely this penalty. If everyone had been 5 per cent more efficient, the result would have been no better, and the workers' increased deserving would have gained them nothing.

Another requirement of democracy, already noted, is a considerable amount of decentralization, since otherwise real self-government is lost in the grindings of too large and too impersonal a machine, working at too great distances. Another thing which some thinkers have set up as a requirement is an underlying right of revolution, in case the machinery of government becomes so completely the property of a single group that the general will cannot dislodge it in the ways regularly provided. On this highly delicate point two things can be confidently stated. This does not justify revolution by a minority, which is the kind most threatening today. And of our modern republics, those which make freest use of this right of revolution are not the most democratically governed, to say nothing of other qualities by which a government may be judged. There are, of course, two interpretations of this, one being simply that revolutions are most frequent where provocation is greatest. The other interpretation, which contains more of truth, is that the habit of appealing to force is itself hostile to the foundations on which a genuine rule of the majority must rest.

For one of the most essential of these foundation stones of democracy is a willingness to abide by the results of "due process of law" as long as is humanly possible, and a saving imperturbability which is not easily stampeded. Back of this lie an absence of fear and distrust and a spirit of generosity and mutual confidence which is strong enough to stand the strain involved in readjusting ancient rights. This means that people must be able to endure changes that sometimes do them wrong, as judged by those standards they have been brought up to revere and accept without question. This kind of population and this cohesive stability of the popular mind are the last and most fundamental requirements of successful democracy. Without this there can be no "consent of the governed," no matter how good are the vehicles for ascertaining the will of the majority. Some people never consent to anything, and this disease cannot be cured merely by preaching mutual confidence between classes. Such confidence must be earned by both sides, and earned not once, but endlessly. Only thus can democracy trust itself to make use of the knowledge of the specialists; only thus can it be competent and intelligent.

4. INDIVIDUAL DESIRES *VS.* GROUP WELFARE

Having set up a scheme of organization consistent with the requirements of democracy, what shall we try to do with it? What purposes shall we set before us as goals toward which an intelligent people ought to strive? A democracy will naturally set for itself the standard of the good of the greatest number, or the maximum good where each person counts as much as every other. To this test it will subject the dogmas of national power or class interest which dominate the "ideologies" of modern dictatorships—and especially the revealing forms they take in actual policy. The democratic mind is certain to scrutinize such proceedings, asking inconvenient questions as to their necessity or their usefulness to the common people. As a result, many people reach the conclusion that "national interests" are always and solely a cloak for the selfish material interests of particular classes or the aspirations of small groups and refuse to support anything which does not further the corresponding present material interests of the masses.

This represents a wrong scale of social values, only less wrong than that against which it protests. The feeling men have for being members of a strong and respected group represents a real value, in spite of having been perverted and used as a cloak for the ambitious designs of autocrats, bureaucrats, or militarists. And the democratic individualism which serves so effectually to puncture this camouflage is not the final word. In discrediting all patriotic fictions which the logic of mass interest cannot easily corroborate, real values may be sacrificed which the experience of the race approves.

For the ultimate standard is not the pleasure nor even the welfare of persons now on earth; it is posterity. In calculating the "good of the greatest number," posterity outnumbers the present generation many times. And the good of posterity is definitely out of harmony with a disposition on the part of the present generation to calculate and follow their present material welfare too closely. Those who carry this to its extreme too often do not have any posterity at all.

Natural selection promoted the ends of posterity at the cost of untold suffering to the living. Now that we control natural selection, we must learn to care for the needs of posterity deliberately, something we have hardly begun to do as yet. On the other hand, posterity does not demand the sacrifice of the really essential interests of those now on earth, for the very adequate reason that it is only through us that posterity can ever come into being at all. If we are not sound, then posterity is threatened. But it is quality that counts, not quantity. It is not everyone in the present generation who is vital to posterity, but some unknown quota of us—perhaps even a small minority—who will hand on something of value. It may be physical offspring, or it may be a heritage of ideas or tools, of ideals or traditions. The world has been strangely careless of perpetuating the physical descent of those who have left an outstanding mental or spiritual heritage. In any case, the present individual is of value, not so much in his own right as in his role of a vehicle for posterity. Viewed from this standpoint, many of the things we most cherish dwindle into relative insignificance, and things we tend to neglect loom large.

5. THE DESIRABLE HUMAN TYPE

But what kind of values should we try to preserve for posterity? It is plain at the start that externals are wholly secondary and personal qualities are everything. Possessions mean nothing unless they mean a better human type. And the desirable type is defined, not in terms of enjoyments received, but in terms of activities engaged in and capacities developed, of sound bodies, sound minds, moral stability, stamina, and social sympathies.[1] Incidentally, this sort of development makes for happiness, which seems to be best attained as a by-product of the pursuit of other ends. Men should develop as many of their capacities as possible. Some, such as fighting and sex, cannot in the nature of social living be indulged without restraint, and these should be diverted into harmless channels. For our impulses have a very elastic capacity for finding substitute outlets, other than literal gratification, which save the individual from the internal strains which accompany the complete balking of any of the more general and fundamental impulses or groups of impulses. In order to bring this about, we need to know human nature better than we know it now, and especially to learn what kinds of "balking" produce harmful results, and what are the possibilities and limits of substitute outlets.

6. OTHER GENERAL OBJECTIVES

How are we to translate these ideals into a definite program in a world already quite fully occupied with getting its daily living and staving off its daily perils? With democracy as a governing aim, it is hard to make the other ends at all specific without inviting the charge of attempting to prescribe in advance things which the people must be left to settle for themselves. What we can do here is to point out some

[1] See, for instance, Dewey and Tufts's *Ethics*, in which this is the dominant standard of valuation.

of the general purposes to which most people already subscribe, at least nominally, and give them as much definiteness of meaning as possible. Where there are conflicts of standards, we must recognize that fact and try to exhibit clearly what issues these conflicts involve.

Another task is to develop the possible agencies which a really democratic social control will need to use. The political state is clumsy, rather inhuman, and unduly centralized. More mobile agencies exist in every walk of life: neighborhood, trade, and professional organizations. They control the individual in the interest of a group, but the group is too narrow and its interests are too often in conflict with those of the community at large. These agencies must be used, but they must also be socialized; real organs of common action must be built of the raw materials available in trade unions, employers' organizations, cooperatives, professional associations, and the like. And here is work enough to keep everybody busy for some generations to come. This, along with education, should go far to care for one other vital need: the development of a well-informed and healthy public opinion.

With these first general aims of policy there can be no serious disagreement; but as we go on to others, we shall find that they do not easily harmonize with one another, and that this lack of harmony becomes more evident precisely in proportion as we succeed in giving these general purposes the definiteness which goes with a specific program. The dominant ones may be summed up for convenience under eight heads. They include "efficiency" and abundance, liberty, "equality of opportunity," equitable distribution of goods, leisure, security, the development of the individual, and "progress," or a sense of improving conditions. As far as these conflict with one another, the result must be in the nature of a compromise or an attempted reconciliation. Among the things difficult to harmonize are liberty and security, for reasons obvious to any observer of motor traffic and no less evident to students of business cycles; also liberty and collective efficiency; while efficiency in modern large-scale industry is not easy to reconcile with either the development of the mass of individuals or an equitable distribution of income.

As for reconciling efficiency with liberty, the simplest way would be to give each person that kind of control we call "ownership" over the land and materials he works on and the tools he works with. He would need to be deprived of the liberty of parting with this ownership, but otherwise he could be left to produce as he saw fit. If production had never developed past the handicraft stage, we might possibly, some day, achieve this ideal and with it attain democracy, equality, and fraternity. But the efficiency of large-scale production has rendered this forever impossible as a universal goal and has put in its place the freedom of some to associate themselves together for the purpose of owning and administering (through some form of delegated agency) the equipment and goods on which other people work. This makes for inefficiency in so far as the hired workers do not put their hearts into their work as the proprietor-worker does. But this element of inefficiency is so far outweighed by the economies of machines and massed organization that no one thinks of it for a moment as an argument against organizing business in large corporations; merely as an irritating and unwelcome circumstance for which one blames the spirit of the times. Thus liberty and efficiency are reconciled by giving free rein to the investors' liberty to unite many investments under the control of a few of their number in an organization which becomes the "employer"; the employer's liberty to employ both capital and labor on the most profitable terms; and the empty-handed man's liberty to choose his employment from among these employer organizations.

This way of reconciling liberty and efficiency has resulted in new and troublesome kinds of insecurity and in vast inequalities, including a considerable inequality of opportunity. The insecurities of modern industry include industrial accidents and diseases, the danger of bankruptcy which constantly threatens small tradesmen and small employers, and the chronic unemployment which arises from the business cycle as well as from the seasonal and casual nature of much of our modern work, and which falls with concentrated force on certain classes of laborers.

From all this it does not follow that life is growing less secure, for the world has vastly reduced the older insecurities of famine, pestilence, and (in democratic countries) the irresponsible tyrannies of the ruling classes. The trouble is subtler than that; it is a change in the quality of insecurity. Nor does it follow that all insecurity is a bad thing; witness the fact that insecurity of some sort is of the essence of adventure, and that the lack of adventure is one of the most widespread complaints against the life to which most of us are condemned in modern society. To some extent, the trouble is with the essentially contradictory nature of man himself.

What, then, is the right kind of insecurity? In general, it is the kind which invites us to do something about it and gives us a chance to make that something effective. If it arises from human conflicts, they should be conflicts of equals or something approaching it. Exposure to the arbitrary operation of overpowering forces for which other persons are in any way responsible—this is a destructive type of insecurity, not a constructive type. For this reason the insecurities resulting from large-scale production have a destructive element in them, especially the business cycle. Even among the more constructive risks, it is only natural to urge that the perils with which one gambles shall not involve an undue destruction of life, limb, health, or economic independence—not more than the adventurous spirit of the individual really demands. On the whole, while there is no effective demand for absolute security, there are many chances to eliminate risks which serve no useful or constructive purpose, and the benefits to be gained will easily justify some moderate encroachments on individual freedom of the formal sort. The result will be more real freedom in the end.

As for inequality of income, nearly everyone is agreed that some inequality is a good thing, but that at present we have altogether too much, while few would be able to agree as to what constitutes an equitable system. The aristocrat, who is still heard at times, is probably right in his claim that it is better that some should have the means of a really generous existence, even if there is not enough to provide it for everyone. But this could rarely be used as an argument for incomes in excess of, let us say, $20,000 per year. On the other hand, we are effectually committed to the principle that there should be some sort of minimum based on human needs, and that if there is to be a competitive struggle it should take place above this minimum, and not below it. Some would introduce the principle of needs into the regular payment of wages, giving the man with a dependent family more pay than the bachelor for the same grade of work.[1]

The basis of the individualistic system of distribution is to pay according to the commercial worth of one's contribution to the earnings of some business, contribution being made either in person or by lending the use of one's property. While the majority acquiesce in this general plan, nearly all agree that the largest rewards it provides are needlessly large; that many important contributions have little or no commercial value and hence get small rewards; and that it is fair to reduce the inequalities by progressive taxation. Remedies are limited, however, by the general reluctance to give up the system of private enterprise and private bargaining.

Something may be done by utilizing the laws of supply and demand. By providing a well-balanced assortment of educational opportunity, making managerial brains more plentiful and mere "hands" scarcer, class differences in incomes can be somewhat reduced, and this is well worth attempting.[2] But nothing can prevent certain strategic occupa-

[1] See Paul H. Douglas, "Factors in Wage Determinations," *Amer. Econ. Rev.*, Sup., XIII (March, 1923).

[2] See T. N. Carver, "Some Probable Results of a Balanced Economic System," *Amer. Econ. Rev.*, Sup., X (March, 1920) 69–77.

tions, such as banking, industrial management, law and, to an extent, medicine from exhibiting tremendous differences between the winnings of the most successful and of the failures. Where one man makes or mars the efficiency of a thousand men who work under him or whose health comes under his care, or tools and materials representing a thousand men's work, differences of efficiency become a thousand times as important. The only way to prevent this from leading to great inequality of rewards is to prevent such persons from getting the full commercial value of their services, that is, to place them under some other system than that of free commercial competition. The alternative is to recapture excessive earnings through taxation, but this faces practical difficulties. To that extent individualistic liberty is inseparable from a very large degree of inequality.

These inequalities can perhaps be endured as long as they do not destroy "equality of opportunity." This phrase expresses one of our most sacred ideals and represents the only condition on which we should for a moment tolerate a régime of competitive freedom. Yet when one examines the phrase, one sees at once that there is not and never can be any such thing as complete equality of opportunity, short of collective bringing up of all children, and this democracy has not yet approved.

What, then, is the ideal we really hold by? One writer has named it "equity of opportunity" and added to it the principle of putting opportunity where it will do the most good.[1] But where will opportunity do the most good? In the hands of a few, so that they may furnish us with enlightened and effective leadership? Perhaps, but the vital question is: On what principle are the few big chances to be divided? What is called for in the twentieth century is a reasonable minimum of opportunity, open to all alike, including a chance to win more liberal opportunities by proving one's capacity to make good use of them. The world cannot afford to waste the talent which lies in the children of the undistinguished masses. This minimum of opportunity needs to be sufficient to eliminate the most insuperable handicaps, to place a reasonably successful lot within reach of all who can make good use of their opportunities, and to make it possible for distinguished ability to go to the top, whatever its start in life.

Aside from the question of opportunity, inequality is attacked by progressive taxation and by a considerable list of policies grouped under the general head of the "social minimum." The attempt is definitely made to see to it that, whatever mistakes and failures the individual may make, they shall not lay him so low as to cripple his possible

[1] See A. B. Wolfe, *The Trend of Economics*, p. 481.

powers of recovery. Consistently with this ideal, charity and social work in general are taking on the character not so much of relief as of rehabilitation.

As for the developing of the individual, this is not entirely easy to reconcile with the type of work which large-scale mechanical industry demands of its routine workers. Education can do something to help, especially self-education on the part of organized labor itself; and a great deal may be accomplished by the right kinds of recreation (which will not develop of its own accord in modern industrial cities). But the situation will not be satisfactory until industry itself comes to the realization that its most important product is men and women— the men and women who work in it and who may be learning to be good cooperators or may be degenerating into hopelessly unassimilable characters.

7. PURPOSES CALLING FOR AN INNER CHANGE IN INDUSTRY

From the standpoint of those who are impatient for far-reaching reforms, democratic gradualism has one serious weakness. It assumes that business is to go on being an affair of private self-seeking and definitely sanctions the business man in adopting this rôle and then tries to control him by external force, after it has arrayed against itself the whole power of customary business morals. Under such conditions, control is necessarily ineffective—so runs the criticism—and business remains primarily acquisitive. Any such institution is doomed unless it can somehow be saved from itself, and it can be saved only by something which will change its basic motivating character.

The one greatest social advantage of such a system is supposed to lie in the development of the individual, but does it accomplish even this end? In the first place, the development is largely confined to the favored few; and, in the second place, even if the majority were developed into successful pursuers of the dollar, this would be developing them in the wrong direction. If only we trained the individual for a better system of control, we could make that better system possible, instead of training people for the system we have and thereby making a better system virtually unattainable from the start. Since human nature has been trained to be contrary to any other system than individualism, any other system appears to be "contrary to human nature," whereas it may be merely contrary to human nurture. And the acquisitive type of business on a large scale is already proving itself to be contrary to human nature in several important respects—chiefly in failing to command the honest effort of the workers—and as a result it is in real danger.

The most important objective of any right policy is to give human nature a chance to show whatever fitness it may have for the highest and best system of control we can conceive, and the one which appeals most directly to the best motives rather than actually stunting them by placing everyone in a competitive struggle where he is virtually forced to develop a selfish attitude, whether he has it naturally or not. This calls for a system of control which begins within the individual himself, making it his main business to render efficient service, instead of leaving this to be an incidental by-product of the chase after profits. "Production for use, not for profit" must be the ruling principle of any system that hopes for permanence in the modern interdependent industry.

More specifically, the argument runs that business cannot assure full employment so long as it is so organized that it is necessarily ruled by the balance sheet. It will unavoidably at times fall into a deadlock in which output shrinks because demand has shrunk, incomes shrink because output has shrunk, and demand shrinks because incomes have shrunk. Then need for goods and power to produce them may both exist but be prevented from coming together, unless industry is so organized as to produce directly for needs and not for the balance sheet. So runs the indictment, and it has enough truth in it to challenge the most earnest consideration.

8. CAN INDUSTRY ADAPT ITSELF?

The central issue seems to be whether private industry can become an affair of "production for use and not (primarily or exclusively) for profit," together with the further and very practical question whether any other scheme would do it more successfully. "Production for use" is not unknown in private industry, and the very large money prizes often go to the man who thinks of his work first and the reward second. The obvious substitutes for private enterprise do not guarantee that selfish private interests will be abolished, or that they will not get in the way of efficient service and warp the social purpose of the organization. The political appointee may owe his first allegiance to a party organization engaged in selling promises for the purpose of staying in power, just as the business man solicits purchases for the purpose of staying in business; and the most important difference between the two may be that the industrial manager is under a quicker and surer compulsion to live up to his promises and "deliver the goods."

The change which is contemplated might be approached in three ways: by public order establishing a collectivistic system or production, by voluntary experiments in producers' and consumers' cooperation, or by progressive change in the constitution of private industry itself. For the first of these this country is clearly not ready at the present time. The second has a considerable history behind it, marked by many discouragements and much promise, especially in the field of consumers' cooperation, which has reached an enormous growth in some European countries and established an assured place for itself. The third is hardly beginning to be tried seriously. What are its possibilities?

It goes without saying that it would not do away with production for profit, or the necessity of at least avoiding losses, unless it went so far as to metamorphose private industry into something totally different. It could not positively insure full employment, but it might be accompanied by measures for mitigating business cycles and distributing their burdens more justly, which would reduce this evil to manageable proportions. Could it prevent profits from standing seriously in the way of the workers' loyalty to the industry and the industry's loyalty to the consumers whom it serves and to the public to whom it is responsible for the general results of its policies? Any attempt to answer this question is exposed to all the risks attendant upon prophecy, but there are certain elements underlying this prophecy of which one can be fairly sure.

First, if private industry does not meet this test, its tenure is insecure and its outlook for the future is dark. Second, private industry has tremendous vitality and considerable power of adapting itself when the choice is to adapt or perish. Third, if guilds or consumers' cooperation, or both, come to hold a strong and successful place in the industrial system, private industry will have to meet their competition, doing as well by its workers and its customers as the other systems do, and not allowing its morale to suffer by comparison with theirs. Fourth, the outcome will be vitally affected by any effective measures that may be taken toward reducing inequalities of wealth, controlling the business cycle, assuming a fair share of responsibility for unemployment and other similar reforms calculated to lessen the worker's distrust of the organization which employs him. Fifth, the government can accomplish something by friendly cooperation but can hardly prescribe compulsory forms of partnership between employer and workers, or between industry and consumers. Sixth, the business corporation has by no means reached its final form and ultimate development. Seventh, the essence of private enterprise lies, not in the present form of the corporation organized for profit, but in the principle of voluntary association for the furthering of legitimate economic interests. In the corporation, directive authority, financial responsibility, and profits and losses are virtually all concentrated in the hands of those who have furnished a part only—often a rather small part—of the capital used by the enterprise. But while this concentration was natural and perhaps necessary in the adventurous and irresponsible days of corporate pioneering and buccaneering, it is evident that conditions are changing. Among the symptoms are the campaign for consumer ownership of public-utility securities, the growth of standing treaties between laborers and employers which become virtually an unofficial part of the constitution of the corporation, the movement toward "partnership of labor in industry," and the increasing number of enterprises reported as having been actually handed over to employees in one way or another.[1] All these are symptoms of an unmistakable movement.

9. CONCLUSION

In all this discussion of purposes of control, one oppressive fact stands out. The goals we *need* to define and set for ourselves are long-run affairs and call for more knowledge and foresight than we have available to bring to bear, while the objectives of our actual policies are sadly shortsighted and superficial. If it were not for the power of inspired minorities, it would seem a sheer waste of time to try to settle what the more far-reaching purposes of social control ought to be. While we are wrestling with this handicap, we may perhaps take a grim sort of comfort from the fact that the human race is very hard to kill. In the end, we must never expect to be satisfied, for the simple reason that it is not in our natures. Man is the animal which is "adapted to maladaptation";[2] his aspirations outrun his performance, and his problem of adjusting himself to the results of his own inventions is as endless as the inventions themselves.

REFERENCES FOR FURTHER READING

CARVER, *Essays in Social Justice*, Chaps. i, vi, x; pp. 112–124.

CLARK, J. B., *Social Justice without Socialism*, 1914.

CLAY, HENRY, *Economics for the General Reader*, Chaps. xxiii–xxv.

COLE, G. D. H., *Economic Planning*, Chap. i, 1935.

COOLEY, *Social Process*, Chaps. xix–xxi.

CUNNINGHAM, *Growth of English Industry and Commerce*, Secs. 283–284.

HAMILTON, W. H., *Current Economic Problems*, 3d ed., Chap. i C.

HITLER, ADOLF, *My Battle* (Amer. trans.), 1937.

HOBSON, J. A., *Work and Wealth*, Chaps. i, xii, xxii.

HOUSER, J. D., *What People Want from Business*, 1938.

LIPPMANN, WALTER, *The Good Society*, pp. 352–390.

MARSHALL, L. C., *Readings in Industrial Society*, Selections 411–414.

[1] This appears often to mean salaried employees only; nevertheless, the movement is significant.

[2] See Hocking, *Human Nature and Its Remaking*, p. 214.

PIGOU, *Wealth and Welfare*, Chaps. i, ii, iv.

ROBBINS, L., *Economic Planning and International Order*, Chap. xi, 1937.

SMALL, "A Vision of Social Efficiency," *Amer. Jour. Sociol.*, XIX (1913–1914), 435.

SMART, *Second Thoughts of an Economist*, Chaps. ii–iv.

SUMNER, WILLIAM G., *Protectionism*, Secs. 44, 123–127.

TAWNEY, *The Acquisitive Society*, Chaps. vi, x, xi.

WYAND, C. S., *Economics of Consumption*, Chap. xix, 1937.

PART II

GENERAL INSTRUMENTS OF CONTROL

CHAPTER V

THE LEGAL FRAMEWORK OF ECONOMIC LIFE

1. INTRODUCTION

The great function of law is to establish and maintain the rights, duties, and liberties of men living together in society, primarily in matters which require the pronouncing of formal judgments and the backing of them up by the ultimate force of the community. It is to tell people what they *must do* and what they *must not* do, and the fruit of it, in the democratic-liberal type of society, is to establish conditions in which they *may do* whatever is essential to their welfare. If the system is to work successfully, conditions must be such that most people not only *may* but *can* do this. The law affords a framework of prescribed behavior within which the voluntary behavior shall take place. Its commands extend from things so important that life is not safe without them to things so unimportant that people are willing to do as they are told and feel no material constraint. Its proper field is that in which certainty of human behavior is worth the cost of compulsion; and this may be either because the behavior is very vital or because the cost of compulsion is very small. Often it merely affords standard forms for voluntary actions.

Law arises out of the need of settling disputes; hence its very nature is the defeating of certain interests that others may prevail. Ultimately it becomes an instrument for furthering purposes and ideals prevailing in the community, but always it faces the necessity of defeating certain interests. Dean Roscoe Pound notes four stages in the evolution of the juristic ideal of justice; first, the mere keeping of the peace; second, the maintenance of the *status quo;* third, a maximum of individual self-assertion; and, fourth, social justice.[1] The first is primitive law. Our present attempts at the control of the labor relation appear to be largely in this stage of development, though the best forms of collective bargaining represent approximations to the fourth stage. The relation of primitive law to justice or welfare is mainly involuntary; it must

[1] See "Liberty of Contract," *Yale Law Jour.*, XVIII (May, 1909), 458 ff.

conserve them to whatever extent may be necessary to maintain order and stability. Even a selfish government violates this rule at its peril. It must pay some attention to those principles which are essential to enable human beings to live together, and to this extent law is a social study whether it wants to be or not.

The second stage is the medieval age of law, in which people's customary stations in life were thought of as divinely appointed, and whatever was suitable to these stations was therefore right. The third stage is the democratic-individualistic stage, which dominated the nineteenth century. No one is born to a station in life, but all are born to an equal and absolute liberty to carve out their own stations—this in a period when the opportunities for doing that thing were unrivaled. Here the glory of the law is that it is the same for all, and there is a tendency to forget what earlier judges remembered: that in bargaining between parties of vastly unequal resources, formal equality at law does not produce an equal bargain.[1] The fourth stage, that of social justice, implies a justice based on a real study of social relations and the social consequences of its rules, rather than on a too sweeping dogma of the supreme worth of absolute liberty. It softens the ideal of maximum self-assertion to maximum self-realization, recognizing that this is cramped by undue self-assertion on the part of others and that it is best promoted by rules that are not the same for all but are differentiated according to the injuries to which people's economic position renders them liable. This differentiated justice is called for, not by the different stations to which men have supposedly been called by birth or divine decree, but chiefly by the relations they have voluntarily assumed toward others or simply by the need of differentiated functions in our complex society.

Our main inquiry will be how the law controls men in the business of getting a living, and how intimately the character and efficiency of the business system depend upon the quality and humanity of the law, the accessibility of its remedies, and the orientation it receives from the fundamental ideas underlying the whole system of jurisprudence. The law can go far to make or mar the success of the financial and industrial structure.

If this study does nothing else, it should serve to combat certain prevalent errors, fallacies, and superstitions about the relation of government to industry. Most glaring is the notion that in an individualistic system the state does nothing in the way of controlling business. Less obvious is the fallacy implied in the view that government

[1] Cf. Lord Northington's opinion in *Vernon* v. *Bethell*, 2 Eden 110, 113, cited by Pound, *op. cit.*, p. 471.

merely "protects" rights of person and property, the fallacy consisting in the implied assumption that government finds these rights ready-made. This leads to ignoring the part government and changing business practices play in defining and shaping these rights, in creating and altering them. Akin to this is the further idea that, because some sort of order and ownership are indispensable to any civilization, therefore the existing system of property rights is justified. This ignores the possibility that there may be more than one kind of orderly ownership. Common ownership is a possibility not to be ignored, while there are indefinite possible variations in the "bundle of rights" which constitutes private property. On the other hand, granting that our existing law does not embody an eternal system of "natural rights," it does not necessarily follow that it is wholly unnatural, or that natural rights, in some sense or other, have no existence. Nor does it follow, because change is necessary and inevitable, that there is no value in stability. The significance of these points will appear as the argument advances.

2. GENERAL CHARACTERISTICS OF LAW

A law is defined as a rule of action backed by that compulsory power which is an essential mark of sovereignty. Compulsion implies power capable of imposing virtually unlimited penalties. As far as this means the ultimate use of force, division of this power means divided sovereignty, and disputed division, anarchy. The state exercises formal sovereignty and is supposedly supreme as to forcible coercion. A rule implies something general in its application, not a special act for the benefit or injury of one person or one arbitrarily selected group. The general processes of law are to make known the will of the sovereign; to enforce it in the name of the whole society upon its members; to regulate the use of this compulsion so that it may be uniform rather than arbitrary, and not a respecter of persons (this is a large part of what is meant by "a government of laws and not of men"); to lend customary morality the force of compulsion where needed; and to educate this morality and to turn against newly discovered evils the force of moral reprobation that goes with illegality.

This double relation between law and morality is an interesting one.[1] The things the law forbids are prevailingly well-recognized evils which common morality has long condemned. This helps good people to develop a righteous horror of any illegality, and this can be used in turn (if it is not overworked) to transfer their moral condemnation to something they had not realized was wrong, by making it illegal.

[1] For discussion of this point see Pound, "Law and Morals," *Jour. Social Forces*, Vol. I, pp. 350, 528.

3. BRANCHES OF THE LAW AND THEIR CONFLICTS

The main sources of the law are three: custom, adjudication, and legislation, and these three sources are of coordinate importance. The law of commerce received its shape by being built upon the customs prevailing in the mercantile world. Custom also comes to have the force of law in other cases, although nowadays the court generally tries to discover some legal decision recognizing a given custom and furnishing a precedent more tangible than custom itself. However, when a dispute arises requiring interpretation of a contract on some point not specifically provided for, the court will assume that the intention was to follow the "custom of the trade" and so will give that custom the force of law.

Many persons fail to realize to what a large extent law is made by the decisions of the courts. New issues are continually coming up which are not exactly covered by existing statutes or previous decisions. In such cases the courts try to apply some recognized principle to the new situation, but in so doing they frequently develop what are really new doctrines. Thus the law evolves, and new laws are virtually made to meet new needs without any legislative action. This process, however, does little to change existing law where existing law applies, and in general it moves too slowly to meet all needs. Moreover the remedies which a court is in a position to bring to bear are largely negative in character, punitive rather than preventive and constructive. Hence legislation is needed to produce more rapid and certain results, to record the will of the people and prevent the courts from usurping sovereignty, to take action which looks to the future and is not retrospective, and to enlarge the scope and constructiveness of the remedies applied. A new doctrine of law laid down by the courts is always laid down by the very act of being applied to a particular case, and hence it is nearly always retroactive, affecting not only the case in hand, but other existing rights.[1] Such conditions make radical changes more than usually unjust and conservatism more than ordinarily advisable.

Legislation for the future is free from this difficulty and therefore can fairly take up the main burden of changing the law, leaving the courts to develop a natural professional bias toward conservatism. But when a statute is passed, the courts still have something to say. With respect to such legislation the courts in this country have three functions: to determine whether it is constitutional, to give effect to it if it

---

[1] This would not be true of court actions looking to the future. Examples would be an injunction to restrain the doing of something which is merely threatened, and a mandamus proceeding to require positive action from an officer of a corporation.

is constitutional, and to "interpret" it in the process of deciding precisely what effect it is to have in a given case. This last process is often unexpectedly far-reaching; in fact, few people realize how powerful the law of custom and court precedent is in resisting attempts to change it by legislation.[1] Outstanding cases are the changing interpretation of "combinations in restraint of trade" under the Sherman Anti-trust Act, the putting to sleep of the "long-and-short-haul" clause of the original Interstate Commerce Act, and the commodities clause of the Hepburn Act of 1910, under which railroads were forbidden to carry coal mined by themselves but continued to do so. When a law whose essential character is to establish theories different from those of the common law is "interpreted in the light of" that same common law, this means interpreting it so as to be in harmony with the common law if the meaning of words can possibly be so stretched as to bring this about (and sometimes when it cannot). Naturally, the effect is frequently to emasculate the law or limit its application to a small part of the field it was expected to cover. These same common-law doctrines are also read into the Bill of Rights of the Federal Constitution and thus become the supreme law of the land.

This judicial resistance can often be overcome by repeated efforts of the legislature, restating the law so as to overrule enfeebling interpretations, obviate constitutional objections, and—not least important—prove to the court that the legislation expresses a genuine and vital social need and not a passing whim of professional reformers or a temporary legislative majority. And it may be, on the whole, a healthy thing that movements for far-reaching change in our social and economic structure should be compelled to prove their vitality in this way. On the other hand, if genuine needs are permanently balked or their realization too long delayed, the result may be to allow discontent to accumulate until the pressure becomes dangerous and the belief spreads that our supposed government by the people is an illusion.

This friction has been responsible for a variety of proposals to limit or abolish the power of the courts to declare legislative acts unconstitutional, from Theodore Roosevelt's proposal for the "recall of judicial decisions" to Franklin D. Roosevelt's "court-packing" bill. These will be discussed later.[2] A moderate number of crucial decisions have carried by a vote of five to four, indicating that the law in the case, as law, cannot be clear and unmistakable, since eminent jurists are so evenly divided on it. Moreover in police-power cases—a very

[1] See Hoyt, "The Economic Function of the Common Law," *Jour. Polit. Econ.*, XXVI (1918), 168–199.
[2] See below, Chap. X, Sec. 5; also Sec. 5 of the present chapter.

important group, as we shall soon see—the law is such as to leave the court free to follow its judgment of the economic and social needs of the situation. In deciding whether to permit an extension of the police power or not, the court is essentially making new law, not interpreting the meaning of the written constitution. Hence the color of reason in the claim that this is a legislative function, on which the court should not have power to overrule the expressed will of the regularly constituted legislative body. These conflicts between different branches of law are among the things with which the layman has little patience.

There are various types of law. Most fundamental for English-speaking peoples is the "common law," by which is meant the general body of case law enforced by English courts of law, as distinct from those of equity, admiralty, etc. It follows old statutes and can be modified or overruled at particular points by new ones. Another important branch of the law is equity, which represents an attempt to do essential justice in cases where the regular legal tribunals and remedies for some reason fail to do so. In particular, it can substitute more effective and sweeping remedies for wrongs, and it can take notice of an expected wrong before it occurs, by the issuance of an injunction. When it was first established, equity was naturally quite free from the precedents of law, but in the course of time it has built up its own precedents and is hardening itself into them so that a second liberation may become necessary. Statute law consists of the enactments of the legislative bodies, while the law of written constitutions, in countries which enjoy their benefits, is the supreme law of the land. Be it noted that the "law of written constitutions" includes not only the instrument itself but also that more voluminous constitution which consists of the body of interpretation built up by the courts, and which is in some respects quite independent of its supposed documentary guide. We shall see what this means when we come to discuss the police power.

The law also covers a variety of subjects. Among these are property, contract, inheritance and bequest, personal rights and liberties, injuries (including torts and crimes), bankruptcy, corporations and associations, weights and measures, legal tender, and negotiable instruments. When the wide variety of relationships represented in this list of subjects is considered, and especially the many ways in which conflicts of interest might arise, it seems fair to conclude that no simple theory of law can be adequate to describe everything it does. Simple theories have been attempted, however, especially the theory of "natural rights" which has dominated English jurisprudence for over a hundred years, from the time of Blackstone nearly down to the present.

4. THE BLACKSTONE THEORY OF NATURAL RIGHTS

Blackstone's theory of natural rights was in harmony with the general trend of enlightened thought in his period, which was the end of the eighteenth century. For him there existed a natural moral law, laid down by the Creator of the universe, and it was the business of legal bodies to discover this law, declare it, and enforce it with temporal penalties. Its basis was simple: eternal justice can be attained only by observing the happiness of the indiviudal, while if the voice of justice be obeyed, individual happiness will follow.[1] And as man was endowed at creation with free will and "discernment to know good from evil," his chief natural right is the right of liberty to pursue his happiness as he will. Political or civil liberty consists of as much of this complete natural liberty as can possibly be preserved in a society; subject to the least possible restraint consistent with the general advantage, natural liberty being diminished only to increase civil liberty.

These . . . were formerly, either by inheritance or purchase, the rights of all mankind; but, in most other countries of the world being now more or less debased and destroyed, they at present may be said to remain, in a peculiar and emphatical manner, the rights of the people of England. And these may be reduced to three principal or primary articles; the right of personal security, the right of personal liberty, and the right of private property: because, as there is no known method of compulsion, or of abridging man's natural free will, but by an infringement or diminution of one or other of these important rights, the preservation of these, inviolate, may justly be said to include the preservation of our civil immunities in their largest and most extensive sense.[2]

In some respects Blackstone's theories seem surprisingly adequate today, while in other respects they appear quite obsolete. In particular, when he speaks of natural rights in the most general terms, he is referring to the benefits the individual secures from them, and he is really expressing the fundamental needs of human nature. These do not seem to have changed radically, though we may nowadays define them more broadly, and they are certainly exposed to new perils. But law as a working instrument does not deal with general human needs

[1] *Commentaries on the Laws of England* (Amer. ed.), Introduction, Sec. 2, p. 40.

[2] *Op. cit.*, Book I, Chap. 1, p. 138. A subtle fallacy lurks behind this statement. The protection of existing property rights may hamper the rights of newcomers to acquire property or may, if carried to extremes, protect the employer in abridging the personal security of his employees. Thus Blackstone's proposition *appears* to mean that individualism **protects all** essential rights, but this **appearance breaks down upon analysis.**

so much as with specific duties, wrongs, and remedies, and it is here, and especially when it comes to remedies, that Blackstone's views really are essentially obsolete. In civil cases, the well-nigh universal remedy in Blackstone is an action for damages by the injured party.

In order to see the inadequacy of this system as a basis for an entire scheme of law, one need only consider what the control of public health would amount to on this basis. The supposition would be that people would not spread infections on account of the likelihood of being sued for damages by anyone who caught a disease. The milkman would protect his milk—a fairly plausible case, since the milkman is under suspicion if a typhoid epidemic starts; but even so, the suspicion is often hard to verify. And would the yellow-fever patient, for fear of private damage suits, see to it that he did not get bitten by mosquitoes because the same insects might later bite someone else and the resulting infection be traced to him?

If this system of penalties proved ineffective, we should have to fall back on the incentive of private gain, set in motion by people who desire protection and are willing to pay for it. Suppose in a city of one hundred thousand people there are ten thousand who realize the importance of mosquito extermination and the poorest of whom are willing and able to pay one dollar a year for this protection, and suppose that the job can be done for ten thousand dollars—a favorable series of assumptions. Then we should have a number of competing mosquito exterminators offering their services—to whom and on what terms? If there are ten million mosquitoes, they might offer to destroy any number a given householder would pay for at the rate of one dollar a thousand, subject to the slight difficulty that the killing of one thousand insects is not worth one dollar to any householder; it is not worth his while to pay for anything short of the wiping out of substantially the whole ten million. Or the exterminators might canvass the whole city to get enough subscriptions to finance the entire campaign, in which case the cost of salesmanship would make the enterprise prohibitive. But if all these obstacles were overcome, still the private exterminator could not succeed without the power to restrain the liberty of private individuals—the ninety thousand who are not interested in the campaign—to keep their premises in a condition which enables mosquitoes to breed. And this can be done only by public authority, which acts without waiting to prove that the mosquitoes bred on Mr. Smith's land have conveyed malaria to Mr. Robinson, after biting Mr. Jenkins next door, who got the disease from Mr. Brown, via Mr. Jones's mosquitoes. This case seems fanciful simply because we have transported the regular methods of private business into a field where they very clearly do not belong. How large is this field? Can we generalize the principle involved?

Another typical case is the common-law doctrine (now happily obsolescent) of liability for industrial accidents.[1] Still more broadly, all novel conflicts of interests give rise to injuries for which no one can be held exactly blameworthy because they are not clearly foreseen; and we have seen that it is from just this type of injury that modern industry is most characteristically suffering.[2]

By way of protection against such injuries, the individualistic system offers the remedy of private action for damages, administered by courts which are slow to develop enlarged theories of liability under which persons are to be penalized, because they would act retroactively and thus involve real injustice. And they are governed by the general principle that there shall be no liability without fault. For the classes of injury of which we are speaking, such a remedy is clearly inadequate; it is not enough to make people refrain passively from committing any conscious wrong. There must be a deal of positive action, some of which may interfere with what used to be the legitimate scope of personal liberty, or even take some of the rights or privileges which were formerly a part of private property.

Without disputing whether security, liberty, and property are in some sense or other natural rights, it is clear that the duties and remedies which go with them are in need of a deal of revising from time to time, in order to keep up with the development of economic relationships, and that no system of specific duties and remedies can possibly embody for all time the requirements of ultimate justice. This question will be made clearer by an examination of the legal meaning of "rights" and "liberties" in general.[3]

5. THE MEANING OF "RIGHTS" AND "LIBERTIES"

What are rights in the legal sense? Property and contract are rights, or bundles of rights, but they turn out on examination to be rather complex relationships between a number of parties, involving an assortment of duties, liabilities, powers, and immunities which require a high degree of discrimination to unravel. In particular, jurists distinguish between rights in the strict sense and something else which we may call liberties. The distinction is all the harder to keep clear because our liberties (or some of them) are protected by rights, so that we "have a right to" certain of our liberties. However, if we can gain

[1] See Chap. vii, Sec. 1, below.
[2] See Chap. iii, above, and Chap. xxx, Sec. 2, below.
[3] We shall return to the search for "natural rights" in Chap. viii, Sec. 4, below.

a clear conception of these two different things, we shall have gone a long way toward understanding the difference between individualism and paternalism as economic systems, for one mark of paternalism is that it makes absolute rights out of things which individualism leaves in the realm of liberty. We shall see in a moment what this means.

Every right implies a two-sided relationship in which one party owes the other a duty and the other party benefits thereby.[1] This relationship, viewed from the standpoint of the beneficiary, is a right in the strict sense. I have rights only as far as other people have duties toward me. (The question whether, to deserve my rights or keep them, I *must fulfill reciprocal duties toward others*, is a separate issue, though, of course, a vital one.) As far as people have no duties toward me or anyone else, they are free: liberty begins where duty ends, and *vice versa*. This means that my rights set the boundaries upon others' liberties.

But to have liberty, one needs something more than mere absence of duty. If others are free to interfere, one's liberty may become well-nigh useless, and hence it must be protected by rights to noninterference on the part of other people. In common speech no distinction is made between these rights and the liberty which they protect, and such protected liberties are commonly called rights. In fact, most of the so-called rights of an individualistic economy are really protected liberties, and the duties they involve are summed up in the general negative duty of noninterference.[2] When a person speaks of a right to *do* something, as distinct from a right to *keep* or to *receive* something, he is nearly always speaking of a liberty. But not all liberties are protected, as we shall see in a moment.

Have I a right to marry or merely the liberty of marrying? To find whether I possess a right to a given thing, I must find whether anyone

[1] On this general matter see W. N. Hohfeld, "Some Fundamental Legal Conceptions as Applied in Judicial Reasoning," *Yale Law Jour.*, XXIII (1913), 16; *ibid.*, XXVI (1917), 710; "Terminology and Classification in Fundamental Jural Relations: A Symposium," *Amer. Law School Rev.*, IV (1921), 607; W. W. Cook, "Hohfeld's Contribution to the Science of Law," *Yale Law Jour.*, XXVIII (1919), 721; A. L. Corbin, "Legal Analysis and Terminology," *ibid.*, XXIX (1919), 163; Roscoe Pound, "Legal Rights," *Internat. Jour. Ethics*, XXVI (1915), 92. This method of analysis is used at length by Commons, *Legal Foundations of Capitalism*, pp. 91 ff., where a fuller bibliography will also be found.

[2] The fulfillment of contracts is, of course, a positive duty, but it is a compulsion voluntarily incurred and is commonly looked on as an extension of liberty. It makes the liberty of exchange more valuable to the very person against whom enforcement proceedings may be taken. His promise becomes more valuable because it is enforcible, and he can get more in exchange for it.

has a duty to furnish me that thing. And no one has any duty to become my wife or to find me a wife. Certain officials have duties to carry out the necessary formalities, provided I have found a willing partner. When that is accomplished, *we* have a right to marriage, but *I alone* have none, only a liberty which requires the cooperation of someone else for its successful exercise. If I own a house and lot, have I a right to raise a garden? No, I am merely free to raise one if I can; but I have a right, if I do attempt to raise one, that no one shall destroy or damage it. Perhaps you could destroy it by merely failing to rid your own garden of noxious parasites, in which case I may acquire a right to protect my garden by compelling you to spray yours, while you will, of course, have the same right of protection against me.

Has a laborer a right to work? He clearly has a liberty to work, and the liberty is protected, in theory, at least; but as long as no one has a duty to furnish him a job, getting a chance to work is not a right in the strict sense. It is a liberty of that precarious sort which requires the positive cooperation of someone else; in this respect it is like the liberty to marry. Perhaps the nearest thing we have to a recognized right in a job arises when workers strike, and anyone who takes their job is regarded as a trespasser and branded with the epithet of "scab." This attempt to establish a right of exclusion or quasi-ownership is, of course, quite without legal basis; in fact, the law is on the side of the liberty of the scab to take the job, and against the striker's right to hold it vacant at will.

Besides the protected liberties, commonly spoken of as rights, there are unprotected liberties of various sorts and degrees of exposure. They may be roughly classified as (1) exposed liberties, (a) those exposed against all comers, (b) those exposed against particular parties; (2) liberties of joint action, which necessarily imply the positive cooperation of other parties, (a) those dependent on no one particular person but liable to defeat if no person at all can be found to cooperate (liberty to acquire economic goods is prevailingly in this class), (b) those dependent on particular persons, such as liberty to buy a monopolized article, to work for a particular employer. Here one person can defeat the liberty, and if the thing in question is a general necessity, it will not be left in the realm of liberty, but one party will be given a duty to furnish it and the general public a right to receive it.

The liberty to work for a particular employer is seldom or never a necessity, though a chance to work for some employer or other is absolutely necessary for the great majority of people. There is a well-defined tendency to protect the more general liberties which are essential if a person is to have a chance to get the things he needs; but the more specific liberties—to get particular things or to bargain with particular organizations—are not commonly protected. For one thing, they usually involve using someone else's property, and this, of course, requires his consent. Furthermore, they are subject to what we call competition. If I do not think the Ford car is a "good buy," other makers of low-priced cars are eager to convince me that theirs is better, and that is ordinarily all the protection I need. Or if I want to work for Mr. Ford, and he will not hire me, there are other employers; while if I will not work for him on his terms, he can look for other employees. His refusal does not deprive me of all chance of a job, nor does my refusal deprive him of all chance to fill his vacancy. That is the kind of protection each of us has under the competitive system. The chief specific liberties which are protected effectively are the liberties a man has to use his own property as he will, as far as they do not depend on getting the help of somebody else to work it for him.

A few examples may help to illustrate what is meant by some of these generalizations. Take, as a simple case, the liberty of going to the theater. The freedom to go is protected, but the freedom of getting a seat is exposed to the liability that other people may already have bought up all the seats available. Or take the liberty of seeing a sunset from one's front porch. Practically speaking, the general public cannot do anything which seriously interferes with this, but it is exposed to the danger of adjoining property owners' putting up structures which will shut off the view. Presumably, they would not put up structures merely for that purpose, but any considerable structure they put up will have that effect. In some jurisdictions, such things as spite fences are forbidden either by court-made law or by statute.[1]

It may help to visualize how much is involved in a relatively simple matter of rights and liberties if we present a diagram (Chart I) showing certain of the principal relationships involved in a typical case. The central relationship will be a contract between two parties, *A* and *B*, involving the transfer of a piece of real estate. There are three main stages in this transaction: before the contract is made, after it is made but not yet fully executed, and after the transfer is completed. To start with, both parties must have rights of ownership in valuable things: one must own the real estate, and the other must own cash enough to make at least a partial payment. Besides this, they both possess the general liberty to transfer their rights of ownership. We may take up the transaction at the point at which the purchaser *A* has made to the owner *B* the payment which "binds the bargain." *A* now has a contractual right against *B*, and *B* has the corresponding

[1] Freund, *Standards of American Legislation*, pp. 107–108.

right to keep the first payment if *A* goes back on his agreement. At this stage the rights and duties may be roughly represented as in Chart I, *O* representing the appropriate officials of government.

As for the rights of ownership which are thus transferred, they require another diagram (Chart II) to indicate some of their main features. Here *P* represents the general public.

CHART I

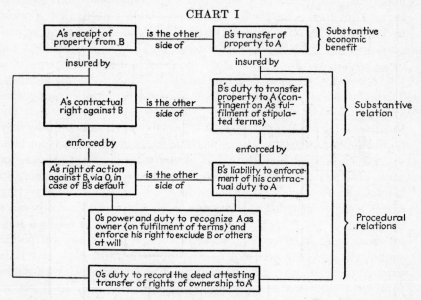

One of the very interesting features of the scheme of relations here crudely outlined is the liberty the owner enjoys of protecting his property himself, if he can. This liberty is not unlimited but is proportioned to the offense. A householder may shoot a burglar breaking into his house at night and be free from punishment, but an ordinary trespasser he may merely eject. Another point of interest is the fact that, while most persons think of their rights in terms of the economic or personal values they can secure, these stand at two removes from the ultimate legal procedure which constitutes the kernel of rights in the strict legal sense. The economic values depend on substantive relations between persons, and these in turn on procedures of legal enforcement.

This whole subject of rights and liberties contains vastly more than can be summed up at this point, and its meaning will develop as we go on to discuss property, contract, and other rights. As far as we have gone, one thing that stands out is the fact that in order to learn the real meaning of rights as instruments of control, we must look at the duties and prohibitions which they involve. The duties are both positive and

CHART II

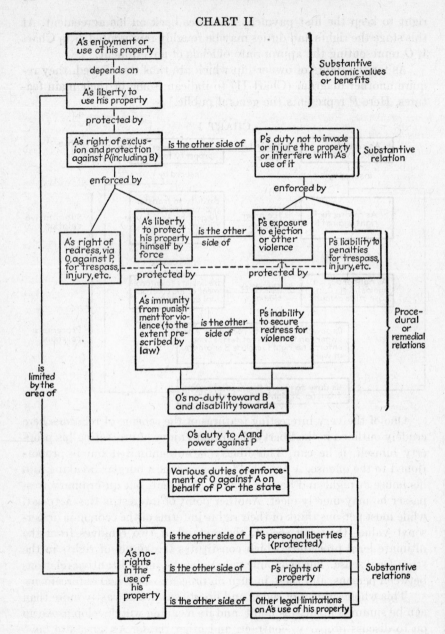

negative, and since the principal economic relationships are those of liberty rather than right, the principal duties are the negative duties of noninterference.

This conception is itself not easy to define. To avoid injuring our neighbors, we must often do something positive ourselves. It may take quick action to turn an automobile and avoid a collision,[1] or to prevent our premises from becoming a source of contagion. And the exact line between injuring a person and conferring a benefit upon him is one which cannot be drawn with absolute sharpness, though it is fairly clear in most cases. There are certain general injuries and benefits for which no effective responsibility can easily be traced, and here the burden of protecting the public falls on the community at large.

In general, the furnishing of actual economic goods and services is not a matter of duty, but of liberty, although there are significant exceptions, such as education and the parent's duty to maintain his child. Public-service companies have a duty to serve all comers alike. And the public assumes a duty to relieve destitution, and to transmit property by inheritance or bequest. These are some of the chief cases in which there is a definite duty to furnish the things we call "economic values." However, there are a great many conditional duties which a person incurs when he undertakes a particular economic function and enters into a particular relationship. For example, any employer must meet certain safety requirements in his buildings and machinery.

Another thing which is clear is that the acquisition of property is not a right (with the exceptions just noted), but a liberty, and it is a liberty of the most exposed sort, because it depends on the positive cooperation of other individuals who are under no definite obligation to do anything at all. Once a person has acquired property, he has rights in it, but he has no right to acquire it in the strict sense. Evidently one of the very delicate questions in the economic functions of law centers in the degree of protection given to some of these exposed liberties on which the acquisition of property depends. In general, these liberties are protected against interference by the violence of third parties. The worker's liberty to get and keep a job is exposed to the liberty of other workers to induce the employer to hire them instead, and to the liberty of the employer to curtail employment or to discharge a particular worker; and its chief protection is the competition of employers. The liberty of the consumer to acquire goods is similarly exposed and protected. If we wish to go further, we must, for example, limit the employer's liberty of discharge or the producer's liberty to

[1] See Hale, "Coercion and Distribution in a Supposedly Non-coercive State," *Polit. Sci. Quart.*, XXXVIII (September, 1923), 475.

curtail production or keep goods off the market; or we must supply jobs or goods publicly where a private supply fails. In such matters there is no absolute standard by which a correct balance can be determined with mathematical accuracy.

6. INALIENABLE RIGHTS AND LIBERTIES

The Declaration of Independence speaks of mankind as possessing certain inalienable rights, including life, liberty, and the pursuit of happiness. But does the legal system make these things inalienable in point of fact? And can any legal system make them absolutely inalienable? To turn this into a reality instead of an aspiration requires control through law to prevent people from alienating these things. And this restraint of itself takes away part of their liberty, so that it appears that absolute liberty is a contradiction in terms. As for the "pursuit of happiness," there is no effective way to prevent people from accepting casual work which deprives them of the opportunity to establish stable family life, or wrecking their minds or spirits, so that happiness is hopelessly out of reach. But it may be possible to define the more simple and tangible economic conditions of property and opportunity without which the pursuit of happiness could not mean anything, and to see to it that no one is deprived of these minimum requisites for the establishment of a successful life. Even this, however, is possible only within very narrow limits.

There are a number of typical ways in which the law may prevent persons from alienating property or liberty. An entailed estate is one which the owner cannot sell, and the device of a trusteeship accomplishes the same result and in addition can be used to protect the income, in a measure, by vesting the management in responsible persons, under whatever limitations the maker of the trust may deem prudent. There are in various jurisdictions limitations specifying certain property which cannot be seized for debt and therefore cannot be alienated in that particular fashion, although the owner can sell it if he wishes to. Bankruptcy itself sets a certain limit on alienation in that it prevents a man from losing his future liberty and economic independence.[1] It enables him to wipe the slate clean by turning over his present possessions (with the exemptions already noted) and to make a fresh start with his economic liberty unimpaired. Another illustration is involved in the whole legal doctrine prohibiting contracts in restraint of trade, where that term is used to mean that a man binds himself not to pursue his calling thereafter.[2]

[1] See below, Chap. vi, Sec. 4.
[2] See below, Chap. vi, Sec. 3.

Another instance arises out of our Constitution, which prohibits slavery or involuntary servitude (except as punishment for crime). In defining this, the courts must necessarily draw a line between legitimate contracts of employment and those which involve involuntary servitude. They have ruled, among other things, that a contract to perform personal services cannot be enforced "specifically"; that is, a person cannot be compelled to perform the exact service he has agreed to.[1] He may be sued for damages if he refuses, but he cannot be held in bondage to a literal fulfillment of his promise. This ruling has far-reaching economic results. It means that labor contracts are almost unenforceable, since a suit for damages is of so little effect against a laborer. Thus the laborer's liberty is made partially inalienable.

As we shall see when we come to study contracts, the essence of a contract is that it binds both parties and makes them liable to definite measures of enforcement, so that they are not free to go back on their word; they have signed away some of their liberty. And the freedom to sign it away is a very valuable privilege, because it enables them to do business on a much wider scale. They can be trusted by people who do not know them personally, but who rely on the ultimate power to enforce their agreements. Therefore liberty can be alienated to a certain extent, and one of the most delicate functions of the courts is to decide just how far this can be allowed to go.

At the present time, legislation is building up a great many limitations on free contract in the interest of what we may call the "social minimum." The intention is to make this social minimum in some sense an inalienable right. In some cases there is set up a definite duty to supply this social minimum to everyone, though this absolute guaranty covers little more than the public school and the poorhouse. Such things as a minimum-wage law are of a different character, because they do not make it anyone's absolute duty to pay the minimum wage to any particular person. A person may lose his minimum wage by losing his job, in which case he falls back on whatever form of relief or other substitute an enlightened state may furnish to meet such cases.

Another illustration of social regulations preventing people from alienating their rights is found in the realm of personal injuries. Broadly speaking, there are certain acts which are not injuries unless they are done to a person against his will, and there are other acts which are injuries under any conditions. If I enter a man's house and live in it, I am not necessarily injuring him; it all depends on whether he consents. He has a right to keep me out, but he can alienate that right for

[1] There are some exceptions to this as to most general legal principles.

a specific term by renting me a room. His consent makes all the difference between a legitimate act and an offense. But suppose, for some reason, he should consent to let me cut off his hand; I should still be guilty of an offense, in spite of his consent, and his agreement would be void. No court would recognize it as a contract. He is not free to give up his right to a sound body—at least, not in this way. By making it a crime for me to maim him whether he consents or not, his right to bodily security is made inalienable.

But only to a certain extent, because he remains free to work in my factory at a machine which might possibly take off his hand through some accident; and in that case the common law would hold that he had assumed whatever risks were incident to the usual operation of the machine and had no claim for damages unless I had been definitely negligent. The injustice of this rule has led to the more modern system of compulsory compensation: an attempt to go farther and make the right to compensation, at least, an inalienable one. To be effective, it needs to be backed up by a provision that the employee cannot free the employer from his liability by a special contract, or else it could be virtually nullified by this practice of "contracting out," in which the employer is able virtually to compel his employees to sign away their statutory rights.

It becomes clear that "inalienable rights" are really a very complex structure of regulations, and that they are matters of degree, with shifting boundary lines between what can be alienated and what cannot. What are the things that ought to be made inalienable? Health, strength (or compensation for the loss of them, adequate to save the family from economic shipwreck), education, liberty, opportunity— these are the main items in the list. Yet naming them does not tell us what we must do to make them inalienable, how far we can hope to succeed, and the limits beyond which we should not attempt to go. Even liberty, which affords the clearest case, cannot be made wholly inalienable. The only general rule is that wherever people lose their hold on these necessities—meaning the substance of them, and not merely the form—and wherever the results are disastrous, there safeguards should be set up even at the cost of limiting formal liberty of contract, up to the point at which the safeguards bring with them more disastrous consequences than the evil against which they are directed. As for methods, one of the foremost is to limit freedom of contract by imposing conditional duties on the employer: "If you hire workers, you must furnish such-and-such safeguards." But in many cases the state itself must stand ready to furnish positive economic goods and services.

REFERENCES FOR FURTHER READING

ANDERSON, B. M., JR., *Social Value*, pp. 137–144.

BLACKSTONE, *Commentaries on the Laws of England*, Introduction; Chap. i.

CARVER, *Principles of National Economy*, Chap. v.

CLARK, J. B., *Essentials of Economic Theory*, pp. 10–11.

CLAY, HENRY, *Economics for the General Reader*, Chap. xxi.

COMMONS, *Legal Foundations of Capitalism*, Chap. iv.

ELY, *Property and Contract*, Part II, Chaps. i, ii.

HALL, J., *Readings in Jurisprudence*.

HOHFELD, "Some Fundamental Legal Conceptions," *Yale Law Jour.*, XXIII (1913), 16; XXVI (1917), 710.

KNAPP, *The State Theory of Money*, Chaps. i, ii.

POUND, ROSCOE, *The Spirit of the Common Law*, Chap. vi; "Social Problems and the Courts," *Amer. Jour. Sociol.*, XVIII (November, 1912), 331–341.

———, "Legislation as a Social Function," *ibid.*, XVIII (May, 1913), 755–768.

———, "Political and Economic Interpretation of Jurisprudence," *Amer. Polit. Sci. Rev.*, Sup., VII (February, 1913), 94–105.

———, "Juristic Problems of National Progress," *Amer. Jour. Sociol.*, XXII (May, 1917), 721–733.

SPENCER, HERBERT, *Social Statics* (Appleton ed.), pp. 62–90.

SPENCER, W. H., *Text-book on Law and Business* (2d ed.), Part I, 1938.

SUMNER, WILLIAM G., essay on "Rights," *Earth-Hunger and Other Essays*.

TAYLOR, H., *Contemporary Problems in the United States*, Vol. II, Chaps. ii–v, 1934.

VEBLEN, *Theory of Business Enterprise*, Chap. viii.

CHAPTER VI

SOME FUNDAMENTAL LEGAL INSTITUTIONS

1. PERSONAL SECURITY AND PERSONAL LIBERTY

As we have already seen, neither personal security nor personal liberty is an absolute right. Every day people are killed by automobiles, buried in coal mines, or injured in various ways by industry. We have a "right" to personal liberty, yet people work under such dangers because they feel that they cannot help themselves; they are not free to do otherwise. What seems to set the limits on the working content of these rights? In the case of personal security, one of the dominant forces seems to be the necessity of allowing production to go on. We do not consciously say that so many tons of coal are worth so many lives, but we do feel that we are dependent on coal and must have it, and that while we should like to have it at a minimum sacrifice of life and may make any "practicable" restrictions to that end, still the mining of coal must go on and the restrictions must not be such as to cripple the industry. One of the things which is making possible increasing protection to life and limb is the growing productiveness of industry itself, which enables it to bear burdens which it did not conceive it could endure fifty to one hundred years ago. This advance of efficiency may also make it possible to give the laborer protection without making him pay for it in the shape of an actual cut in wages, the cost coming out of the growing productiveness of the industry.

Another line of development is the broadening of the idea of personal security into the field of intangible values, such as reputation and privacy. There is a case on record of a girl whose photograph was used against her will for advertising purposes, and who had no redress because the negative was the property of the photographer.[1] Thus the case was settled on a basis of tangible property, where the more important interest was an intangible personal one. This led to the passing

[1] 171 N.Y. 538.

of a statute in New York protecting this right,[1] and even without such a statute, a progressive court today might protect a person against this abuse.[2] Reputation is protected by the law of libel, and the law of libel is itself limited by the need for preserving essential freedom of speech. As a result, criticism of the public acts of officials is not limited to statements of fact whose truth can be proved but may extend to matters of opinion, provided the opinion is held honestly and in good faith; but this does not protect false allegations of fact.[3] Criticism of public characters runs riot in this country—more so than in other countries.[4]

Personal liberty is largely guaranteed by the right of personal security. All alike are free from injuries by violence or threats of violence, and all have equal access to the courts for redress, at least in theory. Actually the costs and delays of the law amount to depriving the poor of equal access to justice. And legal justice affords no more than formal liberty. A person may possess this and still have no real liberty of action. The substance of liberty, as distinct from the mere form, has an economic basis. It depends, in the first instance, on knowledge, especially (in the economic field) knowledge of the market and knowledge of how to produce something with a marketable value and how to dispose of it at a fair market price. A person who does not have a job or any other source of income, and who does not know where to get one and how to go about canvassing the market effectively, does not possess the substance of liberty. That person is in a position to be exploited and to be forced to make contracts which are essentially made under duress.

In addition to this equipment of knowledge, a person needs some reserve funds in order to be able to hold off from the market and see if the second or tenth or twentieth bargain that offers will not be better than the first. When pockets are empty, this search may mean real privation. Often one of the chief obstacles to a real canvass of the market consists of the costs of transportation, in which case "liberty and the pursuit of happiness" may require a free ride on the railroad. If this is not forthcoming from public funds, the employer's private interest may be strong enough to furnish it. But when the employer foots the bill, his interest in the case is likely to end when he gets enough labor, without regard to what happens to the laborers after he

---

[1] For cases upholding and construing this statute, see 104 N.Y. Supp. 1102; 109 N.Y. Supp. 963. It was held not to prohibit the common practice of publishing a picture in a single issue of a newspaper, without the subject's consent.

[2] See dictum in *Corliss* v. *Walker*, 64 Fed. 280.

[3] See 59 Fed. Rep. 530; 55 Fed. Rep. 456.

[4] See Ely, *Property and Contract*, pp. 375, 386–387.

is through with them. For example, in this country various ways have been found for getting harvest hands into the fields without requiring them to pay their railroad fares,[1] but there was no system for getting them back into an effective labor market after the harvest was in.

It is evident that, in order to guarantee the reality of liberty and not merely the form, the government must bear a large responsibility, one on which it is not easy to set definite limits. It begins with education and it continues with the furnishing of various sorts of market information and, in general, seeing to it that the market is a real one, that is, a place where supply and demand can come together with real effectiveness. More than this, real liberty requires that there should be a certain minimum level of economic welfare on which everyone can fall back, in order to prevent him from being under compulsion to accept whatever the market offers at the moment. A man should not starve if he refuses the first job offered or the second.

But this requirement is a difficult one to meet, especially in a society where the bulk of industry is in private hands and where there is a settled fear of undermining the initiative and responsibility of the individual. For there is real danger of demoralizing large numbers of people if they are guaranteed anything like a satisfactory standard of living without being required to meet the competitive standards of work in order to obtain it. If this is a requisite of economic liberty, then such liberty is something the world is not ready to guarantee. It would certainly not be wise to do so without any limitations and safeguards, for it is quite true that there are a great many people who will not work reasonably hard and faithfully unless they are spurred by the fear of losing the job. So far as this constitutes economic compulsion, we are not yet ready to do without it.

Finally, it is a perfectly commonplace fact that everyone's liberty must be limited in order to keep him from infringing on the similar liberty of other people. This principle may be interpreted in two ways which have very different economic effects. One way is to make the *same rules for all* and to maintain them even when there is so much inequality between man and man and so much difference between their functions—the things they desire to do and the ways in which they affect each other's interests—that the same rules no longer have any real equality about them. As a French writer has remarked, "The law in the majesty of its equality alike forbids rich and poor to sleep on park benches."

---

[1] In this case the railroads themselves have enough interest in getting the crop moved to make them willing to help, for example, by giving the men passes to their own work camps, with the expectation that most of them would desert to the harvest fields.

Moreover, this interpretation of the principle does not define any set of specific rules. It *could* refer to a system of anarchy and mutual warfare, in which all are equally free to engage. It *does* refer to a system of settled enjoyment of property and free exchange, and the limits on liberty which it contemplates are those consistent with such a system. But even this permits a wide variety of rules. Competition may be "fair" or "unfair"; various degrees of fraud, deception or combination may or may not be permitted. Does the principle outlaw wasteful methods of extracting oil or the draining of oil from under others' lands, methods of farming which lead to soil erosion or dust storms, and methods of farming or lumbering which aggravate floods? Does it permit "yellow-dog" contracts, closed-shop agreements, fixing of resale prices by manufacturers, or the indulgence by business in unsound speculative booms which result later in general paralysis of business which deprives millions of the opportunity to work? Does it automatically grant corporations the same privileges as individuals? The principle in itself defines no rules for such matters.

The other way of interpreting this rule is to recognize that our modern specialized society calls upon people to enter into relationships with each other in which the part played by one is essentially different from the part played by the other, the things one can do to injure the other are essentially different from the things the other can do to injure the first, and therefore each must be subject to *different* limitations in order to prevent abuses and produce essential fairness. This calls for substantial reciprocity of obligations, but not for formal equality; and this reciprocity should be judged by the aggregate resultant of the whole scheme, and not by the effect of any one provision or transaction.[1] A single act of one-sided legislation in favor of labor *may* be justified on the ground that the relation is otherwise one-sided in favor of the employer. This principle of reciprocity makes for a progressive system of rights, adapted to the actual needs of industry, and capable of insuring the substance of equal liberty. The rule of literal equality, on the other hand, is purely formal. It is adapted to a homogeneous society such as has hardly existed since the time of reliable historical records, and it tends to leave room for serious encroachments on the reality of liberty under modern industrial conditions. The latter rule promotes "maximum self-assertion"; the former, "social justice."

But the search for a differentiated social justice, while unavoidable, is unavoidably dangerous. The rule of formal equality is relatively easy to apply, but the principle of substantial reciprocity calls for dis-

---

[1] This is among the standards set up by Freund (see his *Standards of American Legislation*, Chap. vi, esp. pp. 239–245).

criminating judgment and by that very fact opens the door to class legislation and political group favoritism. This may occur without any intent to be arbitrary and unfair, simply through failing to make legislation as comprehensive as it should be, caring first for the groups whose needs are most strongly put forward or whose protest is most forceful. The judicial temperament is admirably adapted to put a check on such abuses, and it has actually served that purpose in the United States, acting under the rule which requires laws to be nondiscriminatory, sometimes even vetoing legislation which later judgment approves. But the courts themselves recognize that they cannot simply substitute their ideas of social justice for those of the legislature. Social justice is not to be measured by a yardstick, of a judicial or any other variety. There must always remain a large margin of discretion of a sort which is properly legislative.[1]

2. PRIVATE PROPERTY

Most people think of property as a tangible thing which somebody owns. But the important question is What is this thing we call ownership? Ownership consists of a large and varied bundle of rights and liberties. The rights consist chiefly of rights to exclude other people, and the liberties consist of a general undefined freedom to use one's property in any way which does not infringe on the rights or protected liberties of other people, or which is not forbidden by some specific provision of law. The economic substance of ownership consists of the benefits one can derive from one's property, and these depend upon the things he is free to do with it. And these in turn are bounded by the law, which lays down the things one may not do; hence the law determines the real content of property. This boundary line of property rights is a shifting one, and the real meaning and character of ownership may change quite considerably while it still remains "private ownership."

To take a simple case, the law may give the private owner of the land the right to use its surface as he sees fit but reserve the right to take out any valuable minerals which may be found below the surface. This may remain a public right, and people may even have the liberty to go on to other people's land to search for minerals (always making compensation for any damage done). Another interesting case is that of oil lands, where the oil will flow from place to place to such an extent that wells drilled on one man's property can draw a considerable amount of oil from under the property of others. Our traditional American system of meeting this difficulty is simply to prevent owners

[1] Cf. Freund, *op. cit.*, pp. 272–273.

from boring wells within a certain minimum distance from their boundary line. And since this does not suffice to protect surrounding owners, they are frequently forced to protect themselves by boring "offset wells" wherever anyone else has bored on the other side of their boundary line. Thus they are under a certain amount of compulsion if they wish to protect their own property from being taken by someone else. This clearly works toward wasteful boring and unduly rapid extraction of a limited natural resource. Exploitation of a pool as a unit permits a rational rate of extraction and is at least not positively opposed to conservation.

We have already seen how the public health justifies limitations on liberty for the sake of preventing the spread of contagions, and the same principle applies to Canada thistles, the foot-and-mouth disease, and all the pests and parasites against which orchards are sprayed— hence the justice of compulsory spraying. The general underlying theory is that anyone is free to use his property in any way which does not injure others, but the boundary line of this liberty is inevitably hazy and changes with changing industrial technique. Many obvious injuries of a very substantial sort are possible and carry no legal redress.

Every building is subject to the possible construction of other buildings which will shut off view or light or air to some extent. This cannot be absolutely prevented, but a system must be worked out which meets two fundamental conditions: first, the natural exploitation of the land must not be prevented; and, second, the limitations must be known and must be the same for every owner, regardless of who builds first. Thus a reasonable building code will require that certain spaces shall be left open to preserve a certain minimum of light and air. It may limit the height of buildings in proportion to the width of streets and provide that beyond a certain height the building must not cover more than a given part of the land area. Naturally, the kind of protection required for residence districts is very different from that required in areas of huge office buildings. A special case occurs where houses are customarily built in solid blocks on very narrow lots, with a party wall. Here the first one to build is at a disadvantage unless he can put the party wall half on his neighbor's property and require his neighbor to pay his share of the cost. This imposes a burden on the neighbor, but it may be the lesser injustice and is required in certain places.

Another interesting case is that of heavy industry. Does the building of a factory injure the surrounding property owners or improve their property? It depends entirely on what the surrounding property is being used for, and in the long run on what its most natural and economical use is destined to be. As a result, it is not possible to prevent all injury by a general ban on certain kinds of use; the use may be legitimate enough in itself, and yet it may be out of place. Thus injury may arise from incongruous uses of property in a given neighborhood. Therefore one of two things must result: either the property owner must be given unlimited leave to prey upon other property values by exploiting his land in incongruous ways, or else there must be different regulations for different zones or neighborhoods. But a system of zoning is something which could never be carried out by purely judicial machinery, no matter how earnest or intelligent the courts might be in their endeavor to prevent property from being so used as to injure the legitimate interests of surrounding property owners. The common law of property reaches its limit at this point, and a different system needs to be substituted.

There are some special forms of property in our modern industrial society which are less tangible than real estate and call for some special mention. They include knowledge, the good-will of a business and other intangible assets, and the so-called "property" which a man has in his own labor. Knowledge is an extremely difficult thing to appropriate because it involves limiting other people's liberty to do what they want with their own tangible property: for example, to take their own materials and work them up into a machine which falls within the specifications of another man's patent. Knowledge of common matters which cannot be shown to be unique, like a patentable invention, is virtually impossible to protect legally after the fashion of private-property rights. The best safeguard for the original possessor lies in the time and effort it takes for others to pilfer his knowledge. If it is a matter of daily news, by the time it is plagiarized its priority value is gone; and if it is a matter of a difficult technique, as, for instance, that of "scientific management," it takes a very substantial amount of time and effort to learn the technique and thus appropriate the other person's knowledge, and it can never be done with absolute completeness.

As for the good-will of a business, viewed as a form of property, this raises no particular questions until it becomes a matter of selling it. And then it becomes clear that the thing which a man sells when he sells the good-will of his business is a contract limiting his own freedom to compete with the person to whom he has sold out. The chief question of control which arises here is the question to what extent a man should be allowed to limit his own future liberty to compete.[1] Another question arises as to the recognition of good-will as something on which the concern is entitled to earnings, in case the earnings become subject to public regulation. The justice of this depends largely on the question

[1] See above, p. 86.

whether the good-will cost the concern something to build up. In the last analysis, good-will consists of a disposition of the public to buy goods from this concern rather than from other concerns, and a concern may have to spend money in building up this kind of disposition, actually investing capital in the preferences of its customers. But this has little meaning in a noncompetitive industry, such as are most of the public utilities which are subject to regulation. Here the customers have no chance to show a preference, because they have no choice. Good-will is primarily a competitive concept.

The intangible value of a franchise is similar, in that it is a protection against competitors, and this constitutes its chief value. It differs in that it is itself a contract whereby the state or municipality agrees to keep competitors out, not merely an individual preference on the part of the customers, which may be overcome at almost any moment by some unforeseen event.

A person's own labor is property only in a limited sense. Others cannot take it without his consent, and he is free to use it in any legal way, but he cannot sell it except under very narrow limitations. He can sell the current use of his time, but nothing more. So far as labor is property, it is, to an important extent, inalienable.

Having shown what a many-sided and elastic thing property is, we may be in a position to raise the question of the justification of private property. Evidently it makes a great deal of difference what kind of private-property system we are considering. Some kind of private ownership in some kinds of things appears to be absolutely indispensable. The chief question lies in the private ownership of land and industrial capital; and here the answer depends a great deal on the limitations imposed on the owner's use of such property, in the interests of the community.

Those who urge that private property is a natural right are chiefly referring to the fact that it is natural for a man to have complete control of the tools of his work and to receive the whole fruits of it; and, furthermore, that this gives him the greatest possible incentive not only to work hard, but to conserve his own capital assets. It is proverbial that the small farmer who owns his farm will care for his equipment and make his land fertile, while a tenant will let them run down in spite of the most careful watching. (One task of the law of leases is to require proper care of the owner's property, and to fix the tenant's rights in his own improvements.) But this justification of private ownership clearly does not justify ownership by an absentee landlord or by any kind of landlord, for that matter. Nor does it justify private ownership of large collective enterprises as it is now carried on.

In the case of land, it can be argued that if the owner is free to use his land but is not free to rent it, then if he is incapacitated, or has some legitimate interest calling him away temporarily, he may suffer a serious injustice[1] and may be forced to give up other legitimate interests, or he may be induced to stay on the land and cultivate it when he is no longer able to do it efficiently. Thus a reasonable freedom to rent may involve the lesser evil. On the other hand, where agriculture has settled into a system of large estates with absentee owners and an impoverished tenantry, it seems to be universally agreed that the community has an interest in changing the system and giving the tenants an opportunity to own their own land. Such a reform is likely to include financial aid, to which the tenants have a right in their capacity as tenants of a given piece of land. This further calls for some limitation on the landlord's freedom. Otherwise he may either evict the tenants or raise their rents until he has absorbed the full value of any aid the state may have given them. In other words, the owner's rights are limited, and the tenants acquire a certain interest at the expense of what was formerly the absolute ownership of the landlord.

Historically, this ownership was itself generally created out of an earlier system of feudal status in which the lord did not have the absolute rights of a modern private owner but was limited in his rentals and exactions by the "custom of the manor" or other similar customary limitations. Absolute private ownership of land, as we know it, is not by any means a universal and immemorial institution. In developing and modifying it, we shall certainly not go back to the feudal system, chiefly because that operated as a bar to experiments in improved methods of cultivation. Changes are likely to occur in the direction of promoting ownership by the cultivators, but without absolutely prohibiting all renting.

In the matter of large-scale industrial enterprises, the inefficiency of diffused and democratic control furnishes a strong reason for concentration of ownership or at least of direction. And large masses of workers apparently need, for the sake of "discipline," to be under the management of someone who represents an independent interest and is not the elected representative of the workmen themselves. This is true in general and at the present stage of development, and it constitutes the strongest argument for the control of industry by large stockholders, through their representatives. Thus the dominant reason for allowing corporate ownership with concentrated control is that otherwise it would be impossible to get together large enough

[1] The Code of Hammurabi, Secs. 27–31, contains interesting evidence of arrangements which must have imposed hardships of this sort.

masses of capital for the needs of modern production and still manage it efficiently. And if this were forbidden, the small investor would have far less chance than he has now, and the profits of industry would be much more narrowly confined to a few rich people.

Nevertheless, this right of corporate management of industry is not by any means an absolute or natural right. It rests on special grants from the state and is naturally subject to the ultimate power of the state to impose whatever limitations are necessary to prevent abuses. And abuses always tend to arise whenever there is a great joint interest for which a few are necessarily responsible and in which many are vitally concerned. The fact that the laborer does not own the product of his own work will never cease to be a serious disadvantage, although under present conditions it seems to be more important that the managing interest, or the interest which controls management, should have this ownership, because a business would lose more by weakening the incentives of the management than it loses now by weakening those of labor. But this condition is capable of being reversed at any time when labor develops the ability to organize industry under its own direction and still maintain discipline and efficiency.

Thus private-property rights must needs be subject to continual limitation in the interests of the common welfare. The more sophisticated forms of industrial property, such as corporate ownership and absentee landlordism, are not natural in the traditional sense and require more control by society than the simple ownership by a worker of his land or his tools. And if it is not possible to develop adequate limitation of the rights of private ownership, there is serious danger that it may develop into forms which no longer make for efficient social production. In particular, the enlarging conception of the inalienable human rights of the workers constitutes a limitation on the rights of private property which is gaining more and more recognition, as we have seen in connection with accident liability and the "social minimum" in general. The scope of property rights is visibly changing.

The evolution of such an institution as private property takes place in different ways. In the first place, it develops of itself, chiefly by way of meeting new situations to which existing doctrines are not adequate and which compel the courts to develop new theories, commonly by adapting older doctrines. In this way the scope of rights and liberties contained in private property may be either expanded or limited. Such change, however, is slow, and any rapid change requires the more flexible process of legislation, which may enlarge or restrict the liberties of persons or of property without regard for precedent, except as the courts make it necessary.[1] The most striking recent changes in the institution of property have come through legislation.

Other limitations on the rights of private property have already been mentioned. Under the right of eminent domain, the state can take private property for a public purpose but must pay the owner the full value of what it has taken, together with any damages resulting. Under the police power, property may be taken without compensation, though not without limits.[2] And in that large and growing class of industry which is held to be either of a public character or affected with a public interest, the rights of private property are limited by the underlying requirement that the industry shall render service to the public at a fair compensation. Property in such cases does not include what it includes in private industries, namely, the right to whatever earnings the owner can extract from the market. The property of the public utility is held subject to a prior claim on the part of the public, and the property rights of the owner protect him only within the scope of reasonable charges. This subject will be taken up more fully in later chapters.

3. CONTRACT AS AN INSTRUMENT OF CONTROL

A contract is commonly thought of as an agreement, but it is a great deal more than this. It is an agreement for a mutual exchange ("contracts without a consideration" are void), and one of its essential characteristics is that it is enforced.[3] The limiting of contracts to agreements for mutual exchange operates to confine the institution of contract to the realm of business dealings. And the quality of enforceability makes possible the development of impersonal business relations on a large scale and makes contract a powerful instrument of social control. The mere refusal to enforce a given kind of agreement frequently acts to bar it out of the realm of business—a fact which goes to show how intimately business depends on the continual exercise of positive social control in matters which are so habitual that we tend to forget that they exist at all.

The power to enforce carries with it the power to interpret, and the legal conception of a contract includes not merely the agreement itself but the entire body of law governing its interpretation and enforcement,

[1] See Sec. 5, below; also Chap. x, Sec. 1.
[2] See Chap. x, Secs. 1 & 2, below.
[3] Certain types of agreement are not enforced, and one way of speaking of this, in many cases at least, is to say that these are not contracts at all. Some of them are business agreements possessing all the usual earmarks of contracts, save that their effect is "contrary to public policy" (for example, "contracts in restraint of trade"). Thus there are some "contracts" which lack the quality of enforceability.

so that social control becomes an integral part of the contract itself. This element in contracts is capable of change but is subject to conditions making for stability. In interpreting contracts, custom plays a large part, as we have seen, while changes in the conditions of enforcement are subject in the United States to the constitutional provision that no state may pass any law "impairing the obligation of contracts." As a result, legislative changes cannot be made to invalidate existing contracts, though this does not prevent a given kind of contract from being outlawed for the future.

A list of the kinds of contract which the state will not enforce, or agreements which it holds void, presents an interesting variety. It includes agreements made under duress; and we have seen that in the economic sense, at least, this is a very elastic term. It also includes agreements made by a large class of parties not competent to bargain, including minors, imbeciles, and others. It also includes agreements made by the officials of a company when acting beyond the powers which the company possesses. Another class of cases in which the courts are required to draw a rather delicate boundary line consists of contracts resulting in personal servitude. Here the chief limitation, as we have seen, consists in refusing to enforce specifically any contract for personal service.[1] The practical result is that the labor contract is virtually for an indefinite term, terminable at the will of either party. Hence it can also be changed at any time by striking a new bargain; but as long as the worker continues to turn up for work and the employer continues to let him in, the terms of their relationship are governed by the contract they have made.[2]

Contracts in restraint of trade are also void, and this includes two separate classes of agreement. One occurs, as we have just seen, when a man sells the good-will of his business and gives effect to this by agreeing to stay out of the trade himself. If he merely agrees to stay out of a particular market or area, the court will enforce the agreement; but if he deprives himself of the privilege of exercising his trade entirely, the court will not enforce the agreement. The original reason for this was the danger that a person might become a public charge if he were deprived of his customary means of livelihood.[3] A second meaning of the term "restraint of trade" consists of restraints on competition which have a monopolistic character.

Another class of cases occurs where there is a legal liability and the law prohibits the individual's "contracting out" of the liability to

[1] See above, p. 87.
[2] See Commons, *Legal Foundations of Capitalism*, pp. 284–285.
[3] See above, p. 86.

which the law subjects him. As we have seen, this is necessary in some cases in order to make certain rights inalienable.[1]

Another thing which the legislature does is to establish certain conditions which must be met by anyone who, by means of contract, enters into a given relation, such as the relation of employer to employee. The two parties are not free to do as they like in the matter of safety appliances and sanitation, hours of work, time and place of payment of wages, or even the wage rates themselves, where a minimum-wage law is in force. Everyone is left as free as before to enter into this relation or not to enter into it, or to choose with whom he shall enter into it, but limits are set on his freedom to determine the terms of the relation itself. After all, this freedom has not been exercised to any great extent in the past history of the human race, since free contract has dealt far more with the exchange of property than with the establishment of more or less lasting relations between man and man. The latter is a comparatively recent development.

In fixing the terms of such relationships the legislature's action may be of two grades. It may determine such things as sanitary conditions and safety appliances in factories and make its rules binding in spite of specific agreements to the contrary on the part of employers and employees. Or it may merely establish certain conditions in the absence of specific agreement to the contrary. An instance of this, in a different field, is afforded by the legal-tender legislation of the Civil War, which made paper money legal tender but did not prevent people from making contracts specifically calling for gold. By the exercise of this power to prescribe part of the conditions of contract, the scope of free contract is limited and a relation is set up which might be described as a "standardized relationship" or as "status entered by contract." It is not a status determined by birth; nor does it give the individual full power to determine his own status, merely to choose with whom he will enter into relationships, and to determine part of the terms of the relationships, the rest being prescribed by law.

On the other hand, we have recently developed a system of bargaining in which labor for the first time has a really effective say as to the general conditions surrounding the work. Where the laborer bargains as an individual, he can do little except to find out the wages and hours and general type of work and either accept or refuse them. But the modern wage contract does vastly more than this, and it is enabled to do so by the fact that it is not an individual contract. The workers bargain as a unit and through representatives who become specialists in the problems they have to meet, and who are thus able to make their

[1] See above, p. 88.

bargains take real effect on the status of the worker in all its varied aspects. Thus in the field of labor bargaining, free contract is enlarging its scope in certain respects (though it is a collective contract and not an individual contract) at the same time that its scope is being limited in other respects by the action of legislatures.

4. BANKRUPTCY AND ITS MODERN DEVELOPMENTS

Debtors used to be put in prison; now they are so considerately treated that it is even possible for a dishonest man, with proper precautions, to make bankruptcy a profitable profession. This change has taken place gradually. The original purpose of bankruptcy laws was to secure full realization of assets and just distribution among creditors, so that the debtor might not fraudulently transfer or conceal assets and the favored creditor or the one who first levied process should not be able to waste assets belonging equally to all or secure full payment at the others' expense. This was the character of the first English bankruptcy law, that of Henry VIII, passed in 1542. Not until 1705 was provision made for the release of the debtor from the undischarged balance of his debts, and not until 1826 in England (1841 in the United States) could the debtor voluntarily go into bankruptcy and so avail himself of this privilege of discharge.[1] Effective uniformity of bankruptcy proceedings in this country was not established until the Federal Act of 1898.[2]

At present, the discharge of the debtor has become the most obvious characteristic of bankruptcy laws. Its effect is virtually to make financial liberty an inalienable right by enabling a person who has failed in business to make a fresh start without being buried under a mass of accumulated debts which would banish all hope of ever again achieving financial independence. The old system led to evasions; the bankrupt resuming business ostensibly as trustee for his wife or other relative and a straightforward release came to appear preferable.[3] A debtor may turn over all his property (with certain exemptions) for the benefit of his creditors and be discharged from all further legal obligations. This procedure of relief acts as a limit on the obligations of contracts, and all credit transactions are impliedly subject to this limitation.

As for the property which the creditors cannot take, it may include a homestead or the tools of the debtor's trade; both of which exemp-

[1] *Remington on Bankruptcy*, Students' Treatise, pp. 1–3.
[2] *Ibid.*, p. 3.
[3] *Ibid.*, p. 6.

tions could be justified on grounds of protecting the community from the danger that the individual may become a public charge.

A new and far-reaching development of bankruptcy came with the modern corporation and the privilege of limited liability. Here the corporation is treated as a person separate from the individual members or shareholders. It can satisfy its debtors by turning over its corporate property, and there is no further claim against the members.[1] In this respect the corporation differs from the typical partnership, in which the personal estate of any or all the partners is liable for the debts of the firm. If a stockholder turns over part of his personal fortune to meet the debts of a company in which he is interested, he is commended as an example of business honor beyond what the letter of the law requires.

But even limited liability does not give the modern corporation the amount of immunity which the character of its business appears to require. The bankrupt company does not usually give up its property to its creditors but instead goes through a "receivership." Legally, this is an action in equity wherein the court appoints a competent person to act as its servant in disposing of the property so as to secure the best results for all concerned, in proportion to the character of their claims. This means that the claims are adjusted instead of being enforced to the letter. One of the industrial facts which is at the bottom of this practice is the large amount of fixed capital in industry, together with the fact that the creditors are commonly not competent as managers to operate this fixed capital any better than the present managers, if as well. Thus they could not realize on their debts by taking over the property. Their interest requires, first, an impartial determination as to whether the property is worth continuing to operate—that is, whether it can be made to earn a return on anything above its salvage value at a forced sale—and, second, an adjustment of debtors' claims which will set the company free to operate as profitably as may be possible.

It may be to the interest of a first-mortgage bondholder to allow the company to borrow money in order to put a run-down plant in decent working order, or to complete an unfinished traffic connection which may furnish a bankrupt railroad with vitally needed business, even if this involves giving the new creditor a claim which takes precedence

[1] There are, of course, exceptions. National banks in the United States are subject to "double liability," meaning that the liability of the corporation is backed by a further liability of the stockholder up to the par value of his holdings. Stockholders in industrial companies who have had issued to them stock purporting to be "fully paid," but which is not fully paid in reality, are liable to assessment for the shortage.

over the old first mortgage. In fact, receivers always have the power to raise capital by issuing "receiver's certificates," which take precedence over all other claims. The legal ground for this is that they represent the costs of a court action, but the economic justification lies in the fact that it is to the bondholders' interest to secure new capital in this way if they cannot induce the stockholders to furnish it. In other words, the creditor cannot afford to exercise his full legal rights.

One can easily see that such an elastic system is capable of great abuses on account of the vast discretion exercised by the receiver. He is often a high official of the company—and, indeed, he should be someone familiar with the business. The so-called "friendly receivership" is at times unduly friendly to the previous management, which has run the company into bankruptcy, and gives them, through the friendly receiver, a new lease of life coupled with a moratorium on their previous pressing obligations. In general, if our institution of bankruptcy errs at the present time, it errs on the side of laxity. However, this corresponds to the character of modern business, in which investors are able to divide their resources, making themselves safe by putting their eggs in many baskets rather than by putting them all in one and watching that one. As a result, many eggs get broken, but the consequences are not so serious to the individual investor.

5. THE CONSTITUTION AND THE POLICE POWER

The development of the system of rights of person and property may take place by evolution from within or by enactment from without, that is, by legislation modifying previous rights and liberties. If the labor contract is to be safeguarded, if costs of industry now borne by the workers are to be laid on the industry itself, if property values in cities are to be protected by zoning, statutes and ordinances must do the work. If rights are to be made inalienable, people must be prevented from alienating them, which means depriving them of just so much of their liberty by legislative action. But in our American system, legislation must be within the constitutional powers of the legislative body, and the Federal Constitution contains a Bill of Rights safeguarding liberties of person and rights of property. Thus the development of legal rights from without is subject to some limitation by that same judicial point of view which governs the development from within.

Under the Constitution, the Federal Government possesses a specific list of delegated powers, together with the "implied powers" incidental to the proper carrying out of the powers specifically granted. All powers not granted to the Federal Government are reserved to the states and to the people, and the states thus come to be the residuary claimants of all undefined legislative power. This is, of course, exercised within the limits set by the Bill of Rights in the Federal Constitution, most prominent of which in the past twenty-five years has been the provision of the Fourteenth Amendment whereby no state can "deprive any person of life, liberty or property without due process of law, nor deny to any person within its jurisdiction the equal protection of the laws." Property and liberty being, as we have seen, bundles of rights and privileges, any regulation is really a taking of liberty or property, and therefore its fate hinges upon the judicial definition of "due process." And here enters that much-discussed conception, the "police power of the state." The courts have held that proper exercises of this power are valid and meet the test of due process, but as to what the power includes and what are proper exercises of it, the judges differ among themselves, and divergent conceptions of the nature of this power clash in our jurisprudence. One is probably safe in saying that the police power consists of the undefined remainder of legislative power, as far as it is restrictive and as far as it is permitted under the Bill of Rights.[1] It represents what the courts will permit the states to do in limiting liberty and altering the rights of private property; it is the substance they have given to the phrase "due process of law."

Aside from businesses affected with a public interest, it consists chiefly of the power to protect the public safety, public health, and public morals, but it is not rigidly confined within these limits. There is no reason at law why it cannot be greatly enlarged, if the economic needs of the public require it and if the court can be shown the reasonableness and cogency of these economic needs. The court has proved that its judgment is swayed by the weight of economic evidence. It has not moved so fast as progressives thought necessary, but it has moved. Short of constitutional amendment, the most important factor in hastening the movement is that novel proposals should have behind them an economic philosophy, and one which will appeal to the judicial mind as reasonable. Since the judicial mind leans strongly toward regarding liberty of contract as a natural right, such an economic philosophy, to be effective, must admit the general presumption in favor of liberty and show adequate reasons for making an exception. But this whole matter will be gone into in more detail in a later chapter. All that is attempted at this point is to show how vitally the interpretation of the Constitution and the definition of the police power enter into

[1] See W. W. Cook, "What Is the Police Power?" *Columbia Law Rev.*, VII (May, 1907), esp. pp. 322, 326, 335. This is probably the best brief discussion of the meaning of the police power.

the evolution of our scheme of rights and liberties of property and person.

REFERENCES FOR FURTHER READING

COMMONS, *Legal Foundations of Capitalism*, Chap. vii, Secs. 2–3; Chap. viii, Sec. 1.

DAGGETT, *Railroad Reorganization.*

DE LAVELEYE, *Primitive Property*, Chaps. i, xxvii.

DEWING, *Corporate Promotions and Reorganizations.*

ELY, *Property and Contract*, Part I, Chaps. iii–xiii; Part II, Chaps. i–vi.

FREUND, *Standards of American Legislation*, Chap. ii.

HAMILTON, W. H., *Current Economic Problems* (3d ed.), Chap. xii.

MARSHALL, L. C., *Readings in Industrial Society*, Chap. xiv.

NOLEN, *City Planning*, Introduction, Chap. iii; cf. also Chap. xv.

ORTH, *Readings on the Relation of Government to Property and Industry*, Chaps. i, ii.

POUND, ROSCOE, "Freedom of Contract," *Yale Law Jour.*, XVIII (May, 1909), 458 ff.

———, "Legal Rights," *Internat. Jour. Ethics*, XXIX (October, 1915), 92–116.

Property: Its Duties and Rights, by various authors, Macmillan & Company, Ltd., London, 1913.

REMINGTON, HAROLD, *Elements of Bankruptcy Law.*

SELIGMAN, *Principles of Economics*, Chaps. ix, xi.

SPENCER, W. H., *Text-book on Law and Business* (2d ed.), Part II, 1938.

CHAPTER VII

LAW AND ECONOMIC LIFE: SOME
GENERAL PROBLEMS

Law and the costs of industry, 108—Coercion in a supposedly free community, 111—Changes in the law, and the newer "rights," 118—Are there "natural rights"? 119—The value of stability, 122—Conclusion, 123.

1. LAW AND THE COSTS OF INDUSTRY

The costs of industry have two different aspects or dimensions: the financial expense borne by the business enterprise, and the sum total of burdens ultimately falling on everyone in the community as a result of the operations which this enterprise carries on. The latter consist ultimately of sacrifices incurred by human beings or damages suffered by them. Some of these the industry has to pay for, and these payments constitute its financial expenses. The object of an industrial enterprise is to economize its financial expenses, while the object of the community is to economize the ultimate sacrifices and damages borne by all its members. The financial expenses serve as representatives, on the books of private enterprise, of these underlying community costs; and the efficiency of private enterprise as a system for producing a maximum of valuable things at a minimum true cost to the community depends in no small degree on how well the financial expenses serve their purpose as representatives of the true costs.

And this depends in turn, more than anything else, on the quality and completeness of the system of law under which industrial processes are carried on. For this determines what damages cannot be inflicted upon an individual without his consent and thus gives him the rights on which his demands for compensation must necessarily be based if they are to have any effective standing. Where this simple protection is not adequate to the needs of the case, the law may prohibit certain damages from being inflicted at all, regarding them as injuries to the public and not merely to private individuals. Thus the state may forbid a smoke nuisance, or it may forbid a twelve-hour work day in mines or in bakeshops, if the legislature so decides and the courts permit. Or the law may prescribe the terms and methods of compensation for particular incidental injuries, as we have seen in the case

108

of industrial accidents. Thus, in one way or another, the law plays a vital part in determining whether private enterprise is to be predatory and socially wasteful to an inordinate degree, or whether it is to be in the main serviceable and socially efficient.

The traditional theory of the matter seems to be that, since no one can injure another without the other's consent, therefore the sacrifices of industry are all voluntarily undergone and compensated at a rate which is at least sufficient to purchase this consent and in that sense to "make it worth while" to undergo the costs of production. If the compensation is inadequate or seems so to a soft-hearted observer, that (says the individualist) is a matter of the private judgment of the person who incurs the sacrifices, and not a public issue. The industrial system gives the individual sufficient basic protection for his person and his liberty of bargaining, so that if he is exploited, it is his own fault and not the fault of the system. This theory has failed to satisfy the demands of progressive social policy, and many measures involving quite different theories have made their way into general use and have come to be regarded as essential features of an enlightened economic order. These measures include sanitary regulations and safety-appliance acts, systems of compulsory accident compensation, prevention of child labor and control of the hours of work for women and for all workers in trades where long hours give rise to special dangers, minimum-wage regulations, regulations in the interest of conservation of natural resources, the zoning of cities to prevent the destruction of values resulting from incongruous uses of adjoining property, and insurance against unemployment.

If these various policies have any common principle underlying them, it is hard to discover, except the negative principle of refusing to accept as a measure of costs the terms of the bargain which the industry is able to make with those who incur voluntary sacrifices in the course of production, and the very general positive principle of trying to make industry either cover its true costs more perfectly, or where that is not practicable, avoid wanton waste in those items of cost which cannot be charged against it or those which appear to be undervalued in the market for one reason or another. One way of looking at some of these policies is to regard labor as a productive resource of the community at large. From this standpoint, it appears clearly to be bad economy for industry to pay tender attention to the conservation and maintenance of its capital and to allow its labor power to be wasted or destroyed, merely because the laborers have not the intelligence or the strategic economic position to drive a bargain which would adequately protect them.

In case of sanitation, safety devices, child labor, and hours of labor, the purpose of control is simply to prevent injuries. But the reason why legal prevention is necessary is that industry, if left to itself, would have no adequate motive to prevent them, because it either would not have to pay for them or would not have to pay anything adequately measuring the real loss to society. Whether through ignorance, inertia, or sheer necessity, workers will work under conditions which shorten their working lives or injure their future efficiency, and they are not able to charge any adequate premium for such kinds of work. This might perhaps be treated as nobody's business but the workers', save for the fact that their children and other dependents have an interest in their working efficiency, also their future employers, or the taxpayers or contributors to charity who must pay for the rescue work which may become necessary, or the businesses out of whose product the funds for relief must come—in short, there is a "public interest" in the avoidance of such wastes.

The same principle extends to wage rates which are too low to maintain the worker in a condition of reasonable efficiency, or any arrangement which is likely at any time to plunge a family into dependence, such as the old common-law system of liability for industrial accidents. The modern system treats these injuries not as matters of fault between man and man, as did the common law, but as costs of industry, to be borne (or at least compensated in regular and predictable fashion) by the employer as the "representative of the industry," the person by whom the costs of the industry should naturally be paid. It may be said that the workers should use their bargaining power to secure adequate protection for themselves: they should demand an accident-insurance system from their employer as part of their regular wages. Perhaps they should do this, but they have not done so in the past, and if any of them had the power, it would be the best-organized and best-paid class of laborers—precisely those who need the protection least. As for the others, their failure might be charged to lack of intelligence, but others more intelligent do no better; and if they had the intelligence, they still lack the economic power. The machinery of free contract cannot fully protect this particular cost of industry.

In the case of city zoning, there is another kind of parasitic injury to be guarded against, due to the fact that neighborhood real-estate values are an organic whole, and that the use made of one lot affects the value of all the surrounding property for better or worse. The factory or garage, legitimate and necessary enough in itself, ruins the value of the residence district into which it intrudes. Here is a case where property can be used to injure others, and where the general law of property cannot forbid such injury by a general prohibition without forbidding uses which are in themselves perfectly legitimate. It cannot forbid factories, and it does not want to, for they are quite commendable things, in their proper place. The outcome is a system of localization of industry which gives each type of use its place and aims to minimize these damages and increase the aggregate use value of all the properties to their owners and to the public.

In this connection it is interesting to note that somewhat the same result can be secured by mutual consent and free contract, through the device of a "real-estate restriction." This commonly originates with a single owner of a tract which is to be subdivided and sold for residential purposes. Each buyer accepts limitations on his manner of using his lot, in consideration of all the other buyers' accepting similar limitations, of a character tending to maintain the quality of the neighborhood and the value of the property. Such agreements can do things which government itself has not the power to do, for they can censor architecture, require an owner to spend not less than a given sum on his house, and in general limit the use of private property in the interest of harmony and beauty, subjects to which the police power of the state has not yet been extended.

But it is impossible to exhaust this topic. Enough has been said here to show how vitally the costs of industry depend on the legal system, and some of the ways in which modern developments of law are striving to eliminate unpaid costs and in general to make industry pay its costs more fully and at a more equitable and socially economical rate.

2. COERCION IN A SUPPOSEDLY FREE COMMUNITY

From the standpoint of coercion the traditional keynote and ideal of our system is to use legal coercion to prevent economic coercion, as far as possible, and to keep economic relations as free as possible. But after what has already been said, it need hardly be pointed out that the simple protection of property and maintenance of formal liberty will not be enough to carry out this ideal, and that formal liberty needs to be limited in order to prevent substantial economic coercion. The state, by common consent, actually removes a great many things from the sphere of "free" bargaining, because free bargaining would result in the weaker party's being under undue pressure to accept terms which are not good for him or for the community. But can the state hope to stamp out economic coercion? It has lately been suggested that all bargaining is a form of coercion, and that when popular thought draws a line between "coercion" and "voluntary inducement," it is really drawing the line between justifiable and unjustifiable coercion.[1] On the other hand, Carver maintains that our system is essentially voluntaristic.[2] While no such issue of language can ever be settled finally, it helps illuminate the facts to look at them in the light of different usages. In this case, such a study serves to emphasize the fact that the boundary line between economic coercion and voluntary inducement is a very hazy one indeed, one that can never be located with anything like precision.

We have already seen that mankind is nowadays born under compulsion to exchange, and that one man's refusal to deal with another— or rather, to continue his customary dealings—may actually be a heavier penalty than many of those wielded by government; for example, the loss of one's job is typically a heavier penalty than a fine for speeding. We have seen that monopolies are admitted to have coercive power, meaning, in the first instance, power to coerce the customer into paying a higher price than is economically necessary. To this it should be added that the key to monopoly is the power to keep out rival producers in the face of the inducement offered by the profits of those already in the business, when these profits are more than enough to attract new enterprise into the field, if it were free to come. Thus the coercion of monopoly is two-sided.[3] We have also seen that, even if there is competition, a customer needs to be in effective touch with the market to get the benefit of it. Lacking this, he is still exposed to the same generic kind of exploitation, though in lesser degree. And when two monopolies are dealing with each other, there is an anomalous situation, a sort of mutual coercion, the chief feature of which is that the outcome does not follow any definite economic law. Something of this sort occurs when a labor monopoly and an employers' monopoly bargain together.

We have seen that the law refuses to enforce contracts made under duress, but the other examples make it quite clear that duress, in the legal sense, does not cover all the things that common sense would call

[1] Cf. R. L. Hale, "Coercion and Distribution in a Supposedly Non-coercive State," *Polit. Sci. Quart.*, XXXVIII (September, 1923), 470–494; also Commons, *Legal Foundations of Capitalism*, pp. 56–59, 83–84, 128, 290 ff.

[2] *Principles of National Economy*, reviewed by Hale, *loc. cit.*

[3] Monopolies are roughly classified into legal monopolies, natural monopolies, and "trusts" or "combinations in restraint of trade." In the first group, the law excludes would-be competitors; in the second group, the nature of the business makes competition hopeless or clearly uneconomical; while, in the third group, would-be competitors are coerced by those in the combination in a wide variety of ways which are not necessary to the business or consistent with the maintenance of socially useful competition. This subject will be taken up more fully in a later chapter.

coercive. The intent of the law is to protect the typical forms of business transactions, as sanctioned by custom; hence it is a foregone conclusion that the legal conception of duress will be confined to things that can be outlawed without undermining customary business methods. This is sensible and necessary where the remedy at the courts' disposal—the voiding of the contract—is too sweeping to be used save in extreme cases. It would do no good to declare the typical labor contract void, even granting that the worker is usually subject to some degree of coercion. In this case and in many others like it, the situation really requires something more constructive and discriminating, such as only legislation can supply. But if, when the legislation is enacted, it is held unconstitutional as an arbitrary interference with liberty, because the court cannot see any economic coercion except what is included in the legal definition of duress, then the legal concept becomes a real evil. Evidently there is need of recognizing two grades of duress: one justifying a court in voiding a contract, and the other justifying legislative action and satisfying the constitutional requirements of "due process of law" which such legislation has to meet.

We have seen that the inevitable shortage of goods carries with it the compulsions of poverty in some form or other, a thing for which no man is definitely responsible. And we have seen that these fall on certain groups in aggravated form and with concentrated weight on account of our social organization, for which, again, no one is definitely responsible, but for which the community as a whole has some responsibility.

Another instance is a strike in an industry where continuous operation is necessary to the community's welfare. If the workers are free to strike, they can coerce the public; and if they are not free to strike, the employer can coerce the workers. Evidently there is no way of avoiding some degree of coercion on one side or the other. The community may have to step in and force both sides to accept a reasonable settlement—preferably by the informal pressures of public opinion, if they are adequate.

Another example of a less powerful kind of pressure is found in the contracts which express companies used to make with shippers, making it difficult for the shippers to secure adequate redress in cases of loss or damage to the goods. While there was some competition between express companies, *they did not compete in this matter of the form of their contracts*, so that the shipper had to accept these terms or go without the express service. He could still get goods transported in other ways, but often not without serious delays, so that he was under a qualified compulsion, the chief point being that the prospective chance of loss was always less important to him than the immediate convenience of shipment by express, and he always did sign the unfair contract. People can be coerced in minor matters, simply because it is not worth their while to incur serious inconvenience in order to escape. Wherever contracts are standardized for a whole trade, this form of coercion appears.

Another example is the use of the epithet "scab," a form of moral or social coercion with an economic purpose, and representing one of the most powerful coercive forces in the economic field. In general, labor's coercion of labor is one of the widespread and important forms of economic pressure, without which it is impossible to understand the actual workings of our economic organism. Another example is the discipline of the shop, to which labor regularly subjects itself. This, however, raises no particular problem so long as the underlying contract is not unduly coercive.

Another form of coercion by labor is sabotage. Here the worker expresses his dissatisfaction with the job, not by leaving, but by remaining at work and doing all the harm he can without detection, "accidentally on purpose." This is, of course, a violation of contract as well as an injury to property and might be regarded as coercion simply because it attacks these legal rights; but there is a deeper reason, because sabotage attacks the conditions without which organized production cannot go on at all. But if the workers should all exercise their free and legal right to refuse to work, then industry could not go on either. One may ask, "Why, then, does one kind of refusal spell coercion and the other liberty?" The answer is that if *all* workers refused to work, they would have coercive power, like any combination that puts an end to competition. But they do not all combine. If some do, the employer is left free to try to find others who will accept his terms; and one of the significant things about sabotage is that it puts well-nigh ruinously prohibitive obstacles in the way of this canvassing of the market and gives a few workers power to block production where others might be willing to cooperate. Of course, the "willingness" of these others may be a euphemism for the compulsion of unemployment, and this may need to be redressed by some compulsion on the other side. But, even so, sabotage will still be an intolerable policy, not because it is coercion, but because it is not the right kind. It is ruinously costly and next to impossible of direction to any constructive and definite end; and it is the sort of tactics which enable minorities to coerce majorities. It is chiefly a revolutionary weapon; but if a revolution were brought about by its aid, it not only would impoverish the nation while the struggle was going on but would render the work of reconstruction well-nigh impossible; for each minority faction would have learned to use this weapon against the others, and in the face of this, no common will could be effectively carried out.

Can we build up a definition in harmony with these various instances? Coercion is always the use of a penalty, or threat of one, to induce people to act as they would not act otherwise, but the nature of the penalty varies, marking off the fields of forcible coercion, economic coercion, and moral or social coercion. Forcible coercion is supposed to be the monopoly of the state, with reservations in favor of private rights to defend person or property. But the state's favorite penalty, the money fine, is a curious hybrid. It is an economic penalty, with force in the background to insure submission, but a large part of the effect may arise from a moral or social stigma.

What we think of as economic coercion acts mainly through the power to withhold access to goods or services, where the person from whom they are withheld needs access to these particular goods or services so much that he is, or feels, "dependent" on them in some substantial degree. Under primitive conditions, the property owner's right to exclude others protects him in his personal use of his property. In modern industrial property the owner masses his holdings with others' into a vast engine which is of no use to him except as he can get workers to operate it; and his power to exclude them serves mainly as the basis of his bargain with them for their services. It is not the sole basis, however. If he lost the power to exclude them from his physical property, they could not themselves make much more use of it than the owner; they still need his business organization, through which the property is able to yield an income. The result of the change would merely be a new basis for bargaining, in which each could now prevent the other from making effective use of the property. The "sit-down" strike might be taken as an illustration.

Some power to withhold is essential to any system of bargaining. We bargain for something we have power to bestow; and without power to withhold, the power to bestow is economically meaningless. But "withholding" covers a variety of economic facts, though it is not easy to separate them in practice. It is one thing to exclude Smith in order to hire Jones, because I think Jones is a better worker, and another thing to exclude all workers and shut the plant down. It is one thing to exclude Smith when there are other employers waiting to hire men, and another thing to exclude him when there are millions of qualified workers unemployed, and I am virtually excluding him from opportunity to work for an indefinite period. It makes a great difference whether Smith has a family and a home or not, and whether or not he can market his ability without going to some distant place. Evidently the thing is a matter of degree.

Moreover, the one exercising coercion may not himself be free. An employer who forces workers to accept a reduction in wages may have no option except to do this or go bankrupt. The ultimate compulsion may come from the condition of the economic system over which he has, as an individual, no control. And compulsion is not confined to the present type of economic system; an isolated self-sufficing farmer must produce or starve and may not be able with his best efforts to secure a satisfactory living. Under our system, the inescapable compulsions of economic life are passed along by individual agents, mixed with their own discretionary acts, and the whole resultant transformed by the character of our present economic structure.

It is possible, in principle at least, to distinguish arbitrary personal coercion from impersonal compulsions for which no one individual is responsible. Where business enterprises compete effectively, no one of them can arbitrarily coerce the customers, though they are under a general compulsion to pay enough to induce some producer to serve them. But where monopoly exists, the customers are dependent, to the extent of their need for the product, on being served by this particular concern. "Businesses affected with a public interest" clearly involve this kind of dependence, either because they are natural monopolies or because the public is not in a position to get the full benefits of competition.[1] And where the market is not perfect, other businesses exhibit the same kind of dependence, though not legally recognized as belonging to this class.

In general, the law sanctions compulsion such as is exercised by the economic system in general, though not personal coercion exercised by a single arbitrary power. Thus it draws the line at coercion of consumers by a monopoly but permits the compulsion exercised by the force of competition and permits the producers on whom it falls in the first instance to hand it on to their wage earners and their customers, believing that in the aggregate this makes for plenty and cheapness and so minimizes the compulsions of nature. Some such handing on of economic pressure is inescapable and represents the fundamental facts of natural scarcity.

But while nature itself makes some such compulsion inevitable, nature does not dictate the particular form it must take. This is gov-

---

[1] The requirement that they shall deal with goods or services of common necessity defines the field within which these businesses lie but does not identify the particular group within this field which is legally set off for special treatment. Clothes are a necessity, but tailors are not therefore "affected with a public interest."

erned by our economic system, which concentrates certain burdens in such a way as to make them unnecessarily serious. For example, the nature of agriculture makes it necessary either to find some alternative work to occupy the winter months, or else to waste a great deal of time. In the days when every farm carried on household manufactures, these filled in the winter season very simply and naturally; but when manufactures moved off the farm and into the factory, the factory no longer dovetailed its operation with the farm work. The farmer does not time his demand for goods as he used to do when he made them himself. Manufacturing for the farmer is now carried on when the farmer has need for the goods or money with which to buy them, not when he has time with which to make them. The result is a seasonal irregularity which is not compensated and which falls with serious force on certain classes, especially harvest hands, though it affects many other workers in seasonal industries. Those who cannot raise themselves out of the ranks of casual labor are compelled to accept this concentrated burden of irregularity. The form this compulsion takes and the concentration of the burden are not the inevitable result of the nature of agriculture; they are produced by our existing economic system.

In short, it seems that we must accept the fact of economic compulsion, but that our responsibility does not end here. There is a public interest in seeing to it that this pressure is converted into an incentive to do the thing that will be most effective in lightening the burden for all concerned. But this pressure is handed on to workers via employers, who thus become, in a sense, beneficiaries of the compulsions of nature and trustees for the community, to see that this force is turned into the most constructive channels. This works well as far as the interests of the employer are in harmony with those of the community, but we have seen enough to be well aware that this harmony is far from perfect. The workers are in a position to be compelled to do things that are bad for them, if the employer thinks those things are to his interest, and he, being also under some pressure, may take a short-run view of his own interest and that of the workers as well, with unfortunate results. He may force his workers to sacrifice interests that should in the long-run interest of the community be made inalienable.

So far as poverty makes people work hard without exacting more pay than industry can reasonably afford, it works in a useful direction, though as things are, this force misses its maximum effect because it works most strongly at just the time when the product of industry is limited by a business depression, a condition which hard work on the part of individual workers does little or nothing to remedy. But so far as workmen are led, for instance, to accept the conditions of casual labor just as they are, or any other injurious industrial conditions, the effect is not constructive and needs correcting.

As between different methods of bringing this about, preference should be given to using the power of the state to redress inequalities of bargaining power and relying on the parties most immediately concerned to work out their relations in the way that seems to them most appropriate. Economic pioneering, in particular, can best be done in this way. This is the great element of truth in the position of the advocates of a voluntary economy, as against one which is ordered in all its details by the compulsory power of the state. But when this voluntary pioneering has been done, it often needs to be backed up by the power of government to make its results effective; and where the social interest is clear, government is not always justified in waiting for the results of voluntary pioneering.

3. CHANGES IN THE LAW, AND THE NEWER "RIGHTS"

Our legal system is evolving. As we have seen in connection with the costs of industry, new ideas of economic responsibility are being enacted into law, modifying the individualistic common-law doctrines. Private rights and liberties, never absolute in character, have been more and more qualified by the recognition of social claims; and private remedies, such as the suit for damages, are being supplemented or supplanted by collective insurance or collective prevention or both.

In this conflict between the old legal doctrines and the new, the old have a great advantage in being formulated in compact and cogent maxims such as only time can develop and usage sanctify. For usage develops their meaning, twining around them just the right threads of association, so that they convey to the mind just the right pictures of conditions which the mind accepts as representative. Thus is built up the "stereotype"—to use the term coined by Walter Lippman[1]— which the orthodox mind accepts as a substitute for the complex realities of the legal system, and which carries with it a corresponding stereotype of the economic facts and human relations with which the law has to deal. Progressive social education consists largely in scrutinizing these stereotypes and getting at the facts behind them. No matter if the all-sufficiency of the formula disappears upon analysis; it may still do its work if no substitute is ready to take its place. And the newer forms of control, not having that deceptive appearance of

[1] See *Public Opinion*, Chap. vi and elsewhere.

homogeneity which attaches to "liberty" in the abstract, do not fall into simple stereotypes with the same happy facility.

Among the attempts to supply this need is that of Professor Ely.[1] He describes certain phases of the modern movement by saying that we are developing new rights akin to the rights of property, and that if the older rights of property have been forced to give way, it has been to make way for newer rights of a generally similar character. Among these he mentions the right to be well born, the right to health as well as education, the right to reputation, to privacy, and others.

These are rights of persons, not of property, and therefore their growth is naturally at the expense of some of the former rights of property owners to use their property as they saw fit. In one important respect, these new rights are not similar to property rights or even to the personal liberties of adults in an individualistic system but are more like the rights of children and dependents in general. The rights of property do not give anyone a positive duty to furnish anyone else with food or clothing or any other economic goods. True, the state has the duty of furnishing the property owner with clear possession of his property, but this is a duty which it does not owe to everyone, merely to property owners. As we have seen, the *acquisition of property in general* is not a right, but a liberty.

But these newer rights call on the state or some other body to furnish positive economic goods and services. In that respect they differ from the older traditional rights in the direction of paternalism, and we may as well recognize the fact and call it by its true name. Is this development alarming? Not unless it is carried so far that the ordinary individual's responsibility for his own economic success dwindles to a point where he actually has less burdens than are good for him and less than he can reasonably be asked to handle. So far, it can hardly be said that we have reached that point, since the difficulties of modern life constantly outrun the advances of social legislation.

Are these newer rights a violation of the older "natural rights" of personal liberty, or are they themselves natural rights? Probably we can answer this question better after we have looked at a more fundamental question, namely, whether there are any such things as natural rights.

4. ARE THERE "NATURAL RIGHTS"?

In attempting an answer to this question, two points in the foregoing argument are of dominant importance: the evolutionary point of view toward social arrangements, and the analysis of rights into

[1] See *Property and Contract*, pp. 367–379.

duties, remedies, and the resulting benefits to the person in whose favor the duties are enforced. Furthermore, to answer this question we must know the precise meaning of "natural rights," and the harder one tries to give the term a precise meaning, the more difficult the task appears. It cannot refer, as Blackstone suggested, to the rights people would enjoy in a "state of nature," living apart from all their fellows,[1] because the very meaning of rights involves the relationships and obligations of people living together in society. And since these relationships and obligations change with changing ways of living and working, they cannot possess that quality of permanence which seems to be part of the idea of a natural right, as the term has been actually used.

Another possible meaning of natural rights is a system of obligations which is virtually self-enforcing because it follows those ideas of fair conduct which are so generally held that any transgression will rouse the victim to a sense of just resentment and resistance, in which he will be backed up by the sympathy and active aid of the whole group. Ross has described a natural order of this sort very suggestively, making clear three vital facts.[2] First, such a system can maintain itself under special conditions of a simple sort which are bound to be temporary: for example, American frontier communities in the days of the forty-niners. Second, the law of such a system is primarily a law of equal combat, where both the weapons and the rules are the same for both sides, but *this does not determine the nature of the weapons or the character of the rules.* The natural "sense of justice" may attach itself to rules of any level of enlightenment or barbarism and the use of any variety of weapons. Third, such a system is totally inadequate to the needs of modern society. Preserving equality of legal weapons in an economic struggle does not keep the struggle from being predatory, does not prevent injuries to innocent bystanders, and does not even produce an equal combat when organization makes the combatants unequal in size and resources. It fails to provide for our modern impersonal relations between unequals and our frequent conflicts between the needs of the community and the average citizen's simple standards of man-to-man fairness. Such vestiges of this natural order as persist under modern conditions can be summed up in the maxim attributed to Turgot: "Economize coercion." Go along with the customary stand-

---

[1] *Commentaries on the Laws of England* (Amer. ed.), Introduction, Sec. 2, 43; Book I, Chap. i, p. 124.

[2] *Social Control*, Chap. vi. Cf. also Chap. vii, where he shows the limitations of such a system and the need of something more definitely organized and planned to serve the common interests.

ards of justice as far as possible, and antagonize them as little as possible. Where change is needed, educate the people to it and, if possible, present new rules as extensions of familiar and accepted principles. But this does not give us a system of natural rights.

One hint we have already gained from reviewing the ideas of Blackstone, who appears quite sound when he is speaking of "rights" in the shape of actual benefits which people receive and enjoy, but whose position begins to appear obsolete and inadequate as soon as he goes on to the procedural relations, the system of wrongs and remedies, which serves to protect these substantive benefits. To put it in another way, there appear to be certain *natural needs* of humanity which are, for all practical purposes, permanent, but the system of legal rights needed to protect these human needs changes with changing methods of work and conditions of living.

These human needs include the requisites of efficient production and may be extended to include not merely food and shelter but the whole range of necessary incentives. One such natural right is the right of the producer to receive the fruits of his individual efforts. Another is the right to subject one's self to coercion by binding one's self in enforceable contracts. These two needs or rights are in conflict with each other, for the right of contract allows a man to enter a factory where his individual product is untraceable[1]—a fact which may stand as typical of many conflicts between these natural needs of humanity. They cannot all be fully satisfied.

But satisfaction is relative, and with each human need there is a certain minimum of which people cannot be deprived without society's suffering serious consequences. The exact boundary line of this minimum is impossible to draw, but there are plenty of cases in which there would be no doubt, in the judgment of intelligent persons. We may say, if we choose, that everyone has a natural right to this minimum, in a certain sense. When the term is used in this way, two fundamental propositions stand out. One is that *natural rights in this sense must necessarily be inalienable; hence liberty cannot be a natural right to the extent of making it possible to alienate any of the others, and to cut one's self off from meeting one's minimum natural needs.* A second fact is that it requires very different schemes of duties and remedies to protect these minimum needs in different stages of social development, with the result that, *even if there are natural rights in this sense of needs for*

---

[1] That is, untraceable by such simple methods as are available to the common sense of the man in the street. Whether the product is traceable on the basis of "marginal contributions" is a controversial question among theoretical economists, and the answer does not concern our present problem.

substantive benefits, which society cannot afford to see denied, this carries with it no natural system of legal obligations. These must still be treated as adaptable instruments for the attainment of social purposes. There are no eternally natural procedures.

Even the minimum of natural needs is not easy to define. Have the feeble-minded a right to propagate? Have those who are merely stupid a similar right? Or has posterity a right to be fathered by the best stock of the present generation? In answering such questions as this, progress will be necessarily slow; and in the meantime personal liberty will probably be given the benefit of all reasonable doubt.

5. THE VALUE OF STABILITY[1]

One of the prime requisites of a flourishing economic development is that those who take the initiative and assume responsible leadership shall know what to expect and shall be able to count on the consequences of their own acts and those of other persons with whom they have dealings. The consequences of any new practice can never be perfectly foreseen—that is why the business pioneer's experiments are so risky, under the best conditions—and legal uncertainties increase the risk tremendously. New laws are as uncertain as any other new thing. Even their literal construction is in doubt until the courts have passed on it, and their ultimate economic effects are still more in doubt. People do not typically know what they are doing. That is, they do not understand the *why* of it, why it produces certain results. They merely expect a familiar kind of action to be followed by the customary result, because it has worked that way in their past experience. They accept bank notes with confidence, not because they understand the Federal Reserve law—that is reserved for a small minority of bankers and other students—but because everyone else accepts them and finds them safe.

This need of stability is the ground for our constitutional provision that no state may pass a law impairing the obligation of contracts, since contract is the keystone of economic relations. Hence, there arises the business habit of going cautiously in matters covered by any new legislation until its meaning has been construed and its operation tested. Every new law is to some extent unjust, especially new law resulting from court decisions on actions which have already occurred, so that the change in the law is retroactive. And yet every old law is also unjust, to precisely the extent that conditions have changed

---

[1] Cf. Homer Hoyt, "The Economic Function of the Common Law," *Jour. Polit. Econ.*, XXVI (1918), 168–199.

so as to alter the results it produces. The best that can be hoped is to reduce the inevitable injustice to a minimum.[1]

In practice, our system consists of the common law, which follows precedent and protects that justice which inheres in stability; and the statute law, which has the function of preventing the injustices of stagnation and altering the law when new conditions require it. In the resulting contest, each side is protecting one variety of justice, usually at the expense of the other, and the ideal balance has not yet been found. Legislatures deluge the country with imperfectly considered measures, and a legislator will often support an unsound bill for the attainment of a popular object, simply because he knows the courts will kill it and can be made to bear the odium of its defeat, while the legislator gains the credit of favoring the people's interests. If the courts should abdicate their veto powers, one of two things would happen: Either legislatures would be forced to be more circumspect than they are at present, assuming a far greater measure of responsibility for conserving the values of stability; or else the increased uncertainty of business as to the conditions it would have to meet might impair its willingness to invest for a distant future and thus seriously weaken an economic system dependent on voluntary private enterprise.

6. CONCLUSION

The position of law as a means of economic control is by no means a simple one. Arising itself in part out of business practices, it must also control them. It may veto new legislation or yield to it, the decision often resting, in the last analysis, on grounds of the needs of society. The law is bound by precedent, yet ultimately capable of changing to almost any extent which the settled judgment of the community may demand. It is a means to social ends, yet the value of stability makes any standing law or precedent an end in itself and right merely because it exists. The law cannot be reduced to any all-resolving principle, other than the general rule of conserving the most important social values.

That this fact is increasingly realized by jurists is one of the most hopeful features of the situation. The law is becoming consciously an instrument of social control. While the inertia of precedent persists and the value of stability is highly emphasized, nevertheless economic facts are more and more finding their way into legal briefs, and

---

[1] "Injustice" is used here in the sense of hardship which the sufferer has done nothing to deserve, and which results from human arrangements. No human arrangements can eliminate all such hardship, and a system which minimizes it may perhaps be called "just" in the sense which identifies justice with the happiness of the greatest number. This, however, is not the most common meaning of "justice."

the evolution of law in response to changing economic circumstances is coming to be recognized as one of the accepted conditions of present-day life.

REFERENCES FOR FURTHER READINGS

ADAMS, BROOKS, *Theory of Social Revolutions*, Chaps. ii, iii.

BARNES, I. R., *Cases on Public Utilities*, section on "The Public Utility Concept and the Right to Regulate," 1934.

CARVER, *Principles of National Economy*, Chap. vi.

ELY, *Property and Contract*, Part I, Chaps. xiv–xx; Part II, Chaps. vii, viii; Part IV, Chap. iv.

FREUND, *The Police Power*, Chap. i a.

———, *Standards of American Legislation*, Chaps. i, iii, v.

HALE, "Coercion and Distribution in a Supposedly Non-coercive State," *Polit. Sci. Quar.*, XXXVIII (September, 1923), 470–494.

ORTH, S. P., *Readings on the Relation of Government to Property and Industry*, Chap. vi.

POUND, ROSCOE, *The Spirit of the Common Law*, Chaps. vii, viii.

———, "Preventive Justice and Social Work," *Proc. National Conference of Social Work*, pp. 151–163, 1923.

RUBINOW, *Social Insurance*, Part I.

SEAGER, *Social Insurance*.

SPENCER, W. H., *Text-book on Law and Business*, Part III, 1929.

SUMNER, essays on "Equality" and "Liberty," *Earth-Hunger and Other Essays*.

CHAPTER VIII

WHAT IS COMPETITION?

1. INTRODUCTION: RELATION OF COMPETITION TO THE PROBLEMS OF CONTROL

The relation of competition to control is many sided, and while some of its aspects are obvious, others may be worth pointing out. It is a form of private and spontaneous control, maintained and kept within bounds by other underlying forms of control, chiefly the protection of rights of person and property, which we have just been discussing. It is sometimes thought of as merely a corollary of the two basic facts of universal liberty (always within the bounds of law) and the division of labor. For if anyone has found a profitable service which he can render to his fellow-men, others will want to engage in the service and share in the profits; and if they are free to do so, then competition is inevitable. But what if the new producer, once he is in the business, chooses to combine or agree with those who are already there, or they with him, and so extinguish the competition as fast as it starts up? Even under these conditions competition would have some effect, though not what its advocates intend it to have. "Free competition" in the usual sense, however, bars out such combinations or agreements. It exists only when each competitor follows his own financial interests absolutely independent of the others, with no collusion or concerted action of any sort. Competitors are free—except to combine.

Viewed from another angle, competition is an exception to the rule that no one may so use his property as to injure another, for one is allowed to injure his competitors as long as the injuries are merely those incidental to "legitimate" competition. This makes it decidedly incumbent upon us to discover what legitimate competition may be, as distinct from other varieties. The theory is that, when A's competition injures B by inflicting losses upon him or depriving him of income which he would otherwise have had, this can only mean that A is giving the consumers more for their money, with the result that every dollar B loses is matched by a dollar's worth of gain to the consumers, and any net gain A may make is a clear advantage to the community.[1] Whether or not this arithmetic is always completely borne out by the facts, it is clear that, so far as competition does consist in giving the consumer more for his money, the main issue is not between A and B, but between B and the public, and that the interest of the public is paramount.

With a sufficient number of rivals in the field, the public is no longer dependent upon any one, for either the quantity, quality, or price of the goods he sells, and they are better served than if one were in absolute control and followed the usual bent of commercial "human nature." And this without denying that if the one producer's chief desire were to serve the public well, rather than to make money as easily as possible, and if he were fired with a zeal which spurred him to exert his best efforts without the pressure of necessity to compel him, he could probably serve the public better if he did not have rivals to compete with. No one can measure exactly either the wastes of competition or the gains resulting from it and tell for certain which is larger, but even without knowing this, the public will not tolerate the mere fact of being dependent upon the good will of a private monopolist to use his power humanely. Such power amounts to "taxation without representation," and it is regarded as tyranny, quite apart from the weight of the taxes the ruler may impose.

Competition, then, is the option the public has of dealing with anyone who may wish to deal with it, and this option frees it from servitude. But it also frees the producers and dealers from the obligations to serve which would be laid upon them if the public did not have this option. No one dealer is necessary to the public; therefore no one dealer is under obligation to produce, and the shutting down of a plant is a matter of private choice and not of public concern. Moreover, under "proper" competition a plant will not close down so long as it can cover "costs"; hence this freedom of the producer cannot be used to exploit the consumer. Yet if labor troubles close several plants, the consumer may suffer; and if a large plant chooses to close down, its local community may be placed in a serious situation. It remains to some extent dependent on the producers, and to just the extent of its dependence it needs to be able to hold the producers to some cor-

[1] On this point see Pigou, *Wealth and Welfare*, pp. 161–162.

responding duties and responsibilities in the matter of reasonable and continuous service. But it does not have the formal power to do this. Only industries "affected with a public interest" in the legal sense have in the past been subject to a positive duty to serve the public. In ordinary competitive industry the producer's duty to serve, which still exists, though to a less extent than under monopoly, has to be enforced by informal and extra-legal means.[1]

Another thing competition does, which has a substantial bearing on control. Where competition is free and active, each person is supposed to have open to him, as buyer or seller, a number of possibilities of approximately equal attractiveness and representing about what the business organism can afford to offer him. As applied to labor, this casts doubt on the possibility of raising the general level of wages, by deliberate control, above the level an open market would fix. The chief guaranty that this will not go below the minimum of subsistence lies in the fact that industrial output is increasing, from generation to generation. The world is growing richer; it afforded a subsistence to past generations; hence it can afford at least as much to those now living. But this is far from being an absolute guaranty. Particular displaced groups might still starve, but for the intervention of the community.

2. COMPETITION DEFINED

But what is competition? It may be defined, in general, as rivalry for income by the method of giving more than one's rivals give in proportion to what one asks in return, or by making the public think so, or by making them at least act as if they thought so to the extent of buying one's goods in preference to those of one's rival. Presumably the successful competitor is giving people what they want, or at least making them think he is giving them what he has made them think they want. And this is a process to which Lincoln's saying about fooling the people is peculiarly pertinent, including the part about fooling some of the people all of the time.

Competition includes, of course, the making of goods to sell and the getting of things to make them with, including land and plant, materials, power, and labor, and the privilege of operating, in cases

[1] The attitude of the courts toward the Kansas Industrial Disputes Act indicates that they are slow to extend the obligations of service attaching to industries "affected with a public interest" to the general field of industry, or to allow the legislature to make sweeping enlargements of the class of public-service industries. See *Wolff Packing Co.* v. *Court of Industrial Relations*, 262 U.S. 522 (June 1923). More recent decisions indicate a relaxing of this attitude, at least in the matter of power to control prices. Cf. below, Chap. x, Sec. 3.

where that is not automatically open to all. Thus competition extends to many forms of rivalry, most of which may be treated as subsidiary to the basic struggle of business enterprises making and selling goods, but which are, nevertheless, very different from one another. There is buyers' and sellers' competition, one-sided and two-sided competition, competition in price, in quality, in advertising and selling, and in securing access to the means of production. There is competition of consumers for goods, competition of different classes of workers to secure jobs, to hold the jobs they have secured, and to obtain advancement. The character of this competition differs widely with the character of the work, from the unskilled casual laborer to the high-grade professional expert on a salaried basis, while the professional man who is in business for himself differs from all the others, presenting a mixture of business competition with professional standards and obligations, punctilios and restraints. But for that matter, as we shall see, all kinds of competition are subject to some of these informal and self-imposed restraints, violations being stigmatized as unfair or predatory or cut-throat competition.

One current impression of the nature of competition is not borne out by the facts, namely, that it always acts downward, whether on prices or on wages. Buyers' competition acts upward, including that of business concerns and market speculators, and so tends to raise both wages and prices. In the upward swing of the business cycle, competition tends to raise prices more than to lower them, while in a period of depression the opposite is, of course, true. But the great swings of prices, lasting a generation or more, are governed predominantly by other forces. As far as competition stimulates the development of more efficient methods of production, it increases the real incomes of the community in terms of goods; and since it also tends to reduce the profits of business enterprises, this is likely to mean an upward tendency of real wages. This may, of course, be canceled by other forces, but the large increase in real wages which went on steadily throughout the nineteenth century can be attributed to the increase in efficiency of production—which competition helped to accelerate—coupled with the inability of the employer to retain all the benefits for himself, owing to the force of competition. Thus, while competition does act downward and may at times reduce wages to less than a living rate, this is not its only effect, especially in the long run.

3. COMPETITION OF BUSINESS ENTERPRISES

Perhaps the best way to approach an analysis of competition is via its antithesis, monopoly. They are alike in that each is trying to get the largest possible net profit, but under different conditions of marketing their goods, so that the results are different. Each is limited by the fact that if it raises the price of what it sells, it cannot sell as much as if it kept prices lower, and if it lowers the price of the things it buys, it cannot get as much, or of such good quality, as if it kept prices higher. Either limitation will reduce its marketable output and so affect its gross earnings, so that it has to choose between larger sales at smaller profits and smaller sales at larger profits; and it fixes its various prices with a view, not to selling as many goods as it can, nor getting as large a gross income as it can, but with a view to the largest possible net income. But the response of the market to one firm's price tactics is quite different in the two cases.

Every market has some elasticity, so that the total demand will shrink in response to a rise in prices, while the total supply (especially of raw materials) will ordinarily, though not always, shrink in response to a lowering of the price offered. The supply of labor *for any one industry* will commonly behave in the same way, shrinking with a fall in wages, chiefly because labor has the option of going into other industries, so that the industry in question does not have a monopoly of the entire demand for labor but has to meet a qualified sort of competition. When a monopoly raises or lowers prices, it is subject to this elasticity of the general market, and a rise will cause some buyers to reduce their purchases, do without the good entirely, or buy some "substitute." By "substitute" is implied something which is inferior for the purpose in hand by an appreciable margin in the eyes of most buyers, so that they will not change from one to the other on as slight provocation as they would if it were only a question of buying the "same goods" from a rival maker.[1] The monopolist can raise his price without losing all his customers. The theoretical monopoly price is the most profitable compromise between higher returns per unit sold and larger volume of sales. It will be above the added cost of added output and will ordinarily (though not inevitably) be above total cost, yielding a "monopoly profit."

But, with competition, the market for the product of any one producer is far more sensitive than this to any change of his own prices if

[1] Of course, this "sameness" is a matter of more or less. Every competing producer does his best to convince his customers that his goods are different from his competitors', and that the latter are really inferior substitutes, thus lending the demand for his individual product more resistance to the attacks of competitors—making it less elastic. He can, however, never hope to make it as inelastic as if he controlled his competitors' goods as well as his own. The preference for an "Easy" washing machine as compared to a "Thor" can never become so strong as the preference for some machine or other as compared to the scrubbing board.

the other producers do not follow suit. When he lowers his price and the others do not, he may get all the new business and a great deal of his competitors' old business as well, provided he can handle it. Or if they follow suit after a delay or do not cut prices so far, the initiator of the move will still get some of their customers away from them and get more than his proportionate share of the new business besides. Conversely, a producer's demand may fall off even if he has not raised prices, simply because his competitors have lowered them.

It is this more than proportionate sensitiveness of the single producer's sales that is the distinctive earmark of competition; and wherever it is found, some degree of competition exists. As a consequence of all this, the price which results from his individual search for a maximum net return is lower than with a monopoly producing at the same cost, being shifted far closer to the limit beyond which business would be done at an absolute loss or in some cases even beyond this limit.

In practice, of course, different producers have different costs of production. The normal level of prices is one at which a majority of the goods are produced at a profit and a minority at a loss.[1] This minority commonly includes the output of the definitely inefficient or handicapped producers, together with some of the medium-cost group who are, for some temporary reason, having a worse year than usual. In the long run and on the average of fluctuations, prices must be such that normally efficient producers can earn enough to attract capital.

4. GRADES OF COMPETITION

As might be surmised from the foregoing discussion, there are many varieties of competition which require special notice. There is cutthroat competition, due to an excess of producing capacity; there is predatory competition, where the object is not present earnings, but the driving out of competitors and the establishing of a monopoly; there is localized or discriminatory competition, and "unfair competition" of various sorts; and, finally, there is partial or imperfect competition and competition modified by agreements, informal under-

---

[1] Data bearing on this question have been gathered by the Tariff Commission and the Federal Trade Commission and analyzed in a number of articles published during the six years following the World War. The trend of these is summed up by A. B. Wolfe, "Competitive Costs and the Rent of Business Ability," *Quart. Jour. Econ.*, XXXIX (November, 1924), 39–69. The figures need supplementing by data gathered during more normal times, and by more perfect allowances for depreciation and interest on all the capital employed. With all these items reckoned in, price might be found more nearly equal to average cost of production.

standings, or a sentiment against "spoiling the market" by unsound or cutthroat tactics.

Cutthroat competition and predatory competition differ from ordinary competition in that the producers who hold the strategic position and have most influence on the market—typically, large and fairly efficient concerns—do not stop lowering prices at a point which covers all costs, including a fair return on investment, but go below this level, either in the whole market or in some section of it. This situation is made possible mainly by the fact that there are large amounts of fixed and specialized investment in the business which cannot get out, so that when there is not enough demand to keep it all busy at profitable prices, a manager may judge that it is better to let the capital work for less than a fair return than to let it stand idle, earning nothing at all. The same principle applies to many of the operating expenses which do not vary much whether the plant is working at full or at half capacity. This question will be gone into more fully in a later chapter, but it is clear that it creates a delicate situation, susceptible of much abuse and calling for some measures of restraint or control. Out-and-out predatory competition finds its chief discouragement in the anti-trust laws, which aim to take away the prize— monopoly position and profits—without which prospect a business will hardly incur the certain losses of such a struggle.

Evidently the public cannot afford to rest on a simple belief that all competition is good. The situation requires careful differentiation between different types of competition, coupled with wise restraints temperately exercised.

5. UNFAIR COMPETITION

What is "unfair competition"? To most people it would be easier to decide what practices are unfair than to tell why. There would be little question that it is unfair to hire people to spy on a competitor's business or to bring about a strike in his shops, to damage the reputation of his goods by false statements or bogus demonstrations, or to advertise one's own goods as "marked down" when they are not, or to make any other definitely false statements in advertising one's own goods. Bribing of purchasing agents is also a clear case, at least in principle. It is taken for granted that it is unfair for a concern to pose as an "independent" when it is really controlled by a "trust," though this might be defended as merely a way of avoiding the unjust stigma arising from the popular prejudice against trusts. More tangible tactics are the getting of discriminatory railroad rates or favors in car supply—practices which regulation has done much to diminish in the past thirty years—or the selling of goods below cost in the territory covered by a small competitor while keeping prices up in districts where he does not operate. Selling a competitor's goods below cost has also been attacked as tending to discredit the quality of the goods and the fairness of the price the competitor regularly charges.

Other practices complained of include espionage on the competitor's business, a practice which is chiefly useful in connection with other "unfair" tactics. It is of great help to the concern that wishes to concentrate competitive efforts on the particular customers who form the competitor's field, so that the competitor faces a crushing attack while the general market does not get the benefit.

Another group of practices generally condemned consists of intimidating a competitor's customers or agents, to make them cease handling the competitor's goods. This takes various forms, including the making of exclusive contracts with dealers, granting them certain goods which are so strongly established in the market that the dealer cannot do without them, on condition that he refuse to handle the goods of competitors. Another form is inducing customers to break their contracts or cancel their orders, or buying the goods away from dealers to keep them off the market. Competitors' goods may be imitated (a practice of the National Cash Register Company) or purchasing agents may be bribed.

At the other end of the process of production, control of raw materials may handicap competitors. Thus the Aluminum Company of America, as a producer of the raw metal, controls supplies of bauxite ore which no would-be competitor has yet been able to match, while as a manufacturer of aluminum utensils it competes with fabricators who must buy their material from it. The possibilities of this situation are obvious. Patents may be infringed, or where there has been no infringement, fraudulent suits may be brought for alleged infringements, merely for the purpose of hampering a competitor's legitimate operations. In general, the regular conduct of a competitor's business can be interfered with in an untold variety of ways, and the threat of such treatment may be used to scare out competitors or to make existing dealers boycott a rival's goods.[1]

Again, wholesalers feel aggrieved when manufacturers sell to retailers without adding the customary wholesalers' discount and are inclined to regard this as unfair competition, though it could be de-

[1] For a general discussion of these methods, see Stevens, *Unfair Competition;* Franklin D. Jones, *Trade Associations and the Law,* Chaps. i–iii; Eliot Jones, *The Trust Problem in the United States,* Chaps. v–x, sections on the sources of monopoly power; and G. C. Henderson, *The Federal Trade Commission,* Chaps. iv–vi, 1924.

fended as the only way to subject the wholesalers' margins to a real competitive test at all. And among doctors and lawyers, advertising itself is considered unfair competition, or at least unprofessional conduct, while the splitting of fees with those who are in a position to turn business to a member of one of these professions, or to whom he may be in a position to turn business, is still more strenuously condemned. These may be taken as typical examples and should be sufficiently varied to illustrate the main principles involved.

Some of these practices are clear cases of interfering with the competitor, who is supposed to be absolutely free to do his best in organizing his work and putting it before the public. Incidentally, a purchasing agent who takes a bribe betrays his employer, and a labor leader who is paid to call a strike is not only conspiring to injure the employer; he is betraying the men who have elected him to office. Railroad discriminations are also a clear case, because one shipper gets an advantage which is irrelevant to the supposed object and nature of the competitive game in which all are engaged, in which the prize is intended to go to the most efficient producer. He gets a handicap in a race which fails of its purpose unless it is run from scratch; as if handicaps were used in the trials for the selection of an Olympic team.

Of course, all competitors may have an equal chance to pull the wires and secure the rebates, and that equality may satisfy the uneducated and unthinking sense of fairness,[1] but that is not the only test of justice, nor the true test. That would justify the most brutal rules if only both sides followed them. To find *what rules are just rules* to set up for all concerned to follow, we must probe deeper. We must fall back on the purpose of the game from the point of view of the community, namely, the selection of servants to organize and carry on its production who can—and will—serve it most efficiently and on the lowest terms of ultimate expenditure and sacrifice. Anything which violates this purpose is undesirable, though it may not be recognized as unfair. But if business men in general can be brought to see the undesirability and to develop a positive disapproval, then the thing becomes "unfair" in terms of the accepted morals of the trade, because it is an advantage which men of the highest character will not take, and those who do take it gain by being more unscrupulous than their fellows. It is one of the tasks of control to attach the sentiment of unfairness to all practices which violate the social purpose of the game of competition. Under our present federal anti-trust laws, making unfair competition illegal, the Federal Trade Commission can and does draw on the consensus of judgment in a trade for guidance in framing

[1] See above, p. 120.

its own list of unfair practices,[1] though it has been hampered by narrow judicial interpretations. The courts have not adopted the broad social conception set forth above. Under favorable conditions, however, it appears that law and business sentiment may be mutually reinforcing.

6. PARTIAL AND IMPERFECT COMPETITION

Modern analysis is distinguishing a number of different conditions in which competition under normal business motives tends to different results. With a standardized commodity, the producer with even a slightly lower price than his rivals can take all their business away from them, up to the limit of his capacity to handle it. He will then have an incentive to lower his price as long as it is even slightly above the added cost of added output; on one condition, namely, that he does not expect his competitors to meet his reduction at once. If producers are many and small, a reduction by one may not create enough disturbance to force the others to follow suit at once. And a secret reduction (almost necessarily limited to part of the market) will not have this effect. In such cases the incentive to make reductions persists down to the level of added cost. Thus secret price cutting tends toward cutthroat price wars in industries with large constant costs.

But a general and open reduction by one of a few large producers is so sure to be promptly met that the initiator cannot count on taking any material amount of business away from his rivals. Hence, some have concluded that the incentive to make such reductions stops at the same point as if there were a complete monopoly. Actually, such reductions may gain a few large orders and a precarious good-will. They are often made as a response to secret and irregular price cutting by rivals. Moreover, the personal equation enters; whichever producer favors the lowest price will govern the market. And if, either in these ways or because of changes in costs, the price ever gets below the monopoly level, there is no competitive force acting to raise it up to that level. For if one producer *raises* his price, his rivals are under no necessity of following suit—quite the contrary. They can leave their prices unchanged and take his business away from him. Thus the same force does not work in both directions; and price is indeterminate and likely to be slow to change. In the long run, it is likely to be governed by the fact that new producers will enter any highly profitable industry.

The case of agriculture is different, for here producers do not set individual prices and adjust output to sales week by week, as in

[1] F. D. Jones, *op. cit.*, pp. 40–43; Blaisdell, *The Federal Trade Commission;* Henderson, *The Federal Trade Commission*, Chaps. IV–VI.

manufacturing, but put the season's output on the market for what it will bring. And if it does not cover cost, they may or may not restrict output for the next season; and whatever they do is subject to the chances of the weather. Thus agricultural prices tend to fluctuate widely from season to season, with an average range probably below the theoretical competitive level.

In the case of quality products, each producer is sometimes said to have a monopoly of the differences in quality between his product and his rivals'. But if all are free to choose what type of goods they will produce, such a "monopoly" can hardly be the basis for a monopoly profit. The very fact that a small price reduction by one such producer will not automatically take away all his rivals' business means that the reduction is not sure to be followed by the rivals and therefore actually leaves any one producer with more competitive incentive to make such a reduction than in the case of standardized products where producers are large and few. Prices will tend to be above added cost of added output, affording some protection against the danger of cut-throat competition, but are not likely to be above total cost for the industry as a whole on the average of good and bad times ("cost" including the minimum necessary return to capital). For example, the automobile industry is cited in a recent survey by the Brookings Institution as a conspicuous example of effective and serviceable competition in the field of large-scale industry.

A producer whose competitors are all located at a distance has a differential advantage of location, sometimes spoken of as a "limited monopoly," with respect to its near-by selling area; and it has an option how it shall use this power. It may charge lower delivered prices there, because its transportation costs are lower, or it may charge higher delivered prices because its competitors' transportation costs to these areas are higher, if it chooses to follow the principle already laid down, of getting as high a return as existing competition permits. This is done, for example, by nonbase mills under a basing-point system. If the attack on this practice succeeds, it will amount to establishing the doctrine that this form of differential local advantage is "affected with a public interest," requiring such producers to give their near-by customers the same relative advantage they would receive if there were many rival producers at every point of production, though in fact there are not.

"Perfect" or "pure" competition is supposed to bring prices to the level of added cost of added output. But where this is less than average unit cost, such a price spells cutthroat competition and is itself a rather serious imperfection. Some offsetting "imperfections" may produce a healthier condition and a closer approximation to the ideal competitive price which must cover total cost. Evidently, the line between competition and monopoly is impossible to draw precisely; and for officials charged with the heavy responsibility of enforcing the principles of the anti-trust laws, under the "rule of reason," the marking out of a practical borderline is a difficult task.

7. POTENTIAL COMPETITION

A considerable part of the controlling effect of competition is exerted by competition which is not actively in existence. In other words, the expectation of stirring up active competition is enough to restrain business men from following extortionate policies, especially if it is fortified by recollections of painful experiences in the past. This takes many forms, including (1) the expectation that new plants will be built or new enterprises launched, (2) the possibility that producers serving other markets will reach out and invade this one if prices go high enough to make such an invasion profitable, or (3) the possibility of stirring up cutthroat competition among existing producers in a trade where the rivalry is now on a tolerant, live-and-let-live basis. Such warfare may break out if anything is done which exceeds the bounds of what the other members of the trade are prepared to tolerate, and what they regard as legitimate. The first two possibilities tend to prevent combinations and monopolies from becoming too exacting, while the third has an opposite effect, tending to prevent competition itself from becoming too fierce, on account of the fear of reprisals. This last potentiality also tends to weaken the effect of the first, for the building of new mills may precipitate a state of cutthroat warfare. And the fear of cutthroat warfare may deter would-be competitors from building new mills. Thus the third form of potential competition may need to be restrained in order to preserve the effect of the other two forms.

8. THE FORCE AND EFFECT OF COMPETITION

It is a truism of competition that it is a system of mutual compulsion which forces everyone in a business to do what no one of them would choose to do if competition did not compel him. It nullifies the "will of the majority" in the trade, a fact which has often been expressed by saying that one man out of twenty can coerce the other nineteen. This, however, does not convey quite an accurate impression, and it would be truer to say that the consuming public can use one man out of twenty to coerce the other nineteen. The one man cannot coerce the others unless he has the consumers behind him. If competition did not exercise this kind of coercion, it would never reduce prices, weed out inefficient producers, and apply the spur of ruthless necessity to the others, all for the benefit of the public. In fact, if competition followed the will of the majority in the trade—phrase of speciously democratic sound—it would not be competition, but monopoly. Rule by the majority in a trade is precisely the thing the public is most anxious to prevent.

Yet social students of business often mention the tyranny of the twentieth man as a ground justifying common action; though it is always plain from the context that the real ground is the fact that this tyranny is used to force a serious burden on the trade without gaining any commensurate benefit for the consuming public, for instance, forcing barber shops to keep open on Sundays when the majority in the trade want to close. The real reason must lie in something about Sunday closing, hours of work, or similar matters of trade practice which makes it seem reasonable that they should be determined by the will of the majority in the trade, while output and prices must not be so determined, or the public will rise in revolt.

One reason is that if the workers assume added burdens in *these* matters, the public cannot easily be made to pay for them, or to pay anything remotely equivalent to the added sacrifice imposed on the workers. A barber *might* charge double rates for shaves on Sunday, but he might as well keep his shop closed. Laborers, in general, are not in a position to bargain for extra pay for trade practices which make their labor conditions unduly burdensome, unhealthy, or dangerous. Consumers sometimes vote for such conditions with their dollars, not knowing what they are voting for, whereas if the issue were openly put before them, they might vote the other way. Yet even with the evidence before them, consumers are but human, and the family budget is an inexorable thing, so that cheap goods are likely to win out, even against the consumer's better judgment. Thus the preference actually expressed by the consumer's dollar is not in such cases entitled to serious consideration as against any definite and material interest of the producers, though one should never act without inquiring what, if anything, will be the cost to the consumers.

Of course, the force of competition in such matters, as in all others, falls much more mildly on the enterprises which have a fair margin of profit than on those which are struggling for bare survival. This leads to another effect of competition, namely, that it is impossible for the whole trade, whatever its good will, to follow the example of the most humane (and most prosperous) employers. It is not necessarily true that what one man can do, all can do. Hence the unpopularity of the too conspicuous promoter of "welfare work," as well as his attempts to avert this unpopularity by showing that his methods are self-supporting on a commercial basis, so that his competitors could follow them if they would and improve their finances rather than otherwise.

9. COMPETITION AND THE WORK OF PRODUCTION

Does competition tend to improved quality of goods and more efficient methods of organizing work, or does it mean an unhealthy pressure in the direction of skimping quality, starving the wage earner, and spending too much on advertising and selling, so that the true efficiency of production is impaired rather than promoted? This is a serious question.

Competition is commonly classified into that which centers in price and that which centers in quality, the difference hinging generally on whether the quality of the product is definitely standardized, fairly uniform throughout the market, and something of which the buyer can judge accurately. So far as the buyer knows what he is getting, competition must act either downward on price or upward on quality or both, and so far as the commodity is thoroughly standardized, competition will act chiefly on prices. But where the buyer cannot judge independently of what he is getting, the result is a serious weakening of the principal disciplinary force which keeps competition focused upon good quality and low prices. For instance, where the buyer judges quality by price alone, all the seller has to do for the richer portion of his trade is to raise prices without taking the trouble to improve quality. And where the buyer is as little able to judge quality as this, there is a great deal of pressure to skimp quality past the point of good economy, in order to lower prices.

At the time of the dissolution of the "powder trust," the business of making explosives for the navy was not divided up among rival concerns, because, as one admiral expressed it, those who slept over explosives wanted to know that they were not made by a concern which had first put in the lowest of a series of competitive bids and then economized in every way to try to avoid losing money on the contract. This case is, of course, peculiar in that we have a purchaser who would, if he could, pay enough to be sure of the highest quality but is under tremendous pressure from an appropriation-paring Congress so that he cannot buy as liberally as he would like. Otherwise he would undoubtedly pay for what he wanted and get it, even in a competitive market.

Competition in price should take effect in making the producers organize their work so as to require as little expenditure as possible, not merely of money, but of materials, labor time, and the use of capital. It should also distribute the results equitably and not allow the profit taker to absorb an arbitrary or extortionate amount as his share. If it does not do these two things, the lowering of prices by itself is meaningless, a wholly fictitious advantage to the public. Since most people think of lower prices as an end in themselves and the chief purpose of competition, this contrary statement will at first sight seem absurd and will require careful explaining. The wiping out of undue profits means that prices in one industry must bear the same relation to costs of production that they do in other industries, while the equitable division of the proceeds requires that a given amount and quality of labor, materials, or other factors of production should be paid for at the same rate in different industries and in different plants in the same industry and should therefore always be represented by the same money cost of production.

As far as this condition is approximated, to just that extent it becomes impossible for the employer to lower his costs of production by pushing down the wages of his help, that being taken out of his hands by the force of competition, which compels him to pay the market rate. Hence he can lower his costs of production, not by cheapening the labor or other things which he uses, but only by using less of them to turn out a given amount of product. This represents the competitive ideal. But if the rivalry of industries in selling goods to the public is keener than the rivalry of the same industries in hiring laborers, then it becomes possible to reduce costs by squeezing down wages; and this is, in fact, one of the serious defects in the competitive system. Thus, to return to our theme, competition in reducing prices needs to be balanced by an equally active and vigorous competition in bidding up the rewards of the factors of production, or else it may produce positively harmful results.

If prices in one industry are higher than costs dictate, and the industry pays market rates for labor and other things, then the employers in that industry are getting too much at the expense of the consumer, and prices in that industry should come down. If prices are too high and are handed on to the laborers in that industry in the shape of wages above the market level for labor of that grade, then that labor is getting too much at the expense of the consumers, and wages and prices in that industry should both come down. If employers in general are making too much profit, this can be corrected either by lowering prices or by raising wages and prices of materials. It makes no difference which happens, barring the inevitable transition effects of a disturbance in the value of money. A general fall in prices may be one

way of correcting inequities of distribution, but it cannot by itself
create more goods to divide, and hence it cannot by itself make a
nation rich. The important effect of competition, then, is to stimulate
producers to get more results out of a given amount of labor, materials
and equipment, not to make them accept lower rewards for what they
do turn out, in the sense of lowering the general level of money compensation. Lowerings of money compensation are incidents of an equalizing process, and their value lies wholly in their equalizing effect, not
in any lowering of the general level of prices which may be produced
Any general policy of control should keep this fundamental fact constantly in mind.[1]

Does competition actually stimulate productiveness in this fundamental physical sense? We know that under a competitive system
industry has been revolutionized at an incredible pace and tremendous
increases in physical productiveness have been forthcoming, proving
that competition has not been a wholly unfavorable influence. We
know that in competitive industry it is harder than under monopoly
for a man to gain an important position and continue to hold it,
merely because he is the son of his father; and that innovations which
promise to be useful are eagerly sought after and rapidly imitated—
sometimes, it may appear, even before they have sufficiently proved
themselves. Monopoly tends to be more conservative, weighing the cost
of abandoning established methods and scrapping existing equipment. On the other hand, competition is itself responsible for many
wastes—not the "ideal" competition of economic theory, but the
actual institution with all its inherent crudeness.[2]

There are wastes of advertising, wastes of bargaining and negotiation, undue multiplication of plants and equipment, undue multiplication of sizes and models of goods; wastes of secrecy and uncoordinated
attempts to get information (thus wasting one of the most vital forms
of industrial capital, namely, knowledge). There are perversions of the
quality of the product, spending money where the buyer can see it and
skimping where it will not show, and there are perversions of industrial
effort when the wrong producer wins and the one who would serve the
public best is forced out of business. Some of these are merely the
competitive form of wastes which are inherent in human organization
and human fallibility and would be found under any system. Such
are the wastes of salesmanship and window dressing, whose political
form is even more serious than the economic. And always the problem
is twofold: first, can any other system show less waste and more sur-

[1] Cf. J. B. Clark, *The Distribution of Wealth*, p. 17.
[2] See Van Hise, *Concentration and Control*, Chap. i, Secs. 7–9.

plus? And, second, what changes can be made without costing more than they are worth? For instance, trade associations can and do mobilize knowledge much more efficiently, but will they also undermine competition itself?

Though no evidence could be irresistibly conclusive—not even a protracted trial of an alternative system—it seems fairly clear that while competition has produced a great deal of waste, it has—let us say, up to 1929—more than made up for it by a stimulus to productive efficiency. The most serious question remaining is whether it can continue to work with dominating effect under the changing conditions of large-scale industry; and whether the hybrid system now in force, with many elements of rigidity in prices and wages, can continue to show equally favorable results.

This does not, however, affect the impulse competition gives toward economical production, within the plant, of such goods as the market permits to be produced. Here the person who actively manages a business is typically not the owner, competing with other businesses on his own account, but a salaried official, engaged in the competitive struggle with other businesses merely as a representative of the owners' interests, while the competition in which he is engaged on his own account is the rivalry with other managers for advancement in position and salary, and the general personal rivalry in acquiring a competence. All the other workers are in the same situation, though their more standardized work and pay afford less opportunity for delicate discrimination in rewards. Most of the competition the average worker is in contact with is artificial, consisting of the system of tests, tasks, and incentives set for him by the management. It includes piece-wage systems; competition in records between rooms, gangs, or plants, with or without money bonuses; and the ever-present possibility of being laid off. So the question remains: How well can the wage-and-salary system succeed in passing on the pressure which competition puts upon the owners of a private business, and making the employee behave as if the business were his own? On the whole, it has in the past succeeded surprisingly well, far better than the early classical economists expected; but it is subject to an increasing strain, while the incentives it uses seem to depend less and less on the position of the stockholders as takers of competitive profits and bearers of competitive losses.

The stockholder's work consists in selecting directors and, through them, choosing a manager and exerting pressure on him to exert pressure on his subordinates to do the things that will make the business profitable. Are this choosing and this exerting of pressure materially affected by the fact that the stockholders are expecting to receive competitive profits if the business succeeds? One view is that the stockholder has become a fifth wheel, performing no useful function; while the other view is that the necessity of showing profits vitally affects the problems and conduct of the business manager (as compared to the manager of some nonfinancial undertaking), and that the existence of competition determines what kinds of thing the manager must do to make a record of profits and forces him to use his powers of reward and penalty, promotion, and discharge in such a way as to stimulate progress. A subordinate who takes intelligent initiative in the interest of the business is likely to be rewarded, even if he makes a normal percentage of mistakes and causes an appreciable amount of effort to go for nothing. The management cannot afford to follow the principle of never taking chances, which means never trying experiments, because in a field of active competitors that is the least safe thing it can do, and sure to lead to ultimate losses. A noncompetitive concern *can* make innovations also, but it is not forced to do it as a competitive concern is, and the natural human impulse to let well enough alone is all against it. To sum up, it seems probable that competition still makes for efficiency of production, even in large corporations. The assumption that it is totally obsolete is clearly premature.

On the other hand, there are many resistances which the force of competition does not break through, settled differentials which it does not modify, or adjustments which it should make and does not. In particular, when wage rates fluctuate, the effect is not always evenly distributed over the whole force. When wages go up, new men get more than old, though they are worth less; and when wages go down, the man who has a family and cannot leave may be the first to be demoted. Here the benefits of competition are unevenly divided. Some get them and others do not, and the result does not in the long run make for efficiency, however much it may spare the treasury of the concern for the moment.[1] The concern saves money wherever it can be done without precipitating immediate trouble, instead of spending it wherever necessary to provide healthy long-run incentives to efficient work. Another resistance which competition does not break through is the refusal of labor to do more than a certain amount, either under union rules or under a general sentiment against doing too much in a day. This leads us to the subject of the competition of laborers to get the job, to hold the job, and to gain advancement in it.

[1] See Slichter, *The Trend of Economics*, Section 9.

10. COMPETITION OF LABOR

Passing at once to the question on which hinges a possible demand for control, we may ask, Does the competition of laborer with laborer have an elevating or a degrading effect, and is it a thing which requires limitations and safeguards? Such rivalry falls broadly into two types, which may be described as competition in giving more, and competition in accepting less. One aspect of this we have already seen, namely, the difference between competition which merely lowers prices and competition which increases the physical efficiency of production. It is peculiarly important in the case of labor, because the labor power of a man or a woman is such a variable thing and capable of being developed or stunted to a surprising degree, and also because the principle of the social minimum sets a certain limit on the extent to which labor is allowed to compete by accepting less, rather than by making his services worth more to his employer.

If labor were literally a commodity, it might make little or no difference whether ten dollars' worth of it were embodied in one person or in two—merely a difference in the size of the package, so to speak. Even so, fewer and larger packages are cheaper to handle and bring certain economies in overhead costs of supervision, recording, etc., so that the employer is not wholly indifferent to the per capita level of the labor power he buys. But to the laborer, of course, since he is a human being and not a commodity, it is vital.

Under ideal conditions there would probably be no serious conflict between these two varieties of competition. The employer would be forced, as we have seen, to make the most effective possible use of the labor he can get in the market (though he may not have an adequate incentive to give them the kind of training which a long-run regard for their ultimate efficiency would suggest), and competition of laborers forces them to cooperate with the employer in developing output, while their mutual competition fixes wages at the amount necessary to make it worth while for employers to hire all the labor in the market, an amount which increases with every increase in the per capita yield of industry.

The facts do not quite coincide with this ideal picture for various reasons. The inefficient employer, who does not know how to make labor yield all it properly can, can often pay less than the market rate of wages and still get workers of a sort. These are in part inherently poor workers, on whom it would not be economical to lavish the highest grade of training and direction; but they also include people who are merely out of touch with the market. These last may be caught in a vicious circle, becoming inefficient because they are not paid enough to support themselves properly and because they work for poor employers who cannot direct them into efficient ways of working, and being forced to compete in accepting low wages because they cannot do anything else.

But the most powerful as well as the most universal force which acts in this direction is the periodic unemployment which results from general business depressions, attacks all industry, and makes the competition of labor, for the time being, entirely one-sided. It acts as a powerful argument to convince the laborer that it is not to his interest to contribute more product, since the markets cannot absorb it, though for the moment men will usually work fairly well for fear of losing their jobs entirely. But this has an after effect in the shape of a general hostility toward competition in the speeding up of output, so that the ultimate result is a compromise between the fear of being marked for early dismissal if one does too little, and the very real possibility of working one's self out of a job prematurely if one does too much at a time when jobs are for the moment plentiful.

A third cause of hostility to competition in doing more work lies in the abuse of the "pace setter." The very fast worker becomes a cause of cutting the wage scale for all and making them do more work for the same pay as before, while the immediate benefit goes to the particular employer who has succeeded in speeding up his work. This benefit is not even handed on to the consumer in any way that works at all quickly or that can be proved to work at all. If the speeding up took place in all plants at once, throughout an industry, competition would naturally hand the gain on to the consumers in the shape of lower prices and larger supplies, and laborers in general would benefit as consumers (except in the rare case of luxuries made by standardized machine processes and yet so very aristocratic in character that laborers do not use them). This benefit to labor in general might not be an adequate consolation to the laborers in the particular industry, but at least it would not arouse their hostility as it does when they feel that the entire benefit goes into the pockets of the employer.

If the same thing happened in all industries, one after another, giving time for the market to absorb the surplus product or for the industries to put their products in new forms adapted to the increased producing and buying power, then the result would be an unqualified gain to labor. It would take the shape of more goods at lower prices, or more leisure, or both, with a strong probability that any losses in money rates of pay would be won back as the speeding up became

the system of middlemen of which they are a part, and the wholesaler knows that it will extend its scope as soon as it grows strong enough. Furthermore a producer does not like to antagonize the existing dealers, with whom he must do the bulk of his business, and they are antagonized by the development of a system of direct selling or of cooperative buying far more than by the rise of new competitors of the same kind as themselves. It violates that natural sense of fairness which, as we have seen, depends chiefly on equality of rules and weapons among combatants, but which has little to do with the question as to which is most serviceable to the public. Thus the regular dealers are likely to feel that predatory competition on their part is justified by the exigencies of the case. This opposition is a serious force which has to be overcome by any new system, so that its first weak beginnings frequently do not get a chance to survive on their merits.

12. COMPETITION AS A TEST OF FITNESS FOR INDUSTRIAL SURVIVAL

As a weeder-out of inefficient concerns and methods, competition works wonders, rendering a service which we should be very slow to undertake to do without. One of its strongest points is its heartless impersonality, enabling it to carry out sentence of economic dissolution where any human judge would find extenuating circumstances or would hold that guilt was not proved beyond reasonable doubt. But while it works inexorably, its decisions are not infallible. One struggling concern which deserves to survive, by right of the efficient quality of its productive management, may succumb to unfair competition, while another which ought to perish on account of inefficiency may manage to continue its existence for an indefinite time by finding labor which it can hire at less than market rates and thus make the labor bear the burden of the employer's incompetence. An artificial rail-rate structure may maintain production at a point where it is wasteful and ought to be abandoned; an informal alliance to protect the customary wholesalers' and retailers' discounts may prevent the introduction of a less expensive system of distribution; or a "Pittsburgh plus" system of quoting steel prices may lay an artificial handicap on the building up of steel-using industries outside the Pittsburgh district. Thus the test of competition does not automatically coincide with the public interest, and as a result it needs to be controlled and directed in order to make it a better and better test.

This control may be regarded as an extension of that first and "natural" control, based on the protection of property and the enforcement of contracts. These are supposed to outlaw gains made through steal-

148   GENERAL INSTRUMENTS OF CONTROL

ing or cheating and to lay the foundations for rivalry in service; but
much more is needed to complete the structure and make it weather-
proof and thiefproof. The forms of control and the particular abuses
prohibited are continually new, and they must always be new, since
eternal vigilance is the price of free competition as truly as of any
other form of liberty.

REFERENCES FOR FURTHER READING

ANDERSON, B. M., JR., *Social Value*, pp. 144–147.
BLAISDELL, T. C., *The Federal Trade Commission*, Chap. i, 1932.
BURNS, A. R., *The Decline of Competition*, Chap. i, 1936.
CARVER, *Essays in Social Justice*, Chaps. iv, v.
CHAMBERLIN, E., *The Theory of Monopolistic Competition*, 1933.
CLARK, J. B., *Philosophy of Wealth*, pp. 64–69, 119–125, 187–190, 203–208.
———, *Control of Trusts*, esp. Chaps. v–vii, 1912.
CLARK, J. M., *Economics of Overhead Costs*, Chap. xxi.
COOLEY, *Human Nature and the Social Order*, pp. 262–281.
HENDERSON, G. C., *The Federal Trade Commission*, Chaps. iv–vi, 1924.
JONES, ELIOT, *The Trust Problem*, pp. 66–83, 114–115, 145, 151–152, 174–176,
    251–254, 358–363, 419–438.
JONES, F. D., *Trade Associations and the Law*, Chaps. i–iii.
MARSHALL, L. C., *Readings in Industrial Society*, Chap. xiii.
MEADE, J. E., *Economic Analysis and Policy*, Part II, Chaps. i–v, 1936.
NIMS, *The Law of Unfair Business Competition*.
RATZLAFF, C. J., *The Theory of Free Competition*, 1936.
ROBINSON, J., *The Economics of Imperfect Competition*.
SELIGMAN, *Principles of Economics*, Chap. x.
SLICHTER, S. H., in *The Trend of Economics* (R. G. Tugwell, ed.), Selection ix.
STEVENS, *Unfair Competition*.
VAN HISE, *Concentration and Control*, Chap. i, Secs. 7–9.

CHAPTER IX

AN ECONOMIC CONSTITUTION FOR THE STATE

1. INTRODUCTION

We have now surveyed, very briefly, the chief landmarks in that vast area of control which most persons do not recognize as control at all—the control which underlies the system of individualism. Beyond this lies the formal and purposive control exercised by the state, which is the only thing most persons think of as social control at all. "The state" is a generic term which in this country can be taken to cover both state governments proper and the Federal Government, which between them exercise the powers that are vested in a sovereign commonwealth. The legal constitutions under which they exercise their powers of control have been attacked as being out of touch with social and economic needs. Their "bills of rights" safeguard individualism too jealously to suit modern progressives. Can we not, then, frame an economic constitution, expressing those powers the state needs to have on economic grounds, independent of inherited legal doctrines?

The groundwork for such a structure has already been laid in the chapter which discussed whether business is a matter of private right or of public interest. The grounds of the public interest in business constitute the basis of the state's economic right to interfere. As the reader will remember, we started with the list of conditions essential to the satisfactory working of individualism and then concluded that a public interest existed wherever these essential conditions were not met. The result was a surprisingly long list of exceptions to individualism, so numerous as to touch practically every economic process at more than one point, so that all industry appeared to be "affected with a public interest" of some sort or other. With some rearrangement and a few additions the list of exceptions to individualism may be summed up as follows.

2. GROUNDS FOR PUBLIC ACTION UNDER STRICT INDIVIDUALISM

First come the powers implied in the functions which government exercises even under a strictly individualistic system:

(1) Public defense. In time of war this justifies a virtual suspension of individualism for the duration of the emergency, but even in time of peace the requirements of preparedness may justify the steering of economic resources into different channels from those which free competition would dictate. Protective tariffs are partly based on the desire for national self-sufficiency in case the ordinary sources of supplies are cut off: both military supplies and the necessities of life for the civilian population.

(2) The protection of person and property. As far as this can be accomplished by general prohibitions against assault, trespass, and damage, it involves no departure from individualism. But cases arise where the essential end in view can be secured only by a more active, anticipatory, and discriminating system of control—for instance, a public-health service or the zoning of cities. The state needs to have power to make such extensions of the basic institutions as may be necessary to accomplish the essential purpose of preventing anyone from injuring others in person or property wherever this can be done without unduly crippling the freedom of private enterprise in legitimate production. And liberty, especially substantive rather than formal liberty, cannot be made what it is supposed to be—an "inalienable right"—without limiting people's liberty to alienate it. Restraints on liberty are a part of the protection of liberty.

(3) Regulating the appropriation of goods which are not yet private property. This covers oil and natural gas, fisheries and game, and the entire administration of the public domain. Here the government has in the past had some of the greediest and most unscrupulous of the private interests to combat if it were to conserve the essential interests of the commonwealth with efficiency and honesty.

(4) Controlling inheritance and bequest. The principles of individualism do not dictate any particular system, and the system which a given state chooses will inevitably have far-reaching effects on the distribution of wealth and economic opportunity and will react on the incentives to accumulation and the amount of productive effort put forth.

(5) The raising of public revenues. This cannot be done without some effect on industry, even if the government is doing its best to produce as little disturbance as possible. This being the case, such

effects as are inevitable had far better be in harmony with social policy than opposed to it. And if there are purposes which can be furthered by measures which will incidentally raise revenue, the objections to this interference with the "natural" course of events are minimized, since there must be some interference in any case.

3. FURTHER GROUNDS FOR PUBLIC ACTION[1]

Beyond these basic powers lie others more far-reaching, arising out of the fact that the conditions necessary to successful individualism are lacking. These further necessary powers cover the following cases:

(1) Monopoly, complete or partial, and cases in which the individual is not in a position to get the advantage of such competition as may exist. The prevention or control of such conditions is a necessary function of government.

(2) Maintaining the level of competition as a healthy rivalry in service to the public. This includes those cases in which a law is needed to enable the will of the majority in the trade to have its way in such matters and to free the trade from the tyranny of a minority whose standards are low (always taking care that the will of the majority is not allowed to weaken proper rivalry in price and productive efficiency).[2] The prevalence of imperfect competition makes this public interest potentially applicable to most industries and trades.

(3) Cases in which the individual is not competent for the responsibilities which individualism lays upon him. Individualism does not assume that the individual is perfectly intelligent, for a nation of such individuals could organize a socialistic state successfully and avoid the admitted wastes of individualism, but it assumes that he has enough intelligence to look after his own interests in direct exchanges better than some outsider can do it for him, and also to learn by his mistakes, thus converting them into essential incidents of the only life worth living: the life of a being who makes decisions and takes the consequences. Wherever the people do not live up to this standard of competence, the presumption is that they need to be sheltered from individualism's extremest rigors. Cases of this sort may be divided into several groups:

(a) The individual himself may be of low mentality or may lack the "economic virtues" in some respect or other. Most of these persons

---

[1] A considerable part of the material for the "fourteen points" contained in this section is drawn from John Stuart Mill's discussion of the "grounds and limits of laissez faire" in his *Principles of Political Economy*, Book V, Chap. xi; also from Henry Sidgwick's *Principles of Political Economy*, Book III, "The Art of Political Economy."

[2] This point was discussed in the preceding chapter, Sec. 8.

are perfectly able to do self-supporting work, but not to choose occupations wisely, or to determine what working conditions are safe enough to be acceptable, or, perhaps, to budget their expenditures or bring up their children to be good economic citizens. In a compact community which surrounds its members with a stiff mold of custom, even the mentally feeble might stand erect enough, though if the mold were shattered they would be ready to collapse at a touch. Individualism may or may not be breeding increased numbers of weak types, but it is certainly shattering the molds that have sustained them, with disastrous results in all too many cases. As Cooley has said, "With freedom goes degeneration."[1]

(b) The nature of the decision may be such as people in general are not competent to make. This includes, in a sense, any decision which will lead to changes in one's own personality, but chiefly decisions destroying freedom for the future. This covers not only such things as selling one's self into slavery, or agreeing never again to practice one's calling, but also almost any irrevocable decisions, and especially any bargain which tends to put one at disadvantage in future bargaining.[2] If liberty looks to the substance as well as the form, it will include health and freedom from the worst kinds of poverty. And the most essential condition of substantial liberty is within the individual—a well-rounded development of the powers and capacities he possesses. This means that he should use them in a well-rounded way. Any use of liberty whose result is to stunt these powers, atrophy them, or put them in bondage is using liberty to destroy liberty just as surely as if a person sold himself into slavery. It is manufacturing what Aristotle called "slaves by nature." And until people learn not to use liberty in such ways, they will need some protection from themselves, in the interests of the greatest liberty. And there are many cases in which the damage is so evident and serious that even such a clumsy agency as the state is justified in trying to improve matters.

(c) Another type of decision is that in which people act in other people's interests. Here three considerations enter: first, there is no longer a presumption that the person acting is the best judge of the interests of the person to be benefited; second, the beneficiary tends to become dependent unless great care is taken to prevent; third, the private giver, who may have pauperized the beneficiary, has no continuing obligation to bear the resulting burdens, and in general he may act capriciously.

[1] Cooley, *Human Nature and the Social Order*, pp. 433–434; cf. also Chap. xi.
[2] Cf. Marshall, *Principles of Economics*, Book V, Chap. ii, Sec. 3; Book VI, Chap. iv, Secs. 3, 6; 5th ed., pp. 335, 562–563, 569.

(*d*) Another case is the complex decision in which many different elements of value are bound together in one act of choice. Here, unless the individual has time and opportunity to canvass a wide range of alternatives, there is a presumption that some of these values will perforce be neglected, especially if the decision is a hurried one. An automobile is a complex "bundle of utilities," but there is ample variety to choose from and the buyer usually makes an extended canvass. Buying groceries with trading stamps thrown in is not so complex a purchase as that of an automobile, but the trading stamps intrude an unnecessary and extraneous element and make the market a poorer place for the measurement of separate values. The labor contract, however, is the one whose complexity raises the most serious issues. It creates an enduring relationship with a thousand and one important possibilities for good or harm to the worker, but all he can be expected to cover by any specific agreement with his employer is the position to be filled, hours of work, and wages. The other things are necessarily secondary when the workman is out of a job and looking for work, and the market cannot be said to measure their importance effectively. They include safety, sanitation, the ultimate physical and mental effects of the work and the working conditions, stability of employment, and the chance for advancement—all of them of enormous importance. Only through organization can the worker make his demand for these things effective; otherwise the competition of the most needy and ignorant minority can be used to depress conditions for all. And organization is not universal.

Here again the state can do something, but before we decide to give it forthwith complete power over the terms of the labor contract we should remember one thing. If the labor contract is a complex decision, the choice of a public official is far more so and for that reason is an even poorer mechanism for expressing what the citizens really want. The market may tie too many values together, but this is nothing to the confusion of issues, deliberately cultivated as a political fine art, which surrounds the typical election. Hence the political machinery should not supplant the economic but should be used, first of all, to strengthen it at its weakest points and prevent the most obvious abuses, that is, unless we are prepared to go over outright to a socialistic system.

(*e*) Finally, the individual may not be in a position to protect his own interests on account of external circumstances, chiefly lack of information. The buyer does not know what is in the patent medicine or what kind of materials are covered up by the plaster of the house he is buying. The small manufacturer cannot afford a laboratory to test his materials. The worker who moves from place to place in search of a job cannot know the state of the market well enough to save himself from being victimized by private employment agencies. In fact, of all private businesses except that of patent medicines the private employment agency is perhaps best able to thrive on the marketing of false pretenses. If the buyer were in a position to prevent this, he would not need the service at all.

(4) Delegated agencies or associations. Does it follow, because an individual will work more energetically and faithfully for his own profit than for a common fund that a corporation will do the same? Not at all. Where the corporation is concerned, the question takes a different form, namely, will a man promote the interests of a joint enterprise better if the enterprise is private than if it is public? In general, the answer seems to be that he does. The difference between private and public organization is far less than it once was, but there is still a difference, and it tells on the side of efficiency for the private company. Hence the general presumption in favor of private enterprise holds good, even for large corporations. But that is by no means the whole story.

The internal organization of the corporation is full of possibilities of abuse. The members need protection against each other. A share of stock is one of the most complex of commodities, and the market position of the small investor gives him little chance to know what he is getting and to purchase fidelity in his board of directors as he purchases warmth in his winter overcoat. The relation is one of trusteeship, and chances to make money at the expense of the company are varied and tempting. Publicity must be had for the essential facts, and standards of honor appropriate to trusteeship must be developed and enforced—a task in which government must share. But there is no need to argue that the state, which creates the corporation, may properly control it to any extent, limited only by economic expediency.[1]

(5) Victims of change and catastrophe. In the face of disasters like the San Francisco fire, the Halifax explosion, or the Tokyo earthquake we do not think of applying individualistic principles to the work of providing for the needs of the victims. Where the need arises from a disrupting of the regular framework of life, something against which the individual could not be expected to have made provision, relief does not carry the stigma of charity, no one asks if it will pay, and those who take advantage of the victims' helplessness to overcharge them are clearly seen to be offending against common humanity. Does not

[1] Much of this work is better handled by informal methods. See Chap. xii, below, pp. 217–218.

the same principle properly apply to the victims of our wholesale economic changes and upheavals? Clearly it does, with the additional provision that the real need is a fair opportunity for work, rather than relief, and that any industries which cause particular upheavals—for example, by adopting improvements which displace labor—have an economic obligation which individualism does not enforce. Here, then, is work for the state, and for an enlarged social consciousness in industry. This merges into the next topic, that of the social minimum.

(6) Human wreckage and the social minimum. Despite our individualism, there can be no doubt that we do believe in distribution according to need, up to the point of providing for the absolute necessities of life. We feel it intolerable that anyone should be left to starve. Perhaps we should save society a great deal of trouble if we were harder hearted, but that is beside the point. We are committed to preserving the weak. From a crude policy of doles we have advanced to principles more in harmony with sound individualism, as follows: (a) Prevention is better than relief. (b) Rehabilitation of victims is the only sound goal. (c) Let industry bear its full responsibility. These combine into the policy of the "social minimum," and it is within the proper powers of the state to promote this policy by any means consistent with successful private enterprise. This justifies relief work, "social security," and also minimum-wage laws, within the limits of the "penumbra" of the law of supply and demand[1] for labor of normal efficiency and with due provision for any unemployables who may be created.

(7) Economic guidance. This has already been touched on, but it deserves a heading to itself. All forms of economic guidance are, actually or potentially, "affected with a public interest." One important phase of this is the guidance needed to make a good market, one where supply and demand can come together effectively. This may or may not be adequately taken care of by individualism. Honest labeling, truth and economy in advertising, and impartial testing of goods for the benefit of the public are all appropriate objects of state policy. So also are research and education in sound farming methods or efficiency in any other industry, but especially where the producers are too small to carry out effective research themselves. The Bureau of Standards is an important agency in this field but appears at present to serve small producers better than consumers. This principle does not justify control of the basic agencies for diffusing news and forming public opinion. Here liberty is essential to democracy.

---

[1] Cf. below, pp. 163–164; also Chap. xxix.

(8) "Equality of opportunity." This may be regarded as a part of the social minimum, and the most important part. It means that the fundamentals of economic opportunity should be inalienable and justifies such interferences with liberty as may be necessary to keep these fundamentals from being alienated.

In respect to this fundamentally important matter, individualism is a paradox. It presupposes equal opportunity and it creates inequality at every turn. So the state, having started its citizens off in life with "equal opportunity" as far as it can do so without reversing all the results of past competitive struggles, may be forced to go farther and to interfere with the workings of individualism, as far as the inequalities it produces constitute a serious handicap to the continued satisfactory working of the system. It may be, for instance, that the land—and with it the fundamental opportunity to produce—comes to be held too largely by the rich for their pleasures and too little by the poor for their livelihood. The rich will not use it all for lawns, game preserves, and private golf courses, but what they do not use in such ways as these will be worked by hired laborers or tenants, neither of whom are likely to develop it as effectively as small private owners, according to the views of individualism. Or perhaps the sheer high price of farm land may become a serious obstacle to the would-be farmer-proprietor and tend to keep him indefinitely in the status of tenancy. Under such conditions the state may take measures to control the distribution of land and the system of land tenure, in the interest of making equality of opportunity a real thing in agriculture. Or perhaps there is inequality of access to credit under the banking system; or perhaps the sheer concentration of inherited wealth becomes so great that the resulting inequality of opportunity—always an unfortunate fact—becomes a truly serious evil, and measures are taken to mitigate it. All these might be justified under the general principle of equal opportunity.

(9) Unpaid costs of industry. Such costs occur wherever there are interests which the general system of legal rights does not cover—interests which can be invaded without consent or compensation. Real-estate values may be damaged, as we have seen, by nuisances or merely by incongruous uses of adjoining property. Rights in water also need special protection. Or it may have the same effect if the remedies available to the common-law system are inadequate to the purpose (this is true of injuries to the public health). Or the individual may, through sheer lack of bargaining power, be unable to translate his technical legal protection into actual economic protection of an effective sort. Workers, for instance, do not have to work under dangerous con-

ditions unless they are paid enough to "make it worth their while" and to secure their free consent; but this does not give laborers the strategic economic position to exert an "effective demand" for safe and satisfactory conditions. Thus the worker may be paid for his actual labor, but the risks of injury, of occupational disease, or of unemployment, considered as separate costs, may not receive any compensation at all, or nothing approaching the money value of the risks as an insurance actuary would estimate them. In the broadest sense, any general evil resulting from industry has such diffused effects as to fall on innocent parties without compensation and so comes under this principle. Damages of this sort also occur in the use of the air and the ether, and the spread of infections and agricultural pests. The state has an interest in minimizing all such evils.[1]

(10) Inappropriable services, and the furthering of joint interests. This covers all cases in which the person who renders a service cannot, for any reason, appropriate it in such a way as to be able to sell it to the recipient. The two largest classes of cases are: (a) all kinds of unpatentable knowledge, and (b) the diffused effect on real-estate values of any economic expansion or industrial improvement (there are also many uncompensated damages in this field). Irrigation and city planning afford typical examples of joint interests. This subject has been developed in earlier passages.[2] In all such cases the state has a duty, since it cannot take for granted that private incentives will bring forth as much effort as is worth while in such directions. Where the effort is forthcoming, the state need do nothing; but where private enterprise lags, the state has a clear license and duty to fill the gap. Furthermore, wherever it can locate the unearned benefits resulting from such uncompensated services, it may subject them to special responsibilities or special tax burdens. This applies not only to land values but to values of many other sorts.

(11) Actions which neutralize each other. First let it be stated as emphatically as possible that such neutralizing of efforts does not, always and necessarily, constitute an evil and a waste which must be utterly stamped out if we are to have a socially efficient system of production. In fact, it is impossible to imagine any free community where people can find out what they want without an expensive conflict of ideas. But wherever we find such head-on collisions of human effort, the community has an interest in reducing the lost motion to a minimum and—still more important—seeing to it that the net result-

---

[1] See above, pp. 34–36, 42, 44, and especially Chap. vii, Sec. 1, "Law and the Costs of Industry."

[2] Cf. especially pp. 78–79, above.

ant is what the community really wants: the selection and survival of the most efficient methods and the most desired goods. And where there is no prospect that control would do any appreciable good, there things should be left alone, since control is, in and of itself, a thing to be avoided.

Among the activities which neutralize each other are competitive armaments and competitive advertising (which have some things very much in common), the whole contest of wits which goes with bargaining and negotiation, the waste of "cross freights," where substantially identical goods are shipped in opposite directions at the same time, similar wastes in the wanderings of labor in search of jobs, and, in principle, the whole field of "invidious consumption" and of purely conventional consumption in which people's wants are governed by what other people have and their satisfactions are lessened by the growth of others' possessions. In all these instances the interest of one individual is one thing, the interest of other individuals is directly opposed, and the interest of society is something different from either and is often not realized or formulated.

(12) Unused capacities. The general law of demand and supply presupposes that there is a certain amount of labor power which people normally wish to use in "gainful occupations," and a certain amount of funds put into the form of productive capital, and that the rewards paid for these are enough to equalize demand with supply: that is, to call the full supply into use. Without going into abstruse analysis, it is clear that the facts of unemployment of labor and capital, as we regularly see it in times of slack business, represent a real failure of this principle, constituting a valid ground for public interference. The case is largely covered by other principles already discussed, and there is no need to enlarge upon it here or to argue all possible objections to it. The chief limit is our imperfect knowledge of how to devise effective means of control.

(13) The interests of posterity. The market discounts future values at compound interest for a period of perhaps two generations, beyond which commercial principles virtually cease to set any value on the future. But if, as has been suggested, the interests of posterity are paramount over those of the present generation, then this scale of values is false from the social standpoint, and the state has a duty to see that the needs of future generations are not unduly sacrificed to present profits. This justifies the conservation of natural resources, and possibly other policies of similar purport.

(14) Other discrepancies between private and social accounting. "Social accounting" is an unfamiliar conception, but the thing it

describes has a very real existence.[1] The principles of uncompensated costs, of unpaid services, of unused capacities, and of conservation, all involve a revising of the market's reckoning of costs and values in the light of a fuller social accountancy. (a) Complete social accountancy would undertake to set a true social value on all the human values and costs of industry, revising the values set on them by the individuals concerned. In many cases there is fairly solid ground for doing this, as we have seen in discussing the competence of the individual, though there will probably always be a margin of doubt and controversy in such social valuations. (b) A considerable measure of social accountancy is possible, by using only the measures of things already found in the market, but recombining them, so as to give a more complete picture than is found in the books of any one concern. Here it is not so much a question of finding the total income and outgo as of tracing the change due to any particular policy or transaction. A few instances will help to show what is meant.

If the nation comes to regard the health of its workers as an element in its resources for national defense, or even as a part of its national industrial capital, it will naturally want to conserve this national asset, and there will be hardly any stress of poverty so great that the nation will feel that it cannot afford the cost of such conservation. Individuals may be so poor that they literally cannot afford to conserve their health, but the nation is never so poor as these poorest individuals, either in goods or in the range of policies and expedients which are open to it; hence it can afford to conserve health where the individuals themselves cannot and can set a higher money value on it than the individuals are in a position to do.

Another instance is the value set on different levels of human ability. In the market the valuation is mainly competitive, and each employer is forced to pay approximately what a man is commercially worth to him in order to get his services away from rival bidders. This gives very large rewards to the highest grades of efficiency and thus incidentally affords a very strong stimulus to those with ability to develop it to the utmost in the service of business. But is this stimulus necessarily the best and most economically arranged for bringing out the talents society needs? If the nation were the only employer, free from the compulsions of competition, could it perhaps hire the talents of a captain of industry for the salary of a cabinet officer? On this point two things can be said with confidence. First, an omniscient state could arrange a scale of rewards which would call forth more energy than at present at less aggregate outlay in material stimuli.

[1] Cf. J. M. Clark, *Economics of Overhead Costs*, pp. 25–34, 383, 397–403, 411.

Second, no large state yet seen on earth has given evidence of sufficient collective wisdom to devise a system which would work anything like as effectively as the competitive struggle does. Third, in spite of its limitations, a state may command enough wisdom, without wiping out the competitive system, to see where its worst wastes and perversions lie, and to modify it here and there in the direction of the system which the all-wise state would establish. There are many devices which can be used without committing the unpardonable sin of "violating economic law." As a matter of fact, industrialism as we know it contains a vast multitude of modifications of precisely this character, from public parks and free medical clinics to progressive inheritance taxes, minimum-wage laws, and family wage systems.

Another large class of cases is of the following sort: A retail clothing concern suddenly feels the need of retrenchment and curtails its orders for garments. It saves itself the whole price it usually pays and reduces its expenses that much. This is a part of the process by which the whole impersonal business machine decides whether it is worth while to go on making and marketing clothes or not. This question ought to be decided according as the costs which the economic system as a whole could save by making fewer clothes are greater or less than the value of the garments. The dealer, of course, decides it according as the costs which his own establishment would save by curtailing purchases are greater or less than the amount he can get for the garments in the market. And the two tests do not coincide. The business community does not save as much as the dealer does by the curtailing of output. The dealer saves the entire wholesale price of the clothes, but the people who make the clothes do not save this much, chiefly because a large part of their costs are "constant" and go on just the same whether more clothes are made or fewer. So the business system may cut down the making of clothes at a time when a joint survey of costs would show that there is more to be lost than gained by such curtailment. Hence anything within reason that government may do to promote the stabilization of business and employment is justified as tending to correct a demonstrable discrepancy between private and social accounting.

In general, wherever increased or decreased production brings less than proportional change in costs, there is likely to be a discrepancy between private interest and social interest as to how far production should be pushed.[1]

---

[1] This type of case affords a considerable portion of the material in A. C. Pigou's books *Wealth and Welfare* and *Economics of Welfare*.

But it will be impossible to detail all the possible forms which social accounting may take, for new ones will be continually developing. And our social constitution will do well not to delimit its scope in too much detail, for that would hamper its development. There should be some blanket provision broad enough to leave room for future developments, even though their character may be totally unforeseen.

4. SUMMARY OF POWERS CONFERRED ON GOVERNMENT

By this time, it is evident that our economic constitution has conferred powers on the government which are very far-reaching indeed. They include measures for the public health, social insurance, the protection of the "social minimum," and even a qualified wardship for the great masses of people of low-grade mentality. The state may control the internal affairs of corporations, provide for honest labeling and for the publicity of essential business facts almost without limit. It may control industrial disputes to the extent of its power, always subject to the freedom of the worker from "involuntary servitude." Where stoppage of operation creates a genuine public peril, the force of public opinion will give public awards greater force than they would have in ordinary cases, resulting in a qualified power of compulsion. Such industries may come to be regarded as "affected with a public interest" by reason of the necessity for continuous operation, justifying whatever kinds of action are appropriate to this need, while keeping them clearly distinct from the "public-service industries" now recognized, in which the public interest is largely in preventing monopolistic extortion and the measures of control are correspondingly different. The state may promote the development of trade ethics, may draw the line between fair and unfair competition, and may even set minimum standards of quality in cases where the consumer is not in a position to protect himself from serious injuries. It may control or take over advertising, assume responsibility for substantially anything in the field of economic information and research, and insure the conditions of a healthy market in which supply and demand may meet in the freest and most complete fashion. It may control tenures of property and the distribution of wealth as far as is consistent with the continuance of a system of private enterprise. Any uncompensated costs or damages it may undertake to prevent, compensate, or repair, and any "inappropriable services" it may subsidize, stimulate in any other way, or take upon itself. It may zone cities and tax unearned increments. Finally, lest anything be left out of the specific enumeration, it will retain that undefined realm of the police power, capable of being extended to cover anything of vital public necessity.

Altogether, the valid grounds of public action are so many and inclusive that, if the state were to act upon all of them, stretching them to their utmost reach, there would be little of individualism left. Therefore if we are designing a system whose purpose is limited to controlling private industry, implying that there is to be some private industry left to control, we must make some reservations and set some limits on the expansion of the powers of government.

5. LIMITATIONS ON THE POWERS OF GOVERNMENT

Perhaps the most fundamental limitation on control arises out of the fact that the paramount human value is liberty. Hence liberty should be limited only to increase liberty, that is, the true and effective sum of liberty for the people as a whole. And liberty, as we have seen, is limited just as surely by ill-health or poverty as by actual servitude. We must deal with the substance, not merely the form. Here, of course, we face difficult problems of definition and a still more difficult task in judging the relative importance of different kinds of liberty, where it may never be possible to construct a satisfactory common measure. Control should limit itself to cases which are clear, in the judgment of reasonable men. In deciding where to stop, the decisive consideration is the amount of liberty that is left to the individual. He must be left to decide his own destiny just as far as he is capable. He must be driven, if necessary, to as large an exercise of liberty as he can profitably make, but not beyond this point. State control should reach its limit, not when the number of liberties that are taken away appears too large, but when the number that remains becomes too small.

A second general limitation on the growth of state control is that it should preserve a healthy balance between the public and private occupations, in terms of the numbers, intelligence, and power of those engaged. Neither should gain such complete ascendancy as to rob the other of its fair share of talent, else the other will degenerate and both will be the worse. In the United States, since the Civil War, if either side has had too great an ascendancy, it has been private business. At present (1938) this may to some extent remain true in terms of ability, but the growing number of public employees, and still more of public financial beneficiaries, is having unfortunate effects on the tone of politics.

A third general limit lies in the great value of voluntary organization rather than compulsory, wherever it is capable of handling any matter of common interest. It is flexible; it can experiment without committing the whole of society; it economizes compulsion; and it gives the most effective kind of minority representation, for each minority can organize in its own way.

Fourth, the presumption should always be against allowing the state to substitute its judgment for that of any individual in matters which primarily concern him, unless the state's judgment is fortified by some systematic and impartial reckoning of the importance of the interests at stake—something deserving of the name of "social accounting"—or by a standard of human welfare which has scientific authenticity, as, for example, a medical verdict on the requirements of human health. The machinery we call "political" is often a poorer instrument for weighing the true worth of conflicting interests than the machinery of the market.

In the fifth place, since every business is affected with a public interest of one sort or another, and since these various types of public interest call for very different sorts of action to protect them, the state should always be limited to the particular kind of control which the particular public interest calls for in each class of cases. Where "natural monopoly" exists, one kind of control is necessary; where public health is endangered, another; and where continuous operation is necessary to the public safety, still another. No power of control should ever be presumed to exist unless there is specific need for the exercise of that specific power. The exercise of power must correspond to the particular interest involved.

Sixth and last, special duties and obligations should accompany certain kinds of control which are in peculiar danger of "violating economic law." Where the state regulates prices, wages, or other costs of production in such a way as to interfere materially with the law of supply and demand, some safeguards must be imposed in order to see that the public is not deprived of the quantity and quality of goods and services which it needs and is willing to pay for, under guise of protecting it from the extortionate exactions of the producers. The Supreme Court already exercises some such safeguard, though its power is defined in different terms. And if the state fixes economic values at a point such that supply and demand are actually out of equilibrium, such action must always be accompanied by some definite and adequate substitute machinery to perform the essential function which the forces of supply and demand formerly performed. If prices are lowered below the competitive level necessary to call forth the desired supply, some substitute stimulus must be furnished, or the shortage made good by government. If wages are raised to the point at which workers become unemployable, the state must take up the obligation to rehabilitate the unemployable worker or furnish him employment. There is—and this is of vital importance—a "penumbra" within which the law of supply and demand is indeterminate; and while it does not veto changes within these limits,[1] they are exposed to a peculiar danger.

Railroad earnings may be below the necessary supply price of adequate capital and enterprise; and railroads will not stop operating and will not even wholly stop raising new capital; yet the service will be starved, and efficiency and even safety will ultimately suffer. Wages may, by the state or by strong unions, be set above the level at which the workers affected can find full employment; yet it may never be possible to isolate the unemployment due to this particular cause among all other causes and trace it to its source. Where the law of supply and demand has a considerable penumbra, the outer borders of it are necessarily vague and uncertain. Legitimate limits may be passed without our knowing it. The critical point is bound to be a matter of doubt and obscured by controversial claims of interested parties.

On a broader scale, the fear that a multitude of successive restraints will weaken the enterprising spirit of private business is justified, even though this spirit of enterprise has survived many shocks in the past, which business men claimed would be fatal. Fear of the policies of an unpredictable and apparently hostile government can contribute to reduce willingness to make large capital outlays on the faith of an uncertain future. This is a particularly serious matter where the end in view is to stimulate business activity and escape from a depression. And no one can tell with certainty when this subtle and elastic limit has been reached or passed. It remains true, however, that as long as we rely on controlled private enterprise, it must be left that minimum of liberty—presumably a variable quantity—which at any given time and place it requires for health and vigor.

Within these general limits, the state may properly exercise an almost undefined range of powers. The matter is well summed up in the words of Woodrow Wilson: "Government does not stop with the protection of life, liberty, and property, as some have supposed; it goes on to serve every convenience of society. Its sphere is limited only by its own wisdom, alike where republican and where absolutist principles prevail."[2] With this philosophy there is one practical difficulty.

[1] See F. W. Taussig: "Is Market Price Determinate?" *Quar. Jour. Econ.*, Vol. XXXV, pp. 394–411.

[2] Woodrow Wilson, *The State*, p. 647.

The less the wisdom of any given state, the less likely is it to recognize the limits of its own wisdom. There is need of some independent check. In the past, the American courts have served in this capacity—perhaps too effectively. If, as seems likely, judicial checks are much relaxed in future, there will be more need than ever before for the check of an alert, responsible, and public-minded citizenship.

6. THE WISDOM AND COMPETENCE OF THE POLITICAL STATE

The modern political state is a thing in evolution; it is already very different from anything known to the founders of British individualism or the framers of the American Constitution, and in another century it will almost certainly become something very different from what it is now. Its organization grows with the multiplicity of its functions, and its departments secure the services of specialists: chemists, agricultural experts, health experts, engineers, accountants, statisticians, and even economists. Thus the intelligence at its command grows, and thus it earns the right to an increase in the scope of its powers. It labors, however, under certain serious handicaps.

First, its resources are limited in comparison to the "interests" it strives to control, and its experts are typically pitted against higher-paid experts, presumably of greater ability. Second, the ultimate control lies in the hands of people who are not specialists: cabinet officers, legislators, and especially judges. The legislator receives plenty of expert guidance (or pressure) from interested parties, and the judge hears volumes of interested testimony but no disinterested counsel.[1] Thus at the points where critical policies are decided, we find persons who have not the expert's facilities for weighing the values represented by the conflicting interests in the case. Third, and as a result of this, questions are likely to be settled by popular clamor, by judicial conservatism leaning on an outworn economics, or, worse yet, by the political process of "log rolling," in which each group of legislators buys support for the measures in which its own constituents are interested by supporting other measures in which the constituencies of other groups are interested, and no measure receives the benefit of an impartial and courageous judgment of what the common interest demands. It is this sort of vote trading which called forth the cynical remark that the tariff is a "local issue"; and the present institution of an expert tariff commission, acting in an advisory capacity, has as yet only partially remedied this evil. Fourth, the game of politics is one

[1] This point was treated in a very able paper read by Prof. K. N. Llewellyn before the American Economic Association, December, 1924. See *Amer. Econ. Rev.*, pp. 672, 676–677, December, 1925.

in which a good issue is an asset not lightly to be sacrificed; and it may be better politics to keep it unsettled and go through the motions of fighting for the public interest and shifting the blame for failure on the opposition or the courts, rather than to bring about a reasonable settlement which, precisely because it is reasonable, does not carry a spectacular victory for the financial interests of the majority of voters. This is perhaps most often seen in local politics in connection with the question of rates and service of public-service companies. The evil rests largely on the inability of the voters to master the technical intricacies of such cases and to see clearly what is, and what is not, reasonable and practicable.

As a result of these and other weaknesses, the actual working of political control is full of fakes and perversions, and the arguments which furnish social justification for control too often become mere pretexts to cover the conferring of privileges on some private interest. There are valid reasons for protection in some cases, but those reasons do not explain the actual history of our tariff.[1] The real justification which exists for subsidies to railroads in new territory does not prevent the energies of railroads from being diverted from sound railroad building to corrupt subsidy grabbing if a liberal subsidy policy is once established. Assuredly consumers have a right to know what they are buying, but is this the sole reason for the passage of laws requiring butter substitutes to be colored green? Or is the safety of the public the only force behind the railroad full-crew laws?

Another weakness of the state is a tendency to underestimate the cost of control and, still more, the extent of control to which it is committing itself when it embarks on a new policy. This is, however, not an unmixed evil, since the results may often justify an expenditure which the state would have felt it could not afford if it had known in advance how great the burden would be. Here the most serious evils are probably the intangible ones. In the first place, where there is a more or less limited amount of energy available for enforcement, a new law may divert some of it from the enforcement of those already on the statute books.[2] This may be minimized by setting up separate agencies of enforcement, but this in turn produces overlapping, waste, and shifting of responsibility. And the basic scrutiny of public opinion cannot be too much departmentalized and remain wholly healthy and impartial. Few issues hold the headlines long, and politics can usually drag red herrings across the trail. Second, successful control rests

[1] See F. H. Taussig, "How Tariffs Should Not Be Made," *Amer. Econ. Rev.*, I (March, 1911), 20–32.

[2] See paper by K. N. Llewellyn, *op. cit.*, pp. 666–669.

largely on the willingness of "good" concerns to cooperate, and this willingness may be exhausted by too great a multiplicity of exactions. This might perhaps be minimized by consolidating the work of fact finding, so that inquiries would not overlap and duplicate each other so much as at present. Third, the energies of business itself are partly diverted from the pursuit of efficiency in management to propaganda and political strategy. Fourth, the state may embark on a policy of formal and compulsory control without realizing how far it will ultimately be forced to go; whereas if it had possessed the gift of prophecy, it would have found the voluntary methods of informal control more suitable and, in the last analysis, more effective. And the decisions of the state, like those of the individual, may be irrevocable, and correspondingly dangerous.

These weaknesses are not fatal, but they reinforce powerfully the general presumption in favor of restraint in the state's exercise of its formal powers of coercion. But how are we to convert these general considerations into concrete rules? How translate them into a legal charter which will give government precisely the proper scope and impose precisely the correct limits? Frankly, there is no sure method. Rules to this end cannot be framed so as to be "fool-proof." They must be intrusted to some body which has discretion enough to follow them in the spirit without being bound by the letter. But this kind of discretion is, on the whole, more legislative than judicial. If we are to give our legislatures enough power to meet the needs of our time, we must trust them with discretion, subject to an intelligent public opinion, in setting limits upon themselves; for there is no way in which constitutional rules can be laid down and intrusted to the courts to apply, in such a way as to permit everything that is wise and prohibit every law that is foolish.

REFERENCES FOR FURTHER READING

CLARK, J. M., "The Basis of War-time Collectivism," *Amer. Econ. Rev.*, VII (December, 1917), 772–790.

————, *Economics of Overhead Costs*, Chaps. ii, xviii, xix.

FREUND, ERNST, *The Police Power*.

HAMILTON, W. H., *Current Economic Problems* (3d ed.), Chap. xv *b*.

MILL, JOHN STUART, *Principles of Political Economy*, Book V, Chap. xi.

ORTH, S. P., *Readings in the Relation of Government to Industry*, Chaps. i, iv.

PATTERSON and SCHOLZ, *Economic Problems of Modern Life*, Chaps. xx, xxxi, 1937.

SIDGWICK, HENRY, *Principles of Political Economy*, Book III.

SWENSON, *National Government and Business*, Chaps. ii, iii.

WYAND, C. S., *Economics of Consumption*, Chap. xiii, 1937.

CHAPTER X

THE LEGAL AND THE ECONOMIC CONSTITUTIONS

The actual or legal constitution from an economic standpoint, 168—The police power, 171—Businesses affected with a public interest, 176—Federal powers, 180—Proposed changes, 183.

1. THE ACTUAL OR LEGAL CONSTITUTION FROM AN ECONOMIC STANDPOINT

At first sight it seems that the legal constitution can have nothing in common with such a list of general economic principles as we have just examined. Nevertheless, the two have some features in common—enough to give at least a basis for comparison. They are alike in that both admit a general presumption in favor of liberty and then grant exceptions for particular reasons. Among the exceptions found in both systems are certain incapable and dependent classes of the population, monopolies, certain businesses on which the public is dependent, some instances in which liberty is used to destroy liberty for the future, things which have qualitative effects on human nature (as far as they affect public morals), and a wider scope for public control over the incidental terms of a contract than over its central features[1] of supply, demand, and price.

On the other hand, all these exceptions are far narrower in scope in the actual Constitution than in our tentative economic charter, and there is even in past court decisions a dogma to the effect that interference with basic liberty of contract must always be the exceptional thing in the sense of being relatively rare,[2] whereas our economic

[1] At least, this distinction was used by Justice Sutherland in the course of explaining why the Supreme Court held a minimum-wage law unconstitutional, while laws regulating hours and methods of payment were upheld. The wage he held to be the "heart of the contract," while the other matters were incidental; also, if the wage were controlled, there was no longer a chance for the parties to compensate, through the money payment, for any increased burdens which law might have imposed upon one or the other (*Adkins* v. *Children's Hospital*, 261 U.S. 525 [District of Columbia Minimum-wage Case]). This case has since been overruled in *West Coast Hotel Co.* v. *Parrish*, 300 U.S. 379 (1937), but the importance of this distinction may be expected to persist in diminished degree.

[2] See *Adkins* v. *Children's Hospital, op. cit.*, p. 546, also *Wolff Packing Co.* v. *Court of Industrial Relations of the State of Kansas*, 262 U.S. 522, 533.

charter was so broad as to make the exceptions appear more general than the rule. The fact is that "exception" means a different thing in the two cases. Our economic charter grants an exception to the individualistic rule wherever the conditions of successful individualism are not fully present—with the result that there are some exceptions in substantially every business. The legal code, on the other hand, has stuck to the implied assumption that the conditions of successful individualism are actually present in the great majority of cases. Hence it was inclined to reject any very far-reaching principle of control, merely because it was too general, at least, if it interfered with freedom of contract at its "heart," namely, the money payment involved. (This attitude, however, appears to be changing.) There are other differences, but they will appear as the argument develops.

All that has been said so far applies to our working code of constitutional law rather than to the written document around which it centers. The practice of the code is different from the theory of the document. For in theory the Constitution grants a general undefined legislative power and then makes exceptions by way of specific limitations in the "bill of rights," which are designed to set up safeguards against arbitrary and tyrannical actions. In practice, however, the courts have construed the federal bill of rights so broadly that in effect it creates a presumption against any new extensions of control and then allows the courts to set up a fairly limited group of objects of control, which can successfully overcome this presumption. In legal terms, the presumption created by the bill of rights does not prevent the regulation of service and prices in businesses affected with a public interest or appropriate regulation of other matters properly covered by the police power of the state, chiefly the protection of the public safety, peace and order, public health, and public morals. These four public interests do not define the eternally natural limits of the police power but they do include most of its actual content, which is a matter of historical development, based largely on custom and precedent and on the economic ideas of the judges.

This condition arises out of the interpretation of the Fifth and Fourteenth Amendments to the Federal Constitution. The Fifth says: "No person . . . shall be deprived of life, liberty, or property, without due process of law, nor shall private property be taken for public use without just compensation." (The passage which is omitted is obviously directed against tyrannical action in criminal cases.) The Fourteenth says: "No state shall . . . deprive any person of life, liberty, or property, without due process of law, nor deny to any person within its jurisdiction the equal protection of the laws." These have been so broadly construed as to cover not merely total deprivation of liberty or the absolute taking of a given piece of physical property, but any diminution in the scope of a person's liberty or in the rights and privileges he possesses with respect to his property. Since this is so broad as to include any act of economic regulation, the effect is to require them all to meet whatever standards of "due process" the Supreme Court may lay down.

The court thus assumes enormous power, for it has interpreted due process of law very broadly. This term would naturally seem to refer to the forms of orderly procedure, setting no limits on the subject matter which might be regulated. But under the interpretations of the Supreme Court, it comes about that the regular procedure of an act of a state legislature is due process if the subject matter of the act is within the scope of the police power and is not due process if the subject matter is outside the scope of the police power. In cases which come under this power, the state may destroy property or reduce its value without compensation, but not in other cases (and even here it must compensate if the taking of property becomes the "main thing").[1]

Furthermore, the actual enumerating of powers is not done by the written constitution, but by the courts, for neither the police power nor the concept of a "business affected with a public interest" is found in written constitutions. They are creations of the courts and seem to represent their ideas of the essential needs of the community. These ideas rest partly on custom and partly on what seems to be at bottom a weighing of values—an economic act. The courts' notions of economics have sustained the control of monopolies; but when the labor contract was regulated in the interest of one of the contracting parties, this seemed to the courts an invasion of the natural right of free contract, and they were slow to sustain it except in the case of children. It is chiefly on this issue of the labor contract that the judicial economics appears backward, as judged by the ideas of contemporary social thinkers. These points of legal economics are peculiarly likely to produce a divided court and to be settled by a five-to-four vote, representing a disagreement between the learned judges on matters of economics, or on how far the court should consider such matters, not on points of law in the obvious meaning of the term.[2] This fact has occasioned much severe criticism.

---

[1] See *Pennsylvania Coal Co.* v. *Mahon*, 260 U.S. 393, decided December, 1922.

[2] To 1924 there were about fifty cases in which the Supreme Court held acts of Congress unconstitutional, and nine of these were decided by a majority of one (A. H. Monroe, "The Supreme Court and the Constitution," *Amer. Polit. Sci. Rev.*,

2. THE POLICE POWER

The police power is undoubtedly the greatest unwritten clause of our Constitution, wherefore it becomes rather important to know what it is. Unfortunately there appear to be two contradictory conceptions of it expressed or implied in court decisions and in the writings of legal authorities.[1] One is a power over an independently defined list of objects, which can be used in turn to define the scope of due process of law. The other is the undefined residuum of power reserved by the Constitution to the states (as far as it is of a regulative nature). This, of course, exists only within the bounds of due process. Hence due process defines it, and it cannot possibly define due process. These two contradictory notions may perhaps be brought together by the proposition that the ultimate nature of the power is undefined and that, when a court defines it in terms of safety, health, and morals, or any other list of specific subject matter, the court is merely describing its customary content. Such a list, on this hypothesis, is only a minimum: a summary of powers sanctioned by usage and therefore clearly within the bounds of any reasonable conception of due process of law. But, unless due process is to include only what has been done before, no such list can possibly serve to define its maximum limits. Every implication to that effect should be resolutely combated and constitutionality should be shown to hinge, not on this traditional list of powers, but on the principles underlying due process, principles which have so far not been formulated in general terms by the courts.

The phrase itself is imported from English law, but the English meaning has no application to our situation. In England it applied to executive procedure, such as Parliament might lay down, which, when so laid down, executives were bound to follow. But there is no power in England competent to prescribe what shall be due process for Parliament itself. Hence the American courts have had to create a meaning for this all-important term.[2] As a concept setting limits on

---

XVIII (November, 1924), 748. The situation is well exhibited in the conflicting opinions in the District of Columbia Minimum-wage Case (*Adkins* v. *Children's Hospital*, 261 U.S. 525–571). The vote in this case was five to three against the law, Justice Brandeis (who would unquestionably have sustained the law) not voting. Chief Justice Taft and Justice Holmes wrote dissenting opinions, and that of Justice Holmes, in particular, might be taken as a text for much that is here said.

[1] See esp. W. W. Cook, "What Is the Police Power?" *Columbia Law Rev.*, May, 1907. The outstanding theories are those of Freund, Hastings, and Cook. For a list of authoritative definitions, see Tugwell, *The Economic Basis of Public Interest*, pp. 4–11.

[2] See Cook, *op. cit.*, p. 326.

social and economic legislation it did not come into prominence until the Granger legislation of the eighteen-seventies, and the greater part of its history before the Supreme Court has occurred since 1900.[1] By 1870 the police power of the states was well developed, though vague as to its nature and boundaries, and the court held that it was not taken away by the Fourteenth Amendment. The principle involved is essentially the same as that underlying the great Charles River Bridge Case of 1835, namely, that the natural powers of police and public welfare, for the sake of which governments exist, are not to be taken away as a result of a mere implication, even (in this case) if the implication is in a charter grant which the state has itself made and

---

[1] The contest between the bill of rights and the power of control has gone through various stages, hinging on different clauses of the bill of rights. First came the clause forbidding states to pass laws impairing the obligation of contracts. Under this the Dartmouth College Case had the effect of paralyzing regulation until the Charles River Bridge Case relaxed the bonds. Then came the Dred Scott Case, followed by the Civil War and reconstruction. The first test of the new Fourteenth Amendment was made mainly on the clause protecting the "privileges and immunities of citizens of the United States," in the Slaughter House cases of 1873, in which the court held that this clause did not protect the general economic rights of individuals and allowed the carpet-bag government of Louisiana to grant a monopoly which appeared palpably unjust and excluded over one thousand persons already in the business.

The first great cases hinging on the "life, liberty, and property" clause of the Fourteenth Amendment were over the Granger laws of the early seventies, the leading case being *Munn* v. *Illinois*, 94 U.S. 113. Here the court enlarged the conception of a business affected with a public interest to include the storage of grain and permitted regulation of rates on that ground. Other cases permitted control in the interest of "public safety, health, and morals," and in the last decade of the nineteenth century this definition was expanded into the area of general welfare. This, with some liberalizing of ideas as to what may be justified under the "public health," has made possible the great growth of social legislation since 1900.

Among the laws held unconstitutional during this recent period, perhaps the chief ones are the New York ten-hour law for bakeshops (this decision is now generally considered to have been, in effect, reversed), the Kansas law prohibiting discharge of workers for membership in unions, a federal law to the same effect for railroads, the Kansas compulsory arbitration law creating the Court of Industrial Relations, the two federal child-labor laws, and the District of Columbia Minimum-wage Law. Warren points out that, from 1889 to 1918, out of 422 conflicts between the police power of the states and the Fourteenth Amendment, only fifty-three state acts have been held unconstitutional, two-thirds of these were rate cases in public-service industries, only fourteen were laws affecting the general rights of individuals, and only four aroused serious criticism (see Charles Warren, *The Supreme Court in United States History*, Vol. III, 466, 1923. For other material referred to in the foregoing outline, see Vol. II, pp. 298, 308, and Vol. III, pp. 257–258, 262, 296–303). However, the effect of the constitutional restrictions is out of proportion to the number of laws actually invalidated.

which, under the Dartmouth College Case, has the force of a contract.
The same rule, apparently, applies to the implication contained in
the due-process clause, which is not allowed to block the customary
and proper exercise of the police power. The idea of the police power
appears to be historically continuous with this general power which
was upheld in the Charles River Bridge Case: the power which is to
be granted every presumption simply because it is what government
is for.[1] The totally undefined character of the phrase "due process"
certainly seems to give the court ample latitude for settling doubts in
favor of the power of control, and not depriving the state of this power
by mere implication.

But why does not this residual power to legislate, being granted in
general terms, extend to the protection of any public interest whatever,
and why is not due process satisfied if the measures taken are not clearly
arbitrary, discriminatory, or tyrannical?[2] This is one of the mysteries
of our constitutional law. Probably the courts believed very firmly
that an undue interference with economic liberty was in itself both
arbitrary and tyrannical. One finds fairly recent judicial utterances
stating or implying that acts of legislatures, on their face intended to
protect public interests of some weight, are sheer meddling interference
with the rights of the citizen.[3]

At any rate, courts have assumed the duty of determining what is
undue interference. Their method is characteristic. One major premise

[1] Hastings has shown how Chief Justice Marshall passed from one phrase to
the other between 1824 and 1827, and Judge Barbour, in 1837, used both phrases
with the same meaning, namely, the residual sovereignty of the states (cited by
W. W. Cook, *op. cit.*).

[2] The court reserves the right to determine, not merely whether the object of
control is legitimate, but whether the measures taken are appropriate to the end in
view and are not so "arbitrary, unequal, and oppressive" as to "shock the sense of
fairness" (quotations from *Chicago & Northwestern Railway Co.* v. *Nye-Schneider-
Fowler Co.*, 260 U.S. 35, 43).

[3] See especially Justice Harlan's statement that employer and employee have
an *equal* liberty to determine all the conditions of employment and that any interference with this is "an arbitrary interference with freedom of contract, which no
government can legally justify in a free land" (*Adair* v. *United States*, 208 U.S. 161,
175, decided in 1908). The interference in question was a law protecting the worker's liberty to belong to labor unions. Cf. the idea that liberty of contract cannot be
restricted in the interest of the *contracting party*, but only in that of the health,
safety, and morals of the *public*, implying that the interest of the contracting party
is not to be regarded as a public interest except in special cases where such an
interest is recognized, as in the case of children (see *People* v. *Marcus*, 128 N.Y. 257.
In re House Bill 203, 21 Col. 27, cited by Roscoe Pound in "Liberty of Contract,"
Yale Law Jour., Vol. XVIII, pp. 454, 470). Mr. Pound states that the extreme
theory of liberty of contract expressed by Justice Harlan first appears in state
decisions in 1886, in *Godcharles* v. *Wigeman*, 113 Pa. St. 431.

is that customary types of control, which governments had been exercising without question, were not to be suddenly invalidated by the Fourteenth Amendment. Another premise is that the power to make new laws, and presumably new types of law, is not to be suddenly and completely taken from the state governments; but along with this goes a strong judicial bent toward construing new cases as instances under established rules. This lends force to the attempt to formulate a definition of the (customary) police power of the state, which is seen to include (at least) the protection of the public peace, health, and morals. Reason sanctions this, since these are such important values that they outweigh the disadvantages of interference with private liberty, even in the most individualistic view of society which is humanly possible. But such provisional statements tend, in the law, to be given more importance than their character justifies, by attorneys and judges eagerly searching for a rule or a precedent.[1] Hence they tend to harden into rigid rules. This threatened to be the fate of the definition of the police power, but in the last decade of the nineteenth century it burst its bonds, refused to be confined to "safety, health, and morals," and expanded into the unlimited field of public welfare.[2]

Having been thus emancipated, it seems destined to become again what it was in the beginnings of our jurisprudence: the undefined residual power of the state to control its citizens. And due process for the exercise of this power, as far as it is not simply traditional, seems to mean: "with due regard for the natural rights and liberties of individuals." Or, as Freund expresses it, limitations of liberty "must be capable of justification upon some theory of public interest which is both rational and regardful of individual liberty and property as rights essential to a free state. . . . As regards degree, the principle of reasonableness means that the burden imposed shall not be disproportionate to the benefit sought to be secured."[3] Whether this is or is not the theory which the court consistently holds, the fact seems to be that a law, to convince a court that it is duly "regardful of individual liberty," must overcome a strong presumption on the part of the court in favor of liberty of contract—not absolute liberty, be it noted, but the customary degree of liberty. As a result the courts have been very slow even in allowing the protection of health to be

---

[1] An outstanding instance of this tendency in the field of public-service regulation is the so-called "rule" of *Smyth* v. *Ames* (which is not a rule at all) for valuing the property of regulated companies. Hence the suggestion in Sec. 8, below, to replace this with a rule possessing real but elastic economic meaning.

[2] See Warren, *The Supreme Court in United States History*, Vol. III, p. 466.

[3] Ernst Freund, article on the police power in *Cyclopedia of American Government*, cited in Tugwell, *The Economic Basis of Public Interest*, pp. 5–8.

extended, for example, to a ten-hour law for workers in bakeshops,[1] while they have also gone slowly in allowing additions to the traditional list of three basic values: safety, health, and morals.

It is a well-established rule of constitutional interpretation that an act of Congress or of a state legislature must be construed as constitutional if it is possible so to interpret it. This would seem to call for upholding a law if the theory of public interest on which it is based is within the bounds of what a reasonable mind might honestly hold, but this did not save the Minimum-wage Law of the District of Columbia. It is not always easy, even for a justice of the Supreme Court, to agree that a particular opinion which differs from his own is one that a reasonable man might honestly hold; hence the court gravitates at times toward substituting its own judgment for that of the legislature. The majority opinion in the District of Columbia Minimum-wage Case clearly did this, while the dissenting opinions of Chief Justice Taft and Justice Holmes (which appear to be the better authority) uphold the act, although taking pains to indicate that they were inclined to agree with the majority of the court as to its unwisdom. That, however, they insisted, was a matter within the scope of legislative discretion, which the court should not undertake to supplant.[2] In a later case, the majority of the court accepted the views of the former minority and overruled the earlier decision, permitting reasonable minimum-wage legislation for women.[3] To do the court justice, it has upheld numerous laws which the majority of its members did not approve, thus allowing legislative discretion considerable scope.

Akin to this is the theory of Justice Holmes that the court should accept the verdict of prevailing opinion, where that verdict is clear, strong, and settled, as to the subject matter which may properly be regulated under the police power.[4] This presupposes a theory of public interest supporting the exercise of power and a clear judgment that the public interest is of so vital a sort that there can be no question but that it outweighs the evils of control. This would seem to be well within the limits of Mr. Freund's theory, but the Supreme Court has not accepted it. It is doubtful if the theory of public interest expressed

[1] See *Lochner,* v. *New York*, 198 U.S. 75. This is cited by the court in the District of Columbia Minimum-wage Case, already referred to, though Justice Holmes remarks in his dissenting opinion that the case has been overruled.

[2] See *Adkins* v. *Children's Hospital*, 261 U.S. 525–571.

[3] *West Coast Hotel Co.* v. *Parrish*, 300 U.S. 379 (1937).

[4] The best-known statement of this doctrine is as follows: "It [the police power] may be put forth in aid of what is sanctioned by usage, or held by the prevailing morality or strong or preponderant opinion to be greatly and immediately necessary for the public welfare" (*Noble State Bank* v. *Haskell*, 219 U.S. 104).

in this chapter would be accepted by the court, even as now constituted, though it seems clearly to be such a theory as a rational mind
might accept. Yet in practice the result is not so different from Justice
Holmes' views as the judicial theory would indicate. If the public
opinion back of a measure is strong and settled enough to command
repeated legislative majorities and to pass successive laws in forms
aimed to overcome judicial objections, the judicial veto is likely—but
not certain—ultimately to be circumvented. To some, this delay
appears as an advantage, making for sounder measures in the end; to
others, it appears to delay needed changes to the point of increasing
the danger of violent revolution.

Such, in rough outline, is the police power: a strange mixture of
legal logic, obsolete individualistic presumptions, and real appreciation
of the need of allowing the legislature elbow-room to fight the battles
of the twentieth century.

3. BUSINESSES AFFECTED WITH A PUBLIC INTEREST

Certain industries are set apart from the rest as subject to a four-
fold duty: to serve, to serve all alike on the same terms, to give service
of fair quality, and at reasonable rates. They are accordingly subject
to whatever governmental regulation may be required to enforce these
special duties. On what grounds are these duties imposed on certain
industries and not on others? Legally, these industries fall into two
groups: those rendering a service "of a public character," which
government itself has a duty to render, and private businesses "affected
with a public interest" of a kind and degree justifying this type of
regulation. The first group includes highways and, by extension, rail
transport, also municipal water supply and certain other recognized
"public utilities." The second group includes a wide and growing
variety of services. But this does not explain the grounds on which
these classifications are made.

This is an unsettled question among jurists, various theories being
put forward. The resulting confusion may be simplified by distinguishing two types of theory. One deals with special legal circumstances giving the community a hold on the companies, such as the granting of a
special franchise or permit to use the public streets. These special legal
circumstances may be regarded as of minor importance for our purpose,
simply because, with or without them, a public interest will be recognized if the character of the industry is such as to give rise to it. An
example of the extension of this concept to a new industry is found in
the classic case of *Munn* v. *Illinois*.[1] A refusal to make a new extension

[1] 94 U.S. 113 (1876).

is illustrated in the later case of the Kansas Industrial Disputes Act.[1] This act declared a large assortment of general industries to be affected with a public interest for purposes of preventing industrial disputes (not of price regulation) on the ground that uninterrupted operation of these industries is essential to the public. This act was overthrown by the Supreme Court in a decision which held that, whatever might be the basis of this classification, the courts and not the legislature have the final power to decide upon it.

Among the economic grounds put forward as bases for deciding this question, some are too narrow to account for the actual cases, or to furnish a basis for a rational policy, while others are too broad. All alike presuppose that the service in question is an essential one, but this alone is not sufficient. The narrowest ground suggested is that of monopoly, or rather, "natural monopoly," since the concept has not been extended to cover "artificial monopolies" or trusts. A broader theory is that of "consumers' disadvantage" in bargaining with the industry; another points to a peculiar dependence of the public on the industry (whether as buyers or sellers). Still broader is the theory that anyone who "holds himself out" to serve the public thereby subjects his business to a public interest; while the broadest theory of all holds that, originally at least, all enterprises conducted on a business basis acquired this characteristic. On this theory the legislature would have complete discretion to extend this type of control to any business at all.

It seems clear that the obligation to serve the public at reasonable charges dates back to a time at which the obligation attached to anyone who offered his services to the public in what is now the regular business way. As this was before the industrial revolution, modern businesses of large fixed capital were unknown, and fair prices were not based on a fair return to the capital invested, but on a fair return to the person carrying on the enterprise. It appears to have been an extension of the medieval doctrine of the just price, which was based on the customary standard of living of the worker; and it has been argued that the real obligation of such businesses is merely to maintain customary prices. Modern regulation is different in character and based on different grounds. Today, when only a few selected industries are subject to this special control, we are clearly not acting on the theory that anyone who holds himself out to serve the public subjects himself to it. This theory and practice were swept away by the era of individualism, and the courts, in continuing or reapplying this doctrine in a limited range of cases, must be basing it on a narrower

[1] See *Wolff Packing Co.* v. *Court of Industrial Relations*, 262 U.S. 522 (June, 1923).

ground. The old ground is too broad for the present application of the theory.

One suggested basis is purely traditional, referring to "certain occupations, the public interest attaching to which, recognized from earliest times, has survived from the period of arbitrary regulation of all trades or callings by Parliament or colonial legislatures, e.g., inns, cabs, and grist mills."[1] This group includes only a part of the cases and, being based on custom, leaves us in the dark as to why control of these particular callings survived the general reaction against indiscriminate and "arbitrary" regulation. It appears to include callings likely to be local monopolies, or in which the customers, being travelers, are not in a position to canvass the market and get the benefit of such competition as may exist and therefore are likely to be exploited.

On the other hand, the theory of monopoly, or "virtual monopoly," is too narrow and will not account for all the cases. To constitute a monopoly in the judicial sense, one consolidated organization must be in substantial control of the market, and this is hardly true of railroads, to say nothing of hotels.[2] On economic grounds a business which is naturally monopolistic, that is, one which can render its service most efficiently if organized as a monopoly, should certainly be allowed to do so and be subjected to public regulation. The concept of natural monopoly, complete or partial, probably covers substantially all the businesses "of a public character" but fails to account for a considerable fringe of private businesses "affected with a public interest." The key to this group appears to lie in the fact that they are services which private enterprise cannot be trusted to organize properly. This at least puts us on the right track.

A valuable suggestion is afforded by the theory advanced by Professor Tugwell: that of "consumers' disadvantage." This carries with it a dependence justifying control of service and rates. The concept might need to be broadened to include sellers as well as buyers, for instance, farmers selling cattle in stockyards or selling milk to large distributors. The essential economic fact seems to be that the nature of the business is such that competition, for one reason or another, does not afford the protection to buyers and sellers which it is supposed to afford when working freely, and which their interests require.[3]

[1] *Ibid.*

[2] See Tugwell, *The Economic Basis of Public Interest.* This monograph contains an excellent summary of the various legal theories, on which much of the present argument is based.

[3] See 273 U.S. 429. Justice Stone uses language very similar to that of the last sentence of the paragraph before the preceding, which was written before this decision was rendered.

This may be because there is a monopoly, or it may be that the individual is not in a position to avail himself of the options which competition affords, as in the case of travelers stopping overnight at a hotel. This seems to describe adequately the economic grounds justifying the particular type of regulation we are now considering, namely, the securing of fair prices for a fair product or service. It seems an adequate justification—whether it is the one which actually governed the courts or not—for the cases in which a public interest has actually been found, and to afford a rational basis for future additions to this class.

The recent history of this doctrine is both interesting and important. An attempt to control ticket-brokerage agencies in New York was overthrown by a divided court, Justice Stone, in his dissenting opinion, setting forth a theory in harmony with the views just expressed.[1] Another decision by a divided court held private employment agencies not affected with a public interest, though Stone, again dissenting, said: "Certainly it would be difficult to show greater necessity for price regulation." With this judgment anyone acquainted with the abuses of the highly imperfect market represented by private employment agencies would heartily agree. Finally, in the case of the New York law providing for a *minimum* price for milk, the former minority opinion became, in effect, the majority opinion of the court, and the law was sustained.[2] Whether this means a broadening of the category of businesses affected with a public interest, or an extension of the power of price regulation beyond this category, is a question which may perhaps be left to the jurists.

Within this category the incidental relations, such as that of the wage earners, are not considered, nor the incidental functions other than the sale of the product, such as market information or the educational function of advertising. If these things were admitted as creating a relation of dependence, the resulting public interest would not be limited decorously to a few businesses but might include all industry with respect to these particular relations or functions—not, to be sure, to the extent of regulating their prices. A public interest of this sort would not attach to an entire industry in contrast to other industries, but to certain relations or functions (which most industries share) in contrast to other relations or functions. This would have the effect of merging the doctrine of public interest with the general police power. This may or may not have been the effect of the *Nebbia* case. However,

[1] See 277 U.S. 355.
[2] *Nebbia* v. *New York*, 291 U.S. 502 (1934). Cf. R. L. Hale, "Some Reflections on the Nebbia Case," *Columbia Law Rev.*, XXXIV (March, 1934), 401–425.

it had already been recognized that different types of public interest exist, and that the type of regulation should be appropriate to the needs of the particular type of case.[1] The boundary line between this concept and the general police power, like most such boundaries, becomes in practice rather shadowy and may possibly disappear. So much, then, for the general power of government to regulate industry.

4. FEDERAL POWERS

A further vexed question is that of the division of this power between state and federal governments. Here the natural principle of division is that laid down by one of the framers of the Federal Constitution: "Whatever object of government is confined in its operation and effects within the bounds of a particular State, should be considered as belonging to the government of that State; whatever object of government extends in its operation or effects beyond the bounds of a particular State, should be considered as belonging to the government of the United States."[2] Under this principle, if "effects" were construed broadly, the regulation of business in general would become largely national, since the nation is becoming more and more an economic unit.

In one respect, basic to our prosperity, the Constitution recognizes and protects this unity: the states are not permitted to levy protective tariffs against foreign countries or against one another. In practice, it requires eternal vigilance on the part of the Supreme Court to protect this principle against trade barriers which local interests are ever ready to impose under guise of health or inspection regulations or in other ways. Preference for state-made goods in state government purchases cannot be prevented. And the prohibition-repeal amendment, in protecting states which wish to prohibit or control liquor against imports from other states which do not have equal controls, is so worded as to go further and permit discriminatory burdens of a protective character, thus repealing the prohibition of interstate trade barriers for the liquor business.[3] The promptness with which this has been taken advantage of bears witness to the need of vigorous watchfulness if the principle of national trade unity is to be even partially maintained. It has already suffered material impairment.

[1] Cf. Smith, Dowling, and Hale, *Cases on the Law of Public Utilities*, *passim*.

[2] James Wilson, "Address to the Convention of Pennsylvania," *Elliott's Debates*, Vol. II, p. 424, cited in "The Proposed Child-labor Amendment," by John A. Ryan, D.D., National Child Labor Committee, *Pub.* 323, p. 10, 1924.

[3] See *State Board of Equalization of California* v. *Young's Market Co. et al.*, 299 U.S. 59–64 (1936). Cf. "Death by Tariff," *Fortune*, pp. 32 ff., August, 1938.

The powers actually granted to the Federal Government, as far as they bear at all on internal economic regulation, consist of the taxing power, the commerce power, and power over bankruptcy law, coinage, weights and measures, postoffices and postroads, patents, and copyrights. These have been extended to include protection to industry through tariffs, banking, and anti-trust laws, and to a number of other matters which have no logical relation to the power under which control was justified. In the words of Charles E. Hughes.[1] "There has been in late years a series of cases sustaining the regulation of interstate commerce, although the rules established by Congress had the quality of police regulation. This has been decided with respect to the interstate transportation of lottery tickets, of impure foods and drugs, of misbranded articles, of intoxicating liquors, and of women for the purpose of debauchery." The taxing power has been used, among other things, to stamp out state bank notes, prevent the coloring of oleomargarine to look like butter, and control the sale and use of narcotic drugs.[2]

If this trend continues, Congress may, under these two powers, be able to exercise any control which would be proper to a state, thus setting up a federal police power as extensive as that of the states. The movement came to a temporary halt with the federal child-labor laws, the first of which was passed under the commerce power and the second under the taxing power.[3] Both of these were declared unconstitutional. The Supreme Court expressed the fear that, if this precedent were allowed, the Federal Government might supplant the states entirely.[4] Yet the inability of the state to protect its producers from the competition of goods imported from other states is one of the serious obstacles to the development by the states themselves of such standards of child-labor legislation as are really desirable. The Federal

[1] From an address before the New York Bar Assoc., cited by R. G. Fuller in *Child Labor and the Constitution*," pp. 239–240, 1923. For a discussion of this whole question of a federal police power, see R. E. Cushman, "Studies in the Police Power of the National Government," *Minn. Law Rev.*, Vol. III, Nos. 5, 6, 7, and Vol. IV, Nos. 4, 6 (also separately printed); also Warren, *The Supreme Court in American History*, Vol. III, pp. 457–461.

[2] Fuller, *op. cit.*, p. 241.

[3] That is, one prohibited interstate commerce in the products of child labor of certain defined sorts, and the other laid a 10 per cent tax on the net profits from the sale of goods made by child labor.

[4] *Hammer* v. *Dagenhart*, 247 U.S. 251, and *Bailey* v. *Drexel Furniture Co.*, 259 U.S. 20. One writer contends that the federal power could be successfully sustained on the ground that child labor is "involuntary servitude" within the meaning of the Thirteenth Amendment (J. F. Lawson, *Amer. Law Rev.*, Vol. LVI, pp. 733–746).

Government should have some power adequate to support the states which want good standards, and the most clearly practicable method is to give it power to set minimum standards.[1]

The development of what amounts to a federal police power was resumed, despite setbacks, during the Federal Government's attack on the problem of national depression in 1933 and the years following. Control of intrastate business under the National Recovery Administration was overturned in the Schechter case; yet out of three major objectives of this administration, two have been reembodied in subsequent federal laws. These are the control of wages and hours and the protection of collective bargaining. In the third major division of NRA controls—those over competitive pricing and trade practices—few features commended themselves in the light of experience; and some of them are being carried forward under state legislation. The Agricultural Adjustment Administration was barred as using the taxing power to carry out what was essentially a plan of regulation not directly within the federal power, namely, limitation of crop acreage and raising of prices. Substantially similar control was, however, resumed under the heading of conservation. Under the Social Security Act the power to tax wages and make grants to states has been used for the effective promotion of unemployment insurance and old-age pensions. This may in time come to be the most thoroughly approved of all the New Deal measures.

It is of the essence of depressions that all business is interdependent, whether interstate or intrastate; but the court has—perhaps properly—declined to give the Federal Government general power over intrastate business because of this general relationship, which it is likely to regard as indirect rather than direct and therefore not placing intrastate business under the federal power. It has, however, granted extensions of federal power greater than many cautious citizens approve, and probably as great as we can well assimilate at the present time.

[1] Conceivably, the federal power might be limited to prohibiting the transport of goods into any state unless the conditions under which they were made, as respects child labor, hours of labor, or other conditions vitally affecting expense of production, were as good as those required by the laws of the state into which the goods were transported. But under this system, if it could be called such, every producer would be under as many industrial codes as the number of states into which he shipped his goods. In theory the rule would preserve state's rights and merely stop up a gap in the state's fences, so to speak. But in practice it would be so unworkable that it would either become a dead letter or would compel uniformity among the states and so wipe out their independent power of regulation more completely than would the setting of minimum standards by the Federal Government.

To sum up, the territorial division of powers under the letter of the United States Constitution no longer corresponds with the scope of our economic problems. Amendments increasing federal powers are difficult to frame and unlikely to be approved by the states whose powers would be encroached upon. We shall apparently go on by the method of judicial construction, involving a stretching of existing powers to serve purposes not originally intended. This method has shown surprising and perhaps adequate elasticity but is likely to reach at least temporary limits at unexpected points and places upon the judges a tremendous economic responsibility of what is essentially a legislative or constitution-framing sort.

5. PROPOSED CHANGES

There are clearly two sets of questions raised: as to the scope of the powers of government, and their apportionment between state and nation. On both these questions there is deep cleavage of opinion, running all the way from those who are satisfied with the kind of veto—mainly suspensive—which the courts now exercise, to those who wish a completely unchecked legislative power and hold that the Supreme Court usurped the power it now holds to declare legislative acts unconstitutional. From the administration of Theodore Roosevelt on, there have been intermittent proposals to change this situation. These may be classified as follows: proposals to change the personnel of the court, proposals to overrule its decisions, proposals to require a special majority of the court to hold a law unconstitutional, amendments to the Constitution to permit specific measures, amendments to enlarge the powers of the legislature more generally, and amendment liberalizing the amending process for the future.

Enough has been said to show that, if things are left as they are, the result will not be fatal to all progressive development of social control, though there will be delays, some of which may be serious. The "economic constitution," already set forth, calls for a very considerable widening of the possible grounds of public action.[1] A general presumption in favor of liberty remained even under this Constitution; but the presumption created by the Supreme Court's construction of the Fifth and Fourteenth Amendments is beset by legal logic and does not always guarantee a real weighing of the economic values at stake.

Probably the main object would be accomplished by an amendment, not in the Constitution, but in the economics of the judges, coupled with the adoption of "progressive" views on the scope of the police power and the proper realm of discretion to be left to the legisla-

[1] See above, Chap. ix, Sec. 3.

ture. Then we might expect to see the police power broadened to include a really elastic and adequate theory of public interest.

While this might make possible all needed legislation, many persons would feel that the power of the state rested on an insecure foundation, and that precedents of a less liberal sort would continually confuse and obstruct the carrying out of the new theory, unless it were fortified by further measures.

Proposals to alter the personnel of the court include the "recall of judges," advocated in Theodore Roosevelt's time, and the "court-packing bill" of 1937. This method has been rejected by public opinion, and probably rightly. The second proposal parallels the method whereby the English House of Commons maintains its ultimate supremacy over the House of Lords, through the power of the King, in case of critical deadlock, to create new peers. But in our case there is not the necessity for such an extreme measure, since we have available, as the English have not, other and more regularly constitutional ways of meeting the situation. Where this is true, the personal independence of the judiciary is not a thing to be lightly impaired. Moreover, such a proceeding, like some of the others proposed, is too general in character and not easily confined to the kind of cases which might really justify an overriding of the court.

Another proposal is to give Congress power to pass laws over the veto of the Supreme Court. Such a measure, be it noted, would not help the state legislatures. It would eliminate the encroachments of the court upon the federal legislative power; but unless it were carefully limited to certain classes of cases, it would carry even more serious consequences through abolishing the power of the court within its proper field of judicial action. First, it would free Congress from all the restraints of the bill of rights, and not merely those of a political-economic character. There is surely no reason for removing the ban on *ex post facto* laws, bills of attainder, and other similar abuses. Second, it would enable Congress to encroach on the powers of the states without limit, and even to exercise more power in state matters than the states themselves possess, since it would be free from all constitutional limitations. Such a remedy abolishes all safeguards where the situation calls for the removal of certain specific obstacles— obstacles which should be capable of separate treatment.

Another and less sweeping proposal is to require more than a bare majority of the court to declare an act of Congress unconstitutional— for example, a two-thirds vote. If there is any way of confining this provision to cases in which the court is voting according to its economic judgment, it may be quite logical as an additional way of giving the legislature's economic judgment the benefit of all reasonable doubt. But if it could not be confined to such cases, it would be likely to prove a boomerang. It could easily produce the very strange spectacle of a dissenting opinion vainly upholding the constitutional guaranty of free speech against laws passed in a fever of patriotic fanaticism, the dissent being signed by a majority of the court but overruled by the minority! It is significant that Justice Holmes, who has consistently upheld measures of economic control, has been equally consistent in championing the right of free speech against governmental encroachment.[1]

Another method is to amend the Constitution whenever some particular thing is wanted and is held unconstitutional, giving Congress or the states power to do that specific thing—or perhaps going farther and putting legislation into the Constitution, as did the prohibition amendment. This tendency is in danger of being carried too far, threatening the character of our Constitution as a charter of general powers. A better method, if practicable, would be to maintain its constitutional character by a more general broadening of governmental powers.

This might perhaps be accomplished by amending the Fifth and Fourteenth Amendments, differentiating the due-process clause so as to give different treatment to different classes of cases, maintaining its protections where they are appropriate, and liberalizing its meaning where needed, thus bringing it into greater conformity with economic needs without removing all safeguards on legislative action. The following proposals are made only by way of illustration in order to give concreteness to this general type of policy, but with no implication that they constitute the only right course of action.

A pertinent plan might be to divide the taking of life, liberty, and property into three distinct kinds of taking. The first includes depriving any person of life, of all his liberty, or the complete taking of any piece of physical property (depriving him of all his rights in any bit of property). Here the present restrictions should stand unchanged. The second division covers industries affected with a public interest, in the present meaning of the term. In enforcing the obligation of reasonable rates and service, which rests upon them, there is real need of a more definite rule defining reasonableness in economic terms, and removing certain sources of confusion and uncertainty which have arisen from the rulings of the courts on the subject of "fair value."

[1] See Dorsey Richardson, "Constitutional Doctrines of Justice Oliver Wendell Holmes, *Johns Hopkins University Studies in Historical and Political Science,* Ser. XLII, No. 3, 1924.

A rule of this sort will be proposed in a later chapter. The proposal is of a sort which requires no break with present standard practice, its chief effect being to introduce greater liberty of method in dealing with future investments.[1]

The third division would cover all other limitations upon the scope of personal liberties or of the rights of property, including the right of contract. Such limitations, being implied in all regulative law, would not be forbidden but would be required to be in accord with due process of law. Due process, in such cases, should consist of an act of the legislative body having jurisdiction, based upon a specific constitutional grant of power or upon the existence of a public need or interest which the measure in question is reasonably adapted to promote, and subject to judicial veto when the legislative body has gone beyond the limits of what a reasonable mind might honestly judge to fulfill these conditions. A public interest arises wherever particular conditions are present such that free contract does not produce its normal benefits to any group or groups whose essential interests are involved, and where the resulting evils are substantial enough to outweigh the general presumption in favor of liberty. Such a public interest may attach not only to an entire industry, but to any class of transactions within the operations of the industry, or any contact it has with the interests of the community; and there should be no presumption that it is only rare and exceptional industries that are thus affected. The control justified by the existence of such a public interest should, of course, be limited to such measures as are appropriate to the nature of the evils to be guarded against, and the weight of the presumption against control should vary with the degree of interference with personal liberty or with economic law.

As to the scope of federal powers, the central government ultimately needs such powers as would be adequate to deal with business depressions. But aside from political difficulties, one serious obstacle to drafting an amendment for this purpose is the lack of knowledge or agreement as to what powers would be necessary and adequate for this purpose. Perhaps the most pertinent measure of enlargement of the federal powers would be to provide, as suggested above, that when the power of the states to control their own internal affairs is seriously obstructed by the effects of interstate commerce with states having different standards of control, Congress shall have power, for the purpose of restoring effective control, to set minimum standards, which shall not supplant state laws except so far as may be necessary to make these standards effective. This would give Congress no broader power

[1] See Chaps. xx, xxi, following.

than states are actually exercising. It would not "abolish the states" or encroach upon any field where their regulation is now effective.

Further, and probably first in point of time, comes an amendment to the amending procedure, making it less difficult and cumbrous and removing the possibility that a negligible minority of the people could block the passage of needed amendments. Constitutional amendments should probably be substantially more difficult than legislation, at least in the United States, but the present requirement of ratification by three-fourths of the states appears to carry conservatism unduly far.

REFERENCES FOR FURTHER READING

ADAMS, BROOKS, *The Theory of Social Revolutions.*

BECK, JAMES M., *The Constitution of the United States,* Chaps. xiv, xvii–xix, xxi–xxiv.

COOK, W. W., "What Is the Police Power?" *Columbia Law Rev.*, May, 1907.

CORWIN, E. S., *The Constitution and What It Means Today,* 5th ed., 1937.

————, *The Commerce Power versus States Rights,* 1938.

————, *The Twilight of the Supreme Court,* 1934.

FREUND, ERNST, *The Police Power.*

GOODNOW, F. J., *Social Reform and the Constitution.*

HOLMES, OLIVER WENDELL, in *Noble State Bank* v. *Haskell,* 219 U.S. 104; and dissent, in *Adkins* v. *Children's Hospital,* 261 U.S. 525–571.

ORTH, S. P., *Readings on the Relation of Government to Property and Industry,* Chaps. iii, vii.

PARSONS, *Legal Doctrine and Social Progress.*

POWELL, T. R., articles on the Supreme Court and the Constitution, *Polit. Sci. Quart.*, XXXVI (September, 1920), 411–439; XXXVII (September, 1922), 486–513; XL (March, 1925), 101–126; XL (September, 1925), 404–437.

SMITH, DOWLING, and HALE, *Cases on the Law of Public Utilities* (2d ed.), 1936.

SWENSON, *National Government and Business,* Chaps. iv, v, xii, xvii.

TUGWELL, R. G., *The Economic Basis of Public Interest.*

WARREN, *The Supreme Court in American History.*

CHAPTER XI

DATA AND STANDARDS FOR THE GUIDANCE AND CENSORSHIP OF CONTROL

1. THE NEED FOR STANDARDS

It is clear that the task of deciding what exercises of public powers are justified would be vastly easier if there were some scientific method of measuring the importance of the interests at stake on both sides and determining which are the more important. Unfortunately, standards of this sort seem to be out of reach because the interests which have to be weighed against one another are of such diverse sorts, and no common unit of measurement seems possible. Nevertheless, we can in many cases achieve partial or provisional standards. Even if our efforts in this direction lead to nothing more than the gathering of trustworthy data and bringing them to bear on problems of public policy, there will be an enormous gain over the typical strategy of legislation where no standards of any sort enter.

One of the characteristic methods is log rolling, the game of "you vote for my measure and I'll vote for yours." This game has freest scope where each measure grants a definite, visible benefit to one group at a cost which is indefinite and concealed or diffused over the whole community. Here log rolling serves admirably to secure a majority vote for policies whose aggregate benefits are not worth the aggregate costs involved. If public hearings are held, it is the few with heavy interests who appear, and the unorganized millions of small interests are inadequately represented. Labor is coming to be well represented, as far as it is organized, but the consumer, as such, is still almost wholly silent. And the data submitted by interested parties are often well-nigh useless, owing to biased selection of cases, failure to include crucial items of expense, or merely for lack of adequate assurance that such bias has not crept in.

Even where a standard (or rule) has been set up in general terms, like the Republican principle of gauging tariff schedules by the difference in costs of production at home and abroad, the attempt to apply this via public hearings results in nothing but confusion. It required years of work on the part of the tariff commission to secure comprehensive data, computed on a uniform basis, and to present them graphically, putting the exceptional figures in their proper place and indicating in tangible form what the normal relation between costs and prices actually is, and what cost it is, out of many prevailing at any time in any industry, that has to be covered by the price of the goods if the industry is to be reasonably prosperous. Such data do not tell us what duties are socially justifiable, but they do tell us what duties are called for by the principle to which we are committed. They do not guarantee that we voted for the correct tariff principle, but they can help mightily to give us what we voted for, instead of something deviously or corruptly different.

2. THE JUDICIAL NECESSITY FOR STANDARDS

The courts set up many standards to which legislative and executive policies must conform, particularly standards of due process of law. There is the standard of compensation when private property is taken for a public purpose, and the dead-line of confiscation which must be avoided in regulating the rates of public-service industries. Of another sort is the conventional list of purposes for which the police power may be invoked, and the requirement that a measure must be rationally adapted to promote one of these public purposes, and that it must be nondiscriminatory. And when the modern type of commission is set up, with large discretionary powers over some specialized field of business, the legislature must set up standards for the guidance of the commission sufficient to satisfy the rule that legislative power must not be delegated. This was accomplished, in the Interstate Commerce Act, by providing that rates must be reasonable and not unduly discriminatory, a standard so vague as to seem no standard at all, so that it might seem that this requirement is an empty form. The phrases used have, however, a meaning of a sort at common law, so that the standard is not quite so indefinite as it seems to the layman. On the other hand, the act setting up the National Recovery Administration of 1933 was found lacking in standards. It provided for codes of "fair competition" which were obviously intended to go far beyond any previous legal definition of that term, guided only by very general recovery objectives.

These judicial requirements should, in general, be easily satisfied because of the general rule that the constitutionality of a legislative act is to be given the benefit of all reasonable doubt. But the legislature ought to seek standards for its own guidance within the zone of discretion which the courts leave to it. As Freund indicates, there is need for more standards than can ever be made judicially enforcible.[1]

3. GRADES OF STANDARDS

Standards are of different sorts. In the "rule" of *Smyth* v. *Ames*, applying to valuations for rate regulation in public-service industries, the Supreme Court listed certain evidence which should be considered, without dictating the weight to be given to the different criteria. This is a standard of procedure and does not determine the precise result to be reached. But it does bar out findings which have no rational basis in the evidence and thus sets limits beyond which the findings may not vary. When the court says that regulations in the interest of the public health are justified, even if liberty and property are taken, it is setting up a standard, or scale of values, of what may be called a qualitative sort: values of one kind take precedence over values of another kind. When a case comes up in which the court holds that the taking of property is the "main thing" and the regulation of health secondary and therefore requires compensation, it is setting up a quantitative standard of a very crude sort. It is deciding at what point the health interest ceases to predominate and the property interest outweighs it. When experts are asked whether a given quantity of a given food preservative is actually deleterious to health, or how much money it costs to maintain a human being in physical efficiency, they are definitely in the realm of quantitative standards. To be sure, the mere setting of the standard does not determine whether it is worth society's while to maintain John Doe in physical efficiency, but it does determine whether he is able to do it for himself on the wages he receives, or whether help of some sort is necessary. It helps to tell us how serious the problem of poverty is and what we have at stake in it.

Any such highly technical standard can be reduced to meaning only by technical experts. Presumably they are supposed to do no more than report the facts or apply a predetermined rule, but they will inevitably do more. Within a considerable margin they have the making of the standard. Hence the success of such attempts at control depends largely on being able to secure the services of experts who possess not only integrity but judgment of a high grade. Ritualistic competence is not enough. One of the great difficulties of control is the securing of such a qualified and trustworthy personnel to administer it.

[1] See *Standards of American Legislation*, Chap. iv, esp. p. 272.

The expert knows that his data will play a part in the forming of the standard which any action on the subject implies, and he must inevitably organize his material with this in view. Bare existence costs so much, physical efficiency and decency cost more, and comfort, more yet. Perhaps the greatest service specialists can render to our complicated society is to report facts in just such forms as this. Sometimes the facts virtually permit of but one answer in terms of community action.

In fact, the more one examines the standards actually employed, the more it appears that none of them is or can be perfectly objective, in the sense in which a foot-rule is an objective standard. They all involve some exercise of judgment, and generally at two important points. There is usually a general act of judgment in which it is decided that a certain value is worth protecting, a certain need worth meeting, or a certain damage worth preventing, even at the cost of interfering with the natural course of free industry. There is the particular act of judgment needed in order to decide whether a particular case comes under the general principle: whether $3\frac{1}{2}$ per cent beer is intoxicating; whether a given food preservative is deleterious to health; whether $1,500 a year is a living wage at a given time and place; whether a given "open-price association" is a monopolistic organization; whether a tariff schedule is equal to the difference in cost of production at home and abroad.

One thing on which the expert may shed a deal of light without usurping the power to decide ultimate policies is the question of what results are attainable. Perhaps the chief instances are the verdict of the health expert as to what diseases are preventable and to what extent, and that of the safety engineer as to what industrial accidents are preventable and at approximately what cost. The average length of life in this country has actually been increased over fifteen years since 1855, being now close to sixty years, and a possible average of sixty-five years is confidently asserted, "based upon mortality rates attainable under present knowledge of preventive medicine and public health."[1] In the realm of industrial accidents, prediction is less definite, but experimental data are accumulating (for example, the work of the United States Bureau of Mines) which prove, for instance, that coal-mine explosions can be prevented by the method of "rock dusting." And Dr. John B. Andrews, secretary of the American Association for Labor Legislation, once expressed the belief that "two-thirds of the fatal and serious accidents at the bituminous coal mines of this country could be prevented by the universal adoption of safety methods

[1] See *Statistical Bull.*, Metropolitan Life Insurance Co., December, 1922.

already in successful operation at some of the mines of this country or in Great Britain."[1] Here the standard was set up by combining the best results actually attained in different establishments.

Standards of attainable performance are also becoming more and more prominent in industry itself. In fact, the central contribution of "scientific management" consists in precisely this working out of independent standards of possible performance, so as to make the management no longer dependent, for their knowledge of what their industry is capable of doing, on the worker's knowledge of his craft and his willingness to be lured into doing his best by incentives and stimuli. But in making the management independent of the worker, is it just possible that scientific management will end by making the public independent of the old brand of private management? Will it describe the conditions of efficiency so definitely and objectively that the industrial department of a government may be able to set standards of efficiency for private operation, or for themselves, perhaps, if they choose to operate the industry directly? It is not wise to expect the economic utopia to come tomorrow by this route, since the standards of scientific management are not so completely objective as some enthusiasts have supposed, and new processes will always be unstandardized; nevertheless, the development has significant possibilities.

4. HEALTH

Foremost among the questions which everyone has to refer to an expert are those of health. Under this heading, various general standards appear to have been set up. For instance, the consumer, when he buys regular articles of food, is presumed to want them in a safe condition, and accordingly he has a right to be protected against definitely harmful ingredients or preservatives, definitely inserted in the process of manufacture, or diseased conditions of meat which can best be detected in the process of slaughtering. Here the case for control is clear, because there is no interest on the other side which is entitled to any consideration. Borderline cases occur: when there is doubt whether a thing has an appreciable harmful effect; also when it is not a question of harmful ingredients deliberately put into foodstuffs, but merely of the natural process of spoiling, and the consumer can tell as well as, or better than, the dealer whether the thing has become unfit for use; and also when the harmful effect is inherent in the nature of the thing the consumer wants, so that there is some reason for saying that he deliberately chooses to run the risk of injury to his

[1] See *Amer. Labor Legislation Rev.*, March, 1924, article, also printed separately, under the title "Needless Coal-mine Accidents."

health, and that his liberty is interfered with if he is not allowed to do so. In such a case the line might reasonably be drawn more conservatively, taking action only to prevent such very substantial injuries to one person's health as would appreciably affect the interests of other parties: his family, his employer, or the community at large.

From this we pass to the question of standard hours of labor, standard working conditions in such matters as safety appliances, ventilation, light, seats, and working postures generally, and other matters of similar effect. These are, of course, infinitely varied, and even the length of the working day which is consistent with efficiency varies from industry to industry. The ultimate test is the avoidance of cumulative fatigue, which will shorten the working life of the employee below what seems a reasonable expectation or materially increase the accident hazard or lead to a diminished total output in the long run, even if no bad effects appear over such periods as a month. In some kinds of work the effects may show themselves almost at once, as was indicated by the experiments with a shortened workday in the Zeiss optical works, while in heavier and cruder work the job may not appear to suffer until the worker becomes "old at forty." The pioneer attempt to set up scientific standards for hours of work is Josephine Goldmark's *Fatigue and Efficiency*. Subsequent studies have endeavored to improve the scientific character of the data and the interpretation; and while it is impossible as yet to claim more than fragmentary scientific knowledge as to what length of working day gives the greatest output in the long run, progress is being made in that direction.

5. COST OF LIVING

The cost-of-living standards have already been mentioned. They originated in an attempt simply to discover and make known the amount and severity of the poverty actually existing. Booth, in London, and Rowntree, in York, made studies in which various grades of poverty were distinguished, starting with incomes which stood for positive physical undernourishment. Since these studies were made, the science of nutrition has made great strides, and it seems clear that families begin to suffer from the effects of a badly balanced ration or from the lesser grades of malnutrition long before their expenditure for food has reached the minimum of the earlier studies. This is without taking account of the almost universal fact that people will skimp on the physical necessities to satisfy wants of a social character, so that a wage, to give them the physical necessities, must be enough to buy them some other things besides.

How far should these other wants be recognized in reckoning a living wage where this wage is to be enforced upon industry under minimum-wage legislation? Evidently this calls for a high degree of judgment. Should added wages be granted subject to the condition that the recipient make proper use of them? Henry Ford has actually censored the expenditures of his workmen, exercising a degree of paternalism which no democratic government could hope to impose on the whole population of the United States. No one was compelled to accept the Ford paternalism, but the Ford wage rate was a very powerful inducement. And a government-imposed minimum rate for all industry could not hope, under existing conditions, to rival the rates which the Ford efficiency enabled him to pay.

This brings us to the fact that a standard of human needs is not enough; there must also be a standard of what industry can afford to pay. On this point no systematic studies are available, and it is probable that no general answer to the question can be worked out in definite quantitative terms. The cost of a minimum wage may be borne in various ways. It may pay for itself through increasing the productivity of the worker directly; it may come out of the profits of the producers, in which case it may hasten the weeding out of the least efficient producers; or it may spur them to eliminate wastes and so survive in spite of it. If some producers are eliminated, that may mean diminished employment or it may merely mean absorbing into the more efficient enterprises the workers formerly employed in the less efficient. Or the burden may be passed on to the consumers and so disposed of, provided the minimum wage does not affect too many industries. If the regulation affected every industry alike, the result would be, in a general way, to raise the pay of the lowest-paid classes at the expense of the higher-paid workers and those who get their incomes out of profits or the ownership of property. The question whether a general minimum wage can result in a permanent increase of the general level of prices is one that probably will never be conclusively answered, since the theorists cannot settle their controversies, nor can statisticians isolate the effect of one cause among the multitudes at work in any actual swing of prices.

Evidently the possible combinations of these alternatives are too varied to permit of any simple formula which will embrace them all. In practice, the matter is usually handed over to a board dealing with a given industry in a given locality, and the question of how much the industry can stand is left to the semi-intuitive processes known as judgment. It is safe to say that such a board never sets rates at which a "representative firm" cannot earn a living rate of return on its investment, at least in normal times. But an exact standard in this matter remains to be formulated. It is not even easy to find out the facts as to costs of production, and this is the necessary first step. Afterward it may be found that flexible rules of action will be developed in the course of treating long series of cases "on their merits."

6. ECONOMIC VALUE OF LIFE

One of the least satisfactory of our would-be social standards is that elusive quantity: the value of a human life. This must always mean value in some limited economic sense, since it is clearly hopeless to attempt to fix the ultimate worth of a life in terms of the money yardstick. Even the money values people are willing to sacrifice to save life are not really a measure of what they think the life is worth— still less of what it really is worth. When funds poured in and volunteers crowded to attempt the rescue of Floyd Collins, trapped in a Kentucky cave, it was not simply on that one life that a value was being set. The driving force was the impulse of human solidarity which makes people come to the help of their fellows without weighing values in a nice balance or carefully counting costs in money or effort. This impulse is of vastly more value than any single life, and it would not be worth so much if it were put through a calculating machine before being allowed to express itself. This fact makes it worth while to spend, sometimes, vastly more than the particular life in question is economically worth on any reasonable estimate.

The only money value we can presume to place on a human life is its value as a commercial asset and nothing more. It represents an answer to the question How much can the community afford to spend to save a life and still be richer for the expenditure rather than poorer? The only reason why this question need be raised at all is that not all issues of life and death stir the popular imagination and reach the popular sympathy as did the fate of Floyd Collins. In fact, we are sadly inconsistent in our scale of values (if we can be said to have a scale at all), profoundly stirred by one incident which is picturesque or spectacular and apathetic while the routine risks of industry kill their thousands. This is particularly true when it is a matter of prevention—never so stirring as rescue, but far more effective. No particular victim has as yet been struck down, the mine has not yet exploded, and there is only a cold statistical probability that any particular mine will explode. The action called for does not bring the thrill of encountering physical dangers, but rather all the distasteful incidents of securing the passage and enforcement of a law regulating someone against his will and against his financial interests. In such cases we often, in effect, fail to set even as high a value on human life as would be economically worth while on money grounds alone, inadequate as these admittedly are. And in such cases an estimate of economic worth may furnish just the sort of impersonal incentive appropriate to this impersonal situation.

From this it begins to be apparent that we must interpret this measure in terms of the particular purposes it serves and the particular situations to which it is applied, and not take it as a universal truth. For instance, the economic value of an immigrant is one thing, that of an increase in the birth rate of our native stock is quite another thing (even without raising the question of the relative social desirability of different racial types), while the value of adult lives saved by preventing industrial accidents and diseases is different from either of the other two. A country may well be in a state of development in which added immigrants are worth less than nothing in terms of their effect on per capita prosperity, while it would still pay to spend large sums to prevent premature deaths from accident and disease.

For accidents in industry take people at just the productive period when, if ever, they are worth more to the community than they cost it. The period of childhood is over, when they were an economic burden, and most of them are members of families to whose support they make a net contribution, even those who are not the sole or chief support of an entire household. Even if a family consisted of four wage-earners, each supporting himself or herself and contributing one-fourth to the common expenses, the loss of one member would make the household poorer because the expenses could not easily be reduced by one-fourth to match the loss in income.

The governing principle would seem to be that the value of life itself to the person living it is not a calculable economic quantity: All that can be calculated is the economic loss, resulting from a death, to other persons than the one who has died—chiefly that person's dependents. It might seem superfluous to add that these other persons must be persons who are, or will be, in existence, regardless of whether the death in question occurs or not. In other words, it is not in accord with our governing principle, if a childless man of twenty-three dies, to count as economic loss the support he would have given to the children he would have had if he had lived. The reason for mentioning this is that one of the principal methods of measuring the economic value of life—namely, the person's production minus his individual consumption—involves the inclusion of this economically inapplicable quantity. The result is to give the highest economic value to young producers who have many productive years before them, but who have not yet acquired the dependents to whom this economic value will accrue. The more correct principle, excluding these nonexistent dependents, is more in accord with the natural judgment which sees the greatest economic loss in the death of a more mature employed producer, most of whose dependent children are already born.[1] Such a death might involve an economic loss, on the average, in the neighborhood of $16,000 or more, at present rates of earnings. At other ages the economic loss would be less.

Another proviso would be to the effect that a wife, who earns no money wages but does the housework and cares for the children, is "producing" an amount which might be very inadequately measured by what it would cost to hire someone else to do the same work, as nearly as any hired person could be got to do it. So the economic values of father and mother, added together, may be more than the whole income of the family, which is logical enough, since if both these mainstays were lost, the family would become an actual burden on society until such time as the children should become self-supporting. And yet if the whole family were simultaneously wiped out there might, by the cold-blooded standard we are employing, be no economic loss at all beyond funeral expenses and the trouble of filling one or two industrial vacancies. The whole, in this case, is not equal to the sum of its parts—a further indication that this statistical quantity is one to be used with the utmost caution. No one figure can be set as the economic value of a life, applicable under all circumstances.

Another type of "standard" is concerned with compensation for industrial accidents, unemployment, or sickness; and usually represents a level of compensation which the friends of such systems regard as satisfactory. Here the desideratum is a proper balance between three major elements: to save the immediate sufferer from disaster, to keep down the financial burden on industry or taxes, and to leave sufficient uncompensated suffering to make sure that the individual still has a healthy incentive to do his very best to minimize his own risks, to avoid malingering, and in general to look out for himself to the utmost of his powers. The point where this balance is struck is not exactly a matter for scientific determination, and the published standards cannot be regarded in that light, but it is a matter which can best be judged by the person who has had actual experience in the administra-

---

[1] The author has developed this thesis in *Costs of the World War to the American People*, pp. 207–223, and Appendix B. The best available calculation based on the principle of production minus personal consumption is that of Dublin and Lotka, "The Money Value of Life and Life Extension," *Amer. Jour. Public Health*, XVII (June, 1927), 549–557; also *Statistical Bull.*, Metropolitan Life Insurance Co., August, 1926.

tion of the insurance or compensation schemes. In that sense it is a matter properly to be decided by expert judgment rather than by popular vote.

7. STANDARDS OF MENTAL COMPETENCE

Standards of mental competence appear to be of more use, at present, in education and in selecting candidates for jobs than in policies of social control. Yet there are certain obvious applications which are already common practice, and others which may hold untold possibilities for the betterment of the human race in the future, when knowledge shall become definite enough to justify more resolute policies. Aside from the question of sanity under the criminal law, there is the question whether a particular person is competent to care for his property or whether the court should appoint a conservator. The question whether parents are fit to bring up their children is, to a very considerable extent, one of intelligence, as is also the far more delicate question of whether they are fit to have children at all. This last is a live issue of control by virtue of the fact that some states have laws providing for the sterilization of certain classes of socially dangerous defectives, while private social agencies are giving indication that some effect can be produced by such forms of supervision as they are in a position to exert, without legal compulsion or physical segregation.[1]

One obstacle to the extension of negative eugenics beyond a very small minority of hopelessly unfit is the difficulty of distinguishing the parts played by heredity and environment, and the natural reluctance to impose sentence of racial extinction on a given line of heredity because its past environment has been poor or has simply been such as to place this particular group of traits at a disadvantage, whereas in a different environment they might have proved their value. This is especially likely to happen in the medium grades of ability. On the other hand, it has been pointed out that some hereditary defects are easier to deal with or even cure, as far as the present individual is concerned, than some of the effects of "social heredity."[2] The children of vicious parents are bound to have a vicious environment if they are brought up at home; and if they are taken away, their environment will be inferior for another reason. This might be a reason for saying that there should be no children in such cases, regardless of whether the ultimate source of the defect is hereditary or environmental. The

[1] See "Private Agency and the Feebleminded," *Survey*, pp. 763–765, March 15, 1925.

[2] See A. W. Kornhauser, "Intelligence-test Ratings of Occupational Groups," *Amer. Econ. Rev.*, Sup., pp. 110, 121–122, March, 1925.

history of the Jukes, or of other bad stocks, is a record of dangerous social contagion, whatever the source of the evil.

The most definite quantitative measure of mental competence at present in vogue is the intelligence quotient: the grade made in intelligence tests. This is of assistance in diagnosing hereditary feeble-mindedness, but in the medium grades it is doubtful if it gives any very reliable index of inborn capacity. One thing which is strongly indicated is that low-grade intelligence gravitates to certain occupations so strongly as to create a presumption that a large minority in these particular callings, and perhaps even a majority in some instances, are not fully equal to the task of looking out for their own interests in the strenuous game of economic competition.

They are, presumably, quite equal to the ordinary demands of the work they are called upon to do and so are capable of earning their own support, but they may not be capable of collecting it or keeping it after they have earned it, or of seeing to it that the conditions of work are such as their long-run welfare demands. When the data on this point have been more carefully digested, they may furnish ground for special safeguards in certain groups of occupations, simply on the ground that a large percentage of the workers are not of the mental level which individualism presupposes and requires.

8. CONCLUSION

To sum up, it seems that we are developing at least in the direction of objective standards for deciding the questions which our political machinery is so sadly incapable of handling properly. We think of the worth of food in terms of calories and a balanced content, rather than in terms of taste; we submit materials to the testing laboratory of the bureau of standards, rather than wait to see how well they will stand up in service; we regard fatigue as a physiological condition with determinable symptoms, rather than merely as an unpleasant feeling which must somehow be overcome if adequate output is to be forthcoming; "cussedness" is becoming a pathological state to be diagnosed and treated by the psychiatrist; intelligence is being measured; and even the efficiency of the sacredly private processes of industry are, many of them, reduced to standards of motion and time to an extent which makes it conceivable that workable standards of industrial efficiency may before so very long be available for the use of public commissions for purposes of regulating private enterprise or of operating the properties themselves.

For the most part our standards are still quite imperfect or rudimentary, but even so they are of great value in giving definiteness to issues which would otherwise be the playthings of political pressures, with sentimentalism on the one side and financial group interests on the other.

We have at least something capable of supporting the burden of proof which our individualistic system places upon all proposals to amend the "standard" of the market and the outcome of free exchange. In many cases we have something which we can refer to an expert and receive a fairly definite and authoritative answer, in addition to which we have a growingly competent assortment of experts to whom to refer such questions. The list includes doctors, specialists in public health, psychiatrists, bacteriologists, and the organized records of social workers, as well as engineers and accountants and, last but not least, members of commissions who become experts by specialized labors in the actual field of control. Without the help of such experts, our political machinery would stand helpless before the complexity of its task, and its efforts at control would be reduced to muddling and chaos—and this even admitting that the expert in the economic field is often biased and still more often handicapped by the suspicion of bias. Politicians may distrust them, but they cannot wholly do without them.

REFERENCES FOR FURTHER READING

Amer. Labor Legislation Rev., "The Social Cost of Sickness," pp. 11–15, March, 1916; "Health Insurance Standards," pp. 237–238, June, 1916; "Economic Losses from Industrial Accidents," p. 230, December, 1922; "Safety in Coal Mines," March, 1924.

ARMSBY, H. P., "The Modern Science of Food Values," Yale Rev., n.s., IX (January, 1920), 330–345.

BOOTH, CHARLES, Life and Labour of the People in London.

BUREAU OF APPLIED ECONOMICS, Standards of Living, Washington, 1920.

FEDERATED AMERICAN ENGINEERING SOCIETIES, The Twelve-hour Shift in Industry.

———, Waste in Industry.

FLORENCE, Economics of Fatigue and Unrest.

GOLDMARK, JOSEPHINE, Fatigue and Efficiency.

———, Comparison of an Eight-hour Plant and a Ten-hour Plant, 1920.

HAMILTON, Current Economic Problems, 3d ed., Chap. x C-G.

ROWNTREE, B. S., Poverty: A Study of Town Life.

RUSSELL SAGE FOUNDATION, The Pittsburgh Survey.

TAYLOR, F. W., Scientific Management.

WYAND, C. S., Economics of Consumption, Chaps. xvi–xviii, 1937.

CHAPTER XII

INFORMAL CONTROLS

1. INTRODUCTION

"Formal controls" are primarily those exercised through the official machinery of government and backed by compulsory mandates. But behind the enactment and enforcement of these mandates lies a whole world of forces exercising social control upon the government in a multitude of ways. And it should not be surprising to find that these forces, being powerful enough to affect the action of government itself, can and do act directly without the mediation of government. Custom, tradition, religion, education, propaganda, public opinion, and the *esprit* of a class, an organization, or a profession—all are vital forces and through them all moral forces of various sorts are brought to bear. So important are these informal controls that there are some who believe that we should get on better if we employed no others. Whether this is true or not, the working constitution of industry depends so largely on these controls that without some knowledge of them we cannot possibly understand the world we live in, and why business is a system of order and not of chaos.

Direct control by group opinion has many advantages over state action; likewise it has the defects of its qualities and some serious disadvantages and weaknesses.[1] It is cheap, requiring, for the most part, no monetary support. It is prompt in action; but, on the other hand, when for any reason it cannot act promptly, it often forgets to act at all. It discriminates between case and case according to many circumstances which would appear irrelevant to a court, but which affect the equities of the particular dispute. Is the aggressor rich and the victim poor? Was the temptation such as to rouse the secret sympathy of the observer? Is the real position of the parties different from their ostensible legal position—for example, is the strike breaker accorded the legal treatment due to a free man desirous of working at a trade on terms the strikers have rejected, when he is really nothing of the sort?

[1] See Ross, *Social Control*, Chaps. ii–vi, and esp. Chap. x.

Perhaps he has no desire or fitness to work at this trade and is being paid more than the wage the strikers refused for the purely temporary service of breaking the strike. Public opinion has a keen eye for imposture and does not wait to have it proved to the hilt, as in a court of law. And one's fellow-craftsmen can judge of such things more truly and on less evidence than any court would require. The pressure of public opinion is felt even by those whose misconduct is still their own secret. People may condemn the kind of thing I am doing without knowing that I am doing it, but my own knowledge makes the condemnation strike home.

On the other hand, public opinion often discriminates on personal or sentimental grounds which have little to do with the economic seriousness of the act. It is swayed by the spectacular. It needs a personal guilt to fasten upon and therefore is often reduced to impotent wrath by the evils of impersonal organizations and is a failure when called on to judge right and wrong in terms of distant and intricate chains of economic consequences. While one's own immediate group can be very searching in its penalties, if its own code has been violated, it is often too little interested in the code of the community at large. The offender can retire within the shelter of a friendly circle and escape the wrath of the public. Thus public opinion needs formal institutions to give it consistency, persistence, rational regard for consequences, and the advantages of expert knowledge.

But while informal controls cannot do everything, their scope is indeed wide, including the ultimate control of government itself. The law can seldom convict a director, for instance, of having made an illegitimate profit out of his corporation; but if suspicious transactions are brought to light, he will suffer in reputation. The business man's duty to the community is not standardized, as legal requirements must be, but one who "does his bit" receives his reward. For such purposes, legal compulsion is too crude. And often it is in the nature of the case impossible (as with labor contracts, which cannot be enforced effectively in a free country). It may be that formal action would be peculiarly likely to violate economic law, or that the state has already used up all the energy it has available for the enforcing of its commands, or that the wrongs in question are so intimately tied up with legitimate and necessary operations that it is impracticable to forbid them all.

We have already seen that it is impracticable to prevent by law all damages of economic importance, with the result that there is always and necessarily a margin of "inappropriable values" and uncompensated costs. The law grows by taking cognizance of such

hings, but it cannot treat them all, and the margin beyond its present
·ffective action is a realm of moral responsibility: a field for the play
)f informal forces of control, which may pioneer the way for future
aws or may act in lieu of law indefinitely. Even law itself must have
he aid of these subtler forces: a legal penalty which does not carry
vith it the condemnation of one's fellows is often virtually nugatory
ind is always robbed of its chief effect.

If it could not rely on voluntary obedience in the majority of cases,
·ur system of control would be a dismal failure. We already have
nore laws than we can enforce, and this is bad in every way. If the
aws were enforced, the overgrown area of compulsion would itself
)e a worse evil than to let a few abuses go unprohibited. A happy way
s afforded out of the dilemma when moral forces can be trusted to
)ut some check on abuses with which the law has not dealt effectively.
Most of the control in business must always be moral in character.

?. CODES OF ECONOMIC ETHICS: THEIR GENERAL CHARACTER

As far as people agree in matters of ethics or conduct, they establish
·odes, and such codes, whether or not they embody ultimate ideals or
ibsolute right, are powerful forces for the control of those who come
inder their influence. Those who accept the code fully are coerced
;hrough their own consciences as well as through the pressure brought
:o bear by their fellows. Those who reject the code utterly may feel
10 pricks of conscience in violating it, but they still feel the social
)ressure, except as they can form a morally independent community
.with its own moral code, such as that of professional criminals or
:evolutionists.

And what is a code? It is never a simple thing, and the codes
people subscribe to in public are at best only a part of the codes they
ictually work and live by. At the worst, such codes may contain a
ieal of sheer hypocrisy. They represent an attempt to raise the level
)f conduct. Since modern social groups are not disciplined to the
point of perfect conformity, it follows that the very existence of a code
implies that the actual level of conduct is on a lower average plane
than the code acknowledges.

A code typically contains items of various grades, including things
one *may* do, things one *must not* do, things one *must* do, and things
which carry some positive merit but are not required. Some of the
things have to do with the relations of the members of a trade group
toward each other, and some with their relations to other groups or
the general public.

In connection with the things that may be done, the code may contain an expression of the just and legitimate interests of the group in question as against other groups—for example, labor's idea of its "right" to a living wage and a fair distribution of the national dividend. This has implications, none the less significant for being unformulated, as to the duties of other groups toward labor. The other groups, not having been consulted, may not wholly agree, or they may set up legitimate ambitions of their own which are so expansive that they cannot all be gratified because there is not enough to go around.

While items of this sort are not fully ethical, in the sense of taking into account all the interests and forming one scale of values which harmonizes them all, nevertheless they have a moral character, and they are certainly powerful agencies of control, not merely over the group whose interests they assert and protect, but over the other groups with which these interests come into conflict. These groups know that if they infringe on the standards which any group has come to regard as its settled and customary rights, they will encounter more determined resistance than commonly arises from the ordinary bargaining motives. In the case of labor, even boards of arbitration must often give way to these standards, since labor cannot be forced to work against its will. This is particularly true where these standards have gained a place as part of the recognized "custom of the trade," as in the case of traditional working rules.[1] In much the same way in which the "custom of the manor" served as the tenant's chief safeguard against the exactions of the feudal lord, so these newer customs serve to limit the employer's freedom to organize his shop as he pleases. Where machinery has introduced a wholly new technique, of course these customs are destroyed, but they can be reestablished in less than a generation, and there is growing up a custom of giving the existing workers preferred treatment in the introduction of new processes, thus giving customary rights a certain continuity, even where advances in production cause a complete change in the rules of the trade.

And so, when we find that doctors or real-estate dealers have drawn up a visible code, we must be alert to distinguish the different

[1] For instance, a case arose in the Chicago garment trade in which trade custom decreed that cutters might cut twelve garments at once out of the same cloth, but not if the colors or patterns of the cloth were in any way different. The board of arbitration made a ruling requiring cutters to cut twelve garments of different cloths where the motive was increased output, and the employers were to put the resulting savings into a fund for the workers' benefit; but in spite of these factors it was almost impossible to enforce the ruling, the workers resorting to that most baffling of weapons, a cessation of work without any organized strike.

kinds of items, to see if all are equally well represented or if there are significant omissions or inequalities of emphasis, and especially to read between the lines for the unexpressed and often quite unregenerate working code which underlies the published formulation and which may be far more significant as a working force. We should pay particular attention to the codes which remain unformulated, especially those of different groups within the ranks of labor.

The economic groups which have the most firmly rooted and effective codes are the professions, especially the legal and medical professions, which have strong organizations, have put their codes in printed form, and are in a position to visit serious infractions with penalties which carry some weight. The code of the military officer is even more powerful but has less economic application. Less explicitly formulated, but none the less real, are the codes of scientific research and of the teaching profession, while architects, engineers, and accountants have written codes which they may be expected to develop considerably in the not distant future. After them, in their various degrees come dentists, pharmacists, brokers, advertising agencies, real-estate dealers, and an impressive number of strictly business occupations; also chambers of commerce, Rotary clubs, and other general bodies. There is an unwritten code for the salaried staff of the typical large establishment, and a number of different codes in the world of labor. Some of the written codes probably have little actual moral force behind them, while some callings with strong working codes have not put them in writing. We may expect large developments in these codes to follow the recent enormous growth of trade organizations in practically every field.[1]

3. PROFESSIONS AND THEIR CODES

A great deal is said nowadays about making business a profession, with the implication that business would thereby experience a much-needed regeneration. Since this appears to be a live issue, it is pertinent to examine the recognized professions, even perhaps the unbusinesslike ones, in an attempt to see what are their outstanding characteristics, on what basis their forces of moral control rest, and what are the strong and weak points of their codes. Then we may be in a better position to judge whether business has enough in common with these professions to justify the expectation that it will develop similar features, and also to look for weak points which will need strengthening.

[1] In 1925, ninety-five such codes were on record in the office of the International Rotary Clubs in Chicago, and the number is constantly growing.

In a profession such as law, medicine, or education, there are special features creating a need for an effective sense of obligation on the part of the members, and there are certain other features which facilitate the development of such a sense of responsibility and so make it easy to meet the need. Both together are responsible for the resulting strong professional *esprit*.

First as to the need: The professional man is an expert, selling services of guidance to persons who are in the nature of the case not experts. Moreover, their need is peculiarly vital to their well-being, whether it is the need of the man threatened with a lawsuit, the sick man's need for health, or the adolescent's need for wise and dependable counsel. Thus the customers are in a peculiar relation of dependence on the one who is serving them, and the rule of *caveat emptor* is peculiarly out of place. They cannot afford to wait and learn, if they can, by the trial-and-error method, whether the diagnosis was false or the legal advice disinterested, for the first mistake may prove fatal. They thus become clients rather than customers. Furthermore, doctors and lawyers can render their proper service to their clients only if the clients tell them every essential fact, even facts they would die rather than have generally known. Clearly, these professions are almost under a necessity of building up a reputation for being absolutely safe repositories of confidential information, and there arise delicate questions as to whether the point may be reached at which one's duty to the community requires him to divulge such information.

So much for the elements creating the need for codes of professional conduct. As for the facilitating causes, they consist largely of the common discipline through which all members of the professions have gone. Students are naturally group conscious and keenly alive to all things making for the honor and prestige of the group, and this like-mindedness continues if their lifework is a direct continuation of their training. Even the ceremonials help materially: a medical graduate taking the oath of Hippocrates can hardly be unaffected by the sense of obligations which he is assuming. On the whole, however, the schools appear to make relatively little attempt to focus this force on the development of professional ethics. The results achieved are largely natural by-products of the general character of professional training.

Another feature is the fact that professional services are rendered by professional men in person. In this they differ vitally from the services of the typical man of business. This has two important results: it favors the development of sympathy, confidence, and honorable relations, and it is a fairly effectual obstacle to the growth of large-scale production, thus removing the chief incentive to commercialized methods of sales promotion. This constitutes what is probably a permanent difference between the professions and business.

Out of such conditions spring the actual codes. Here the keynote is an obligation of service which is most strongly expressed in the medical code: "A profession has for its prime object the service it can render to humanity; reward or financial gain should be a subordinate consideration."[1] The specific duties which make up the body of this highly significant code are divided into duties toward patients, duties toward fellow-physicians, and duties toward the public in general. And three-fourths of the entire document is devoted to the duties of physicians toward each other.

This suggests at once the question: Is the code primarily an instrument for promoting service to humanity, or for protecting the craft-interests of the professional group itself? The answer depends, of course, upon the spirit and purpose underlying the provisions. Is it to prevent the jealousies and rivalries of the profession from interfering with the rendering of the best possible service, or is it to safeguard the craft against legitimate competition (including that of heterodox medical sects) and shelter its foibles and mistakes against proper and salutary publicity under the guise of upholding the reputation of the profession? The same things may be said, in general terms, of the codes of the bar associations, and the same questions arise concerning them.

Typical among the articles in question are such as these: Neither lawyers nor doctors must advertise or follow typically commercial methods for promoting the sale of their services. "The most worthy and effective advertisement possible, even for a young physician, and especially with his brother physicians, is the establishment of a well-merited reputation for professional ability and fidelity. This cannot be forced, but must be the outcome of character and conduct."[2] Lawyers are counseled to refrain from stirring up litigation, and from "bold and confident assurances" as to the probable outcome of litigation, "especially where the employment may depend upon such assurance."[3] This seems clearly in the interest of good service. Since the professional man must do his work in person, it is peculiarly unfortunate if his attention and energies must needs be divided between service and salesmanship; and since he cannot develop large-scale

[1] *Principles of Medical Ethics,* American Medical Association, Chap. i, Sec. 1, 1914.

[2] See *Principles of Medical Ethics,* American Medical Association, Chap. ii, Art. I, Sec. 4, 1914.

[3] See *Chicago Bar Association Code of Ethics,* Secs. 8, 27, 28, 1910.

production in the business sense, a competent man can develop all the custom he can handle while still living up to this standard.

A large portion of the legal code has to do with fair conduct of cases, abstaining from undue influence over judges, from citations of authority which are intentionally misleading, from currying favor with juries, suppressing facts, or concealing witnesses favorable to a defendant whom the lawyer is prosecuting, or other "fraud or chicane."[1] The plain drift of these provisions is to eliminate tactics which have nothing to do with the merits of the case and so can only tend to pervert justice rather than further it. This is a problem peculiar to the law; the temptation is enormous, and we should hardly expect that the actual practice in the rank and file of the profession would come very close to the ideals set up in a published code. The latter represents an attempt to combat a very serious evil.

Another group of provisions deals with various forms of the question of whether a member of the profession should tell what he thinks of another member's work when that may tend to discredit the other member, or whether the members of the craft should stick together in such matters. The general spirit of these provisions may be indicated by the following: "Efforts, direct or indirect, in any way to encroach upon the business of another lawyer are unworthy of those who should be brethren at the bar; but, nevertheless, it is the right of any lawyer, without fear or favor, to give proper advice to those seeking relief against unfaithful or neglectful counsel, generally after communication with the lawyer of whom the complaint is made."[2] When a doctor is called in consultation, only exceptional circumstances justify him in examining the patient without first getting the opinion of the physician in charge, or in reporting his opinion other than in the presence of the first physician. "There never is occasion for insincerity, rivalry, or envy, and these should never be permitted between consultants."[3] A consultant should not supplant the physician originally in charge without that physician's consent.[4]

"When a physician does succeed another physician in charge of a case he should not make comments on, or insinuations regarding, the practice of the one who preceded him. Such comments or insinuations tend to lower the esteem of the patient for the medical profession and so react against the critic."[5]

[1] *Ibid.*, Secs. 3, 5, 7, 15–25, 30, 31.
[2] *Chicago Bar Association Code of Ethics*, Sec. 7, 1910.
[3] *Principles of Medical Ethics*, Chap. ii, Art. III, Sec. 2.
[4] *Ibid.*, Sec. 8.
[5] *Ibid.*, Chap. ii, Art. IV, Sec. 4.

Here the profession must steer a course between undue rivalry and undue solidarity. The authors of this code seem to have been chiefly preoccupied with preventing undignified rivalry, and they might well consider the fact that, if the impression gains ground among patients that there exists a tacit collusion to conceal errors or malpractice, the esteem of the profession will suffer immeasurably more than from some excesses of grasping personal rivalry. Fortunately, the truly vast increase in knowledge which the medical profession has achieved within the present generation has placed them in a position in which they can afford to be franker than in past generations as to the limitations of their knowledge, and such frankness appears to be increasing.

Both professions are under certain obligations to render service to those who cannot pay for it: "The poverty of a patient and the mutual professional obligation of physicians should command the gratuitous services of a physician. But institutions endowed by societies, and organizations for mutual benefit, or for accident, sickness, and life insurance, or for analogous purposes, should be accorded no such privileges."[1] "A client's ability to pay cannot justify a charge in excess of the value of the service, though his poverty may require a less charge, or even none at all."[2] Wisely, perhaps, the code makes no attempt to define what the "value of the service" is. It impliedly maintains the doubtful position that the service has a standard market value but indicates that charges may be graded according to the client's pocketbook—yet not graded upward without limit.

This rather indefinite rule is in accord with the economic character of the services concerned. The professional man is in a position to discriminate as much as he pleases, because his services are non-transferable and any particular service occasions, in most cases, no very substantial money cost, since most of his costs are in the nature of overhead. Thus any part of his work which he may do for little or nothing seldom causes him an actual money loss, for he does not often actually turn away more profitable business on this account. But if he had to charge all persons alike, he could not serve the poor or near poor without giving up the chance to make a comfortable living, such as his skill justifies. Hence he should be allowed to discriminate, the chief limit consisting in the fact that it is not consistent with the best spirit of the profession to be consciously trying to exact the last dollar of possible profit out of anyone or any group.

Another feature of the doctors' working code, which is not expressed in the written formulas, is the conduct required of nurses, over

[1] *Principles of Medical Ethics*, Chap. ii, Art. VI, Sec. 1.
[2] *Chicago Bar Association Code of Ethics*, Sec. 12, 1910.

whom the doctors have virtually complete authority. While nurses have written codes of their own, their requirements are in harmony with the standards set for them by the doctors, and one of the noticeable features of these codes is the fact that the nurses' obligation not to criticize the physician is absolute, not qualified by any duty to the patient or to the public.[1] This is capable of abuse, and it would seem that the doctors have an obligation to patients and public not to use their authority over nurses primarily for their own protection. The interests of patient and of public should take first place with both groups.

To sum up, the profession assumes responsibility for the quality and sincerity of its workmanship, for rendering service, to some extent, according to the rule of need rather than the rule of maximum profit, and for maintaining a level of competition which centers in service rather than in salesmanship. It also shows some tendencies toward protecting the selfish craft interests of its members, though the best standards do not consciously or explicitly countenance this.

Much could be said of other professions, but space does not permit. The morale of the teaching profession has not always been high; in fact, in England, at the time of the American Revolution, it was distinctly low, Oxford professors making little pretense of instruction. At present it seems, on the whole, to be fairly satisfactory, including standards of intellectual honesty, judicial rectitude in dealings with students (a standard which needs strengthening against the pressure of various noneducational interests), a willingness to assume unremunerative outside duties, and to refrain from engaging in so much profitable outside employment as to interfere with the work of education. This last is a limitation on the universally conceded right of eking out the educational stipend by writing, lecturing, consulting, and other outside work.

Not being codified, the mores of this profession have a spontaneous tendency to emphasize rights and subordinate the corresponding duties. In connection with academic liberty, for example, too little attention is paid to the questions What must we do to deserve it? What are its responsibilities? There are, of course, different academic liberties, liberty of expression of private opinion, liberty of political action, and liberty of official academic utterance. The first two are virtually absolute, but to earn them the teacher has the duty of keeping them scrupulously distinct from the third. And to deserve the liberty of official academic utterance the teacher must be responsible for the scientific spirit in which the utterances are made—not necessarily

[1] See Heermance, *Codes of Ethics*, pp. 387–392.

avoiding all expressions of opinion, but distinguishing opinion from proved fact. Many features of the codes, both of teaching and of scientific research, await satisfactory formulation.

The professions which sell their services to business present special problems of their own. Engineers, architects, and accountants have a fiduciary relation to their employers, and it is clear how this is transgressed if they are secretly employed by competitors or accept commissions from dealers in supplies when they are supposed to be single-minded in recommending what is best for the employer's interest. Provisions dealing with this issue form one of the most prominent features of codes of this class. An engineer must render an unbiased report on an industrial project, though a favorable report means lucrative employment for himself. Valuation work by accountants, for public regulation or taxation, gives rise to an obvious need for integrity of a higher sort, not merely faithful service to the employer, but a true record as required by the interest of the public. Otherwise the public is left at sea, and regulation tends to remain the football of politics. Engineers have also a peculiar opportunity to further the public interest in industrial efficiency and industrial statesmanship, and this opportunity should give rise to a corresponding sense of obligation.[1]

In the matter of compensation, these professions do not have the same duty as do doctors and lawyers to serve first and think of reward afterward. To that extent they are apparently expected to be more businesslike. But there are evidences of a tendency to keep professional compensation on a basis of standard fees, separate from the profits and losses of the business which is served. Architects may not engage in the building or decorative trades nor guarantee their estimates.[2] The first provision may be interpreted as insuring disinterested advice to the employer, and the second as a protective measure, but their effect remains. The Free-lance Artists hold that they "should not be asked to speculate with or for an advertising agency, or asked to do work on any basis which entails the possibility of loss to the artist through factors beyond his control."[3] The American Society of Civil Engineers and the Society of Industrial Engineers call for acceptance of the stated fees and no other rewards.[4] Such provisions are far from universal, but a certain cleavage is set up between professional fees and business profits and losses, and this affords food for thought in connection with the movement to develop business into a profession. Is pro-

[1] See especially *Waste in Industry*, published by a committee of the Federated Engineering Societies, organized under the leadership of Herbert Hoover.

[2] Heermance, *Codes of Ethics*, pp. 22–23.

[3] *Ibid.*, p. 27.

[4] *Ibid.*, p. 170.

fessional standing inconsistent with pursuit of profit and exposure to loss? In any case, such speculative features must make an important difference in the rights and obligations of the profession.

4. CODES IN THE BUSINESS COMMUNITY

The business man is commonly thought of as having no code other than "getting by" and making profits, or, at best, the code of "common honesty" in business transactions. This is decidedly a misconception of the business man, as it would be of any class at all in organized society. Probably the chief ground of criticism of the business code is not its weakness so much as the narrow perspective of obligations which it includes. Perhaps the best way to get a picture of this highly mixed moral phenomenon is to try to express first the unwritten code, often rather unregenerate, as one sees it at work around one.

Thou shalt boost thy town (says this code) in conversation with citizens of other towns, by supporting all projects aiming to increase its size and wealth or to promote any other ends of civic greatness as the business community sees civic greatness, and by lending time and energy to such projects in such reasonable amounts as community opinion may demand. The legitimate ends include civic beauty and things making for the welfare of the masses, though not things tending to diminish the prestige of the business class or to rob them of any part of their proper position of dominance. It is creditable to discover ways in which a good town may be made still better, but not such serious defects as raise doubts as to whether the town is really a good one or to call in question the business community's standards of what constitutes a good town.

To one who lives loyally up to the spirit of these requirements the business community will reciprocate, and he will gain that kind of good will which is not wholly without profit. With a certain brand of business man this community loyalty seems to concentrate more on the town's reputation than on admitting evils, grappling with them, and so making the town worthy of its reputation. Some evils it is proper to admit, provided they reflect discredit on other classes than the business community itself. One of the weaknesses which the business code needs to overcome is the tendency to be too easily satisfied with outside activities of a civic sort, at the expense of the more important demands of genuine statesmanship in the conduct of industry itself.[1]

Thou shalt pay thy debts, fulfill thy contracts, and give full measure. These things are, of course, required by law, but the law cannot

[1] See Glenn Frank, *The Politics of Industry*, pp. 49–50, 61–64.

easily enforce all of them without the help of the public opinion of the business community. In enforcing contracts, for example, it is limited to the letter, rather than the spirit. The device of bankruptcy can be used to evade the payment of just debts, and customers can cancel orders or return goods on various pretexts or no pretext at all, the seller often fearing to lose indispensable future trade if he alienates customers by insisting on the letter of his legal rights. In times of depression this gives rise to serious evils, and definite movements are sometimes instituted to develop sentiment in favor of living up to one's obligations, even where they turn out to be unprofitable.

Here we have to do chiefly with conflicts of interests arising among business men themselves, which do not involve the more awkward difficulties raised by conflicts between the moral standards of different classes. On the other hand, business honesty is likely to be satisfied with what is customary (in which case people get what they have reason to expect) rather than what is best for all concerned in the long run. The well-established "tricks of the trade" are likely to be condoned for some time after the most forward-looking have seen that they are evils; and by the time sentiment has grown to the point of outlawing them, other evils are needing attention.

Thou shalt believe in thy business and thy goods (it pays). This applies with especial force to the ethics of salesmanship. At its most complacent levels it is close to the psychology of the White Queen, who practiced believing impossible things for half an hour a day and achieved a record of six before breakfast. At its best it stands for a conviction that only the man who is thoroughly interested in his work for its own sake can make the best kind of financial success. It means that "production for use" actually plays a considerable part in our system of "production for profit"—whether more or less than under some more cooperative system can only be conjectured.

Akin to this is the standard which lays the chief stress in business on the making of satisfied customers. An interesting variant is mail-order ethics, which takes for granted that the customer is honest and gives him the benefit of all reasonable doubt, thus going far beyond the requirements of mere fidelity to contracts. Here, of course, the business could not be developed successfully except on such a basis of confidence and generous treatment. Intelligent self-interest requires it. Nevertheless, it argues sincerity when such a rule comes to govern the daily practice of large business enterprises.

Thou shalt compete—so says the law and public opinion, supported by the customary mores of business, approved by a considerable weight of business opinion, and tacitly acquiesced in by the rest of the business world. Thou shalt not compete unfairly—so say all concerned, though there may be differences of opinion as to what constitutes unfairness. Thou shalt not compete with the purpose of wiping out all competitors and so bringing the competition to an end—so says the law—and thou shalt not compete in ways that are destructive to the welfare of the trade—so says the trade itself.

Evidently there is much in common between the requirements of the public and the class code of business itself, and they might be able to agree on the form of precept to be followed, but with subtly significant differences of spirit and substance. The code of a mercantile trade is very likely to regard it as unfair competition to establish direct selling methods which do not protect the customary margins of the middleman and endanger his position. They argue that these margins have approved themselves by experience as necessary to the support of the service they properly render, and that the new devices will come to the same result in the end, but in the meantime trade and service will suffer. This may be true in a majority of cases, and still the public cannot afford to accept it at its face value, for it would result in preventing other methods from ever being put to a competitive test and would protect the insidious tendency to spend more and more on salesmanship and "service," for which the customer ultimately has to pay.

Thou shalt not support radicalism, pacifism, or any other "ism" which attacks the fundamentals of things as they are. This is the first and great negative commandment and it manifests itself in many ways. The second, like unto it, is: Thou shalt not give aid and comfort to the aims and ambitions of labor so far as these are inconsistent with the continued successful conduct of private business, nor introduce undue liberality into any business which is sufficiently large and powerful to embarrass its competitors seriously or tend to make their position and policy untenable. Henry Ford has been hated, in certain quarters, with a virulence which is only to be explained by the fact that he was our most conspicuous violator of this commandment. He was felt to be a traitor to his class, though probably his enemies were not wholly aware of the reason for the peculiar force of their feelings, explaining it to themselves on other grounds.

The Adamson law was also a flagrant violation of this commandment on the part of the government, which should have known better.[1] One practice which undoubtedly offends in some degree, yet seems

---

[1] This law fixed a basic eight-hour day for railroad employees, the effect being to raise wages through overtime provisions and, in effect, to settle a pending strike in favor of the employees.

perpetually immune from condemnation, is advertising. Business systematically stirs up unlimited desires for goods, doing its best to put the clerk on a par with the president of his company in his consumption, and still more in his ambition to consume, and to wake into activity the desire for what one's richer neighbor has. With this goes a restless demand for more income, a demand which is as unlimited as the ambition of advertisers to market goods to ever-widening circles of consumers, and will always keep ahead of earning power, under the wage system or any other. But when labor demands more than business can pay, business men are inclined to condemn this irrational covetousness without connecting it with their own sales propaganda. The code of business has its blind spots—its convenient failures to trace the relation of cause and effect.

Thou shalt not do welfare work without regarding whether it pays, or without at least making a decent pretense of believing that it pays—that is, the large business must not. The employer in a small one-man business may treat his "help" as liberally as he pleases; he is on a more personal basis, and he is not large enough to be dangerous. And while undue altruism is under suspicion, on the other hand there is a growing sentiment against discrediting the trade in the opposite way, by showing too flagrant and open disregard for law, public opinion, or the welfare of customers, labor, or the community at large. This is, of course, bad business and has so proved itself.

Further, it is approved if one wins the sympathy and good will of one's employees without too flagrant generosity, takes a genuine interest in the welfare of one's own men, and tries to turn out a good product. Alongside of the idea that the best product of an industry is satisfied customers is growing another idea, held as yet only by a few employers: that the lives of its laborers may be the most important product of all, and that the satisfied or benefited worker deserves to rank alongside of the satisfied customer as a goal of business policy. This is having its effect on the more purely commercial standards typical of the nineteenth century and will undoubtedly gain much ground in years to come. For no system which is not built upon this principle will find it easy to survive the stresses which the twentieth century has in store for it.

Such, in part, is the code of business: a most curious mixture of the more presentable phases of intelligent private interest, class interest, community obligation, and natural human sympathy, wherein altruism is upheld one moment and apologized for the next, and virtue and expediency are inextricably interwoven. Each trade, of course, has its own peculiar problems, and these find expression in the written codes which are becoming every day more numerous. To these we may next turn.

Such codes typically start with a statement that the business is justified by rendering a valuable service to the community; that it is responsible for rendering this service well; and that this justifies a "fair profit" to the business man. The business is made responsible for a good product and for truthful salesmanship, and the requirement is often laid down that contracts must be of genuine mutual benefit, or even of benefit to all concerned, directly or indirectly. Discrimination in prices is frequently condemned, as is the use of trading stamps and premiums. A number of the codes condemn "profiteering" in times of heavy demand and scant supply, but with no attempt to define what is meant by this term.

One virtually universal provision condemns the attempt to take from a competitor orders he has already secured. This is implied in respect for contracts, since the accepted order is a contract, whether the agreement is in writing or not. A number of codes urge members of the trade not to disparage the goods of competitors, while some merely condemn false disparagement. Selling below cost is generally condemned, as are various practices which operate to conceal the true price charged and tend to veiled cutthroat competition. Among these is the practice of taking used automobiles in trade at allowances in excess of the worth of the cars.[1] One code justifies a refusal to sell below cost as being in the interest of consumers as a class.[2] Discrimination between customers is frequently condemned. In competitive bidding it is not fair practice to revise one's bid, and especially to have a private arrangement by which one is allowed to secure orders by meeting the lowest bid which any of the rivals has made. No ulterior inducements should be given to, or received by, purchasing or selling agents, who should act single-mindedly in the interest of their employer. One manufacturers' code specifically prescribes that the margins of dealers shall be protected.[3]

Relations toward labor are less universally dealt with, one of the most adequate early codes in this respect being that of the International Association of Garment Manufacturers, adopted in 1924.[4] The right of collective bargaining was recognized by federal law in 1933, though not universally conceded in the employers' own formal or informal codes. Fair hours, sanitary conditions, and a friendly

---

[1] Heermance, *Codes of Ethics*, pp. 36–37.
[2] *Ibid.*, p. 96. Provisions of this sort were made formal and were implemented under the NRA. See below, Chap. XXVII, Sec. 4.
[3] *Ibid.*, p. 76.   [4] *Ibid.*, p. 84.

attitude are frequently enjoined, sometimes with the added argument that they are good business. On the other hand, one of the very common provisions is against attempting to hire away a competitor's employees without first notifying the competing employer. Sometimes this qualification is omitted, and the employer is expected to select from whatever applicants may respond to public advertising. There is a delicate question here, involving the worker's right to the full value of his services, and the equitable interest of the employer, who may have been at some expense in furnishing the training and opportunities by which the worker's ability has been built up. Employers may be more willing to invest in the long-run development of employees if the rate of turnover is not unduly swollen by the poaching tactics of other employers, but this interest is secondary to the requirements of adequate and two-sided competition. While the codes do not ignore the claims of the laborer, it is clear that those of the customer take first place.

To sum up, the written codes set a higher standard than the unwritten and lay more emphasis on the obligation of service, but they also lay a deal of emphasis on protecting the interests of the trade itself. There are large sections dealing with rights rather than duties, and serving notice on various groups with which the trade has dealings, as to what the trade considers to be its due, and what treatment it will insist on. The written codes, like the unwritten, are made of decidedly mixed elements.

So far we have been speaking of businesses as units, but what of the different functionaries who play responsible parts in the organized life of the large corporation? The moral code of the corporate director, for example, is in process of development, with the courts backing up its progress by making a certain minimum of faithfulness obligatory. This legal minimum moves forward along with the code of the business men themselves. Should a director speculate in the stock of his own company, so as to make profits out of his superior knowledge of its conditions and future policies? Should he assume that such profits would come out of the pockets of persons who already own stocks of the company and who are therefore his own constituents, toward whom he stands in a relation of trusteeship and in whose interest he is supposed to manage the property? If he should not speculate, where should the line be drawn between this and legitimate buyings and sellings of stocks in which he is required to be an investor?

Should he sell supplies or industrial properties to his own company or do financing for it or cause it to buy things in which he has an interest—for example, from companies in which he is a large stockholder?

In railroads, such dealings were strictly limited by the Clayton Act of 1914, which set a standard far more rigorous than the prevailing code and caused numerous bankers to retire from railway directorates. Or should a buyer accept entertainment from a salesman (we may take for granted that he should not accept bribes or commissions)? Here are matters on which the code is necessarily very vague and leaves much opportunity for abuses on the part of unscrupulous individuals.

5. CAN BUSINESS BE A PROFESSION?

At first sight it seems that business lacks all the essential features of the professions and that it can hope to be one only in name. There is little or no homogeneous training, relatively little confidential personal relation to the customer, and the customer is traditionally expected to decide for himself what he wants, without throwing responsibility on the business to tell him what he needs, so that there is little occasion for the business to assume the responsibilities that go with trained and expert guidance. However, these things are all growing. The marvels of synthetic chemistry place the consumer at a disadvantage in judging the quality of goods and create a need for a responsible attitude on the part of the seller, and the growth of schools of business is furnishing at least a nucleus of men and women who have gone through something in the way of common discipline. More important than this is the school to which the business man has been going, of late years, in his own business. It has introduced him to many professional specialists and many applied sciences, and to the "science of business management," until he has been forced to acquire a deal of formal knowledge, as distinct from the older type of intuitive thinking and unorganized experience.[1] The effects of this are in their infancy, and it is quite as unwise to expect too much as it is to assume that no transformations are possible. Business is becoming organized in associations which can, if they will, perform the same service toward business ethics that the professional associations are performing for law and medicine.

On the other side stands the fact of large-scale production, which abolishes most of the element of personal contact and also cuts the ground from under the dignified professional practice of building up a clientele by service only, with no dependence on salesmanship. Large business cannot be run in that way. Also, there will probably always be a large and influential class in business who have come up from the ranks—which is as it should be but minimizes the effect of any ethics that may be developed in the schools. The pressure of competition

[1] See Glenn Frank, *The Politics of Industry*, pp. 54, 58–59.

is inevitably fiercer than in the traditional professions, with bankruptcy always more imminent, making self-denying ordinances harder to live up to.

For all these reasons we should not expect business, in the near future, to become a profession in the full sense. Nevertheless, the need exists, and some, at least, of the mechanism exists and, last but not least, the stability of the business structure itself depends, in some degree, on using the available mechanisms to meet the need. Numerous individual business men already have a professional spirit in their work which would do credit to any of the recognized professions.

6. THE REQUIREMENTS OF AN ADEQUATE BUSINESS CODE

One of the first requirements of a business code is that it shall be not merely written, but lived. The written code is merely the symbol of something existing in the minds of men, and the symbol may be an empty one if the written code is out of touch with the working convictions of those it is supposed to govern. Even if it is consciously taken as a guide to the working code, it is not the only guide, and its real effect depends upon the intelligence, sincerity, and courage with which it is interpreted (for it takes courage to see meanings which run counter to our interests and prejudices), upon the loyalty with which it is followed, and upon the force of the penalties with which infractions are visited. The code as lived, not merely as written, must measure up to its task of guiding the pursuit of private gain into channels of efficient productive service to the public.

The code, then, must not merely be well drafted; it must have something to build on in the way of an understanding acceptance of obligations. Its requirements must be able to attach themselves to some preexisting sense of duty. And while existing codes are far from perfect in either of these respects, they are coming to recognize the main areas of obligation, and within each area there is a nucleus of working standards, already recognized and accepted, on which the code may build and to which it may attach its more definite formulations. The codes cover six areas of relationships of business: to its customers, to those from whom it buys, to its competitors, to the government, to its workers, and to that sadly ill-defined constituency made up of all those whom its operations affect in any way, directly or indirectly. Needless to say, the duties so far recognized in this last field are decidedly nebulous. In each of these fields there are one or two central obligations which can be simply stated, though it goes without saying that no six principles, or twelve, can cover the entire ground of business ethics, and to give definition and effect, even to a few simple principles, is an endless task.

In the internal relations of the business the basic need is integrity, faithfulness of agents and officials to their trust. Toward the customer the codes recognize the duty of honest salesmanship, equal terms for all, and a good product. Toward those from whom one buys there is the duty of adherence to contracts (which is recognized), and the further duty of taking reasonable pains to follow an ordering policy which does not unnecessarily disturb the operation of the business receiving the orders. This last is beyond the scope of present-day business ethics. Toward competitors, fair rivalry is called for; toward the state, adherence to law in spirit as well as in letter, and voluntary cooperation in proper policies of regulation (the state in its turn *should* be so honestly administered that the qualification "proper" would not be needed). Toward labor, business should be as much interested in the welfare of laborers as it is in that of its customers; for if the customers are patrons of industry, laborers are essentially partners. Toward the larger group of those affected by industry, including laborers and many others, the business has an obligation to see to it that they are not worse off for its operations; to leave them at least as well off as it finds them. This last item is impliedly recognized in some of the codes, but it is safe to say that its full significance does not begin to be appreciated. It involves a tremendous extension of a very elementary obligation.

Every honest business man wants to pay his debts, to meet his money liabilities. If he does this, he is self-supporting. But these money liabilities are only the rather imperfect representatives of the ultimate costs incurred and damages inflicted in the operation of the industry, and the business is not really self-supporting unless it compensates all these ultimate costs and damages and compensates them adequately. In other words, the simple morality of self-support must be given a vastly enlarged interpretation and extended into fields where its requirements cannot easily be defined.

For instance, no business is self-sustaining unless it takes care of its fair quota of the costs of unemployment: the idleness occasioned by its own operations. In the past, unemployment has been regarded as one of those emergencies for which no one is responsible, and which make demands on the generosity and public spirit of those who wish to acquire merit by doing more than their minimum duty. We shall almost certainly fail to accomplish much until we adopt the idea that the industries which furnish irregular employment are responsible for the costs of their labor, including those arising out of unemployment.

This is only one of a number of ways in which industries may fail to pay the full costs of the labor they employ and so be parasites rather than producers.

This applies to industries in which the responsibility for irregular employment is direct and traceable; and might call for such systems of work stabilization and wage protection as private employers could, on their own initiative, employ successfully. Such general catastrophes as the great depression which culminated in 1933 are too overpowering to be adequately handled in this way. The efforts of progressive employers were overwhelmed, their resources inadequate. Moreover, the industries showing the greatest decline did so largely because of unpredictable declines in demand arising from other industries— responsibility was diffused and untraceable. This problem goes far beyond what the informal codes of industry can handle. But as long as an adequate national policy toward it requires a spirit of willing cooperation on the part of industry, so long it will be vitally important that the industrial code should recognize a compelling obligation in this field.

This same need would be met in a more positive way if it should ever come to pass that industry should regard as its main business the furnishing of worth-while conditions of work and opportunities for worth-while life to the people who get their living out of it. It may seem strange to put this ahead of the task of turning out cheap goods in large quantities, and the people in general may never go this far, though the reasons for doing so are stronger than appear at first glance. But when business becomes somewhat accustomed to feeling a sense of responsibility for good products and seems capable of assimilating new duties, the time may be ripe for embodying in the code of business ethics the proposition that the making of men and women is at least as important as the making of goods.

REFERENCES FOR FURTHER READING

Ann. Amer. Acad. Polit. Soc. Sci., "The Ethics of the Professions and of Business," March, 1922.

ARNOLD, T. W., *The Folklore of Capitalism*, 1937.

CALDER, JOHN, *Capital's Duty to the Wage-earner*.

CARR-SAUNDERS, A. M., *The Professions*, 1928.

CLARK, J. B., *The Philosophy of Wealth*, pp. 37–48, Chaps. ix, xii.

CLARK, J. M., "The Changing Basis of Economic Responsibility," *Jour. Polit. Econ.*, XXIV (March, 1916), 209–229.

COOLEY, C. H., *Human Nature and the Social Order*.

DENNISON, H. S., "Business Management and the Professions," *Ann.*, pp. 143–147, May, 1925.

DEWEY, JOHN, *Human Nature and Conduct*.

EVERETT, W. G., *Moral Values*, Chap. xi, Sec. 4; Chap. xiii, Sec. 5.

FRANK, GLENN, *The Politics of Industry, Third Paper*.

HADLEY, A. T., *Standards of Public Morality*, Chaps. i–iii.

HAMILTON, W. H., *Current Economic Problems* (3d ed.), Chap. xv *a*.

HAMMOND, JOHN HAYS, "Industry and the Engineer," *Administration*, pp. 292–293, September, 1921.

HEERMANCE, E. L., *Codes of Ethics*.

JONES, F. D., *Trade Associations and the Law*, Chaps. i–iii.

KELLEY, F. W., *Voluntary Setting-up of Quality Standards in Commodity Production*, Portland Cement Assoc., June, 1923.

LIPPMANN, WALTER, *Public Opinion*.

LUMLEY, F. L., *Means of Social Control*.

ROSS, E. A., *Social Control*, Chaps. ii–vi, x, xii–xxvii.

SMART, W. A., *Second Thoughts of an Economist*, Chaps. v, vi.

TAEUSCH, C. F., *Policy and Ethics in Business*, Parts D, E, F, 1931.

TUFTS, J. H., *The Real Business of Living*, Part II.

CHAPTER XIII

INFORMAL CONTROLS—*Continued*

1. THE CODE OF THE RESPONSIBLE SALARIED WORKER IN BUSINESS

An outstanding characteristic of the code of the salaried man, at least at the higher and more responsible levels, is the fact that he is expected to adopt an attitude of responsible concern for the needs and welfare of the business, and to govern his work accordingly. His hours of work vary with the pressure of business, and in emergencies he may be asked to turn his hand to almost anything, even to taking a workman's place during a strike. He may bargain with his employer as shrewdly as his opportunities permit. But collective bargaining or strikes are beneath his dignity.[1] His bargaining must be untainted by anything that savors of compulsion, or of withdrawing his services at a time when production would be disrupted thereby.

It is evident at once that the code of the salaried group is not a class code, in the sense of expressing the selfish interests of the salaried class itself. Rather, it asserts their associate membership, as it were, in the business class, by way of recognizing the obligations of that class. In fact, the line between the employer and the salaried employee becomes dim when the management of the largest establishments comes into the hands of salaried officials. And the line between responsible salaried workers and wage earners becomes dim at the lower end of the scale as more routine workers are put on a salaried basis and carry into it the code of organized labor. Unionization is reaching into the salaried and professional ranks, but without merging them completely in the code of organized labor or obliterating the group discussed above or its characteristic code.

[1] Since this was written there has occurred the "exception that proves the rule," in the shape of a quasi-strike of engineering employees of the city of Chicago. This was a protest stoppage, intended to last for a few days only, and not until the grievance should be adjusted, as a regular strike would do. The stoppage roused unfavorable comment.

2. THE CODE OF LABOR

Labor's code is probably more varied and heterogeneous than that of any of the other groups with which we have to deal. And it is very far indeed from the code of the salaried workers, being based on a clear-cut cleavage between laborers and employers. Laborers who adopt the employer's point of view do so largely as individuals responding to their personal relation to their employer, not to any code of their fellow-workers.

On its most positive side the code of labor is one of solidarity and mutual help and support. First, perhaps, comes mutual help in time of sickness or other need—the workers do far more for each other than other classes do, and their mutual help means more in terms of sacrifice than the charity of the wealthy. Next comes the rule of sticking together in any dispute with the employer; in particular, the duty of walking out when a strike is called and staying out till it is ended, whatever the cost may be. The strike is definitely a moral phenomenon, calling on the striker to disregard his personal and immediate financial interest for the sake of loyalty to the aims of the group. The rule is, of course, not ironclad, and some allowance will be made, for example, for an old employee who stands to lose a retirement pension if he takes part in a strike. Some degree of mutual help between unions is also a part of the code, though in this matter there is no definite obligation.

Another large part of the code is concerned with not doing too much work. Attitudes on this matter are so various that no short summary can do them justice. Almost universal is the condemnation of the pace setter—the fast worker who earns so much at prevailing piece rates that the rates are cut and the rest of the force has to work harder to make the same living as before. Fairly general is an informal resistance to doing more in a day than a mediocre worker can easily do. This may be fortified by the philosophy of making the work go around and not working one's self or others out of a job—a philosophy which may be based upon mistaken notions of the causes of a scarcity of jobs, but which is a natural "defense reaction" to the evil of unemployment and is not without its moral elements. A better means to this same end, of course, is a definite arrangement by which all go on part time to save some from being laid off. Where the shortage of work is temporary, this is the logical adjustment.

On the other hand, some unions undertake to insure the doing of good and adequate work by their members. It is quite general to take pride in being a good workman, that is, in being *able* to do a good day's work, which is a different thing from being *willing* to do it for any given employer or for employers in general. One may even take pride in doing the work efficiently where that does not too obviously and directly increase the profits of some employer. For instance, a station hand may take pride in getting the baggage on the train quickly. If he were paid according to the number of pieces he loaded in a minute, there would probably soon grow up a code limiting the permissible speed, as a defense against pace setting and rate cutting. Even so, of course, the defense would not be so badly needed in a job where the heavy exertion is intermittent as in one where it lasts through the whole of an eight- or ten-hour day.

Another article of the code is that a striker has a right to his job. Most workers prefer, other things being equal, not to take a position made vacant by a strike, and the professional strike breaker is an outcast. It is because they believe in this right so firmly that many have thought violence justified in defense of it—just as the holder of legally recognized property rights has violence at his disposal for their protection. While one criterion of the general belief in this right is the extent to which laborers in general respect it under no compulsion but the moral force of peaceful picketing, this test is too exacting to be fair. Peaceful picketing has some effect but does not afford the protection to which strikers feel they have a right.

But violence at the command of a single interested group, to protect its interest as against other groups, spells anarchy if it is allowed to have its way. The only way out is the development of standards of conduct of labor disputes which will determine what rights strikers have in tenure of their vacated jobs and will have a clear and general popular judgment back of them. This is a formidable task; it cannot be done quickly and perhaps never completely.

Underlying this theory of the laborer's property right to his job are implied theories of competition and of wages. It is not right, in labor's code, for labor's livelihood to be at the mercy of the competition of the unemployed man in the street. Thus labor rejects the law of supply and demand in its most unmitigated form, though the economic implications of this rejection have not been fully worked out by labor or by any other group. The worker asserts a right to a living wage and as much more as industry can afford to pay. These are undoubtedly some of the things which lie back of the oft-repeated formula that "labor is not a commodity." This may be taken to mean, further, that the labor market is a moral phenomenon; that the standards of a competitive market for commodities should not be applied to it; and that labor itself should be permitted to exercise a greater degree of control over it than would be permissible for producers marketing commodities on a purely commercial basis.

One of the very important phases of labor ethics is the code of the labor leader. The legitimate financial rewards of his position are limited, and he can often make more money by being false to his trust and engaging in industrial blackmail, or taking bribes. If labor is to have the leadership it needs, the leaders must be ready to resist all opportunities to leave the ranks of labor and become salaried officials or business men. Many able men have been lost to the labor movement by this route, but some have refused to be tempted. On the whole, it seems that the code of the really good labor leader calls for heavier economic sacrifices than any we have yet considered, and it should be no source of wonder if the average level of performance is far from ideal. All the more credit that the movement is able to show as large a percentage of intelligence and integrity as it does.

3. REVOLUTIONARY MORALITY

William J. Bryan had a saying to this effect: "When a man says to you, 'I don't think it's wrong to steal,' it's no use to argue with that man; search him." This is at best an effective half-truth and misses the most essential point at issue. The man who takes the trouble to set forth such heterodox opinions will not usually talk about "stealing" —he will not admit that stealing is really stealing because he will not admit that property is rightfully property. And a search of his pockets will reveal little ill-gotten plunder. The only thing to do with him is to lock him up or present him with a soap box.

The genuine revolutionist's code is simple: the revolution is the supreme end; everything that stands in its way is to be overthrown, and the revolution is war, in which everything is fair. Commonly he does not bother to assert the rightness of what he proposes to do; merely that it represents proletarian morals as over against capitalist morals or middle-class morals, and that the proletariat has the power to make its morals supreme. Life and goods are not to be wantonly destroyed—not wantonly, but only as the necessities of war dictate. Fidelity to contracts as contracts is no more required than truthfulness is required of a blockade runner, but loyalty to one's fellow-workers is paramount. This is set above legal honesty, Christian charity (an "inane, powerless, and demoralizing spirit"),[1] and all the other conventional virtues.

Is this the negation of morality? Or is it simply a class morality, as the other moralities we have studied are class moralities, but more

[1] See Arturo M. Giovannitti, *The Independent*, Vol. XXVI, October 30, 1913.

extreme? It exhibits one difference in degree so great as to amount to a difference in kind; namely, it allows for no working relations of mutually serviceable dealing between this class and any other—not until the other classes become merged in the proletariat and cease to exist as separate classes. A less obvious feature is the fact that this dual morality of interclass struggle is necessarily temporary, having no further excuse for existence once the struggle succeeds and the classes are merged. The permanent need, under any system, is for a code of cooperation to govern those who are operating the industrial machine, each performing his subdivision of a function and receiving his part of the work of all the rest.

Such a code, adequate to this many-sided task, is not contained in the phrase "solidarity of workers" or even in the spirit which lies behind the phrase. It will not take us far with the task of deciding who shall do what jobs, how much work each shall do, how much each shall receive if he does good work, and what shall happen if he does not do good work, who shall say what is good work and—most serious of all, perhaps—how authority shall be delegated. For without some delegation of authority the workers may have to spend so much of their time arguing questions of public policy (now merged with business policy) that they do not have a reasonable remainder of time and energy to spend baking bread, making clothes, and repairing locomotives. The Russian Soviet administration showed some traces of comprehension of this fact, after it was forced upon their attention by experience; witness Lenin's statement that since the workers had taken over the functions of the *bourgeoisie* they must now develop the *bourgeois* virtues. Under Stalin, much has been done to develop a cooperative morale under authoritarian management. Differential wage rates (at low levels) are combined with intangible incentives, while "purges" ensure submission, and keep alive the morale of class war.

4. THE BENT OF WORKMANSHIP

The so-called "instinct of workmanship" is an important part of the machinery of informal control. In the first place, it is not an instinct in the strict sense. In the second place, it is a trait the very nature of which is to reinforce from within the suggestions, incentives, and stimuli which we receive from outside. The phrase itself is most misleading. It suggests an independent impulse which drives us to do work and to do it efficiently, apart from other and ulterior incentives: a form of creative urge. But what Veblen, the foremost exploiter of the term, means by it is something different from this.[1] It may become

[1] See Veblen, *The Instinct of Workmanship*, esp. pp. 27–35, 160–161, 172–173, 180, 227.

an impulse to efficiency or to waste, for it is not an independent motive force.

The trait which Veblen is referring to under this term is really the faculty of making an end in itself out of what was originally a means to some other end. It is one of the happiest faculties and the most troublesome and altogether most characteristically paradoxical faculties of the fundamentally paradoxical nature of man. Without it, efficient work would be a psychological impossibility, but with it, numberless perversions and wastes are inevitable, due to mistaking the means for the end and failing to subordinate it as it should be subordinated. Man cannot attend to anything without undue strain and exhaustion unless the thing interests him so that his attention is spontaneous. Voluntary attention, if unaided by any element of spontaneous interest, soon tires. If men are to endure toil, it is imperative that they should be capable of acquiring a spontaneous interest in the work itself, apart from the useful result or the material reward.

To the extent that one is interested in growing a garden because it is a useful thing to do, the instinct of workmanship strengthens his efforts by interesting him in the technique of gardening—and he may end by growing more things than he can use and give them to the neighbors to get rid of them. To the extent that money is to be made by cultivating the desires of the customer, interest is transferred to this and the desires of customers become desirable things to cultivate in their own right. Industry becomes somewhat more human than it would be were it governed solely by the technical man's interest in efficiency as he sees it. And to the extent that money is to be made by predatory competition or parasitic speculation, these activities become worth-while ends in themselves.

To some kinds of work the bent of workmanship may never attach itself. The work may not exercise enough faculties to become interesting, or the person may fail to discover any aptitude for it and may get the repellent sense of failure and baffled effort in place of the pleased desire for more, which accompanies virtually any form of successful activity. Or the work may do positive outrage to some part of one's nature—even to the sense of workmanship itself. Destroying the results of others' work will be abhorrent to anyone whose sense of workmanship is combined with human sympathies which make him enter into the workmanlike feelings of the victims in the case.

Thus, while the bent of workmanship is not inherently an interest in doing what the community needs to have done, it has numerous and varied chances of becoming so. Law and public opinion establish, as we have seen, a rough working approximation to the rule that gain shall be had only by doing useful things. And in conforming because he has to, everyone is exposed to the contagion of workmanlike interest in the doing of the worth-while thing in itself. He cannot conform outwardly without running a considerable chance of being converted from within. On the other hand, if he evades the spirit of the rules, then the game of evasion becomes an end in itself to him. But most people conform.

Clearly, we have here an enormously useful tool of social control. Possibly if law and public opinion were more definite and exacting in setting up the rule that gain shall come only through doing useful work, and especially if they put the rule in positive rather than in negative form, the bent of workmanship would be more exclusively directed to serviceable ends. Does this mean that if we installed a system of "production for use and not for profit" the workmanlike spirit would more than make up for the eclipsing of the gain spirit? Not necessarily. It may well be that for the best results with men of ordinary make-up the various strong appeals need to be used in combination. At any rate, the ordinary man is much happier in following some creative urge, if he knows that he is not unduly sacrificing his natural ambition for personal gain. What we need is the system which will use all these motives in the most effective combination and will reduce to a minimum the destructive conflicts between them. Judged by this test, our present system is honeycombed with imperfections, but it is not clear that any other available system would be less so.

The bent of workmanship plays a further part in control by virtue of the fact that some of the classes who are most influential in guiding the course of control are themselves governed by a strong professional *esprit*. One of the greatest safeguards of our system of attempted self-government is the bent of judicial workmanship in our higher judges—but the judge tends to make the Constitution an end in itself instead of an instrument of service to the nation's ends. The public must learn to interpret the politician's opposition to a settlement of a municipal traction question in the light of the possibility that he may not want it to be settled because his bent of political workmanship demands a chance to dramatize it as a conflict in which he figures as the people's defender, and to make speeches about it which will bring the voters flocking to the polls. And one saving grace is that the politicians, being forced to deal with the public welfare, and not always having axes to grind, can hardly help settling many questions in a workmanlike manner. We are forced to rely altogether too largely on this political craftsmanship because modern questions are too complex for those directly interested to comprehend them in their entirety and compose them with statesmanlike magnanimity.

5. CONTROL OF THE INFORMAL CONTROLS—EDUCATION

These informal pressures to which the individual is subject are obviously powerful and pervasive, but they are also very imperfectly oriented, from the standpoint of the true needs of society. Can they in turn be socially controlled? The task is clearly difficult, not merely because of the inertia of popular ideas and the obstinacy of popular prejudices, but because of a deeper difficulty. For who has the right to presume to say what is the true goal of social policy, if not public opinion itself, the very thing we are proposing to control? And how can any control over public opinion by any person or group be spoken of as social? The person who speaks in these terms usually means one of two things: either converting public opinion to his personal views of social welfare or bringing it to accept the programs which fit in with his own selfish interests. It goes without saying that public opinion should not be controlled by any group interest, and probably not by any one person's idea of the public welfare. The only person who has any such claim is the social genius who can appreciate and harmonize all the conflicting group ambitions, standards, and needs, and there is no practicable machinery for picking out such a genius from the host of eager proponents of social nostrums, save the final judgment of public opinion itself.

The chief need for social control of the informal controls we have been studying lies in the fact that they are themselves group affairs and need to be corrected by having the interests and ideals of other groups brought to bear upon them, and by being forced to harmonize themselves with these other interests and ideals. Concretely, the leaders of each group need to work in constant contact with the leaders of other groups, and the rank and file need corresponding personal contacts if they are to be had. In any case they need contact with a press and periodicals, art and literature, in which they may find a fair representation of all the important forces and interests which play a part in the life of their day. The class press and the cheap art which distorts reality and caters to class prejudices are among the worst enemies of the right kind of social control.[1] Here the end in view cannot be

---

[1] To take a single instance, the writer has seldon seen a moving picture which carried conviction as a sincere effort to portray a rich money maker as he typically is or the process of making a large fortune as it typically is. Gratuitous distortions are no help to the making of difficult social adjustments.

furthered by social control so much as by an honest bent of workmanship in art and journalism.

This is also largely true of another all-important branch of that
underlying sort of social control which works on the sources of social
control, namely, education. Education may fortify class prejudices
or break them down, rouse mental independence or lull it to sleep. It
can go far to make bigots or adaptable cooperators, docile subjects
or capable citizens, to spread a gospel of democracy or service, or to
cultivate a self-centered and self-satisfied snobbery, of either abstract
culture, aristocratic privilege or comfortable middle-class complacency.
It has been controlled in the interests of the church, of a militaristic
aristocracy, of communism, and atheism, and often it has worked
wonders.

But a democracy should beware of attempts to make it serve the
dominant interest, no matter how important it seems or how sincerely
it is believed in. For one thing, such attempts in a democracy are
bound to be bungling affairs, and by destroying the prestige of education they tend to destroy its usefulness for any rational social purpose.
To just the extent that education is known to be subservient to the
interests of "big business," it loses its influence, with the business class
quite as much as with the natural opponents of the business point of
view. If education becomes propaganda, it gives rise to counter-
propaganda and thus weakens the cause it seeks to uphold. It may
be due to these facts that education in the United States has gained
a fairly generous measure of freedom, placing it largely under the
control of the trained educator's bent of workmanship.

What is the proper task of the educator in relation to social control
of things economic? Is his duty done when he has taught respect for
law, Constitution and the flag, and expounded the virtues of property,
the errors of communism, and the beneficence and omnipotence of the
law of supply and demand, with proper reservations (if he happens to
be a Republican) in favor of the protective tariff? All this is not
necessarily wrong; in fact, much of it is good, but it is not enough, and
it tends to turn out fatally one-sided citizens. What is needed is the
making of men and women who will be equipped to play a responsible,
intelligent, and constructive part in the unpredictable changes which
the progress of modern industry is forcing upon us. They must be
morally good, they must be intelligent, and they must be accustomed
to using their intelligence on moral and practical issues. And since the
raw material of these issues consists of the rights, wrongs, and interests
of others, they must be accustomed to dealing tolerantly and under-
standingly with this raw material. They must be ready not only to

assert new rights for themselves, but to make new concessions to the rights of others. All this involves discipline, but it is the discipline of reasoned self-control and voluntary adjustment rather than of unthinking conformity.

The future citizen needs to know the most significant facts, in a fairly well-proportioned assortment, about the world he lives in; how it came to be what it is, and in what directions it is being urged by the logic of events and the pressure of conflicting forces. This implies that he should be given the materials for an understanding of the various sides of controverted questions, and for contact with both the balanced view of the moderate and the insistent conviction of the advocate. He must also learn that human nature and material forces set limits and impose conditions on any attempt to remake the world or solve its problems, and that these must be reckoned with, even if we cannot define the limits in advance by a rigid formulation of "natural law" but must find them experimentally. If these things are done, the particular views of the teacher on particular issues are not of vital moment.

Needless to say, education in practice will always fall far short of this ideal. Educators are specialists, seldom able to view their specialties in their relation to the whole of life, and teaching in the main what they have been taught, which tends to keep them at least a generation behind the demands of contemporary life—perhaps a century or more behind in some respects. All the more is it clear that they cannot hope to save the world by giving their pupils definite prescriptions for all the ills of its economic constitution, and that their only hope is to develop a habit of mind which will survive changing issues, a capacity for meeting novel issues and hammering out workable solutions. And this holds no hope except as pupils have minds with a capacity to "stand the gaff" of independent thinking.

Not that everyone must be a social inventor. But the people at large must be able to pass intelligently on social inventions which are offered for their approval. They must be able to discount propaganda and value sincerity. They must distinguish between principles for which one ought to stand stiffly and extravagant demands which, if insisted on, will block any reasonable solution. They must choose between conflicting prophecies of the results of a proposed measure when they are themselves not competent to make an independent prophecy; and to this end they must be able to utilize partisan criticism, criticizing it in turn to see where it has made its case and where it has failed. The mind that can do these things is competent for the exercise of the ultimate duties of sovereignty in a democracy. It is the ultimate seat of control.

6. CONTROL OF THE INFORMAL CONTROLS—RELIGION

The relation of religion to social control has been, and is, important and is changing in definite and important ways. There has been a movement away from priestly oligarchy and toward democratic religion, away from a self-centered scheme of personal salvation to a spirit of unselfish brotherhood, from an almost exclusive emphasis on the next world to a dominant interest in this, and from definite control of social behavior through a stage of relative indifference to a period in which the task of religion is conceived as the motivation of individuals in accord with a human and social gospel, at once forming ideals and strengthening the power behind them.

Three stages may, roughly, be distinguished: medievalism, Puritanism, and the social religion of today. In the medieval church, interest was centered in personal salvation. But the rewards, and especially the punishments, of the future life were so vividly conceived, and in such material terms, and the priesthood was conceived as having such power over them, that they were able to set up rules of conduct in this life as the means of salvation in the next.[1] "Salvation by works" was the rule, and the code was one of customary justice and of (limited) brotherhood within the bounds of men's customary ranks and stations to which God was supposed to have called them.

The Puritan reaction set up the right of the individual to find the truth in the Scriptures and replaced salvation by works with salvation by faith. This last, an invaluable consolation to the struggling soul whose works are forever inadequate to satisfy any but formal priestly standards, was inevitably carried too far, leading to a relative neglect of works. Interest was still focused on personal salvation in the next world, and the affairs of this world were largely left to the spirit of individualism which Puritanism so powerfully promoted.[2] Meanwhile the spirit of democracy, which Puritanism also furthered, together with the skepticism of science and the inescapable human message of the gospels, were slowly at work, preparing the next stage of development.

The modern Protestant church faces the hardest task of all. It no longer has sufficient authority to dictate specific rules of conduct or, by rewards and penalties, to enforce outward virtue on men who

[1] "Whatsoever thou shalt bind on earth shall be bound in Heaven, and whatsoever thou shalt loose on earth shall be loosed in Heaven" (*Matthew* 16:19; 18:18). The Catholic priesthood was supposed to have succeeded directly to this authority, granted to the apostle Peter.

[2] For the effect of Puritanism on individualism, see Roscoe Pound, *The Spirit of the Common Law*, Chap. ii; and Tawney, "Religious Thought on Social and Economic Questions," *Jour. Polit. Econ.*, XXXI (August, 1923), 461–493.

remain prevailingly selfish. It must make men genuinely unselfish from within, and so far as an object of worship is an essential part of this achievement, this must be found visibly manifest in the world we live in. In other words, men must be made genuinely religious and genuinely good, instead of outwardly conforming through superstitious hopes and fears. The choicest spirits in the past have achieved this in spite of the religion in which they were instructed, while the masses conformed from lower motives and a cruder vision. Now everyone must find "the root of the matter" for himself, if at all. Hence it is no wonder if the church today is struggling and not wholly successful. If it succeeds in finding the religion appropriate to an age of science, many will inevitably feel that it is not religion at all. Hence the conflicts which are shaking the religious world today. One type of socialism finds its chief basis in Christianity, while another type has outlawed religion and "abolished God," because religion stands for the old order and the old morality rather than for materialism and the class war. But the morality of the class war cannot rebuild society. That requires the morality of cooperation; hence the wholesale discarding of religion has its obvious dangers, especially for a system which must be based on brotherhood. Men can be moral without religion, but it remains to be seen whether a whole people can solve the problem of living together without the help of this most powerful force. Therefore the present period of readjustment is one of truly critical import for the safety of civilization.

REFERENCES FOR FURTHER READING

Besides the references given at the end of the previous chapter, the following bear directly on the particular subject matter of the present chapter:

DOUGLAS, HITCHCOCK, and ATKINS, *The Worker in Modern Industrial Society*, Chap. i, Sec. 5; Chap. ii, Secs, 3, 4; Chap. iii, Sec. 3; Chap. v *d*; Chap. xiv, Sec. 4 *c*; Chap. xxvi, Sec. 2.

EDDY, SHERWOOD, *The New World of Labor*, Chap. ix.

GIOVANNITTI, A. M., *The Independent*, Vol. xxvi, October 30, 1913.

HAMILTON, *Current Economic Problems* (3d ed.), Chaps. xi *b*, *i*; xv *d*.

MATHEWS, SHAILER, *The Social Teaching of Jesus*.

McLEAN, D. A., *The Morality of the Strike*.

RAUSCHENBUSCH, *Christianity and the Social Crisis*.

SINCLAIR, UPTON, *The Brass Check*.

SOREL, *Reflections on Violence*.

"The Church and Industrial Relations," *Ann.*, September, 1922.

VEBLEN, T., *The Instinct of Workmanship*.

PART III

ONE MAJOR FIELD: PUBLIC UTILITIES AND "TRUSTS"

CHAPTER XIV

TYPES OF CONTROL: GENERAL SURVEY

1. INTRODUCTION

We next come to consider deliberate policies of social control, over and beyond the underlying institutions hitherto considered. Here no complete survey is possible, since such controls reach into all phases of economic life in numberless and ever-increasing ways, and no sample can illustrate all the principles involved. However, we may take as a starting point a form of control which, from 1870 down to the World War, occupied the center of the stage in the United States, namely, the protection of consumers against exploitation by monopoly and near-monopoly, with emphasis on the problem of price.

In all these cases the main aim of control is to prevent prices from rising too high. There is also, however, regulation aiming to raise prices or prevent them from falling too low. Until quite recently, the main agency of this sort consisted of protective tariffs. Of late, however, there have been many attempts, often with some govern-mental sanction, to "valorize" particular commodities of which one area produced a commanding portion of the world supply, raising their prices and limiting the volume sold. In Germany, industrial cartel policies limiting competitive reduction of prices have had the sanction and sometimes the participation of government, contrary to the American "anti-trust" policy. In this country the great depression starting in 1929 has brought with it essentially similar policies for special "sick industries" and for agriculture, while the National Recovery Administration temporarily sanctioned measures by indus-tries of all sorts to set limits on the "destructive" price competition which the depression brought with it, suspending the application of the anti-trust laws to practices approved by the administration while still disavowing any sanction of "monopoly."

As a result, government is working to raise or maintain some prices and to lower and restrict others, with no clearly defined standards for distinguishing cases and determining proper limits. Much confusion

237

and bewilderment have naturally resulted, and the lack of formulated standards affords much room for considerations that are political rather than economic. It is true that this mixture of policies is not inherently and necessarily inconsistent. In general, the point at which downward regulation of prices begins is higher than the point at which government will initiate price-sustaining policies, at least in terms of the profitableness of the prices to producers, leaving a possible intermediate zone of noninterference. But the matter is not so simple as that; for example, the unprofitableness of an industry does not in itself exempt it from the anti-trust laws.

A deal of the existing confusion arises, in discussions of industrial regulation, from failing to distinguish between different classes of cases, though probably still more arises from the opposite error of refusing to draw up any general principles because each case is a thing by itself and different, in some respects, from every other case. In general, it makes a difference whether the business is a monopoly or not, whether it is completely consolidated or contains numerous independent companies, whether regulation is temporary or permanent, whether special motives other than economic self-interest are available or not, and whether fixed capital is large or small relative to sales.

We may, then, distinguish the following types of regulation: First comes emergency regulation, for which the recent war gave occasion on a huge scale. This is characterized by sudden and great demands, or shortages, violent dislocations of the ordinary directions and proportions of economic effort, which are likely to be largely temporary, and a resulting task of mobilization which is temporary, even if some of the effects may be permanent. Next comes the consolidated "natural monopoly," with which we shall deal at some length in the chapters to follow. Next comes the partial natural monopoly, of which the railroads are the outstanding example. They do not compete actively for local business, but the local rates are affected by the competitive ones and, still more important, under any scheme of rates that can be installed, some roads will be richer and others poorer; there will be competitive advantages and disadvantages. Next comes the "trust," or industrial or commercial combination, toward which the accepted policy in the United States is to attempt to restore and maintain competition and thus influence prices indirectly, rather than to regulate them directly. Other methods of control include the public ownership of industry and the rationing of supplies, which may be a necessary feature of a general policy of price regulation.

A final type of control which must be noticed is the general control of prices which would be necessary under any of the federative-collectivist systems which will be mentioned later. This would, of course, involve greater difficulties than the control of a few special industries, but it would also afford greater powers and opportunities. For it controls the entire field of employment for both capital and labor, and hence it is in a position to alter the competitive distribution of rewards. When only a few industries are controlled, capital in these industries must be allowed to get approximately what it can earn in the unregulated field, or else it will seek the competitive industries and avoid the regulated ones. But if all are regulated, it has no option except to go abroad (and the totalitarian states have found ways of preventing that), and so it may be willing to accept harder terms. Something similar is true of the salaries paid to the higher grades of ability; such men may be willing to work for less than the competitive value of their services if there is no competitive field open to them. How much difference this will make can only be discovered by experiment. Such a system of universal price control is probably not legally possible under present interpretations of our American constitutional guaranties. We may, then, turn to the examination of some of the types of downward or restrictive price control with which we have had experience, realizing that this is only a section of the field.

2. EMERGENCY REGULATION

In the field of emergency regulation there are two fairly well-marked types, best illustrated by the wartime control of prices and the postwar control of rents. In each case the prices in question are competitive, but a heavy demand or a sudden shortage, or both, have forced prices, or threaten to force them, to oppressive levels. This is the natural way in which a shortage corrects itself under the competitive system; the high price stimulates production and checks demand, preventing foods, for instance, from being all used up before another crop is available. Thus it prevents shortage from being turned into actual famine. It also distributes the supply among localities. Thus it renders a real and important service, and hence we should think twice before tampering with its action. There is, nevertheless, justification for control in the special features of the emergency.

The problem is in large part one of industrial mobilization. Under ordinary conditions, with relatively small mobilizations called for and plenty of time allowed, a relatively small rise of prices will produce all the effect that is needed. But under war conditions the mere amount and suddenness of the shortage may bring it about that the price goes higher than is necessary to afford all the incentive needed to the most rapid mobilization of which industry is capable. It may even be that additional supplies are not to be had at any price, and that, from the side of production, the high profits which result render no useful service whatever. The high profits tend to make high wages, and these increase the demand for luxuries. They also stimulate the workers to leave their jobs and hunt for better-paid ones, thus decreasing their effective working time, or simply enabling them to spend less time working and still be richer than before, taking time off to enjoy their luxuries. Thus the nation, in bidding for the goods which are essential to the prosecution of the war, may actually bid against itself, reducing the amount of available labor power and diverting labor to the production of "nonessential" goods.

Again, in ordinary times these effects, which at such times would be moderate in amount, would not be regarded as evils, for leisure and luxuries for workers are among the chief ends for which industrial civilization exists. But when they are immoderate in amount they are bound to be temporary, and more likely to be demoralizing than permanently helpful; moreover they are not equitably distributed. And the emergency of war adds a further objection, namely, that luxuries and leisure are, for the time being, no part of the paramount purpose of the nation. It wants to turn all the energies and resources possible into fighting and furnishing the material means of fighting, and to have as little as possible devoted to other purposes, consistent with this main purpose. This focusing of efforts is limited in two ways. The people require enough consumption to furnish energy and maintain loyalty; and there may be resources which simply cannot be shifted to war purposes within the time available and might as well remain in their ordinary uses. Beyond these limits, luxuries and leisure are a detraction from the dominant national purpose. Large increases in prices and wages, which really enrich favored groups, are inconsistent with this standard. Hence the nation has a reason for striving to confine the disturbance of prices and of wages within the narrowest possible limits.

The typical policy under these conditions is content to leave prices of essential goods high enough to afford something more than the usual competitive profit, so as to offer the incentive which is needed to increased production. Where the supply price cannot be controlled, as in the case of imported foodstuffs, prices to consumers may even be fixed below cost and the difference made up by a subsidy, as Great Britain did with bread.[1] The undertaking was made simpler

---

[1] See Gray, *War-time Control of Industry*, pp. 245–247; also Litman, *Prices and Price Control in Great Britain and the United States during the World-War*, Carnegie Endowment for International Peace, pp. 130–131, 1920.

by the fact that the government already controlled the mills. To stimulate agriculture, the United States Government guaranteed a minimum price on wheat. The dangers of this policy are illustrated by the British guaranteed price for potatoes, which stimulated more output than could be sold at the guaranteed price. Reductions had to be permitted, the government making up the difference to the producer.[1] The United States undertook a policy of maintaining a sliding scale of prices for hogs, based upon the price of corn in such a way as to insure that hog raisers or feeders could fatten hogs on corn with a profit.[2] This last measure proved to be a mistake and was abandoned, since it would have tended to stimulate an unlimited rise in the price of corn, and corn proved to be so valuable that it was necessary to secure the greater food value from it by feeding more of it to human beings direct, rather than the lesser value secured by converting more of it into pork. This illustrates the very general fact that policies of price control do not always accurately gauge the relative importance of alternative uses of essential goods.

Other problems arise from the practical difficulties of ways and means. One rather crude method, employed in the early stages of the war, was to limit prices to a maximum excess above prewar levels.[3] This gives room for the customary differentials between qualities, localities, and seasons but is obviously difficult to enforce. Another method is, without fixing prices directly, to limit the profits of producers to a given percentage on their investment. This is only appropriate where the investment is large, and even so there is no time for a public valuation, so that the existing accounts have to be accepted with all their discrepancies and inaccuracies. Furthermore, the plan may be evaded by the accumulation of reserves of various sorts, kept under cover until control shall come to an end. And it requires that different producers with different costs of production shall sell equivalent goods at different prices—something which could only be done with relatively unstandardized products and probably for a limited time, or where the manufacturer's entire margin makes but a small percentage difference in the price to the consumer, as in meat packing. Last, it requires the producers to fix their own prices, each being responsible for keeping his earnings within the prescribed limit. The plan was used by the United States Food Administration in controlling the five largest packing-house establishments, but for the others, whose investments were smaller and not even approximately known, the

[1] See Litman, *op. cit.*, p. 128.
[2] *Ibid.*, pp. 251–252.
[3] See Pigou, *Political Economy of War*, pp. 120–121.

administration resorted to fixing a maximum percentage margin of profit on sales—still without directly fixing particular prices.[1]

Where prices were fixed directly, probably the outstanding problem arose from the differences in the costs of different producers and different plants. Statistical analysis revealed that such costs were distributed according to a curve of fairly uniform general type, and that unregulated prices were high enough to cover the costs of all but a small portion of the output, commonly from 11 to 15 per cent. This furnished a basis for fixing prices which would not restrict output, but which would not cover freak costs or the costs of gross inefficiency.

A variant requiring different treatment arises where the differences in costs are due to the different qualities of natural resources used, as in the case of coal. High-cost manufacturers may go on producing in the hope of lowering their costs by retrenchments, improvements, or increased output, or overcoming the special misfortunes of what may be an unusually bad season; but there is no corresponding hope of increasing the thickness or accessibility of a vein of coal. Hence, if the output of the high-cost veins is required, the necessary costs must be covered, and the price will afford more than the minimum necessary profits to the owner of low-cost veins. It may be that if labor and railroad cars were concentrated at the low-cost workings, these could supply more coal at less cost than if effort were distributed among workings of all grades, but there was not sufficient time during the war to determine experimentally whether this were true or not, or to determine what were the equitable claims, if any, of the high-cost producers who would be prevented from using their property. And the plan involves an amount of paternalism from which even a war administration might well shrink. Furthermore, even if the least economical workings in each region were closed down, the main resources of each region must be kept in operation, and there remained considerable differences between the typical conditions of cost in the different regions, which could not be eliminated. This situation was met by the United States Fuel Administration by fixing lower scales of prices for coal from thicker veins, thus forcing the owners of the best workings to divide part of their advantage with their customers. This meant, of course, that prices were not graded wholly according to quality, as a free market would grade them, and this could probably not persist in a peace-time economy. As it was, the first scale of prices was attacked as being prohibitively low for some needed workings, and some revisions were made.[2]

[1] See Litman, *op. cit.*, pp. 254–256.
[2] See "Price-fixing by Government," *Unpopular Rev.*, April-June, 1918; also Litman, *op. cit.*, pp. 271–274.

Merely to limit manufacturers' prices would not help the consumer unless dealers were also restrained.[1] This was commonly done by informal methods, local committees making up "fair-price lists." Compulsion was exercised by licensing dealers, with the possibility of taking away the license as a penalty for flagrant "profiteering." Where nation-wide control was practiced, the method was to limit the percentage the dealers were permitted to charge above the prices they paid for the goods. This meant, if strictly adhered to, that goods bought at different times might have to be sold to the same customers at different prices—a "violation of economic law," perhaps, but on the whole a minor one, and not very different from practices which frequently occur in unregulated merchandising. If the dealers are given the benefit of the doubt in fixing margins, a small percentage of unnecessary margin will yield a very large profit on the dealers' capital, since this is small compared to their gross sales. Hence this sort of regulation is not an instrument of precision, capable of allowing the entrepreneur exactly 5 per cent, or 7, or whatever is decided to be the ideal amount. It carries with it the need of limiting the number of dealers' margins that may be charged to the consumer, as well as the size of each.

To sum up, ideal conditions for price control—nowhere fully present —would be those of manufactured goods uniform in quality, durable, and not seasonal in character, produced at fairly uniform cost, and with uniform, reliable, and adequate accounting, so that investment and costs could be accurately determined, and prices fixed accordingly. Different conditions in these respects give rise to different policies. And the actual conditions are so far from favorable that it is doubtful whether control of prices could be even reasonably successful were it not that the emergency gives rise to a feeling on the part of the business community of willingness to cooperate in meeting it. This is, of course, especially true where the emergency is that of war and the feeling is that of patriotic loyalty. This does not wipe out selfishness or abolish economic obstacles, but it does minimize their effects sufficiently to make it possible to secure fairly useful results out of measures too crude to be relied on in ordinary times. And the fact that these measures are temporary makes people willing to put up with minor injustices and to do some things without the economic incentives which would be necessary if they expected to live permanently under such conditions.

Where costs of transportation are material, different prices must be allowed at different distances from the source or sources of supplies.

[1] See Pigou, *Political Economy of War*, pp. 123–124.

Even if a rational system of this sort is worked out, it may not meet all the requirements of furnishing incentive to distribute goods geographically according to need, since a miscalculation might cause a shortage in one place, while the surplus logically available to meet it would have to come from other places where prices were no lower, so that no profit could be made on the transfer unless the price system were departed from.[1] Or, if there is danger of future shortage greater than present prices are allowed to reflect, goods may be hoarded in one place although there is a premium on shipping them elsewhere which would normally be adequate to bring this about.

This brings us to one of the main conditioning factors of emergency price control, namely, the need of taking direct measures to limit demand and apportion supplies. Demand must be limited so that the scant supply shall not be used up as fast as in ordinary times and shortage turned into famine. And supply must be apportioned so that the rich shall not be able to consume as usual and hoard supplies while the poor go without the necessities. In this matter, the law of supply and demand works hardship enough in ordinary times; in serious emergencies it becomes intolerable. This means that supplies must be rationed, by voluntary means if possible, but using compulsion if voluntary means fail.

Other supplementary measures tend to be adopted because emergency control of prices is such an inaccurate instrument, and so incapable of eliminating all socially useless profits. An excess-profits or a war-profits tax serves to take back for the community a large part of the surplus which the community has failed to prevent industry from taking from the consumers. Nonessential industries may have their supplies limited or cut off entirely, especially if the government has taken over the actual ownership or administration of these supplies. Commonly the control and rationing of coal and railroad-transport facilities are enough to determine whether a nonessential industry shall operate full time, half time, or not at all.

The postwar control of rents differs from most of the other instances of price control, in that little or no consideration seems to have been given to the need of an economic incentive to stimulate new building and so break the housing shortage in the only practicable way. This was especially true in Germany, where the postwar control of rents virtually confiscated the property of landlords. Under such a handicap new houses can be built only on some noncommercial basis. The control of rents carries with it the limitation of the land-

---

[1] The sugar situation in this country afforded instances of this general sort. See "Price-fixing by Government," *Unpopular Rev.,* April-June, 1918.

lord's right to evict and virtually gives the tenant some of the rights of ownership in the quarters he occupies. In this country, increases were allowed which ultimately reached the point of stimulating large amounts of added building, but not during the war. While hostilities continued, the nation's demand for building consisted mostly of the demand for cantonments, housing for workers in the new shipyards and other war industries, and other public purposes, so that new private housing was in the class of nonessentials, and there was, for the time being, no purpose to be served by allowing private rents to go high enough to afford an incentive to new construction.

To sum up, wartime control did not prevent prices from increasing enormously, but it set some bounds to the increase. It was inaccurate and wasteful, and few, if any, of the many methods used were sufficiently well developed and complete to stand the test of permanent use. Nevertheless, the policy did accomplish some results, sufficient at least to justify its existence. And its shortcomings were, in part at least, inherent in the character of emergency control itself.

3. CONSOLIDATED NATURAL MONOPOLIES

The "natural monopoly," in the usual sense, is an industry in which competition is necessarily so wasteful as to make monopoly clearly the lesser evil. We may fairly start, then, with the assumption that the cost of production under monopoly is less than it would be under competition which duplicates the service.[1] The task of regulation is to give the consumer as much of this saving as justice and expediency permit. The state must at least see that he is no worse off than he would be under competition, and it will try to leave him as much better off as possible. Without regulation, the monopoly could absorb the benefit of its economies and give the public nothing in return. It could keep prices well above cost, thus preventing the demand from developing to the full extent that is practicable and so limiting the usefulness of its service to the public.

To say that it would "limit the supply of its product" would not be quite descriptive, since it is characteristic of these industries that they do not themselves positively determine the supply of their goods or services. They furnish cars ready to carry passengers but do not govern the number who ride, except as the car supply may be so outrageously inadequate that, even with standing room crowded, there are still people waiting to be carried. Of course, people will not live in places where they are dependent on this kind of service, and in this way the

---

[1] Two telephone companies, each serving half the subscribers, might not be more costly than one serving all, but the service would be far inferior.

company may control supply through controlling demand. Or the company furnishes a tank-full of gas or a potential of current at the end of a cable, and connections, out of which the consumer can take as much or as little as he wishes. In such cases supply, in the sense of output, is not separate from demand, but identical with it.

Even if these industries were not under legal obligation to serve all comers, it is hardly thinkable that they would refuse to do so. The monopolies would not limit supply in that sense. What they would be in a position to do is to furnish inadequate capacity to carry the "peak load," or even to carry normal load without undue crowding, or falling-off in voltage or gas pressure, or in other ways they might furnish service of low quality.

What is the objective of regulation? Certainly it is not the socialistic objective of extinguishing interest and profits, or else regulation would not be limited, as it is, to a few special industries. The objective is usually expressed as adequate service at fair prices, but what is adequate service and what is a fair price? Adequate service, in terms of quality, is probably best defined as whatever the public would choose to buy and pay a fair price for it if it had the option. And fair prices must be adequate, with such degree of efficient management as the public has a right to expect, to cover expenses of production at prevailing market rates and yield enough net earnings to attract whatever capital is needed to render the service as efficiently as possible, with a further reward to the management if they have done anything to deserve it. They may earn a special reward either by reducing costs or improving quality of service beyond what the prevailing state of the art gives the public a right to demand of any management, or by enlarging the usefulness of the service in any special ways. Perhaps the best test of fair prices, in principle, is that they should promote the largest possible usefulness of the service. This requires that they shall be low enough to develop the largest demand for which they are adequate to call forth an answering supply. To call forth a supply the earnings must meet the attractions afforded by unregulated business, and these constitute the chief controlling forces in the finding of fair rates.

Such regulation has three main dangers to avoid. One is that profits may be too high because the regulators are too lenient or are unduly influenced or are hoodwinked by the companies. Another is that earnings may be too low, and capital may be inadequate, enterprise discouraged, and the service starved. A third is that rewards, while adequate, may be fixed too mechanically and without reference to deserving, so that management has no incentive to incur outlays or take risks to improve the service but has an incentive to divert too much of its energies to trying to secure better terms from the regulating authorities—perhaps even to damage business confidence by making their condition seem worse than it is—rather than to concentrate on a determined drive to solve the operating problems of their industry. An incidental evil is the slowness with which commissions can act in adjusting rates to changed conditions, and the uncertainty as to what returns a new schedule of rates will actually yield. These two factors combined have, in recent years when conditions demanded increased rates, worked powerfully to the disadvantage of the companies.

This, then, is the problem of controlling natural monopolies, in its most general terms. The devices used in the practical attack upon this problem will be taken up in separate chapters.

4. PARTIAL NATURAL MONOPOLIES, OR SEMICOMPETITIVE PUBLIC UTILITIES

What are "partial monopolies"? It is sometimes urged that such consolidated companies as gas utilities really compete with electricity or with other substitute fuels. This is what the economist calls "substitution" rather than "competition," but the line between the two is not clean-cut and unmistakable. For our present purpose, however, the distinguishing characteristics of out-and-out monopolies are two: first, such rivalry as exists would not usually prevent an unregulated company from earning more than the minimum necessary to attract capital and enterprise into the business, though there is always the possibility of displacement by a new service—witness the effect of automobiles on street railways. Second, a regulating body usually has it in its power to fix rates for each company under which each company will earn a reasonable return, and it is not necessary to give more to some in order that others shall not receive less. Both of these things are usually true in the field of local public utilities other than transportation, while neither of them is true of our system of steam railroads. Even if unregulated, few railroads could earn an adequate return under present conditions, and some could not do so in the best of times, while no scheme of regulated rates can give every road the rate of return which is thought to be fair. Some will always earn more than others. Railroads are, therefore, only partial monopolies.

The difficulties arising from this are obvious. The higher earnings which some companies receive are due in part to more efficient management, in part to shrewder choice of the original location, and in part to the nature of things, in that some routes are better than others and not all companies can occupy the best routes. Thus the differentials in earnings are partly earned and partly unearned, and there is no known way of analyzing out the two elements. This has its compensating advantages, for it is almost impossible to prevent single companies from reaping gains if they do improve their efficiency, so that there is an automatic safeguard against one of the subtlest dangers of regulation, namely, the deadening of incentives to improvement by a rigid return.

Rates must be fixed with due regard to the situation of the richest roads, the average roads, and the deserving poor—possibly to some extent the undeserving poor also, though the appropriate remedies in their case are reorganization and improved efficiency rather than rate increases. In extreme cases it may be the economical thing to allow a line to be abandoned, but this hardly applies to any but small lines, or branches serving localities which can do their carrying by motor at a lower aggregate cost. Our main arteries of traffic are all worth keeping in operation, whatever the handicaps under which some of them may work.

If rates are fixed to yield an average of 6 per cent to all roads, then any one road which makes improvements will earn more than if it had not made them, for it will reap the whole gain; and even if the resulting economies lead to some slight lowering of rates—which is unlikely in practice—the loss will fall on all the roads and the burden felt by the road which made the economies will be imperceptible.

If the limit which economic law sets on reductions of earnings were a rigid one, rates would have to be much higher than they are, or a large part of our railroad mileage would be unable to operate. But, fortunately or unfortunately, even roads which are earning far less than 6 per cent on their entire investment are still able to offer new capital the rate which the market demands. On some properties, unwisely or unfortunately located, it may seem wisest that the original investment should permanently receive less than the market rate of earnings (preferably accompanied by a reorganization and a scaling down of the capital account) as long as the road can offer new investors the return necessary to attract funds for needed extensions and betterments.

Other ways of dealing with this problem of differences in economic strength include the plan by which the government takes a share of all profits beyond a certain percentage—also the consolidation of weak with strong properties so as to diminish the differences in earning power. The Transportation Act of 1920 included both these measures but, so far, excess earnings have been practically nonexistent, and the obstacles to the projected type of consolidation have balked this part of the program.

5. DIRECT PRICE CONTROL FOR "TRUSTS"

Dissatisfaction with the apparent ineffectiveness of the anti-trust laws has sometimes led to proposals to treat the trusts like public utilities and regulate their prices directly. At present, however, there is too much dissatisfaction with public-utility control to make this seem a hopeful remedy for evils in the field of general industry. The wartime experience in general price control, also, was not promising as a basis for a permanent policy.

In the case of aluminum and possibly one or two others, control by one company is complete enough to permit it to be regulated without much regard for rivals. In most cases, however, there remain a number of large concerns and many smaller ones. Whether these small concerns exist on sufferance of the large ones is hard to determine. The existing anti-trust laws afford the large producers ample motive for leaving many smaller ones in existence. The same would probably be true under direct price control, since the smaller concerns would afford the large ones some actual protection. The small producers' costs of production vary more than those of their large rivals, and some are typically operating at high costs. As a result, the larger producers are frequently able to make liberal profits at prices which afford the typical small concern no more than a living rate of earnings.

Under such conditions, the attempt to protect consumers by fixing prices is obviously a matter of great difficulty. The government would naturally hesitate to fix prices so low as to drive out of business any very large number of the small producers, and therefore it is not in a position to give the consumers any very substantial benefits by this method. Clearly the question is a delicate and difficult one, and it is not easy to say whether the profits of the larger concerns are solely due to superior efficiency or whether they contain some measure of monopolistic exploitation.

6. PUBLIC OWNERSHIP

Public ownership, as a means of protecting the consumer, involves a weighing of a number of quantities, plus and minus. Most fundamental is the effectiveness with which labor and materials are organized to produce the service: the efficiency of operation in ultimate physical terms. In the long run, the system which gets most results out of given amounts of labor, instruments, and materials will yield the largest dividends to all concerned, including laborers and consumers, and to the public. The taxes from an efficiently conducted private enterprise are very likely to exceed the revenue (above interest) of an inefficiently conducted public enterprise and so be more profitable to the state, assuming that it gives the consumers the same value. The chief advantage of public ownership lies in the lower rates at which governments can borrow capital, a saving which may amount to as much as 1 per cent. But this saving is not to be had for nothing. It depends on issuing bonds which are virtually insured against loss, which means that, if the enterprise itself will not pay the interest charges, the state must make them up out of general taxes. This whole matter will be gone into in a later chapter; suffice it to say here that public ownership is far from being a sure source of large gains to consumers or to the general public.

The latest phase of public ownership and operation has a different character and purpose, namely, its use as a "yardstick" for the rates of private companies. This is the outgrowth of a feeling that the system of private operation with public control should be required constantly to meet the test of furnishing service on as good terms as the public could furnish directly. It is felt that without this there is no adequate check on the reasonableness of costs, and that the system of valuing the property and allowing a "fair return" on the valuation is full of loopholes, operating in practice too favorably for the companies. The intent of the yardstick policy is to supplement these weak points of regulation by furnishing standards of reasonable cost and by putting the private companies under pressure to meet the cheapness of public service, under the possible penalty of being displaced if they fail to meet a fair comparative test. The idea of public production of commodities in competition with trusts has also been suggested as a means of controlling their prices; and the Tennessee Valley Authority—itself the outstanding yardstick experiment—actually secured a reduction in the price of cement for its dams by proposing to build its own cement plant.

The problems involved in this form of control will be discussed in a later chapter.[1] It presents many possibilities of usefulness, and also of error and loss, and may prove to be one of that numerous group of controls which raise more problems than they solve.

REFERENCES FOR FURTHER READING

Amer. Econ. Rev., Sup., Papers and Discussion, pp. 114–142, March, 1913; pp. 233–279, March, 1919.

ANDERSON, B. M., JR., "Artificial Prices a Menace to Economic Stability," *Chase Econ. Bull.*, May, 1924.

[1] See below, Chap. xxiv, Sec. 5.

BACHMAN, *Government Price-fixing*, Chaps. i, ii, 1938.

BAKER, CHARLES WHITING, *Government Control and Operation of Industry in Great Britain and the United States during the World-War*, Carnegie Endowment for International Peace, 1921.

BARNES, I. R., *Cases on Public Utility Regulation* (rev. ed.), The Public Utility Concept and the Power to Regulate, 1934.

BAUER, JOHN, *Effective Regulation of Public Utilities*, Chaps. ii, iii.

CAMP, "Agriculture and Price Stabilization," *Jour. Polit. Econ.*, pp. 282–314, June, 1924.

CLARK, HAMILTON, AND MOULTON, *Readings in the Economics of War*, Chaps. vii–ix, xi.

GRAY, *War-Time Control of Industry.*

HAMILTON, *Current Economic Problems*, Chap. iv *e.*

HANEY, "Price-fixing in a Competitive Industry," *Amer. Econ. Rev.*, pp. 47–56, March, 1919.

HARTMAN, *Fair Value*, Chap. ii.

JONES and BIGHAM, *Principles of Public Utilities*, Chap. ii, 1931.

LITMAN, *Prices and Price Control in Great Britain and the United States during the World-War*, Carnegie Endowment for International Peace, 1920.

MILLER, *Railway Transportation*, Chaps. v–viii, xxx–xxxiv.

PIGOU, *Political Economy of War*, Chap. ix.

Quart. Jour. Econ., August, 1918, pp. 567–634, 664–667 (various authors).

RIEGEL, "Fire Insurance Rates," *Quart. Jour. Econ.*, pp. 704–737, August, 1916.

SHAUB, "The Regulation of Rentals during the War Period," *Jour. Polit. Econ.*, pp. 1–36, January, 1920.

SLICHTER, S. H., *Modern Economic Society*, Chap. xvii, 1928.

SMALLEY, *Railroad Rate Control*, Publications of the American Economic Association, Vol. VII, No. 2, Chap. i, May, 1906.

SURFACE, *The Stabilization of the Price of Wheat during the War*, United States Grain Corporation, 1925.

TAUSSIG, "Price-fixing as Seen by a Price-fixer," *Quart. Jour. Econ.*, pp. 205–241, February, 1919.

TINSLEY, J. M., *Public Regulation of Milk Marketing in California.*

CHAPTER XV

THE CORPORATE BACKGROUND OF REGULATION

1. INTRODUCTION

In the field of corporate organization there are four main aspects which bear directly on the control of prices. One is the location of responsibility, for purposes of command, enforcement, and, if necessary, punishment, in the impersonal organization of the corporation. Another is the reaction of capitalization on price policies. A third is the division and incidence of the burdens of regulation as affected by the organization of the company; and a fourth is the location of responsibility for efficient conduct of the business, which bears on the reaction of regulation on efficiency and the proper place in which to apply stimuli of pressure or reward.

2. THE LOCATION OF RESPONSIBILITY

There are only two methods of controlling a corporation: to hold the corporation as such responsible, or to locate the responsible official, agent, or employee and fix the responsibility on him. In matters of price fixing, the first step is to determine what prices should be, and to order the corporation, as a corporation, to carry out the findings. When it comes to the penalizing of violations, there is more room for differences of policy, and the state is likely to be driven by necessity to choose, not the ideally just means, but any means which gives promise of results.

A corporation cannot be imprisoned. It can be fined or deprived of the right to do business, but fines may be paid ultimately by the customers, and the seriousness of the offense seldom justifies depriving the company of its charter. Hence it is not always easy to find just the appropriate penalty. This difficulty is not a serious obstacle to the enforcement of orders fixing prices directly, but it does create some awkward problems in the indirect control of prices through the maintenance of competition and the suppression of unfair tactics.

The corporation can, in effect, give evidence, in the shape of its official books and records. But other kinds of evidence must be gotten

252

from officials and employees; and where it is evidence of illegal things which they themselves have done, they can take shelter behind the constitutional immunity which protects any person from being compelled to testify against himself. This has led to the frequently used practice of compelling the individual to testify and guaranteeing him against prosecution on account of anything revealed in his testimony. This often leaves the punishment of the corporation as the only practicable resource.

3. CAPITALIZATION AND PRICE POLICY

Does "watered stock" raise prices? The man in the street often assumes without question that it does, while many economists assume, almost without question, that it cannot, since prices are governed by the forces of demand and supply, competition, substitution, and cost of production; and stock watering does not affect these forces.

A share of capital stock is a certificate, usually bearing a certain par value and certifying that the amount of this par value has been paid into the treasury of the company when the stock was originally issued. If stock is issued as fully paid when it is not, the recipient may be held liable for the shortage. This is the primary meaning of watered stock.[1] Aside from this, the par value on the stock carries no definite money rights. The holder of a share of common stock holds an undivided interest in the assets and earnings of the company in the proportion which his holdings bear to the total shares outstanding, and that is all. Even if the stock was originally fully paid in cash, there is no guarantee that the assets it represents are worth that amount now. They may have shrunk in value, or the company may have lost money. That the mere issuing of stock of a given par value does not enable a company to earn and divide the equivalent of interest on that amount may be verified by the most cursory glance at current stock reports.

Besides the common stock, there may be preferred stock and debentures which carry a claim to a definite rate of payment ahead of the common stock, but no right of action if there are no earnings from which to pay it. And there are mortgage bonds: definite promises to pay so much principal and interest, backed by the right of foreclosure if payment is defaulted. Similar in effect is the leasing of property, since the owner can take it back if the terms of the lease are not met. But even these prior securities cannot call earnings into existence where there are none.

[1] For our present purpose there is no need to settle all the controversial questions involved in setting up an ultimate standard of correct capitalization, if indeed this be possible.

Where capitalization goes beyond the amount actually invested, the volume of securities is not so much a cause of earnings as a symptom of expectations—which may or may not be fulfilled. This is especially true of competitive industries, which must take prices as they find them. A monopoly has more option, and the burden of a large volume of securities may lead to a more grasping policy than would otherwise be followed, especially if the securities are of the fixed-income variety. But this is problematical, and in any case the chief evil in the practice lies in the fact that the investors and the public are deprived of reliable information as to the assets of the business, to which they have a right. They may go to the reports issued by the companies, but the book value of the assets in these reports is necessarily inflated to balance the inflated volume of capital liabilities and so will do them no good unless they are keen enough to detect this inflation.

One kindred practice, the issuing of stock dividends by a going concern, commonly has still less to do with price policy. It is usually a sign that liberal earnings are already coming in, and that the company expects to divide them more generously in the future than in the past. If a considerable part of the earnings have been turned back into the business for some time previous to the cutting of the "melon," that means an increase in the physical investment, which helps to justify the increased capitalization. The abuses of this practice affect chiefly the investor rather than the consumer and arise mostly from concealment of the financial state of the business.

Overcapitalization may have served to conceal exorbitant profits, and so to protect unduly high prices from detection and public attack, but the public is by now as keenly on the lookout for the one as for the other and has means of detecting both. Where rates are regulated, it is always on the basis of an independent appraisal of the property, in which the par value of securities is given little or no weight. This can be made more effective where the accounts of the companies are also controlled as the Interstate Commerce Commission controls the accounts of the railroads.

If times become hard, overcapitalization may lead a company to divide more than it can afford, starving reserves and postponing or neglecting maintenance. This may result in inefficiency and ultimately react somewhat on prices, though this is not its primary effect.

4. RELATION BETWEEN DIFFERENT TYPES AND ISSUES OF SECURITIES

Fluctuations in the earnings of the business are concentrated upon the common stock, and the bondholder's income is unchanging. This commonplace fact has a much-neglected bearing upon methods of regulation. Regulation has proceeded with the corporation as if it were a person, has tried to fix a reasonable rate of earnings on this basis, and has often tacitly assumed that the division of these earnings between the various classes of security holders is a matter of private arrangement which does not concern the public. This is far from being the case.

Suppose that increased income is needed because of a shrinking dollar and a rise in interest rates. Suppose that the general level of prices, and with it the reproduction cost of public-utility property, have risen 25 per cent, and interest rates have gone up from 5 to 6 per cent. A commission might hold that an original investment of $100 now had a right to $7.50 yield (6 per cent on $125) instead of $5.00 as before. Is it no concern of the commission's that the bondholders would get no increase, and the stockholders would get it all, their income being doubled or trebled, according to the proportion of stocks and bonds outstanding? Or should the compensation for the shrinking dollar be based merely on the stockholders' equity in the business, since they are the only ones who will get it in any case? The importance of this question is illustrated by the fact that numerous utility stocks made large speculative gains in the period of postwar prosperity, instead of maintaining the character of conservative investments.

Another issue of unsuspected importance may be illustrated in this way: Suppose that no stocks could ever be issued for less than their full par value, in cash; in other words, suppose the evil of overcapitalization is utterly suppressed. Suppose that the fortunes of business bring the market value of some stocks below par all of the time, and of all stocks some of the time. How will companies in this position secure additional capital? They cannot issue stocks in the open market for lack of willing buyers. If they borrow, they narrow the margin of earnings above debt charges, and thus narrow the margin of safety of their bonds and make both bonds and stocks less secure than before. If this goes on indefinitely, not only will stocks be unsalable at anything approaching par, but bonds can find a market only on unduly burdensome terms, because of the unbalanced state of the capitalization. Bonds will then be sold at a heavy discount, and it is worse for the financial stability of the companies to issue bonds below par than stocks.[1]

This can to some extent be circumvented by devices such as the issuing of bonds and stocks together. Otherwise the result would be

[1] See *Report of the Railroad Securities Commission*, headed by A. T. Hadley, 1911.

that, in order to bring about financial stability in the long run, the government would be forced to grant earnings sufficient to keep the market value of stock up to par, regardless of whether the original investment justifies any such value. Par value of securities would become the standard governing regulation, just or unjust. And not merely the average road, but the poorest, would need to be enabled to sell its stock at par.

The difficulty here illustrated was one of the important factors in the situation of railways and public utilities in the critical period preceding and following the World War. The proportion of bonds in the capitalization had grown far beyond the 50 per cent which had formerly been considered a safe ratio. This was, in part, due to the fact that the regulating bodies of the various states had placed obstacles in the way of the sale of stock below par and so made it difficult for many companies to sell stock at all. Other causes have contributed, especially the desire of the stockholders to keep control, as the property grows, without making additional investments. Thus bonds increase, and both bonds and stocks become more speculative. If this tendency were to go unchecked, it would lead to a deadlock from which the only escape would be a drastic reorganization and scaling down of the capitalization of many companies, coupled with a change of policy for the future which would prevent the same dilemma from arising again.

In a forced reorganization, holders of old securities suffer, while new capital has to be offered the market rate, except as funds can be raised by assessing the present stockholders. In either case, there are discrepancies in the treatment of holders of securities of different issues, and the rate needed to attract new capital need not be paid on the entire investment. When a property is very prosperous and stock could be sold above par, the right to subscribe at par is granted to the existing stockholders; and if they do not wish to exercise it themselves, they may sell it for a price, so that the new stockholder pays a premium representing the present worth of the future excess earnings, and the older investor puts this premium in his pocket. Similarly, when new issues of stocks or bonds are sold cheaper than the old, the device enables the company to offer the market rate to attract new capital, even though the property cannot earn this rate on the whole investment, and the older investors have perforce to be content with less. But for some such factor of elasticity, regulation would hardly be possible at all. The government would be forced to allow an exorbitant profit to the strong companies in order to let the weak ones secure the capital which is absolutely necessary to meet the growing demand for service. As it is, a company which is only earning 4 per cent may offer 6 per cent to new investors—at the expense of the older ones.

But this possibility has its dangers as well as its uses, for there is no guarantee that its use will be limited to cases in which justice requires that the older investors suffer in this way. An unjust and short-sighted government might conceivably fix rates so that even efficient companies would be forced to issue new securities far below par, the old investors accepting a corresponding shrinkage of their returns below a fair yield. Under such conditions a company would make as few capital expenditures as possible, and the service would suffer from slow starvation. In the long run, even new investors might become shy, fearing to be squeezed in their turn. But in the meantime much harm and injustice might have been done. Though there is a natural economic law limiting the power of the state to fix rates unreasonably low, it is not immediate or rigid in its action. For this reason, if for no other, it is probably not wise to allow unlimited liberty in the issuing of securities below par.

5. THE RIGHT TO GOOD FINANCING

Evidently the investor's right to a return is conditional, not only on reasonably economical construction and operation, but also on a reasonably sound and properly balanced capitalization. The public has a right to pay no more than the moderate yields which a good capitalization makes possible, and the companies and commissions have a duty to cooperate to this end. A good capitalization, moreover, is not merely one in which the volume of securities is limited to the investment actually put into the property, or to the valuation on which the regulated company is to be allowed a fair return. It is obviously desirable that capitalization should agree with valuation as closely as possible. But this consideration must give way at times to more important things, including a sound balance between stocks and bonds, and the necessity of leaving safe ways of financing open to companies whose stock, for whatever reason, will not sell at par.

6. HOLDING COMPANIES

Holding companies have long been criticized as a means whereby a relatively small amount of capital can control a large amount, and whereby capitalization is expanded and stockholder's equities (in the holding company) made thinner. These objections can be obviated if the holding company acquires substantially all the stocks of its sub-

sidiaries instead of a bare controlling interest, and if it does not issue
its own bonds on the basis of the common stocks it holds.

A more recent criticism is to the effect that this unduly easy method
leads to combinations which have no rhyme or reason geographically
or economically but are mainly means of financial expansion and of
escape from regulation. It is suspected that income is, in effect, diverted
from operating companies and placed beyond the control of regulating
commissions. In the field of electric power especially, holding companies render services to operating companies and receive payments
from them. Such payments should, of course, be subject to the same
sort of regulation as the charges the operating companies make to
consumers. These criticisms have led to the so-called "death-sen-
tence" provision of the Public Utility Holding Company Act of 1935
under which the Securities and Exchange Commission has ultimate
power to dissolve such companies. This is probably chiefly important as
a leverage to bring about voluntary reorganizations which may
eliminate the worst evils of the system.

REFERENCES FOR FURTHER READING

BARNES, I. R., *Cases on Public Utility Regulation* (rev. ed.), sections on Control of
Security Issues and Capitalization, and The Holding Company and Inter-
corporate Relations, 1934.

BERLE and MEANS, *The Modern Corporation and Private Property*, 1932.

BONBRIGHT and MEANS, *The Holding Company*, 1932.

CLARK, J. M., "Railroad Valuation as a Working Tool, *Jour. Polit. Econ.*, pp. 276–
282, April, 1920.

DEWING, *The Financial Policy of Corporations*.

DIXON, F. H., *Railroads and Government*, Chap. xx.

HEILMAN, "Control of Interstate Utility Capitalization by State Commissions,"
Jour. Polit. Econ., pp. 474–488, May, 1916.

———, "Development by Commissions of the Principles of Public Utility Capitalization," *Jour. Polit. Econ.*, pp. 888–909, November, 1915.

———, "Capitalization of Public Utility Consolidations," *Amer. Econ. Rev.*,
pp. 187–194, March, 1917.

JONES, ELIOT, *Principles of Railway Transportation*, Chaps. ii, xvi.

JONES, ELIOT, and VANDERBLUE, *Railroads: Cases and Selections*, Chaps. xix, xx,
xxii.

JONES and BIGHAM, *Principles of Public Utilities*, Chaps. xi, xii, 1931.

MILLER, *Railway Transportation*, Chaps. xi, xii, xxi.

RAILROAD SECURITIES COMMISSION, *Report*.

RIPLEY, *Railroads: Finance and Organization*, Chaps. i–iv, vii–ix, xx.

SHARFMAN, I. L., *The American Railroad Problem*, Chap. viii, Sec. 3.

———, *The Interstate Commerce Commission*, Part III, Chap. xiii.

TAYLOR, H., *Contemporary Problems in the United States*, Vol. II, Chap. xv, 1934.

VANDERBLUE and BURGESS, *Railroads: Rates, Service, Management*, Chap. xxiv.

WILSON, HERRING, and EUTSLER, *Public Utility Regulation*, Chaps. x, xi, 1938.

WOOD, *Modern Business Corporations*.

CHAPTER XVI

THE LEGAL AND ADMINISTRATIVE BACKGROUND OF PRICE CONTROL

1. INTRODUCTION

The powers and limitations under which control of prices is carried on are determined largely by the governmental background. This includes the police power of the state, the concept of a business affected with a public interest, the constitutional guarantees which set limits on the regulation of such businesses, the legal doctrine of fair value which determines the extent of the protection afforded by the constitutional guarantees, franchises, and the relative positions of legislatures, courts, and commissions, and of federal, state, and municipal governments. The police power, the concept of public interest, and the constitutional guarantees have already been discussed, and the doctrine of fair value will be taken up in a later chapter, but the other matters may be discussed briefly at this point.

2. FRANCHISES

One of the most important opportunities for regulation consists in the fact that local utilities must secure a franchise or permit to carry on their business and to use the public streets for the purpose. This instrument has its dangers, however, for a franchise is held to be a contract between the city and the company and gives the company property rights which the courts will protect. The Dartmouth College Case made it appear that such rights created by a corporate charter or a franchise were absolute property and could not be altered subsequently to the disadvantage of the company holding them. But this has been modified by later decisions, a recent Illinois case holding that a city cannot contract away the police power of the state to regulate rates and service.[1] Most franchises at the present time contain fairly adequate reservations and safeguards, but some anachronisms persist.

[1] See *State Public Commission ex. rel. Quincy Railway Co.* v. *City of Quincy*, 290 Ill. Rep. 360. In New York the power to raise rates depends on the time when the franchise was issued! If the franchise was granted after the passage of the

259

Franchises may be perpetual, or for a definite term, or indeterminate, with provision for termination on specified conditions. The perpetual franchise is an intolerable signing away of public rights, and such franchises are no longer granted. Even with regulatory powers reserved, terms may need to be altered or relations with a particular company may become so impossible that a change is imperatively needed.

The definite-term franchise presents a dilemma. If the term is longer than twenty or twenty-five years, it is open to the same objections as a perpetual franchise, in lesser degree. In recognition of this, the state constitution of Illinois, for instance, forbids the granting of franchises for more than twenty years. But a grant as short as twenty years acts as an obstacle to the free investment of capital, except during the first years of its term. Machinery may have a normal life of twenty years or more; buildings, wharves, and similar structures last far longer, so that the company's rights would end while it still had property with much unexpired usefulness, even if the plant were built once for all on receipt of the grant. But such a plant must grow continuously with the needs of a growing community, and it is hardly reasonable to expect millions to be invested under rights which have only ten years, or five, still to run.

This situation would be intolerable were it not that the relation between the city and the companies is based on something more stable than the grant itself, namely, their continuing mutual need of each other's cooperation. A large city cannot afford simply to order a company off the streets, and companies are willing to make some investments because of the knowledge that they will be allowed to use them, and that as long as they are so allowed, their constitutional guarantees continue to protect them against confiscatory regulation. But the more satisfactory plan is to make the grant correspond with the nature of the service. This means to make it continuous, but with provisions which make it possible to change the terms or substitute a different company or take the plant over into the hands of the public, leaving the company a right to such just compensation as will make them willing to invest capital in whatever amount the service may need at any time, even though the public might exercise its rights the next day. This is the principle of the indeterminate franchise or terminable permit, which is coming into use as a solution of this dilemma.

---

public-service commission law, any rates fixed therein are subject to control by the commission; also in certain other cases. The situation is decidedly confused. See John Bauer, "Control of Public Utility Rates in the State of New York," *Amer. Econ. Rev.*, p. 872, December, 1920.

Typical provisions of such franchises are that the grant may be terminated "for cause," or for cause provided by statute, and that the property may be purchased at any time for its fair value—presumably substantially equivalent to the value which is taken as the basis for regulating rates. Just cause for termination of grant should include violation of the terms of the permit, or persistent and incorrigible failure to provide reasonably adequate service. As for compensation, it seems probable that terms of compensation may be fixed by agreement which are different from, and more definite than, the judicial doctrine of fair value; and would be recognized by the courts as binding. It would seem highly desirable that the courts should uphold such agreed terms unless unforeseen conditions cause them to work intolerable hardship on one or the other of the parties. Not only have the preferences of the parties a right to be considered, but the theory of value is in such an unsettled state that there is great need of a chance to experiment with different principles of valuation and observe their results. And a thing which would be unjust if it came without warning may be perfectly just if it is known and agreed to in advance.

3. DIRECT LEGISLATIVE REGULATION

Legislatures are not equipped for the task of rate regulation.[1] Few, if any, of their members could acquire the specialized knowledge and experience necessary, and regulation requires a nonpartisan weighing of objective facts and a willingness to come to whatever conclusion the facts warrant, while legislators are too often elected on the basis of such promises of action as would commit them before they ever heard the evidence on a specific case. Rate matters must be acted upon with a promptness which cannot be secured by a body whose program is already so overloaded that important bills are rushed through in the closing days of a session with little consideration, after which the members go home to look after their fences and are not available for emergencies which may arise. The fact that the docket of the Interstate Commerce Commission is so crowded that its decisions are seriously delayed means, *a fortiori*, that a legislative body could not handle such business at all. Rates once fixed could hardly be revised, no matter what the need.

Direct legislative rate regulation is, in this country, limited for the most part to certain maximum rates for railroads, which are well above any of the rates now charged. The British Parliament has also

[1] An excellent demonstration of this is given by Professor L. D. White, "The Origin of Utility Commissions in Massachusetts," *Jour. Polit. Econ.*, XXIX (March, 1921), 177–197.

passed schedules of maximum rates, but active control has long been in the hands of a commission or special tribunal.

4. COURTS AS A RELIANCE IN REGULATION

It would be quite possible to pass laws setting up requirements such as are contained in typical modern public-utility acts and leave them to the courts for enforcement. Many commonwealths have for long periods relied on no other machinery, though now substantially all states have commissions. The shortcomings of courts in this rôle are only less great than those of legislatures. The cost of suits before a court is prohibitive to those who need the protection the most; hence some body is needed which will take the responsibility and bear the cost of a fair hearing and decision without throwing on the plaintiff the cost and delay of a court action, with fees to expensive attorneys. In short, the purely passive rôle of the court is not appropriate here, and a body is needed which can take a more active attitude.

The crowded docket of the courts is another difficulty, giving rise to a need for a body which can spend all its time in hearing this class of cases. Furthermore, a court, even more than a legislature, is unspecialized, hearing cases on all conceivable subjects, and getting its education in mechanics, industrial chemistry, psychiatry, or what not from the expert witnesses, whom the court cannot meet on equal terms. Not being overly credulous, it may take refuge in excess of caution. Hence arises the need for a body which shall specialize in these problems until they become expert in them, and expert not after the fashion of those trained in the service of the private interests, who necessarily (and honestly) take the private interests' point of view.

Other difficulties might be cited, but it is sufficiently evident that some different agency is needed wherever the problem of railroad and public-utility regulation arises on a large scale, involving numerous companies, considerable numbers of large cases requiring enormous records, and innumerable individual complaints not worth the cost of an expensive lawsuit. These needs have brought into being that great governmental innovation of the past sixty years, the regulating commission.

5. ADMINISTRATIVE COMMISSIONS

The commission is nominally an administrative body, charged with carrying into effect the law as passed by the legislature. In fact, the crucial economic features of the law are generally summed up in the one word "reasonable." In applying this term the commissions must give it whatever definiteness of meaning it possesses in reference o the characteristic modern issues. In practical effect, the commissions combine the legislative, executive, and judicial functions. Their great growth carries with it a very considerable departure from he theoretical separation of powers on which our republican form of government is supposedly founded. Were it not that the subject matter is strictly limited, that the legislature can always take back the power it has given, and that the courts hold the ultimate right of judicial review, there might be danger of replacing popular government by bureaucracy.

The Interstate Commerce Commission is at present our most respected and possibly our most powerful commission.[1] Established in 887, with little more than a shadow of power, it has steadily advanced until, since the act of 1920, it exercises power over substantially all phases of the business of interstate common carriage.[2] It forces accounts o be kept on a system which it has itself drawn up; it controls the issuance of new securities; and it is charged with bringing about the consolidation of the railroads of the country into a new alignment of systems. The courts accept the findings of the commission as final in matters of fact, if supported by evidence, and the reasonableness of a rate is held to be a matter of fact, at least up to the point where the issue of constitutionality is raised.

The commission has justified its enlarged dignity by hard and conscientious work, a high level of impartiality, and, on the whole, a considerable amount of statesmanlike wisdom. During the period of increasing prices from 1910 to our entrance into the war the commission, acting under a provision which placed the burden on the companies of justifying increased rates, failed to make its rate rulings anticipate the increasing costs of operation. As a result, earnings during this period were probably inadequate, as was inevitable in the circumstances. After the war the commission was, with good reason, cautious in feeling its way up to a level of rates sufficient to earn a fair return on the property, and before this goal was reached, the competition of motor transport grew so severe that no system of rates the railroads could fix would bring them the recognized fair return. Rates which would otherwise have been high enough to do so would, under these conditions, have diverted traffic to the motor carriers and so defeated the end in view.

This raised a new issue, for the commission, charged with fixing rates so as to earn as nearly as possible the fair return, undertook in

[1] Of the New Deal agencies, the agricultural administrator would seem to outrank it in present power, and the two great labor agencies have enormous potentialities, while the Federal Trade Commission is a close rival.

[2] For a more detailed discussion, see Chap. xviii, Sec. 4, following.

some cases to substitute its judgment for that of the carriers as to what level of rates would bring the largest net earnings. Proposed increases were denied or partly denied, and some experimental reductions in passenger fares were ordered in the hope of stimulating traffic. Whether the commission would have taken this position, if its whole background had not been that of protecting shippers against high rates, is a question which can hardly be answered. Some critics would take this particular power from the commission, leaving the companies to judge what rates will be most advantageous, where no rate will earn the legal "fair return."

It is hardly fair to point out, as some do, that we have here what is generally held to be the outstanding example of a fair and judicial commission, yet the industry it controls is prostrate. Wage conditions, motor competition, depression, and other circumstances, rather than merely the inherent tendencies of commission control, have combined to determine this result. In general, the commission's attitude has been fairer than most men would have dared to prophesy. That it should continue this high standard has become an absolute public necessity, so important are the powers with which it is now intrusted.

On the whole, the commissions seem to have been able to protect themselves from the pressure of political demagoguery, though in Illinois a commission was abolished and another created, with a different name, apparently for the one purpose of ordering a five-cent fare on the Chicago street-car lines at a time when five cents would not cover operating expenses. The Federal Trade Commission has roused more criticism than the Interstate Commerce commission on the score of partiality, though it must be said that the criticism has come from both sides. Its status of prosecutor of the public's case and umpire at the same time makes an impartial attitude difficult and illustrates the objection to the undue merging of powers. When to this is added the tendency to make the commission's findings of fact final, or final if supported by evidence ("fact" often covering the essential economic judgments), and when records of cases become so voluminous that evidence for almost anything can be found, possibilities of future trouble appear unless the impartial character of such commissions is vigilantly preserved.

6. CONCLUSION

Other legal questions of great interest and importance include the issue of state control *vs.* municipal home rule in municipal utilities and the division of power between state and federal governments in matters of nation-wide scope. But these and other issues raise problems of a political, rather than an economic, character, and we must pass on to the more strictly economic basis of regulation, namely, the nature and behavior of costs of production in regulated industries.

REFERENCES FOR FURTHER READING

BARKER, H. G., *Public-utility Rates*, Chap. i.

BARNES, I. R., *Cases on Public Utility Regulation* (rev. ed.), sections on The Public Utility Concept, and the Power to Regulate, Federal and State Jurisdiction, The Courts and Commissions, Certificates of Convenience and Necessity, 1934.

BAUER, JOHN, *Effective Regulation of Public Utilities*, Chaps. i, xiv.

BLACHLY, and OATMAN, *Administrative Legislation and Adjudication*, 1934.

DAGGETT, S., *Principles of Inland Transportation* (rev. ed.), Chaps. xix, xx, 1934.

DIXON, *Railroads and Government*, Chaps. xii, xviii.

HARTMAN, *Fair Value*, Chap. i.

JONES and BIGHAM, *Principles of Public Utilities*, Chaps. iv, xiii, 1931.

JONES and VANDERBLUE, *Railroads: Cases and Selections*, Chaps. xix–xxi.

LANDIS, J. M., *The Administrative Process*, 1938.

"Milk Distribution a Public Utility," *Survey*, February 24, 1917.

MILLER, *Railroad Transportation*, Chaps. xxviii–xxix.

ORTH, S. P., *Readings on the Relation of Government to Property and Industry*, Chaps. iv *d*, v.

SHARFMAN, I. L., *The Interstate Commerce Commission*, Part I, Chap. vii; Part II, Chap. x; Part III, Chap. xi; Part IV, Chaps. xvi–xviii.

TUGWELL, R. G., *The Economic Basis of Public Interest*, 1922.

VANDERBLUE and BURGESS, *Railroads: Rates, Service, Management*, Chaps. ii–v.

WHITE, "The Origin of Utility Commissions in Massachusetts," *Jour. Polit. Econ.*, pp. 177–197, March, 1921.

WILSON, HERRING, and EUTSLER, *Public Utility Regulation*, Chap. iii, 1938.

CHAPTER XVII

COSTS: THEIR BEHAVIOR AND SIGNIFICANCE FOR CONTROL

Outstanding accounting concepts, 266—Economies of increased output: short run, 268—Long-run economies of increased output, and natural monopoly, 270—Short-run expectations vs. long-run results, 271—Complementary products and the principle of joint cost, 271—Business fluctuations and costs, 272—Illustrative problems, 273—Conclusion, 276.

1. OUTSTANDING ACCOUNTING CONCEPTS

When the term "operating expenses" is used in connection with the problems of regulating prices, it is assumed to mean all those outlays which, together with taxes, have to be covered before the return on the investment begins. It refers to outlays for the operation of the business, not for additions to capital or other nonoperating purposes. It includes maintenance, sometimes depreciation, and all the actual work of turning out the product. In each department, for any given accounting period, it includes the book value of materials utilized during that period, and the wages of labor employed on account of the work of that period. In most cases, this means simply the wages paid and materials utilized during that period for work chargeable to operating expense, but under some systems of accounting a portion of the indirect costs may be carried over as a deferred charge from periods of less than average output, to be made up when output rises above the average. Many railroads charge an equal amount each month for maintenance of way, though the amount actually spent varies with the weather conditions of the different seasons.

One of the commonest indexes of the behavior of costs is the "operating ratio," or ratio of operating expenses to income from operation. Where the investment is no larger than the annual operating income, as with many typical manufacturing industries, the operating ratio can be well above 90 per cent and still leave enough to cover taxes and a liberal return on the investment. But where, as in the case of railroads before the war, the investment was not far from five times the annual gross earnings, it required some thirty cents out of every dollar of gross earnings to furnish 6 per cent for taxes and net income combined, so that the operating ratio could not rise much above 70 per cent without financial hardship to the roads.[1] The ratio has shown an upward trend during the history of the roads, due largely to an increasing volume of business done per dollar of investment. For Class 1 roads in the year 1924 it was 76.12 per cent. The future normal relation may lie between 70 and 75 per cent, if the roads can ever achieve a fair net income. At present, the ratio is close to 100 per cent, and many of the roads are bankrupt.

The operating ratio is of great significance from the standpoint of regulation. Where the investment is small, relative to gross earnings, and the normal operating ratio high, regulation might take away, let us say, one-third of the investor's net income without lowering prices materially to the consumer. Moreover, some unforeseen increase of unit costs or unfavorable change in commercial conditions might wipe out all the net earnings and turn them into a loss before the machinery of regulation could make the necessary correction in prices. Or if regulation should result in relaxing efficiency and so increasing costs, the loss, which the consumer would ultimately have to pay, might easily outweigh the gain from taking part of the investor's return. Hence even if earnings were unreasonably high, it might not pay the consumer to try to take away the excess by regulating prices downward.

Where the operating ratio is lower, the possible gain to the public is larger, relative to the possible loss, though even with railroads a reduction of net earnings from 6 per cent to 5 per cent would be neutralized by a 7 per cent increase in costs of operation. Thus regulation has the most favorable opportunity in industries with low operating ratios and large capital investment, and it is not a coincidence that these are the industries in which it is in regular use at present.[2]

In manufacturing cost-accounting systems, costs are classified into direct and indirect, the direct costs being those which are visibly devoted to particular units of output and can be charged to them on the spot. In public-service industries, few costs are direct in this sense, and this classification is of little use. Responsibility for outlays cannot be even approximately determined by this system of direct charging but must be worked out by subsequent analysis of the figures. In electric utilities, certain costs are governed primarily by output and

---

[1] In comparing railroads and manufacturing, it must be remembered that the railroads' gross earnings correspond to the "value added to materials" by manufacturing, rather than to the gross sales of the plant. Thus the large difference in typical operating ratios is partly apparent rather than real.

[2] See Ross, "The Case for Industrial Dualism," *Quart. Jour. Econ.*, XXXVIII (May, 1924), 384–396; also Kotany, "The Socialization of Industries," *Amer. Econ. Rev.*, Sup., pp. 127–139, March, 1924.

are classed as output expenses, while certain others, like billing and meter reading, are governed by the number of customers and are classed as consumer costs. Others are determined by the capacity of the plant and are known as capacity costs.[1] With railroads, costs are allocated on various bases between freight and passengers, or between state and interstate business, and certain percentages of the different main accounts are regarded by the experts as "constant," and the rest as "variable."

Actual cost accounting involves the allocation of all the indirect costs, currently, as they are incurred, in such a way as to furnish a cost figure for every item of product. Cost accounting in this sense is practically unknown in the field of public utilities. Under the Federal Coordinator of Transportation years of study were devoted to devising an approximation to such a system which might serve as a guide to the fixing of freight rates for different commodities and different hauls. The result is still tentative and experimental. It would measure approximate difference in costs occasioned on the average by a limited number of important traffic characteristics, such as less-than-carload loading, revenue tons per car, percentage of empty back haul, and distance hauled, all costs being allocated on the basis of one or another of these traffic characteristics. But many other factors affecting costs remain to be estimated outside the formula, as well as the important question how much of the costs are constant and how much variable.

2. ECONOMIES OF INCREASED OUTPUT—SHORT RUN

With a plant of a given size, temporary increases or decreases in volume of output cannot affect the interest on the fixed investment, which is thus a constant cost if it is regarded as a cost at all. Depreciation is also constant, as far as it is due to time and not to use, and it is usually reckoned at so much per year, that is, as a constant expense, whether it actually varies somewhat or not. Repairs and maintenance have certain constant elements due to weather; supervision and general office expenses vary little in the short run; and most of the main classes of expenses do not vary so much as output, at least up to a certain point, and this fact is sometimes expressed by saying that a certain portion of them is constant. As output increases, however, a point is reached at which the variable expenses begin to increase faster than output, owing to congestion and delays, overtime, night shifts, the taking on of green hands, increased spoilage of materials, or other

---

[1] See H. G. Barker, *Public-utility Rates*, Chap. iv, and elsewhere; also G. P. Watkins, *Electrical Rates*, Chaps. iii, iv, and elsewhere.

auses which vary from industry to industry. If this is carried still urther, the increase in these items may outweigh the economy due o the fact that the constant costs are becoming less per unit of product, and average cost per unit may begin to increase, or a point may be eached beyond which output cannot be pushed at any cost. Thus here is a rate of output which brings maximum efficiency for any plant, and we may, for lack of a better term, call this its "normal apacity." No business can work all its plants at this point all the time, ince output is necessarily changing, though some units, with capacity ess than the minimum output, may be kept working at their best rate and the fluctuations concentrated on the others. When a plant is vorking short of this point, increased business lowers average cost per unit, and the amount which it adds to costs is less than the average, Hence, if this output could be sold by itself at a special price, the price ould be set lower than any existing price, and lower than average ost, and still increase the profits of the company.

This is clearly not a permanent condition, but with modern industry it is chronic. One result is that such an industry can increase its rofits by discriminating, if thereby new business can be attracted vhich would not come at the prices already charged, and if the reductions can be confined, or largely confined, to the new business, so that he old business remains as profitable as before. But if this new business is taken away from competitors, they may retaliate, and the low rices may spread, perhaps to the whole market. Thus prices in general nay go to a level dictated by variable costs only, and no one may be ble to cover his constant costs. Yet no one can escape by refusing to ut prices, for he would merely lose business, and his constant costs vould go on in any case.[1] This is the condition known as "cutthroat ompetition," and it is a constant peril for industries with large constant costs. When businesses of large fixed capital were new, price vars of this sort were frequent and disastrous, but at present business appears to have built up a successful scheme of defense against them.[2] Discrimination remains a problem, however, both in the semicompetitive public utilities and in the natural monopolies where competition no longer exists.

[1] In strict accuracy it should be noted that the costs which would go on even f a plant shut down entirely are not exactly equal to what we may call the "constant component" of costs when the business is working, for instance, at 60 per ent of its full capacity and has a chance to increase this to 70 per cent. For most ractical purposes this discrepancy may probably be ignored, as the adjustments re only approximate in any case.

[2] See Eliot Jones, "Is Competition in Industry Ruinous?" *Quart. Jour. Econ.*. XXXVI (May, 1920), 473–519.

3. LONG-RUN ECONOMIES OF INCREASED OUTPUT, AND NATURAL MONOPOLY

A business usually adapts its capacity to its market, or its expecte market, with a view to being able to handle the "peak" withou permanent loss of business due to turning away customers, or withou incurring disfavor by failing to meet its reasonable obligation to th public. Where goods may be stored, or orders deferred, the peak doe not have to be served on the instant, as in the case of service-renderin industries. But in any case a general growth of business will call fc a larger plant. When the plant is enlarged, the costs which we hav previously classed as constant are increased along with the "variabl costs," and in some instances they may grow even faster.[1] Averag costs may be lowered, but for a different reason from that which go erned in the previous case. There are many mechanical reasons wh larger units are, up to a certain point, more efficient than smaller.

All industries gain efficiency in this way up to a certain size, bu in most cases the gains cease, or cease to be decisive, long before th one plant has absorbed the entire market. Combination of plants i one business organization ("horizontal combination") also bring opportunities for gain, but the opportunities are not always success fully taken advantage of, and these commonly cease to be decisive lon before the stage of monopoly is reached. Thus competition remair economically possible in most industries. But where the economies increased size remain decisive, up to the point of absorbing the entir market, the business becomes a "natural monopoly." Competition impossible or intolerably wasteful, and the public must secure to itse as much as it can of the advantages of large-scale efficiency (whic should properly be no one's permanent private property) by regulatio of prices and service.

The telephone is an interesting partial exception, since here cos increase faster than the size of the exchange, or group of exchange But it is still wasteful to have two companies serving one communit for obvious reasons. The service is not so good if one is connected wit only half of his fellow-subscribers, and if he obviates this by takin both services, cost and inconvenience are both increased. Railroac are another interesting instance. Terminals commonly reach the poir of maximum economy while the main line still has spare capacity, an main lines reach their best utilization while branches and feeders ar

---

[1] Thus larger electric generating units cost less per unit of power than small ones, but the economy in operating expenses is even greater. See P. M. Lincol *Proc. Amer. Inst. Elec. Eng.*, pp. 1937, 1942–1943, 1913.

still in the stage of markedly decreasing costs. While the largest systems have probably grown as large as the utmost attainable efficiency requires, still without absorbing all competitors for through and long-distance traffic, there is a limited natural monopoly of local traffic. To parallel every line would mean prohibitive inefficiency. If new lines are to be built, they should, where the terrain permits, be interspersed between existing lines in the territory between the main terminals and large sources of traffic, so as to give direct service to a new series of local points. Over the traffic of these points they will, of course, have a qualified monopoly.

4. SHORT-RUN EXPECTATIONS *VS.* LONG-RUN RESULTS

In the actual development of business, as of other things, the long-run consequences often come not so much as the result of far-sighted planning as from the cumulative effect of a series of things done from short-run motives. And even where there is long-range planning of facilities for future growth, as there must be in any reasonably well-managed public utility, the immediate policy of traffic development may not be consistent with the long-run facts but may be governed by the immediate fact that the plant has spare capacity and that added traffic will add nothing to the constant costs. This may lead to the making of rates, to develop traffic, which yield little toward the constant costs, at the same time that the management is incurring heavy interest charges and the necessity of maintenance, depreciation, and other costs in order to provide for the growth of business.

The situation is certainly confusing, since it may be only at rare times that the capacity of the plant is taxed, and yet any increase in business may make necessary a larger plant in order to insure the proper handling of the next expected peak. For instance, it seems probable that a deal of low-grade freight has been handled by American railways for less than it really costs the roads, because only the short-run variable cost was considered, and the necessity of added plant to carry the growing business was not taken into account, at least not by the particular traffic officials responsible for the reduced rates. The two grades of fact somehow failed to get correlated.

5. COMPLEMENTARY PRODUCTS AND THE PRINCIPLE OF JOINT COST

Another peculiarity of costs, which in some cases merges into the economy of utilizing unused capacity, arises from complementary products produced at joint cost. This is the case of by-products, or any products which can be produced more cheaply together than apart, the economy not depending on the mere increase in total output, but on having the various complementary products in the proper proportions. Eastbound and westbound freight are complementary in this way, but freight and passengers are not. Economy comes from having balanced amounts of eastbound and westbound tonnage, but it does not come from having to provide separate sets of terminals for freight and passengers and to handle trains of widely different speeds, whose schedules interfere with one another. If roads could specialize, handling only passengers or only freight, they would diminish costs; hence freight and passengers are not complementary.

The separate cost of producing one of a group of complementary products, if the others are already being produced, is very low; the cost of producing it alone is very high; and the price is naturally somewhere between these two levels, the exact level being governed by demand and not by cost. The entire joint process should yield enough to cover its total cost, and the price for each product should be fixed at such a point that the market takes them in the same proportions in which they can be most naturally and most economically produced, so that no materials or facilities are wasted, provided this can be done at a price which will cover the extra cost of working up each product, over and above the cost of the joint process.

To apply this to railroads, westbound freight rates, when empty cars are moving in that direction, should be whatever will fill the empties, if it is enough to cover the added cost of hauling them filled over hauling them empty. And additional eastbound tonnage is not worth taking unless it pays the cost of the double haul, for which it is really responsible. Of course, the natural geographical division of labor will not make itself over for the convenience of the railroads, and if bulky materials move from west to east and valuable manufactures from east to west, no freight-rate system will be potent enough to balance the tonnage. Attempts to do so might amount to cutthroat competition for westbound tonnage, which is naturally able to stand fairly high rates, and so sacrifice valuable revenues without accomplishing its object. Hence, while the roads make material concessions in rates where the policy may be of material help in balancing the tonnage, they make no attempt to follow the principle of joint cost to its logical conclusion.

6. BUSINESS FLUCTUATIONS AND COSTS

Business fluctuations result in the wastes of unused capacity and offer opportunity to increase output with existing equipment and at a corresponding reduction in costs, if only the fluctuations can be ironed out. They are of different kinds, short and long, predictable and unpredictable, inevitable, and capable of modification The electric utilities exhibit, for instance, regular daily and seasonal cycles which are quite predictable, and the daily ones, at least, are so short that violent discriminations in charges might be made between afternoon and evening hours without embarrassing the treasury of the company when dividend time came around, as it would be embarrassed if the same means were used to stimulate business to fill in a business depression. Some systems of charges actually involve charging different rates for different hours' use of the same current, but usually the same end is sought in more indirect ways. But all are based on the principle that off-peak business costs the company less than business which comes on the peak and should receive corresponding concessions in rates. Where the fluctuations are irregular and cannot be predicted, it is impossible to work out a systematic scheme of this sort. The street-car rush hour is an instance in which no leveling-out is possible or desirable, and if it were, no practicable change in the rates charged would furnish sufficient incentives to bring it about. The most practicable measure of mitigation is to have different industries distribute their opening and closing times over half an hour or more and so spread out the peak. Reductions of fares for off-peak hours would have no effect and would merely make a present to the shoppers at the expense of the clerks who wait on them. Where discriminations are made, they consist of reductions at the times when workmen are going to and from their work (which are peak times) and have nothing to do with the principle of joint cost.[1]

7. ILLUSTRATIVE PROBLEMS

One current problem involving to a high degree the principles we have been examining is that of the organization of the transportation system of the nation into a consistent whole, including highways, railways, waterways, and air routes, so as to secure the economy which comes from using each kind of instrument for the service for which it is best suited, and devoting to each the amount of funds which can be more useful there than anywhere else. This is, of course, bound up with the policy of charges laid—whether in the form of prices, fees, or taxes—on the users of each kind of service. One plan, long obsolete, was that of toll roads. This is open to fatal objections. Besides the unduly large expense of collection, the tolls prevent the full utilization of the roads, barring off traffic which cannot pay the toll, when most

---

[1] The writer has elsewhere gone into these matters in more detail (see *Economics of Overhead Costs*, Chaps. viii, xvi).

of this traffic would probably cause no appreciable damage and occasion no additional outlay on the roads but would be a clear gain, socially. Hence the proper policy is that of a free highway, supported by taxes. But we are having to revise this theory again since the great growth of a new kind of traffic, enormous in volume, destructive to all the former varieties of road construction, and demanding highways which cost nearly as much per mile as standard-gauge railways. The motor, furthermore, is competing with the railways (as well as cooperating by bringing them traffic), taking many kinds of short-haul freight, and making very serious inroads on the passenger business. Is this an economical shift, or is it due to the fact that the cost of motor traffic to the motorist does not measure the full cost to the community? How much should the motorist pay, and what is the best means of making him do it?

The socially economical charge on the motorist should, if possible, cover the same items as the railroad rate. This includes maintenance, depreciation, and interest on the highway, and some contribution toward the political functions of government, corresponding to the taxes paid by the railroads. The volume of automobile traffic is so vast that this burden would be no heavier a fraction of the total cost of motoring than are the corresponding items for rail traffic, and in all probability, considerably lighter.[1] The distribution of this burden presents a delicate problem. Responsibility for highway costs is joint, depending partly on number of vehicles, partly on weight, partly on character of tires, and partly on speed. Not all roads can be built to carry as heavy loads as are economical on some much-used routes. Should overloading be kept within bounds by a system of fees, or by direct regulation? Some control is essential to prevent the cost of highway traffic from being unduly swollen by premature wearing-out of roads.

A more familiar problem is the classification of freight on railways. To what extent should it be on the principle of "what the traffic will bear," and how far should it be governed by considerations of cost? If all lines were four-track lines, fully utilized, it would not pay to bid for any low-grade freight which could not be made to pay its full quota of constant costs, including interest on the plant. But most lines are not heavy-traffic lines, and the classification must be made for all the lines of a region as a whole. The natural result is a compromise, but the element of cost is far more fundamental, relative to the element

[1] The writer has elsewhere made an analysis of the two budgets on a common basis (see *Economics of Overhead Costs*, pp. 300 ff.). The figures are, of course, not up to date, but the present figures would more strongly support the conclusion here drawn.

of what the traffic will bear, than many observers suppose. Many of the low rates are also the sources of largest net earnings, as in the case of coal.

Coal offers another interesting problem, for it has been suggested that the railroads should make seasonal reductions in rates in order to stimulate the off-season movement and so use the plant more efficiently and make it possible to carry more coal with the present equipment. The question clearly hinges on a number of surrounding conditions. How responsive would the traffic be? This would depend on how many other agencies beside the railroads were taking measures and making concessions to the same end. Railroad rates alone would not afford sufficient incentive to produce any substantial result. What percentage increase in traffic might be expected, and how much would the roads lose on the traffic they already carry in the off season? Would the increase in off-season business be a net increase, or would it be merely a transfer from the present autumn peak? These are some of the data that would be needed for a satisfactory answer to the problem, and they suggest the character of the answer which would probably emerge.

Another interesting application of the theory of increasing economy on railroads was made in connection with the Plumb plan for public purchase and joint management with the employees. It was prophesied that rate reductions could be made self-sustaining through the economies resulting from the increased traffic which they would call forth, and reductions of 40 per cent were confidently predicted at a time when the rates in force were insufficient to yield anything approaching a customary fair return. Numerous questions arise here. What would be the response of traffic to a 40 per cent decrease in rates? What would be the long-run economy resulting from this growth of traffic? These are, of course, matters of conjecture, but some rough indications may be had.

A generally accepted formula counts as constant half the operating expenses and all the return on investment. This is, of course, only true in the short run and within the capacity of the existing plant, and the long-run economies would be far less than this formula would indicate. On the basis of this formula, traffic would need to be considerably more than doubled, without adding a car or a locomotive, let alone extra yard tracks, engine houses, stations, etc., in order to produce the predicted result. If we count the long-run constant costs as about one-third of the whole (a liberal estimate), a simple calculation will show that traffic could grow to an infinite amount and still not make possible a 40 per cent reduction of rates—an interesting conclusion.

Another interesting problem is that of "dumping" surplus goods in foreign markets or other insulated markets, at lower prices than those charged at home. Is this proof of monopoly, or is it merely a natural result of the attempt to use spare capacity and reduce costs by distributing the constant costs over a larger volume of output? The answer may possibly depend on whether the goods are dumped only at intervals, when a surplus exists, or continuously, being produced in large amounts for the low-price market. The second kind of dumping is much more likely to be a symptom of monopoly than the first. Of course, any dumping at all means that competition is not equally active in the two markets, but in the case of intermittent dumping of surpluses this may be due merely to the fact that the producers in the home market have developed defenses against cutthroat competition, such as are found in almost any "competitive" market, and may not signify any greater degree of monopoly than is implied in this practically universal condition.

8. CONCLUSION

The economies of increased output have one very important effect: they mitigate the tendency of a monopoly to raise prices and restrict output and increase the probability that it will follow a policy of large sales and relatively small profits per unit. It is even theoretically possible, though perhaps not probable, that a monopoly might, without regulation of its prices, charge less than competing producers would, making its monopoly profit entirely out of the savings of consolidation, in both the work of physical production and the wasteful outlays of competitive salesmanship. The public, of course, would not be wise to trust to this probability and cease all attempts to maintain competition, but there is much consolation in it for the possible ineffectiveness of many of our attempts at public control.

REFERENCES FOR FURTHER READING

BARKER, H. G., *Public-utility Rates*, Chap. iv.

BROWN, H. G., *Transportation Rates and Their Regulation*, Chap. i.

CLARK, J. M., *Economics of Overhead Costs*, Chaps. i–vi, xiii–xvi.

JONES, ELIOT, *Principles of Railway Transportation*, Chaps. iv, v.

KOTANY, "The Socialization of Industries," *Amer. Econ. Rev.*, Sup., pp. 127–147, March, 1924.

MOULTON, H. G., *Waterways versus Railways*.

PARMALEE, "The Separation of Railway Costs between Freight and Passengers," *Quart. Jour. Econ.*, pp. 346–362, February, 1920.

PUTNAM, "Joint Cost in the Packing Industry," *Jour. Polit. Econ.*, pp. 293–303, April, 1921.

RIPLEY, *Railroads: Rates and Regulation*, Chaps. ii, iii.

ROSS, E. A., "The Case for Industrial Dualism," *Quart. Jour. Econ.*, pp. 384–396, May, 1924.

VANDERBLUE and BURGESS, *Railroads: Rates, Service, Management*, Chap. vii.

WATKINS, G. P., *Electrical Rates*, Chaps. iii, iv.

CHAPTER XVIII

THE HISTORICAL BACKGROUND OF PRICE CONTROL

Origins of the modern movement, 277—The evolution of judicial protection to property, 1876–1898, 279—The practice of valuation, 281—Federal control of railroad rates, 281—State regulation, 287—Other phases of control, 288.

1. ORIGINS OF THE MODERN MOVEMENT

The modern phase of public control of prices began a decade after the Civil War. Between the medieval efforts at control and those of the present day intervened a period of individualism which swept away even the memory of the exact policies followed and lessons learned. At the same time, the Industrial Revolution so altered the organization of production that the experience of the earlier period would hardly be of much use to modern regulators, even if it were available. The new movement in this country began virtually with the "Granger laws" of the early seventies, marking the first serious attempt at state control of railroad rates. Massachusetts had a commission of the "advisory" type in 1869. Earlier limitations were imposed in the charters of the first railways, sometimes limiting the rate of net earnings or dividends, but more often fixing maximum rates and fares. One such limitation fixed 20 per cent as the maximum net earnings, and typical maximum freight rates were from six to eight cents per ton-mile.[1] While some of the earliest roads found these rates insufficient, the progress of the art soon reduced costs so far that rates fell below the legal maxima. The latter are chiefly of importance as asserting the right to control.

About 1870 the Middle West experienced a revulsion of feeling against the railroads. Up to this time there had been an eager scramble for rail facilities to help the settlement and development of the great frontier areas of the Mississippi basin. States and the Federal Government had granted enormous amounts of land; nation, states, and local communities had issued bonds; and countless individuals had subscribed to railroad securities for the sake of the service, together with the development and prosperity which they foresaw as a result. The

[1] Haney, *Congressional History of Railways in the United States to* 1850, pp. 210–215.

roads were built where traffic had yet to be developed, and they often
stimulated premature settlement which could not possibly prosper.
Farmers bought farm implements on credit but could not pay for them,
and freight rates furnished a visible explanation of their inability to
market their crops at a profit. Investors in railroad securities also lost
their money; towns were bankrupted;[1] and too often it was found that
the funds had been wasted or diverted into promoters' pockets, leaving
the properties struggling to sustain the burden of badly watered
capitalization. Towns which had paid for the benefits of a railroad
station did not always get even that, and if they did get it, were often
disappointed in the results unless they had a second railroad to give
them the benefits of competition. Otherwise they often saw freight
hauled past them to competitive junctions at lower rates than they
paid for a shorter haul, while mercantile business naturally gravitated
to the junction towns. Those who suffered from these discriminations
figured that, if the railroad could voluntarily make the low competitive
rates, these must be remunerative, and if so, the higher rates paid by
local shippers must be exorbitant. While this argument was based on
a failure to understand the principle of constant costs, there were
plenty of solid grounds for discontent.

Five years of overrapid expansion culminated in the panic of 1873,
after which it was five years more before a sudden and enormous increase in our exports of wheat and flour marked the emergence of the
Granger region from the worst of its tribulations. The New York
Central and the Pennsylvania had both secured through connections
to Chicago in 1869, and the same year witnessed a rate war in which
the Chicago-New York rates, formerly $1.88 first class and 82 cents
fourth class, reached for a short time the low level of 25 cents on all
classes. Grain rates fell from 60 cents in 1873 to 30 cents in 1875, and
fluctuated between 45 cents and 20 cents in two months of 1876.[2]
Average freight revenue per ton-mile fell from 1.92 cents in 1868 to
1.1 cents in 1882, and following years saw further reductions. Even
more than these low, if unstable, freight rates, improved harvesting
machinery helped to put the western farmer on his feet. But improvement required time, and meanwhile the middle seventies were a very
dark epoch indeed.

The Granger agitation of these years had the railroads for its chief
target and resulted in the establishment of a number of state commis-

[1] B. H. Meyer mentions the town of Watertown, Wisconsin, with 7,553 people
and a railroad debt of $750,000, or $100 per capita (*Bull.*, University of Wisconsin,
Vol. XII, p. 362, cited by Ripley, *Railroads: Rates and Regulation*, p. 37).

[2] See Ripley, *Railroads: Rates and Regulation*, p. 22.

ions, notably in Illinois, Iowa, Wisconsin, and Minnesota, and the
assage of legislation fixing maximum rates.[1] While the popular clamor
or lower freight rates took little account of the carriers' needs, the
aws were more discriminating, in that they struck an average between
he high local rates and the low competitive rates, on the theory that
he roads could make as much money as before by eliminating the
ifferentials. This, it appeared, the roads were unable to do, as long
s competition continued unchecked.

The resulting issues were fought through the courts in a series of
ases which have established the main outlines of the legal doctrines of
tate power and judicial review.

2. THE EVOLUTION OF JUDICIAL PROTECTION TO PROPERTY, 1876–1898

The Granger laws came before the Supreme Court in a series of
ight cases, decided in 1876, of which *Munn* v. *Illinois* is the leading
ne.[2] This case had to do with rates for the warehousing of grain, and
he court not only upheld the state's power to regulate but declined
o review the reasonableness of the rates fixed, holding that the remedy
or unreasonable regulation lay in the political machinery of govern-
ent, not in the courts. A minority opinion, however, upheld the need
f safeguarding property against confiscation. In 1884, in the Spring
alley Water Works case, the court gave the first hint of judicial
ntervention, and in 1886, in the Railroad Commission cases, it stated
hat the power to regulate "is not a power to destroy, and limitation
 not the equivalent of confiscation."[3] In 1888 it again expresses doubt
f its power to review state-made rates,[4] but in 1890, in the first
Iinnesota Rate cases, it definitely asserts the right to review the
easonableness of rates.[5] Again a minority opinion is heard, asserting
hat under the doctrine of the majority the courts would supplant the
ommissions as arbiters of reasonableness. Standards for the deter-

---

[1] Illinois in 1871 passed a law fixing maximum rates and forbidding discrimina-
ons, but in 1873 transferred rate-making power to a commission. Wisconsin and
wa passed maximum-rate laws in 1874 but abandoned mandatory control tem-
orarily in 1876 and 1878, respectively. In the decade following 1873 a number of
her states established commissions with broad powers, but Illinois was the only
ranger state to maintain this policy unbroken (see Miller, *Railway Transportation*,
. 708–709, 712–713).

[2] 94 U.S. 113 ff.

[3] 110 U.S. 347; 116 U.S. 307.

[4] *Dow* v. *Biedelman*, 125 U.S. 680.

[5] *Chicago Milwaukee & St. Paul Railway Co.* v. *Minnesota*, 134 U.S. 418, 456.

mination of reasonableness, however, are lacking from these earlier decisions.

In one of the Texas Railroad Commission cases, in 1894,[1] rough data were presented indicating original cost of $40,000,000, cost of reproduction of not less than $25,000,000, and capitalization of $25,000,000. Here the inadequacy of earnings (during the depression following the panic of 1893) was admitted, and the lower figures of investment were sufficient for the purpose in hand. In 1898 the famous case of *Smyth* v. *Ames* was decided, setting the mold to which valuation proceedings have had to conform ever since. The case concerned the Nebraska maximum-rate law, in which the legislature had fixed rates 29½ per cent lower than those previously in force. Assuming that these rates would reduce net earnings by this same percentage, and that the operating ratio on the intrastate freight business was not less than 10 per cent higher than that for the roads' entire traffic, the court found that the net revenue from the new rates was, for nearly all the roads, a minus quantity. It was suggested that the proper test was whether the new rates reduced the aggregate revenues of the roads below a proper figure, the intrastate freight receipts of the Burlington, for instance, being only one-twentieth of the aggregate revenues of the entire road. The court squarely rejected this, holding that the domestic business must be fairly remunerative by itself.[2]

The decision in this case did not require the choice of a definite method of valuing the property or investment of the carriers, but the court went on to state that the companies had a right to a fair return on the fair value of their property, which was being used for the public service, and to give a list of data which must be considered in determining this fair value. This statement has been given the force of a judicial precedent, though commonly this weight is not accorded to statements which are not necessary to the settlement of the case in hand, and though the pronouncement in question is not definite enough to constitute a rule which commissions may confidently follow. This matter will be taken up in a later chapter; for our present purpose it is sufficient to note that this marks the beginning of a period in which rate regulation is required to be based upon an estimate of the fair value of the property, and in which physical valuations play a central part in such policies of control.

[1] *Reagan* v. *Farmers' Loan and Trust Co.*, 154 U.S. 362; other cases, pp. 413, 418, 420.

[2] *Smyth* v. *Ames*, 169 U.S. 466. For an excellent summary of this case, see Smalley, *Railroad Rate Control*, Publications of the American Economic Association, 3d ser., No. 2, pp. 59–65, 1906.

3. THE PRACTICE OF VALUATION

Valuations of property for taxation and for condemnation are familiar enough, though systematic "physical valuations" of large plants did not begin until 1900, when Michigan took the lead in the field of tax valuations, utilizing Henry C. Adams' well-known theory of intangible values based upon earnings as an addition to the tangible values of the physical property. Sound enough for the purpose of taxation, this element of value has no place in rate regulation; but the appraisal of the tangibles, whose value for taxation is doubtful, has a great deal of meaning as an index of fair rates.

Still earlier, beginning in 1893, Texas made a pioneer valuation of its railroad properties, for the immediate purpose of controlling capitalization, and the Massachusetts anti-stock-watering law of 1894 placed on the railroad commission of that state the duty of determining the value underlying new security issues. These different purposes have so intermingled in valuation work that, as Ripley says, "Comparatively few states have attempted physical valuation solely in connection with rate regulation." In 1907 the railroad commission of Minnesota was ordered to make an inventory for use in the contest over its two-cent-fare law and commodity-rate law, passed in the same year. By this time the courts had established the practice of having a thorough canvass of facts made by a master in chancery, and these masters' reports constitute some of the pioneer valuations.

In 1913 the Interstate Commerce Commission, after repeatedly urging the need of a federal valuation of the railroads of the entire country, was charged with making one, in accord with the general terms of the "rule" of *Smyth* v. *Ames*.[1] The commission has made compromise valuations largely based on cost of reproduction (not at postwar prices) with deduction for depreciation, some allowance for intangibles, and occasional recognition of other special conditions, as when a slight stretching of the cost figures would just cover the amount of a bond issue.

4. FEDERAL CONTROL OF RAILROAD RATES

While the rate wars of the seventies and eighties brought such heavy reductions in the general level of charges that this was no longer a grievance of the first magnitude, the abuses of discrimination were, if anything, intensified. Open wars were so disastrous that roads took to secret devices for cutting rates, giving rebates to favored shippers

[1] The cost of the work up to 1925 was approximately $100,000,000, of which the companies bore the larger part. This amounts to one-half of 1 per cent on a total appraisal of not far from $20,000,000,000.

in the hope that these shippers would "scoop the business" and the road granting the rebate would benefit thereby. Pooling organizations had made considerable headway in eliminating direct competition in rates, and in removing the opportunity to profit by secret rate cutting. The Southern Railway and Steamship Association, under the able leadership of Albert Fink, was the most successful of these.[1] But a people bred in the theory of competition as the consumers' only adequate safeguard, and distrustful of their power to protect themselves through government regulation, were not ready to sanction this way out of the difficulty.

Accordingly, in 1887, after many proposals and much consideration, the Interstate Commerce Act was passed, requiring rates to be reasonable, forbidding all undue discriminations, and establishing the Interstate Commerce Commission as an enforcing and interpreting body. For sixteen years the commission was virtually on probation, its scanty powers defined so narrowly by the courts as to give it no chance to do serious harm to anyone, except the recipients of discriminatory favors. The prohibition of unreasonable rates, so the courts held, did not give the commission power to fix rates for the future. The long- and short-haul clause, forbidding a lower rate for a longer haul than for a shorter haul included within the longer, "under substantially similar circumstances and conditions," was held not to apply where the longer haul was competitive and the shorter haul was not. As this circumstance furnished almost the only reason the roads had for making such a discrimination, the clause was effectively put to sleep. In 1903 the Elkins Anti-rebate Act put more teeth in the law as regards personal discriminations, but the commission was still without general rate-making power.

The first great enlargement of the commission's powers came with the Hepburn Act of 1906, but the effects of this were not immediately felt, and it was not until 1910, after the passage of the Mann-Elkins Act, that the work of the commission had any serious effect in limiting the earnings of the carriers. This first period, from 1887 to 1910, may be defined as the period of "regulation of discriminations," and the net effect was probably to increase the earnings of the roads rather than to diminish them. Rebates and concessions from the published rates were not profitable for the roads as a whole, though under competition any single road would lose money to its rivals if it did not give these favors to shippers who were in a position to bargain with competing carriers for their business. And the roads were not sorry to have some body able to protect them from themselves and from each other.

[1] See Ripley, *Railroad Problems*, Chap. iv.

During the first ten years of this period, prices in general were falling, and railroad operating expenses and rates fell with them, while net earnings steadily increased. Ton-mile earnings fell from 19.9 mills in 1870 to 7.24 mills in 1899, after which they rose slightly, reaching 7.63 mills in 1909. After prices began to rise, the economies of increased traffic continued to cause a fall in railroad operating expenses, so that until 1910 the railroads continued to show increased earnings without material increase in rates. From 1911 to 1917 operating expenses approximately kept pace with traffic, and net earnings fluctuated, falling off from the high point which they reached in 1910, but rising in 1916 to the highest point they have reached. In this same year, ton-mile earnings reached their lowest point, 7.16 mills. This represents the turning point. From this time through the period of postwar prosperity, the economies of increased traffic were swallowed up by the increase in prices and wages, making increased rates imperative, while earnings, in spite of such increases as were allowed, fell off sharply.[1] This period from 1910 on, then, is the period of effective limitation of earnings and falls into four subperiods: that from 1910 to the establishment of federal operation on January 1, 1918; that of federal operation and guarantee of the earnings of the companies; the decade following the Transportation Act of 1920; and the subsequent crisis. It is only in the third subperiod that the full machinery of control has been in operation (including the federal valuation of the roads), under anything like normal conditions. Therefore our experience with genuine control of earnings has been very short and can only be regarded as experimental.

The full machinery of control is elaborate, many sided, and ponderous. The act of 1906 gave the commission full control of the accounts of the carriers, going so far as to forbid them to keep any records or memoranda other than those prescribed by the commission. Together with the subsequent act of 1910, it enlarged the jurisdiction of the commission to include express and sleeping-car companies, telegraph and telephone companies (as far as concerns their interstate business), pipe lines, and other outside organizations which play an essential part in transportation. The act of 1906 gave the commission the power to fix rates for the future on complaint, and to make general rate inquiries on its own initiative, while the act of 1910 completed

[1] This movement has been briefly analyzed by the author in his *Economics of Overhead Costs*, p. 261. The course of ton-mile earnings is shown in Miller, *Railway Transportation*, p. 629. Ton-mile earnings are only a rough measure of changes in rates, on account of variations in the proportion of high-grade and low-grade traffic.

this power by giving it the right to fix rates on the basis of its own investigations. It also resurrected the long- and short-haul clause, eliminating the qualification which had resulted in the emasculation of the original one of 1887.

But the most potent weapon contained in this act was the power to suspend increases of rates proposed by the carriers pending an inquiry in which the carriers were required to show positive reasons why the increases should be allowed. This made it necessary for the carriers to furnish evidence of the fair value of their properties—an essential fact which the commission had not sufficient power by itself to elicit. In placing the burden of proof on the carriers to justify any increase of rates, it did more than was generally realized, for the rise of the price level continued, with the result that increased nominal rates were necessary in order to make up for the shrinkage of the dollar in which the shipper paid them. Thus the roads had to sustain the burden of proving that they should not receive a continually shrinking amount of real value in exchange for their services. The element of time also worked against them, for relief continually ran behind the proved need for it, and necessarily so, under the conditions created by the law and the movement of prices, even with the best intentions on the part of the commission.[1]

In the emergency of the war it became abundantly evident that some more rapid and elastic method was needed of adjusting rates to costs, and one that could act in anticipation of possible future needs which could not, in the nature of the case, be demonstrated with the definiteness called for by the existing law. And the event proved that, even with such machinery at work, it might not have been practicable or desirable to increase rates as fast as costs increased. This was probably sufficient reason for temporarily guaranteeing the earnings of the roads, while another cause lay in the need for pooling equipment, routing of traffic by the short st or least congested routes, joint use of terminals, reduction of passenger service, and other policies which infringed on the competitive interests of particular carriers for the better service of the nation's needs. All of these factors made government operation necessary.[2] During this régime the commission was deprived

---

[1] See the 1911 rate-advance cases, 20 I.C.C.R. 243, 307; the 5 per cent case, of 1913, 31 I.C.C.R. 351; 32 I.C.C.R. 325; and the 15 per cent case of 1917, 45 I.C.C.R. 303. The commission showed a reasonable willingness to grant relief, as far as the need should be positively demonstrated, as the law required.

[2] For this subject, see Dixon, *Railroads and Government*, Chaps. viii–xiv; Sharfman, *The American Railroad Problem*, Chaps. iii–v; and Cunningham. *American Railroads*, Chaps. iii–xx.

of its power to suspend rate increases, and local committees of railroad and shipping interests were set up to deal with inequities resulting from the horizontal percentage method of increasing rates—the only method which could be put into effect instantly.[1]

In June, 1918, freight rates were increased 25 per cent, which, with changes in minimum weights and other rules, resulted in increasing many rates far more than this percentage. Passenger rates were raised to three cents per mile, with one-half cent additional for Pullman service. But increases in wages and other costs resulted in steadily dwindling net earnings until, during part of 1920, they were a minus quantity, and for the entire year, after paying taxes, the net operating income was three-tenths of a cent for every dollar of earnings.[2] The treasuries of the roads were saved by the federal guarantee of an amount equal to the average net operating income of the three years ending June 30, 1917; and the privilege of this guarantee was extended for six months after the resumption of private operation in March, 1920, in order to furnish a breathing spell in which rates might be brought to a paying basis.

This extension of the privilege of guarantee was one of the incidental features of the Transportation Act of 1920, which ushered in the present period, the period of comprehensive regulation. This act was a truly remarkable document, and its bulk and scope bear eloquent testimony to the way in which the task of regulation tends constantly to enlarge itself as more and more related problems are seen to be essential parts of the central task. The act set up a Railroad Labor Board for handling of wage disputes, gave the Interstate Commerce Commission full control of the issuance of securities, and required its consent for extensions and abandonments. The control of rates was for the first time placed under a definite legislative rule of rate making, backed by a federal valuation of the properties of the carriers and including specific recognition of the problem of the rich and poor roads.

Perhaps the most ambitious project contained in the act was the provision for consolidating the roads into systems which should maintain competition within each region of the country, preserve established

[1] Where the existing differentials between localities are customarily established in cents per hundred pounds, and commercial competition has adjusted itself to this relation, a horizontal percentage increase changes the differentials. Such a change may or may not be called for in any given case. If the percentage system is modified so as to preserve existing fixed differentials, this produces new inequalities, as compared to other places whose differentials are fixed on a percentage basis.

[2] Sidney L. Miller, *Railway Transportation*, Chap. xxii, 1924, has excellent tables and graphs of the course of earnings and expenses through this period.

routes and channels of commerce, and be of approximately equal strength. The purpose of this, as we have seen, was to take care of the weak roads by combining them with stronger ones, so that their financial needs might be met without the necessity of making rates so high as to yield an unduly large profit to the stronger companies. The Interstate Commerce Commission was required to prepare a plan of consolidations and to encourage and permit consolidations in harmony with this plan. However, no power to compel consolidations is as yet provided.

The attempts so far made have revealed great difficulties. Inequalities of earnings can at best be mitigated, not removed. And no system will willingly assume the burden of the larger weak roads. Even more serious, perhaps, is the danger of weakening the force of market competition and the freedom of traffic interchange at secondary centers, where some systems now terminate, by carrying all systems into a few great centers, already seriously congested.[1] In fact, the program of consolidation would have effects and raise problems which appear to outweigh in importance the original governing objective: that of diminishing inequalities of earning power between railroad systems. Changes of ownership would result in changed traffic routings and changed earning power. The most logical additions to round out a particular system into an effective unit are not likely to be just the ones best calculated to equalize its earning power with those of other systems; and of the two considerations, the former is likely to be the more important and has bulked large in the actual attempts to carry consolidations forward. This illustrates a frequent characteristic of measures of social control: the means adopted to solve one problem leading on to others which may ultimately dwarf the first.

Under this rule of rate making, rates were raised materially in 1920, but the depression of 1921 reduced both traffic and earnings and at the same time made it apparent that the business of the country would not, for the time being, bear rates high enough to yield the statutory return. In 1922 occurred the strange phenomenon of a reduction in rates of about 10 per cent although clearly the existing rates were not yielding a fair return. The carriers themselves admitted the need of a reduction, feeling that it would promote a recovery to normal business activity and thus would be to their advantage and minimize their losses, offering a lesser evil than higher rates and continued depression. The rule of rate making, however, made no provision for action on such grounds as this, and the commission justified its ruling

[1] See papers and discussion by Ripley, Daniels, Haney, and others, *Amer. Econ. Rev.*, Sup., March, 1924; also Splawn, *The Consolidation of Railroads.*

by the hope that the rates would prove sufficient, under normal conditions such as might be expected to prevail over a reasonable term of years in the future, to yield a fair return. This hope was not realized, though the reduction apparently served its immediate purpose of aiding the recovery of business and thus bringing the returns nearer to the fair level than they would otherwise have been.

During the greater and more obstinate depression of the thirties, the roads were too weak to make similar sacrifices again, while nothing they could have done would have sufficed to bring about a prompt recovery like the rebound from the depression of 1921. In this case, freight-rate increases were unavoidable. In passenger fares, increases appeared hopeless, owing to competition by both highway and air. Here the Interstate Commerce Commission tried the other tack and ordered the eastern roads to reduce passenger coach fares to two cents a mile in the hope of increasing rail travel. Part of this reduction has recently been restored, the rates being provisionally raised to two and one-half cents. Regulation has been divorced from the standard of fair return and is feeling its way in uncharted territory. In California and some other western states, interstate rail and truck rates are being revised with a view to making them "competitive" on an equal basis, the truck rates being raised. It is hoped that this may eliminate the cutthroat competition and bad labor conditions prevalent in trucking.

5. STATE REGULATION

In the meantime the states had been active in the control both of capitalization and of rates. Massachusetts had long maintained the policy of limiting the capitalization of public-service companies to their actual investment. Other states attempted to lock this door after the horse had been stolen: in other words, to bring the capitalization back to an investment basis after much watered stock had been issued. This policy, notably in the case of Texas, went so far that it was for some time impossible for companies in that state to raise new funds in the normal way, and the result was an increase of floating debt, the raising of funds by affiliated companies outside Texas, and a considerable limitation on railroad extensions which might otherwise have been made. On the whole, however, the control of capitalization has been salutary, protecting investors against many corporate abuses.

The states have also controlled classifications and rates for intrastate business. The recession from mandatory control following the Granger movement was only temporary; in 1885 Minnesota reverted to a policy of positive control, followed by Iowa in 1888, and Texas in 1891, and at present a majority of the states have commissions with power over rates of both railroads and public utilities, some of them including utilities owned by municipalities. Freight rates are rarely fixed by direct legislation, but in the decade following 1900 a wave of two-cent passenger-fare laws passed over the states, some of these laws remaining in effect long after interstate fares had been raised to three cents. In 1914, however, the Supreme Court, in the Shreveport cases, decided that when a state-made freight rate produced discrimination against interstate traffic, the power of the Federal Government over interstate commerce extended to the removal of the discrimination, even though this involved the setting aside of the state-made rate on intrastate business.[1] In case of conflict, then, the federal power is supreme. In this case the Texas commission had been using the Texas rail rates to produce a differential amounting to a protective tariff for Texas jobbing centers against competitors in other states.

By way of compensation for such conflicts the states have served as experiment stations, rendering a very real service. The lessons of experience are often obscure, but they do serve to set up danger signals marking the most unmistakable and costly errors, while successful policies may be copied with reasonable confidence that they contain no unsuspected or unintended jokers.

6. OTHER PHASES OF CONTROL

This meager sketch of the development of control necessarily omits many issues of large scope and importance. Among these are the political aspects of the struggle—the struggle of the utilities for the control of the state, as well as of the state for the control of the utilities, the changing aims and tactics of the companies in this field, and the far-reaching reaction of these highly specialized problems on the traditional mold of our republican form of government. Nor is there space to describe the great growth of the local public utilities, or the community's endlessly growing dependence on them, or the recent metamorphosis which promises to turn the burning of coal for power into an enormous interstate public utility through the system of "giant power," which appears to be in its infancy. The postwar crisis among the public utilities, especially street-car lines operating under a fixed five-cent fare, and the resulting experiments with plans of service at cost, and trend toward public ownership—all these must be taken for granted, as must the whole matter of control of service as to safety, quality, adequacy, and economy and efficiency of promo-

[1] *Houston East & West Texas Railway Co.* v. *United States* and *Texas & Pacific Railway* v. *United States*, 234 U.S. 342, 23 I.C.C.R. 31.

ion, construction, and operation. The outline here presented may erve as a background on which particular problems may be fitted nto their place in the general scheme and may be seen, not as problems solated in time and space, but as parts of a vastly interrelated movenent which is still going on and whose terminus no one can predict.

REFERENCES FOR FURTHER READING

BARNES, I. R., *Cases on Public Utility Regulation* (rev. ed.), Sec. 18, The Federal Power Commission, 1934.

CUNNINGHAM, *American Railroads.*

DAGGETT, S., *Principles of Inland Transportation* (rev. ed.), Chaps. v–x, xxix–xxxv, xxxix–xl, 1934.

DIXON, F. H., *Railroads and Government.*

HAMILTON, *Current Economic Problems*, Chap. vii c.

HANEY, *Congressional History of Railways in the United States.*

HUBBARD, J. B., *Current Economic Policies*, Chap. viii, 1934.

JONES, ELIOT, *Principles of Railway Transportation*, Chaps. iii, x–xiv, xxv–xxvi.

JONES and BIGHAM, *Principles of Public Utilities*, Chap. i, 1931.

OLDHAM, *A Plan for Railroad Consolidations.*

RIPLEY, *Railroads: Rates and Regulation*, Chaps. i, xiii–xx.

——, *Report to the Interstate Commerce Commission on Consolidation of Railroads.*

SHARFMAN, I. L., *The American Railroad Problem*, Chaps. ii, x–xii.

——, *The Interstate Commerce Commission*, Part I, Chaps. i–v.

SPLAWN, W. M. W., *The Consolidation of Railroads.*

TAYLOR, H., *Contemporary Problems in the United States*, Vol. II, Chaps. ix, xi, xii, 1934.

VANDERBLUE and BURGESS, *Railroads: Rates, Service, Management*, Chap. xxvii.

WILSON, HERRING, and EUTSLER, *Public Utility Regulation*, Chaps. iii, xii, 1938.

CHAPTER XIX

DETERMINATION OF COSTS AND EARNINGS

1. THE IMPORTANCE OF CORRECT INFORMATION

The importance of knowing the facts before undertaking so delicate a task as the regulation of prices needs no argument; nevertheless, it will be worth while to indicate the particular evils that arise from misinformation, and some of the questions of principle and method for which answers must somehow be found. Companies may have a definite interest either in understating or in overstating their earnings, and these interests are always in conflict with the interest of the public in correct reporting of the companies' standing, for the benefit both of investors and of the authorities charged with regulating prices.

A company still in the hands of the promoters, who wish to make a quick market for its stock in order to get rid of their holdings at a profit, may pay out part of its capital as dividends. This is likely to be done, not directly, as the promoter of a bogus scheme does, but through the more refined methods of postponing maintenance, neglecting proper depreciation charges, failing to write down the value of depreciated or doubtful assets, or other methods of understating costs or losses and correspondingly overstating earnings. Or the earnings may be alternately exaggerated and concealed, in order that insiders may make a profit in the stock market, speculating both for a rise and for a fall. Large expenditures may be charged to operating expenses when they are really additions to capital, or unnecessarily large amounts may be accumulated in reserves for depreciation or other contingencies. Thus expenses may be made to seem larger than they are, and earnings correspondingly smaller, and a "secret reserve" may be built up. The corporation income and excess-profits taxes afforded an added incentive to this kind of concealment.

With the regulated company, other incentives appear. The chief one is to conceal earnings, building up secret reserves which the company may later reveal—preferably without revealing their source—and demand to be allowed to make a fair return upon them. Or if earnings have been padded at the expense of the property, the attempt may be made to keep the shrinkage from being deducted from the valuation on which the company's returns are calculated. And where a given rate case has to do with only a part of the company's output, it is important to see that this class of services is charged with its fair proportion of the indirect expenses, and no more.

2. INTEREST: COST OR INCOME?

The question whether interest should be treated as cost or as earnings is a controversial one among accountants, and the answer makes a considerable difference to the technique of accounting; but the purposes of regulation can be served under either nomenclature. The traditional accounting procedure is to treat interest as earnings, and this is a natural and convenient course, from the standpoint of general accountancy, the dominant purpose of which is to show what the earnings have been and how much the company is free to divide without trenching on its capital. This is also convenient enough for most purposes of regulating the general level of rates and earnings, where the natural procedure is, first, to find what the earnings have been, and then to decide whether this amount constitutes a fair return.

On the other hand, for the purposes which govern cost accountancy, where it is a question of allocating burdens to different parts of the output and seeing that each pays its fair share, it is important to know how much of the capital investment each portion of the business is responsible for, so that each may pay all the burdens which are incurred on its account. Thus the "consumer costs" of an electric utility properly include interest on meters and service installations, while the "capacity costs" include most of the interest on the rest of the fixed plant. Business which increases the peak load should bear its share of the capacity costs, while off-peak business does not have to cover any fixed share of these items in order to be a source of gain to the company. In speaking of constant and variable costs, it is convenient to include these items of interest, though it is quite possible to take account of them separately, and speak of constant and variable operating expenses and constant and variable capital burdens.

The Federal Trade Commission, in its investigations of costs of production and profits, does not include interest as a cost, and the reasons appear sufficient and convincing for the purposes it has in view. Interest on bonds and other debts is of no significance for its purposes, since different companies with the same capital investment may have widely different proportions of funded debt, and their costs would thus vary for reasons which have nothing to do with the fairness of their prices or earnings. The whole capital investment is the important thing for this purpose, regardless of how it is raised. But the books do not show this on any uniform or accurate basis, and the commission has no valuation of general manufacturing and commercial properties by which to check the values as shown in the books. Hence it does not have the data necessary to a correct reckoning of interest as a cost.

Moreover, for the properties with which it deals, no fair rate of earnings on investment has been determined. The properties it has to do with are not public utilities, but supposedly competitive properties, and its study of earnings is only a part of the evidence bearing on the question whether some degree of monopoly power exists. If it charged interest at any given rate, its reports would carry the implication that any return above this rate was unfair: an evidence of monopoly. It is not in a position to make such a finding, at least not until it has considered a great many facts beyond its mere preliminary survey of costs and earnings. And in any case the courts have the final say in this matter. Hence the most appropriate thing is to keep clear of the question of valuation and fair return, leaving that for separate determination. After earnings are reported, it remains to consider whether, in view of all the other evidence, and of the special circumstances of the business, they afford evidence of undue control of the market.

Thus there need be no quarrel with the system which does not treat interest as a cost, even though one is firmly convinced that it represents one of the sacrifices of production in the economic sense, just as truly as wages. The chief thing is, in interpreting any findings, to be quite clear on which basis they are computed.

3. THE RELATION BETWEEN THE INCOME ACCOUNT AND THE BALANCE SHEET

One thing which must be kept in mind is the fact that everything that is done to the income account has its corresponding effect on the book value of the assets as shown in the balance sheet. This is well illustrated by one method of taking care of depreciation, which is simply to write down the appropriate amount as an expense. The result is that the net earnings appear that much smaller than they otherwise would, that much less is available for dividends than would otherwise be the case, and the company must keep that much more assets which do not appear as surplus. The assets are there, but they are balanced by a liability created in the shape of a "reserve for accrued depreciation." This may be added to the liability side of the balance sheet or subtracted from the asset side.

4. DEPRECIATION AND BOOK VALUE

Whenever operating expenses are inflated by charges which do not belong there, the natural result is to undervalue the capital, and vice versa, whenever an expense which is properly replacement is treated as an addition to capital, the property is overvalued. Thus accounting practices have a twofold effect. One of the most vexed phases of this fact concerns the "reserve for accrued depreciation." In a composite property like a railroad or any large public utility, parts of which are of different ages and which will never wear out all at once, like the one-horse shay, this reserve will never all be needed for actual replacements. For the actual cash requirements of replacing plant items as they wear out or become obsolete, some reserve is needed, but not the full amount resulting from the accounting practice described above. Furthermore, this accrued depreciation does not represent any falling-off in the physical efficiency of the plant. Hence it is argued that this represents an arbitrary accounting requirement rather than a necessity for the sound conduct of the industry, and that to deduct this amount of depreciation from the value of the property for purposes of finding the value on which the company has a right to a fair return is unjust to the owners.[1] The extreme form of this contention is that no depreciation should be charged because in a properly maintained plant the replacements come at a regular rate and the property does not depreciate.

Against this extreme position, serious objections arise. It may be that replacements ought to be made with sufficient regularity to make reserves unnecessary for the mere purpose of financing them, but that is no guarantee that this will be done. And even if the cash is found as needed, there is still the question of the correct reporting of the annual earnings and of the value of the property in view of the probability that there will be some years in which replacements are heavier and some in which they are lighter; some years (or series of years) in which deterioration is not being fully made good, and others in which it is being more than covered. Deterioration, in present technical efficiency, is not the decisive consideration, for an old machine may

[1] See esp. A. A. Young, "Depreciation and Rate Control," *Quart. Jour. Econ.*, XXVIII (August, 1914), 630. The opposite contention is well set forth by John Bauer, *Efficient Regulation of Public Utilities*, Chap. vii.

work as well as a new one and still have lost most of its value. It has little service life ahead of it and must soon be replaced. The working life of plant units grows shorter, and their value is reduced thereby, whether the loss is being made good by replacements or not. The earnings for the year are the earnings above the using up of values which has occurred, not the amount above the replacements which happen to have been made. The plan of trusting the company to carry out its replacements on an even schedule offers too much opportunity and temptation to ease the budget in a bad year by skimping on replacements that should be made, or to conceal the earnings of a very good year by unnecessarily large outlays on this account. The technical condition of the property might be too much governed by the financial fluctuations of the business, and the statement of earnings for a given year might mean relatively little.

These, then, are the two sides of the case, and the issues raised are by no means simple of solution. Clearly, there should be a depreciation account which should record the changes in the condition of the property from year to year and act as a check on the discretion of the management in the scheduling of replacements. It thus seems clear that the depreciation charges must take effect on the book value of the property, in such a way that if the units of one property are, on the average, two-thirds of the way to the scrap heap and those of another are only one-third worn out, the book value of the first property will show a larger deduction for accrued depreciation, sufficient to measure the greater worth which it actually possesses in view of the lighter replacement expenses which will be necessary in the coming years. This does not mean that the property with the older units may not be, at the present moment, in as good technical operating condition as the other, able to handle the same output at as low a cost. But this condition will not continue so long, and the worth of the plant lies in its whole capacity for future service, not in the service it will render in the present year alone.

But should the deduction be fully two-thirds of the difference between the cost of the units new and their scrap value in the one case, and one-third in the other, as it would be under the straight-line method of figuring depreciation? Or should we accept the contention that a property in average wearing condition is worth as much as when it is new? If the latter is the case, then it ought logically to follow that the plant whose units are only one-third worn out is worth more than a new plant. If this is the case, the extra value may come from two sources: the physical seasoning which a new plant goes through in its first few years, or the building up of business connec-

ons—which takes time and usually involves a period of low income—
nd all the other elements which go to make up the value of a "going
oncern" as over against the value of a mere physical plant, whose
usiness connections (which are necessary to its full usefulness in
rvice) are still to be built up. It makes a difference which of these
the source of the extra value, for the seasoning is a physical matter
nd expires with the physical units to which it is attached, while the
oing value attaches to the organization and continues through the
newing of the physical units.

It is not possible to give a final answer to this question here, but
ne conclusion is plainly indicated. If, by valuing a plant in average
earing condition with no deduction for accrued depreciation, an
llowance for going value is embodied in the physical value of the
lant, then a further separate allowance for going value in addition
the worth of the physical plant is a duplication, is illogical and
njust to the public. It would seem more satisfactory, if such an
llowance is to be made, to make it separately, in such a way that
will appear in its true light, and not to merge it in a purely
chnical appraisal.

The seriousness of this controversy is mitigated by one circum-
ance. Owing to the fact that some kinds of units are nearly perma-
ent, and also to the continuous growth of population and the demand
r the service of public utilities, the typical plant is, on the average,
onsiderably less than halfway to the scrap heap, a majority of its
nits being relatively new. For this reason it is possible, as the en-
neers say, to keep a plant in about "80 per cent condition." Thus the
epreciation would be roughly balanced by a 20 per cent allowance
r going value, such as has sometimes been made; and even if it is not
lly covered, any injustice which may occur is reduced to minor
roportions.

5. FURTHER ASPECTS OF DEPRECIATION

Current charges to depreciation are, at best, estimates of something
hich can never be known with perfect accuracy in advance of the
tual breakdown or retirement of the thing in question. They are
ased on an estimated life which may be twenty or twenty-five years
r heavy machinery and fifty years for buildings, or even more for
me kinds of heavy concrete work, though there is usually more than
little doubt whether any present structure will be wanted fifty years
om now, even if it remains physically serviceable. Where similar
nits are installed in considerable numbers, like freight cars, experience
akes it possible to predict approximately how their retirements will

be distributed, some succumbing in a few years, while others w
remain in service well beyond the standard time of retirement.

In view of these uncertainties the more conservative practice is
handle the account in such a way that, if any units are retired befo
the depreciation reserves on their account have accumulated the f
difference between book value and scrap value, the shortage shall
charged to retirements for that year. Other systems may be us
where large numbers of units are concerned, but the principle shou
be maintained that errors in fixing depreciation rates should be co
rected when the ultimate replacement has to be made, or soon afte

What would then be the effect of such errors? Under some circu
stances they might be virtually self-correcting. If depreciation we
grossly underestimated, there would be a postponing of expenses a
also an overvaluation of the property. Ultimately, the postpon
expenses would have to be met, but in a large composite plant th
might involve no more burdens than the depreciation charges wou
have amounted to in any case, and while they would be somewh
more irregular, the effect of this might not be serious.

If each unit of the plant turns out the same amount of produ
the total burden per unit of product, if depreciation is overstated, w
be slightly heavier at the start and slightly lighter afterward; while
depreciation is understated, it will be lighter at the start and heav
afterward, the variation being about twice as great in the latter ca
as in the former. Prudence is in favor of giving the benefit of the dou
to the system under which the burden grows lighter with time. T
implies resolving all doubts in favor of heavier depreciation charg
rather than lighter. This would help to ease the burden of any unfo
seen obsolescence that might occur. This fact has reconciled co
servative managements to the system of charging depreciation, sin
they then have less to lose if some invention unexpectedly render
large part of their plant obsolete. On the other hand, the busin
may be better able to bear these burdens in its maturer years, when
clientèle has grown larger. Apparently, wisdom in this matter is n
an affair of mathematical formulas.

6. COST OF MATERIALS FOR WHICH ALTERNATIVE USES ARE AVAILABLE

The question whether materials should be charged at cost or
market value is one which has figured in recent attempts to cont
prices, though not so much in relation to public-utility rates as in t
emergency regulation occasioned by the war. Should corn fed to da
cattle be reckoned at the cost of growing it, or at the prevailing mark

price? The same question applies to hides and other intermediate products of packing houses, when transferred to the by-product departments.

If all the prices of all the products were regulated so as to conform to their costs of production, the question would lose most of its significance. But if the market price of the intermediate products yields a substantial profit, an important issue is raised. Customary accounting would value the materials at cost, under the rule of "cost or market, whichever is lower," but if prices of milk are based on this accounting, the farmer may sacrifice the profit on his corn if he feeds it to his dairy herd and so may actually lose money on the dairy part of his business, in the sense of being poorer than he would be if he abandoned this branch of production. A balance must be preserved between the profitableness of different uses of the same resources, and if the demand for milk calls for the feeding of corn to dairy cattle, the producer should realize the same gain from this use of the corn as from any other.

One practical consideration entered in to modify the conclusion in this particular case, namely, the likelihood that corn would be used which was not up to market quality but could be fed on the farm with satisfactory results. Such corn should not be charged at market price, but it would be impossible to prevent it if any corn were allowed this privilege. And even on the principle of market value, corn on the farm would be worth less by the cost of getting it to market: something very difficult to ascertain, especially under the abnormal conditions of war and in the short time which the emergency allowed for preliminary investigation. Here, again, no perfect solution seems possible, and the result was bound to be of the nature of a compromise.

In public-utility regulation this issue would arise with reference to such things as coal mined by the company for its own use. Here it should be possible to determine a fair market price, with proper deductions for any savings in cost of transportation, and so prevent the abuse of the market-price principle. This would leave the company whatever profit on its coal-mining operations it would be able to get if the rest of its business were not regulated. If this were not done, it would have an incentive to sell its own coal in the open market and buy it back, or buy other coal for its own use, and so evade any attempt to absorb the profits of the mining activities under guise of regulating the price of its public-utility service. Something in this direction the company might endure, rather than break up its established arrangements, but within quite narrow limits. Most such coal properties are held by separate corporations, and the coal transferred at a price. Where this is the case, and where the companies are under the same control, the chief public interest is in seeing that the price is a fair one, and not a device for transferring profits from the regulated industry to its unregulated departments and so escaping regulation.

7. THE PROBLEM OF REINVESTED EARNINGS

The principles involved in the reinvestment of earnings may be illustrated by a simplified problem. Suppose a company, capitalized at $100,000, which has, during the ten years of its life, divided an average of 6 per cent on this capitalization, or $60,000 in ten years. The company is suspected of monopolistic tactics, and in its defense the dividends are cited, as evidence that the profits have been only moderate. To this it is replied that the company is overcapitalized—half its capitalization at the time of organization was water, and the stockholders have never been assessed to make good the shortage. The company admits that this is the case but claims that there is now no overcapitalization, because money spent on betterments and additions to the property has equaled the amount of the original water, while no further securities have been issued, so that the present capitalization represents actual investment. Admitting the facts as stated, what rate of return has the company been earning on its investment? Is it 6 per cent, or 12 per cent, or more?

The investment is now $100,000, but it clearly has not been this much throughout the whole of the ten years. Furthermore, the money spent for additions and betterments came from somewhere, the only possible sources being the issuance of new securities, assessments on existing securityholders, and earnings. Since it did not come from either of the first two sources, it must have come from the third. We may assume that, on investigation, the company is forced to admit this fact, and it is thereby established that the earnings have been $110,000 during the ten years, and not $60,000. If the additions and betterments were evenly distributed throughout the period, the investment was increased $5,000 each year, and the average amount was $75,000. Average earnings have then been $11,000 per year on an average investment of $75,000, or $14\frac{2}{3}$ per cent per year. An uneven distribution, either of earnings or of betterments, might modify this average, but for the purpose in hand we may ignore such irregularities as not affecting the principle of the case.[1]

This illustration makes it abundantly clear why it is of the utmost importance to have an accurate separation between replacements and

---

[1] For an early case illustrating this principle, the reader is referred to the briefs in the Standard Oil case of 1911, before the Supreme Court, where statements of income, constructed on this principle, were agreed to by both sides.

betterments, since betterments may be used to conceal earnings from the eye of the public. It is sometimes urged that betterments should not be regarded as the investment of the owners, being paid for out of the consumers' money, but should be treated as the investment of the public, on which the owners should not be allowed any return. On this point it seems certain that the courts would hold that the earnings, once allowed to the company, are their property to do with as they see fit, and that, if they choose to invest them in their own property rather than in some outside investments, they should not thereby lose what was theirs. As far as past methods of regulation go, this seems the only possible answer. But does it dispose of all the equities of the case, or settle the question for all possible methods of regulation for the future?

As to the equities, the company's hands are clean if they made plain what they were doing at the time they took earnings not needed by the stockholders and invested them in the business. Then, if the public allowed this to go on, they tacitly sanctioned it. But in the past such facts have, typically, not been laid before the public. The betterments have frequently been charged to operating expenses in the accounts, which means that the earnings out of which these betterments came were concealed. Thus the companies did not give the public the chance of deciding whether it would sanction these earnings, and some companies may have escaped regulation in this way. This affects the equities powerfully, though it may not be a sufficiently tangible consideration to alter the holding of the courts.

It has sometimes been proposed that the companies should be deliberately allowed earnings enough to pay the investors a sufficient cash return, and to provide for additions to the property besides. If this should be done, the equities would be clearly altered. This amounts to assessing the consumer for the upbuilding of the property, and the resulting increase should, if possible, be treated as his investment and not that of the companies. One difficulty with this is that the stockholders lose their incentive to leave earnings in the business voluntarily, and thus a desirable source of capital is discouraged. Making betterments out of earnings is, in itself, not culpable. It only becomes an evil when used to conceal the earnings and so escape proper regulation. Therefore, if such a plan were tried, the public's share in the investment should be limited to the amount of the extra rates, beyond a fair return to the investors, which the consumer has paid for this specific purpose, and any amounts which the owners leave in the business, out of their own fair returns, should be regarded as their own investment. The administration of any such plan presents obvious difficulties.

The earnings and the investment are the same in either case. Under one plan, part of the earnings might be regarded as belonging to the public, and as constituting its contribution to the property. But under neither plan should any part, of either earnings or investment, be ignored or concealed. This is the real evil to be guarded against.

The income statistics of American railroads present some interesting features in the light of this discussion. They show a remarkably persistent increase in rate of return through the period for which we have figures, down to 1917. Such an increase has undoubtedly taken place, but there is some reason to suspect that the statistics exaggerate it. The earlier rates of earnings were almost certainly larger than shown, on account of overcapitalization. Later, many roads built up their properties by charging betterments to operating expenses, making no secret of the practice. In this period it is quite possible that the actual earnings were larger than the figures show.

Another still more important question concerns the relation of all this to the fair rate of return. A fair return is, in the last analysis, whatever is necessary to attract capital. But investors will be satisfied with a smaller cash dividend if they know that part of their money is going to build up the property, and that this will bring them more income in the future. Property which is increasing in value, whether for this cause or any other, will sell for a higher price in proportion to its present cash yield than property which has no such prospect. If, then, this process of building up properties out of earnings were to be stopped, it would be found that the market demanded larger cash yields than would otherwise be required to attract capital with the same freedom. A rational choice of policy should take account of this differential. Under either policy, capital can be had for a lower rate of return than before the Great Depression. Commissions and courts should be prompt in adjusting their ideas of a fair return to take account of this, whether or not it proves to be a permanent change.

8. IS APPRECIATION INCOME?

This leads to another unsettled question, namely, whether increases of value which come, not in money earnings, but through revaluation of the existing property should be counted, for purposes of regulation, as part of the fair return to be received by the company. The outstanding instance is the appreciation in land values which goes to the company under the regular practice of valuing land at the present market value of similar or adjoining lands. If the company is allowed earnings on this value, then the granting of the increase has quite the same effect as an increase in physical plant. It is not present cash

nd cannot be divided at once, but it is a money benefit to the investors
hich has a present value and is an added inducement to them to
vest in this kind of property.

There are two logical ways of treating this, which have the same
ltimate effect. One is to count it as income.[1] This is not in accord
ith accounting practice and would be difficult to administer fairly,
specially as revaluations do not take place every year, so that the
icrement would not come in regularly. It is also difficult to predict
r the future. The fact that a company's land has doubled in market
alue in the past ten years is no proof that it will continue to appreciate
t the same rate in the two years or five years to come. If it does,
is not certain that the company will find it practicable to realize
t once the increased cash earnings to which this appreciation would
heoretically entitle it. The increased land value is ordinarily a symp-
m of a condition of the market which would make possible larger
ales and increased net earnings without increased rates, and the
icrement may be easily realized if it comes in this form. But other
ictors may counteract the economy of increased sales and make it
ecessary to raise rates if the company is to realize a money return on
he increment in land value, and this may be inexpedient, even if a
ommission would allow it.

Another policy is not to treat this appreciation as earnings, but to
ecognize it as an advantage accruing to the investor which makes it
nnecessary to allow him as large a cash return on that part of his in-
estment as would otherwise be necessary. Thus, in one of the early
ases, the Minnesota court held that $2\frac{1}{2}$ per cent was a fair return on
ertain city terminal lands which carried this prospect of appreciation,
s other investors in similar lands earned even less cash return.[2] Either
method will serve the ends of equity, and the second is probably pref-
rable as being more in line with orthodox accounting practice.

REFERENCES FOR FURTHER READING

DAMS, H. C. *American Railway Accounting.*
ARNES, I. R., *Cases on Public Utility Regulation* (rev. ed.), Sec. 5, "The Regula-
  tion of Accounts," 1934.
ONBRIGHT, J. C., *Valuation of Property,* Chaps. ii, vi, 1937.
LARK, J. M., *Economics of Overhead Costs,* Chaps. xiv, xx.
AVENPORT, H. J., "Farm Products and Cost Accounting," *Jour. Polit. Econ.,*
  pp. 354–361, May, 1919.

[1] Commissioner Maltbie took this position in *In Re Gas and Electric Rates of
e Queens Borough Gas and Electric Co.,* New York Public Service Commission
irst District, decided June 23, 1911.

[2] *Steenerson* v. *Great Northern Railway Co.,* 69 Minn. 353, 72 N.W. 713, esp.
18–719. Decided in 1897.

DUNCAN, C. S., "The Chicago Milk Inquiry," *Jour. Polit. Econ.*, pp. 321–34
    April, 1918.

FEDERAL COORDINATOR OF TRANSPORTATION, *Report on Cost Finding in Railw*
    Freight Service for Regulatory Purposes, 1936.

FEDERAL TRADE COMMISSION, Reports on *Newsprint Paper, Canned Foods, Co*
    War-time Costs and Profits, Southern-Pine Lumber Companies, Shoe and Leath
    Costs and Profits.

HOOPER, W. E., *Railroad Accounting.*

INTERSTATE COMMERCE COMMISSION, accounting bulletins; also *Annual Statist*
    of Railways.

JONES and BIGHAM, *Principles of Public Utilities*, Chap. x, 1931.

MILLER, *Railway Transportation*, Chap. xvii.

SALIERS (ed.), *Accountants' Handbook*, Secs. 5, 11, 13, 24.

VANDERBLUE and BURGESS, *Railroads: Rates, Service, Management*, Chap. xxvi.

WILSON, HERRING, and EUTSLER, *Public Utility Regulation*, Chaps. iv, viii, 1938.

YOUNG, A. A., "Depreciation and Rate Control," *Quart. Jour. Econ.*, pp. 630–66
    August, 1914.

CHAPTER XX

FAIR VALUE AND FAIR RETURN—THE
LEGAL DOCTRINE

1. THE FUNCTION AND POWERS OF THE COURTS

The courts have the ultimate authority to enforce upon public-service companies the obligation of adequate service at reasonable rates, but, as we have seen, their character is not well adapted to this task under present-day conditions, and it has been taken up by administrative commissions created by statute. The courts now assume a different function: that of interpreting the law and deciding whether the acts of commissions are in accord with it. This includes, of course, the Constitution, which is the supreme law; and the constitutionality of rate regulation hinges chiefly on the Fifth and Fourteenth Amendments. These provide, as the reader will recall, that private property shall not be taken for a public purpose without just compensation, and that no state shall deprive any person of life, liberty, or property without due process of law. The courts have held that extreme and unjust regulation may constitute a violation of these provisions.

In exercising the powers thus assumed, the courts are governed by the established doctrines of constitutional interpretation, one of which is that an act of legislature is to be deemed constitutional if it is reasonably possible so to interpret it. The general power of the legislature to control private actions in the common interest is to be given the benefit of that margin of discretion within which reasonable minds may differ. The legislatures, however, have spoken only in the most general terms, handing over the definite formation of policies to commissions, whose actions may not carry the same presumption of constitutionality. The courts have gone so far as to say that the reasonableness of a rate fixed by the Interstate Commerce Commission is a matter of fact and not of law, and that, under the law as it now stands, the holdings of the commission are final on such matters if its procedure has been legally

303

correct. This rule does not apply, however, to the question whether a rate is constitutional or not. This is a matter of law, which the courts must determine in the last resort.[1]

This distinction between reasonableness and constitutionality is logically doubtful, for reasons rooted in the underlying status of public-service industries. The very starting point of regulation is the principle that the property of the company is held, and its business liberties are exercised, subject to the obligation to render fair service to all at reasonable charges. Property being, as we have seen, a bundle of rights and liberties rather than a physical thing, the property of the public-utility owners is of a different sort from property in a purely private industry. It actually includes less, and therefore the constitutional guarantees which protect it against regulatory action are not protecting the same thing, for the public right to a certain kind of regulation is definitely reserved and qualifies the property rights of the owner.

The simplest way of looking at this seems to be that the property rights of the company cover the right to charge reasonable rates, but no more. If this is correct, then regulation begins to take property at precisely the point at which it forces rates below a reasonable level; above that point it is not a taking of property. In that case, confiscatory rates and unreasonably low rates are one and the same, the only practical difference consisting in the degree of certainty required for proof, and the question which party is to be given the benefit of the reasonable doubt that arises in matters involving discretion and judgment.

Another possible interpretation, leading to essentially the same conclusion, is that any regulation is a taking of property, but that the police power of the state includes the right to whatever taking may be inseparable from enforcing the public's right to reasonable rates; and a reduction of rates which sincerely attempts to carry out this purpose, guided by a rational weighing of the appropriate evidence of reasonableness, constitutes the due process required by the Constitution. Beyond this, the point is reached at which even the police power does not justify the taking of property without compensation. Here again constitutionality depends on (1) the reasonableness of the rates fixed, and (2) the degree of discretion to be permitted to the regulating body in judging such reasonableness.

---

[1] The distinction between reasonableness, a legislative question, and constitutionality, a judicial one, is made in *Smyth* v. *Ames*, 167 U.S. 466, that potent source of confusion in the theory of rate control (see also Vanderblue and Burgess, *Railroads: Rates—Service—Management*, pp. 51–52).

However that may be, the courts maintain the distinction between reasonableness, a legislative matter, and constitutionality, a judicial one, though the precise difference remains undefined. A court which thought 8 per cent on investment a fair return would probably sustain rates yielding 6 per cent and might possibly uphold lower rates if justified by special conditions, but it would almost certainly condemn rates yielding only 4 per cent as confiscatory. This simply means, if the foregoing theory is correct, that 4 per cent on investment is so clearly unreasonable, in the mind of the court, as to exceed the discretion properly allowable to the legislature and to overcome the presumption in favor of the constitutionality of any act of the legislative power. Unconstitutionality, on this theory, is simply a departure from reasonableness which is incontestably clear, and to the disadvantage of the private owner. This power of review was not assumed by the courts without disagreement and hesitation, as we have already seen in tracing the development of the doctrine.[1]

2. THE "RULE" OF VALUE IN SMYTH V. AMES

The legal doctrine in this matter has long been governed by the case of *Smyth* v. *Ames*, in which the court defined reasonable rates as rates yielding a fair return on the "fair value" of the property and enumerated a list of criteria which might be taken into consideration in determining fair value, though taking pains to state that other facts might also be considered. "And in order to ascertain that value, the original cost of construction, the amount expended in permanent improvements, the amount and market value of its bonds and stock, the present as compared with the original cost of construction, the probable earning capacity of the property under particular rates prescribed by statute, and the sum required to meet operating expenses, are all matters for consideration, and are to be given such weight as may be just and right in each case." The phraseology in which reproduction cost is referred to is significant, suggesting that this is—as it had been up to that time —a check on original cost rather than an independent standard of fair value. The background of this case, as of all the earlier ones, was the period of falling prices which lasted from 1873 to 1897. From then on, the character of the issue changed as the world entered on a period of steadily rising prices, culminating in the enormous increases resulting from the World War.

In framing a policy for the future, if our legal fetters permit such a thing, it will be well to remember that the future course of prices remains uncertain. This has a vital effect on the wisdom of the repro-

[1] See Chap. xviii, Sec. 2, preceding.

duction-cost standard of fair value. In the first period this standard was invoked by the public as a check on the inflated book values which accompanied overcapitalization, and on other extravagances embodied in the "original cost." In the second period it was taken up by the utilities, for the obvious reason that it gave them an increased valuation in harmony with the increase in price levels and the shrinking purchasing power of the dollar. In the third period its effect is conjectural, and this uncertainty is in itself a disadvantage to the utilities. Some which have suffered lean years would be content if they could earn a return on "prudent investment." These facts appear to be weakening the companies' opposition to the prudent-investment standard.

The formula quoted above, with its bare list of heterogeneous elements, and with all the uncertainty as to the intended relation of these elements to the appraisal of the property, appears in the original case of *Smyth* v. *Ames* to have been only a dictum.[1] But it has been accepted as a "rule" of fair value by persons predisposed to seek and find a rule whether one exists or not. Its effect is to leave the basis in doubt between original cost, with subsequent additions, and cost of reproduction, for the other data suggested are of incidental character. The rule has also been construed as requiring commissions to make an estimate of reproduction cost as well as of original cost, and to give them both genuine consideration. While this process of weighing is not one of mere averaging, and the court avoids indicating what weight should be given each element, still if it becomes apparent that one element was given no weight at all, there arises a presumption that the rule of the court laying down due process of law has not been followed.[2] The position in which this places any rate-making commission is a very difficult and ambiguous one.

3. THE DEVELOPMENT OF THE REPRODUCTION-COST HYPOTHESIS

The development of the conception of reproduction cost has gone through two main phases. The first was the elaboration of hypothetical conditions under which the imaginary reconstruction of the property was to be carried out. This was done largely by engineers and from the

[1] Only reasoning essential to deciding the case in hand has the force of precedent. Other parts of judicial opinions, while indicative of the court's attitude, have not the force of law. Cf. above, p. 280.

[2] See *St. Louis and O'Fallon Ry.* v. *U.S.*, 279 U.S. 461, 487 (1929). In this, the initial ruling on the Interstate Commerce Commission's valuations under the Valuation Act of 1913, the court held that not enough weight had been given to reproduction cost.

utility standpoint. The assumption appeared to be that reproduction cost was an independent standard of value, and not a mere check on particular abuses of original cost, and the logic was that of discovering what it would cost literally to reproduce the properties, rather than the logic of a search for evidence bearing on the just return to be allowed to owners who would never have any actual occasion to reproduce their properties. The second phase came with the settling of particular issues involved in this hypothesis, and the result was to eliminate many elements suggested by literal logic but having no proper relation to the task in hand, and to recast the concept in a form more suitable to its original character of a check on actual cost. It has gone far toward becoming an estimate of what original cost might reasonably have been, with allowance for subsequent changes in prices and unit costs of construction. The prices used are typically not those of a single year, but an average covering a sufficient term of years to have some claim to be considered normal.

The utility engineer typically assumes the rebuilding of the existing plant rather than an equally efficient substitute. This does not mean installing generators of a type no longer made, or ties of a wood no longer available:[1] in such cases he will use substitutes of a kind that is now to be had. But it does mean that he will not question the location and general arrangement of the plant and the number, capacity, and general character of its units. The cost of an equally efficient substitute plant has at times been considered by commissions, and a federal court has held that this may be considered but cannot be a controlling feature of a valuation.[2] This latter standard is, of course, more conjectural than the cost of reproducing the existing plant, though some conjecture is involved in either case. If we are seeking evidence of value, as it is found in other industries, the cost of the modern substitute plant may often govern the present worth of an older competing plant, which might be less than that of the modern substitute in proportion as its operating costs were higher or its service inferior. But the cost of reproducing the identical plant has no economic meaning at all in the field of general industry, unless it happens to be the "representative" plant whose cost governs competitive price.

This suggests the question What is the logical relation of cost of reproduction to fair rates for public utilities? Three hypotheses suggest themselves: One is that it is the best index of the normal value

[1] Texas Midland Valuation case, where treated pine timbers were substituted for the now unavailable *bois d'arc*, Vol. I, Ref. 1, p. 43, cited by Vanderblue, *Railroad Valuation*, p. 15, 1920.

[2] See *Spring Valley Water Co.* v. *San Francisco*, 165 Fed. 667 (1908); cf. also *Capital City Gaslight Co.* v. *City of Des Moines*, 72 Fed. 829 (1896).

of plants in competitive and unregulated industries, and that it is the business of regulation to give the consumer the benefits he would enjoy under competition. Another is that the plant furnishes a service which, if it were not there, the public would now have to furnish or pay someone else for furnishing; and that the worth of this to the public is what it would cost to replace the service, either if the existing plant were destroyed, or if it should go out of service and a substitute should have to be built. The chief difference between these two variants of the second assumption lies in the implications regarding the value of the land used, where that is uniquely adapted to the service it renders. The third assumption is simply that the return of the owners should vary with changes in the price level.

The first assumption is logical but is not the only logical assumption on which to base regulation and therefore should not be set up as a rigid standard in an issue of confiscation, where the legislature is to be given the benefit of choice between all possible reasonable methods, and the court should prohibit only what is clearly outside the bounds of reason. This assumption, as we have seen, is more likely to justify using the cost of a modern substitute plant, with possible deductions, than that of the identical plant now in use.

The second assumption does not correspond to the obligations the company has assumed, or to the common sense of the situation which would be created if the company should withdraw from service. It would then lose its rights to operate, and the value of its plant to the owners would be reduced to scrap value. To the public, the worth of the plant itself would be the cost of an equally efficient modern substitute, but the worth of the land, if uniquely adapted to its present use, could not be rationally determined under this hypothesis.

The third assumption, that of giving the investor an equivalent for changes in the price level, does not call for reproduction cost at all, but rather for original cost or prudent investment, multiplied by an index of price changes. There seems no reason why this should be confined to the changes in the cost of constructing this particular kind of equipment, for the investor is not going to spend his income for these things, and an index of general prices will serve his interests better. And it applies logically to the stockholder's equity, not the whole plant. This might give a value which would be fair to the investor and, while foreign to the usual modes of approach to fair value, cannot be said to be wholly without reason.

The issues may appear more clearly if, in the light of this general introduction, we examine some of the specific items claimed as elements of value under the reproduction-cost hypothesis. One of these was an allowance for paving over mains, where the mains had been laid before the streets were paved. On the subsequent paving of the streets by the city, the cost of cutting and relaying the pavement becomes a literal part of the imaginary reconstruction of the property. The claim is utterly logical, granting the assumptions. The only flaw is that these assumptions have nothing to do with the finding of a reasonable reward for the rendering of the service. They calmly put upon the public the burden of an order of procedure in building streets which is reprehensibly wasteful and one which no administration in its senses would follow or allow to be followed. And even if it were a fairly frequent practice to pave the streets first, there is no sufficient reason why a community which is able to arrange for the more efficient method of installation should pay the cost of the less efficient one, while the company pockets the difference. This claim has no easily discernible competitive analogy and cannot be defended on the score of the forces which govern normal competitive values. And it has, quite properly, been disallowed, in spite of the fact that it is an element in the literal process of imaginary reconstruction.

Another claim arises in valuing land. According to the hypothesis advocated by the utilities, the company reconstructing the plant has to acquire land by condemnation, paying the present market value of surrounding lands, together with consequential damages and other costs of condemnation, bringing the total up to several times the market value of the surrounding lands. Justice Hughes rejected this claim, as far as railroads are concerned, in the Minnesota Rate Case, pointing out that the surrounding lands have their value because the railroad is there, and criticizing the whole process of imagining the road gone and then paying for the lands at the value the road's presence gives them, plus multiples for damages to values which would never exist if the road were destroyed. This, he said, is "mere conjecture" as to matters "wholly beyond the reach of any process of rational determination."[1] The court was willing, in this case, to appraise land at the market value of adjoining land, as a way of giving the companies a share in the increased values they had caused, but not, apparently, because the reproduction hypothesis logically required it.

This whole difficulty is thrown into relief by the further question whether allowance should be made for the cost of buildings which might be supposed to occupy the land. This has not been done, even though buildings had to be wrecked in the original construction.[2] This

[1] Second Minnesota Rate Case (*Simpson* v. *Shepard*) 223 U.S. 349.

[2] See Whitten, *Valuation*, pp. 141–143. The claim was made in re Metropolitan Street Railway Reorganization 3, P.S.C. (New York), 1st Dist., decided February

outlay is typically less than the subsequent increase in the value of the land itself, and certainly the exact buildings which were wrecked when a railroad was built forty years ago or more have no logical relation to the present cost of reproduction. If hypothetical present buildings are to be considered, we would have such absurdities to deal with as the cost of acquiring and wrecking a hypothetical fifteen-story hotel, hypothetically built for the purpose on the site actually occupied by a one-story car-barn in the heart of New York City.

This extreme case involves two principles. First, the public has a right to a reasonably efficient use of land and economical choice of sites; and where this calls for moving a plant to a cheaper site or building large office buildings above the space used for railroad-terminal purposes, the company should be required to do it and the public should be charged with only that part of the cost of the double structure properly allocated to the railroad use. The company might reasonably be penalized in its valuation for perpetuating such anachronisms, certainly not rewarded by a valuation greater than they would have if they made the change. The cost of reproducing anachronisms has no relation to present value on any rational basis. Second, in less extreme cases the objection raised by Justice Hughes still applies, as well as the general principle of the case of paving over mains. The only economical—the only conceivable—way of developing the most valuable uses of land is to install *first* the necessary public utilities. The extreme reproduction hypothesis burdens the public with the cost of an inconceivably wasteful order of construction and allows the company to pocket the difference between this and the order actually followed. Where it is inconceivable that the public should wait until the present for the first building of its utility property, present reproduction in itself violates the rule that the public has a right to reasonable economy of construction, and logical consistency in following that hypothesis cannot make the result reasonable for the purpose in hand.

The logical difficulties of the hypothesis are further illustrated by the question whether trees, embankments, streams, quicksands, and other such conditions should be imagined as they were when the property was actually built, or as they are now. Mr. Alvord argues for original conditions, and Whitten considers them more equitable,[1]

27, 1912. Here the company presented no data as to buildings actually torn down at the time of construction. The Interstate Commerce Commission's reproduction hypothesis assumes the land vacant (see Vanderblue, *Railroad Valuation*, p. 12, 1920.

[1] Alvord, in *Trans. Amer. Soc. Civil Eng.*, LXXIII (1911), 388; Whitten,

while the Interstate Commerce Commission has used present conditions in its valuation work, the result being favorable to the companies in some cases and unfavorable in others, and the net balance unfavorable in the opinion of Professor Vanderblue.[1] The rule of original conditions would eliminate paving over mains and hypothetical buildings, but it would include an allowance for the added cost due to piecemeal construction. Reproduction under present man-made conditions is often difficult to imagine, but it is a still greater strain on the imagination to conceive a railroad cutting its way through virgin forests, the land under which is worth the price of highly developed farm land, into a large terminal city which is only there to serve the people who are living where the virgin forests are supposed to be, and where the road must pay the high prices for land to which the actual dense settlement gives rise. This gives the company the benefit, at the public's expense, of two kinds of difficulty, one of which an actual road might have to meet, but never both, since they could not possibly occur together. One excludes the other.

Other difficulties, also, are illustrated by the Interstate Commerce Commission's reproduction hypothesis. The company must organize, secure a charter, and make surveys, but the land it finally selects is miraculously vacant and the surveys do not involve "suppositious groping around the country." The road is then built with the aid of all the existing means of transport except the road under consideration, so that construction may begin in several places, whereas the original line was necessarily built from one end, and the time of the work may be shortened. Here a purely arbitrary element enters in, for, "Had the Texas Midland been absorbed, say, by the St. Louis Southwestern, the latter road would not, as now, be available to haul men and materials."[2]

But the road built after all the other lines were in place would be burdened as well as benefited, for the younger line has commonly to pay the whole cost occasioned by crossings, though this may take the shape of a bridge for the other line's tracks to cross over. Then, if each road were successively assumed to be the youngest one, all these costs would be counted twice in the aggregate valuation of an entire district. The commission has avoided this by departing from the strict

---

Valuation, pp. 77–81. Alvord uses this to justify inclusion of costs of clearing, excavating, etc., which might not have to be done if construction had waited till the present. Whitten's approval is to be construed in the light of his preference for actual cost over any kind of reproduction-cost hypothesis.

[1] Vanderblue, *Railroad Valuation*, pp. 17–18, 1920.

[2] *Ibid.*, p. 13.

reproduction hypothesis and charging the bridge to the line which uses it.[1]

Many other points might be considered, but these will serve to indicate the inextricable tangles into which the logic of reproduction cost unavoidably falls when applied to natural monopolies. It would seem clear that the useful thing to do is not to make a complete and literal appraisal on this basis and then try to decide what weight the result as a whole should have in determining fair value, but rather, on the basis of present experience with the issues raised, to decide what features of reproduction cost have a bearing on fair value, and not to waste time and money in canvassing other features. This would be more in character with the mental picture which must have been in the minds of the members of the Supreme Court when it laid down the rule of *Smyth* v. *Ames*. They could not have foreseen all the irrelevant intricacies which the reproduction hypothesis later developed but had in mind certain general features which seemed to have some claim to relevance.

4. ORIGINAL COST PLUS ADDITIONS

The relevance of original cost is plain; it is the thing the investor invested and for which he expects a return. Additions are, under fair conditions, simply further acts of investment by the owners.[2] The chief objections urged against this standard have been the inclusion of wasteful expenditures and the difficulty or impossibility of discovering what the actual expenditures have been. The first is met in principle by adopting the rule of prudent investment. The second can be overcome with far less resort to doubtful estimating than characterizes the reproduction-cost standard. Added to this is the fact that the amount, once determined or estimated, can be kept up to date by the regular operation of correct accounting. The estimating does not have to be repeated with every rate case.

Original cost may be difficult to discover because the records are inaccurate. When a company waters its stock, it is forced also to make a book showing of assets to balance the inflated volume of securities, and this is very likely to mean the inflation of the book cost of plant and equipment, making the figures worthless and an independent canvass necessary. Or the records may be lost, especially if the property has been transferred and the original company has gone out of business. But the seriousness of this is mitigated by the fact that property which has been retired need no longer be considered. In most

---

[1] Vanderblue, *Railroad Valuation*, pp. 18–19, 1920.

[2] See Chap. xix, Sec. 7, preceding.

cases its book value is represented by an equivalent amount of the cost of the new property with which it was replaced. The company has a right to a return only on property now used and useful in the public service. Under ideal accounting conditions the original cost plus additions would be identical with the actual cost of the property now in existence. When special methods of accounting are followed which give rise to a discrepancy between these two figures, it is quite logical to hold that actual cost of present property is the true measure of original cost plus additions, and that if the books' measure does not agree with this, then it is the books that are incorrect.[1] Whatever the answer to this may be, actual cost of present property is a far better index of what is wanted than can be had for any of the quantities on which the cost of reproduction hinges and involves far less speculation, even where it has to be estimated.

Abandoned property is not included, except as special dispensation may be granted to meet the equities of a special case. But some parts of the property may have disappeared, like filling poured into a quicksand, so that an inventory would not now reveal them; hence an inventory should always be supplemented by a history of the property, as far as it is to be had.

5. INTANGIBLES

An estimate of original cost may also include intangibles. These include organization expenses and might include the whole cost of establishing the business as a going concern. In principle, advertising employed to build up good-will, beyond the amount necessary each year to maintain what has been built up, might be regarded as a capital charge: an investment in intangibles. But the slippery nature of the resulting assets argues extreme caution in any such allowance, even to the point of refusing to admit it at all. The Wisconsin Commission has included under this head the deficits incurred during the developmental period, as a cost of establishing the business as a going concern. While this has not been allowed by the Supreme Court as an element of value, it is clearly something any new company faces and for which a prospect of compensation is required, whether in the valuation or in the rate of return. It represents, of course, a sacrifice by the investors rather than a value, but so do all the quantities in an estimate of either original or reproduction cost.

Going value, like other values, may be gauged by cost or by earning power. The cost measurement, in the shape of the Wisconsin rule, has

---

[1] Vanderblue takes this position (see *Railroad Valuation*, pp. 74–77, 1920; see Chap. xxi, Sec. 4, preceding).

been rejected by the courts. The earning-power measure is too obviously out of place in a procedure which questions the company's right to its present earnings, with the result that no clean-cut basis is left for going value to rest on, and it is introduced on a vague and ambiguous footing. It is typically based, not on earning power directly, but on various factors which take effect on value via earning power, this phase of their relationship being naturally kept in the background. In the following chapter an attempt will be made to outline a theory of going value which will have both consistent economic meaning and a useful relation to the task of regulation, distinguishing between earnings value, service value, and cost or sacrifice, and also between monopolistic and semicompetitive industries.

6. FAIR RATE OF RETURN

On the "value" of its property the company has a right to a return such as the market affords on other businesses and other investments, with due regard for risk or stability. Commissions have often allowed 7 or 8 per cent, but the courts, in considering the issue of confiscation, draw the line some 2 per cent lower than this in typical cases, always with the proviso that the company's right to its return is conditional on its being able to earn it at rates which are "reasonable to the public."

In estimating returns, a year is the period usually considered. Seasonal deficits are viewed merely as symptoms of what may be expected for the entire year. On the other hand, liberal earnings in past years cannot be offset against low earnings in the present, but present rates must be made reasonable without regard to the past.[1] Similarly, prior deficits have no claim to present or future compensation as far as the courts are concerned,[2] though, as Professor Ruggles points out, commissions can hardly ignore them.[3] Economic forces make it impossible, for the reward must be enough to offer some compensation for the prospect of early deficits, or capital will not be forthcoming. Professor Ruggles also thinks the way is open for legislation specifically providing, in the interest of stable rates, methods of applying the excess earnings of prosperous years to make up for shortages in bad times.

A commission may, of course, allow a liberal rate of return as a reward for efficiency. This would increase the value of the property as a going concern, but only as long as the extra return continued to

---

[1] *Newton* v. *Consolidated Gas Co.*, 258 U.S. 165, decided March 6, 1922.

[2] *Galveston Electric Co.* v. *City of Galveston*, 258 U.S. 388; *Georgia Railway & P. Co.* v. *Railroad Commission of Georgia*, 262 U.S. 625.

[3] "Rate Regulation and Fair Return," *Jour. Polit. Econ.*, Vol. XXXII, p. 543.

be allowed. Conversely, the United States Supreme Court has upheld a commission which required a gas company to make a rebate to consumers because of poor service.[1]

Obviously, the question whether the property is actually worth the amount of the "valuation" on which rates are based depends entirely on the rate of return allowed. With a 4 per cent return it would be worth less than the valuation, while with an 8 per cent return it would ordinarily be worth substantially more. There appears to be a tacit presumption that the rate should be such that the property will be worth the amount of the valuation, in the absence of special reasons to the contrary, but this is not definitely expressed, and in any case the courts distrust the stock-market quotations as evidences of value, because they are exposed to so many purely speculative influences. A property may be worth the same amount under a strict valuation and a liberal rate of return as under a liberal valuation and a low rate of return—a fact which makes it clear that the valuation which is taken as the base from which to calculate rates is not the same thing as the value actually allowed to the owners of the property.

For clearness in dealing with this question, two quantities should be recognized: the base on which the rate of return is calculated and the amount which the property ought to be worth under fair rates. With monopolistic industries it is possible to make these two approximately coincide, but with semicompetitive properties the actual earnings of the different units and their relative worth are governed by commercial forces which cannot be controlled or even calculated with any exactness. Even with monopolistic utilities, elements of value which are of a transitory character or are dependent on the management are best taken care of through the rate of return, rather than through the rate base or valuation, for that is assumed to be something fairly permanent, and representing the property rather than the commercial conditions surrounding it or the efficiency with which it is handled.

7. SUMMARY AND CRITICISM

The legal theory of fair value is undeniably groping and confused. The courts, as befits their function, have not laid down definite rules for the future, to which all cases must conform, but have dealt with each case as it came before them according to the circumstances surrounding it. This is natural, for the task of laying down definite methods of valuation is for legislatures and commissions, and the courts have merely to decide whether the methods used are within the bounds

[1] Ruggles, *op. cit.*, p. 553.

of reason and the proper discretion of the legislative arm of government. But, in practice, the courts' deliberately indefinite pronouncements were made binding on legislatures and commissions (whose proper function it is to make definite rules for the future) in such a way as in effect to debar them from exercising that function and from setting up definite standards of valuation. The result was a perversion and stultification of the system of division of powers between courts and legislatures.

Political pressures have undoubtedly urged commissions to fix rates as low as the courts permit, thus adopting the judicial rule of confiscation as their own rule of reasonableness, and wiping out the zone of reasonable discretion which ought, in theory, to exist.[1] This has probably led the courts, in turn, to move the confiscation point up until they come too near to substituting their own ideas of reasonableness for those of the commissions. There has been provocation for this, but the result is to encroach on what should be the proper field of action of responsible legislative bodies, and to impose the backward-looking, judicial type of ruling on a situation requiring the forward-looking, legislative-administrative type of ruling for its proper treatment. The results have been hampering, if not stultifying.

The logic of the judicial theories—for they are not one theory—is confused by the use of the term "value" in a sense for which no definition can be found.[2] It cannot mean value in the commercial sense, for that depends on earnings and cannot be used to determine whether the earnings are reasonable, but no other meaning is forthcoming, and the result is a constant effort on the part of the utility interests to insert commercial value in various disguises, and great embarrassment for the courts in striving to combat unreasonable efforts of this sort. The emphasis laid on original cost and reproduction cost has shifted in baffling fashion, and the resulting uncertainty is not a blessing to the utilities themselves, to say nothing of the public. Probably the greatest need of the situation is an opportunity to lay down rules for the future which will be certain.

One of the ablest students of this question, John Bauer, has seen, in some of the most recent decisions, the hope that the courts may sanction such rules if confined to future investments, without insisting that they conform to all the standards set up for the ordinary

---

[1] Justice Brandeis notes this tendency; see *State of Missouri ex. rel. Southwestern Bell Telephone Co.* v. *Public Service Commission of Missouri*, 262 U.S. 276, 296.

[2] See J. C. Bonbright, *Valuation of Property*, for the standard discussion of different meanings of value adapted to different purposes.

rate case which applies to the past.[1] In short, he sees a possibility of achieving certainty by agreeing on some valuation or other for the existing properties, and making additions to it on a basis about which no fundamental issues are left in doubt, leaving only matters which sound accounting and statistics can handle. This hope may prove unduly optimistic, but its grounds should surely be tested before accepting that unwelcome conclusion.

Justice Brandeis, in his minority opinion in the Southwestern Bell Telephone Case, gave a table of the standards used in 363 cases, which showed that original cost had, on the whole, played a larger part than reproduction cost in past cases. A majority of the 363 cases employed some past valuation, with subsequent additions at actual cost.[2] In this opinion (in which Justice Holmes concurred) Justice Brandeis squarely rejected *Smyth* v. *Ames*, stating: "The so-called rule of *Smyth* v. *Ames* is, in my opinion, legally and economically unsound," and holding that the thing devoted to the public use is the capital invested, rather than the "value of the property." The majority of the court, however, still officially held to the vague rule of the Ames case.

8. SOME RECENT DEVELOPMENTS

In recent years there has been widening dissatisfaction with the results of rate regulation under judicial restrictions. It has seemed to "common sense" that there was something wrong when companies which were clearly in a prosperous economic and financial condition could still show that their rates were, by judicial standards, below the confiscatory level.[3] This result was sometimes due to outside operations, not subject to regulation; but there appear to have been cases which could not be explained in this way. The present movement toward public operation, and the use of public rates as yardsticks to control or influence private charges free of judicial rules, is an outgrowth of this dissatisfaction. The common-sense view has finally found its way into Supreme Court opinions, and in 1934 two decisions

---

[1] See "Recent Decisions on Valuation and Rate-making," *Amer. Econ. Rev.*, Vol. XIV, pp. 254–263; also comments by R. L. Hale, D. R. Richberg, and W. L. Ransom.

[2] See separate concurring opinion of Justice Brandeis, in *State of Missouri ex rel. Southwestern Bell Telephone Co.* v. *Public Service Commission of Missouri*, 262 U.S. 276, 289 ff. (1923). The opinion is a dissent, in principle.

[3] Cf. minority report, *New York State Commission on Revision of the Public Service Law*, pp. 192–194, 1930.

were handed down which might, if followed up, revolutionize the judicial rule of fair value.[1]

In the Chicago telephone case the court upheld rates as nonconfiscatory without in any crucial matter disputing the finding of a lower court that the rates were confiscatory by conventional tests. The decision was based on other grounds of reasoning. The company's capital stock, capital reserves, and surplus had all increased, while an 8 per cent dividend had been maintained. Its fixed capital had doubled in eight years and its credit was excellent. "This actual experience of the company is more convincing than tabulations of estimates. In the face of that experience, we are unable to conclude that the company has been operating under confiscatory intrastate rates. Yet, as we have said, the conclusion that the existing rates have been confiscatory—and grossly confiscatory—would be inescapable if the findings below were accepted."

This decision, however, appears to be a "sport" among Supreme Court decisions on this subject. Subsequent decisions have seemingly reverted to the traditional standards of valuation.[2] And there the matter rests for the present, while the center of interest shifts to the complete circumvention of the court via yardstick experiments, which are probably more seriously disturbing to property values than an outright reversal of *Smyth* v. *Ames* would be.[3]

REFERENCES FOR FURTHER READING

BARKER, *Public Utility Rates*, Chaps. v, vi.

BARNES, I. R., *Cases on Public Utility Regulation* (rev. ed.), Secs. 8, 9, on The Present Fair Value Doctrine and Valuation Methods, 1934.

BAUER, JOHN, *Effective Regulation of Public Utilities*, Chap. v.

———, "Recent Decisions on Valuation and Rate-making," *Amer. Econ. Rev.*, pp. 254–282, June, 1924.

BERNSTEIN, E. M., "Public Utility Rate Making in Depression," *Quart. Jour. Econ.*, p. 113, November, 1937; also comment by J. D. Sumner, *Quart. Jour. Econ.*, p. 713, August, 1938.

BONBRIGHT, J. C., *Valuation of Property*, Vol. I, Parts II, III; Vol. II, Chaps. xxx–xxxiii, 1937.

DAGGETT, S., *Principles of Inland Transportation* (rev. ed.), Chaps. xxii–xxiii, 1934.

---

[1] *Lindheimer* v. *Illinois Bell Telephone Co.*, 292 U.S. 151; also *Dayton Power & Light Co.* v. *Public Utilities Commission*, 292 U.S. 290. Cf. also R. L. Hale, "The New Supreme Court Test of Confiscatory Rates," *Jour. Land and Public Utility Econ.*, pp. 307–313, August, 1934; and "Conflicting Judicial Criteria of Utility Rates," *Columbia Law Rev.*, XXXVIII (June, 1938), 959, 974–977.

[2] Cf. *West* v. *Chesapeake & Potomac Telephone Co.*, 295 U.S. 662 (1935), Stone, Brandeis, and Cardozo, dissenting.

[3] Cf. below, Chap. xxiv, Sec. 5.

HALE, R. L., "The Physical-value Fallacy in Rate Cases," *Yale Law Jour.*, pp. 710–731, May, 1921.

HARTMAN, *Fair Value*, Chaps. iii, v.

JONES and BIGHAM, *Principles of Public Utilities*, Chap. v, 1931.

Lawyers' Reports, annotated, pp. 599–682, 1916 F.

SHARFMAN, I. L., *The Interstate Commerce Commission*, Part III, Chap. xii.

SMALLEY, *Railroad Rate Control*, American Economic Association Publications, Vol. VII, No. 2, Chaps. ii–vi, May, 1906.

SOUTHWORTH, S. D., "Some Recent Problems in Public-utility Valuation and Regulation," *Amer. Econ. Rev.*, pp. 606–613, December, 1922.

TAYLOR, H., *Contemporary Problems in the United States*, Vol. II, Chaps. x, xi, 1934.

VANDERBLUE, *Railroad Valuation*.

WHITTEN, *Valuation*, also Sup., 1914.

WHITTEN and WILCOX, *Valuation* (rev. ed.), 1928.

WILSON, HERRING, and EUTSLER, *Public Utility Regulation*, Chaps. v, vi, 1938.

CHAPTER XXI

FAIR EARNINGS AND FAIR VALUE FROM THE ECONOMIC STANDPOINT: TWO PHASES OF ONE FACT

1. INTRODUCTION

Since the logic of the legal doctrine of fair value is generally admitted to be in an unsatisfactory state, and since some writers think there is a possibility of clarifying matters for the future, it may be worth while to attempt to define the principles of fair return on economic grounds, independently of legal rulings on fair value. If this proves possible, it may shed light on the question what needs to be done in the legal realm in order to make a sound economic solution possible.

The starting point is the principle that the property of the private company is held, and its business liberties are exercised, subject to the obligation to render fair service to all at reasonable charges. Therefore fair regulation must be legal, and no private-property rights can stand in the way of this basic fact. A second basic proposition is that the value of any property, in the basic meaning of the term, is what it will exchange for in a representative market transaction. Where the property is unique and transfers are infrequent, an estimate must be made of what someone would be willing to give for the property, as well as what the owner would be willing to forego in order to keep it. This is the basis of that hypothetical transaction between a willing buyer and a willing seller, which figures so largely in legal valuations. An impartial estimate of this sort might be spoken of as a fair value, meaning a fair estimate of the actual value. This value, for an industrial going concern, is based upon present and prospective earnings; and if these are reasonably steady and certain, the value will capitalize the earnings at a rate not far above the current rate of interest.

Value thus depends on earnings, and earnings cannot be governed by value; or rather, the value is simply what the earnings are worth.

320

They are two dimensions of the same thing.[1] The problem of regulation is the problem of determining what the earnings (and the corresponding value) ought to be, as distinct from what they are. It assumes that both the earnings and the corresponding value may be unreasonably large, and that both may need to be brought down to a reasonable level. Hence the power to regulate (which is our major premise) is the power to alter the value of the property, or it is nothing at all. This affords a basis for another definition of fair value, namely, what the value ought to be, under fair earnings. This is the only species of fair value that can logically be used to describe the standard to which rates ought to conform. It contains no solution; it merely states the problem.

We are now ready to define the terms on which the discussion of this subject hinges. Fair return (and the corresponding fair value) is that return (and that corresponding value) the prospect of which furnishes sufficient incentive to capital and enterprise to secure both in adequate amounts, in fair rivalry with the unregulated field of employment. This is the basic test of reasonableness. The return should be conditional on reasonable efficiency and economy of construction and operation, and the investor should, if possible, have a chance to increase his return by marked efficiency and assume the risk of having it reduced by marked inefficiency, but the average prospect must be enough to induce him to incur this uncertainty, as well as to invest his capital. The attractiveness of any prospective return depends largely on its certainty, and therefore uncertainties should be reduced as far as possible, consistent with adequate incentives to efficiency. In this matter the public has a right to the benefit of whatever form of incentive will call forth adequate service at the smallest total burden to the consumer, in the long run. Whatever system of returns meets these conditions is a reasonable system, and the corresponding value of the property is a fair value.

In the process of determining fair returns, the regulating authorities may make use of an estimate of the investment, or some other capital sum, as a "rate base." This may or may not coincide with the ultimate fair value; usually not, for reasons which will soon appear. There are some elements affecting fair value which can best be allowed for through the rate of return, rather than the rate base, and some which can hardly take effect through anything but the rate of return. The rate base will naturally cover some of the most significant evidence of fair value, but not necessarily all. This rate base may be spoken of as

[1] This expresses the main fact for the present purpose, though considerations of sentiment, for example, might have some effect on value apart from earnings.

a valuation, if we keep in mind that it need not be intended as a complete measure of the fair value of the properties and does not show what value has actually been allowed to the owners in the fixing of a schedule of rates. To find this last we must look to the earnings which the rates actually produce.

2. THE RANGE OF POSSIBLE INCENTIVES

The incentive about which difficult issues arise is the incentive to the investor. Active management is rewarded by salaries, and while it is within the province of the regulating authority to see that these are reasonable, this is usually left to the discretion of the directors. If systems of premiums for efficiency are evolved, to be paid to the salaried officials, these might be subject to the same possibility of scrutiny, but there could be no objection to them in principle. The directors, under our American system, receive their chief reward in their capacity as stockholders. The investor, then, is the real problem. For what is he to be rewarded, and to what valuable service is he to be stimulated? What is his function? It is the providing of capital funds and the placing of them in this industry, subject to whatever risk it may involve; and also, or so says the traditional theory, some basic functions of direction. About this last there is nowadays not a little disagreement, some holding that the typical stockholder, as such, is an absentee income taker and no more, all the work of management being performed by others.

Without elaborating all angles of this controversy, certain things can be clearly seen. The small stockholder is a passive absentee, but the control, nevertheless, vests in stockholders: large ones with enough voting power to count. They choose the directors, and in large part they choose themselves. And the directors have not only the determination of basic questions of policy, but also the choosing of the active managing officials.

This last is a function which can never become negligible, no matter what developments of corporate organization may take place. It is better to choose the right man for general manager than to choose the wrong one and place him under the most perfect scheme of efficiency premiums that could be devised. Whoever does this choosing should have reward enough to make it worth his while to pay serious attention to it; and he should be a person, or preferably persons, of such caliber that his time and attention have a high value. Even so, this service could probably be secured at a price which would make very little impression on the earnings of a large company. But it is also in point that the reward for this service should vary, automatically if possible, according to the success with which it is performed. This means that the large stockholder (if he is intrusted with this function) should, where practicable, be exposed to losses from bad management and have a prospect of profits from good management, even if he is not himself the manager. In short, the stockholder still performs important functions of direction, and the prospect of profit or loss is still an appropriate incentive to the proper performance of them, though not a cheap one and not the only one possible.

In the matter of risk, the regulated industry is in a peculiar position, for the reason that the risk which falls on the investor is, at least in part, under the control of the public authorities. They may make the rules of regulation such that the return will be uncertain and speculative, or more certain and less speculative, or they may guarantee the return and thereby eliminate risk altogether for the investor. None of these tactics has much effect on the uncertainties inherent in the industrial processes themselves, but they alter the distribution of these uncertainties between the consumers, the investors, and the government. The effect on the investors is, however, as we have already seen, conditioned by the terms and amounts of the different types of securities by which the corporation distributes the uncertainties of its income between the holders of mortgage bonds, debentures, and preferred and common stock. Hence the government is not free to do absolutely anything it desires, unless it takes control also of the securities themselves and alters the customary terms of bond issues.

In general, the more certain the return, the cheaper can capital be secured, though this is by no means always the case if the possible losses are averaged in with the returns yielded during normal successful operation. Companies are exposed to the chance that the developing state of the arts may destroy the value of their plant, or a large part of it; and the public has so far felt that it cannot afford to assume the danger of such losses, preferring to pay the companies enough to make them willing to assume it. In practice, however, the public is at times compelled to protect the companies in order to bring about desired modernizations of the plant, since the company will prefer to keep old equipment in service if a replacement would compel them to sacrifice the whole remaining value of what they now have. Thus in 1907 the city of Chicago secured an agreement with the surface lines to install underground trolleys in place of their cable-car equipment and in return allowed them to add the whole cost of the new plant to their capital account without deduction for the plant which was retired. In this case the addition to the capital account did not affect the fares, which were fixed at five cents, but it constituted part of the price which the city would have to pay if it purchased the properties during the life of the ordinance, and it was indirectly taken into account when the rise of prices following the war made the five-cent fare inadequate and caused the Illinois Public Utilities Commission to raise fares to eight cents (later reduced to seven).[1] A company may be allowed, then, in special cases, to include the value of abandoned property in the valuation of the plant for rate-making purposes. The rules of fair value give the companies no right to this.[2] If granted at all, it should be for a limited time, the company being required to write off the value by regular amortization charges.

Thus it may prove impracticable to place upon the companies all the losses to which they have theoretically exposed themselves, and this furnishes an added reason for putting the incentive offered to the investor in such a form as to reduce his risks to a minimum. On the other hand, if all risks are removed, the investor loses the incentive to take proper care to secure efficient and progressive management, as we have seen. The ideal system would be one which would eliminate risks of a purely speculative character, or those due to forces over which the investor has no control, and would leave a differential return which would measure the worth of his performance. Such a system has not yet been devised.

What are the risks to which the investor is subject? They differ in different types of industry, some being unavoidable and others dependent on the policy of regulation followed. A semicompetitive industry is subject to the risk that other enterprises may cut rates or take away part of its business. Risks of this kind are to a large extent dependent on the efficiency and progressiveness of the management, though there are some uncertainties as to the advantages of the location chosen and the development of the market naturally tributary to a particular company. Of the uncertainties which affect monopolistic and semicompetitive enterprises alike, the chief ones are those incurred in starting a new enterprise. There is a chance that the demand will not develop to a point at which it will be commercially possible to make any system of rates which will yield a fair return on the investment, as many railroads in sparsely settled territory have found to their cost. A monopoly price does not always yield a profit.

[1] See *In the Matter of the Application of Chicago Railways Co. et al.*, Illinois Public Utilities Commission, No. 9357, decided November 5, 1920. The commission did not specifically include this amount in their valuation, but they recognized it as an argument justifying them in including a substantially equivalent amount as "going value," thus bringing the total up to the amount of the purchase price provided by the ordinance of 1907.

[2] See Whitten, *Valuation*, pp. 190–195.

In such a case there is an added possibility that the company will not be allowed to charge the utmost price that the market would permit. While the usual standard of reasonable rates is such as to yield the company a fair return, the courts have held that the companies have not an absolute right to a normal return if this cannot be earned without fixing rates so high as to be unreasonable to the consumer.[1] This implies that other considerations than the return to the investor may govern reasonableness, at least to the extent of setting a maximum beyond which rates may not be raised. What determines this maximum, under existing law, is somewhat uncertain; but it is chiefly controlled by the customary range of rates charged by other companies for similar service, as indicating the range of rates from which the company in question presumably expected to secure their fair return, and within which range the consuming public had fair reason to expect the company's charges to fall. Inability to earn a fair return at such rates, then, is one of the risks taken when a new enterprise is started, the probability depending largely on whether a potential demand already exists, or whether it will have to be built up.

Other uncertainties include changes in the costs of labor and materials. While these will, if they continue, give cause for corresponding changes in rates, this adjustment may be considerably delayed, and the company will gain or lose in the meantime. On account of this lag, periods of rising prices and costs are likely to bring reduced earnings to the companies, and vice versa.

Another uncertainty which must be recognized is the uncertainty as to the regulating policy of the government itself. There is always a party favoring stricter control, and the moderate attitude of the majority in one legislative body cannot bind the next. The chief stabilizing element is the protection afforded by the courts, but even this is not absolutely predictable. This very protection is played upon by demagogues who advocate intolerably strict measures, knowing that, even if these measures pass, the courts will refuse to sustain them and will thus bear the odium of defeating the popular will, while the demagogue gains the credit of having fought for the people against the corporate interests. This kind of uncertainty is reflected in the value of securities on the exchanges and sometimes materially lowers their prices and increases the rate of yield on their market value, reflecting the high rate the new purchaser requires to make him willing to invest. In spite of these deterring elements in the situation, public-utility securities have generally been regarded by

---

[1] This principle is found in *Smyth* v. *Ames*, 160 U.S. 466; also in *Reagan* v. *Farmers' Loan and Trust Co.*, 154 U.S. 362.

the market as stable investments, selling at higher prices and lower yields than those of competitive industries in general. The present experiment in "yardstick" control, combined with the threat to holding companies, has materially altered this situation.

Other uncertainties may be involved in the method of calculating the fair value of the property. Of the standards which figure prominently in regulation, actual investment is most certain. In its qualified form—prudent investment—it carries some uncertainty as to what will be regarded as prudent, though this is not likely to be serious. It is so interpreted as to rule out nothing except what would be clearly indefensible on ordinary business principles. And all doubt can be removed by setting up a body of experts to pass upon expenditures before allowing them in the valuation, and so settling the question of prudence in advance. Cost of reproduction is subject to change and uncertainty, of two main sorts: changes in the cost of this kind of equipment as compared to other things, and changes in the general level of prices. The latter means, not a change in the value of this property, but a change in the length of the money yardstick in terms of which this value and all others are measured. With regard to this a dilemma arises. Reproduction cost, in such a case, though changing in number of dollars, is stable in terms of value[1]—but it is a kind of stability which people do not expect or fully understand, and hence it cannot give them the benefits which stability ought to bring. They will still issue bonds calling for a fixed number of dollars; and as long as this is done, uncertainty, miscalculation, and injustice are bound to remain.

Granted that a company is to be allowed to earn a given amount, it may still make a difference in what form the allowance is made: whether embodied in the valuation of the property or merely in the rate of return allowed on the valuation. The two may have the same effect on the immediate earnings, but the valuation is harder to change and carries greater assurance of stability. Any value which the community is willing to give the company as a permanent possession may as well be included in the valuation, where it will be esteemed more highly by the investors; but any value which the community is willing to grant only provisionally or during good behavior must be kept out

[1] This assumes that an index number exists whose base line represents a stable amount of value. The securing of such an index number involves not merely statistical difficulties of computation, but that most abstruse question: What is the ultimate standard of value, and does any such standard exist? No one index number can fulfill the equities which this question implies, for all groups at once in a changing society, but any good index number will give a substantially stable base line, compared to the fluctuating dollar.

of the valuation and taken into account in the rate of return. This supports the contention already made, that the "valuation" is not necessarily a measure of the fair value of the property in its present use and should not be expected always to contain every element of fair value.

If the valuation is not the final test of the value which the commission proposes to allow to a company, what is the test? Is it the market value which results from the rates fixed, and is it the duty of the commissions so to fix rates that the market value of the property will be a just value? The only available market value is that of the securities which are traded in on the exchanges, and while these exchanges afford, in the long run, the best gauge of the actual value of a going concern, over short periods the sales recorded are often far from representative. Distrust of the policy of government may make investors unwilling to pay as much as before for a stock yielding 6 per cent cash dividends. In other words, the market will capitalize the cash returns at a high rate, the new purchaser demanding this high return as a premium for risk. Must the government adopt this high rate of return? This would be clearly unnecessary, since the only reason why it is so high is that the market thinks it has reason to fear the fixing of a return far lower. The mere willingness of the government to fix rates sufficient to bring market values to par would at once lower the rate at which the market capitalizes the earnings, with the result that the market would meet the government at least halfway.

3. A SUGGESTED PLAN OF CONTROL: THE GENERAL BASIS

The foregoing discussion indicates that there is not one correct plan of control, but a number of possible options, each of which would satisfy the test of reasonable and adequate return. Therefore, in going on to suggest the outlines of a plan, the purpose will be to illustrate principles, with the assumption that details will be altered in practice. The plan here outlined attempts to make the rewards as little speculative as is consistent with proper incentives to efficiency, and to differentiate between the absolute monopoly and the semicompetitive industry according to their different circumstances. For the sake of greater freedom in following principles, it is assumed that the plan is applied to future enterprises or future investments which are made with a clear understanding of the conditions. If concessions need to be made to investments made earlier, under different conditions, and with different expectations, these may be considered separately.

Since the bondholders receive a stipulated rate of return, regulation within ordinary limits will not affect them. Fair return will include the interest the company has agreed to pay, within the limits of reasonable business discretion in fixing rates and determining the proportion of debt in the capitalization. Both these matters should be placed under public control, and authorized interest rates on authorized bond issues should be regarded as fair, in the absence of actual bad faith. The further problem of fair return centers in the stockholders' equity in the property. If bonds have been issued at a discount, that is to be treated as a deferred-interest charge, to be amortized at a regular rate during the life of the bond, and in calculating the stockholders' equity the deduction for indebtedness will not include the unamortized part of the par value of the bonds. Otherwise, if a going concern issued $100,000 of bonds at 90, the stockholders' equity would be reduced at once by the $10,000 they have agreed to pay at maturity, in excess of the money they have received from the issue.

The stockholders' equity in plant and equipment is to be measured at the actual cost, unless a positive showing is made of waste or imprudence on the one hand or of special economy on the other. Where practicable, a board may be set up to exercise a continuing check on capital expenditures, and anything which they authorize may be regarded as prudent, in the absence of positive bad faith. Gifts, or expenditures made by the public or by any body not sharing in the earnings, are not to be regarded as part of the stockholders' equity for the purpose of reckoning their fair return. They are presumably made to improve the public service by furnishing funds which the stockholders would not or could not furnish, but not to increase the stockholders' private profits. For example, if any further land grants should be made to railroads, that part used by the road itself would not be counted as the stockholders' investment, though if the public should see fit to give land for miles on both sides of the tracks, with no conditions attached, as was done with many of the western pioneer lines, this would be perforce regarded as an affair quite separate from the public service and not subject to regulation. The public wisdom can probably be trusted to make no such grants in the future. A more pertinent issue is the funds contributed by the public in the work of grade separations, the need for which is assuming enormous proportions.

4. A SUGGESTED PLAN OF CONTROL: COMPLETE MONOPOLIES

In monopolistic industries, where the return can be controlled at will, it should be based on the stockholders' investment and should be sufficient to make the equity worth not less than the amount invested (counting land at market value) under reasonably efficient operation.

For a new company it is likely to be impossible to bring the earnings immediately up to this level, or at least not without making rates so high at first as to be out of proportion to their permanent level, constituting an undue burden on the early users and a handicap to the needed development of the use of the service. Hence it may seem desirable, and in accord with the public interest, to be content with lower earnings for a short term of years—possibly two, and certainly not more than five. In this case the lower earnings at first must be made up for by higher ones later, so that present cash earnings plus future prospects may be worth what the stockholders are being asked to invest. It will follow that when the waiting period is over, the stockholders' equity will be worth more than the original cash investment; in other words, it will have a going value due to having built up its connections and the demand for its service and established itself as a going concern.

In most arguments for the allowance of going value it is merely asserted that a going concern is worth more than a bare physical property without a developed business, without meeting the argument that the added worth comes from added earnings, and that it is the reasonableness of the earnings that is in question. Thus the concern appears to be attempting to lift itself by its bootstraps, and no public interest is shown in the allowance of the extra earnings on which the going value is based. There is a public interest in the case, however. The mature company has the power to make larger earnings than the new company without raising rates, and the public can take advantage of this to allow the company to defer part of its fair return to a time when it can be paid with the least burden to the consumer. As much as is necessary for this purpose, and no more, is a proper allowance for going value. In calculating how much the mature property ought to be worth—its fair value in that sense—this much going value may properly be taken into account.[1] But it should not be confused with the investment in the property itself. It assumes that rates will be such that a new property will not be worth its cost if immediate cash earnings alone are taken into consideration.

An additional inducement may be afforded by allowing land to be figured at its market value (without multiples for hypothetical costs of condemnation), on the assumption that if the value rises, it will be a

---

[1] This is substantially the principle of the rule of going value originated by the Wisconsin commission, which has done so much pioneer work in the field of regulation, except that it is here proposed to take account of it in the rate of return and not to include it in the rate base, which is limited to the investment properly chargeable to capital account.

symptom of a growth of population which will make it possible to earn a return on at least this much added value without raising rates. If this is done, investors should be willing to accept a smaller rate of cash return in consideration of the prospect of future gain; or the prospect may balance some of the risks they undergo.

If practicable, earnings should be liberal in periods of business prosperity, building up reserves (not counted as company investments) to make possible reduced rates during depressions, or at least to avoid the necessity for increases. This is, however, admittedly difficult. If the general level of prices rises or falls, it may be provided that the return shall rise or fall with it to an extent sufficient to give the stockholders the same yield as before in terms of present purchasing power. That is, if the dollar should shrink 10 per cent, the stockholders' return would be increased $11\frac{1}{9}$ per cent. The bondholders, having already contracted for a steady income in terms of dollars, could not be affected by anything the government might do, and there would be no justice or expediency in giving the stockholders the extra return on the bondholders' share of the property as well as on their own.

Under certain conditions the cost of reproducing a plant of equal service value may be substituted for the actual cost of the existing plant, or parts of it, or other departures may be made from the investment basis of measuring the stockholders' equity. Where it becomes desirable, for reasons that could not be foreseen in providing for depreciation, to replace or relocate a plant or a stretch of railroad or any other equipment, before it has been written down to scrap value, the company may be allowed to make the replacement and still keep on their books the unexpired part of the value of the abandoned property, to be written off at the same rate as if it had not been abandoned. This might call for some control over depreciation rates. The plan virtually permits the company to charge the unamortized part of the abandoned property to the consumers on the installment plan. Strictly, when replacement becomes economically desirable, the existing equipment has depreciated to scrap value, whether the accounts show that fact or not. But the public has in most cases no independent means of discovering the facts and must depend on the enterprise of the company and the efficiency of its engineers. But then if the company loses the value of any property it decides to abandon, it is penalized, not for the actual depreciation of the property, but for revealing it and making it good. Hence the rate base should be so handled that the company will not lose by doing the right thing.

On the other hand, if the facts are known and the company refuses to make a needed reconstruction, it would not be illogical to penalize it by reducing the value of the existing plant to what it is actually worth in the light of the existence of a more efficient possible substitute. If there is now available a cheaper plant of the same service value, the cost of the cheaper plant measures the value of the older and more expensive one. If, as is more likely, the modernized plant is not absolutely cheaper but will do the same work at less operating expense per unit, the value of the old plant is the cost of the new, less the capitalized value of the savings in operating expenses, and this may easily be less than nothing. Where the new equipment will do more work, as well as do it cheaper, there is the added complication of reckoning the old plant as equivalent to a certain portion of the new, a problem in allocation which would have to be settled differently according to the circumstances of different cases. In similar circumstances the land might be valued at what an equally effective site would cost, where a good site could be had for so much less than the value of the land now occupied that the economy of the service demands a relocation in the public interest, and where the company refuses to make the change.

This problem of modernization furnishes one of the strongest reasons for insisting that depreciation be charged as an expense and a corresponding reserve accumulated in the capital account, for then the company has less to lose by any abandonment. The policy of trusting the management to take care of replacements as they became necessary, without depreciation charges, would be fatally weak at this point. While depreciation should be charged, appreciation due to seasoning may also be recognized in appropriate cases, to the extent of actual expenses, beyond ordinary current maintenance, which are incurred during the early part of the life of the property and do not have to be incurred again.

As for the vital matter of efficiency of operation, where methods have become standard in the industry the company may be ordered to adopt them, but before they have reached this stage other incentives are necessary if anything is to be added to the managerial "instinct of workmanship." One possibility would be to establish one section of the regulating commission with the function of interchanging suggestions with the management, devising tests of the economy or gain resulting from any innovations (not already standard practice), and apportioning the gains between management, stockholders, and consumers, the stockholders to receive their share in the shape of an increase in their standard rate of return, for a limited term of years, probably not over five in most cases. If the innovation takes the shape of an economy in operation, this increased return can be earned without increasing rates; and if it increases the effectiveness of the plant, there is an adde service value received by the consumer in exchange for what he pays. Needless to say, one of the duties of this section of the commission would be to avoid foisting extravagances of service on the consumer in the guise of improvements.

5. A SUGGESTED PLAN OF CONTROL: SEMICOMPETITIVE INDUSTRIES

With semicompetitive industries (railroads being at present the chief instance), some modifications of this plan would be necessary.

In the first place, clearly, standards of fair return are academic matters unless competitive conditions permit a fair return to be earned. At present, they do not, and the railroad problem is of a different sort. Capital structures must be revised to permit the roads to survive some lean years. Costs must if possible be reduced, possibly by consolidations (though that remains a knotty problem). The possible necessity of a reduction of wages must, however reluctantly, be faced, as an alternative to governmental subsidies or public ownership of an industry which is bound to prove a bad investment. Some of the competing truck charges may be found to be parasitically low, and measures may be taken which would result in raising them, though that is an uncertain source of relief. As to rates, the chief problem is whether the commission, having the duty to fix rates which will come as near as possible to earning a fair return, should substitute its judgment for that of the carriers as to what rates will best accomplish this end, and whether it may require lower rates than the carriers propose (as we have seen that it has done), either on this ground or on the ground that business, in a depression, cannot stand the rates the carriers feel they need. In the present desperate state of the roads, there is much to be said for leaving this to their own discretion.

The following plan applies to more normal conditions, if they can ever be achieved. While a check on the economy of capital expenditures may never be out of place, it is probably less urgently needed in this class of enterprises, since the company which is economical gets a competitive gain as its reward and does not have to give the entire benefit to the public. It gets its plant cheaper or gets a better plant, and the earnings are governed by the pressures of competition. What governs rates, inevitably, (if the competition of other forms of transport permits a fair return on investment) is the investment of all the roads, or of some representative road, and no road, except by coincidence, will earn exactly a fair return on its individual investment. For the same reason the problem of a deliberate allowance for going value takes on diminished importance. For similar reasons there would be no need for additions to the standard rate of return to stimulate improvements. The forces of competition would see to it that the road that improved its efficiency would thereby increase its earnings, while the road that allowed its efficiency to decline would see its earnings reduced. This affords a stronger and more automatic stimulus than any that a commission could devise.

But these differentials in earnings are due not merely to technical efficiency, but also, in large part, to the fact that some routes are naturally better than others. The best routes will earn more than is necessary to attract capital and stimulate efficiency, that is, more than a "fair return"; while the poorest will earn less, and much of their original investment will be lost so far as hope of return goes. The strongest lines will have an unnecessarily large going value, while the going value of the poorer roads will be a minus quantity.

These differentials may be considerably reduced by a wise policy of consolidations, but they cannot be wholly eliminated. The most desperately weak units are small properties, and they are usually of use to stronger properties with which they interchange traffic. Hence the stronger properties have an interest in them, which might furnish a motive to voluntary consolidations in such cases. Even without consolidation, much aid is given and received between such related lines. Consolidation of major systems with each other is a more difficult and doubtful task. The plan here proposed is equally applicable, whatever is done in the matter of consolidations.

The persistence of these differentials does not satisfy ideal standards of justice, but perhaps the real objection is not to the greater value of the richer properties, which results from economic law, but to the assumption that it all belongs to the private owners of these properties. Since it is really in large part the result of social conditions, society might set up a claim to a share, as was done under the Transportation Act of 1920, by "recapturing" half the earnings above 6 per cent on the valuation.[1] This does not distinguish the part due to the company's own efficiency from that due to social causes but simply takes half of both and leaves the company half. Thus anything it can make by its own efficiency is its own up to 6 per cent on the valuation, and half of anything beyond that. The strong roads will still have a going value for their owners. For the purposes of the illustrative plan we are discussing, any sharing of profits would begin with a given rate on the investment account, since we have no other valuation. It should,

---

[1] This provision was repealed in 1932, having become inoperative. It could only have effect when conditions make it economically practicable for the roads to earn a fair return, on the average.

of course, be recognized that the average return to the owners is less than the average earnings of the properties by the amount the government takes. Therefore, if the owners are to receive an average return of 6 per cent, the average yield of the properties must be more.

To sum up the principles of this plan, it undertakes to see to it that at the time the investor puts his money into the enterprise he gets a prospect of earnings whose present value is equal to the amount he puts in; recognizing that the earnings may be smaller at first, and that both earnings and the resulting value may be larger when the company has reached maturity, the increment constituting a going value.

In the case of railroads a new kind of going value enters, which may be a plus or a minus quantity, namely, the unavoidable commercial differentials between the earning power of different properties, which cannot be eliminated by fixing higher rates for the poorer companies than for the richer, because that would only take from the poorer companies their competitive business and would leave them poorer than ever. In this going value the community can fairly claim a share. It is not practicable to allow the weakest roads returns which will make their properties worth the full amounts invested in them, but even in weak roads new capital will have to receive such a prospective return. To bring this about, new stock may be issued for less than the present stockholders paid, or there may be a reorganization in which existing investors accept a reduction of their claims. The hardship will often be mitigated by the fact that many of the present holders have bought at prices which discount the low earning power of the property.

In this situation it is not important, for the mere fixing of rates, to find the ideal fair value of each individual property, since the owners will not receive that value in any case. The actual investment is sufficient. If some investments are imprudently made, those properties will gain nothing thereby, and the results will be averaged in with extra-shrewd and extra-economical investments, in determining the aggregate investment in an entire region, on which the level of rates is based.

There can be little doubt that this plan, reasonably applied, would offer sufficient inducements to capital, and some stimulus to efficient management, without selling the public as slaves to the exploiters. Other plans of valuation could be employed, such as the cost of reproduction under not too abnormal conditions and prices. The fluctuations due to the use of this standard would, of course, be concentrated on the stockholders' interest, the bondholders' share being fixed by contract, with the result that neither would get a return varying in proportion to the cost of reproduction of the properties, if this be taken as indicating how the investors' return ought to vary. When one looks, not at the property in the abstract, as if it owned itself (which it plainly does not), but at the equities, interests, and shares of the actual persons who do own it, the reproduction-cost method of valuation appears decidedly less appropriate.

6. TREATING PAST AND FUTURE INVESTMENTS DIFFERENTLY

From one point of view it might be urged that any system of control which is announced beforehand is just, as far as concerns capital invested after the system was announced. If the capital accepts the terms, they must be satisfactory. This is not strictly true, for the terms may be such that unforeseen contingencies will bring ruin, as did the five-cent street-car fare at the time of the war; or capital may come in on unjustly harsh terms for the sake of keeping the service going and rescuing some part of the value of the investment already made. But it is true that terms known in advance *may* be just when the same terms would be unjust if they were imposed without warning on investors who had been led to expect something different. For this reason it might quite possibly be just to follow some such plan as the one sketched above for all future investments, and to value the present plant on a different basis or on no basis at all save that of an agreement which will satisfy both parties. That a mixture of principles of valuation is not unheard of is attested by the fact that in a majority of rate cases the valuation is some previous valuation plus subsequent additions at cost, no matter what the basis of the previous valuation may have been.[1]

Could this be carried to the point of definitely adopting for all future investments a system based on prudent investment, with modifications, while valuing existing properties on any kind of compromise basis which the law will sanction? If this is legally possible, the way is open for regulation to be placed on a basis of reasonably certain and calculable rewards, such as are suited to attracting capital on the most reasonable terms. Otherwise the course of regulation will be marred by uncertainties in the future as it has been in the past.

REFERENCES FOR FURTHER READINGS

BARKER, *Public Utility Rates*, Chaps. vii–ix.
BARNES, I. R., *Cases on Public Utility Regulation* (rev. ed.), Sec. 13, "Rate Regulation: Critical Appraisal," 1934.

[1] See Justice Brandeis' opinion (already referred to) in *State of Missouri ex. rel. Southwestern Bell Telephone Co.* v. *Public Service Commission of Missouri*, 262 U.S., 276, 296.

BAUER, *Effective Regulation of Public Utilities*, Chaps. iv, vi–xii.

—— and GOLD, *Public Utility Valuation*, 1934.

BERNSTEIN, E. M., *Public Utility Rate Making and the Price Level*, Chaps. iii, iv, vi–x, 1937.

BROWN, H. G., "Railroad Valuation and Rate Regulation," *Jour. Polit. Econ.*, pp. 505–530, October, 1925.

CLARK, J. M., "Railroad Valuation as a Working Tool," *Jour. Polit. Econ.*, pp. 265–306, April, 1920.

CRAVEN, LESLIE, "Railroad Valuation," address before American Bar Association, Public Utility Section, August 28, 1923.

HAMILTON, W. H., *Current Economic Problems*, Chap. vii *d, e.*

HARTMAN, *Fair Value*, Chaps. iv, vi–ix.

INTERSTATE COMMERCE COMMISSION, *Tentative Plan of Railroad Consolidations, with Report to the Commission by W. Z. Ripley.*

JONES, ELIOT, *Principles of Railroad Transportation*, Chap. xv.

JONES and BIGHAM, *Principles of Public Utilities*, Chap. vi, 1931.

JONES and VANDERBLUE, *Railroads: Cases and Selections*, Chaps. iv–vi.

RIPLEY, *Railroads: Finance and Organization*, Chap. xi.

RIPLEY, HANEY, COUNTY, and others, *Amer. Econ. Rev.*, Sup., pp. 43–108, March, 1924.

RUGGLES, "Rate-making for Public Utilities," *Jour. Polit. Econ.*, pp. 56–57, February, 1924.

SALIERS, "Cost, Fair Value, and Depreciation Reserves," *Amer. Econ. Rev.*, pp. 272–282, June, 1920.

SHARFMAN, I. L., *The American Railroad Problem*, Chap. viii, Secs. 1, 2, 4.

——, *The Interstate Commerce Commission*, Part III, Chap. xiv.

SLICHTER, S. H., *Modern Economic Society*, Chap. xviii, 1928.

SMALLEY, *Railroad Rate Control*, American Economic Association Publications, Vol. VII, No. 2, Chap. vii, May, 1906.

SMITH, N. L., *The Fair Rate of Return in Public Utility Regulation*, 1932.

VANDERBLUE and BURGESS, *Railroads: Rates—Service—Management*, Chaps. viii, xxii.

WHITTEN, *Valuation* and *Supplement*, 1914.

—— and WILCOX, *Valuation* (rev. ed.), 1928.

WILSON, HERRING, and EUTSLER, *Public Utility Regulation*, Chaps. xiii–xvii, 1938.

YOUNG, A. A., "Depreciation and Rate Control," *Quart. Jour. Econ.*, pp. 630–663, August, 1914.

CHAPTER XXII

REGULATION, SERVICE, AND EFFICIENCY

1. INTRODUCTION

Service and efficiency are coordinate parts of any attempt to control prices; first, because it does the buyer no good to pay a lower price if the quality or quantity he gets for his money is lowered in the same proportion, giving him gas, for instance, of four-fifths the former heating power for four-fifths the former price. Second, it does the buyer no good to compel the producer to accept half the former net earnings if he gets in exchange a management half as efficient, for the poor management will add more to the costs of operation than the regulating commission can take away in reduced earnings. It will also be likely to waste money in capital installations, so that, paying a lower rate of return, he may still have nearly as large a total burden of capital charges as before, to say nothing of increased operating expenses. Or the management may err on the other side, failing to furnish enough producing capacity to serve the demand, and this can easily be a far more serious matter than a moderate amount of overcharging by a company which is effectively eager to do all the business it profitably can. When grain spoils because the railroad cannot furnish cars to carry it or elevator space to store it, or when mines and mills lie idle because the railroads cannot find cars enough to haul the coal, there is a direct loss of wealth which costs the country more than if the same goods moved at rates a fraction of a mill per ton-mile too high.

Not that we are in imminent danger of a disastrous breakdown of our public-utility services. When critics of governmental paternalism wish the most horrible examples of this sort, they go to the records of public operation, rather than private operation under public regulation, and tell of community development crippled in Australia (which seems somehow to have survived and even prospered) or of red tape and inefficiency in the British telephone system.[1] The danger

---

[1] See Pratt, *The State-Railway Muddle in Australia;* and Holcombe, *Public Ownership and the Telephone in Great Britain;* also Yves Guyot, *Where and Why Public Ownership Has Failed.*

337

in our regulated industries is not so much that of glaring abuses as that of a slackening of efficiency that works little by little, or of an increasing number of companies that fail to come reasonably near the standards set by the best organizations. Or there might be an increasing tendency to be content with providing for the existing or average demand and neglecting to make the additional provision necessary to be ready to handle future growth or those peaks of demand which call for reserves of capacity if they are to be handled without cutting down the activity of business in general.[1] The inefficiency we have to fear is the kind which is difficult to prove but is none the less serious in its effects.

Quite apart from the effects of regulation, conditions in the public-service industries tend toward certain kinds of inefficiency. While the best and most progressive organizations undoubtedly set a high standard, those which fail to do so are not eliminated, as in a competitive industry, since they have a monopoly of the whole or a part of their field. Thus the average standard tends to be lowered by the survival of a large number of relatively inefficient plants, and one writer has found evidence in the statistics that the level of efficiency varies more from company to company than in competitive industries, and also that the concerns which make the poorest showing in one year are more likely to continue the same poor showing indefinitely, rather than being able to pull themselves up into the average group or better, as a considerable number seem to do in the competitive field.[2]

The effect of regulation on this condition is not simple and hinges on the kind of regulation employed; on the adequacy of the return allowed; on the extent to which the return can be made to hinge on the efficiency achieved; and the effectiveness with which it is reinforced by direct supervision, the setting of standards, and other direct means of promoting good operation. The utilities have lived through a period of speculative adventure and gambling promotion in which the management was often more interested in the stock market than in the plant and service. The speculative interest came to center largely in the great holding companies and should be reduced through the efforts

[1] The need for such reserves, unused most of the time, is itself an element of inefficiency which may be reduced by greater stabilization of the activity of business in general; but as long as it exists, maximum production depends on the existence of such reserves.

[2] See C. S. Morgan, *Regulation and the Management of Public Utilities*, Chap. ii. Compare with this Secrist, *Competition in the Retail Distribution of Clothing*, Northwestern University Bureau of Business Research, 1923. Differences in efficiency appear to be widest in the smaller utility concerns. This point is discussed in the author's *Economics of Overhead Costs*, p. 321.

of the Securities and Exchange Commission. Operating properties are in the hands of experienced managing and engineering staffs whose attention is presumably not divided between the plant and the stock market.

The chief difficulty arises with monopolistic utilities, since the semicompetitive concerns, as we have seen, can increase their individual profits by economy of operation, rates being fixed with reference to an average or representative company. The monopoly may feel that its rates will be adjusted to give it the same rate of return whether it makes improvements or not, so that the public will get the entire benefit. Even so, in times of rising prices, it may take some pains to keep down its expenses by economies of operation rather than be forced to the expense, delay, and uncertainty of a procedure for increased rates, and for the same reason it will ordinarily take some pains to see to it that its efficiency does not fall off so much as to make increased rates necessary if its fair return is to be maintained. But these motives are not enough to insure a really progressive policy.

Another fundamental point is that efficiency has more than one dimension. It is a ratio between results and expenditure and is measured not only by the economy of the means of production but by the adequacy of the results secured, as to both quantity and quality. And there is a certain antagonism, not so much between these two dimensions of efficiency as between the plans of control calculated to give each the most natural and self-acting stimulus. If rates are fixed for a considerable term of years, the company has every incentive to lower its costs of operation for the sake of increasing its profits, and to that end it also has an incentive to cheapen the service, running few cars and old ones or furnishing poor gas, until the regulating authorities call a halt or until popular dissatisfaction reaches a point at which it threatens to become expensive to the company. Here the company has an automatic incentive to economy, but adequacy must be cared for by direct supervision.

On the other hand, if a company has a guarantee of an adequate return, it has no money incentive to economy, and the public interest therein will need to be protected by positive supervision, so far as it is protected at all; but the natural desire for popular approval will lend a certain incentive to good and adequate service, so long as it does not cost the company anything in the way of deduction from its fixed return. This kind of incentive, needless to say, is most effective with a publicly operated concern. The typical case of a regulated utility is neither the one thing nor the other, and neither economy nor adequacy is sufficiently taken care of by such automatic incentives as can be brought to bear. They depend partly on direct supervision and partly on the willingness and enterprise of the management itself.

The relation of the rate of return to efficiency is twofold, depending on both the amount of the return and the way in which it is differentiated. Aside from differentiation, a niggardly return will make it impossible to render good service, even if the company desires to do so, by making it impossible to attract the necessary capital. A reasonably liberal return will make this possible but will not in itself afford a strong incentive; and a lavish return will afford a positive incentive to spending money on more elaborate equipment than the public should be asked to pay for. A return graded according to efficiency would afford the perfect solution, but it is doubtful whether the ordinary commission has good enough standards of measurement available to make such a policy practicable.

2. ADEQUACY OF RETURN AND ADEQUACY OF SERVICE

It would serve no useful purpose to attempt to enumerate all the elements which enter into the efficient operation of a utility plant. But certain ones have a special relation to this problem of adequate return, because they call for added investment. Of the many uses to which added capital can be put, some are more profitable than the average of the existing investment, some may be about equally profitable, and some are less profitable or yield no direct profit at all. The Pennsylvania Railroad has had a policy of using funds reserved out of earnings for capital expenditures which they classed as "unproductive." "Productive" and "profitable" are to be taken in the sense of rendering increased service without change of rates, profitable implying that the yield is more than operating expenses. The highly profitable classes of expenditure include the rehabilitation of obsolete equipment, or equipment which is so decrepit that the cost of maintenance and repairs is exorbitant, the installing of new improvements which will increase the efficiency of the whole existing plant, the completion of traffic connections which will bring a railroad large traffic, of which it is seriously in need, and other things of like effect. A mere increase in the number of units already installed is not likely to be more profitable than the original investment, though the increase in size may be taken advantage of to secure some economies—usually moderate in amount. Such an increase may be less profitable because the added capacity it represents may be called into use only a small part of the time.

However, if the utility receives the same return on its investment in any case, then any use it may make of capital is profitable—to the company's treasury—as long as the commission can be persuaded that the capital is "used and useful" in the public service and therefore is entitled to a return. While commissions will not include plants built many years ahead of demand, or land held merely for future speculation, still they are inclined to be liberal in including reserves of productive capacity, reserves of coal, and construction in advance of demand within reasonable limits.

Among other outlays that are less profitable than the average come branch lines into very thinly settled territory, which cannot furnish the main line enough traffic to make up for their own deficits, passenger stations (here again there is an indirect profitableness, for shippers ride on trains, and the satisfied passenger is likely to turn freight to the road), grade separations, and, in general, any improved device for which there will, for the present, not be enough use to pay a return on its cost. For most of these there is a social demand not strictly proportionate to the number of units of paying traffic which they bring to the line, beyond what would have been carried in any case. A good company is a company able and willing to make some, at least, of these less profitable outlays; presumably those having the greatest worth to the community, as far as that can be judged.

Now the natural or automatic incentive to make these various classes of outlays varies with the rate of return allowed. It may be worth while to examine the natural effects of economic self-interest in a number of simplified cases, because that is one of the major forces with which public policy has to reckon; always keeping in mind that actual cases are less simple and that other motives and pressures are available besides bare economic self-interest. First, we may assume a semicompetitive industry, such as railroads, where rates are fixed on the basis of a fair aggregate to all the roads in a region, and any profits any one road may make as the result of improvements will not result in any appreciable reduction in its rates. The profitableness of improvements will depend, then, solely on their capacity to bring in more business or to furnish facilities to handle the natural increase, or to reduce the unit cost at which business can be handled.

Consider, first, a road earning less than the standard return. It will not pay this road to raise capital except for improvements of greater profitableness than the average. In former years it might have built feeder branches; but at present it is more likely to abandon its most unprofitable branches and rely on motor vehicles as feeders. As to reserve capacity, such a road will have a tendency to make scant provision, relying on being able to keep on its line in times of pressure an extra amount of cars belonging to other roads. Certain roads consistently use more cars than they own. Large shippers may also be led to furnish cars for their own use, thus easing the strain on the road's finances. As long as other organizations can furnish a reserve supply of cars, this situation may not be serious, though it is clearly not ideal.

If the earnings are just equal to the return necessary to attract capital, the situation is far better, though the road will have some difficulty in making enough provision in slack times, which are always relatively unprofitable, to be prepared in advance for the extra demands when they come. By building up reserves in the more prosperous times, however, this may be taken care of. The road will still have difficulty in making the less profitable extensions and will be under some pressure to issue an undue amount of bonds in order to secure capital cheaply enough so that it may produce more than it costs.

If the earnings are more than the necessary return, the road will be able to provide reserves and build feeders. In order to provide enough cars for itself in busy periods, it may even build somewhat more than enough for its own requirements, knowing that other roads will try to keep such of its cars as they have on their lines, and that it will not be practicable to insist on their return. While the road will still have no positive incentive to make the really unprofitable betterments, it will be in a position to consider indirect results, such as the growth of business in normal times which may result from being able to take good care of its shippers in times of pressure, or from making thoroughly good provision for passenger traffic.

The situation is different with a monopoly whose returns are fixed on the basis of its valuation, and whose valuation is increased by any useful additions to its investment. Here any investment is lucrative to the company, though in practice it may, as we have seen, shrink from taking advantage of its theoretical rights if that involves an action to secure an increase of rates. If its rate of return is kept below the amount fixed as necessary by the market, then no investment will yield a profit equal to its cost. If the return is equal to the market rate, the company is able to make the less productive additions at the expense of its other patrons but it has no positive incentive. If it is in a stage of decreasing costs, it will be able to make a number of the less profitable additions along with the more profitable, without being forced to ask for an increase in rates, and it will be very likely to make them. If the return is more than the market rate, the company has a positive incentive to make extensions and other added investments, whether they are needed or not, and there is need for a public check on capital expenditures in order to avoid waste.

The making of additions, however, does not depend solely on the financial interest of the companies. Commissions may be granted the power to order them to be made, as far as they are reasonably needed for the public service. This includes such things as branch lines, grade separations, and signaling systems required for the public safety. In a semicompetitive industry any road might suffer a loss from such expenditures if it were required to spend more money in proportion to its gross earnings than the other roads in the same region, so that the task of the commission will be easier, and the equities better preserved, if such relatively unproductive expenditures are fairly divided between the roads. There is also an important distinction between additions which merely involve added service and those in which the commission assumes to tell the management how its property should be operated in the interests of economy and efficiency. The Interstate Commerce Commission has said that it is not the management of the roads and cannot order economies to be introduced. Gains which are unmistakably within the reach of the companies may be taken into account in fixing rates,[1] but problematical gains resulting from untried experiments are not in this class, and the utility commissions are hardly in a position to order companies to make such experiments. This leads us to the next question: that of standards of construction, service, and economy which are available for the actual work of regulation.

3. STANDARDS OF CONSTRUCTION

The control of construction serves the three ends of adequacy, economy, and safety. As to adequacy, there is no question of the right of government to require a utility to install facilities which may be essential to adequate service, including, of course, the raising and spending of capital funds for that purpose. It is certain also that there is a limit on such requirements, a point beyond which they would be held confiscatory. But the location of that point is uncertain. It is not necessary that every separate extension should pay a full return on its cost; and with regard to abandonments, at least, the Interstate Commerce Commission has held that the fact that a branch is not, by itself, earning enough to cover operating expenses is not conclusive that the road should be allowed to abandon it. The branch may, of course, be feeding a lucrative traffic to the main line. The general rule, as expressed in the act of 1920, is that the commission may not require continued operation at a loss, unless required by charter provisions. The same act gives the commission the power to require extensions,

[1] On this point see especially the 1911 Increased Rate Case, 20 I.C.C.R. 243, 279, and the Five per cent Case, 31 I.C.C.R. 351, 406–414.

if the expense is not such as to impair the ability of the carrier to perform its duty to the public. The extent and character of extensions are left undefined, and Vanderblue and Burgess take the position that the provision is of doubtful constitutionality unless construed to apply only to construction incidental to a service which the carrier has already "held itself out" to perform, and not to new services which it had not contemplated rendering. Under this interpretation the commission might require the construction of feeders and enlargements of existing terminal facilities, but presumably not an extension of the main line beyond its present terminus. In any case calling for large capital expenditures, such as a major operation on a large city terminal, it is virtually unthinkable that the commission should proceed without the voluntary assent of the carriers. The technique of compelling people to lend money was fairly well developed during the Middle Ages, but that of compelling them to borrow represents virtually an untried field. The limit on this power, then, is somewhat vague, and it may be much affected by the public sense of what is reasonable.

On the negative side, it has long been the practice to require a "certificate of public convenience and necessity" before permitting any new railroad enterprise. The need for this arose from the amount of wasteful duplication of lines which marred the development of our railway net, some of the lines being built for nothing but their nuisance value to other existing lines. By the act of 1920 this function was centered in the Interstate Commerce Commission, and that body is now in full exercise of it. As an instance, it has faced the interesting and delicate problem whether to permit the building of a new trunk line across Pennsylvania, connecting with certain other lines which now lack a through connection. Extensions, as well as new projects, must pass the scrutiny of the commission.

Economy of construction is ordinarily left to such checks as the self-interest of the company may set up. The state has an interest in the matter, however, since part of any reasonable scheme of control of security issues is to see to it that the funds raised go into the working property and are not diverted or diluted through secret commissions and the like. Where an attempt is made to keep capitalization down to the actual investment, the obligation is still more definite to see that the intent of the state's policy is not evaded by fraud or lack of ordinary business economy in construction. A more remote check consists in the possibility that an extravagant cost will not be recognized in the valuation for rate making.

Such a conjectural future check is of little force compared to a check exercised at the time the money is spent, together with a continuing check, through the accounts, on the subsequent changes in the property. This can be accomplished in special cases—for instance, expenditures which go into the purchase valuation of the Chicago surface lines are passed upon, as they are made, by the Board of Supervising Engineers. But the amount of work involved is so great that the practice is not likely to become general. Such a system places an enormous responsibility on the board, since costs, once authorized, can hardly be questioned afterward; and if the board fails of its very difficult duty, the damage is well-nigh irreparable.

In the case of railroads, compulsory building of cars and loco-motives does not seem to have followed on the heels of compulsory construction of track extensions, and there seems to be no standard of adequate supply in the matter of rolling stock other than that implied in the general obligation of the company to serve the public demand. This does not mean every single demand, for it is recognized that the heaviest peaks will not and cannot instantly be met. To do so would probably require not only more cars but more trackage in yards, or even on the line itself. The streets would have to hold nothing but street-car tracks to serve every passenger as he wants to be served, at the rush hour. The cost of such 100 per cent adequacy would be out of proportion to the burdens imposed by a moderate amount of enforced waiting. As we saw in discussing costs, the machines' demand that we move, not when we wish to move, but when the machines can move us, is a very reasonable demand. Sometimes the peak load is not necessary and inevitable, but rather the result of the fact that people will not plan in advance to provide for their needs on a schedule which industry can meet without undue disturbance. This lack of planning bears a large share of the responsibility for the unnecessary and harmful ups and downs of American business and industry.

That the maximum demand cannot reasonably be met is recognized by the resort to rules for the distribution of freight cars when there are not enough to go around. The roads have also gained recognition for the practice of embargoes, though this is limited to emergencies, to be used only as a means to the carrying of the maximum possible amount of freight, and is under the supervision of the Interstate Commerce Commission.

4. STANDARDS OF SERVICE

The public-utility services are, on the whole, peculiar in the readiness with which they may be reduced to standards. The number of thermal units per cubic foot of gas—now substituted for the earlier candle-power measurement—can be determined by a calorimeter, and the amount of impurities by quantitative analysis. The voltage of electricity is a simple measurement, and unsteadiness of voltage makes itself known instantly to the user. Whether water is safe to drink or not is gauged by a count of bacteria, and the element of judgment involved is of the sort which must always be left to the medical profession. Gas and electrical meters are commonly required to be accurate within a small fixed percentage of error. In the working out of all these standards the best results can only be had with the help and cooperation of the technical and professional associations in the field.

Safety is perhaps the chief ground of regulation of the service of carriers, especially railroads. The loss of life from the old link-and-pin coupling has been done away with by a standard type of automatic coupler, and other safety measures include ash-pan specifications and boiler inspection, gates or grade separation at crossings, electric headlights, the experimental installation of automatic stop devices on single divisions, the hours-of-service law of 1907, the limitation of speed by certain localities, and numerous other measures. These, however, are not directly linked with the regulation of prices and must be passed over here in spite of the interesting and difficult questions involved, especially in keeping such regulation free from undue influence by special interests, each with its appliance to sell or other axe to grind.

5. OPERATING EFFICIENCY IN RELATION TO A FAIR RETURN

Is it possible to gauge the efficiency of operation of a public utility by objective tests, and definitely enough to furnish sound basis for awarding one company, for instance, 8 or 9 per cent return for unusual efficiency, and another 4 per cent by reason of inefficiency? The difficulties are discouragingly great, and no perfect measure is to be found, but we are getting accustomed, in cases in which perfect measures are not to be had, to trusting to imperfect ones or, rather, trusting the regulating bodies to use imperfect measures justly. The bare figures of operating expenses mean nothing as an index of economical operation. In the first place, some plants have lower operating expenses because they have invested capital funds in expensive improvements. Figures for hydroelectric plants and coal plants are not comparable, since hydroelectric plants have a heavy investment in waterworks and extraordinarily low operating expenses. In the second place, the larger plants are vastly more economical than the smaller, simply on account of size, and there would be no justice in penalizing all the small plants and rewarding all the large ones when some of the small ones are operated as efficiently as their size permits, and some of the large ones are culpably inefficient. In the third place, some plants serve more densely peopled areas than others, and the latter have to cover more ground and invest more in transmission mains to secure the same volume of business for the central plant. Or the same result may occur through lack of enterprise, through failing to secure a normal percentage of the residents as customers. In the fourth place, the coal available in different localities is of different qualities and different prices, and so on indefinitely.

In attacking these difficulties the best weapons are physical indexes, rather than money outlays, as these indexes are not affected by differences in prices. As a first corrective, it is quite possible to obtain statistical curves showing the normal effect of size on these various units of expense, other things being equal, and of density of population, other things being equal. The other special conditions might be allowed for separately, and an intelligent judgment might be formed as to the normal amount for a given item of cost in a particular type and size of plant under particular conditions. By canvassing a large number of representative items, a fair measure of total efficiency might be secured, in terms of a percentage of normal.

One of the most interesting approaches to this subject, that of Dr. C. S. Morgan, follows a different method and rates the comparative standing of different companies in each of twenty-six statistical items having some bearing on efficiency, in financing, operation, or sales. By summing up these ratings he produces a final rank for the eight companies on which he tries his experiment.[1] Needless to say, such comparisons should be confined to plants of similar size and general characteristics, or else the ranking should be modified at some point in the process by an allowance for size; otherwise the largest plants will show a consistent tendency to make the best efficiency record. Telephone companies would, of course, be an exception to this. Other characteristics also should be allowed for, if possible.

Such rating scales might work some injustice between companies in spite of all that could be done to allow for differences in conditions. A more conservative method of using them would be to allow each company a standard return at a time when its efficiency appears to be satisfactory, and then for a term of years to allow a differential scale of returns, according as the company's rating scale shows more or less efficiency than in the standard year. This would need to be accompanied by a right to revise the whole scale of returns at any time when

[1] C. S. Morgan, *Regulation and the Management of Public Utilities*, Chap. ii, esp. p. 58.

methods of production change so radically that the results of the former scales are no longer just.

A plan similar in principle, which has been in use for a considerable time, is known in this country as the "Boston sliding scale," though it has been used longer and more widely in England. It is applied to gas companies, and instead of an index of operating efficiency, it uses simply the price charged for gas. Return increases as the price is lowered. This has the merit of simplicity but is doubly liable to become obsolete, being subject not only to changes in the arts, but also to changes in the purchasing power of the dollar. It is suited to a condition in which the art is progressing, but not by too radical transformations. It tends to exhaust its effect as a company gets nearer the minimum cost practicable under existing conditions, or it may give a large premium for some general change in the art, for which the management of this company is not at all responsible.

The study and comparison of records which accompany an efficiency rating scale can hardly fail to have a good effect, apart from any money incentives which may be employed. Such study always reveals the fact that every company has something to learn from some of the others in some parts of its work. Even the most efficient are not best at everything.

6. HOW FAR SHOULD CONTROL GO?

The control of efficiency is peculiarly far-reaching, for it means that the government takes a share in the functions and responsibilities of management, and the question may well be raised whether the benefits supposed to be derived from the initiative and independence of private enterprise may not vanish when well-nigh every decision is subject to scrutiny and review. This is a large and difficult question, to which no simple answer is possible. Is it possible that the government, to control the utilities effectively, must virtually duplicate the work of management, and that it might as well manage them directly, and avoid the duplication?

This deserves consideration in a separate chapter dealing with the choice between public control and public operation. Suffice it to say here that: (1) even within the private organization of a huge modern enterprise, there is an increasing amount of this scrutinizing and reviewing of decisions, and a growing system of checks and balances, so that unless the initiative of private enterprise has enough stamina to combat such conditions it cannot survive the results of its own growth. (2) Public officials may be more zealous in setting standards for others to conform to than they would be in reforming their own methods were they in actual charge of operation. (3) Private enterprise has, on the whole, a very good record of accomplishment, even under modern conditions in which the emphasis is shifted from competitive to cooperative methods and incentives. As a result, the burden of proof is still on the advocates of public operation. (4) Until the government is ready to assume this burden of proof, it is better to put up with some unsatisfactory conditions rather than to extend regulation so far and so fast as to break the morale of private enterprise and cause it to feel discouraged and helpless. (5) There is probably no fixed limit to the amount of supervision which the morale of private enterprise can withstand. Given time, it can accommodate itself to things that would seem intolerable if imposed suddenly.

REFERENCES FOR FURTHER READING

Annals, pp. 262–306, May, 1914.

BARNES, I.R., *Cases on Public Utility Regulation* (rev. ed.), Sec. 14, "Rate Regulation: Operating Expenses," Sec. 17, "Service Regulations," 1934.

BAUER, JOHN, *Effective Regulation of Public Utilities*, Chap. xiii.

BUSSING, I. C., *Public Utility Regulation and the So-called Sliding Scale*, 1936.

HOLMES, *Regulation of Railroads and Public Utilities in Wisconsin*, Chap. xviii.

JONES, ELIOT, *Principles of Railroad Transportation*, Chap. xix.

────── and BIGHAM, *Principles of Public Utilities*, Chap. ix, 1931.

────── and VANDERBLUE, *Railroads: Cases and Selections*, Chaps. xiii–xvii, xxi.

MORGAN, CHARLES S., *Regulation and the Management of Public Utilities*.

RUGGLES, "Railway Service and Regulation in Port Terminals," *Amer. Econ. Rev.*, pp. 438–446, September, 1921.

SHARFMAN, *The American Railroad Problem*, Chap. vii.

VANDERBLUE and BURGESS, *Railroads: Rates—Service—Management*, Chaps. xiii–xxi.

CHAPTER XXIII

THE QUESTION OF RELATIVE CHARGES

Differential rates based on constant costs and a divisible market, 350—The general rule of comparative cost permits some differential rates, 352—Scientific electrical rate systems as an illustration, 353—Railroads and the rule of comparative cost, 355—Stimulating new business *vs.* securing an increased share of existing business, 356—The infant-industry principle as a justification for discrimination, 357—Preservation of established business, 358—Other considerations, 359—Systems of differential freight rates, 359—Should a long haul ever be charged less than an intermediate short haul? 362—The problem of "Pittsburgh plus," 365—Conclusion, 367.

1. DIFFERENTIAL RATES BASED ON CONSTANT COSTS AND A DIVISIBLE MARKET

Edison claims to have originated the device of making money by selling goods below cost in a foreign market: the device now known as "dumping."[1] His plant was working at part capacity and, in response to his inquiries, his experts estimated that it could turn out 25 per cent more lamps at only about 2 per cent increase in cost. Accordingly (against the advice of his associates) he began selling lamps abroad at less than the foreign cost of production, utilized his spare capacity, and increased his earnings. If he had tried to achieve the same end by cutting domestic prices he would not have fared so well, since to sell one new lamp he would have had to reduce the price on four lamps he was already selling. And if he had tried to sell his extra 25 per cent at home at a price low enough to take them off the market, while keeping up his price on the ones he was already selling, he would have encountered difficulties calculated to tax Edisonian ingenuity. His best chance would have been to devise new kinds of lamps with totally new uses, such as pocket flashlights or bulbs for Christmas-tree illumination. But to develop such uses calls for more than merely manufacturing goods and setting a price on them: it is a large task of technical development and creation of demand, in which the lamp itself is a minor feature. It is far simpler to invade some new region and seize a part of the existing trade there by underbidding.

[1] Cited in Marshall, Wright, and Field, *Materials for the Study of Elementary Economics*, p. 421, from *Wall St. Jour.*, December 20, 1911.

This case illustrates the essential basis of the theory and practice of differential rates. When added output can be had at considerably less than proportionate increase in costs, the producer has an extra incentive to cut prices. If he has an assured market at the prices he is now charging, he is not likely to cut far into the market, for he will soon reach the point at which the profit on added sales will not make up for the reduction of earnings on the business already in hand. Only if some competitor threatens to take away a large part of his existing business is he likely to be drawn into a war of heavy price cutting to defend it. But if he can attract new business at reduced prices while keeping all his former business at the old prices, then he can gain by the transaction as long as the new business pays anything more than the actual increase in costs which results from it, beyond what the costs would have been if the added business had not been found. Thus occurs the paradox of profitable sales "below cost"—that is, below average cost, or below the amount which a typical cost-accounting system would allocate to the goods, but not below the added cost occasioned by their production. The profit depends on this margin above additional cost, and on keeping the reductions in price pretty closely confined to new business. Hence the market must be of a sort that can be divided up into parts, or classified in some way, so that goods can be sold cheaper to some than to others.

Where the producer sells a homogeneous commodity, of known quality and easily transported from place to place, classification is not easy. But the public utilities, with which we are concerned, sell services, or commodities, delivered from fixed pipes or wires in such a way that the delivery is an essential feature. Here the company can discriminate as much as it pleases, the chief limits being set by the resentment of customers or the disorganization of the market which results when every sale is a matter of personal higgling or when everyone suspects that others are getting goods on more favorable terms than himself, that these favorable terms are profitable to the company, and hence that the price he is paying is exorbitant. Back of these forces stands the regulating power of the state, in case discriminations cannot be defended by the tests of justice and public usefulness. In general, discrimination must be accompanied by some difference in service which the ordinary man can understand, and it must tend to increase the usefulness of the industry to the public and, as far as the rates affect the competitive standing of the producers who pay them, any discrimination must be consistent with fair competitive rivalry in which the fittest may survive and the public may have the benefit of their services.

2. THE GENERAL RULE OF COMPARATIVE COST PERMITS SOME DIFFERENTIAL RATES

We naturally think of a nondiscriminatory rate as so many cents per kilowatt-hour, or per thousand feet of gas, or per telephone call. With railway freight rates, people have quite generally been educated up to the point of realizing that a rate of so many mills per ton-mile would be a very discriminatory rate indeed, since the long haul costs far less per ton-mile than the short haul. Less-than-carload freight costs more than carload, partly because the railroad loads and unloads it instead of the shipper, as with carload freight; and partly because the loading and unloading of a mixed car is itself more expensive, and the car often has to be stopped and unloaded en route in order to sort the contents into carloads bound for single destinations. Furthermore, carload freight nearly always shows a higher percentage of paying weight to dead weight. If a balance of empty cars moves regularly in one direction, it costs less to move added freight in that direction than in the other. Hence freight rates must be highly differentiated if they are to approximate an adjustment based on the relative costs of the different classes of traffic which they cover.

Costs of single shipments cannot be discovered at all and need not be, for rates are not made for single shipments. A commodity rate covers all the traffic between given destinations in a single important commodity, and a class rate covers a large group of less important commodities. The rate from one station to another is only a part of some regional structure of rates in which one cannot be changed without affecting many others. In any practical question of rates, then, what the rate-making authorities need to know is the aggregate cost of the traffic affected by the system of rates in which a change is contemplated, or its relative cost as compared to other classes or groups of traffic. Such relative costs can be estimated—roughly, it is true, but closely enough to furnish a basis for rate policies. Thus there is no sufficient ground for the idea that rates cannot, in the nature of the case, have anything to do with cost. A great deal of the differentiation of rates is based on differences in the cost of handling the business. Hitherto, costs have been taken account of in special studies when special rate questions arose. If the tentative system of cost accounting formulated under the Federal Coordinator of Transportation comes into general use, it will furnish continuous information, with greater certainty that all costs are allocated. Many factors affecting costs, however, will still remain to be dealt with in special studies, if at all.

The same thing is true, under different conditions, in the other public utilities. In the furnishing of electrical current, the investment is largely governed by the capacity of power units and mains, and this in turn depends on the maximum demand or peak load, rather than on the total amount of current sold. Maintenance, depreciation, and interest on this investment are "capacity expenses," and current taken at off-peak hours adds nothing to these expenses and need not pay anything toward them in order to be self-sustaining. Current taken at peak hours, on the other hand, must bear its shares of these capacity expenses in order to be worth taking. In making rates it is not ordinarily practicable to charge one rate at ten in the morning and another at five in the afternoon, but there are classes of business, such as church lighting, which are likely to put a fairly heavy load on the plant at the peak time without taking a very large aggregate amount of current, while there are others, such as power used in industries, which use current regularly through the day, resulting in a large aggregate consumption with a relatively small peak demand. The use of electricity for cooking, water heating, and domestic machinery improves the character of the residence demand, increasing the total use without proportionate increase in the peak load, and thus reducing the average cost per kilowatt-hour. Thus the cost of different types of business varies greatly.

Similarly, in telephone service there are differences in the cost of one-party, two-party, and four-party lines, while the extra cost of additional calls is less than the average cost of the entire service. With water, the fire-hydrant service calls for large investment in connections and in extra capacity in the mains and hence is quite an expensive service, but the total amount of water taken is insignificant.

The comparative-cost rule, then, requires, not an equal unit charge in terms of the natural unit of service, but a highly differentiated system of rates, the governing principle being that each class of business shall pay the costs for which it is really responsible, as far as that is practicable. This is partly a matter of justice as between consumers, but there is another and even more important reason for it when the utility sells to producers a service which forms an important part of their cost of production. For then a producer's success in the competitive struggle may depend on paying equitable rates as compared to his competitors.

3. SCIENTIFIC ELECTRICAL RATE SYSTEMS AS AN ILLUSTRATION

Ordinarily, the rule of comparative cost requires that the overhead or constant costs should be distributed uniformly over the output. This conflicts with the principle of maximum utilization, which urges that no chance should be lost to attract added business which will yield anything at all above its additional cost. In electrical rate systems these two principles can be, to a considerable degree, harmonized, because it is not necessary to charge each user a uniform rate for all his current. As a result, he may be made to pay his fair share of the overhead burden, while the last unit of current he takes may cost him no more than its actual additional cost to the company. The most logical system of this sort divides the rate into three parts: a consumer charge for billing, meter reading, and similar items; a "readiness-to-serve" charge, based on some index of the amount the customer is likely to add to the peak load on the plant; and an output charge for the actual current used. More commonly, the first two parts of the rate are merged in a high rate per kilowatt-hour for the early units consumed, which is so arranged as to accomplish substantially the same result in a way that seems more simple and does less violence to the prejudices of the consumers.[1] The customer who is responsible for a larger share of the peak load must use more current before getting the benefit of the lower rate, thus virtually paying a larger readiness-to-serve charge.

The crucial thing in such a system is the index used to represent the consumer's "peak responsibility." If he makes a special contract not to use current at the peak hours, the matter settles itself. Usually the criterion as between individual consumers is the capacity of their fixtures, while if studies show that the peak burden from this class as a whole is, for example, one-half of the aggregate individual capacities of all its members, the capacity charge will be correspondingly reduced. In some cases a meter may be used which records the consumer's peak use of current, or even a meter which runs at different rates at different hours. None of these methods is perfect. They often fail to give the individual consumer an opportunity to lower his rate by reducing the demands he makes on the plant at the peak, but at least they afford a method of taking care of the capacity costs in such a way that they do not swell the charge the consumer has to pay for added current beyond his ordinary consumption. And they reduce the rate to the "long-hour" user, who takes a large amount of current in proportion to the capacity of his fixtures and takes most of it at off-peak hours. The results of such rate policies, and other policies looking to the development of business to utilize the off hours, can be seen in the very great increase in the effective utilization of modern power plants.[2]

[1] The law sometimes requires that there shall be no charge except for current actually supplied.

[2] See Watkins, *Electrical Rates*, p. 22, for a diagram showing, for a typical large plant, an increase in the load factor (ratio of average to maximum load) from 50 per cent to over 80 per cent, but with a relapse to less than 70 per cent after the end of the war. A load factor of 80 per cent undoubtedly means night work in industry.

But rate systems are not wholly constructed on such scientific principles. Often power rates are lower than others simply because the manufacturer is in a position to generate his own current, sometimes as a partial by-product of his other operations, and a low rate is necessary to secure his business. This is simply the principle of charging what the traffic will bear. It is a proper principle to apply, if the plant has spare capacity even at the peak; but if this is not the case, and the added business calls for added investment, care needs to be taken lest the business taken at extra-low rates may not be worth what it costs.

4. RAILROADS AND THE RULE OF COMPARATIVE COST

This rule is particularly important for railways because their shippers are so very dependent on rail rates for the opportunity to survive and prosper. When the railroads gave low rates to competitive junctions and charged other points more, even for shorter hauls, they made it virtually impossible for the noncompetitive points to develop successful jobbing enterprises, or any other business which was done on a sufficiently small margin to make transportation rates a decisive element in costs of production. Many places felt that they were being deprived of their "natural advantages of geographic location." Places where railroad lines meet are, of course, natural centers of production and distribution, but a junction of branch lines of one system or affiliated roads is just as much a natural center as a junction of competing lines, as far as the cost of transportation is concerned. From this standpoint, rates paid by shippers in localities which are competing should be proportioned to what it costs the railroads to handle their traffic, rather than to the strength of the competition which may prevail between the railroads.

This principle would allow roads to classify traffic almost without restrictions, though such related commodities as wheat and flour, or livestock and dressed meats, should be charged such rates that the road makes the same profit on the raw material as on the product made from it.[1] The location of flour milling and meat packing may depend on such adjustments, low rates on the raw material and high rates on the finished product having a tendency to push the manufacturing process nearer to the centers of consumption. Roads would

---

[1] This does not mean the same profit per hundred pounds, but the same profit from 100 pounds of the raw material as from the amount of finished product into which 100 pounds of raw material goes. Where a number of materials are used, coming from different directions, and the product is distributed in different directions, this rule cannot be applied with any definiteness, but in some cases it is important.

also be permitted to make low rates in the direction of empty-car movement and, if they desired, low seasonal rates to develop off-season business or to stimulate shippers to move their goods with greater regularity. In general, rates would increase with distance on a tapering scale, since the long hauls are less costly per mile than the shorter ones. But the effect of distance on costs is often an uncertain quantity, and a great deal of latitude would naturally be left to the roads to increase rates with distance or to disregard distance over considerable areas, as is done, for example, with rates on milk into the large cities. In these and other ways there would still be much room for charging what the traffic will bear.

5. STIMULATING NEW BUSINESS *VS.* SECURING AN INCREASED SHARE OF EXISTING BUSINESS

When a low rate makes it possible for the utility to render a service which otherwise could not be rendered at all, utilizing some of its spare productive capacity for the purpose, the utility gains the difference between the rate and the additional cost of producing the service, the user gains the difference between the rate and the maximum amount he would have been willing to pay rather than go without the service, and there is no corresponding loss to anyone. But when the low rate makes it possible for one set of producers to render services which competing sets of producers were perfectly able and willing to render, then the first set of producers gain, as before, the difference between the rate and the additional cost of handling the business, but their competitors lose the gain they formerly made, measured by their former gross earnings from this business minus whatever reduction of costs they are able to accomplish as a result of no longer having this business to handle. The consumer gains the amount of the reduction in the rate. If the costs traceable to this service are the same for either group of producers, the gains and losses exactly balance. In other words, the profit made by the company which succeeds in diverting business to its line is a gain without corresponding benefit to the community. But the matter does not stop here, for the discriminations may stimulate the growth of business in favored localities although the total cost of production and transportation—meaning the cost to the carrier—is greater than it would have been somewhere else. When this happens, the losses are greater than the gains, and even the consumer is likely to lose, in the long run, from being served by producers who may not be the very best who might have served him. Such a system places a premium on the concentration of manufacturing and trading in large centers where important main lines come together and may have been partly responsible for the overgrowth of large cities and the relative backwardness of smaller places. The present movement toward taking industry out of the congested centers should certainly be given a fair chance, and it cannot have a fair chance unless industry can move out without having to pay higher freight rates for equivalent service.

To sum up, the discrimination which develops new business is a clear social gain, but that which merely serves to divert business from one competing line to another, or build up industry and trade in one place rather than in another, serves no social purpose and does a probable balance of harm. The worst of these discriminations have been done away with, and under the long-and-short-haul clause local points have quite generally been given equal rates with the junctions next beyond them.

6. THE INFANT-INDUSTRY PRINCIPLE AS A JUSTIFICATION FOR DISCRIMINATION

The principles of community interest in this matter of discriminating rates are the same as those involved in the question of free trade *vs.* protection, being concerned with manipulating the money cost of moving goods in order to further the national interest and promote the most desirable geographical organization of industry. One of the principles which must be recognized as modifying the simple rule of comparative cost is the principle that a rate may be justified by the conditions it will help to bring about in the future, even if it could not be justified by the conditions existing before it goes into effect. A low rate may build up an industry which will ultimately furnish a large enough flow of traffic to make the rate remunerative, while if it had to pay in proportion to cost in the early stages, when traffic is small and cost is high, it could never get a start.

The "basing-point" system of rates, formerly used in the south, gave certain points low competitive rates and charged all other points the rate to the nearest basing point plus the local rate to the destination, even though the basing point was beyond the other. Thus one haul was charged the price of two, giving an enormous stimulus to ship goods in to the basing point and out again. The result was to develop a considerable volume of business to a single destination, which is cheaper to haul than more diffused business which has to be handled by way freight. Thus the system may actually have stimulated a more efficient concentration of business by deciding in advance which places should have the opportunity to grow into mercantile centers of really efficient size, when there was not enough business for all to do so, and giving the chosen places in advance the benefit, in rates, of the superior economy which the rates themselves would enable them to develop. Here is a case in which favoritism may really be the secret of efficiency —for a time and under particular conditions. But these conditions may be outgrown in time. The favored centers may grow until the efficiency of concentration is marred by the wastes and evils of congestion, and economy begins actually to require the keeping of traffic out of the larger centers, not the concentrating of as much as possible in these already congested areas. This is decidedly true in the northern and eastern part of the country, where special belt lines are beginning to be used to route through freight around congested terminals instead of through them. To sum up, the infant-industry policy is a delicate thing, calling for very great wisdom in foreseeing the future needs and development of the country, and is extremely liable to error.

7. PRESERVATION OF ESTABLISHED BUSINESS

Another of the general principles governing the social interest in rate making is that existing channels of trade and locations of production are to be given the benefit of all reasonable doubt, since the livelihood of communities has come to depend on them, not to speak of the value of large capital investments. Where cities are in close competition with each other, especially in types of business in which a small difference in rail rates might be decisive, business adjusts itself to the existing rate differentials, whatever they may be, and any change is a misfortune. Hence these relationships should be preserved, as far as possible, through all changes in rates, unless it becomes perfectly clear that they are unjust or uneconomical in such a substantial degree as to warrant the injustice and economic loss which would result from a change. Furthermore, the need of preserving established interests throws an added light on the infant-industry principle. It means that if the infant should disappoint expectations, he may meanwhile acquire a "vested interest" in protection and thus become a permanent burden.

One outstanding example of established interests which need special treatment in order to be able to survive, and which are granted special treatment, is the situation of the New England region. Originally a center of population and manufacturing, the westward movement of population has left it in a byway, working at a disadvantage in length of hauls. The industrial regeneration of the south, which followed the period of reconstruction, meant the growth of cotton mills with the material at their doors, and a relatively short haul across the Ohio to the Middle Western centers of population. Such competition the New England mills can hardly meet without favorable rates to offset in part the handicap of greater distance. Should such help be granted? What is the limit beyond which it should not go? These are delicate and serious questions. A clearly uneconomical location should probably not be sustained permanently, but the disaster of a sudden closing down of major industries should be avoided at almost any cost. Where a change is really called for, it is likely to be less wasteful if it is made gradually, as it might be under the spur of reduced profits, rather than suddenly, as it would be if forced by imminent bankruptcy.

8. OTHER CONSIDERATIONS

The problem of relative rates is so many sided that no formula can anticipate all its developments, and hinges on circumstances too numerous to mention. Rates should be stable enough to give industry and trade a reasonable sense of security but should not be absolutely rigid. They may well afford to give some regard to purely social considerations, especially where it is not clear that this would involve any sacrifice of strictly economic efficiency. Thus they may undertake to promote whatever distribution of population may be socially desirable —if we ever find out what this is. How large should cities be allowed to grow, for their own good? Are industrial suburbs desirable, as compared to independent communities of moderate size? These and other similar questions will repay all the thought which can be given them, even if it is impossible to arrive at definite answers. There is no danger that the rail-rate system will ever be used to force us into some theoretically predetermined mold different from the form in which we are developing naturally. But there may be some danger that desirable experiments may not always receive rate adjustments which will give them a fair chance to hold their own and prove their worth.

But we have generalized sufficiently. The issues at stake can best be seen in definite cases or specific problems. A few of these we may next examine.

9. SYSTEMS OF DIFFERENTIAL FREIGHT RATES[1]

Fifty years ago the system of "charging what the traffic will bear" in fixing freight rates meant no system at all, but chaos. Published

---

[1] One of the best brief analyses of these regional systems is found in Vanderblue and Burgess, *Railroads: Rates—Service—Management*, Chaps. ix–xii (see also Eliot Jones, *Principles of Railway Transportation*, Chap. ix; and Miller, *Railway Transportation*, Chaps. xxiv, xxv).

rates were full of discriminations, but even the published rates meant little or nothing, since shippers of any importance seldom paid them. They were the points of departure for secret rate cutting, and little more. Competitive rail junctions received low rates while the intermediate points paid as much as the road could exact—often more than it would cost to haul the goods past their destination to the next competitive junction and back again. Water competition was met by even lower rates than rail competition, especially ocean competition—where the roads entered the struggle at all. And rates were continually changing. Out of this chaos there has come a structure of rates, bafflingly complex and many sided, but nevertheless a system whose main features can be described.

In the first place, local rates have come to be made up on tapering scales based on distance, with a fixed component, corresponding to the terminal costs. This same general principle, with modifications, applies to through and competitive traffic in some regions. These rates are based on distance (with an allowance for terminal costs), but only approximately. The boundaries of rate zones are likely to be fixed by railroad crosslines, and points on these crosslines, which have for years been rivals on an equal footing as concerns rates, are kept on an equal competitive footing with each other regardless of minor discrepancies of distance.

In the southern region, as we have seen, rates were fixed by combination on certain basing points, that is, by adding the rate to the basing point and the local rate from there to the destination, whether the shipment passed through the basing point or not. The basing points included the important sea and gulf ports, the "fall-line" towns at the head of navigation of the rivers, other points with actual or potential water competition, competitive rail junctions, and some few which seem to have been arbitrarily selected. The ports received lower rates than the other basing points, as was necessary to meet the low costs of ocean shipping. The causes of this system appear to be mainly competitive, but its results are to be understood in the light of the situation of competing wholesalers and jobbers.

The jobber located near the consuming area, competing with larger jobbing houses located at the points of manufacture, earnestly desires a rate system under which he can ship goods in to his warehouse and then out again to the local retailer without paying more for the double haul than his rival does for his single one. If he can buy in carload lots, he can often secure the necessary economy in this way, as his rival must ship the whole distance at less-than-carload rates. But in the south at the time the rate structure was acquiring its distinctive character, few jobbers could handle carload lots. Under these circumstances the basing-point system was defended as the only way in which any successful jobbing centers could be built up in that region. If the basing points had not been favored, their prosperity would not have been diffused among their smaller neighbors but would have gone to the northern manufacturing centers, or to the seaports. With the growth of population and manufactures, and corresponding ability to ship in carload lots, this problem has changed its form, and the Interstate Commerce Commission has made important modifications in the system, under the long-and-short-haul clause. Concessions were made, however, where the rate at the basing point was justified by water competition, over which the Interstate Commerce Commission had no control.

The main feature of the transcontinental rate system has for years been the low rates from coast to coast, made to meet water competition, while the western intermountain region paid rates equal to the coast-to-coast rate plus the local rate from the Pacific coast to the inter-mountain point. If not the full local rate, a somewhat smaller differential was added. Intermediate points at the eastern end of the haul were accorded quite different treatment, commonly paying the same rate as the seaports on commodity traffic both eastbound and westbound. This rate blanket in some cases extended as far west as Omaha. Since 1910, the Interstate Commerce Commission has increasingly applied the revived long-and-short-haul clause to this situation.

Class rates on transcontinental business carry a relatively small amount of traffic and are treated differently from commodity rates. One delicate feature of the whole situation was the question whether, for example, rates from Chicago might be made lower to the coast than to intermountain points, when rates from eastern seaports were so made, in order to put Chicago on an equal footing with the eastern seaports in competing for the western markets. This has been the subject of more than one ruling.

Other regions have their own characteristic rate structures. In all these adjustments it is understood that the rate to any competitive point is the same via all the principal routes, and that if the rate is supposed to be based on distance, it is commonly the short-line distance that governs. Longer routes are at liberty to carry goods at these same rates; but if they are materially longer, they may not find it to their interest unless they can secure relief from the long- and-short-haul clause. Otherwise it might be too expensive in terms of reduced revenue on intermediate business. This opens up an interesting series of questions.

10. SHOULD A LONG HAUL EVER BE CHARGED LESS THAN AN INTERMEDIATE SHORT HAUL?

One of the many problems to which the Interstate Commerce Commission has been forced to find some answer is the question whether a more distant point should ever be charged less than an intermediate point. If the reader will imagine himself in the position of the commission and undertake to solve the issues involved, he may gain some respect for their difficulty. The purpose underlying the law is to prevent rates from being grossly out of accord with comparative costs, as far as regulation can prevent this, and we may accept as our starting point the principle that the nearer point should not normally pay a higher rate.

Let us look first at the case of two lines of equal length, connecting common termini, each serving its own intermediate points. Here, if the rule were enforced from the beginning, it would tend to prevent the competitive rate from being cut as low as it otherwise might be, since rate cutting is made more expensive. Thus the principle would not hurt either road but rather tend to save them from themselves and from each other. After the system of discrimination has become established, a subsequent application of the long-and-short-haul rule is likely to mean reducing the intermediate rates without raising the through rates, thus resulting in a loss of revenue which might have to be made up for, in the long run, by an increase in the general scale of charges. But this is within the control of the commission and raises no great difficulty.

If both carriers are railroads, subject to the orders of the commission, the rule is capable of being enforced without serious hardship. If one of the routes is a competitive deep-water route, the situation changes. Nothing the commission can do will prevent the competitive point from getting lower rates than intermediate points. If the railroad is forced to obey the long-and-short-haul rule, it will simply be unable to compete for such traffic as the water carriers are adapted to handle, since the cost of deep-water carriage is too low to be met if the railroad must extend the cut to a material part of its other business. If it is allowed to meet the water competition without lowering its local rates also, it may be able to take a share of the business at rates which will more than cover the added cost, but it will hardly be able to threaten the existence of the deep-water route.

If the water route is a navigable stream, its costs will be higher than those of a deep-water route, and it may easily be that the railroad can force it out of business if allowed to cut rates to the water point without regard to its intermediate stations. Should this be permitted? The boat lines must be able to cover their total expenses and yield something on the investment, and they must do it almost entirely out of traffic subject to rail competition, while the railroad need cover only the additional cost of this particular business and has relatively large amounts of other traffic not exposed to this kind of competition. Is this fair to the boat lines? If the added costs of handling this traffic are correctly figured on a long-run basis, including interest on any rolling stock, terminals, or other investment which this traffic may require, and if this additional cost is less than the costs the boat lines have to cover, then it can fairly be said that the cheapest way for the community to get this particular freight moved is to take advantage of the surplus carrying capacity of the railroad and the low additional costs of utilizing it.

But great care should be taken that the added costs are not underestimated, as there is a strong tendency to do, ignoring costs which increase only in the long run. There should be some assurance that, if the boat lines are forced out of business, the railroad does not proceed to put up rates again until the public gains none of the benefit of the low additional costs which have enabled the railroad to win the contest. This last is the reason for the provision of the act of 1910 to the effect that, if a railroad lowers its rates in competition with a water route, it cannot subsequently raise them again except on a positive showing of justification other than the elimination of the water competition.

If the reader, in his temporary rôle of Interstate Commerce Commissioner, decides the case in the way indicated and grants relief to the railroad, he must be prepared to find the waterway advocates stigmatizing him as a servant of the railroad interests, even though the railroads, in view of some of his other policies, might indignantly refuse to consider him in that light.

If one of two competing railroads is materially longer than the other, still another situation arises. One way of analyzing it is to point out that the junction is nearer the common market than some of the intermediate points on the longer line, and on the distance principle it should have lower rates. This advantage is not seriously affected by the fact that a roundabout rail line may bid for a share of the traffic. If the junction rate is reasonable, the intermediate point on the longer line, being really a more distant point, should pay more; and if the law gives it equal rates, the law is creating a discrimination rather than preventing one.

But granting all this, should not the roundabout line stay out of the competition and leave the business for the more direct line which can presumably handle it at less cost to the community? If the direct line cannot handle all the business, the indirect line is needed, and also it will be able to get some of the traffic without meeting the rates of the shorter line. But in practice this occurs only in relatively rare periods of great congestion, and in ordinary times the shorter road would be able to handle all the tonnage and the longer road would have none unless it did cut rates. The longer road is then rendering an emergency service which is of value all the time, though most of the time it merely stands ready to serve. If this service is really needed in the emergency times, it ought to be worth what it costs to render, including the "idle overhead" which goes on while the freight is not being carried. But how can the road which furnishes this readiness to serve be paid for the service? By far the simplest way is to let it compete on the most favorable terms possible for a share of the competitive freight. Thus, in such a case, it seems justifiable to let the longer route enter the competition without lowering its intermediate rates, always assuming that these are not otherwise unreasonable. This may mean that some freight moves by a somewhat more costly route, but this seems by far the most available and least obnoxious way of subsidizing a real transportation service. It is better than forcing the freight to go the shorter way and then paying the resulting saving over to the longer line to compensate it for its standby service. It may be, in some cases, that the roundabout line has so much traffic of its own from other sources that it has less spare capacity than the more direct route. In this case the foregoing argument does not hold, and there is no clear social justification for granting relief, other than the difficulty of drawing the line in such a case.

Another consideration is the possibility that the roundabout line may be one of the weak roads whose existence is the cause of so much perplexity in determining fair earnings. If a weak line can add to its revenues by engaging in roundabout competition, it may help to make the present system of regulation workable and to avoid the necessity of more radical remedies. Relief granted to weak roads, if it has this effect, may well be worth a moderate amount of waste from roundabout haulage.

Under these conditions what should be the rule as to this practice? It appears that roundabout lines should be granted relief in some cases, at least. Among the essential conditions should be (1) that the competitive rates should be reasonable, on the basis of cost or distance by the short lines; (2) that the intermediate rates on the roundabout route should be reasonable by a similar test; (3) that the roundabout line should do no more than meet the existing competitive rate; (4)

that this rate should pay something more than the added cost of the traffic to the roundabout line, figured on a long-run basis; (5) that the roundabout line is not a strong line with heavy traffic, but a line with more spare capacity, and preferably a lower rate of earnings, than the line with which it is competing. The Interstate Commerce Commission has actually followed a policy of granting relief quite generally, but always requiring as minimum conditions the first four of those mentioned above.

These are only a few of the multitude of problems of relative rail rates. Equally perplexing, though different in character, are the issues appearing in the field of general industry.

11. THE PROBLEM OF "PITTSBURGH PLUS"

Under the "Pittsburgh plus" system of price fixing, condemned by the Federal Trade Commission in 1924, steel was sold by the United States Steel Corporation at the Pittsburgh price plus freight to destination, and other companies followed this system even where the steel was made in other places, such as the Chicago district, and did not actually pay the freight from Pittsburgh. This system has been attacked as a discrimination against steel-using industries located in or near the Chicago district and getting their steel from that source. They paid more for their steel than their competitors in the Pittsburgh district, though the steel might actually cost less. The system also tended to maintain the sales of Pittsburgh steel by making it as cheap to the buyer as steel from any other source, though it might not be so cheap to make and transport.

In defense of the system it was urged that the Pittsburgh steel was needed to supply the total demand in the western markets, and the price had to be high enough to move the steel westward. In support of this contention figures were cited showing that the westward shipments of steel exceeded those in the other direction. However, it appeared that some steel did move eastward in spite of the less favorable terms on which it could be sold there than farther west. The western producers were willing to "dump" some of their product in markets tributary to Pittsburgh at far lower margins than their own market afforded. The preponderance of westward shipments might be maintained partially because the price system made it easier for Pittsburgh to sell steel westward than for the Chicago district to sell eastward. The condition urged as a defense of the price system was a condition which might not continue to exist if the price system itself did not sustain it.

After the Federal Trade Commission's order against Pittsburgh plus, it was replaced by a system with multiple bases; different ones for different products, but usually including at least Pittsburgh, Birmingham, and the Chicago district. Base prices at Chicago and Birmingham, however, continued to be materially higher than those at Pittsburgh. In 1934 the commission reported adversely on the revised system as a form of price fixing, while the NRA recommended constructive reforms. In 1937 the commission instituted an action against the essentially similar system in the cement industry. In July, 1938, while a general governmental inquiry covering monopoly was getting under way, the steel structure was changed by eliminating or reducing the price differentials between the principal bases, and adding a number of new ones, prices being revised downward.

The chief objection to the multiple-base system remains, however, namely, the freedom of both base and nonbase mills to reach out into the territory nearer to other mills and meet the other mills' delivered prices in this territory, although this yields them less, after deducting freight, than they received in their own near-by territory. This is called "absorbing freight" and is attacked as discrimination. It is claimed that, if the producers were truly competing, they would concentrate on the more lucrative near-by business rather than reaching out for low-yield sales and thus would cease to absorb freight. A more valid criticism is that the competitive incentive to lower base prices is reduced because a mill can increase its sales at less sacrifice by maintaining its base price and pushing its freight-absorbing sales. This involves less sacrifice because in the latter case the reduced yield is confined to the new business which the mill thereby secures and does not have to be extended to the whole market. The result is wasteful cross-freighting and a multiplication of selling expense.

The system has perplexing ramifications too numerous to discuss here; and any ruling that may be made will have far-reaching effects, since the practice of freight absorption is widespread in industry. An economist's judgment will naturally hinge on a comparison of effects under the present system and possible or proposed alternatives. The latter include limiting or forbidding freight absorption, and giving the buyer the privilege of taking delivery at the mill instead of only at destination.

To forbid freight absorption would mean that a producer could increase his selling area only by reducing his base price, provided others did not make an equal reduction. The immediate effect would probably be to precipitate price wars which would drive prices down to cutthroat levels. The ultimate effect might be a form of stalemate in which no one would reduce prices because others would be sure to meet the reduction. Unrestricted selling f.o.b. mill would probably bring on price wars and lead ultimately to some form of truce. It is a doubtful and debatable question whether these measures would, in the long run, promote desirable and healthy competitive conditions, while they would necessitate costly relocations of plants. On the other hand, reasonable limitations on freight absorption, while raising some problems of administration, would afford a more moderate strengthening of competitive pressures on prices and also reduce the wastes of cross-freighting, without going to destructive extremes. But any form of competition in these industries must necessarily be "imperfect" on account of the unavoidable characteristics of the industries themselves.

Many industries discriminate in the sense of disregarding transportation costs or accepting lower net yields on sales where this is necessary to meet competition. The law permits discriminations made in good faith to meet an equally low price of a competitor, but not such as are intended and calculated to extinguish competition or unduly to limit it. The distinction is hard to define in objective terms.

12. CONCLUSION

To sum up, it appears that problems of relative prices exist in all types of business. The considerations governing such policies are sometimes in conflict. The maximum utilization of existing facilities may conflict with the rule of selling to different customers at prices based on the relative cost of serving them, while too zealous attempts to dispose of surplus products may interfere with the conditions of healthy competition, both among customers and in the industry itself. And the dominant consideration, both in the public-utility field and in general industry, is a rate or price policy which shall be consistent with fair and healthy competition, both in the industry itself and among those who, as customers, must use its services and pay the prices it charges.

REFERENCES FOR FURTHER READING

BARKER, *Public Utility Rates*, Chaps. x–xvi.
BROWN, H. G., *Transportation Rates and Their Regulation*, Chaps. iv–vii, x, xi.
CLARK, J. M., *Economics of Overhead Costs*, Chaps. xiv, xvi, xx.
———, *Standards of Reasonableness in Local Freight Discriminations*, Columbia University Studies in Political Science, 1910.
———, "Basing-point Methods of Price-quoting," *Canadian Jour. Econ. Polit. Sci.*, IV (November, 1938), 477–489.
COMMONS, "Delivered-price Practice in the Steel Industry," *Amer. Econ. Rev.*, pp. 505–519, September, 1924.

DAGGETT, S., *Principles of Inland Transportation* (rev. ed.), Chaps. xvi–xviii, xxi, xxiv, 1934.

FETTER, F. A., *The Masquerade of Monopoly*, Part III, Chap. xv.

HADLEY, A. T., *Railroad Transportation.*

JONES, ELIOT, *Principles of Railway Transportation*, Chaps. vi–ix.

JONES and BIGHAM, *Principles of Public Utilities*, Chaps. vii, viii, 1931.

—— and VANDERBLUE, *Railroads: Cases and Selections*, Chaps. vii–xii.

MILLER, *Railway Transportation*, Chaps. xxiii–xxvi.

RIPLEY, *Railroads: Rates and Regulation*, Chaps. iv–xi, xix.

SELIGMAN, "Railway Tariffs and the Interstate Commerce Commission," *Polit. Sci. Quart.*, Vol. II, No. 2 (separately reprinted).

SHARFMAN, I. L., *The Interstate Commerce Commission*, Part III, Chap. xv.

VANDERBLUE and BURGESS, *Railroads: Rates—Service—Management*, Chaps. ix–xii.

WATKINS, G. P., *Electrical Rates.*

——, "The Theory of Differential Rates," *Quart. Jour. Econ.*, pp. 682–703, August, 1916.

CHAPTER XXIV

PUBLIC CONTROL VS. PUBLIC OPERATION

How and why public ownership comes about, 369—Gains from public owner-ship commonly exaggerated, 370—Comparisons of efficiency favor private opera-tion, 372—Ownership without operation, 375—Public enterprises as yardsticks, 375—Conclusion, 376.

1. HOW AND WHY PUBLIC OWNERSHIP COMES ABOUT

Public ownership may come about for a variety of reasons, and at different stages in the development of an enterprise. If private capital is scarce and timid, the enterprise large, and its benefits likely to be diffused, the government may be the only organization able and willing to furnish the necessary capital. This condition frequently prevails in the development of countries like India. Or a compromise plan may be followed, the government guaranteeing the earnings of private capital. This calls for such full control, if the government is to protect its interests, that it is likely to lead to public ownership even if it is not accompanied, as in the case of the French railways, by a provision that the roads shall revert to the government at a definite future time. In the United States, except for the early period of railway develop-ment, private capital has been ample and has needed little artificial encouragement. Where public ownership has been adopted in this country, it has been a substitute for the system of regulated private enterprise.

It may have been adopted for positive reasons, to insure pure water, or adequate service of other sorts, and incidentally to prevent exploitation of the public by the companies. It may come for military reasons, such as the building of strategic railways, or for financial reasons, to yield the government a revenue independent of taxes or legislative appropriations, though this last is not likely to appeal to the legislature of a republic. It may be sought to avoid the building up of a dangerously great private money power, and the strain on political institutions resulting from the struggle to regulate it. It may be under-taken to promote policies of conservation, where this involves a sacri-fice of present profits and where the weapons of regulation do not appear strong enough to force unwilling private owners to incur this sacrifice. It may come in cases where the government wishes to dis-

courage consumption rather than to encourage it, as with liquor and
drugs. Or the government may become the owner of things it does
not want, as a result of extending credit to private owners of homes,
farms, or other properties. This has happened during the recent
depression.

Or it may come simply as a way out of the dilemma of regulation when this appears to have reached a deadlock. If regulation is
thought to leave rates too high, public ownership may be undertaken
as a yardstick, as is now being done in the field of electric power.
Or if earnings under regulation become inadequate, public ownership
may appear the only way out, as has often been suggested in the case
of the railroads. It may even be invited by private interests as a
means of realizing on their investments without incurring the odium
of an increase in rates when economic conditions make an increase
inevitable, the responsibility being shifted to the government for
either raising rates or shouldering a deficit. It may come, like many
things human, not so much from a rational anticipation of benefits
as under the compulsion of finding some way of escape from present
difficulties, thus changing the character of a problem rather than
solving it. This, indeed, is to some extent characteristic of most
measures of economic control.

2. GAINS FROM PUBLIC OWNERSHIP COMMONLY EXAGGERATED

There is a great attractiveness in the idea of owning one's own
service and ceasing to pay profits to private capital. The fact is, of
course, that the paying of a return to private capital does not cease
the moment ownership is transferred but takes on a new form. The
private holder of the company's stocks and bonds becomes a bondholder of the government, and his income is safer than before, even
though it may not be quite so large. Other methods of financing may
be used, but only to a limited extent. The government can borrow
more cheaply than a private company can raise its capital. This
constitutes the chief, and often the only major item of economy in the
case, and even this may properly be subject to certain deductions.

The two chief methods of financing are by issuing "full faith and
credit bonds," which must be paid out of taxes if the revenues of the
utility service are not sufficient for the purpose, or by issuing bonds
whose claim is limited to the earnings and assets of the particular
service in question. In order to make such bonds safe and marketable, special machinery has to be provided whereby the rates will be
automatically adjusted so as to produce sufficient earnings. Even this

would not be enough except in the case of a well-established utility or one serving so sure a market that there is, humanly speaking, no possibility of a situation arising in which no rates the utility could charge would produce the required amount of net earnings. However, it appears possible to make securities of this type marketable at rates of yield perhaps 1 per cent or more below the rate required of a private enterprise. The typical American city operates under a constitutional limit on the amount of indebtedness it may incur and is usually so near the limit as to make public ownership of large utilities impossible unless it is granted the right to borrow additional amounts for lucrative enterprises, the loans to be supported by the enterprises and not to be a burden on the general city finances.

In addition, it is considered conservative to provide for amortization of the debt in from twenty to forty years. Private companies commonly make no such provision, and the necessity for it is a debatable point. It affords a safeguard against unforeseen obsolescence which might leave the city with a worthless property on its hands and its bonds still outstanding. In the private company this risk is borne by the stockholder, whose additional rate of return is, in part, compensation for it. The addition of a reserve to care for such contingencies would reduce the apparent saving of the city in its lower interest rate. If the city is amortizing its bonds on a thirty-year basis, it will not, in thirty years, have unencumbered ownership of its entire property, since continuous new additions will have been necessary and the investment will, in a typical growing American city, have more than doubled during that time. But the city might fairly expect, in that time, to become unencumbered owner of half the property, and to be in a better position than the average stockholder in respect to its margin above fixed charges.

The city enterprise will not be obliged to pay taxes, but it might fairly be called upon to do so, and in figuring the balance of advantage from public ownership a correct answer cannot be had without deducting the equivalent of the taxes the property would have paid in private hands. Where only a few small properties are taken over, this may easily be ignored, but any general policy of public ownership will make such inroads on the available taxable property as to raise a serious question whether the strained financial system will be able to endure the loss unless it continues to receive some equivalent revenues from the same source.

If all these factors are taken into account, the gain from public ownership may be estimated at less than 1 per cent on the investment; while if the community hopes in time to own its property free of debt, it must devote virtually the entire saving to amortization. All of which leads to the conclusion that, if the community hopes to gain anything immediate and measurable from public ownership, the main reliance must be on superior economy and efficiency of operation. Lower rates, more elaborate service, or better wages, if they do not have this for a foundation, are fictitious gains, coming ultimately out of the pockets of the taxpayers.

3. COMPARISONS OF EFFICIENCY FAVOR PRIVATE OPERATION

When the question is asked which is more efficient, private or public operation, the answer must be that neither system is always superior to the other, both showing conspicuous successes and conspicuous failures. Among the successes of public operation may be named the Prussian railways in the days before the war, the noted Glasgow street-railway system and, more recently, the Ontario hydro-electric system, which owed its early success so largely to the devoted service of an engineer of large abilities, the late Sir Adam Beck. The city of Cincinnati is a successful owner of a steam railroad—a unique position among American cities—but the road is operated under lease as part of the system of the Southern Railway.

Comparisons of actual results are difficult, owing to differences in the nature of the service rendered, and to various local conditions; therefore it is still possible for advocates and opponents each to claim superiority for their favorite system. On the whole, however, the evidence appears to indicate that private management is more enterprising, keeps costs down more vigilantly, and has more backbone in resisting appeals to laxity or undue liberality, whether from laborers, consumers, or other interests. And as a result, the advantage in efficiency appears to be with private enterprise more often than with public operation. Private companies pay higher salaries to the highest officials, though the salary scale for the lower grades of officials on American railways is noticeably meager compared to the responsibilities involved, as judged by the standards of private and competitive industry. With smaller prizes before them, and promotion more generally on a basis of seniority, the officials feel relatively little incentive to take any chances on innovations. In fact, the logic of their position urges them to play safe, taking as little initiative as possible in order to avoid responsibility for any new policies which may turn out to be mistakes. A good manager can combat this tendency and even overcome it, but it persists in the average run of cases.

Liberality to labor is one of the most frequent reasons for high operating costs in publicly operated plants. This may be a matter of

conviction and deliberate policy, though it may also be mere demagoguery or a weak following of the line of least resistance, and it is
often probably an unconscious mixture of the two. But the effect is
the same on the budget. It requires a deal of financial backbone for a
public enterprise, which cannot be bankrupted in the same sense as a
private company, to stand out stiffly against giving favorable treatment to large and needy classes of citizens and voters, when their
needs can almost always be made to seem more important than the
state of the budget of a public enterprise.

Success depends largely on the building up of a competent professional staff with a spirit of loyalty to the service and free from
political interference. Back of this, naturally, is the need for a disinterested, honest, and large-minded public administration, but to
place the utility services of a city at the mercy of the character of the
mayor and city council is to court disaster, since even the best administration is likely to be turned out at the next election, and good
administrations in large American cities are relative rarities. Federal
administration appears to rank higher, but, even here, our political
world has not yet been made wholly safe for public ownership. Hence
it becomes all the more necessary (as it is good policy even under a
good government) to separate the industrial from the political functions of government and to place the industrial functions, as far as
possible, under the type of check common to the economic field and
protect it, as far as possible, from the characteristic political types of
influence.

This must not be taken to imply that sinister political influences
are not found where city governments attempt to regulate privately
owned utilities with huge property interests at stake. But the large
interests seem to be becoming less crude in their methods and more
open in their ways of seeking to influence the holders of political power.
Moreover, their very size and permanence tend to make them adopt
a long-run point of view, which is likely to be a temperate point of
view. In this field the struggle for grossly exploitive privileges is
diminishing. Large operating profits are not usually expected. But the
other interests, laborers and consumers, who would expect to come
into their own under public operation, have not learned the lesson of
moderation, and the political leaders who might make capital for themselves out of serving these interests (or appearing to serve them) have
no such permanence as the private company, and therefore, if they are
to extract profit out of their position, they must do it rapidly, while
they have the chance. If one must be exploited, it is well not to have too
many changes of exploiters. Finally, while political influence is an evil

under private operation, it is not primarily the kind of evil which directly attacks economy and efficiency of operation. Its natural tendency is toward exploiting the consumer and sharing the profits among stockholders, high officials, and those with large political influence. But when the consumers (and laborers) become the exploiters, the situation is more dangerous to solvency and efficiency. Exploitation by the many is likely to be more devastating than exploitation by the few, whatever may be the relative justice of the two cases. The hope of success appears to lie in the completeness with which municipal administration of public utilities can be divorced from "politics."

On the other hand, the differences in organization and incentives between private and public enterprises are decreasing, and the efficiency of the two may be coming closer together. With unions limiting the power to discipline labor, commission inquiries taking away the possibility of quick and unhampered decision which used to be the glory of the private business man, promotion by seniority becoming general, and checks and balances introduced at every turn, private enterprise is no longer private in the former sense. It still differs from public enterprise in the same direction as before, but not to the same extent. And the cost of the work of the regulating commissions themselves is something which can be reduced (though probably not wholly eliminated) under public operation.

In the case of railroads, terminals may be unified, duplicating passenger services and wastefully circuitous freight hauls eliminated, and equipment standardized to a greater extent than now prevails. But the standardization of locomotives during the World War was probably a mistake and has not been continued. The gains are likely to be overestimated and can easily be swallowed up in the ways already indicated. On the other hand, where public and private power plants serve the same area, as at present in Seattle, the shoe is on the other foot, and the duplication causes heavy wastes.

Public ownership has been advocated as a way out of one of the most baffling difficulties of regulation, namely, the difference in efficiency between different plants, mines, or railways. The government could average its costs and base prices on the average. True; but how is it to secure the best properties without paying a price for them in which their superior efficiency is capitalized, so that the total cost, including interest on the purchase price, would be brought to something like equality?

In times of emergency public ownership has decisive advantages in its powers of cutting through the established red tape of regulation, and securing quick adjustments. In other times the burden of proof is upon it to show special circumstances indicating why it may be expected to make a more favorable showing in the industry in question than it has done, on the average, throughout its history.

4. OWNERSHIP WITHOUT OPERATION

Some ends would perhaps best be served by a system of public ownership and private operation under lease. The private company would not be obliged to stake huge investments, and therefore the lease could be for a much shorter period than the shortest practicable franchise, permitting a far more positive control. Facilities could be furnished and the company required to operate them, with the result that the public could have as adequate service as they were willing to pay for. If one company proved impossible to deal with satisfactorily, operation could be handed over to another without any transfer of the ownership of the property. One incidental effect would be to make a clear separation between the return on the fixed investment and the reward for managerial efficiency. The problem of fair rates would be cast in a new form, and judicial doctrines as to the "value of the property" would offer no obstacles to whatever rate policy the public might deem desirable.

5. PUBLIC ENTERPRISES AS YARDSTICKS

The case of public ownership most in the public eye at present (1938) is the yardstick experiment in the Tennessee Valley. Here the conditions are favorable to public efficiency, though less favorable to a fair comparative test of costs. Dams serve flood control, navigation, and power; and the last, being hydroelectric, involves a minimum of operating expenses and correspondingly reduces the dangers of inefficient operation. But the problem of cost allocations affords an obstinate focus of controversy. Back of the enterprise lies the feeling that regulation under judicial restrictions has been too liberal to the companies, and also that the companies have been slow in utilizing possibilities of serving rural communities and developing added use of current by rates which might be below initial cost but would justify themselves by the added use they would stimulate. The power is to be sold to local public distributing systems, which may in turn be assisted by Federal Public Works funds, which are to be granted only if existing private properties have refused "fair" offers. The decision as to fairness, both of TVA rates and of offers of purchase to private companies, is shifted from regulating commissions and courts to administrative officials— Mr. Lilienthal and Mr. Ickes—and this change may have great significance.

The rates have been much lower than those of private companies, being aimed to yield something over 4 per cent under capacity operation. At present, working at about one-third of capacity, the enterprise is failing to cover costs, claiming that it is being prevented by lawsuits from disposing of its full capacity and thus justifying its rates. As already noted, the cost estimates and allocations are hotly contested. The administration is now under congressional inquiry and the results cannot be definitely appraised.

The outcome illustrates the difficulty, first, of insuring that the cost accounts and charges are fairly comparable with the burdens private enterprise has to bear; and, second, of making their fairness clear beyond reasonable doubt or controversy. And the second task appears more difficult than the first. If politics does not vitiate the first objective, it appears well-nigh inevitable and it should obscure the second. The first chairman of the TVA board enunciated highly reasonable principles but was in a minority on the board and has disavowed the actual results.

Incidentally, the administration secured reduced prices for cement for its dams by proposing to build its own cement plant, thus applying the yardstick principle in the field of manufacturing. Here again the question of fairness remains controversial. The cement producers have not accepted the reduced price of cement as a fair standard—merely as a lesser evil than the building of a public plant, in an industry already afflicted with excess capacity. They held the administration's estimates of cost much too low but were willing, like any producers with large constant costs, to take business at less than average cost rather than lose it entirely. Thus this experiment, while suggestive, fails to prove the case, one way or the other.

6. CONCLUSION

To sum up, it appears that public ownership and operation are not impossible or necessarily disastrous, but that it is not a thing to be welcomed as an easy panacea for the ills and vexations of the program of regulation. Ultimately, it is probable that these services will be operated by some organization more directly representative of those whom they serve and who invest their daily labor in them, as well as their capital, but the development of such an organization is likely to be a matter of long evolution. The present form of political government shows few symptoms of being the proper agency to fill this need, or even of developing into the proper agency. And so, though no one can tell what the future will bring forth, the wise policy in regard to public ownership and operation seems to be to make haste slowly.

REFERENCES FOR FURTHER READING

BIGGAR, "Government Ownership and Private Ownership of Railways in Canada,"
    Jour. Polit. Econ., pp. 148–182, February, 1917.

———, "The Ontario Power Commission," *Jour. Polit. Econ.*, pp. 29–56, January,
    1921.

BRITISH COAL INDUSTRY COMMISSION, *Report on the Coal Industry*, 1919.

BYE and HEWITT, *Applied Economics* (2d ed.), Chap. xxvi, 1934.

COOK, W. W., "Industrial Democracy or Monopoly?" *McClure's Mag.*, January,
    1912 (separately printed).

CUNNINGHAM, *American Railroads*, Chaps. iii–xx.

DEWEY, R. L., "The Failure of Electric Light and Power Regulation and Some
    Proposed Remedies," *Amer. Econ. Rev.*, Sup., XXI (March, 1936), 242.

DIMOCK, M. E., *Government-operated Enterprises in the Panama Canal Zone*, 1934.

DIXON, F. H., *Railroads and Government*, Chaps. ix, x.

DUNN, S. O., *Government Ownership of Railways*.

FEDERAL COORDINATOR OF TRANSPORTATION, *Report*, 1934.

FEDERAL ELECTRIC RAILWAYS COMMISSION, *Report to the President*, August, 1920.

GUYOT, YVES, *Where and Why Public Ownership Has Failed*.

JONES, ELIOT, *Principles of Railway Transportation*, Chaps. xxi, xxii, xxiv.

JONES and BIGHAM, *Principles of Public Utilities*, Chap. xv, 1931.

KEEZER and MAY, *Public Control of Business*, pp. 238–240, 1930.

SHARFMAN, I. L., *The American Railroad Problem*, Chaps. iii–vi.

SPLAWN, W. M. W., *Government Ownership and Operation of Railroads*, 1928.

TAWNEY, "The British Coal Industry and the Question of Nationalization,"
    Quart. Jour. Econ., pp. 61–107, November, 1920.

TAYLOR, *Contemporary Problems in the United States*, Vol. II, Chaps. xiv–xvi, 1934.

WALDMAN, LOUIS, *The Great Collapse: Higher Fares or Public Ownership*.

WALLACE, D. H., *Market Control in the Aluminum Industry*, pp. 360–365, 485–489,
    1937.

WILCOX, DELOS F., *Analysis of the Electric Railway Problem* (a report to the
    Federal Electric Railways Commission), 1921.

WILSON, HERRING, and EUTSLER, *Public Utility Regulation*, Chap. xix, 1938.

CHAPTER XXV

THE PROBLEM OF "TRUSTS"

1. MOTIVES TO COMBINATION

A "trust" may be defined as any industrial unit, combination, or combined action, not in the field of recognized public utilities, possessing a degree of monopoly power sufficient to injure the public interest and to call for measures of prevention or control. As to what monopoly means, we shall have more to say later. Monopolies are at least as old as Joseph's reputed corner in Egyptian wheat, but the modern trust movement began in the seventies of the last century, the newly established petroleum industry affording one of the conspicuous opportunities. The movement reached its greatest prominence in a wave of trust promotions which marked the closing years of the nineteenth century and the opening of the twentieth. It may be, however, that more recent forms, less obvious and less conspicuous, are even more far-reaching in their effects. In fact, the character of the problem is changing and coming to center in trade practices intermediate between "pure" or "perfect" competition and outright combination or monopoly.

The outstanding motives to combination include monopoly profits, defense against cutthroat competition and economic instability, promoters' profits from the organization of combinations, as distinct from their operation, the economies of combination, and the lust of economic empire—the desire of industrial organizers to extend their power for the sake of extending it. These motives appear in very varying proportions, and different forms of combination serve different purposes. Of the first, monopoly profit, nothing need be said at this point, though we shall later have occasion to analyze its nature and limits, the bases on which it rests, and the tactics necessary to achieve and maintain it. This motive is clearly opposed to the public interest.

But what of the claim that combination is necessary to protect industry against the evils of cutthroat competition? Cutthroat competition, as we have seen, is the result of an oversupply of fixed and specialized investment and may be defined as a condition in which prices are forced below "cost," so that even the efficient concerns cannot earn a reasonable return for their investors.[1] There were numerous conspicuous examples of this during the early years of some of the modern machine industries, though the most extreme cases were the wars of railroads and steamboat lines, which are outside the field of the trust problem. Studies made prior to the recent great depression indicate that competition in the field of general industry had not been so ruinous as frequently claimed, and that representative concerns had been able, on the average of good and bad times, to make fair profits.[2] It may be that this protection has been brought about by methods which were not strictly competitive, and that the figures simply mean that competition has not been allowed to do its work unchecked. This question may reduce itself to the issue of whether competition is still to be called competition when it is checked by a "sentiment against spoiling the market," or by cost-accounting systems and customs of basing prices on them in such fashion as to "protect the overhead," or by similar defense reactions embodied in the mores of business. Or is "oligopoly" (few competitors) to be classed with monopoly or with competition?

In normal times it appears that these natural or informal checks are, in the main, sufficient safeguards against cutthroat competition, except in the case of agriculture. They may, in fact, be more than sufficient. During violent depressions, however, they tend to break down. And under the short-lived National Recovery Administration various forms of cooperative action were permitted, aiming to set limits on "destructive" or "cutthroat" competition.[3] But with few exceptions, publicly authorized collective action by industries as a protection against cutthroat competition does not appear to have justified itself.

Promoters' profits as a major motive to combinations appear to belong largely to a past era when combinations were new, and their powers and prospective profits were exaggerated in the minds of the investing public. During this transition period promoters were able to float huge issues of "watered stock," representing the expected

---

[1] See above, Chap. viii, Secs. 4, 5; also Chap. xvii, Sec. 2.

[2] See Eliot Jones, "Is Competition in Industry Ruinous?" *Quart. Jour. Econ.*, pp. 473–519, May, 1920.

[3] See below, Chap. xxvii, Sec. 4.

earnings of combination in excess of the previous earnings of the constituent companies, and to grow suddenly rich by marketing the substance of things hoped for in an optimistic market. Subsequent experience has taught that it is peculiarly unsafe to count this variety of chickens before they actually break the shell. The economies of combination figured largely as a promoters' "talking point," but they have probably never been a major force in the actual forming of combinations.

2. FORMS OF COMBINATION

The early combinations were characteristically in the form of "pools," in which the participating companies entered into an agreement to apportion output or fix prices or to divide net earnings, the distinguishing feature being some system of payments into and out of a common fund, so administered as to take away any gains which an individual member might make by price cutting or other competitive tactics. This form of organization was so clearly directed to preventing competition and raising prices that combinations were soon driven to take refuge in other forms. In Germany the term "cartel" is used to describe a form of association similar to the pool, but closer, usually with a common selling organization.

The form which gave the trust its name consisted of an arrangement whereby the stockholders of the various companies handed their stocks over to trustees, receiving instead certificates of interest in the entire assortment of securities which the trustees held. Their original interests were thus effectively scrambled, and the trustees gained absolute power over the constituent companies through voting their stock. The courts held that a corporation had no power to hand over its corporate functions to such an unauthorized board, or to form what amounted to a partnership with other corporations, and this device was brought to an end.[1] The State of Ohio was still struggling to make the "unscrambling" of the Standard Oil trust a reality when the properties were reorganized into a holding company. This form of combination was first made possible by the New Jersey acts of 1889 and 1893 and accomplished the same kind of joint control as the former trust, but under specific authority of law. It soon became a favorite form of organization, though some combinations preferred to absorb the properties of the constituent companies outright, thus forming a completely consolidated corporation.

[1] North River Sugar Refining Company Case, 121 N.Y. 582 (1890); Standard Oil Case, 49 Ohio 137 (1892).

Looser forms of combination included the "community of interest" in which the same individuals were influential stockholders in a number of companies, and the companies were represented on each other's boards of directors or had directors in common. There were also informal agreements or understandings, or such tactics as the "Gary dinners," at which members of the steel trade discussed the state of the business, the result being a clear implication as to the proper policy to pursue in the joint interest, but without any definite agreement. At present nearly all trades are organized in trade associations, which perform many highly useful and necessary functions, and which typically have legal counsel present at their meetings to see that their proceedings do not overstep the bounds of legality. Another form of organization is the "open-price association," in which the members exchange information while still presumably competing with each other.

In still another field are found the agricultural cooperative marketing associations, such as the California Fruit Growers' Association, in which the growers market their fruit through a central organization but do not, presumably, control either the supply or the price. Spasmodic combinations of growers of various crops have at times attempted to limit the crop for the definite purpose of raising the price, but they have typically found it necessary to use coercion on recalcitrant individuals, by "night riding" or otherwise, in order to make the limitation of supply effective. The most prominent instance was in the tobacco fields and represented a measure of defense against the tobacco trust, which had a buyers' monopoly.

Another arrangement which has some effect in restricting competition is the system by which manufacturers of branded and advertised goods attempt to control the price at which the goods shall be resold by the dealers. This, of course, prevents the dealers from competing by way of cutting their margins but does not extinguish competition between the manufacturers themselves, so that the final price which the consumer pays is still affected by competitive forces. Not all these forms of combination, or trade methods, are clearly monopolistic, but all limit competition to some extent, and in connection with all of them the question has been raised whether they do not transgress the principle of the anti-trust laws.

The general effect of the policy of the American states and Federal Government has been to drive combinations from the looser and open forms, like pools or cartels, into the closer forms like corporate consolidations, or else into those very informal and secret forms of which proof is difficult or impossible to establish. A further effect has been to prevent holding companies and consolidated corporations from attempting to acquire complete control of an industry, or so large a percentage as to give them clear and indisputable domination of the market. Thus a limit has been set, if a somewhat indefinite one, on the growth of consolidations. The attitude developed by the courts has been that of going behind the forms to the substantial nature and effect of the combination. They ask whether the intent, natural tendency, and effect are substantially to diminish competition, to the injury of the public.

The forms mentioned above, excepting the agreements for resale-price maintenance, are in the field of horizontal combination, or combination of natural competitors in the same stage or stages of a chain of industrial processes. Some mention should also be made of vertical combination or integration, the combination of successive stages under one control or management. This has numerous effects on the character and extent of competition. It furnishes an assured source of supply of materials or an assured outlet for one's product and minimizes the necessity of going into a competitive market to find these particular things. But it leaves the integrated concerns competing with each other in the production and sale of their product to the final purchaser and thus does not, in itself, establish monopoly. It does, however, tend to introduce large-scale operation into stages of the process in which small-scale operation was the previous rule, especially where a large manufacturer establishes his own system of selling establishments alongside of the independent retailers. And if one vital link in a chain of processes is monopolized, integration makes it possible to extend the control over the other links in the chain also. Thus the Aluminum Company, with its fairly complete monopoly of the production of the metal, had the manufacturers of aluminum utensils at its mercy; while a railroad owning coal mines may, if it is permitted, give its own mines such an advantage over independent properties as to put an end to fair and adequate competition in mining and put itself in a position to absorb the independents on its own terms. Thus integration extends the powers of a monopoly but does not of itself create one where none existed before.

3. COMBINATION AND EFFICIENCY

The effect of combination on efficiency is at least as various as the forms of combination. The looser forms have probably little effect, except as they may so lighten the competitive pressure as to permit some inefficient concerns to survive that would otherwise succumb. Joint selling organizations may greatly increase the efficiency of this department of the business, especially where the separate sellers are agriculturalists who cannot easily attend to the far-reaching details of effective marketing. Horizontal combination in general affords opportunities for economies, chiefly in research, purchasing, the saving of cross freights, and the specialization of plants, but the history of such combinations does not show that these opportunities have actually resulted in material savings.[1] Integration and consolidation bring advantages, within limits. As between large and small concerns, the large ones show less variation in efficiency, and their average is higher than that of the small concerns, largely because the very inefficient concern seldom grows to large size.

But of one thing one may be sure: the attempt to absorb or extinguish all essential competition in a naturally competitive industry, and to maintain that position while raising prices above the competitive level, is in itself an expensive luxury and makes for inefficiency, not efficiency. Such a policy invites the building of mills for the express purpose of forcing the "trust" to buy them, and the trust must either pay a good price and burden itself with an excess of productive capacity, purchased at a nuisance value, or must intimidate the interlopers, or destroy them by expensive price wars. If it merely aims at a commanding position in the industry, without absolute power over prices, it may limit itself to efficient producing units; but if it wishes to go farther, it must take in the less efficient or take measures to render them harmless as competitors.

It is probably this fact which sets the limits on the exactions of industrial combinations and serves to explain why they practice so much moderation. Early experiments have shown that a combination could not maintain too grasping a policy without being overloaded or forced to adopt predatory tactics which were bound to bring public condemnation and the penalties of law. Thus the extreme policy of the early trusts has been succeeded by a characteristic policy of moderation.[2]

Combination for export trade deserves separate mention. The difficulty and expense of canvassing a foreign market are greater than for a home market, and the volume of sales which must support these costs is usually less. This difficulty is recognized and compensated, to some extent, by the consular and foreign-trade services of the various governments. But the exporters may feel that such public services do

[1] See Dewing, "A Statistical Test of the Success of Consolidations," *Quart. Jour. Econ.*, pp. 84–101, November, 1921. Cf. also Louis D. Brandeis, *Business—a Profession*, essay entitled "Trusts and Efficiency."

[2] See esp. Jones, *The Trust Problem in the United States*, pp. 262 ff.

not meet all their requirements and may wish to combine their forces in order to maintain an effective selling organization without too great an expense. This is, in itself, an element of efficiency and does not, in itself, destroy competition, since there is still the foreigner to meet on his home ground. These considerations account for the passage in this country of the Webb law, which permits combinations for foreign trade only. One of the chief objections lies in the question: If producers combine their operations in the foreign market, are they not less likely to continue to compete actively in the home market?

Another and broader phase of efficiency is the question of serviceableness in the carrying out of definite public policies. This end can most readily be furthered if the industry is organized into a unit. Where the government is still actuated by mercantilistic principles and feels that the promotion of export business is in a peculiar sense a national interest, combination may most effectively promote this end, possibly with the government itself as a participating member. This policy has been quite generally followed in Germany, where the government has favored the growth of cartels and has itself been a member of the principal ones. Or if the government has a definite policy of stabilizing prices or production, it may promote this policy in the same way. Or if it wishes industry to be conducted in time of peace so as to be most readily mobilized for the national emergency in time of war, the same method may be used effectively. These elements are largely accountable for the difference between the prewar German policy and our own, and they have been much intensified under the stricter governmental control of the Nazi state. German industry, though less efficient than American in the productive power of its individual units, demonstrated a collective efficiency in the prompt meeting of the needs of the war emergency which our industries were not able to equal.[1] This need we are attempting to meet by the preparation of plans for wartime mobilization, with how much success only the test of another war can definitely determine.

4. COMPETITIVE *VS.* MONOPOLY PRICES, PROFITS, AND OUTPUT

The objections to trusts may be summed up in the statement that they deprive the public of all the advantages of competition. These have been discussed at some length in a previous chapter.[2] For the present purpose the important things are that "normal" competition tends, in general, (1) to lower costs, the incentive to improvements outweigh-

---

[1] Cf. Clark, Hamilton, and Moulton, *Readings in the Economics of War*, Secs. 13, 14, 21, 22.

[2] See above, Chap. viii.

ing the wastes of salesmanship; (2) to reduce profits to the lowest level which will balance supply and demand; hence (3) to give the lowest prices and the largest output which private enterprise can afford; (4) to distribute the community's stock of labor and capital into whatever channels afford the greatest opportunities for gain; and (5) to give labor as much as industry, in general, can afford to pay for its services.

As over against this, the key to the meaning of monopoly lies in the power to control supply, and hence to maintain prices and profits above the competitive level. This is naturally regarded as a reward for giving the consumer less for his money rather than more, and reducing the usefulness of the industry to the community, rather than increasing it.

The theory of pure monopoly assumes that certain industries are monopolized while others remain competitive. The monopolists raise their prices to the point which yields the largest possible aggregate net profit. This is limited, among other things, by the price of available substitutes, but this limit may still permit a considerable amount of exploitation. The increase in price necessarily cuts down the demand, with the result that fewer goods can be produced and sold than under competition. As a further result the monopolized industries furnish less than the normal demand for capital and labor, and these must find employment in the field remaining open to competition. Thus the competitive field is crowded and the worth of capital and labor in the open market is reduced. The effects of monopoly, then, are not confined to the monopolized industries, or to the high prices paid for monopolized products.

Of course, a monopoly might choose not to use its power to oppress the public. It might merely protect the trade against cutthroat competition and be content with a normal rate of return on its investment. Instances of such pure self-denial are rare in business, however. Even to a manager starting out on this beneficent principle, there would be an almost irresistible temptation to accumulate a reserve for future contingencies and, having accumulated it, to regard it as an investment entitled to a return, and possibly to start accumulating further reserves. And in any case, under the moral code of our time, such power over the welfare of one's fellow-men does not belong in the hands of private individuals, no matter how it is used.

The law of pure monopoly price is not a thing we should expect to see exemplified in practice, except for a few patented articles, for the simple reason that, long before such complete control of supply could be attained, the government would act under the anti-trust laws. Even without government action, it is seldom possible for any organization to keep complete control of the supply of any one commodity, once they begin to use their control in such wise as to make the profits of that particular business look conspicuously attractive to all and sundry who might like to enter and share them. What we really need to know, for the sake of a wise trust policy, is the relative levels and behavior of prices, profits, and wages under three different conditions: normal competition (if such a thing exists), such hybrid conditions as persist in the face of our attempts at control, and combination as it might be if the government should follow the advice of the skeptics and cease its well-meant efforts to interfere with the natural tendencies of business. As to the last, if the government took its hands off so completely that it ceased even to try to prevent unfair competition, the answer is simple. Prices and profits would be just as high as they could be without stirring up such resentment as would make the government revert to its policy of control. The public would be mulcted as much as it would stand, and profits would reach the limits of public patience before they reached any limits of the economic variety.

Under such circumstances combination would probably become so general that nearly every business would have its trust, with the possible exception of agriculture. There would then be little question of supply being limited in some industries and unlimited in others. If all raised prices, the effects would neutralize each other. And if all but agriculture did so, there would be only two major sources of real gains for the monopolies, namely, the fattening of profits at the expense of labor and of the farmer. If labor were so strongly combined as to possess monopoly power of its own, the natural result would be an inconclusive deadlock or an unholy alliance, from either of which we may well pray to be delivered. We have had quite sufficient foretastes: of deadlock in the coal industry and of unholy alliance in the building trades.[1] It seems clear that the only possible course is to continue to oppose monopolistic combinations. The question remains whether the utmost efforts of government can prevent a considerable amount of exploitation.

Of late, another phase of the price problem has been coming to the fore, namely, the idea that "administered prices" (which are not necessarily monopolistic) show a stickiness or stability which is in itself contrary to the public interest.[2] It is pointed out that with

[1] Written in 1925, when conspicuous examples in these fields were fresh in the public mind.

[2] This idea has been spread mainly through the writings of Gardiner C. Means, though the problem of sticky vs. flexible prices was earlier emphasized by F. C. Mills, *The Behavior of Prices*, *passim*.

some commodities (chiefly agricultural) price fluctuates more than output, and with others (chiefly manufactured) output fluctuates more than prices. This is undoubtedly a fact, though the available statistical measures are imperfect and liable to exaggerate or minimize the true degree of fluctuation. As to their interpretation, one basic consideration is the fact that demand for staple agricultural commodities fluctuates relatively little, and the chief fluctuations come from the supply side and largely from the weather. There is nothing here corresponding to the violent fluctuations of demand for durable manufactured goods, which cause operation in extreme cases to fall to one-third or even one-sixth of capacity. Under such conditions, while freer movement of prices would probably mitigate slightly the fluctuations of output (even that is disputed), no conceivable flexibility of prices could possibly bring about the kind of relationship prevailing in agriculture. There is here an inchoate standard of public policy, not yet sufficiently well formulated to serve as a definite guide to present policy, but affording possibilities for the future.

5. OTHER REASONS FOR OPPOSING COMBINATION

One serious objection to monopolistic combination, implied in what has already been said, is the probable slackening of economic progress. When it becomes possible to increase profits by merely raising prices, there is not the same keen urgency about searching out ways of reducing costs and improving products. It is true that a trust, like a competing producer, can always make more money if it can reduce its costs. But whenever a proposed innovation involves any element of uncertainty, the tendency of a secure monopoly is likely to be to let well enough alone and play safe; whereas the competing concern is forced to take some chances, and a policy of always letting well enough alone is the most dangerous one it could adopt. Furthermore, in figuring whether an improvement will reduce costs or not, the monopoly is likely to charge against it the book value of the equipment which it will send to the scrap heap,[1] without always recognizing that the progress of the art may already have reduced the real value of the old equipment to less than its book value—perhaps to nothing at all. A competing producer, on the other hand, is sometimes overready to follow a new and imperfectly tested idea or to scrap equipment which still could give service. This is especially true where it is a question of

---

[1] This point is aptly illustrated by the testimony of C. H. Jones on the United Shoe Machinery Company, cited in Jones, *The Trust Problem in the United States*, p. 180. On the other hand, monopoly does not inevitably mean stagnation; witness the technical progressiveness of the Bell Telephone organization.

developing the quality of the product rather than merely reducing costs of production. Both sides are liable to errors, but on the whole the errors of overprogressiveness seem more in accord with the community's long-run interest than the errors of overinertia.

Another objection comes from those who like to see many men own their own businesses, regarding this as the individualistic ideal, and objecting to a system in which the goal of the typical successful man is a salaried position in some huge organization. This, however, is as much a protest against large-scale production as against combination, and large-scale production has come to stay, despite all laments of "historic homesickness." More important in this connection is the manner in which the independent business man is persuaded to relinquish his status: the tactics used to drive him out of business or absorb him. As long as there are capable men who prefer to work as "independents," the trust cannot control supply unless it can bring some undue pressure to bear on these outsiders.

6. SOURCES OF MONOPOLY POWER

The power to control supply may rest on a large number of factors. The aluminum combine has a well-nigh insuperable advantage arising from having had first choice of ore supplies and power sites.[1] The United Shoe Machinery Company made use of certain essential, patented machines, which shoe manufacturers could not do without, to force them to buy their other products also. The Standard Oil Company secured discriminating treatment from the railroads and also followed the policy of cutting the price of oil to a ruinous level in the particular market in which a comparatively small competitor was operating, while keeping prices up elsewhere, until the competitor was beaten, after which the price rose again. At present, competitors cover sufficiently wide areas to make this weapon far less decisive. At one time the American Tobacco Company, having some brands which every dealer must have, offered dealers 10 per cent discount from retail prices if they would agree not to handle the goods of competitors, and $2\frac{1}{2}$ per cent if they handled all goods on equal terms. It was claimed that a dealer could make no profit on $2\frac{1}{2}$ per cent discount, so that the arrangement was in the nature of coercion rather than inducement.[2] The National Cash Register Company kept a "morgue" of the machines of defunct competitors and used it to intimidate any who

[1] See D. H. Wallace, *Market Control in the Aluminum Industry*, 1937.

[2] See the Lexow Report, pp. 991–992, cited in Jones, *The Trust Problem in the United States*, p. 152. For the other practices mentioned, see the records of the various cases, cited in Jones, *op. cit.*, pp. 66–82, 471–491. See also Stevens, *Industrial Combinations and Trusts*, Chaps. vii, x, xii, and *Unfair Competition, passim.*

might contemplate entering the trade. They also secured their rivals' machines and sold them themselves, to prevent sales by the rivals, or made machines to resemble those of competitors, and followed most of the known methods of focusing competition on the particular customers to whom their rivals were trying to sell, using espionage to gain the necessary information or taking competitors' employees into their pay.[1] Independents in some businesses have mysteriously failed to secure credit. These are examples, but the methods of unfair competition are too varied and resourceful ever to be catalogued with anything like finality. The tariff has also simplified the problem for some combinations by eliminating the foreigner as a serious threat, though the tariff alone does not explain monopoly. The impression gained from a rapid survey of such instances is, first, that competition has a great deal of vitality and, second, that there has been, during our earlier trust history, an amazing fertility of invention devoted to methods of competition calculated to down the competitor, no matter what his productive efficiency and his economic right to survive.

The effect of such measures in building up a monopoly needs no pointing out. But the modern trust does not want to absorb or drive out all its competitors. It does not typically wish to control much more than half the market, for fear of bringing on a government suit. The problem of such a concern is different, if it still aspires to make more than a competitive profit, that is, more than its superior efficiency would automatically bring it. Its aim is to establish a "live-and-let-live" form of competition, rather than to drive out competitors. It must sustain prices at a level which would enable some of the independents to make fair profits and expand their business, but it must prevent them from expanding fast enough to cut seriously into its own volume of sales. It can afford to let them expand slightly faster than it does itself (as frequently happens), but only slightly faster. It can reestablish its position by occasionally absorbing some efficient independent, as the Tennessee Coal and Iron Company was absorbed; but this must not happen too often. The trust may be able to keep prices well above costs if the independents are either afraid to cut the trust's price for fear of reprisals or at least are impressed with the wisdom of extreme caution in that respect. The possibility of unfair competition, rather than the actuality, may act to keep the independents from cutting under the trust's price and making serious inroads on its business. This is the present form of the "law of monopoly price" in the field of general industry, if this law is in operation at all. It amounts to backing up the "sentiment against spoiling the market" by the

[1] See court order, cited in Jones, *op. cit.*, pp. 478–479.

force of trade discipline exercised by the strongest concern or concerns in the trade, with the understanding that any serious inroads on the price policy of the dominant concern are considered to be a spoiling of the market. The force which such trade discipline can exert depends largely on the extent to which the independents are protected against genuinely unfair and predatory competition. With such weapons eliminated, trade discipline can still exert some force and can possibly raise prices somewhat above the theoretical competitive level, but only within rather narrow limits. Or "price leadership" may be accepted voluntarily, or prices may be stabilized somewhat above the ideal competitive level by the natural weakening of competitive incentives arising from the certainty that a price reduction will be instantly met.

7. METHODS AND POLICIES OF PUBLIC CONTROL

If it is assumed that the government is committed to the principle of protecting the public against monopoly, two main types of policy are possible, which may be characterized as direct and indirect control. Indirect control aims to keep alive the force of competition and to trust this force to protect the consumer, while direct control would permit combination and substitute the ultimate power of government regulation for the force of competition as the means of insuring fair quality and fair price to the consumer. Such control might remain latent if the combinations limited themselves to restraining the worst excesses of cutthroat competition, without raising prices near to the debatable zone of fairness. But the power would have to exist. It would extend the principle of public-utility regulation to the field of general industry. The decision between these two types of policy is one of the major issues of economic control before the American people.

The plan to which we are committed at present is that of indirect control. It has two main phases: one looking to the prevention of combinations or the dissolution of those already formed, and the other looking to the prevention of coercive tactics and the maintenance of fair conditions of competition. The one looks at monopoly as a state of being, while the other proceeds on the assumption that monopoly is as monopoly does, and it attacks the policies on which monopoly power is based. The two are complementary, both being necessary to a successful program of indirect control. While this policy has not been completely satisfactory, there are many reasons for being slow to abandon it in favor of the other. Chief of these is the fact that the change would be likely to be irrevocable. It is easier to keep industrial units apart than to "unscramble" them after they have once combined, and a policy of permitting combination would almost certainly result in such a growth of mergers that, if we should subsequently change our minds and desire to return to the plan of indirect control, the necessary unscrambling would prove to be virtually impossible. Before committing ourselves to direct control, then, we should do our best to visualize its ultimate consequences, as well as to try out all the possibilities of the plan we are now following.

Monopoly has long been illegal at common law. In 1890 the Federal Government enacted the Sherman law, forbidding, in the field of interstate commerce, all contracts, combinations, or conspiracies in restraint of trade, and all monopolies or attempts to monopolize. Most of the states have laws of similar character. The peculiar phraseology used is borrowed from the common law and has been construed in harmony with common-law doctrines, at least since the famous "rule of reason" decision in the Standard Oil Case of 1911. In 1903 a federal investigating bureau was established, known as the Bureau of Corporations, and its reports proved to be of considerable value. In the same year the Elkins Act made more effective the prohibition of personal discriminations in railroad rates. In 1906 the commodities clause of the Hepburn Act struck at the coal combines by making it illegal for railroads to carry their own goods for sale in competition with independent producers (exception being made of lumber).

In 1914 the federal statutes for the first time made definite provision for the control of trade practices in the Clayton Act and the act establishing the Federal Trade Commission. The Clayton Act forbade unfair competition in general terms, as well as defining certain outstanding practices. Discrimination of monopolistic intent or tendency was forbidden, but not discriminations "made in good faith to meet competition." It also forbade the acquisition of stock by holding companies, where this tends substantially to lessen competition or create a monopoly, and forbade interlocking directorates between companies which are legally required to compete. It also stated that labor unions are not violations of the laws against combinations (though they are not specifically exempted from prosecution if their *acts* are monopolistic) and placed certain limits on the use of the injunction in labor disputes. The Federal Trade Commission was given power to enforce the provisions of the act as far as they apply to corporations in the field of general business. It also succeeded to the investigating powers of the Bureau of Corporations.

In 1918 the Webb-Pomerene Act was passed, legalizing combinations for export trade only. In 1921 control over packers and stockyards was vested in the Secretary of Agriculture under a special act, and in 1922, under the Capper-Volstead Act, the same was done for agricultural cooperative marketing organizations. The Robinson-Patman Act of 1936, aimed especially at the bargaining advantages of chain stores, forbids discrimination of monopolistic tendency, when not justified by differences in cost, but still permits the defense that the lower price was made to meet an equally low price of a competitor. This, in brief outline, is the principal legislation under which the campaign against trusts has been carried on.

8. DISSOLUTION OF COMBINATIONS

The chief instances of outright dissolution by court decree have been the cases of the Standard Oil Company and the American Tobacco Company. In the Standard Oil Case the holding company simply distributed to its own stockholders the stocks of the constituent companies which it held. This left a large number of technically separate companies, but with identical stockholders. In the tobacco-trust case this plan was modified by giving one group of holders a majority in one of the major parts into which the combination was divided, and a minority in the other. In later cases greater effort has been made to see that the properties are put in the hands of really separate groups of persons, but the courts have not set this up as an absolute requirement. The shortcomings of the stock-distribution method of dissolution are obvious.

Far more numerous than the judicial dissolutions have been the "consent decrees," of which the International Harvester Company Case may be cited as an example. The company agreed to sell certain of its lines to independent parties. This decree was criticized by the Federal Trade Commission on the ground that the brands to be sold were not holding their own with the two chief brands—the McCormick and Deering—which the company was to retain, and that the brands which were to be disposed of cost more to manufacture and hence could not compete successfully. The commission asked that the Deering and McCormick brands be placed in the hands of totally separate parties.

A different principle is illustrated by the decree of 1920 against the meat packers. The five largest packers were maintaining separate organizations since the dissolution, in 1912, of the National Packing Company, through which the Swift, Armour, and Morris interests had held certain properties in common. Thus there was no tangible merger to be dissolved. They were, however, forbidden to own public stockyards-market companies, stockyard-terminal railroads, stockyard-market newspapers, or public cold-storage warehouses (with certain exceptions), and from engaging in the distribution of a large list of foodstuffs not essentially connected with the business of meat packing.

Here we have a far-reaching decree directed against vertical combination rather than horizontal. One principle involved is that a producer shall not control market facilities or essentially public services connected therewith which have to be used either by independent and competing producers or by those from whom the producer buys his raw material. The market in which cattle growers sell must not be controlled by the buyer. The other phase of the decree arises from the fact that the packers have utilized their existing distribution service, with its large investment in refrigerator cars and other facilities, to extend their business into many lines whose only connection with packing houses is the fact that the same distribution system can be economically used by all. Here a private facility has reached out into what would ordinarily be a public service, though it is still mainly a private facility. The packers insist that they must handle their goods themselves in order to be sure that they receive proper treatment. The advantage, or "monopoly," in handling other food products is an incidental result. This situation presents a difficult dilemma. California growers complained that the cutting off of the packers' service deprive them of their market without furnishing a substitute and left them worse off than before.

Another way of describing the issue is to say that we have two systems of distribution: the private, or exclusive, and the general, open to all competing products in any of the customary divisions of trade. Into these general systems of distribution—such as the typical independent retail store—the exclusive principle should not enter. They should be neutral. This principle is at the bottom of the objection to the exclusive agreements made with dealers by the American Tobacco Company. It is a phase of the general public interest in seeing that markets are places where the purchaser can canvass and compare goods in the most effective fashion.[1] Usually the goods can be distributed by one or the other system—exclusive or general—on terms which are fair to all; but in the packers' case, just examined, the two methods appear to be in a head-on collision.

The trust dissolutions have not resulted in a spectacular and instant rescue of the consumer from the evils of monopoly, but that was hardly to have been expected. One of the chief results has been of a preventive character; combinations have grown careful not to expand to the point at which they will have to be dissolved again. This preventive effect is undoubtedly a gain. Incidentally, it is un-

[1] See Chap. ix, Sec. 3, preceding.

doubtedly more difficult, after dissolution, for the constituent interests to organize campaigns of predatory competition; and this is probably the greatest gain from dissolution. Dissolutions are, however, less and less sought after, and emphasis is shifting to the control of trade practices.

9. CONTROL OF TRADE PRACTICES

Dissolution has never been relied on as the sole remedy for monopoly but has always gone hand in hand with orders to refrain from unfair tactics toward competitors. The shoe-machinery and cash-register cases are instances in which the courts refused to dissolve the companies; their state of being was unobjectionable, and only their actions were condemned. Such orders are far more numerous than actual dissolutions. The orders of the Federal Trade Commission under the unfair-competition provisions of the law reveal such an amazing variety of objectionable methods as to suggest the question whether a company can be forced to compete fairly if it does not want to. Undoubtedly there will always remain some chances to deal underhand blows; but with the more dangerous or fatal ones effectively barred, a competitor can probably manage to survive the rest, if he is one who deserves to survive at all. As we have seen in an earlier connection, the commission has enlisted the help of the trades themselves in drawing up standards of fair and unfair competition. And this, to the extent that it develops, is real industrial self-government, and better than any form of governmental compulsion.

Moreover, the part played by unfair competition in the trust problem has changed from a means of extinguishing competitors to a sanction of trade discipline, held in reserve most of the time, and serving mainly in the form of occasional reprisals to induce rivals to conform to the live-and-let-live types of competition. Thus, even if attempts to prevent it are not wholly successful, it does not threaten the same black menace of economic servitude which alarmed thinking Americans in the eighties and nineties of the last century, but something which would have seemed to them much less serious. However, standards change; and if the price stability associated with live-and-let-live forms of competition does, as is charged with some reason, tend to intensify depressions, that may make it as serious an evil as any we face in this field.

And these live-and-let-live forms of competition need to be scrutinized on their own account, whether or not they are backed up by the threat of unfair tactics. As examples we may cite basing-point systems (already discussed)[1] and open-price systems, both of which are on the border line of legality. As to the latter, the conclusion drawn from studies of such systems under the NRA is that their effect on prices depends, on the whole, more on the underlying conditions of the industry or trade in question than on the form of the system itself. Where the market is not well organized, producers may learn of fields they would gladly enter and learn what they must do to enter them effectively, and thus competition may be increased. On the other hand, where there are few and large producers, the system may serve to increase the certainty that a reduction of price will be instantly met, and thus to reduce or remove the characteristic competitive incentive to make such a reduction. A "waiting period" after a change is announced and before it goes into effect is particularly suspect, first, as affording a chance for rivals to exercise persuasion on a producer to withdraw an announced reduction before it goes into effect and, second, to make it quite certain that, if the reduction is not withdrawn, it will be met the moment it does go into effect and therefore will afford the initiator a minimum of opportunity for competitive gain in sales at the expense of his rivals. The steel code under the NRA even declared it to be "unfair competition" for a producer to have an agreement with a customer whereby he secured the customer's trade in return for initiating a reduction in price. Unfair competition was here used in a different meaning from the one we have given it in these pages and in effect included any tactics tending too strongly to depress price at a time when industry as a whole was unable to cover full costs. This meaning was peculiar to the NRA period, when the antitrust laws were temporarily in abeyance.

In general, the purely informative type of open-price system, with no commitments as to future action via a waiting period or otherwise, is generally held to be legal, though it does afford some protection against cutthroat competition. Additional features, making it appear that the device is part of a plan to raise or maintain prices, are likely to cause the plan to be held illegal.[2] This illustrates how delicate is the line which the public authorities must draw, and to which business must try to conform, often in advance of clear controlling decisions.

One very real difficulty in this field of trust policy lies in the fact that the law hinges on combination or combined action, while many of the most important issues now center in trade practices which may have grown up without definite combined action; and, as we have seen, undue weakness of competitive forces may arise from the natural

[1] See above, Chap. xxiii, Sec. 11.
[2] See Burns, *The Decline of Competition*, pp. 43–64.

conditions of an industry, for which no one is to blame.[1] This is why anti-trust law actions sometimes seem, to an economist, to have some difficulty in laying hold of the present economic realities. There is need of adjusting trade practices constructively to secure the most salutary economic results, somewhere between cutthroat competition and exploitation or undue restraint and stability, rather than merely preventing acts of combination. In any revision of our present policy, this need should somehow be met.

If the charge is made that there is still some exploitation—as there always will be—and that therefore our policy has failed and we should forthwith change it, we should do well to consider that other policies might also show some failures and might be even more costly and less likely to "economize coercion."

10. POLICIES OF ABANDONING COMPETITION

Proposals to abandon the attempt to restore or maintain competition are not new and come from various quarters. One type comes from spokesmen of business interests, concerned only with relaxing controls and neglecting the matter of adequate public safeguards. It is possible that in some cases an unregulated monopoly would serve the public better than enforced competition; but the public would not tolerate the degree of dependence on private discretionary power which this would involve. As a matter of general policy, it is not a debatable issue.

Another type is advocated as a conscious measure of approach to a socialistic system, that is, as a phase of the policy of abandoning the control of private business in favor of the kind of control that goes with ownership and the abolition of private business. This is a debatable issue, but it belongs at a later stage of our discussion, along with the general question whether the whole system of control of private business is a hopeless failure. At present we may limit ourselves to policies including an adequate degree of social control in a private but noncompetitive system.

There have been two periods of strong advocacy of such a policy, or possibly three. One began in the first decade of the present century and lasted until the World War. Distinguishing features of this period, bearing on the issue, were the early discouragement with attempts to dissolve trusts, especially the apparent futility of the Standard Oil and tobacco dissolutions of 1911, growing interest in conservation, and the early and more hopeful period of commission control in the

[1] See above, Chap. viii, Sec. 6.

field of public utilities, marked by the Railroad Acts of 1906 and 1910. A second period, hardly applicable as an index of permanent policy, was that of the World War itself, during which combined action was a means of furthering the prompt carrying out of war policies, emergency price controls were carried out on a basis that would not have been permanently practicable, and the motive of patriotism afforded a powerful if unreliable force not ordinarily available. The third period arose out of the recent great depression and reached its climax in the codes of the National Recovery Administration. It was dominated by ideas of the "anarchy" of competition as causing or intensifying depressions and by somewhat vaguely defined notions of "planning" and "stabilization," and also by an economic situation in which monopolistic exploitation in the ordinary sense was not likely to occur in any case, so that the public-utility type of price limitations was not likely to be called for. Public-utility control had by this time entered on a period of bafflement and controversy and did not afford such an apparently promising model as twenty years previous. One might also mention the period of postwar prosperity, during which there was much interest in "rationalization," and some progress toward standardization of goods involving joint action of producers under leadership of the Department of Commerce, but without the formation of trusts or cartels for the purpose.

During the first period a strong case was made for the policy of direct rather than indirect control. It was charged that competition had failed to control either price or quality; that it was wasteful, including tragic wastes of natural resources; that the most highly competitive business—retailing—was the most wasteful of all; and that the possibility of successful direct control was already demonstrated in the field of railroads and public utilities.[1] These claims, however, shrink somewhat under a realistic and comparative scrutiny, especially in the light of later developments.

As to price and quality, there are failures to be charged against both policies. The automobile was becoming a thing of silent smoothness and nearly "fool-proof" reliability, while the street car still jarred the passenger and deafened the bystander. It is competition and not regulation that has given us the light-weight streamlined train. In the

---

[1] See especially Van Hise, *Concentration and Control*, Chap. i, Secs. 7–9; Chap. v, Secs. 5, 6. This is a fairly moderate expression of this point of view. It is worth noting that the author was President of the University of Wisconsin, which had played an important part in the development of one of the most distinguished state railroad and public-utility commissions. He had also a special interest in conservation.

public-service industries there are standards of quality, as far as they go, which simplify the task of regulation enormously. But what is the standard for cigars, clothing, or other style and quality products?

As to price, we should face the problem of valuation of the prop-. erties and control of accounts for businesses, including many small members which could not afford an elaborate system suited to the larger units. And the baffling dilemma of the strong and weak producers would appear in aggravated form, since any fair price would amount to sentence of death to some producers—often to many. Even before the New Deal it was evident that prices of some farm products would have to be regulated, including tobacco, livestock, and any other products sold to combinations. Familiar methods would be out of place here, and many mistakes would be inevitable. And by what standard should prices of manufactured products be made to fluctuate between good and bad times? Unit costs often rise in bad times, but prices should presumably fall. This implies losses, which in turn implies profits in good times sufficient to make up a fair average. Here again, no simple standard is possible, and many mistakes would be inevitable, even with the most incorruptible commissions—which are not to be taken for granted.[1]

Not only are prices bound to fluctuate, but the differentials between different localities will not follow any absolutely uniform system. One of the things unregulated prices do, and with which regulated prices must not interfere, is to send goods from any place where there may be a surplus to any other place where there may be a shortage by the simple and effective stimulus of a price differential. These differentials would need continual revising, a task which would call for many local committees, effectively coordinated under one supreme head. The central body would be almost certain to fall behind its docket, with the result that necessary movements of goods would be delayed. One way of visualizing the outcome is to imagine the wartime policies of price control made permanent, without the help of patriotic loyalty on the part of those controlled, and with an attempt to shave the margins of net earnings closer than was possible during the war. The result would be an even more burdensome growth of bureaus than we experienced during the war, and their work would probably satisfy no one.

It is doubtful if those who advocate this policy realize the vast extent of sheer paternalism and interference into which the government would rapidly be drawn if this program were adopted. Such a

[1] For other related problems see Burns, *The Decline of Competition*, Chaps. xi, xii.

policy would certainly not economize coercion. The control of prices is precisely the kind of control which cannot be left to that most desirable of all forms of agency, industrial self-government.[1]

Following recent experience, one might expect this policy to eventuate in experiments in control by the method of public competition with private enterprise. This would be subject to all the difficulties already mentioned in discussing yardsticks,[2] but in an accentuated form, since here public and private enterprises would be competing for the same markets and not dividing the field. One reason for doubting that this policy will become general is the probability that it would, in serious earnest, be fatal to the continuance of private enterprise. One hesitates to make this statement, for two reasons. First, it has so often been made without warrant in opposition to almost any increase of public control, that, like the cry of "Wolf!" in the fable, it has lost its force. In this instance, however, it appears to be justified. Second, the objection is not all-conclusive, since private enterprise is not a paramount end in itself. But it is not wise to take measures which may lead to its collapse unless the issue is vital enough to justify the step, and unless we are sure we are willing to take the consequences.

Recent developments have added much to the argument without vitiating the points which have just been made. Newly elaborated theories of imperfect competition have appeared, which are highly significant; but there are not yet (among economists) any theories of perfect control. Experience under the NRA accentuated the fact that a "normally" competitive business is probably nonexistent but revealed a good deal of fairly powerful competition, even if not uniformly modeled after our ideal stereotype. Some of it seemed at the time unduly powerful. These imperfections are an organic part of competitive institutions and cannot be analyzed out by law; but law can modify them, especially if it recognizes what it is doing—that it is striving to reduce the imperfection of competition and to bring about the best available compromise between cutthroat warfare and rigidity or exploitation. It is unrealistic to suppose—if anyone does— that perfect competition can be established if all elements of combination are broken up; but it also seems unrealistic to abandon one policy

[1] This paragraph stands as written in 1925. So far as it applies to the later NRA experiment, only minor exceptions seem to be called for.

[2] See above, pp. 375–376. It is interesting to note that Dr. Wallace, the author of the recent excellent study *Market Control in the Aluminum Industry*, compares various alternatives of direct and indirect control and on the basis of the comparison is inclined to favor control through public competition. His comparison, however, hardly deals with the imponderables of this policy, to which the present writer attaches much weight.

for another radically different one, merely on a showing that the results of the first are not perfect. That leaves out the imperfections of the second.

This is not written to belittle the imperfections of modern competition. They are serious. It is probably safe to say that they are growing, though not so much as many think. In simpler days the only local grist mill, wagon maker, general store, iron foundry, or barber must have had a generous measure of partial monopoly power. Industrial units were smaller, but so also were markets. It seems certain, however, that these imperfections are a growingly serious matter to our growingly vulnerable economy. What is argued for, here, is merely a realistic and balanced comparison of ways and means in dealing with them.

11. TRUSTS AND LABOR

The relation of labor to trusts is a story in itself, and a difficult one to tell. There is the difficulty of generalizing upon the facts which can be seen, but there is also the greater difficulty arising from the fact that the most important relations of cause and effect belong among the "things which are not seen." Wages paid by a trust are frequently higher than those paid by the independents in the same industry, but that is not the whole story. A more important question is the effect of trusts on wages in general, in all occupations, and not on money wages alone, but on wages in terms of purchasing power. If a trust raises prices of things labor buys without raising money wages correspondingly, there is a decrease in real wages. And a trust may divide its profits with its own laborers at the expense of labor in general.

Monopoly undoubtedly brings some increase in power to bargain with labor, partly because a strike may help the combination to limit supply without assuming responsibility for the resulting shortage. This increase in bargaining power seems more likely to be used to resist the growth of organization than to lower wages.

Labor may itself follow monopolistic policies, though the mere fact of collective bargaining is not in itself monopolistic, nor even, perhaps, the policy of the closed shop. Monopoly should be judged, here as elsewhere, by the test of whether it limits supply, excluding some portion which would be furnished if competition were free. The closed shop becomes monopolistic if the control of entry into the union is used to limit entry to the trade, keeping out qualified persons who desire to work, or limiting apprentices to such an extent as to reduce the number who can become qualified to less than the trade can employ at the rates it can afford to pay. It goes without saying that, before condemning any given restriction on apprentices, one would need to be sure that it actually goes far enough to accomplish monopolistic results. In order to make it just to demand that labor give up every trace of control of supply, the same demand should, as a matter of course, be made on the employers.

12. CONCLUSION

To sum up, in view of all the uncertain quantities and vast possibilities of trouble in the policy of direct regulation, if generally adopted, it seems the part of prudence to continue in our present general type of policy. Effort can probably be better spent in strengthening its weak points than in going over to a wholly different system. Chief among these, perhaps, the law needs to recognize that imperfect competition is inherent in modern industry, and to take constructive measures to improve such forms of competition, aside from attacking combinations in restraint of trade. The problem of trusts is many sided, elusive, and changing, and it requires the combined action of the states, the nation, the citizens, and the trade itself, with its organizations, to hold the interests in a tolerable moving equilibrium until the next phase of industrial evolution shall dictate the next change of policy. The question will not be "solved," in the sense of ceasing to exist as a problem. One "solves" such questions chiefly by handing them over to some new agency, and the agencies will always bear watching. Eternal vigilance is the price of freedom to compete, as well as of other varieties of freedom.

REFERENCES FOR FURTHER READING

BLAISDELL, T. C., *The Federal Trade Commission*, 1932.
BRANDEIS, L. D., *Business—a Profession*, essay on "Trusts and Efficiency."
BURNS, A. R., *The Decline of Competition*, 1936.
CASSELS, J. M., *A Study of Fluid Milk Prices*, 1937.
CHAMBERLIN, E., *The Theory of Monopolistic Competition*, 1936.
CLARK, J. B., and J. M. CLARK, *The Control of Trusts* (2d ed.).
CLARK, WRIGHT, and others, Papers and discussions on price-fixing for trusts, *Amer. Econ. Rev.*, Sup., March, 1913.
DAUGHERTY and others, *Economics of the Iron and Steel Industry*, Parts I, II, IV, 1937.
DENNISON and GALBRAITH, *Modern Competition and Business Policy*, 1938.
DURAND, E. D., *The Trust Problem.*
EDDY, A. J., *The New Competition.*
FEDERAL TRADE COMMISSION, *Reports.*
FERNLEY, T. A., *Price Maintenance.*
HAMILTON, W. H., *Current Economic Problems*, Chap. viii.
—— and others, *Price and Price Policies*, 1938.
HANDLER, M., *Cases and Materials on Trade Regulation*, Chaps. iv, v, ix–xv.

HANEY, L. H., *Business Organization and Combination*.

HARING, A., *Retail Price Cutting and Its Control by Manufacturers*.

HENDERSON, *The Work of the Federal Trade Commission*.

JONES, ELIOT, *The Trust Problem in the United States*.

JONES, F. D., *Trade Associations and the Law*.

LYON and ABRAMSON, *The Economics of Open-price Systems*, 1936.

NOURSE and DRURY, *Industrial Price Policies and Economic Progress*, 1938.

PATTERSON and SCHOLZ, *Economic Problems of Modern Life*, Chaps. xxi, xxii, 1937.

SEAGER and GULICK, *Trust and Corporation Problems*, 1929.

SIMONS, H. C., *A Positive Program for Laissez-faire*, 1934.

STEVENS, *Industrial Combinations and Trusts*.

———, *Unfair Competition*.

TAEUSCH, C., *Policy and Ethics in Business*, Parts B, C, 1931.

TAYLOR, H., *Contemporary Problems in the United States*, Vol. I, Chaps. xxvii, xxviii.

TIPPETS and LIVERMORE, *Business Organization and Control*, Parts II, III, 1932.

VAN HISE, *Concentration and Control*.

WALKER, *History of the Sherman Law*.

WALLACE, D. H., *Market Control in the Aluminum Industry*, 1937.

PART IV

THE NEW ERA: DEPRESSION AND COMPREHENSIVE CONTROL

CHAPTER XXVI

BUSINESS CYCLES AND DEPRESSIONS

1. INTRODUCTION

The assumption by government of the burden of dealing with the problems of business cycles, depressions, and unemployment of labor and capital marks, as has been noted, a new era in the social control of business. To the imaginary observer from Mars, it seems unthinkable that a people should at one time be actively and hopefully employed, producing goods enough to furnish relatively ample provision for their needs, and then should suddenly find themselves, with the same needs and the same productive powers and resources, unable to use the resources to provide for the needs, so that a large part of their members is deprived of the opportunity to work and reduced to destitution.

It is no longer possible to regard these calamities as acts of God, to be endured; they are failures of our human arrangements, to be remedied, if we are to retain our customary collective self-respect and satisfaction with our system. We are inevitably adopting something of the attitude of a mechanic toward a machine that does not work properly. He may try to adjust the timer or install a new carburetor; or he may undertake to redesign the machine. The analogy is, of course, not perfect, since our economic system is more than a machine. As a machine, it is bafflingly complex; no mechanic designed it and none understands it completely. And it is not a mere machine, but a living and growing organism.

For a real remedy, hardly any price seems too much to pay—hardly any price. And a remedy of sorts can be had—at a price. A completely socialistic system could—so runs the weight of evidence—substantially remove the kinds of paralysis and unemployment which afflict us most today. The price would apparently include the following elements:

(1) The costs of revolutionary change, including possibly civil war, with a period of hatred, injustice, and suffering, and an aftermath

of slow and difficult rebuilding, after the necessary elements of rebuilding, in the way of solidarity, mutual confidence, and willingness to use existing abilities, have been shattered.

(2) Fresh types of waste, substituted for the wastes of business rivalry and bargaining. These would include the wastes of democratic deliberation on many technical and economic matters, or the wastes and ineptitudes of bureaucratic supervision in a vastly multiplied form, or possibly a combination of both.

(3) Partial stagnation of progress based on free voluntary innovation and experiment, especially in the technical and economic fields, though possibly not so much in the fields of science and such applied activities as public health.

(4) An almost certain sacrifice of those forms of liberty we care most about, namely, liberty of thought and expression, of religion and culture. Complete economic socialization could hardly fail to carry with it these added results.

At a lesser price, something can be done, though no one can tell exactly how much. This lesser price would involve increased controls, at least at certain strategic points, possibly reduced independence of action in the business field generally, and increased correlation, voluntary or otherwise. At present, and in view of these unexplored possibilities, the price of complete socialization appears too high, and the less radical course is being followed. To understand what it involves, one must understand something of the nature and causes of these most baffling partial breakdowns of the system of business enterprise.

2. OUTSTANDING CHARACTERISTICS OF DEPRESSIONS

Despite the doubts of some skeptics, there are such things as general ups and downs in what may properly be called the general state of business activity, as distinct from mere chance combinations of chance ups and downs in the various separate industries and trades. One industry affects another, and most are affected more or less, directly or indirectly, by the same basic conditions. These movements have a rough sort of regularity and show certain common elements, though no two are exactly alike. The most common pattern apparently occurs at an average rate of about three cycles to a decade, the shortest being about two years and the longest about five (prior to the great depression of 1929–1937). At times, it seems that about every third one is more violent than the others, giving some evidence of a longer cycle about three times the length of the short one. Evidence of still longer swings is found by some observers.

Agriculture has its own movements, having relatively little connection with those of the rest of the system. Large crops commonly bring low prices and small crops high ones, and there is some evidence of a tendency to overcorrection of supply in the subsequent season on the part of the growers of some crops, operating toward the perpetuation of swings. In the rest of the field, prices and volume of physical production and sales generally move upward or downward together. The volume and velocity of circulation of bank deposits and rates of interest behave in the same general fashion; also prices of securities and the volume of trading in them. Employment naturally moves with the physical volume of production, while wages show a certain tendency to lag, especially on the upturn.

Different types of prices move differently. In agriculture, fluctuations come largely from the supply side, and demand is for the most part inelastic, so that a given percentage increase in output is accompanied by a larger percentage decline in price. In manufacturing, where output is controlled currently by the producers according as the market will take it at a price covering cost, relatively large changes in sales and in output can occur without equally large changes in price. Prices may not be far above costs in prosperous times and cannot go far below costs in depressions, while costs themselves contain constant elements and in the aggregate show considerable stability. Hence prices cannot move so violently as physical volume of sales or output often does.

The most intense movements of physical volume come in the durable-goods industries and in construction generally. Luxuries are also quite sensitive. The purchase of these types of goods can be easily postponed and is postponed when income is scant or prospects are discouraging. If consumers simultaneously find it necessary to retrench on house room, the current demand for housing construction may be dried up almost completely. Or it may be tripled or quadrupled if the reverse happens.

When bank credit is expanding and being actively used, this means that some people or business organizations are spending more than their realized incomes, and the total of effective monetary purchasing power in the community is increasing.[1] The result is an increase in the total flow of wealth, measured in money; and as not all of this increase

[1] This does not refer to purchasing power in the sense in which all goods constitute ultimate power to purchase other goods, but to purchasing power which can be used to make money payments without previously selling goods for money. That is the important form for our present purpose, though there are rural communities where relatively little money circulates and there is a good deal of bartering of goods and services.

is absorbed in higher prices, it means that the flow of real wealth is increasing, though in less degree. But credit which expands, beyond a moderate long-term rate of increase, must later contract; and when this happens, the movement is reversed.

3. CAUSAL FACTORS

The causal factors in this complex process are not only numerous, they are of different kinds or grades. There are movements, changes in rates of movement, or disturbances, originating outside the business system; and there are the reactions of the business system to these factors. Of the two, the reactions of the business system, though not originative in character, may be the more important in determining the character of the result. More in detail, there are fluctuations which we may take, for our purposes, as originative. There are neutralizing or equilibrating responses (like an increase of production in response to an increase in demand); and in connection with them there are factors obstructing them and factors tending to make them go too far and breed a reaction. There are enabling factors, making possible fluctuations in total economic activity which would otherwise be impossible. There are factors which propagate disturbances from one part of the economic system to another. There are factors which intensify their effects in the course of propagation, causing them to act cumulatively within wide and uncertain limits. The actual result is a complex of the action of all these various sorts of factors.

Human affairs do not naturally move in straight lines on a statistical chart. The introduction of a new commodity or a new process of production tends to move more nearly in a growth curve, first accelerating and then decelerating toward a saturation point or toward a more moderate and fairly enduring rate of long-run growth, in harmony with the growth of population and of per capita real income. Growth of population is not steady; and the approach to a stationary population in the world at large is a force of great economic importance, requiring far-reaching readjustments. A rapidly growing population requires more current production of capital equipment and durable goods, in order to be equally well supplied, than does a stationary one.

Wars, crop movements, and changes in international commercial and financial policies are major disturbances. The postwar shift to managed currencies and the accompanying unprecedented restrictions on international trade are among the greatest causes of present difficulties. The sudden transformation of the United States from a debtor to a creditor country (resulting from the World War) required us to accept more imports if our debtors were to be able to acquire the funds to buy our exports; and to this need we have not yet adjusted our minds or our economic system.

The economic system has certain mechanisms for reacting to disturbances, and some of these are supposed to tend to restore an equilibrium. One of these correctives is the "law of demand and supply." This depends for its full effectiveness on the assumption that the community spends its income as it receives it fairly completely, either for consumption goods or for capital goods via the process of saving and investment. Then if increased demand causes more to be spent for one thing or one class of things, just that much less is spent on others. If, with progress, there is growth in total producing and spending power, this growth is unaffected by particular shifts in demand from one thing to another. Things which are in increased demand bring higher prices, others lower, resulting in increased output of the one and reduced output of the other. Payments for the means of production move correspondingly, till labor and resources have been impelled to shift from industries in which demand has shrunk to those in which it has expanded, prices return to a normal relation to costs, and equilibrium is restored.

As a picture of our actual system, this description is inaccurate at almost every point. Spendings for the products of current production do not necessarily equal income; and a change in the demand for one thing is not automatically balanced by reverse changes in the demand for other things. If it is an increase, it may cause an increase in total spendings, which become increased income in the hands of those who receive them. This would naturally eventuate in further increased spendings. This secondary spending will naturally be diffused over the whole field of industry; so that as a result of spending more for one thing, the community (soon thereafter) spends not less, but more, for other things also. The process involves credit expansion and so rests on a temporary enabling factor; but unless the credit expansion is followed by contraction almost immediately, before the secondary spendings materialize, the cumulative expansion will have started and will naturally become in itself a basis for a further credit expansion on which it can sustain itself. By the time a credit contraction does occur, the cumulative process may have gone far; and the subsequent contraction may go equally far.

Not every spending of money has these portentous effects. In general, when consumers increase their purchases of one thing, they commonly buy about that much less of other things. But not if the new thing is a durable good, financed on the installment plan or through some other form of credit. Then total demand will increase.

And an increased demand for railway equipment, steel mills, or other capital goods is virtually certain to act cumulatively. Business men who want funds for expanding their businesses *may* economize as one way to secure the funds. But they will not secure them all in this way. A larger part will come out of the elastic credit mechanism, with the kind of results just described. Thus the community as a whole will consume more and not less at times when its productive equipment is being increased at more than average speed, and when *some* business men are skimping their normal consumption in order to raise capital funds.

Thus the elastic credit system is a major factor in preventing the "normal" equilibrating forces from maintaining an equilibrium. It enables cumulative swings to take place. Further factors are the relative rigidity of some prices and wage rates, and the immobility of much capital and labor. When an occupation contracts, labor does not quickly move out of it into something else. Indeed, if the shrinkage is of the kind indicated above, there is little reason for it to do so, since other occupations are contracting also. In such a case, some workers may find or make other places, but not all. Trades peculiarly subject to these fluctuations tend to keep available labor enough to handle the peaks (with some overtime if the pressure is heavy) and give them part-time employment at other times or lay off those they can replace most easily. There is much resistance to general reductions of wages in time of general slack employment; and if indiscriminately applied, such a reduction would be a doubtful remedy, though reduction may be called for in some industries. Thus labor, quite naturally on the whole, adopts the attitude of maintaining its wage demands, where it is strong enough to do so, and accepting unemployment, rather than acting on the principle of supply and demand and reducing its wage demands until the whole supply of labor is absorbed. Since no one knows where that point would be, and it seems certain that for numerous occupations no wage rate, however low, could bring full employment in the face of the forces of depression, it is useless to meet this situation by merely preaching a rigorous adherence to the law of supply and demand. Some working compromise with this principle seems inevitable.

Again, if money borrowings increase, giving rise to credit expansion, the natural equilibrating force would be an increase in the rate of interest, stimulating savings and checking borrowings, until the two should reach equality, thus checking credit expansion, and doing it promptly enough to forestall any cumulative swing. Clearly, the rate of interest does not accomplish this as things are at present. And it is probably not in itself a powerful enough instrument to bring this about, even if most stringently controlled with this purpose in view.

Thus the main equilibrating forces appear either to be obstructed or to be inadequate to maintain equilibrium, in the face of the originating, enabling, propagating, and intensifying factors which have been briefly indicated; and cumulative swings are a natural result. Numerous other factors contribute to the actual outcome. Successful innovations come at intervals and are followed by waves of imitation in which the innovation is generally adopted. Moods of optimism and pessimism succeed one another and take effect on speculative markets and on investment for future income. These moods may to some extent have independent origins; but they may also be results of the factors already analyzed. A rise in prices may under certain conditions stimulate demand rather than check it, if it is taken as an indication of further rises to come; and a decline may have the opposite effect. This does not wholly counteract the more normal effect of price changes on demand; but it may constitute a seriously disturbing eddy in the main current.

The effects of past cycles may return to create future disturbances, as when large amounts of capital equipment installed in a past boom reach the age of retirement at about the same time and thus tend to create a concentrated demand for replacements. And the effect of general changes of prices is likely to be a perversion of the normal function of price as a guide to production. If the price of one thing rises relative to other things, that means that more of that thing should be produced, and producers are correct in expanding their equipment to take advantage of the resulting profits. But a change in the general level of prices may produce profits merely because wage costs and interest charges have not yet caught up; and the proper reaction of producers may be to speed up the rise in wages. If then they expand productive equipment instead, they may be doing the wrong thing, and starting a cumulative disturbance destined later to be reversed. Professor Irving Fisher has explained business cycles as largely a "dance of the dollar."

4. POSSIBLE LONG-TERM MALADJUSTMENTS

Some students hold that the business system has within itself tendencies to long-run maladjustments leading naturally to progressive prostration. These forces might be expected, if they exist, to lead to chronic partial paralysis; or they might under certain conditions be neutralized for a considerable time, culminating ultimately in a depression of unusual severity. Some observers claim that the mere taking of profits tends in itself to stagnation through removing purchasing power which should be utilized. The obvious answer is that the purchasing power going into profits is not removed but goes normally into consumption or investment; but this does not wholly meet the case, since there is no guarantee that it will all be so used at any given time.

A more discriminating form of this theory runs as follows: As people acquire larger incomes, they tend to save an increasing proportion of the increasing total. Any increase in per capita national real income would naturally produce this result unless the distribution were so radically altered that the low-income groups (who consume more and save less) were to receive more than the whole increase in total national income, and the high-income groups were to receive a smaller total than before. This outcome is practically inconceivable under the operation of normal business forces. Increased income, then, tends toward a disproportionate increase in savings. But the field for investment in the products of industry does not show any corresponding progressive upward trend. On the contrary, some observers think that it is tapering off to a reduced rate of growth. This might mean that less of our income from past production would be spent to energize current production, with the result that the increase of production and of real incomes would be checked, and an equilibrium would be reached in which we should use only part of our full powers of production. But the theory has also been used to explain the postwar period in which production expanded enormously for a decade, until the great revulsion which began in 1929. Is the theory consistent with these facts? Can an excess of savings occur during a great boom and cause only a delayed reaction?

It seems possible that it can, if one further important factor be taken into account.[1] The studies of the Brookings Institution assume that the excess savings were dissipated in the securities markets. But this process of dissipation will repay further analysis. If we assume that more savings are flowing into these markets than are flowing out of them, through the issuance of new securities by businesses which will spend the proceeds for capital equipment, the excess will naturally result in bidding up the price of existing securities. This results in speculative profits to the previous owners. If they reinvested their profits, the bidding-up process would naturally continue until an amount of these profits, equal to the original excess of funds flowing in,

---

[1] Large amounts were loaned abroad and used to buy our exports, thus activating American industry as if they had been spent at home, though in the end we had many bad debts to show for it. This was a special and temporary circumstance.

had been taken out and spent, when equilibrium would be reached without either stimulating or contracting general industry.

But there is another factor. The securities are used as a basis for loans; and as the total market value rises and speculation is stimulated, the volume of loans tends to increase, with corresponding banking expansion. Thus the boom resulting from an original excess of savings amounting to one billion dollars might add many billions to the total market values of securities and go on until two or more billions had been taken out and spent, the difference being made up, or more than made up, by banking expansion. Thus an excess of savings could lead to an excess rather than a shortage of consumers' spendings, indirectly financed out of credit expansion. Meanwhile prices of securities could reach an irrationally high level relative to actual and prospective earnings, and somewhere the boom would reach a limit, and the expansion be reversed. Something very like this happened in the postwar period of prosperity in the United States. If it happened even in part for these causes, it may be that waves of speculative fever are not to be adequately explained or dealt with solely as forms of psychological aberration exploited by issuers of unsound securities; there may be more material maladjustments underlying them. The case is not proved, one way or the other; but it seems worth the most serious examination.

5. NATURAL OR AUTOMATIC RECOVERY

Depressions in the past have always ended in recovery, but thought is divided as to whether this is due to natural readjustments within the business system, or waits for some outside factor to set expansion in motion. At some point or other, businesses resume capital expenditures, whether because plant has come to need modernizing (for in a severe depression it is not even fully maintained, and this cannot last forever), or because confidence in the future has been regained, or because declining wages and other costs have restored the possibility of profits, or because some new opportunity for profitable investment has arisen. Then the process of expansion starts once more. One factor in setting limits on the decline is probably the fact that families with shrunken incomes manage to maintain a living rate of consumption by using up reserves, thus spending more than their incomes, at the same time that others are, in effect, spending less, since such savings as continue to be made are not fully utilized for the purchase of investment goods.

At the depth of the depression of 1932–1933, confidence in automatic recovery had greatly weakened. The movement had gone so far, and there was so much excess productive capacity, that a revival of capital expenditures seemed remote. The consumers who had been maintaining some sort of consuming power by using up their reserves had exhausted these reserves and reached their limit. Nowhere in the world did conditions afford a prospect of any effective outside force of revival. Fear of ultimate collapse was widespread.

Moreover, of those who thought there would some time be a recovery, many did not welcome the idea that it would be a recovery of the familiar sort, destined to lead to another collapse. Thus those who took the helm in 1933 faced a twofold task: immediate rescue work, and attempting to build on a safer basis for the future. In all this there was one consolation. The unprecedented severity of the depression was not clear proof that the economic system was tending toward worse and worse collapses, though many held this discouraging view. Much of the intensity of the slump was clearly traceable to the aftermath of the World War and its disruption of national financial and economic systems and of normal relations between economic areas. If a recovery of any sort could only be brought about, and if no further wars intervened, there was some prospect that future fluctuations of business might be milder, at least for a measurable time, and afford us a breathing space for reforming our lines of defense against them

6. PROPOSED MEASURES: MONEY, CREDIT, WAGES, PRICES

Measures proposed for dealing with depressions are almost innumerable—and difficult to classify. Some observers look to immediate general recovery, some to the rescue of particular sick industries or groups of industries, some to long-run stabilization, while some accept the fact of depression and look to lightening the incidence of the burden where it falls most heavily.

One group of proposals would act through the money mechanism, stabilizing the general price level through some form of managed currency. Professor Irving Fisher has long advocated an automatic system whereby the metal content of the currency would be increased when the index of prices rose and decreased when it fell, thus maintaining the general level of prices constant within a small margin, and eliminating disturbances due to the dance of the dollar. However, there were doubts whether anything that might be done to the metal content of money, even if accompanied by changes in its quantity, could in itself control movements in the volume, velocity, and value of the means of payment by which most business is carried on, namely, bank deposits. Moreover, one country alone could hardly stabilize successfully; and other countries with irredeemable currencies would have to use other means of control. Even so, it would not be possible to stabilize each country's internal price level and also stabilize the rates of exchange between them, since the course of values in the various countries has some independence of movement. Much could, no doubt, be done to mitigate fluctuations; but to this end it would seem necessary to go beyond the actual money mechanism and into the field of control of credit.

One form of monetary policy is governed by an immediate opportunism, namely, the outright depreciation of a country's money, with a view not so much to raising domestic prices (which lag heavily or indefinitely in such cases) but to taking advantage of this very lag between the domestic purchasing power of money and its value in the foreign exchanges to stimulate exports from the devaluing country. Exports could sell at reduced prices in the currencies of the countries to which they were sent and still bring in as much or more in the currency of the exporting country. This is, of course, not a means of general stabilization, but a temporary stimulus for one country only. In fact, it is one of the milder forms of trade warfare; and when adopted deliberately as a measure of policy, it can easily lead to retaliation.

Control through credit aims to restrict credit in boom times and make it cheap and easy in dull times. The ideal goal might be variously expressed as eliminating marked expansions and contractions of credit; or bringing about a rate of interest which will stabilize the total flow of spendings, including consumption and investment, by retarding investment (and stimulating savings) when consumption rises, and *vice versa*. Some proponents of this idea have even contemplated a negative rate of interest at times. Control via credit, like other forms, faces difficulties. The use of credit can be restricted when there is too much demand, but it is not so easy to increase it when there is none, or practically none. The easiest terms of credit imaginable may not stimulate businesses to borrow and invest when they would only be risking losses by so doing. As it has been expressed, "You can pull with a string, but you can't push with it." This is only one instance of the very general truth that social control of private business works better at pulling back than at pushing forward—better at restricting than at stimulating. This is one reason why the present phase of control, whose central problem is one of general stimulation, is the most baffling we have yet encountered.

Even the restriction of credit may be circumvented by "bootleg" methods—supplies passing through channels not controlled by the central banking institutions. But perhaps the chief difficulty is that of being certain when a boom is going too far—certain enough to take the heavy and unwelcome responsibility of restricting prosperity. Some growth of business is normal, and some long-term expansion of credit is normal. But how much, at any given time? While statisticians can pass lines of secular trend through past time series, when they carry these lines up to the current moment the lines are always doubtful and subject to future revision. In 1929 students of these matters saw no reason to suppose that industry in general was overexpanded in rate of output, stocks of goods, or supply of productive facilities; though they were clear enough that too much credit was flowing into the stock market. It may be that mere quantitative control of the amount of credit is insufficient without being supplemented by qualitative control of the kinds of uses to which it is put.

As to wage policy, the lack of definite standards is clearly shown in the fact that we had at the same time proposals to reduce them, to maintain them, and to increase them. Those who proposed to reduce them were looking at the immediate effect in reducing costs and replacing business deficits with profits. Those who proposed to maintain or to increase them were looking at the effect on consumers' purchasing power; and so far as they considered business deficits and profits, they held that the only way to restore profits was through increased volume of sales, even if in the initial stages profits had to be reduced or deficits further increased. And there were those who thought that wages should be maintained in the consumers'-goods industries, which would as a group receive them back as purchasing power, but reduced in the capital-goods industries. For demand for capital goods depends, not directly on consumers' purchases, but on producers' expectations of profit; hence it cannot be increased by maintaining consumers' purchases *at the expense of producers' profits*, but only by reducing the costs of producing capital goods, so as to make it possible to offer them at bargain prices.

The high-wage theory of prosperity has played a prominent part in the recent crisis. It is, of course, true that modern mass-production industry depends on a wide and liberal distribution of incomes for the sale of its products in adequate volume; it could easily condemn itself to depression by a grasping policy of low wages and attempted high profits (which on those terms would not materialize). But since private business depends also on the willingness of producers to take risks for the future, it will not expand on the basis of wages which are so high as to threaten or wipe out the prospect of earnings to capital. It is not true, then, that any and all increases of wages, without regard to amount or circumstances, are a force for business expansion.

Paying higher wages does not in itself increase purchasing power but merely transfers it. It may transfer it from those who will spend it slowly, or will not spend it all under existing conditions, to those who will spend it all (or nearly all) and spend it promptly. Then the immediate effect would be an increase in total spendings, and a resulting business expansion, with one important proviso. If it goes so far that the shrinkage of prospective business earnings stops practically all investment spending, this may outweigh the increase in consumer spending and bring on a contraction instead of an expansion. The adjustment is a matter of balance between two factors which are, under our system, equally necessary. If, after an increase of wages, the balance between wages and profits is restored by raising prices, then there is no increase in real purchasing power. Increased wages do not automatically create something out of nothing.

Another group of measures looks to increasing the purchasing power of particular groups who are at or near the point of destitution or financial prostration. This includes the raising of farm incomes and incomes of other sick industries, putting a floor under particular prices which are unduly depressed by cutthroat competition, putting a similar floor under the lowest wage rates, and also unemployment insurance or, pending its establishment, outright relief to the destitute unemployed. It is also one phase of programs of public works and relief works or work relief. The funds may come out of increased prices paid by other groups, or out of taxes on consumption; in this case the real purchasing power of these other groups is reduced. But their real spendings may or may not be reduced equally, and thus the net effect may or may not be an increase in the aggregate of real spendings. Or the funds may come out of increased income taxes. In this case there is perhaps a larger chance that total real spendings will be increased; since a considerable part of the added tax revenue may come out of reduced savings (which do not at such a time result in reduced investment spending) rather than out of direct reductions in consumption. But it must always be remembered that any substantial increase in revenue from income taxes must necessarily come out of incomes of moderate size, since the rates in the upper brackets are already so high that there is little room for increase there. Therefore it comes largely out of groups who will be forced to reduce their consumption materially as a result, even though they may make up part of the taxes out of reductions in savings. Or the funds may be borrowed; in this case a considerable part will at such a time probably come out of purchasing power that would otherwise be unused, thus increasing total spendings. Or, finally, the funds may come out of outright inflation of the currency; in this case total money spendings will be increased, and the question whether total real spendings will increase will depend on whether the inflation results in a proportionate increase in prices. It is clear, then, that the effect of such policies on total business activity may vary very much according to circumstances.

The general price level as affected by the monetary system has already been discussed, with the emphasis on stabilization as a means of stabilizing the effective demand for goods and thus preventing business ups and downs. When people think in terms of particular prices, and especially when they think of meeting actual business fluctuations, their ideas are not likely to be integrated with conceptions of general monetary policy. It is clear that a general rise in prices, when it comes about naturally as a result of increased demand, is both a symptom of business expansion and a cause of further expansion. But it is not clear that prosperity can be induced by reproducing the symptom artificially, without the prior condition of increased demand for goods. Yet some believe that when prices have been heavily reduced by a depression, improvement can be brought about by simply raising the prices. Others believe in stabilizing prices in the face of fluctuations of demand, which is a different thing from attempting to stabilize total effective demand and thus bring about a stable price level as a result. Others think that the proper policy is to keep particular prices as flexible as possible, letting them move freely in response to changes in demand. This theory is consistent with a desire for a stable price level but implies that this can be salutary only if it is founded on stabilized demand and results from it naturally, not if it is brought about artificially and without regard to the movements of demand.

Another idea is to reduce the discrepancies between the more rigid and the more flexible prices, by making either the first more flexible, or the second less so, or both. Our present agricultural price policy is based on this idea, accepting as a fact the comparative rigidity of industrial prices and attempting to bring the course of agricultural prices more nearly in line with industrial. But the idea is not limited to agricultural prices. Where other prices have gone below costs, this is thought of as destructive competition, and especially as tending to depress labor standards and prevent the desirable maintenance of wages. To sum up, ideas as to desirable price policy are decidedly mixed, not to say chaotic.

7. CAPITAL OUTLAYS: DEFICIT SPENDING AND "PUMP PRIMING"

One prominent and important policy of stabilization looks to steadying the total amount of capital expenditures of the economy, chiefly by increasing public works during depression and reducing them during prosperity, though the attempt to stabilize private industrial expenditures may also figure. President Hoover, in the early stages of the depression, attempted to induce private industries to maintain their capital outlays, with some slight temporary success. In order to have the desired effect in stabilizing general industry, increased public works during depression should be so financed as not to lead to correspondingly reduced expenditures elsewhere. Other normal public expenditures must continue, and normal private expenditures must not be unduly reduced by increased taxation. This calls for deficit financing during depressions, with surplus financing during prosperity. The original idea did not contemplate any increase in the total outlay for public works over a period of, let us say, ten years—merely changing the timing of works which would have been carried out in any case. Our actual policy, initiated in 1933 in the depth of the great depression and without any previous deliberate postponing of public works, could not have produced anything like the desired effect without going beyond these limits. And the accumulated deficits, from this and other causes, have gone far beyond what any single period of prosperity is likely to be able to make good.

The use of public works as a business regulator faces great difficulties. There are rather narrow limits on the number of projects which are really needed but can be carried out about as well at one time as at another. The amount of such projects is not sufficient to neutralize more than a minor fraction of a really substantial depression. It is not possible to get projects under way at a moment's notice. Even if there has been advance planning with a view to minimizing delay, plans may need to be reexamined and perhaps revised. Careful scrutiny of contracts takes time and is necessary if scandals are to be guarded against. Large projects get under way slowly, commonly have to pass through a preliminary period of relatively small expenditure, and may not reach the point of full expenditure and full employment for a year or two after they are started. Then it may not be good engineering to suspend or slow down operations if the stabilization policy happens to require it, as it well might by that time. Projects requiring the cooperation of several states or other jurisdictions find a further assortment of snags to delay them. This applies where the Federal Government uses grants or loans to state and local projects as a means of inducing them to work in harmony with a nationwide timing policy. These projects then have to be scrutinized by two governments instead of only one. Prior planning may mitigate these difficulties but can hardly overcome them completely.

The stimulative effect of such a program in a depression is a complicated matter, and one which is often reckoned too simply. Deficit spending, especially for public works, has been expected to "prime the pump" of private business by distributing increased purchasing power. This idea needs careful scrutiny, as it tends to confuse two kinds of effects, only one of which can fairly be thought of as pump priming. This term implies a force stimulating a revival *which can then sustain itself.* It is important to distinguish this from a merely temporary stimulus to tide over a depression until revival comes about from *other* sources. A temporary stimulus can fairly easily be brought about. True pump priming is more difficult and doubtful.

In the first place, the assumption is that deficit spending represents an increase in the total spendings above what would otherwise take place, whereas spending out of increased taxes does not. This seems in general justified in time of depression, provided the deficit spending does not go to the length of impairing business confidence. The funds are borrowed at a time when business is not taking and using all the loanable funds available. But if government takes funds which business would otherwise take and use, there is no net increase. And if deficits, by impairing business confidence, impair the willingness of business to take and use such funds as the government is not using, there may even be a net decrease.

In the second place, those who receive the money increase their spendings, though probably on the average by less than they have received; those to whom they disburse it increase their spendings in turn, and so on; until the aggregate increase in the flow of money income and outgo may in a year's time be two or three times the amount of the government's deficit spending.[1] This will ordinarily mean an increase in real incomes, though some part of it may be absorbed by increased prices. But if part of the increased income is saved and not spent for food, clothes, increased merchants' stocks, increased factory equipment, and the like, then the expansive effect will be limited in both time and amount and will quickly dwindle away and disappear if the public deficit spending stops. Something of the sort appears to have happened in 1937.

[1] This is the basis of the theory of the "multiplier" developed by R. F. Kahn and Professor J. M. Keynes.

See R. F. Kahn, "The Relation of Home Investment to Unemployment," *Econ. Jour.*, June, 1931; J. M. Keynes, *The Means to Prosperity*, 1933; also references in J. M. Clark, *Economics of Planning Public Works*, U.S. Government Printing Office, p. 85, 1935.

One more thing is required if the pump of business is to take hold: business must begin to take the idle loanable funds and invest them in the products of current industry. Only if it does this can deficit spending stop without causing a shrinkage of business; only if business acquires and puts into circulation more than the savers are holding out, can it develop a self-sustaining revival. A certain amount of this increased business investment will take place fairly automatically: if sales increase, stocks of goods are likely to be increased. But this alone is hardly enough. Not unless the expansion extends to durable productive equipment can the pump be said to be fully primed. Demand for consumers' goods must expand enough to call forth a derived demand for productive equipment, or this latter demand must arise through obsolescence or in some other way, before the deficits pile up so high as to frighten business for the future. Otherwise business will meet current demand with as little durable investment as possible, and the pump will remain unprimed.

This involves something very like a dilemma. A revival of consumer demand normally brings about a revival of capital outlays when it occurs naturally; and government spending can act to revive consumer demand. But if business expects the public spending to be temporary, it may not be prepared to invest for the future as freely as it normally would in response to the same increase in consumer demand, because the revived demand does rest on a temporary foundation. If business expects government spendings to be permanent, it may be deterred by the prospect either of a dangerous piling-up of public deficits or, as an alternative, of burdensome taxes when the need of balancing the budget becomes too urgent to be ignored. These considerations may not wholly prevent a revival of capital outlays; but they do create some doubt as to whether it will be vigorous enough to accomplish the pump-priming purpose of the program. Some students of the matter have thought that the revival of 1933–1937 showed the characteristics which this analysis would lead one to expect, namely, a cautious and restricted revival of outlays for durable capital, and a sharp recession when deficit spending rather suddenly ceased.

To sum up: government can bring about a temporary expansion of business activity by deficit spending (or partially neutralize a contraction), but to initiate by this means a revival which can go on afterward under its own power requires a combination of favorable conditions which seems unlikely to be found in a really serious depression. First, deficit spending must be ample. Second, there must be assurance that it will not go on until the financial structure is fatally overburdened. Third, there must be assurance that it will taper off gradually so as not to precipitate a second recession. Fourth, the program must not be started until business activity has fallen materially below normal (itself a difficult point to determine) and then must go into effect with a promptness which is extremely difficult for large public works, even with the help of advance planning.

8. OTHER PROPOSALS

Other proposals include the outright printing of money for distribution to consumers, with some provision for later redemption which is expected to come out of the increased flow of incomes resulting. One proposed method of redemption is by a sales tax: not in itself a desirable form of taxation, since it burdens business operations and is regressive in its incidence. One of the most ingenious proposed methods (voted on in California in 1938) is the issuance of scrip in the form of money, to which tax stamps must be attached at regular intervals until the accumulated taxes equal the face value of the money and can be used to redeem it. This plan affords a strong incentive to spend the money as quickly as possible, since its value, in effect, shrinks the longer it is held. But the acceptability of such scrip remains doubtful; also its effect on prices if it circulates.

One simple proposal, which does not pretend to be a measure for revival, is to share work by part time and also share wages. This would distribute the burden of unemployment but would leave the aggregate to fall on the workers, being in effect an enormously heavy tax laid on those least able to bear it. A considerable amount of this may be unavoidable, but it can hardly be a substitute for other methods aiming to distribute the burden more equitably.

Another proposal, which was experimented with in various ways during the recent depression, is to let the unemployed produce goods of which they stand in need and distribute them among one another, putting them as far as possible on the basis of a self-sufficing barter economy. Many goods and services were thus produced, by private "self-help" organizations or with government cooperation, but no such group ever secured in this way anything near the full quota of goods needed for subsistence. Among the many difficulties of such schemes, one is the danger of permanently separating these groups from the general economy, and preventing their members from ever becoming a source of demand for the products of private industry, such as might enable private industry to expand sufficiently to reemploy them. This danger could materialize in serious form only if such plans became more comprehensive and successful than they have actually become;

but the fear of it is presumably one reason why more effort has not been spent in this direction.

9. CONCLUSION

These, then, are some of the main proposals for dealing with the problem of depressions, whether by long-range stabilization, immediate stimulation, or distribution of the burden. Many are logical, some are well thought-out and highly ingenious, but all face substantial difficulties. They represent much of the raw material which was available in the public mind for the use of the two administrations which have successively grappled with the problem since the crash of 1929. For these administrations, nothing of the nature of long-range planning was possible. Their task was one of improvising defenses under fire.

REFERENCES FOR FURTHER READING

BROOKINGS INSTITUTION, *The Recovery Problem in the United States*, Part I, 1936.

BYE and HEWITT, *Applied Economics* (2d ed.), Chap. ix, 1934.

CLARK, J. M., *Strategic Factors in Business Cycles*, 1934.

———, *Economics of Planning Public Works*, Chaps. i–iv, 1935.

CONDLIFFE, J. B., *War and Depression*.

DOUGLAS, P. H., *Controlling Depressions*, Part I, Chaps. i–iv, 1935.

FAIRCHILD and COMPTON, *Economic Problems*, Chap. viii, 1930.

VON HABERLER, G., *Prosperity and Depression*, 1937.

HACKER, L. M., *American Problems of Today*, Chap. vii, 1937.

HANSEN, A. H., *Business Cycle Theory*, 1927.

———, *Full Recovery or Stagnation*, Parts I–III, 1938.

HARROD, R. F., *The Trade Cycle*, 1936.

KUZNETS, S., *National Income and Capital Formation*, 1937.

LEDERER, E., "Technical Progress and Unemployment," *International Labour Office, Studies and Repts.*, Ser. C, No. 22, 1938.

MILLIS and MONTGOMERY, *Labor's Risks and Social Insurance*, Chaps. i, ii, 1938.

MILLS, F. C., *Economic Tendencies in the United States*, 1932.

———, *Prices in Recession and Recovery*, 1936.

MITCHELL, W. C., *Business Cycles: The Problem and Its Setting*, 1937.

NEISSER, H. P., *Some International Aspects of the Business Cycle*, 1936.

PATTERSON and SCHOLZ, *Economic Problems of Modern Life*, Chap. ix, 1937.

PIGOU, A. C., *The Theory of Unemployment*, 1933.

ROBBINS, L., *The Great Depression*, Chaps. iii, iv, 1934.

ROSS, J. A., JR., *Speculation, Stock Prices, and Industrial Fluctuations*, 1938.

SLICHTER, S. H., *Modern Economic Society*, Chap. xx, 1928.

———, *Towards Stability*, Chaps. i–iii, 1934.

SMITH, J. G., *Economic Planning and the Tariff*, Chaps. v–vii, 1934.

TAYLOR, H., *Contemporary Problems in the United States*, Vol. I, Chaps. i–iii, vii–ix, xv–xix, 1934.

TIMOSHENKO, V. P., *World Agriculture and the Depression*, 1933.

TWENTIETH CENTURY FUND, *The Townsend Crusade*, 1936.

CHAPTER XXVII

DEPRESSION AND EMERGENCY CONTROLS: THE "NEW DEAL"

1. PREPARATORY PHASES

While the New Deal truly marks a new era in public policy toward business in this country and is part of a new era for the world at large, it did not come into being all at once by a single act of invention. Like other major events in history, it was built up to and prepared for. The changes that took place in 1933 were large ones, but the new policies were not so utterly different from what had gone before as some are inclined to consider. Some were new to this country, but not to the rest of the world. And some of the most spectacular were a matter of carrying previous endeavors beyond the limits at which they had formerly stopped.

The economic controls employed during the World War contributed something, but hardly a workable model for the "war against depression," though some people thought of them in this light. The problems were radically different; in fact, they were in some respects opposite to one another. During the war there was no lack of motivation to actuate industry to the full; it was even embarrassingly ample; and one of the problems was to prevent this stimulus from leading to an unrestricted boom in the production of general consumers' goods. That would have been a nonessential luxury at such a time. The aim was to divert as much as possible of the available resources to war purposes. The stimulus centered in public spending, with no regard to deficits, under conditions in which loans would be absorbed as a patriotic duty and without raising any question as to soundness or solvency. To furnish goods to meet this demand, producers stood ready to install productive equipment as fast as they could find the funds, and the material things in which to invest them. And for purposes of essential war production, the government stood ready to see that funds were available. In this case, the probable temporary character of the government war spending was no bar to private willingness to invest capital.

Under conditions of depression, it was possible to reproduce the factor of public spending, though on a less lavish scale; and also to furnish loans to industries which might want them. But it was not possible to reproduce the other factors favorable to a confident and vigorous response on the part of private enterprise. The wartime machinery for attempting to see that wages were adequate but not exorbitant was also a pertinent precedent, assuming that we knew what kind of a wage structure would best combat depression; but the psychology of all groups concerned, as bearing on compliance, was different. It does make a real difference whether the government wants to get as many supplies as possible for its own uses, with as little stimulus as possible to private production for private consumption, as was the case during the war, or whether it wants to produce as much stimulus as possible to private production and private consumption with as little government spending as possible. All the machinery for allocating limited supplies of essential resources among conflicting uses, which played so large a part in the wartime controls, had no application to the depression. Where the actuating motives of private industry fail and the result is partial paralysis, the problem is essentially opposite to that of war.

The war did introduce us to the idea of unprecedented public deficit spending, to its stimulative effects on industry, and to the fact that it need not lead to immediate national collapse. It also introduced us to the uses of the Federal Reserve System as a general instrument of stimulus and control. It also accustomed the country to the idea of special emergency controls going beyond ordinary limits, of the usefulness of semivoluntary combined effort in such cases, and of national responsibility for labor conditions and the standard of living. But beyond these rather general matters, its contributions were hardly specific.

The Hoover administration may be said to have marked out and entered upon most of the main fields of effort later occupied by the New Deal, going considerably beyond the nineteenth century type of piecemeal and restrictive control, and demonstrating the limitations of what could be accomplished in these fields without making a more radical break from precedent than this administration was prepared to make. It was not, as its friends and enemies often joined in representing it, devoted in practice to "rugged individualism." Rather, it went far in sounding out the possibilities of voluntary cooperative effort, of moderate public deficit spending, of liberal credit facilities, and of one form of assistance to agriculture. Without this reconnaissance work, the country would hardly have been convinced that the need justified a bolder policy. It would not have been prepared to support the more adventurous experimenting of the New Deal.

By conferences, President Hoover attempted to promote work sharing, stabilization of wage rates, and maintenance of private capital expenditures. The last was the most difficult and could only have succeeded on the assumption, which was at first entertained, that the depression was to be relatively mild and short. As it was, some who made capital outlays in response to this appeal probably found later that they had made a financial mistake, as the depression deepened and lengthened, and the amount of excess productive capacity increased. The Reconstruction Finance Corporation was designed to place capital funds at the disposal of needy businesses which could not get them through the regular private channels. The Federal Reserve System was also undertaking to pump funds into the markets, finding open-market purchases of government securities the most effective instrument.

President Hoover approved of the principle of anticyclical timing of public works and had caused a study to be made of the question.[1] In the spring of 1932, a bill was introduced for the spending of $2,200,000,000 on public works, with emphasis on the self-liquidating type; but this failed of passage. Meanwhile total public works, including state and local, declined heavily. Two billions seemed a great sum, yet the emphasis on self-liquidating works would probably have prevented the funds from flowing out nearly as rapidly as the total amount suggested. And it was small by comparison with the astronomical amounts that would be needed to offset the shrinkage in capital expenditures by states, localities, and private business, in this unprecedented depression. The amounts required for this last purpose were represented in proposals to spend ten billions. At such extreme measures it was inevitable that the government should balk. It was reasonably mindful of the need of balancing budgets, and still owed some two-thirds of a war debt which had seemed staggering when it was incurred, and when we first began to think in terms of billions and tens of billions. Through the first three years of the Great Depression, from 1929 to 1932, it continued to believe, in the light of experience, that recovery would come in due time, and would come more safely without such a perilous attempt to promote it by artificial means.

[1] National Bureau of Economic Research, *Planning and Control of Public Works*, 1930.

The administration also undertook to support the price the farmer received for wheat and some other crops, assuming the burden of holding the unsold crop off the market, and the risk of ultimate disposal. It did not, however, supplement the price-sustaining program with control of supply. At the end, the Federal Farm Board inclined to regard the latter as necessary, but President Hoover was not converted. Under this program the government incurred large losses and was left with a surplus on its hands which could not be disposed of in the open market without danger of breaking the price which the government was still anxious to sustain. Ultimately, under the succeeding administration, some supplies were disposed of in connection with relief and other activities, without putting them on the open market.

The administration was desirous of avoiding undue price declines in general, thinking that they went to destructive lengths and tended to intensify the depression. But it set up no formal organization to combat this tendency. As to relief for the destitute, the need was recognized, and some federal funds were furnished, but administration was left to state and local agencies, with resulting inequalities.

2. MARCH, 1933

By March of 1933, the country was in the midst of a general banking suspension. The depression was at its deepest, with the national income (in current dollars) at little over one-half of its 1929 level, and numerous industries operating at one-third of capacity or less. Confidence in automatic recovery had weakened and in some quarters disappeared. Consumers who had been living on their reserves had reached the end of their resources; and if natural recovery rested on their continued consumption, it was not to be thought of without more effective aid than was then forthcoming. Similarly, the ability of businesses to maintain dividends out of reserves had dwindled to the vanishing point. Existing productive capacity was so far in excess of demand, even allowing for depreciation during the lean years, that there seemed little prospect that concerns so embarrassed financially could see their way to initiate a revival through increasing their capital outlays. Confidence, as well as funds, was lacking, and attempts to restore it by the method of issuing optimistic statements had worn out their welcome so thoroughly that they appeared to produce a contrary reaction. The "new-era" psychology, which in the late twenties had pictured a state of supposedly depression-proof prosperity, was now reversed and pictured a new era in which normal recovery could no longer be looked for, and ultimate collapse was a possibility. Restoration of morale was one of the greatest needs, and this could only be based on doing something fresh and positive. Any hopeful endeavor, even if mistaken, might have been better at such as time than sitting, enduring defeat and contemplating disaster.

This need the New Deal met. It did many things that were worth doing, and many whose usefulness was and is subject for the bitterest controversy; but the first of its outstanding accomplishments was intangible, and its importance can never be accurately estimated. It broke the defeatist psychology. It did it in the only way in which it could have been done—by putting something positive in its place. A master stroke from this standpoint—whatever it may have been by other criteria—was the enlistment of the cooperation of business under the NRA. Business found itself absorbed in doing something positive, and in a mood of hope. This lasted long enough to tide us over what had every appearance of being a really critical danger point. When critics marshal argument to show that the New Deal retarded recovery instead of furthering it, it will be well to keep in mind this intangible achievement.

The manner in which the immediate banking emergency was handled contributed to this result. After the closing of all the banks, a brief survey of the situation was followed by the announcement that all sound banks would promptly reopen. This was done, general panic was avoided, and the normal financial mechanism resumed operation, with the feeling that a strong and resolute hand was at the helm. In this setting the many-sided attack on the main problem of depression was formulated.

Major elements of this attack included monetary devaluation, a large program of public works, federal responsibility for relief, agricultural valorization with control of crop acreage, prevention of soil erosion and some resettlement, and two great composite enterprises: the National Recovery Administration and the Tennessee Valley Administration. The latter was at once a public-works project, with flood-control and navigation aspects, a project of federal generation of electricity involving rural electrification at low rates and a yardstick for private utilities, and a project of planned economic development of the watershed area. The former combined work spreading through shortened hours, increased wage rates, and permission to business to organize and protect itself against destructive competitive practices and destructively low competitive prices. Other elements of the general program included special controls for oil and bituminous coal, control of securities issues, an attack on uneconomic holding companies, unemployment insurance and old-age pensions, and a reduction of trade barriers through international treaties.

In such a brief survey as the present, it is clearly impossible to deal adequately with all the many parts of this program. Some of its outstanding features may be discussed in broad and general terms, but not traced in detail. Yet there is need at least of indicating the amount of the detail involved in some of these policies, since that is in itself one of the most important general features of this great and ramifying regulatory campaign.

Was there a common principle, or a few common principles, running through the whole? There was the principle of adding to the total flow of purchasing power by deficit spending. There was the principle of giving more purchasing power to numerous particular groups in ways which involved, not an inflationary expansion of the total, but a burden laid on other groups. Some of these grants of assistance offset one another, at least in part. To a large extent the assistance went to those in greatest need, while the burdens were distributed widely and presumably on the average fell on groups whose need was less. Or the assistance went to those who would spend the money surely and promptly, while the intention was that the burdens should fall at least in part on groups who would spend less surely and less promptly. Either of these is a logically defensible principle.

Yet once a widespread distribution of special favors is contemplated it is a commonplace of our form of representative government that some kind of log-rolling is almost sure to arise whereby favors to special interests can secure support enough for passage, more or less regardless of whether they could justify themselves on a valid principle of community benefit. To this danger the New Deal was preeminently exposed, and it would have been a political miracle if it had wholly escaped. Despite these dangers, the New Deal was much more than a blind attempt to give everybody something and contained many elements of enduring value.

Along with measures looking to immediate recovery or rescue of destitute groups or imperiled interests, there were others looking to sounder conditions for the future, or to the improvement of conditions not directly connected with the emergency of the depression. Some of these involved restrictions or unfavorable effects on certain business interests and as a result, regardless of ultimate justification, were calculated to retard immediate recovery rather than to promote it. Even without considering these measures, the net effect in stimulating recovery is generally to be sought in a balancing of plus and minus components—a balancing which in some cases becomes rather thin and precarious. It is possible in economic life for two plus two to equal five instead of four, as witness the fact that business itself accomplishes this feat during a revival. But the five is not clear gain: only the extra one. And in some cases the sum may turn out to be three instead of either four or five.

3. MONETARY POLICY

The outstanding feature of the New Deal's monetary policy was the deliberate devaluation of the dollar by about 41 per cent in terms of gold content. This was accomplished after a period during which the dollar was cut loose from gold and moved uncertainly on the exchanges, being apparently maneuvered downward, gradually and with fluctuations, to about the desired degree of depreciation. During this period the policy was announced of a dollar which, when used to pay debts, would on the average give the creditor about the same purchasing power that the debtor received when the debt was contracted. Since existing debts were contracted at widely different times and at widely different price levels, this standard left some latitude. Thus the public at no time during the process knew just what was going to happen. If it had, of course, the dollar would have jumped at once to about its final value, and there could have been no period of gradual change.

This standard of equality between debtor and creditor presumably referred to the purchasing power of the dollar in the domestic markets; but the devaluation had little discernible effect on the domestic price level, taking effect almost exclusively on the foreign exchanges, which naturally followed the change in the metal content. Thus the devaluation did not bring about the kind of equity in debt repayments which the announced standard called for; but it did afford this country whatever advantages in international trade may come from a decline in our exchanges. The actual intentions and expectations of the administration must probably remain somewhat conjectural, since it is of the essence of this kind of manipulation that the government cannot take the public into its confidence. It is not improbable that the administration expected a larger increase in domestic prices than materialized, though it could hardly have expected them to keep pace with the foreign exchanges. The policy was adapted to enabling us to raise domestic prices moderately, while still affording our exports an advantage in foreign markets, rather than subjecting them to a handicap.

Since the period of irredeemable paper money during the Civil War, many contracts have been drawn to protect the creditor against being paid in depreciated currency and call for payment "in gold coin of the present weight and fineness." In order to make devaluation effective, these "gold clauses" had to be abrogated. As far as government debts were concerned, the Supreme Court held that this was repudiation of the government's obligation, but that when a sovereign nation so repudiates, there is no remedy.

Another phase of our monetary policy, or excrescence on it, was the program of purchasing silver. As a measure for improving our own currency structure, it is difficult to see how this served any rational purpose. The price of silver had been greatly depressed relative to gold, yet as a measure of assisting a depressed industry by valorizing its product, the burden of the purchases by our government was out of all proportion to the magnitude of the domestic production which was thereby assisted. It was claimed that the measure would increase the purchasing power of the silver-using countries, including presumably their power to buy our goods. This claim seems demonstrably erroneous. It ignores the fact that their exports to us, which are their only real means of purchasing and paying for our own exports to them, were calamitously handicapped. China was driven off the silver standard, and other silver-using countries were seriously injured. As concerns our trade with these countries, silver purchase was calculated to add to the effect of our own currency devaluation but apparently went so far as to defeat its own end. It is clear that the measure was adapted to securing political support from our western silver mining states, whose voting power in the Senate is grotesquely out of proportion to their population. What other purpose it served, if any, is difficult to discover.

After our currency devaluation, this country joined with England and France in an informal arrangement for stabilization of the exchanges of the three countries. This was a constructive measure, though not strong enough to stand extraordinary strains.

4. THE NATIONAL RECOVERY ADMINISTRATION

One of the major pillars of the recovery policy was the National Industrial Recovery Act, which combined the provision for an unprecedented program of public works with the establishment of the National Recovery Administration for industry and trade generally. Since the latter was more prompt in getting under way, under the driving leadership of General Johnson, it may be discussed first. Under it, industries and trades were invited to set up codes of fair competition and to organize code authorities to carry them out. When properly set up and approved by the administration, the provisions of these codes constituted standards of fair practice which were legally enforceable, though comparatively little in the way of legal enforcement was actually done.

"Fair competition" was not defined in the act, and for definitions of the purposes to be served, one must look to administration statements. A pregnant indication in the act was the provision that actions in accordance with properly authorized codes should be exempt from the anti-trust laws, though there was added (to satisfy objections to this exemption) the provision that such codes should not set up monopolies. The implication of this pair of provisions was that there was a border zone of practices which were either illegal under existing constructions of the anti-trust laws as constituting undue restraint of trade or tending to monopoly, or were of such doubtful legality that business would not be safe in undertaking them, yet which did not clearly constitute monopoly. The practical effect was, first, to shift the power of drawing the line from the Federal Trade Commission and the Department of Justice, with their traditions of combating monopolistic tendencies, to the new administration, animated by the purpose of cooperating with industry, and permitting it to mitigate the most destructive extremes of competition. Secondly, it permitted doubts to be resolved by an administrative determination in advance. Finally, the much-discussed Section 7A protected labor's right to organize and bargain collectively by representatives of its own choosing.

The background of the act helps to explain its purposes. It was an attempt to combine, and if possible harmonize, a number of objectives of quite different characters and origins. Work sharing was an obvious contributing element. The objections to it on the ground of the unjust burden on labor were met by the wage-raising features, which themselves derived their main support from the theory of high wages as a means to prosperity through increase of purchasing power. Minimum-wage rates were to be so set that the reduction of hours would not leave any group of laborers below a living standard, while there was a less definite purpose to see that laborers in general should not suffer a reduction in real earnings per employed worker, and that the total real-wage distribution should increase with the increase in numbers employed resulting from the shortened hours. The protection afforded to collective bargaining was a symptom of the intention to rely on this force to see to it that wage rates above the minima moved in proper harmony. This provision was welcomed by labor as a charter grant of a right which labor had long held was properly universal, but which had been far from being universally attained.

The "trade-practice" features of the program had an independent background in the long-standing movement to revise the anti-trust laws, and the growth of a more tolerant attitude toward associated action in industry. The war had promoted this attitude, trade associations having cooperated with the War Industries Board, and Mr. Hoover's successful efforts as Secretary of Commerce to promote standardization had been built on associated action. The frontier of the anti-trust laws had moved into the field of trade-association activities and practices, tending to restrict or to regularize competition; and not all of them had been condemned. But the borderline was uncertain, and business felt keenly the danger which this uncertainty involved.

When the depression came, many business men believed that destructive and extreme competition was one of the main causes of the prostrate state of business; and also that it acted as a lever to depress wages and labor conditions. At this point the case for relaxing the anti-trust laws made contact with the case for high wages. President Roosevelt, in a statement announcing the NRA, referred to the claim of businesses that they could do much in the public interest if they had the right to organize free from the prohibitions of the anti-trust laws and announced that they now had that right. This should presumably be regarded as an instance of his general policy of experimentation, giving business the chance to give concreteness to its rather general claims, and to show what it could do.

These, then, were the main elements which were pieced together to make the NRA. It was recognized that, if business increased its total wage disbursements and recouped itself by raising prices, the effects would be largely neutralized. And it was recognized also that there were businesses which could not bear the increased costs without thus reimbursing themselves. But it was urged that no business should more than reimburse itself for actual increased costs, and that, as far as possible, business should in the first instance absorb the increased costs without raising prices, taking its gain in the form of increased volume of sales. If the increased public outlays for public works and other purposes came into circulation soon enough, they also would make for increased demand and increased sales and would enlarge the total real income available for all parties, if not absorbed in increased prices.

The actual timing of events, however, did not favor this desired outcome. Public-works funds were slow in flowing out, for reasons already indicated. And in the summer, before the NRA codes were operating, there was a sharp and temporary boom of an anticipatory and speculative sort, due to businesses stocking up with goods before the anticipated rise in costs of production and prices. Whether this anticipation of a rise was due to the monetary policy or to the expected effect of the codes themselves, or to both, can only be conjectured. Output, employment, and hours increased at a speed that could not possibly last, and prices rose, though less markedly. The boom soon spent itself, about two-thirds of the ground gained being lost in the early autumn, except for prices, which were by this time rising under the influence of the codes. One result was to confuse or destroy the possibility of testing the operation of the NRA theory of the effect of increased purchasing power due to increased wage distributions, with prices lagging behind. The major codes got under way while the speculative boom was evaporating, and there was no valid base line from which to judge their effect.

Pending the working out of particular codes, and to get the general program in motion, industries were invited to subscribe temporarily to the "President's Reemployment Agreement" or so-called "blanket code," affording a sample of the kind of results the administration had in mind. It included minimum scales of weekly earnings, maximum hours of thirty-five per week for manufacturing and forty for "white-collar" trades, prohibition of employment of workers under sixteen years of age, and agreement to refrain from price increases not necessitated by increased payrolls. It also included an agreement not to buy from nonsigners.

This last provision added force to the "blue-eagle" drive, and some 2,300,000 employers signed, covering some sixteen million employees out of a possible twenty-five millions in occupations subject to the act. One effect of this was to subject them to the labor provisions of the program, which increased costs, and to give them a strong incentive to secure codes of their own, in order to embody in them the controls over trade practices, and thus secure the countervailing advantages of this other side of the program. This created what was very probably an unexpectedly insistent demand on the part of business for codes. No one had apparently realized how many units there were into which industry would have to be divided, how unanimously they would press for codes, and what varied and difficult problems each code could raise. The result was to put a crushing burden on an administrative organization itself in the process of formation.

This NRA organization had to be enormously expanded, and there was no obvious constituency to draw on to obtain men with enough practical knowledge of industry, yet detached enough, to be capable of representing the public interest against powerful industrial pressures.

A corps of able and devoted workers was gotten together but was apparently soon diluted with political-patronage appointees. The codes were proposed, and later administered, by business groups, few of which included internal representation of labor and consumers. That responsibility fell upon the administration, which set up labor and consumer advisory boards. Proposed codes were passed through their scrutiny and that of the legal and code-analysis divisions and were revised by negotiation with the industry, but the pressure for prompt codification curtailed the intended scrutiny and left little leisure for haggling over numerous doubtful items. Many such codes were passed provisionally, subject to observation of their results. The staff worked day and night, but the task was too vast to be handled satisfactorily.

As to hours of labor, one central difficulty was that of leaving enough elasticity so that production could always meet demand and not be restricted, without opening the door to evasion of the basic purpose of shorter hours. Many devices were tried, none being entirely satisfactory. In durable-goods industries, which were most heavily depressed, hours were already so short that little further decrease could reasonably be required. The actual shortening resulting from the codes cannot be accurately isolated, but it may be roughly estimated that resulting reemployment was in the general neighborhood of two million workers out of possibly twelve or thirteen millions unemployed.[1] Any attempt to absorb all the unemployed in this way (as was proposed in some quarters) would have been disastrous. The remaining unemployment continued to be very unevenly distributed.

As to wages, a typical problem was that of geographical differentials between north and south, and between large cities and small towns. In general, a compromise was struck between those who wanted the existing differentials fully maintained and those who wanted them abolished; but this did not settle the issue. Proper allowance for regional differences in costs of living proved baffling, though wage differentials clearly went beyond any measurable difference in living costs, representing differences in the real standard of living. The collective-bargaining provisions were perhaps most thorny of all, forcing the administration into the question what organization should be recognized as representing the workers' choice, or whether more than one might be recognized in the same establishment or industry.

---

[1] The Brookings Institution study estimated 1¾ millions reemployment. The total of unemployment is uncertain, and its real meaning more so. If one worker loses his job, that may start two other members of his family, besides himself, looking for employment.

Trade-practice provisions were of bewildering variety. Some merely forbade practices which were already contrary to law, having the effect of enlisting a new type of agency in enforcement. This showed some useful results. At the other extreme were a limited number of codes aiming to limit production through limiting machine-hours or through quota systems suggestive of foreign cartels, or limiting new installation of productive capacity. These most ambitious provisions were generally of less effect than their character would indicate. In the lumber trades, they apparently resulted in increased output at first, because output quotas were liberal, while the producers felt safe in producing up to them. This led to unsold stocks, followed by stricter limits on output.

More typical were provisions aimed to prevent sales below cost, and thus to "put a floor under prices." Crucial questions here were "Whose cost?" And "how inclusive a cost figure?" Prohibiting each producer from selling below his own individual cost would do more harm than good unless a high-cost producer were allowed to meet the prices made by those with lower costs. And "fair representative costs" left much to arbitrary judgment and might raise prices unduly. Liberal allowances for overhead might include profits which should not be protected. Costs without adequate allowance for overhead might reduce prices to a cutthroat level if the minimum became the standard, as tended to happen in some cases. In merchandising, actual purchase cost of goods sold plus a conservative-percentage mark-up had some usefulness in limiting destructive price cutting. In the light of experience, few of these provisions approved themselves, aside from prohibitions on outright "loss leaders" and the temporary fixing of minimum prices in a limited number of cases in which a special emergency was declared to exist.

Many codes contained open-price systems, frequently with "waiting periods," giving all producers time to meet a reduced price as soon as it went into effect, and thus reducing or eliminating the competitive advantage to the producer initiating the reduction. Terms of sale were standardized and customers classified—thus bringing to a head the conflicts of interest between different trade groups, especially those between wholesalers and manufacturers who sell direct to retailers. The wholesaler wants his margin protected when the manufacturer sells direct; and the manufacturer who sells direct and also through wholesalers wants to be sure, if he does protect wholesalers' margins, that they will not turn around and split them with the customer and thus undercut the manufacturer's direct sales. This is only one of numerous cross currents of conflicting interest developed in the distribution system. In general, NRA was not favorable to crystallizing distribution under a mandatory scheme of classification with fixed price-differentials; but it did not develop a clear and consistent policy on this and other features of the problem.

The NRA ultimately developed a formulated policy toward code provisions tending to fix prices, but only shortly before its sudden demise. This policy approved only a small fraction of the total mass of provisions embodied in the codes. As each item in the policy was determined, it acted as a bar to subsequent approval of codes containing disallowed provisions or to the implementing of those already approved but not implemented (chiefly by the approval of a system of cost accounting).[1] But it did not repeal code provisions and implementations already approved. The only logical next step would have been to attempt to remove these by a general revision of the codes. This would have precipitated two critical issues. Would the announced policy carry the support of the whole administrative personnel of NRA itself? And would business consent to retain the cost-raising labor features of the codes while being deprived of the compensating trade-practice features, or would the result have been a general abandonment of the code system? In this and in the growing difficulty of compliance and enforcement, the NRA may have been approaching a crisis, apart from the Supreme Court decision which brought it to an end. On May 27, 1935, it was held unconstitutional as an improper delegation of legislative power and an extension of federal control over intrastate business.

It had given a lift to the morale of business at a crucial time, had spread work sufficiently to find jobs for something like two millions of workers, and had taken a considerable remnant of workers under sixteen out of industry. But as an attempt to stimulate production by increasing the distribution of purchasing power to wage earners, its effects were obscure and doubtful. It revealed many of the difficulties of the control of hours and wages but did not develop standards of minimum-wage determination, especially such as might be applicable to a permanent policy as distinct from one for a temporary emergency.

5. THE SEQUEL OF NRA

Following the overthrow of NRA its labor objectives soon came to life again in new form. The collective-bargaining features were reenacted in stronger form in the Wagner Labor Relations Act, with the National Labor Relations Board to enforce it. The patent one-sidedness

---

[1] This barrier was not ironclad: it created a strong presumption, but exceptions could still be made.

of this act is causing a strong demand for its amendment. Furthermore, the board has become involved in the struggle between the American Federation of Labor and the rival Congress of Industrial Organizations and has been charged by the federation with partiality in this struggle. The prohibition on coercion by employers is extended to what they sincerely regard as the mildest and most legitimate persuasion on a matter in which they have an obvious joint interest, and as depriving them of normal rights of free speech. The act contains no provisions whereby the employer may bring before the board corresponding acts of coercion or intimidation on the part of labor, or other departures from a fair and unbiased expression of the workers' preference. The brief of the National Labor Relations Board before the Supreme Court in the Fansteel Metallurgical Company Case is reported as containing the contention that misconduct of employees (engaging in a sit-down strike) must not be allowed to affect their right to reemployment.[1] If this contention were to prevail, apparently the right of labor to protection against discharge for union activity would extend to activity that is in itself illegal.

It appears that there should be serious consideration of the question whether, in this act, the idea of differentiated "social justice," as contrasted with individualistic equality before the law, has not exceeded proper bounds and abandoned the essential element of reciprocity.[2] The right which it aims to protect, however, is fundamental and sanctioned by popular judgment. The Supreme Court has ruled that the board must follow the essentials of "due process of law," even if not required to follow the rules of evidence and procedure which prevail in a court. And the ultimate extent of judicial review will undoubtedly be influenced by the degree to which the board adopts attitudes and procedures appropriate to its quasi-judicial function.

To replace the controls of wages and hours in the NRA codes, there is now a federal wages-and-hours act, applying to employers engaged to a substantial extent in interstate commerce. This, in general, carries a basic minimum wage of 25 cents an hour and a maximum week of 44 hours for the first year of its operation, the figures changing to 30 cents and 42 hours for the second year, 30 cents and 40 hours for the next five years, and 40 cents and 40 hours thereafter. For the first seven years committees are to be set up to fix for the various particular industries "the highest minimum wage rates which (each committee) determines, having due regard to economic

---

[1] *New York Times*, p. 16, October 24, 1938. The Court has since denied this contention.

[2] Cf. above, Chap. v, Sec. 1.

and competitive conditions, will not substantially curtail employment." These rates are to operate in the zone above the temporary basic minima but are not authorized to go above the final 40-cent rate. After this final rate goes into effect, rates fixed by special committees expire, but special rates between 30 and 40 cents may still be fixed where the Administrator find them necessary to prevent substantial reductions in employment. This shifts the burden of proof, though the unconditional minimum remains at 30 cents. These provisions contain a somewhat dubious recognition of the limits set by "economic law"—dubious partly because of the latitude expressed in the word "substantially," and partly because there remains an absolute statutory minimum which disregards forces of supply and demand. This is contrary to the procedure followed in such states as have minimum-wage laws, which do not fix unconditional statutory minima. It seems likely to be found unsound in practice. There is also a provision of doubtful meaning which may be construed, not only to peg any existing wage rate which may be above the minimum, but to raise it by adding the overtime penalty wherever the hours are such that the overtime rate would apply. Aside from this, economic pressure is likely to result in raising rates which are above the minima, in order to preserve existing differentials.

There should be serious consideration of the question whether the limits on hours will prove too rigid and undiscriminating, even though they may be exceeded by paying time-and-a-half for overtime. They may not prove suited to all occupations covered and may at times create bottlenecks tending to limit production. There is a normal tendency, with increasing productive power, for labor to take part of the gains in the shape of more goods and part in the shape of shorter hours and more leisure. But this is a very different matter from work spreading in a depression and involves a different sort of standard. Limits on hours of the sort calculated to spread a limited amount of work should not be made permanent, unless we are prepared to abandon the ambition to get our economic system working to approximate capacity, and producing the standard of living (and of leisure) of which it is capable. One result of the multiplicity of New Deal measures is the fact that this act has not received the amount of public attention and scrutiny which its importance calls for.

To replace the trade-practice features of the NRA codes, there is now something very like chaos as to policy. There is an attempt to sustain prices of coal and crude oil, an anti-trust drive in other fields condemning some practices which were code-sanctioned under the NRA, a setting-up of voluntary codes in some trades, subject to the laws against monopoly and without positive public sanction or enforce-ability, and some state laws permitting resale price fixing and enforcing private agreements to that effect. Governmental policy is acting up-ward on some prices and downward on others; and no adequate and comprehensive formula has been offered by which to tell which prices are too low and which are too high. In recognition of the need of orientation, a national inquiry has been instituted into the general operation of the economic system, with special reference to problems of monopoly and near-monopoly, and with a view to formulating a much-needed policy.

6. PUBLIC DEFICIT SPENDING

Perhaps the chief New Deal policy of a definitely stimulative sort was a policy of deliberate deficit spending in huge amounts, partly dic-tated by necessity but also consciously intended to "prime the pump" of private business. Beginning as it did at the bottom of an unpre-cedented depression, it had to be done without prior accumulation of reserves to aid the financing, and without much preparatory planning of public works, though some efforts in this direction had been made under the previous administration. The theory underlying this program has been examined in the preceding chapter, including its possibilities, limitations, and difficulties.

Under this heading may be gathered the programs of public works, relief work, and outright relief, including such organizations as the Civilian Conservation Corps, whereby outdoor work was provided for successive groups of three hundred thousand young men for whom no private employment was available. Along with this went, at least temporarily, the idea of the split budget, under which ordinary outlays were to be kept within revenues, but not extraordinary emergency expenses. This was by way of affording assurance that the deficits would be temporary, but it can hardly be said to have succeeded in this aim. And it led for a time to some curious results when unimportant forms of "made work" were being carried on by the emergency organizations, while really important regular activities were being crowded out, owing to reduced revenues, or were financed through the back door out of work-relief funds.

Federal deficits did not begin with the New Deal. Students of the subject have estimated that for the three calendar years 1931–1933, inclusive, the Federal Government's contribution, via deficit spending tending to expand the total flow of incomes, was about one and three-quarters billions a year, while for the three succeeding years it was about three billions a year, decreasing sharply in 1937.[1] On this basis the New Deal spending program increased the rate of expansionary spending by about two-thirds above what it had been in the years immediately preceding. These figures are closely related to total fiscal deficits, but not identical with them, especially after the social security tax began to be collected. This reduced the net expansionary spending without reducing the nominal fiscal deficit, since the funds were impounded in reserves.

The course of public and private construction in the United States from 1915 to 1937 is shown in the accompanying chart. Public construction for the country as a whole had fallen in 1933 to about 60 per cent of its 1930 peak.[2] From this point it expanded, accelerating to a peak in 1936 which was nearly double its lowest point. During the four years 1933–1936, public construction was practically equal to private construction (including public utilities), though normally private construction has been three and one-half to four times the amount of public. In 1934, and again in 1935, public construction was about three-quarters of a billion larger than in 1933, while in 1936 the excess rose to about two billions, making a total excess for these three years of about three and one-half billions above the 1933 rate of expenditure. This may be compared with the amount of $3,300,000,000 which was appropriated in the National Industrial Recovery Act. Some of this appropriation went into outlays not counted as construction; nevertheless, the result may be taken as illustrating the difficulties of rapid expansion of public works.

Private construction, which in 1933 had fallen to one-fifth of the high average of 1925–1929, showed very little increase in 1934 and then rose rapidly to 1937. In this year, for the first time since 1932, it was substantially more than public construction but was still only about half the average of 1925–1929. The total of private and public construction was then about two-thirds of the average of the former high period, falling short by nearly five billions. Liberal loans by the Federal Housing Administration appear to have been responsible for much of the recent gain. Public construction had proved totally inadequate to make up the shrinkage in private construction.

[1] Arthur D. Gayer, *The Influence of Fiscal Policies upon Fluctuations of Investment*, paper read at joint meeting of American Economic Association and American Statistical Association, December 30, 1937.

[2] From U.S. Department of Commerce, *Construction Activity in the United States*, 1915–1937, p. 24. The exact figure is 58 per cent. Other estimates differ slightly.

The forms of disbursements which can be more quickly increased are relief and unemployment benefits, which will increase fairly automatically as business reaches a state of depression and decrease as it recovers. To produce a stabilizing effect on business, changes in disbursements should not be matched by simultaneous and equal changes in taxes. Ideally, from this standpoint, the revenues should be collected in prosperity only, and the disbursements made in depression only, thus doubling the stabilizing effect on business. But there are

CHART III

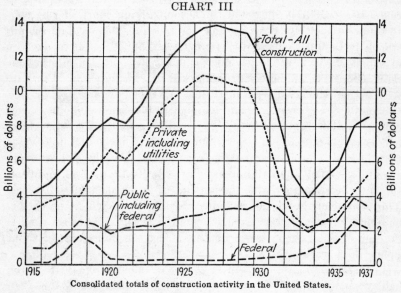

Consolidated totals of construction activity in the United States.

NOTE.—Classifications include new construction, maintenance, and work-relief construction. Federal includes outlays for federal aid for highways, Public Works Administration grants, and work-relief construction, as well as direct outlays by federal agencies. *From U.S. Dep't of Commerce, Construction Activity in the U.S. 1915–1937, p. 2.*

difficulties, starting with the difficulty of determining, for this purpose, where depression shall be said to end and prosperity to begin. Depression may become in some degree chronic; unemployment appears to be so already. In this case this method breaks down, though fluctuations might still be mitigated appreciably.

The actual New Deal policy inevitably began with outright deficit financing of relief. For the future, provision was made on the principle of contributory social insurance, under the Social Security Act. This act, whatever changes may be found necessary in its specific provisions, may take rank as the soundest in principle and the most enduring contribution of the New Deal to our economic structure. It had for some time been evident that unemployment insurance of some sort was needed and was bound to come. The act provides a federal payroll tax, calculated on the principle of building up reserves adequate to provide for future payments, and grants to states which establish unemployment-insurance systems meeting specifications laid down in the act. Old-age annuities, some payments to dependents of deceased breadwinners, and some health services are also provided.

Among other controversial points, the reserves have been attacked as being unnecessary and at present fictitious, being invested in government debts representing current deficits. If the social-security taxes were lumped with other government revenues and the debts to the social-security fund ignored, the result would have been a substantially balanced budget in 1937. This meant a virtual cessation of expansionary deficit spending, coming suddenly; and the business recession of 1937 has by some people been attributed to this cause. Any sudden cessation of public deficit expenditures is likely to have this result unless accompanied by an equally strong revival of private-capital outlays. The obvious danger is that a government, once embarked on the policy of deliberate deficit spending, will find it hard to stop. The recession of 1937 led to a renewal of deliberate deficit spending, which cannot safely go on forever. We have learned—or think we have learned—that deficit spending can stimulate business. This is an expensive lesson to learn and may prove to be a dangerous one, unless we also learn the limits of safety.

Some investigators hold, indeed, that an indefinitely continued policy of this sort is necessary to absorb an excess of savings above what business will absorb; otherwise we shall not spend all the income arising from normal economic activity, and industry will lapse into chronic stagnation. If the diagnosis were correct, the remedy would be only temporary. Taxes must ultimately increase and neutralize the stimulative effects, except as they might be so distributed as to alter the distribution of the remaining incomes in such a way as to cure the assumed tendency to oversaving by cutting down the largest incomes out of which the heaviest savings come. But it is not clear how much farther it is practicable to go in this direction than we have already gone. One obstacle is the enormous and increasing volumes of tax-exempt government bonds which are available as a refuge for the high-income groups. This suggests the elimination of tax-exempt bonds, but there is some doubt as to how much this would accomplish.

7. AGRICULTURAL CONTROLS

Among the most controversial of the New Deal policies have been the successive programs of aid to agriculture, which was in a truly desperate state. During the World War there had been great prosperity and expansion, temporarily reversing a long-term trend toward relative contraction. The results were high land values and the incurring of heavy burdens of debt. After the war, this expansion of demand vanished overnight; and in 1929 the postwar dislocation of normal international economic relations culminated in a further crash of world markets. Whatever the adjustment which this required of American farmers, it was too great and sudden for them to make successfully by themselves.

Under the original Agricultural Adjustment Act, farmers were induced to restrict acreage of distressed staple crops by payments, financed out of "processing taxes" on the manufacture of the resulting products. This was calculated to meet the weakness of previous attempts at sustaining farm prices, which had only resulted in increased surpluses. Restriction of acreage, however, did not prove a sure method of restricting output. After this law was declared unconstitutional, the program was tied to the principle of soil conservation, and payments were still made, but out of general revenues. Use was also made of the method of buying excess supplies, and also of crop loans, the government assuming the loss if the price went below the amount of the loan, and holding the resulting surplus.

The chief goal, or limit, of the program was first defined as "price parity" or a ratio between prices received by farmers and prices of things they buy, equal to the average ratio for the years 1909–1914. This ratio, according to the Brookings study, represented a peacetime peak,[1] higher than that necessary in the long run to call forth adequate supplies of farm products. With this period as 100, the ratio had averaged above 110 during 1917–1920, had dropped to 82 in 1921 (when both classes of prices fell abruptly), rose to 89 in 1922, averaged about 95 during 1923–1929, and fell again to 64 in 1933. Under the valorization program, combined with unprecedented droughts in 1934 and 1936, it rose to 73 in 1934, to 86 in 1935, and 91 in 1936. In 1936 the standard was changed from parity of price per unit to parity of real income per person. This would take account of reductions in crops raised, and also of benefit payments from the government.

To the idea of "parity" was added the idea of the "ever-normal granary," following the droughts of 1934 and 1936. This means carrying over part of the supply in years of large crops—presumably more than would be automatically carried over—until a reserve has been built up

---

[1] See Nourse, Davis, and Black, *Three Years of the Agricultural Adjustment Administration*, Brookings Institution, Institute of Economics, p. 451, 1937. The figures following are from table, p. 22.

which will insure that the consumer does not suffer in subsequent years of short crops. After this reserve has been established, it should be prevented from growing unduly large by control of production. Critics have pointed out that the great droughts of 1934 and 1936 were weathered without hardship to consumers, and with some help from imports, indicating that the deliberate accumulation of special reserves would be an unnecessary burden and expense for the purpose announced.

The results of the first three years of the policy have been appraised in a study by the Brookings Institution.[1] In general, it was found to have succeeded in its immediate objective of giving the producers of the controlled crops a larger income than they would otherwise have had, the gain coming from benefit payments and from increased prices, in varying proportions for different products. In the case of wheat and some other crops, drought reduced output substantially and occasioned imports, so that the restrictions of acreage turned out to be a mistake. Control of production and price was, naturally, more successful with crops produced for a domestic market than with those whose price was governed in a world market. Total benefits for the first three years were estimated in the Brookings study at 780 millions to cotton growers (more than half from cash payments), 356 millions to wheat growers (practically all from cash payments), and 320 millions to producers of corn and hogs. Here it was estimated that the processing taxes reduced the price received by the farmer, and the total net gain was less than the amount of the cash payments.[2] Tobacco producers also benefited largely. In a general way, the neediest areas appeared to have gained the most.

The result was increased prosperity for merchants and others in the benefited areas and an increase in their demand for industrial products. This was presumably partly offset by reduced purchasing power of those who had to pay higher prices for agricultural products; but the effect of this factor on industrial production seems impossible to measure. Growers who did not cooperate in restricting acreage appear to have gained more than those who did cooperate. Some later phases of the program were more nearly compulsory in character. The program was charged with having brought to an end America's supremacy in the world cotton market; to which it was replied that

[1] Nourse, Davis, and Black, *op. cit.*

[2] *Ibid.*, pp. 292, 300–301, 306–307. The figures include only the estimated effect on prices and output attributable to the AAA program, as distinct from other causes. Such estimates are extremely difficult and involve a considerable margin of judgment.

other world conditions were responsible for this result, and that our policy merely made the process less ruinous than it would otherwise have been.

Large surpluses were piled up in the hands of the government, were disposed of following the drought of 1936,[1] and have now (1938) piled up once more. Some have been sold in regular markets, some disposed of by international barter, and large amounts were distributed to persons on relief. The last method has roused little criticism, but the dumping of surpluses on world markets appears to be a dangerous and undesirable policy. At present the administration is considering disposal in this country at less than market prices to low-income groups of the population. Most of these methods of disposal involve losses to the government. Meanwhile the prices of wheat, corn, and cotton have declined, standing at or near their depression-low levels; and there is some restiveness among growers.

The cost of the program to the government, including benefit payments and administration, was estimated at 1,700 millions for the first three years, including commitments to January 1, 1936. Something like half of this amount came out of processing taxes.[2] Agriculture has received a subsidy of about half a billion a year, and the act of 1938 promises to bring a substantial increase. The interests in receipt of these subsidies have become active and powerful pressure groups, and it will not be easy to bring the subsidies to an end, despite some disillusionment with the results. The permanent maintenance of uneconomical production on a large scale has become a real danger. The policy might conceivably have been justifiably used as a temporary measure to ease an inevitable transition, if the goal at which the transition should aim could have been defined and reached. But this appears a baffling task, if not an impossible one. One basic difficulty is the fact that the United States has become accustomed for a long time to maintaining a level of money values higher than that of the rest of the world. This works a hardship on the grower of export crops, whose income is dependent on world prices. Some students of the question look toward a reversion to a policy of education and persuasion, possibly with more positive controls held in reserve as a last resort.

Other phases of agricultural policy included taking out of cultivation land too poor to afford a living, and organized resettlement.

---

[1] There were exceptions, particularly purchases of cattle which drought-stricken farmers were unable to feed.

[2] Nourse, Davis, and Black, *op. cit.*, p. 417. This includes a rough allowance for a reduction in the import duty on sugar, made to offset the processing tax.

Incidental agriculture was involved in projects for "subsistence home-steads," where industrial workers could cultivate modest plots in slack time. But these must be passed over.

8. SECURITIES AND HOLDING COMPANIES

Generally rated as measures of "reform" rather than of recovery are the activities of the Securities and Exchange Commission. Stricter supervision of the issuance of securities is a reform for which little argument need be made, but it requires moderate and wise adminis-tration. The commission has required fuller information from com-panies issuing securities, with increased responsibility imposed on those issuing statements for the accuracy of the information contained. The reports, however, are not in a form easily usable by the ordinary investor. The commission has wide discretion in the approval of issues and reorganizations. Stock-exchange rules have been voluntarily reformed, and margin trading has been revolutionized by radical increases in the margin requirements.

As to its effect on recovery, the increase in the liabilities and responsibilities of issuers and sponsors of securities, and especially the uncertainty (largely temporary) as to what these liabilities were, undoubtedly acted to retard somewhat the raising of capital and was thus a factor unfavorable to immediate recovery. It was the kind of reform which could best be made in a period of rising business activity, but which at such a time would not be likely to be made at all. Much the same is true of the attempt to dissolve public-utility holding companies which do not represent economically integrated aggregates of properties. The collapse of the Insull system served to headline some of the dangers in this field.

If stricter control of securities issues is regarded as a remedy for depressions, it is presumably on the double theory that with sounder and more conservative capital structures, industry would be less likely to collapse; and that with better information for investors and less scope for speculative manipulation, the stock markets are less likely to be subject to wild booms and crashes like that of 1929, and thus will have less tendency to aggravate booms and depressions in industry. As to the first, it does appear that industry needs smaller burdens of fixed debt charges in order to avoid aggravating the effects of a decline in business by bankruptcies and reorganizations. But while this would make business safer when demand falls off, it would seem to have no direct tendency to stabilize demand. As to the second theory, it prob-ably has some force, though its importance can easily be overrated. It is probably concerned with a secondary rather than a primary factor.

It seems clear that stocks tumbled in 1929, not because they were inherently bad in any sense that a regulating commission could cure, but primarily because they had been bid up to irrational levels. While this was accompanied by a wave of speculative fever, the present writer feels that this was more a result than a cause; and that a more important causal factor was an excess of funds seeking investment, above the amount of new issues seeking buyers. People expect stocks to rise when they have shown that tendency, and they show that tendency when demand exceeds supply.

One aggravating factor, however, which may be of primary importance, is the pyramiding of the demand by the use of credit, when stocks are bought on a narrow margin; and this is being controlled. As a result, a given excess of buyers' funds in the market may have less effect in bidding up prices and hence be less likely to lead to a violent reaction. On the other hand, when a considerable block of securities has to be liquidated at one time, it is harder to find immediate buyers for it all, and the price is likely to be more depressed if bargain-hunting speculators are unable to multiply their purchases by buying on a relatively thin margin. There has, it is said, been a loss of liquidity. This might also tend to reduce the price at which a large new issue could be sold, slightly raising the cost of capital to industry.

To sum up, these controls appear to have had some retarding effect on immediate recovery, some of which may have been of a more than temporary sort. And they appear to have, if well administered, possibilities of reducing the scope of general runaway booms and thus exercising a salutary, if limited, effect on future industrial stability, to the extent that this is affected by the securities markets. There are also possibilities of increasing fluctuations of certain sorts. In general, a disturbance coming from the side of demand would probably have less effect, while one coming from the side of supply might have more.

These are a few of the outstanding features of the New Deal. Others include far-reaching attempts at land-use planning, regional planning under the Tennessee Valley Authority (its yardstick for electrical rates has been mentioned in a previous chapter),[1] home loans and a policy of stimulating low-cost housing, the attempt to salvage the remains of opportunity for international trade by a policy of commercial treaties with individual countries, and the taxation features of the program. In this last field, special importance from the standpoint of the control of business attaches to the special tax on undistributed profits, and the progressive features of the corporate

[1] See above, Chap. xxiv, Sec. 5.

income tax, both of which were modified under criticism. Both presumably had a tendency to retard recovery.

9. CONCLUSION

The impact of this period in the administrative, political, and judicial realms was no less far-reaching than in economic matters. An enormous administrative machine was built up, with appointment largely free of civil service restrictions, and with a great increase in the field of political patronage. This trend may be reversed by extending civil-service requirements over the bulk of the new positions. What cannot be reversed, or greatly diminished without abandoning present policies, is the enormous increase in administrative government in the hands of boards, commissions, and single administrators with their staffs. This is changing the character of our governing system and, as far as can be seen, the change is permanent and constitutes one of the major problems of our present era.

These bodies exercise economic controls in matters involving conflicting interests; and as already noted, they combine powers of a legislative, executive, and judicial character, thus departing from the traditional theory of the separation of powers.[1] Scrutiny by Congress is weakened by the increasing number of these bodies and scope of their rulings; and judicial review is limited, not only in this way, but by the increasingly frequent provision that administrative findings of "fact" (including matters of economic judgment) shall be final if supported by evidence.[2] Moreover, the mandates of these bodies are not, like the mandate of a court, to hold the scales even between conflicting interests but, rather typically, to protect certain particular interests which appear to stand in need of special protection. The Interstate Commerce Commission and the Federal Trade Commission have had, naturally and necessarily, the tradition of protecting customers. The National Labor Relations Board is charged with protecting a particular right of labor, namely, the right to collective bargaining. The mandate of the wages-and-hours administrator is in the spirit of

[1] See above, Chap. xi, Sec. 2; Chap. xvi, Sec. 5; Chap. xx, Secs. 1, 7; Chap. xxii, Sec. 3.

[2] The Court's decision in the Columbian Enamelling and Stamping Company Case, announced February 28, 1939 (since the above was written), overruled a decision of the National Labor Relations Board as not supported by evidence within the meaning of the law. The Court construed the requirement as calling for "substantial" evidence. "It means such relevant evidence as a reasonable mind might accept as adequate to support a conclusion." Two justices appointed by President Roosevelt dissented, Justice Frankfurter not voting. *New York Times*, p. 20, March 2, 1939.

going as far as economic limitations permit in raising wages. Agricultural controls are administered, and fresh measures initiated, by an administrative body favorable to the farming interests. The need of review by bodies representing all the interests is increasingly great, but the existing mechanisms seem increasingly ill-adapted to permit it. One partial answer may be some form of separation of powers within the administrative organization.

The habit of voting on a basis of direct financial benefits to be received from government (which is far from new) has gained vastly increased scope and increased power to confuse the issue of the economic soundness of proposed measures. Specialist advisers have, quite naturally, been drawn from the "left wing" of law and economics. And the bulk of more moderate economists cannot denounce what used to be considered demonstrable fallacies with the old whole-hearted certainty, since it has in many cases been shown that there is—or may be—something in them; for example, the immediate stimulative effect of deficit spending. "Economic law" has become less rigid, and we lack standards to determine danger points. It has proved easier to start Congress on the deficit road than to check it afterward.

The personnel of the Supreme Court has shifted, and numerous earlier decisions restrictive of the legislative power to regulate have, in effect, been reversed, thus throwing greatly increased responsibility on legislature and administration for the economic soundness of policies followed. And the latter have not shown sure signs of correspondingly increased capacity to measure up to this increased responsibility. The experimental policy which was announced at the beginning of the New Deal has shown signs of applying experimental tests, not so much to the soundness of the original conceptions of policy as to the adoption of fresh ways and means whereby the original conceptions can be carried out and obstacles circumvented.

Most of these tendencies were in some degree inevitable, though they have been perhaps unnecessarily intensified. Much of what has been done will inevitably persist in some form, regardless of the outcome of future elections. The dangers involved are real but are to be balanced against the possibly greater dangers of attempting too little. We live in dangerous times. The government has at least shown that it realizes the seriousness of the shortcomings of our economic system, is in earnest to do something about them, and will not be stopped by traditional taboos. This general attitude needs to continue, though tempered by experience.

In attempting to assess, as far as may be done, the more general economic results of this program as a whole, it is well to distinguish effects on the amount of production from effects on the distribution and incidence of the burden of the shortage resulting from the depression. Under the former, we should attempt to distinguish, at least as problems, the effect on immediate recovery and the more enduring effects on the attainment of fuller and more stable economic activity for the future.

As to the incidence of the burden, it is clear that the New Deal has a large record of accomplishment in easing the incidence of this disaster on the groups who felt it most heavily. For the future, in the Social Security Act and the Wages and Hours Act, it has set up methods which are sounder and better in principle than the measures it improvised at the start. They will not be found perfect, and there will be need of improvements, more especially, it now seems, in the Wages and Hours Act, which will almost certainly need more definitely economic standards and implementing to insure that it works in reasonable harmony with the forces of supply and demand. These measures, like others, will have reactions on the volume and stability of economic activity. Those of the Social Security Act will in all probability be on the whole favorable, chiefly for the reason that it will tend to make purchasing power more stable than currently earned income. Those of the Wages and Hours Act are more dubious; it may raise some wages above the level consistent with full employment and unduly rigidify them; while the limitations on hours, even with the elasticity allowed, may not suit all kinds of work covered and should be closely watched to see that they do not tend at times to set an uneconomically low ceiling on total production.

As to its effect on recovery, there can be little doubt that the New Deal afforded an initial stimulus. As to its effect over a five-year period, only guesses are possible, as some of the crucial factors lie in the realm of the imponderables. There is a plausible case for the contention that the restrictions and burdens placed on business, and the apprehensions created, have retarded expansion more than the tangible effects of deficit spending have stimulated it. But this can never be proved. As to moderating future fluctuations, the Social Security Act has possibilities, as already noted, and the idea of flexible public works is capable of developing into a more useful instrument than it has yet been, though it is not sufficient to solve the problem. If there were agreement as to the conditions favorable to maintaining, on the average of fluctuations, a rate of production and employment reasonably close to our capacities, it would be less difficult to assess the results of the New Deal from this standpoint. Indefinite deficit spending has already been discussed and may be dismissed as a permanent solution. High wages are one factor (whether as cause or result), but not without limit. Wages are workers' purchasing power, but they are also costs of production; and both rise when wages do. Wages as costs of production can eat up profits, and some of the most important forms of purchasing depend on profits. Unduly high and rigid wage rates can bring stagnation just as surely as unduly high and rigid profit margins.

On this matter a negative conclusion is safest: the New Deal does not show any clear balance of favorable effect. And there are disquieting possibilities. Business is facing increased tax burdens, wage burdens automatically increasing for the next seven years, and some hampering regulations, with apprehensions of more to come, as well as of further currency "tinkering," public competition which it deeply distrusts, or other unforeseen experiments. These things go beyond previous economic limits, and judicial protections have been weakened. Has the sum reached an amount which private enterprise cannot be expected to absorb and still operate with full energy? The crucial point is readiness and ability to take the available capital funds and put them to work, making ample capital outlays for the future, under the regular business incentives. This requires a fair prospect of at least a moderate return. The prospective return does not need to be high, but it must not be a minus quantity. The capacity of business to go forward in this way has not disappeared, and there is no present prospect that it will; but if it is materially diminished, the results may be serious.

It seems fair to assume, first, that there is some critical limit of this sort (though probably a movable one) and, second, that no one can tell precisely where it is at any given time. The resulting dangers are obvious. The importance of the general temper and bias of those in charge of policy increases in proportion as our knowledge of the limits of safety is vague. In this light let us examine the charge, now being made, that we are following a policy which makes private enterprise unworkable or unable properly to fulfill its tasks, and that we are thus drifting into socialism without ever having decided to do so. To this it is added that there is in the administration a minority which wants collectivism and does not actively want regulated private enterprise to succeed. Official policy rejects this aim, but it is vaguely experimental and does not know where the safe limits lie. Under these conditions the minority, which knows definitely what it wants, may hoodwink the majority and lead us so far toward the collectivistic goal that it will be too late to turn back. How shall we appraise this charge?

In such a vast organization as has been built up, there may very likely be a few who, given the opportunity, would deliberately sabotage regulation, aiming to make it unworkable, and so to bring on collectivism. But this element is probably not serious; the greater danger lies elsewhere. There is probably a larger number who aim mainly at securing benefits for the common man and are not actively concerned with whether regulated private business can successfully bear the burdens. In view of the fact, mentioned earlier, that there is a zone within which the administrative official, even a subordinate official, makes the law, it is possible at numerous points for such a group to push applications of regulation beyond economic limits. This danger can probably not be wholly avoided, but it is highly important that those in authority be aware of it and on their guard against it. It is important, that is, if before we commit ourselves to collectivism, the policy of regulated private enterprise is to be given the fullest and fairest chance to show what it can do.

To sum up, the New Deal has done much to alleviate the burdens of depression for those who feel them most severely, both for the present and for the future. It afforded an initial stimulus to recovery, but its later effects on that score are doubtful, and its future effects contain some positive dangers. Whatever the fate of particular measures, it is an outstanding landmark in the struggle to secure an economic system which can justify itself by meeting the essential needs of the people who depend upon it.

REFERENCES FOR FURTHER READING

ACADEMY OF POLITICAL SCIENCE, "Essentials for Sustained Recovery," *Proc.*, meeting of March 25, 1938.

ANDERSON, N., *The Right to Work*, 1938.

Annals, "Revival of Depressed Industries," September, 1927.

BACKMAN, J., *Government Price-fixing*, 1938.

BLACHLY and OATMAN, *Administrative Legislation and Adjudication*, 1934.

BRADFORD, F. A., *Money and Banking*, Chaps. xvii–xix, xxxviii, 1937.

BROOKINGS INSTITUTION, *The Recovery Problem in the United States*, Part III, 1936.

BYE and HEWITT, *Applied Economics* (2d ed.), Chaps. iv, v, xiv, xvi, xix, 1934.

CHILDS, M. W., *Sweden: the Middle Way* (rev. ed.), 1938.

CLARK, J. M., *Economics of Planning Public Works*, Chaps. v–xiv, 1935.

COLM and LEHMANN, *Economic Consequences of Recent American Tax Policy*, 1938.

COLUMBIA UNIVERSITY COMMISSION, *Economic Reconstruction*, 1934.

DAVISON, R. C., *British Unemployment Policy*, 1938.

DOUGLAS, P. H., *Controlling Depressions*, Part II, 1935.

———, *Social Security in the United States*, 1936.

EDWARDS, CORWIN D., "The Relation of Price Policy to Fluctuations of Investment," *Amer. Econ. Rev.*, Sup., pp. 56–68, March, 1938.

GAYER, A. D., *Monetary Policy and Economic Stabilization*, 1937.

———, *Public Works in Prosperity and Depression*, 1935.

———, "Effectiveness of Public Works as a Recovery Expedient," *Index*, pp. 91–105, May, 1936.

HACKER, L. M., *American Problems of Today*, Chaps. viii–x, 1938.

HANDLER, M., *Cases and Materials on Trade Regulation*, Chap. xvi, Sec. 3.

HANSEN, A. H., *Full Recovery or Stagnation*, Part IV, 1938.

HEATON, H., *The British Way to Recovery*, 1934.

HODGE, C. L., *The Tennessee Valley Authority*, 1938.

HUBBARD, J. B., *Current Economic Policies*, Chaps. iii–vii, ix–xi, 1934.

KREPS, T. J., *Business and Government under the National Recovery Administration*, 1936.

LEISERSON, W. M., *Right and Wrong in Labor Relations*, 1938.

LYON, L. and others, *The National Recovery Administration*, 1935.

MILLIS and MONTGOMERY, *Labor's Progress and Problems*, Chaps. vi, viii, ix, 1938.

———, *Labor's Risks and Social Insurance*, Chap. iii.

NOURSE, BLACK, and DAVIS, *Three Years of the Agricultural Adjustment Administration*, 1937.

PARIS, J. D., *Monetary Policies of the United States, 1932–1938*, 1938.

PATTERSON and SCHOLZ, *Economic Problems of Modern Life*, Chaps. viii, xix, xxx, xxxiii, xxxiv, 1937.

ROBBINS, L., *The Great Depression*, Chap. vii, 1934.

ROOS, C. F., *N.R.A. Economic Planning*, 1937.

SLICHTER, S. H., *Modern Economic Society*, Chap. xix, 1928.

———, *Towards Stability*, Chap. iv, 1934.

SPRAGUE, O. M. W., *Recovery and Common Sense*, 1934.

STEWART, B. M., *Planning and Administration of Unemployment Compensation in the United States*, 1938.

TAGGART, H. F., *The Cost Principle in Minimum Price Regulation*, 1938.

TAYLOR, H., *Contemporary Problems in the United States*, Vol. I, Chaps. v, vi, x–xiv, xx, xxiv, xxix–xxxiii, xxxvi–xxxviii; Vol. II, Chaps. xvii, xx–xxv, xxxvii, xxxviii, 1934.

THOMAS, NORMAN, *The Choice before Us*, Chap. vi, 1934.

TWENTIETH CENTURY FUND, *The National Debt and Government Credit*, 1937.

———, *The Security Markets*, 1935.

UNITED STATES ADVISORY COUNCIL ON SOCIAL SECURITY, *Final Rept.*, December 18, 1938.

UNITED STATES COMMITTEE OF INDUSTRIAL ANALYSIS, *Report on the National Recovery Administration*, 75th Congress, 1st session, House Doc. 158, 1937.

UNITED STATES SOCIAL SECURITY BOARD, *A Brief Explanation of the Social Security Act*, 1936.

WALLACE, HENRY A., *New Frontiers*, Chaps. vii, viii, x, xi, xiii, xvi, 1934.

WESTERFIELD, R. B., *Money, Credit and Banking* (rev. ed.), Chaps. xx–xv, xxxviii–xlviii, 1938.

CHAPTER XXVIII

ECONOMIC PLANNING

1. WHAT IS PLANNING?

Economic planning, both actual and proposed, is of many kinds and degrees. The kind which forms the main subject of this chapter lies in the realm of proposals, nowhere realized with any approach to fullness. It arose from the basic idea that depressions are a result of the unplanned character of our economic system, and that the way to cure them is to introduce comprehensive planning into the scheme of controlled private enterprise. This idea was prevalent before the New Deal; and the New Deal itself is regarded as in part an experiment in national economic planning, though lacking some of the characteristics which advocates of this movement regard as essential. Indeed, no program hammered out under pressure of an urgent emergency can have the full character of planning, which involves deliberate preparation for the future. The improvisation and the almost inevitable piecemeal character which marked parts of the New Deal policies are the antithesis of planning as the planners conceive it. Nevertheless, some people think we have already gone a long way on the route to planning; and of these some think we have not gone far enough, while others are sure we have gone much too far, and in the wrong directions. No one, apparently, thinks we have gone just far enough. And the question remains what economic planning really is, and what it implies.

The kind with which we are mainly concerned has one dominant purpose: to eliminate undesirable fluctuations of industrial activity and to make reasonably full use of our powers of production to support an adequate standard of living, on a sound and enduring basis. This does not call for absolute and rigid stabilization—that is a straw man, easily disposed of. There is probably no reason why, when there are great railroad systems to be built or other large additions to our national equipment to be made, we should not temporarily work harder and turn out more than at other times. But the need for ordinary consumers' goods does not fluctuate in this way. It is irrelevant and intolerable, from the planning standpoint, that the production of such goods should reach its maximum only when we are unusually busy building railroads or skyscrapers; and should fall to levels that mean privation when these tasks subside, though consumers continue to have just as many needs and producers continue to have just as much power (or more) to produce goods to gratify them. These irrational and destructive instabilities are the things to be eliminated.

Full utilization of our productive powers is admittedly hard to define, and one of the basic tasks of planning would be to define it. It does not mean turning out twice as many shoes as we have need to wear, merely because we have factories with that much capacity. In principle, it means turning out all the goods for which there is sufficient need to justify the sacrifices of production. We might, within wide limits, adopt as the measure of need the purchasing power a man has in the market, provided the market employs him and pays him what his output is worth. But we certainly should not rate a man's needs at zero because he has no income, if he has no income because the market does not afford him opportunity for employment. In principle, full employment would stop at the point where more leisure would be worth more than more products; but it would not sanction an enforced stoppage, short of that point, due to failures in the market mechanism.

One of the large unsettled questions is whether planning, reasonably adequate to this purpose, necessarily means socialism or a completely regimented form of fascist economy. If we are to plan, is our choice limited to one of these alternatives? Some people frankly say that successful planning involves socialism; others are noncommittal or agnostic on this point; while some envisage planning which need not wipe out private enterprise, though they admit that the system which would embody this compromise remains to be worked out, and that concrete proposals are only first steps. If the organization for planning is to be democratically determined, it cannot, paradoxical though it may seem, itself be planning in advance by any one group. Yet the propriety of talking about planning as a distinguishable program would seem to rest on the uncertain possibility of working out some practicable compromise. For if planning necessarily means either socialism or fascism, then it is misleading to talk of it as if it did not but were something that could be independently adopted. In this uncertainty the whole idea is at present imbedded. Socialism may be the most extreme form of planning; but what is the least extreme form? Where can planning be said to begin?

Individualism was not planning, partly because the system, in general, "just grew"; and partly because the social objectives which theorists found it calculated to promote were general and not specific, being defined mainly in terms of plenty of whatever people with incomes might choose to demand, the equating of supply and demand being left to the market. Protective tariffs were more specific, also policies in the administration of the public domain. But they were thought of as "policy" rather than "planning."

Controlled private enterprise of the sort existing in this country before the World War was not planned as a whole, though the limited objectives of the various measures of piecemeal control may have been conceived with due foresight. As far as control entered into the matters of supply, demand, and price, it accepted competitive standards. The New Deal, as already noted, does involve a large amount of planning, such as the acreage controls in agriculture. But as regards the control of depressions, it is in the position of a doctor administering restoratives to a patient and watching while the patient alternately revives and relapses. The doctor may plan his own course in various contingencies, but he could hardly be said to plan the fluctuating responses of the patient's constitution; and it is to control the corresponding contingencies in the economic field (or the principal ones) that comprehensive economic planning has been advocated.

One naturally plans what one administers. This proposition will be central to our discussion. The difficulty clearly comes in attempting to extend planning over what some independent body is to administer; and to plan an economy when what one administers is not the economy, but a government of limited powers, which does not own and administer industry.

Planning does not require or imply omnipotence. One plans the features which one controls, within the limits set by the conditioning factors and contingencies which one does not control. This is as true of a private enterprise as of a communistic state, but the communistic state controls many things which, to the private enterprise, are uncontrollable conditioning factors or contingencies.

Strictly, in a large organization, one part may plan what other parts are to administer, but this implies a head which adopts the plan and orders its administration. If not, can we properly speak of "planning, or are we in the realm of pious wishes? If the wishes are specific enough, and their desirability and practicability clear enough, they may be adopted by organizations not under the planner's administrative control. In this sense it seems at least thinkable that one's planning should extend beyond the scope of what one administers, and that we might have some degree of economic planning for our system as a whole without a communistic state which would administer industry.

Or we may be able to determine results indirectly, by administering the strategic factors which control them. Nonrevolutionary planning, of the sort which is the main theme of this chapter, hinges on these possibilities.

2. TYPES AND ORIGINS OF PLANNING

There are numerous types of planning, both actual and proposed. The actual types illuminate the origins of the proposed types and have contributed various features to the proposals. They also illuminate the different routes by which different individuals have approached the general idea and help to account for the differences in their points of view and emphases. These types may be broadly grouped into limited and comprehensive planning.

Under limited planning comes industry planning, centering in scientific-management planning within plants; and business planning, centering in cartels, or organizations of producers in an industry which plan for that industry an adjustment of supply to demand. The control of acreage and prices in American agriculture belongs definitely with the business type of planning, though administered publicly. Then there is regional planning, including planned development of towns and urban areas, and the more recent planned development of watershed areas, of which the Tennessee Valley Administration is the most conspicuous example. Land-use planning in general, for purposes other than the valorization of particular crops, might be included here. The planning of production and use of resources during the World War might also be classed as limited planning because, though it extended widely over our economic system, it was limited in its objective by the requirements of the emergency which called it into being.

Under comprehensive planning come socialist planning and fascist planning. There have also been a few proposals of the business-planning type which take rank as comprehensive proposals. And, finally, there is the type in which we are most interested, which may for lack of a better name be called "social-liberal planning." All but the two last have been actually applied; these two remain in the status of proposals. Probably the chief value of a survey of these forms lies in the various particular elements which the earlier ones have to contribute toward meeting the problem as this country now faces it. These need to be separated from the elements which are inapplicable.

3. LIMITED PLANNING

World War controls of prices and wages have already been briefly discussed, the chief conclusion being that they have little applicability

to the problems of permanent peace-time economic organization.[1]
Aside from this, there was allocation of limited essential resources to
what appeared the most indispensable uses, on the basis of a unified
statistical canvass of supplies and needs. Shipping, coal, and capital
funds were outstanding and crucial examples, while something of the
sort was attempted with railway transport via priorities and embargoes. The carrying capacity of the roads was, however, an uncertain
factor, and the embargoes were not so much a form of planning as a
confession of its failure, the roads being congested with so much traffic
that they could not move what they already had on their lines, and to
admit more would have further reduced their performance and not
increased it.

Allocation of these factors was important, not merely because
these factors themselves were scarce, but because they were strategic,
controlling the use that could be made of other factors. A factory
that could not get coal could not operate and could not use other
materials. A denial of capital funds for a nonessential plant extension
was important, not so much to conserve scarce capital funds as to
conserve steel, coal, and labor for the most essential uses. The unified
statistical survey of supplies and requirements was a device of permanent value for planning, as distinct from guidance by an unplanned
market. The attempt to organize the labor market and minimize
aimless wandering of workers in search of better-paid jobs was also a
feature of permanent value to any system, planned or not.

City and regional planning was another source of the growth of the
general idea. This interfered little with private enterprise, except
as the direction of growth, and its general character in particular
areas, was conditioned by the framework of streets, rapid-transit
facilities, parks, public buildings, civic centers, and the like, which
the community or communities administered. The control was made
more specific by building and zoning ordinances, but the amount of
each use was not controlled, nor the timing of private developments.
This limited planning does not touch the crux of the problem of
depressions. In fact, city and regional planners are not notably hospi-
table to the idea of having the timing of their public works subordinated to the requirements of the economic system as a whole,
particularly if this involves enforced fluctuations to offset the fluctuations of unplanned private industry. They naturally wish to do things
when the regional plan itself is ripe for them. This difficulty would not,
of course, apply in the same degree to a system in which private
industry itself was planned and regularized in other ways, though

[1] See above, Chap. xxvii, Sec. 1.

even here some limit might need to be set on the fluctuations which public works might show if guided by local or regional plans only. And the element of advance planning is one necessary step to control of timing. Regional planning has contributed this, and also one form of the general device of control of private activities via strategic factors, publicly administered, though the particular form is one that has little relevance to the problem of general economic stabilization.

Broader regional planning by watershed authorities involves generally similar principles, in different forms. It has also gone farther and attempted, in the Tennessee Valley, for example, to influence, without dictating, the development of promising kinds of industries for the region.

Cartels are the prototype of the limited form of business planning which centers on the adjustment of supply to existing demand. This form undertakes to prevent overproduction of particular goods and undue depression of prices and profits, and also, with less success on the whole, to prevent overinvestment in productive facilities. The keynote is the protection of a fair return to the business. But in proportion as such control becomes general, the conception of fair return loses the competitive standard of comparison by which it needs to be governed and becomes a matter of the preconceptions of business-minded men. It is thus likely to become not only too rigid, but higher than is consistent with the true requirements of a balanced and stable economy. The adjustment of the supplies of particular goods to the demands for them is one element which any planning system must contain. It does no harm if it is merely a part of a system which also contains features insuring that total demand shall be in harmony with total power to produce. Otherwise it is open to the just criticism that it represents an "economy of scarcity," tending to limit the national dividend below what we have the power to produce. Adherents of this form of planning sometimes speak of stabilizing production, but their general method does not operate in this direction.

Another approach to the idea of planning, coming from the technical side of industry rather than from the marketing or business side, arose from the growth of "scientific management." This started with the expert planning of specific operations, such as manual loading of pig iron or the speed and feed of machine tools. As the method progressed, it was found that production centers needed to be planned to furnish an environment in which the specific operations could proceed according to plan; then that the operations of the whole plant must be planned and coordinated to furnish an environment in which the production center could proceed according to plan; and it was finally seen that the whole plant could not proceed according to a real plan because the market environment was not under control. Industries plan, but subject to the uncontrolled contingencies of this most obstreperous factor. Thus the idea of planning proceeded in ever-widening circles until some advocates, at least, contemplated the planning of market conditions themselves.

They thus reached a conception of planning in harmony with the ideal of stabilized abundance, and in sharp contrast to the cartel idea of accepting the limitations of the existing market and limiting production in accordance with them. It is perhaps natural that this should have sprung from the technical as distinct from the business approach. If such control of markets should prove at all compatible with a business system, it would be a more far-sighted way of protecting such profits as business can soundly earn, even though they might be far less than the business man's traditional idea of a fair return.

Scientific management has also contributed to the planning movement the idea of planning by a "staff" organization distinct from the "line" or administrative organization by which the plans are carried out, and involving "functional foremanship" which crosses the lines of administrative foremanship. But the exact applicability of this idea to national planning remains uncertain. In a plant, staff and line are under one head. Perhaps too much has been made of the idea that, as authority goes with function, the planning function can be trusted to carry its own authority, and that valid plans leave the executive no real discretion but to adopt them. Where plans are for a plant, and the executive is administering the plant, the identity of controlling interest between planner and executive may sometimes bring this about. But plans for a national economy, to be administered by business units with conflicting business interests, appear to remain a different problem.

4. SOCIALIST PLANNING

Communist Russia has suffered famine and poverty, but it has been substantially free from the forms of unemployment, and of paralysis of existing powers of production, which plague us. This was not enough to make us welcome communism; but when Russia undertook its "five-year plan," the question was asked: "Can we not do something similar for our economy, even if it is not communistic, since it is its unplanned character (as an aggregate) that leads to these attacks of prostration?" This poses the question whether planning without communism can be transplanted and can produce these particular desirable results. As far as an examination of Russian experience contributes to an answer, its contribution appears to be: Russia gets these results, not simply because Russia plans, but basically because Russia is communistically administered. Communistic planning is an incident to the communistic whole.

Contributory evidence in support of this thesis includes the following.[1] The first five-year plan came a decade after the revolution. Its dominant purposes were other than the removal of industrial cycles and unemployment. A government needs a budget; and a budget for a communistic government is necessarily a national economic plan; it cannot be otherwise. The five-year scope of the plan was apparently an incident of the ambitious long-term program of industrialization, which required large diversions of effort and sacrifices of present consumers' income for the sake of future benefits, to accrue when the industrial plant should be built and operating. As forecasts, the successive plans were highly inaccurate, and achieved performance was far from the planned balances—sometimes more and often less. Oversupplies and undersupplies of particular products were frequent; operations were held up because complementary operations failed or fell short. This general matter of inaccuracy should perhaps not be too much stressed, partly because current revisions were possible, and partly because the aggregate balance of government income (which was also the outgo of individuals) and government outgo (which was purchasing power to individuals) was undoubtedly better than the particular balances for particular products. Nevertheless, lack of aggregate balance is evidenced by the fact that this government, like others, practiced inflation.

Moreover, freedom from cycles and unemployment was facilitated in Russia by its very poverty and industrial backwardness. This point, again, should not be too much stressed, since even an industrially backward nation, under private enterprise, would have some cycles and unemployment, especially if it were undergoing industrialization as rapidly as was Russia.

The really crucial factor appears to be this: the Russian state can adopt a budget of balanced supply and demand, in which the demand side is gauged to the country's power to produce, with assurance that three things will happen. First, the production will be undertaken and carried forward—whether precisely according to schedule or not is not decisive. Losses will not stop it as they would under private enterprise; in fact, some losses are planned for. Second, as the production is carried forward, the purchasing power will flow out in something like

[1] On this general topic, see an illuminating article by Arthur Feiler, "The Soviet Union and the Business Cycle," *Social Research*, pp. 283–303, August, 1936.

the designed volume. Third, it will substantially all be used as demand for products. Again, there may be discrepancies and miscalculations, and one may hear—as one does—of goods failing to find a market owing to inadequate purchasing power; but this will not limit the otherwise possible production to anything like the extent to which it was limited in the United States in 1932. A contributing factor here is the fact that the balance of savings necessary to finance the scheduled additions to capital equipment is furnished by the government, private savings affording only a portion. Thus, in general, no more is saved than is needed and will be used. This fact presumably arises partly from the low per capita income, partly from the absence of the really rich, and partly from the collectivist methods of providing for various contingencies for which personal savings are needed under individualism. To sum up, it is not the existence of the plan as such, but the collectivist conditions of administration under which it is carried out, that appear to determine the character of the result.

Power to produce may itself be limited, and very seriously, partly by the nonindustrial character and background of the people and partly by the natural and inherent shortcomings of communist organization and administration, which it would be folly to deny or overlook. But such as it is under communism, power to produce seems likely to be fairly fully realized, without serious limitations from the side of the market.

Russia has contributed to our own movement for noncommunist planning the idea of a goal, quantitatively defined in the form of a budget of technically achievable production and consumption. The methods of realizing or approaching this goal, if not communistic, remain to be worked out. They represent a problem which may or may not be soluble.

5. FASCIST AND NAZI PLANNING

Of planning in fascist Italy and in Nazi Germany it is perhaps not necessary to speak in detail. As in the case of Russia, the element of planning in the systems is incidental to, or an integral part of, a scheme of control by dictatorship. This scheme in its entirety is not likely to be adopted in this country, except possibly as the outcome of a violent revolution, including as it does a régime of complete and ruthless coercion. Yet, without this, it is difficult to see how the features of economic planning could be made to operate successfully. Furthermore, the planning is not dominantly planning for democratic abundance for the people as a whole, but on the whole rather the opposite. This seems clearly true in the case of Germany, which affords the more extreme and thoroughgoing example.

Here the dominant purposes and circumstances bear a strong resemblance to those of World War control, in that the paramount values are national power and aggrandisement, expressed in armaments and public works, and not a high standard of living for the masses.[1] Adequate purchasing power to energize existing productive resources is forthcoming, as in our World War economy, by public deficit financing where necessary. Unemployment has vanished, much as it did with us, assisted perhaps by absorbing large numbers of the people into fascist organizations and activities. The planning element of economic control centers in allocating scarce resources to the most important ends as judged by the prevailing scale of values. This is done far more completely than we did it during the war, thanks to the coercive controls already mentioned. This type of planning is not in itself an energizing force: the energizing element—in which we are most interested—appears to be located elsewhere. If the paramount purpose were changed to one of abundance for the masses, the whole system would be transformed, and different mechanisms would be needed.

Foreign exchange, available to purchase imports, is limited, owing to limited exports, and is strictly rationed, so also are capital funds available for production. Prices of essential commodities are fixed and supplies rationed, more effectively than we have ever done, the whole being enforced by the system of coercive penalties. The development of substitute materials to replace scarce natural products is a problem peculiar to Germany. And public deficit financing—the most tangible energizing force—is prevented from having the serious economic results it would have in a freer economy. It cannot result in price-raising inflation or in the destruction of public credit, where these matters are not left to free private choice. To sum up, it is difficult to see what elements of the present German system we, with our different scale of values, could usefully borrow.

6. COMPREHENSIVE BUSINESS PLANNING

In this country, in the period prior to the New Deal, business planning formulated a few programs which deserve to be called comprehensive. Of these the "Swope plan" was probably the best example. It advocated organizations within industry to adjust supply to demand, recognizing the ultimate power of government to regulate prices.

[1] Cf. above, Chap. xxvii, Sec. 1.

Reasons for avoiding this type of policy have already been discussed.[1] It avowed the purpose of maintaining adequate labor conditions and more steady employment, but it does not appear that the proposed form of organization would be calculated in actual operation to promote this latter end. It contained a truly statesmanlike proposal for an interindustry system of employee insurance; but the main function of this has now been taken over by the Social Security Act. Its general ideas found some expression in the National Recovery Administration, though with a shift of emphasis which would, in some degree or other, have been inevitable.

7. SOCIAL-LIBERAL PLANNING

Social-liberal planning faces a task which is, in its way, more difficult than that of socialist planning, complicated as that is in practice. In fact, it includes these difficulties together with some others peculiar to itself and centering in the fact that it must "plan" what it does not administer. Socialism, already administering production, need merely plan to produce what it knows, in general terms, it can consume; and full utilization of productive powers, barring errors and miscalculations, is a natural by-product. It does not have to concern itself with the causes which produce stagnation in an economy of private enterprise—that has become for it an academic question. But social-liberal planning must alter the operation of an economic system which remains prevailingly private; and to do this it must diagnose precisely these causes of stagnation, and act on and through them to bring about its effects. It may borrow applicable features from any of the other forms of planning, but some of them it must make over for its own requirements.

As to what these requirements are, we may approach that problem via the difference in implication between the terms "planning" and "policy." Policies we have always had, presumably designed with some degree or other of foresight as to their expected results; planning purports to contribute something more definite and more effective. Its essential distinguishing features, necessary to justify this enlarged implication, appear to be a quantitatively defined objective and a unified or correlated program calculated to reach such an objective. Social-liberal planning implies action on such a unified program via general controls that keep within the limits consistent with a healthy private enterprise, more complete controls being limited to certain strategic factors which condition private economic enterprise, these being such as a "liberal" government may administer. Voluntary

[1] See above, Chap. xxv, Sec. 10.

cooperation would also be sought by whatever means might be found possible.

First, as to the quantitatively defined objective. Ideally, this might be conceived as a social budget of supply and demand, in which the demand side includes those potential demands, not now effective, which would be realizable if our productive powers were fully utilized. It would be worth while to try to make such a budget—even if it could not be done with any approach to accuracy—for the sake of the light it would shed on the elements of the planning problem. It would, of course, be compared with the facts as to current actual conditions and performance.

The conception is a fascinating one, but full of difficulties and uncertainties, as previous attempts in this direction bear witness. By what series of steps could the budget be made up? What assumptions would have to be made as to governing conditions, and how would they affect the resulting totals? Would there have to be a number of such estimates representing different assumed conditions? What other elements of conjecture or uncertainty would enter in? And, finally, how could the results be used to make more effective the means of control available to a liberal state?

The process would really start with a general notion of the size and distribution of the possible social income, drawn from the records of our best past performance, and from past attempts to estimate unused capacity. Then might come estimates, for example, of capacity to produce shoes, with due regard to leather, labor (skilled and unskilled), and replacement requirements, ruling out any capacity for which there would clearly be no effective demand. The field of industry might be covered in this way, revisions being likely to be necessary as successive finished products make increased demands on limited basic materials. As limiting factors were revealed which would prevent full utilization of other factors, resources could be assigned to strengthening these weak spots.

In the meantime, one division of the staff would be facing the problem, if the unemployed and partly employed were at work, how much could employers afford to pay them? What allowance should be made for the fact that the unemployed are, on the average, poorer workers than the employed? This affects not only total output (and total real income), but its distribution. If it were possible to produce real income equal to $2,500 per year per worker at present price levels, it would be irrelevant to assume it to be equally distributed, as long as many workers could not produce that much or make themselves worth that much to any employer. Here at once is a vital element which can only be estimated. Various distributions of income might be assumed, but they would need to be consistent with the kind of economy we are contemplating.

The next major question is How will this income be spent? For this, existing budgetary studies afford some basis, though hardly in sufficient detail. A crucial part of the problem would be the amount of savings; and this would be affected by the concentration of income and the taxing system, and also by the kind of social-security system which is assumed to exist. The exact effects of this last can only be conjectured.

By this time the studies from the production side will be facing the problem of the field of future capital requirements, which will again be conjectural. Yet a vital feature of a balanced budget of the sort we are engaged on is a balance between savings and requirements for capital outlays. If savings exceed capital outlays, the result will be either a shrinkage of income, or a speculative inflation of some sort which will lead to trouble later. At this point, the budget makers will be almost forced to assume that planning will solve this problem, and to throw what light their estimates can on the nature and extent of the probable discrepancies which planning will need to bring into balance. And that light will not be very definite.

The labor supply affords other problems. If full employment became available to every head of a family, how many of their wives and daughters, now holding or seeking jobs because the head is unemployed, would leave the labor market? Here is another conjectural matter. One thing the survey would almost certainly reveal at present would be a relative shortage of skilled labor as compared to unskilled, and as compared to the demands of our potentially realizable consumption. It would reveal, for example, a surplus of coal miners, who might not be easily shifted to other occupations.

Public expenditures would, of course, be a part of the picture, including, as one potentially important item, publicly stimulated low-cost housing. If reemployment eased the present pressure on public budgets, there would be a chance to make much-needed expansions in the fields of education and public-health service. The net outcome of the survey would be, not a detailed budget such as a socialist state might draw up, but an estimate of unused capacities for production and consumption, with a considerable margin of error, or perhaps different estimates premised on different assumed conditions. It would also shed light on the adjustments necessary if these potentialities are to be realized.

The second major requirement is a coordinated policy directed toward this goal. The means of coordination would center in a national organization of the "staff" type: a planning board or national economic council, with fact-finding and advisory powers. It would be responsible for formulating the objective already mentioned, and subordinate objectives indicated by its diagnoses of existing conditions and their causes. Its recommendations would depend on their force and reasonableness to command executive and legislative support for measures of public action, or the support of private agencies as far as their voluntary cooperation might be required.

As further means to a coordinated policy, effective connections would need to be set up with private industry whereby desirable policies might be voluntarily adopted. First steps might be of the character of liaison and mutual education. But ultimately, when an adequate basis of understanding had been reached, there would presumably be need of more formal organization within industry. Such organizations would need to be different from, and broader than, trade associations, code authorities of the NRA type, or any organization of business units only, and within a single trade only. The reason is that, to cooperate effectively in this kind of program, they would need to be so organized that their joint interest in expanding production and consumption to their full capabilities would not be balked by the interest which limited trade groups have in limiting production of their own products to what can be profitably sold under existing conditions of demand, restricted as it is by existing limitations on production. Successful planning of the sort we are considering depends on breaking through this vicious circle, and this can hardly be expected from trade-group organizations acting separately.

The third major requirement is action in following out the coordinated policy which, as far as it is authoritative, would take place through the factors which a liberal government administers or controls. It would therefore be, as now, mainly indirect, operating through the strategic conditioning factors and through voluntary cooperation. The hope is that such action would be made more effective by the other features of the program.

The method of controlling industrial activity indirectly, via the strategic factors which govern its course, in itself is nothing new. We are already attempting control via the monetary system, banking and credit policy, public expenditures, taxes, the administration of public property, control of some wage rates and some prices and of the output of some commodities, social security, and many other measures. We know already the principal fact which a planning survey could tell us, namely, that we are operating on a balance of supply and demand far short of what it could be. Two crucial strategic factors we do not control directly, and we should presumably undertake no compulsory control of them under liberal planning, namely, the consumer's choice between spending and saving, and the producer's choice how and when and how much to invest in productive equipment. We can, of course, try the experiment of taxed money, which the holder is expected to spend promptly, to get rid of it before its value decreases—if he can find anyone who will take it—but the uncertainties of such a device seem to remove it far from the realm of planning. As it stands, our means of indirect control are not complete.

Better fact finding and more unified analysis could hardly fail to make our present use of these indirect controls more effective than they now are. Their limitations, however, have been touched on in the two preceding chapters, and perhaps sufficiently to indicate that it will not be easy to overcome them. By such means we can reasonably hope for some steadying of fluctuations and some easing of the obstacles to full utilization, provided we avoid mistakes which could easily have the reverse effect. We may hope for very considerable lightening of the incidence of the burden of depressions on those who feel it most heavily. Such limited improvements may be enough to enable our system to hold together for a breathing spell during which we may work out further evolutionary developments. But they can hardly be permanently satisfactory.

One thing which planning can contribute is greater stability of policy, thereby reducing greatly the uncertainties which are one of the greatest hampering effects of the present situation on voluntary business expansion. It may reveal ways of bringing about a really substantial reduction of the inequality of distribution of incomes, possibly through a taxing system which raises large revenues without resorting heavily to indirect taxation which falls heavily on small incomes and directly limits production, or possibly in other ways. It may find ways of adjusting the business system to a real reduction in the rate of return to capital, such as appears necessary if the total proportion of the national income absorbed by capital overhead is not to be a hampering burden on production. A small return on fairly steady operation would be better than higher returns alternating with paralysis and crippling losses. And, finally, by its investigations, planning may so convince business, labor, and other groups of the seriousness of the situation that they will be ready to join voluntarily in organized measures to promote their joint interest in expansion, even if this involves a partial surrender of the particularistic vested interests which at present operate to protect the financial returns of parts at the expense of the whole.

In this possibility lies perhaps the greatest promise of nonsocialistic planning. To take an outstanding example, if the vital construction industry is to be stabilized, the total burden of costs must be reduced in dull times in order to afford buyers an incentive. These costs include wages and returns to capital in mining and lumbering, making of steel, cement, and finished lumber, fabricating structural shapes, and designing and erecting structures. It is to the interest of all as a whole to make joint concessions, but no one group, by making concessions alone, could make enough impression on the total burden to have any material stimulating effect on demand. As a single group, its interest lies in protecting its rate of return as far as possible. Even simultaneous concessions by all might not be enough without some planned program affording at least a minimum demand for construction which such concessions would bring into being. The basic idea is not new; proposals of the sort have already been considered among some of the groups involved but have not yet overcome the obstacles arising from conflicting interests, or apparent interests.

This problem cannot be solved merely by some ingenious formula. The basis is simpler than that: namely, a common interest. Where that exists and is realized, cooperation can be hoped for, and ingenious formulas, if necessary, can be devised. For instance, forms of wage payment could be worked out which would insure that labor got increased total earnings if the program went into effect, while the added cost to the employer of employing more workers in dull times was reduced. Labor would need to be convinced that its real interest lies in total annual earnings, rather than in hourly wage rates. This can hardly be done merely by preaching the desirability of accepting temporary reductions in bad times. But if this reduction applies only to added work beyond a minimum and is part of an arrangement between producers and large users affording some definite prospect of steadier work, then there might be a chance of its acceptance, unless past conflicts have destroyed men's power to compose differences to their mutual advantage. But such a system will not come into existence of itself; and here is one of the largest kinds of opportunity for a really statesmanlike national planning organization in a system like our own. If such a proposal had the advantage of leadership equal to that which inaugurated the original New Deal, it would have every chance of success.

Employers can see that, if they all simultaneously expanded operations, in just the right ways, the money they disbursed would flow back to them in purchases, and all would be better off. But if one alone did it, only a fraction of the money would flow back to him, and he would presumably be left with unsold goods on his hands. Even if all tried it, there would be doubt as to the proper rate of expansion for different industries, and further doubt as to whether the total of increased disbursements could be counted on to flow back in increased aggregate purchases. It is at points like these that an adequate national planning organization has the opportunity to make its indispensable contribution.

8. CONCLUSION

Planning is no easy panacea; that much is clearly evident. It can easily make serious mistakes. But it contains possibilities of real contributions to our present stage of industrial development. And an economic system in as serious a state as our own cannot afford not to explore and develop these possibilities to the utmost. We are bound to be trying experiments in the coming generation. Those experiments may be planned or may be improvised; they may be designed in the integral interest of the whole or worked out by the pulling and hauling of special-interest pressure groups. And planning is better than improvisation, and integral designing better than pressure-group politics.

REFERENCES FOR FURTHER READING

Annals, "National and World Planning," July, 1932.

———, "Social Problems and Policies in Sweden," May, 1938.

BUNBURY, SIR H. W., *Governmental Planning Machinery*, 1938.

BYE and HEWITT, *Applied Economics* (2d ed.), Chaps. xxii, xxx, 1934.

CLARK, J. M., *Economics of Planning Public Works*, Chaps. xv, xvi, 1935.

DICKINSON, H. D., "Price Formation in a Socialist Community," *Econ. Jour.*, pp. 237–250, June, 1933.

DOBB, M., "Economic Theory and the Problem of a Socialist Economy," *Econ. Jour.*, pp. 588–598, December, 1933.

FEILER, A., "The Soviet Union and the Business Cycle," *Social Research*, August, 1936.

GAYER, A. D., *Monetary Policy and Economic Stabilization*, Chaps. x–xii, 1937.

GOODRICH, C. and others, *Migration and Economic Opportunity*, 1936.

HANSEN, A. H., *Full Recovery or Stagnation*, Part III; Chaps. ix, xx, 1938.

VON HAYEK, F. A., and others, *Collectivist Economic Planning*, 1935.

HEIMANN, E., "Planning and the Market System," *Social Research*, pp. 486–504, November, 1934.

HUBBARD, J. B., *Current Economic Policies*, Chap. xii, 1934.

HUBBARD, L. E., *Soviet Money and Finance*, Chaps. v–viii, xiii–xv, 1936.

———, *Soviet Trade and Distribution*, pp. 24–25; Chaps. xii–xiv, xxviii, 1938.

LANGE, O., "On the Economic Theory of Socialism," *Rev. Econ. Stud.*, pp. 53–71, February, 1937; pp. 123–144, October, 1936.

LERNER, A. P., "A Note on Socialist Economics," *Rev. Econ. Stud.*, pp. 72–76, October, 1936.

LIPPMANN, WALTER, *The Good Society*, pp. 28–44, 91–105, 1937.

LOEB and others, *Report of National Survey of Potential Product Capacity*, 1935.

MITCHELL, W. C., *The Backward Art of Spending Money*, Essays 6, 7, 1937.

NATIONAL PROGRESSIVE CONFERENCE, "Long-range Planning," *New Republic*, Part II, January 13, 1932.

NOURSE and others, *America's Capacity to Produce*, 1934.

PERSON, H. S., "On Planning," *Soc. Advancement of Management Jour.*, pp. 143–149, November, 1936.

PETERSON, G. M., *Diminishing Returns and Economic Planning*, Chap. vii, 1937. *Plan Age, passim*.

ROBBINS, L., *The Great Depression*, Chaps. viii, ix, 1934.

————, *Economic Planning and International Order*, 1937.

RÖPKE, W., "Socialism, Planning and the Business Cycle," *Jour. Polit. Econ.*, pp. 318–338, June, 1936.

SLICHTER, S. H., *Modern Economic Society*, Chap. xxxi, 1928.

————, *Towards Stability*, Chap. v, 1934.

SMITH, J. G., *Economic Planning and the Tariff*, Chaps. i, xi, xiv, 1934.

SOULE, G., *A Planned Society*, 1932.

TAYLOR, H., *Contemporary Problems in the United States*, Vol. II, Chaps. xxxii–xxxvi, 1934.

UNITED STATES NATIONAL PLANNING BOARD, *Final Rept.*, 1933–1934.

UNITED STATES NATIONAL RESOURCES COMMITTEE, *Planning Our Resources*, 1938.

WALLACE, HENRY A., *New Frontiers*, Chap. xvii, 1934.

WOOTON, B., *Plan or No Plan*, 1934.

CHAPTER XXIX

CONTROL AND ECONOMIC LAW

1. THE MEANING OF "ECONOMIC LAW"

When some policy of public control in the economic realm is criticized on the ground that it is a "violation of economic law," what is meant? The phrase is often used loosely, but one can distinguish two degrees of meaning. One is to the effect that the measures of control which go counter to the economic nature of things cannot be enforced. They will be resisted, evaded, defeated in various ways; in short, the economic nature of things will overpower them. Another interpretation is more elastic but no less damning. Unnatural measures of restraint will fail to accomplish their ultimate purpose, or they will do more harm than good, through preventing useful or necessary transactions from taking place. In either case the natural law in question is the law of free exchange, working itself out in the tendency of supply and demand to meet and to adjust price at a level which will bring about the meeting.

The first form of the statement implies that government cannot prevent people from doing what they want. If this were strictly true, a law against burglary would be a violation of economic law and could not be enforced. Yet all apostles of economic law presuppose the protection of property; it is with this that economic law begins. What this idea really implies is that government can prevent people from doing what they wish, when they are trying to harm others without the others' consent, but that the state becomes powerless when two parties both wish to make an arrangement whereby each will get something he desires. Yet even this does not quite fit the case, for the state will continue to protect property, even if the would-be plunderers are banded together in an agreement for their mutual profit in dividing the spoil. In fact, the law of conspiracy makes some things illegal, when a number of persons do them concertedly, which might be legal if one person did the same thing alone. The real kernel of truth in this position is that, when people are accustomed to making their living by arrangements in which the immediate parties seek their mutual advantage and both sides are willing, and where the transaction has been customarily regarded as legitimate business, then any prohibition will meet enormous resistance. Add to this that any persons who may be harmed by the transaction are not direct parties to it and cannot protect their interests by appealing to their common-law rights of person or property, and it is plain that the state is not only encountering great resistance but must also do without the help of one of the strongest forces on which its basic policies rely, namely, the natural and energetic efforts of the wronged individual to protect his own interests. Attempts to enforce such laws are of a peculiar difficulty, and they must expect to encounter an unusually large amount of evasion.

What of the second form of the doctrine, which states that such laws, if they do succeed in their immediate object, will do more harm than good? This, it would appear, is clearly a matter of the wisdom of the regulations. It depends on the success of the state in weighing the interests of the contracting parties against the other interests which may be injured, or in weighing any elements of duress which may give reason for supposing that the true interests of the parties are not being promoted, or in safeguarding the necessary incentives to production during its attempts to prevent profiteering, or in any other weighing of interests which may be called for. To claim that such regulations necessarily violate economic law amounts to claiming that the state cannot be wise enough to foresee the consequences of its own acts, weigh them justly, and devise antidotes to any undesirable tendencies which may result.

This question naturally breaks itself up into two classes of cases: those in which the state is dealing with matters which are incidental to the main transaction, and those in which the "heart of the contract" is at stake and the state presumes to fix the terms of the exchange and dictate the consideration in money or in goods, or to say that the exchange shall not take place at all.

2. CONTROL OF MATTERS INCIDENTAL TO THE CONTRACT

Regulation of matters incidental to the main transaction of purchase and sale includes a very wide range of subjects. Among them are the safeguarding of life, limb, and health as found in factory and building codes; laws as to the time, place, and form of payment of wages; control of liability for accidents and industrial diseases, and even of hours of work where it is feasible for the employer to make up for any reduction of output by a corresponding adjustment of the wage rate, so that the law of supply and demand remains free to operate. Such regulations impose some burdens on industry, and if they went to great lengths they might materially increase the expense of producing goods, making necessary an increase of prices, and thus keeping some persons from buying the goods who would willingly have paid the price which "free" industry would have demanded. Whether this is good or bad depends on whether this deprivation to certain consumers is more or less serious than the evils against which the state is attempting to guard.

There seems to be no all-powerful force making for evasion of this type of regulations. The amount at stake is not usually enough to turn the average honest business man into a law breaker, or to expose him to fatal handicaps if he has to compete with rivals who succeed in evading the law. The life of the business is not at issue. Some policies of this sort may actually pay for themselves in the long run by increasing the working efficiency of the personnel. Even where the cost to the consumer is increased, he may not know what is the cause and so may have no incentive to take the initiative in conniving at evasion. And if the regulation is wise, even where it may increase prices, it is likely to reduce the burdens which fall on consumers in other ways: as taxpayers or as contributors to charities. For a wise policy of industrial control will tend to reduce the burden of salvaging industrial wreckage (which falls on the community in one form or another), to prolong the self-supporting years of the worker's life, and in other ways to pay its way in a general community sense.

Where the control consists of measures to prevent the industry from laying a burden of uncompensated costs on outside parties, it is clearly not a violation of economic law but is just the kind of thing which is necessary to give economic law a chance to work its normal effects. Uncompensated injuries are supposed to be eliminated.[1] The same principle may be extended to cover some of the worker's sacrifices of production, which are bought and paid for by the employer, but some of which may not be paid for adequately, for instance, accidents or occupational diseases, or even unemployment.

As a final extension of the principle, the minimum wage has been defended on the ground that an industry which does not pay a living wage is really imposing part of its costs on other industries, since it is out of the income of these other industries that the living expenses of the underpaid workers must be made up, if they are made up at all.[2]

---

[1] See Chap. iii, Sec. 3, preceding.

[2] See Sidney Webb, "The Economic Theory of a Minimum Wage," *Jour. Polit. Econ.*, pp. 973–998, December, 1912.

And if not, there is a loss of working power which falls as a diffused burden, often handicapping succeeding generations. Aside from the question of the soundness of this position, this type of regulation clearly deals, not with incidental conditions, but with the "heart of the contract," laying hands on the holy of holies of the individualistic system. Is it therefore a violation of economic law? How much difference is there between regulating incidental conditions and controlling the heart of the contract? The distinction is worth serious consideration.

3. CONTROL OF THE "HEART OF THE CONTRACT"

The chief kinds of control which are guilty of the higher economic sacrilege are regulations forcing the price of goods down, or forcing rates of interest down (the much-debated usury laws), or forcing rates of wages up. If the incidental conditions are controlled—so runs the argument—in such a way as to increase the burdens falling on the employer, he may still shift them upon the consumer in higher prices or upon the workers in lower money wages. His property is not confiscated so long as he is free to charge whatever price is needed to cover his expenses or adjust his wage rates to what the market will enable him to pay. And the ultimate questions of value and volume of production are still settled by free contract. But if the money payment is also regulated, this closes the last opening for voluntary and "automatic" adjustment. It may confiscate the business man's property, thus violating the Fourteenth Amendment, and it also suspends the law of supply and demand. This contention was accepted as the law of the land until 1937, when it was overruled. Reasonable state minimum-wage laws are now constitutional, though the issue of federal control of minimum wages remains to be settled.[1] The distinction between control of incidental conditions and of the heart of the contract still appears to have economic importance and will presumably still have some legal importance, via the power the court retains of distinguishing between arbitrary regulation and regulation reasonably adapted to the economic circumstances.

Usury laws afford probably the simplest and best example of control which is typically evaded, and the effects of which, as far as it succeeds, are likely to do more harm than good. The typical law of this class in the United States simply forbids the charging of interest

---

[1] The older view is illustrated by the decision of the Supreme Court (written by Justice Sutherland) in the District of Columbia Minimum Wage Case; *Adkins* v. *Children's Hospital*, 261 U.S. 525, though dissenting opinions by Chief Justice Taft and Justice Holmes carried more weight to most minds. The dissenting view was accepted by the majority of the court in *West Coast Hotel Co.* v. *Parrish*, 300 U.S. 379 (1937).

beyond a fixed legal rate, varying from 6 per cent to 12 per cent in the various states, but making no distinction for different classes of loans. These state laws do not apply to the rediscount rates of the Federal Reserve System, and certain other exceptions are made, as in New York, where rates on call loans are exempted.

These laws are regularly evaded whenever the state of supply and demand is such that there is an unsatisfied demand for funds at the legal rate. Evasion can be managed through the charging of commissions or fees, or by other devices imposing a greater charge on the borrower than appears in the nominal interest rate specified in the contract. Perhaps the chief problem arises, not from the fluctuations of the market rate which result from changes in the relation of supply to demand, but from the fact that different classes of loans regularly require different rates on account of differences in the risk or security of the loan and in the cost of doing the business. Large loans on good industrial and commercial security are in a totally different class from small loans made to consumers, chiefly on chattel-mortgage security or on assignments of wages. Such loans are not put to productive uses in the commercial sense but are used to meet family emergencies; and as they are commonly made in amounts of from $20 to $100, the cost of doing the business is high in comparison to the amounts handled. A rate amounting to 24 per cent per year is quite commonly needed to afford adequate inducement to capital to enter this field, while it appears unwise to set a maximum limit lower than 36 per cent if the law is to be certain of affording adequate remuneration in all cases.

If a rigid limit of from 6 per cent to 12 per cent is applied to these loans, in common with all others, the effect is to drive scrupulous lenders out of the business, leaving it to the uncertain and inadequate reliance of charity, or to the unscrupulous money lender who is willing to evade the law—and who charges in proportion. Since such business must be done in strict privacy, there is no opportunity to establish a true market, and ignorant individuals can be exploited practically without limit, aside from having to pay for the additional risk which an illegitimate business always involves. Under such conditions, charges equivalent to several hundred per cent per year are the common thing. The law multiplies the evil of extortion tenfold.

Does this mean that the law can do nothing for borrowers? By no means. If it allows a rate sufficient to pay the costs of the business, compensate for risks, and leave a sufficient inducement to capital, there is still the possibility that ignorant individuals in urgent need may be charged many times this rate. The best part of protection for such individuals consists in seeing to it that there is an open and legal market in which they may secure funds at a rate in harmony with the forces of supply and demand, but this is not enough to prevent all extortion in individual cases. The law, then, may render a great service in preventing the exaction of charges which are materially above the true market rate. In other words, this is a business in which the rule against unfair discriminations is necessary to a healthy market. Perhaps the simplest method is to fix a legal rate for this class of loans which liberally covers all costs and necessary inducements, and to forbid all charges in excess of this rate. A number of states have adopted this principle[1] on the basis that it is better for the borrower to pay 30 per cent to an honest lender than 300 per cent to a "loan shark."

What of wage regulation? An increase in the rate of wages, in a given trade, for instance, will naturally limit the demand for that type of labor and either throw workers out of employment or prevent them from finding entry into the trade. It tends to do this in some cases by raising the cost of labor relative to machine work and driving the employer to adopt labor-saving devices, but more typically by raising the employer's costs of production, forcing him to raise the price in order to cover the increased costs, with the natural result that the market will not absorb so many goods as before. Thus there will be unsatisfied customers willing to pay something less than the market price, unemployed workers willing to work at less than the wages fixed by regulation, and employers ready to serve as go-betweens to bring this potential supply and demand together.

But is not this something which might be equally true of regulations affecting the incidental conditions of employment? As far as the effect is to increase the cost of producing goods, all the other results might follow precisely as if wages had been raised. Is the regulation of labor conditions more likely to be self-sustaining by virtue of protecting labor power against needless wastes? Perhaps, but the same thing could be said in defense of an increase of wages where they are too low to support the workers in the level of health, strength, alertness, and stamina which the efficient operation of the industry demands. Increases of wages may prove self-sustaining through raising the level of personal efficiency, through furnishing an added stimulus to the employer's search for improved methods, and through hastening the elimination of the least efficient employers and transferring their business to whose who will conduct it more efficiently.[2]

[1] See Franklin W. Ryan, *Usury and Usury Laws*, pp. 135–136. This book is the most comprehensive recent study of the subject and gives references to the earlier literature.

[2] For a comprehensive survey of this problem, see Hamilton and May, *The Control of Wages;* also Ryan, *A Living Wage*, Chaps. xiv, xviii, xix.

Perhaps the outstanding difference between the two types of regulation lies in the fact that, in the control of the "incidental conditions," the increase in cost is more likely to be a negligible, or a moderate, one even in the first instance. It seems probable that the question whether a regulation is or is not a "violation of economic law" is at bottom a question of degree: of how much change in costs or market values it involves. The law of supply and demand is not a thing of precision and inexorable rigidity. Frequently a small change in costs of production has no effect at all on the ultimate price, where the consumer pays one dollar or some other round figure and the dealers' margins adjust themselves so as to take up any slight change in costs or in wholesale prices. The same principle would apply to an automobile listed at $495, $1,390, or $2,985, or other goods priced according to this method. In general, as we have seen, there is a "penumbra" of supply and demand, within which more goods or less may be sold without change in price, or the price be slightly increased or diminished without changing the amount produced and sold. And this is particularly true of the supply and demand for labor. Thus a large increase in wage rates may be a violation of economic law, in the sense in which we are using the term, where a small increase would not be.

4. COMPENSATING MEASURES: DIRECT CONTROL OF SUPPLY AND DEMAND

Even where prices are fixed so low that there is an unsatisfied demand for goods, or wages raised so high that some workers are left unemployed and unemployable, that fact does not necessarily condemn the policy. A community which knows what it is about may reasonably determine that the urgency of the need justifies such measures. What is necessary, however, is that some definite and adequate machinery should be provided for taking care of the discrepancy between supply and demand which the public policy has created. Means must be found for limiting the demand so that a low price shall not lead the market to use up its limited supply too quickly and so bring on worse scarcity. And means must be found to govern the distribution of the goods in the present market between localities and individuals so that it may be on a basis of need, rather than on the principle of "first come, first served," with the first-comers likely to exhaust the supply and leave none for the others. Production, also, should be directly stimulated, where the usual stimulus of price is reduced.

If prices are raised by regulation, as in our present agricultural controls, the case is reversed. Low prices are a result of large output, and increased prices would in themselves stimulate further increase of output and so defeat their own ends. If the control includes attempts to limit output, they present difficulties. They may be neutralized by uncontrolled increases in world output; and if successful, they may lead to shifts of cultivation, artificially increasing the output of uncontrolled crops, or leading to incomplete utilization of resources and labor power. Such controls may be useful in tiding over extreme emergencies, such as American agriculture faced in the great depression, entailing need for adjustments such as the individual farmers could not successfully make for themselves. There is a real tendency to chronic cutthroat competition in agriculture; and as an antidote, crop controls will fight for a permanent place in our economy. But to deserve such a place, they need the further justification of showing that they can improve matters in a way tolerable for the economic system as a whole. In this respect they are at present on very doubtful ground.

In the case of wage regulation, means must be found for meeting the special case of the unemployable in whatever way may appear wisest. Those who are handicapped may be permitted to work for less than standard rates, with or without additional help from the community. Those who can be rehabilitated may be treated as wards of the community to whatever extent may be necessary, the aim being to turn them out able to earn standard wages. And where neither these nor other measures can succeed, the state may actually furnish employment on works of genuine necessity and value. But while this policy of state employment is perfectly legitimate, it is a delicate and difficult instrument to handle, liable to be abused by the lazy and improvident, and a standing invitation to the indefinite swelling of public budgets by the doing of relatively useless things in an inefficient way.[1] Under proper conditions it need not succumb to these evils and is not foredoomed to failure; nevertheless, it is a thing to be entered on with reluctance, after exhausting expedients of a less paternalistic sort.

What shall we say of policies which so disturb the operation of supply and demand as to make necessary such difficult compensating measures of direct control? Are they violations of economic law or not? After what has been said, this question may appear to be somewhat academic. If the compensating measures are not forthcoming or are not effective, then economic forces, lacking the guidance of the customary stimuli and checks, will work disorder and possibly disaster. Furthermore, the compensating measures are neither easy nor cheap; they can hardly ever work perfectly and may easily drift into sheer futility.

[1] This passage stands as written in 1925.

With energy and intelligence, with knowledge of all the dangers, with self-restraint, and especially with the help of an aroused and well-informed public sentiment, the thing can be done in a limited number of cases; and if too much change is not sought from the levels fixed by uncontrolled supply and demand, it can be done well enough for practical purposes—well enough to do more good than harm. In ordinary times consumers will hardly endure rationing of supplies, nor farmers raise wheat or hogs because the government wishes it; and under such conditions far less can be accomplished than under stress of national emergency. But if such controls are made general and unduly disregard the forces of supply and demand, then there is real danger that the system of private business will be rendered unworkable. The advocates of control can fairly claim that the difference between policies which violate economic law and those which do not is at bottom a difference of degree, and not a sharp cleavage between two radically different orders of being. But it is a difference of sufficient importance to make certain policies unavailable except to meet unusual and urgent needs, and to surround them with unusual dangers.

5. INDIVIDUALISM AS A VIOLATOR OF ECONOMIC LAW

Does individualism itself obey the law of supply and demand, meaning those beneficent forms of the law, to violate which is economic sin? If it does, then the case against public interference is strengthened; but if it does not, then government may fairly claim that, where individualism itself violates the laws of economic nature, there is every reason to prefer the government's brand of violations as being at least devised in the public interest rather than in that of irresponsible private concerns.

What of our periodic attacks of economic depression, leading to unemployment of capital and labor on a huge scale? What is this but a gigantic failure to bring supply and demand to equality, resulting in vast wastes of productive power? Supply of productive power exists, demand at existing prices will not call it all into use; the next step should, according to economic law, be a lowering of the prices charged for the productive powers until they are called into use. But the step is not taken, and demand is allowed to remain short of supply.

It may be answered that the goods are not worth producing, meaning that the price will not cover the expenses of production. Prices are lower than usual, and expenses are not enough lower to compensate. Let us examine this common-sense reasoning. Prices are lower than usual, and production waits till they shall rise. If goods were thereby saved to a time when they would be more urgently needed, as high prices may avert a future famine, then the stoppage of production might be useful, even if painful. But, in the first place, productive powers are not being saved for future use to anything like the extent that they are being deteriorated by disuse and lack of proper maintenance, both for men and for machines. In the second place, the high prices of a prosperous time do not mean that goods to satisfy human want are more urgently needed than in times of depression, but rather the opposite. Clothing and shelter are more needed in time of depression than in time of prosperity, and hoarding things in time of depression is a way to make them less useful, rather than more. Prices will not cover the expenses of production; true; but these expenses of production are simply another set of prices charged for the use of the factors of production, and they do not measure the true and ultimate cost to humanity of producing goods as compared to a stoppage of production. If the prices charged for the productive factors are not low enough to call them into use, they are wasted; and almost any use is better than none.

When a man is idle because he cannot find work at a customary "fair wage" of $1 per hour, it is not because the fatigues of an eight-hour day have a fixed money worth of $8 to him, so that if he took less his work would be worth less than it cost him in ultimate human burdens. If the productiveness of industry were permanently cut in two and if the market share of labor shrank proportionately, he would gladly work for half his former real wage. What he is doing in time of depression is to protect his customary standard against being lowered as a result of a purely temporary reduction in the productiveness of industry. This is natural enough, but it does not bring supply and demand together in the present. The employer's situation is fundamentally similar with respect to his unemployed capital, and his policy is very similar in principle. Like the laborer, he does not make the immediate sacrifices necessary to bring supply and demand together, and to call productive powers into use.

When the magnitude of this problem is considered, it seems conservative to state that individualism, as it operates at present, is the greatest violator of the supposed natural law that prices tend to be set at the point which will make supply and demand equal. So far as government attempts to wrestle with this particular evil, it cannot be charged with creating violations of economic law where they did not exist before, no matter what measures it may adopt. It may add new "violations," and some of them may be mistakes and may make conditions worse than before. It is here that the real problem lies.

6. CONCLUSION

To sum up, social control must reckon with the forces of supply and demand but does not stand helpless before them. If it wishes to raise the wages of ditch diggers, it may well try to reduce the supply of ditch diggers by reducing the obstacles which bar men from entry into better-paid occupations. But this need not be the limit of the state's action, nor need it wait passively for the mills of supply and demand to grind out a change in wage rates. It can take the initiative, raising wages as far as it appears they can go without doing positive violence to the law of equilibrium. It can experiment to see how wide the range is within which the forces of supply and demand will not absolutely veto any rate which may be set. And in taking account of these forces, it need not rely on the market's favorite method of bringing them into equilibrium; it may employ substitute methods. These methods are crude, difficult, not wholly to be relied on, but workable and useful if there are really great evils to be prevented and urgent needs to be met. Government can do a great deal of good by merely seeing to it that everyone gets the benefit of the market rate, whatever that is, and thus preventing the ignorant from being exploited on account of their ignorance. And, within limits, the state can influence the levels of values which economic law decrees.

REFERENCES FOR FURTHER READING

CARVER, T. N., "Possibilities of Price-fixing in Time of Peace," *Amer. Econ. Rev.,* Sup., pp. 246–251, March, 1919.

———, "Some Probable Results of a Balanced Economic System," *Amer. Econ. Rev.,* Sup., pp. 69–77, March, 1920.

CLARK, J. B., "The Minimum Wage," *Atlantic Monthly,* pp. 289–297, September, 1913.

———, *Essentials of Economic Theory,* Chap. xxvi.

FEIS, HERBERT, *Principles of Wage Determination.*

HAMILTON and MAY, *The Control of Wages.*

LEDERER, E., "Social Control vs. Economic Law," *Social Research,* pp. 3–21, February, 1934.

MEANS, DAVID MCGREGOR, "Price-fixing by Government," *Unpopular Rev.,* pp. 312–327, April–June, 1918.

ROOT, ELIHU, *Experiments in Government and the Essentials of the Constitution,* pp. 11–22, 1913.

RYAN, F. W., *Usury and Usury Laws.*

RYAN, REV. JOHN A., *A Living Wage.*

SMITH, J. G., *Economic Planning and the Tariff,* Chap. x, 1934.

TAUSSIG, F. W., "Is Market Price Determinate?" *Quart. Jour. Econ.,* pp. 394–411, May, 1921.

UNITED STATES SUPREME COURT, opinion in District of Columbia Minimum Wage Case (*Adkins* v. *Children's Hospital*) 261 U.S. 525.

See also references at end of Chaps. xiv, xxix.

CHAPTER XXX

CAN DEMOCRATIC CONTROL SUCCEED?

The power of economic interests to resist control, 484—A deeper question: the inescapable effects of established industrial methods, 487—Inherent difficulties of political control, 490—Fakes and perversions in social control, 492—Agencies of control: political and nonpolitical, 493—Summary, 494.

1. THE POWER OF ECONOMIC INTERESTS TO RESIST CONTROL

Can we control business or does it control us? The question should not be asked about business alone, save that it is business we have mainly been seeking to control in recent generations. The question should properly be asked about any strong organized economic interest. Nationally organized labor is stronger than most single employers, and may become stronger than all of them put together. The question how democratic agencies can control such organized interests seems sometimes to take the form: How can the weak control the strong, through government or any other agency? Will not the strong inevitably take control of the agency and tame it? In that case they will make sure that it does not hurt them seriously, though if they are shrewd, they will permit it to make a showing, going through ineffective motions and possibly staging some noisy sham battles and deluding the weak into thinking that their interests are being protected.

As a picture of the fate of attempts to control business, this is less true today than it was a generation ago, and less true of the federal than of state and local governments. In some states, public-utility interests have at times gained a sinister measure of political power, admittedly under considerable provocation from attacks which were sometimes unsound and sometimes corrupt in motive. It is only one side of the picture but as such deserves examination.

Economic power rests on a combination of factors, including organization, intelligence, power to command votes, support by public opinion, and at bottom, perhaps, the indispensability of the service the group renders. Indispensability is more than a matter of our inability to do wholly without the services of the group: we cannot wholly do without either labor or "capital." It means also that we must concede them conditions under which their services can be

484

rendered effectively, and to a considerable extent willingly, in any society dependent on voluntary cooperation.

In the case of business, one source of this power is, of course, the protection of government, without which its property rights would be worthless and most of its strength would vanish like a pricked bubble. In this sense the weak voluntarily maintain the strong in possession of their strength, like a barber who holds the shears over some Samson but always lets him escape unshorn. Government cannot simply abolish private property, unless it is ready to face the fact of revolution and rebuild the entire economic structure. It cannot even abolish the right of property to organize in corporations—a right whereby the strong control vastly more property than they own—because large-scale industry has become dependent on working with masses of capital too large for single owners to provide. So the strong remain strong by consent of the weak—a consent which the weak are not exactly free to withhold.

Their strength has shown itself, among other things, in resisting the development of social control and influencing its course, from its source in public opinion through all the stages of political machinery to its final conclusion in the execution of the statutes. Newspapers can be bought and are not likely to advocate policies too hostile to the interests of those who own them, or, for that matter, of those who support them by paying for advertising space. Political-party organizations require expensive campaigns and are vastly helped by having a permanent nucleus of organization and personnel and an army of paid helpers available. All this costs money, and the organization knows that campaign contributions will be harder to get if it antagonizes too many large financial interests at one time. It must get dollars without antagonizing too many votes and get votes without sacrificing too many dollars.[1]

After the election comes the legislative lobby, which is merely a name for the perfectly legitimate practice of interviewing legislators and exerting whatever arguments one has at command to make them see the public welfare as the lobbyist sees it. But the paid lobby gives an unduly heavy representation to just those economic interests which need to be controlled. There are many ways of exerting pressure without descending to the crudities of out-and-out personal corruption. A politician hesitates to antagonize great powers in the absence of some clean-cut and popular issue out of which he can make political capital.

This sort of pressure applies, not only to legislators, but to the officials charged with the enforcement of the laws. Imagine the feelings of

[1] Cf. above, Chap. i, Sec. 9.

a factory inspector or a child-labor inspector, on a salary less than the earnings of many a highly skilled laborer, discovering serious violations of law in the plant of the largest and most powerful company in his state and by no means sure that his superiors will back him up if he makes a complaint. Or imagine his immediate superior, himself a minor political appointee on a low salary, having to decide whether to push a case against the best legal talent (and the largest campaign contributions) in the district. He probably knows that his party has already selected the issues on which it wants to appeal to the people and in doing so may already have antagonized as many financial interests as they consider politically profitable. In this case the underofficial knows that he cannot expect to gain favor by making new enemies. Under the circumstances, it is no wonder that laws are imperfectly enforced; the wonder is that they are enforced as well as they are.

Or if the situation is reversed, and the voting power of some other group, such as organized labor, comes to carry more weight than the powers of business interests, then enforcement may be biased in the other direction, by pressures no less irrelevant to the requirements of even-handed justice or the interests of the community as a whole. In either case, the most powerful interests may gain too much protection. Judicial checks may be weakened by building up the structure of administrative commissions, acting as prosecutors and judges, their findings of "fact" final if supported by any evidence. And thus governmental power, always liable to be unduly influenced by particular groups, may become increasingly irresponsible.

This problem is a grave one, and there is no panacea for the evils suggested, though many things would help. The extension of the merit system, more adequate salaries for high officials, a social attitude which accords recognition and prestige more on a basis of achievement and less on a basis of the money a man is able to spend, the growth of civic associations which will give the unorganized public interests the benefit of services equivalent to those of an expert professional lobby and also assist in the formation of an intelligent public opinion by publishing disinterested information—all these things will help.

Could all this obstructionism be eliminated by eliminating the source of corruption and abolishing private industrial capital? And is this the only effective way out? The question cannot be answered with scientific conclusiveness, but there is strong ground for the view that under no system whatever can liberty and the common interest be safe unless the people in general, as well as their representatives, possess sufficient moral fiber to resist all forms of intimidation and bribery, to stand up against the prestige of massed power and command over the good things of life, and to hold an oath of office above all forms of private advantage. Unless we can develop and maintain these qualities, we shall be in a bad way under any system, and no system will guarantee them automatically or remove all possibility of temptation.

2. A DEEPER QUESTION: THE INESCAPABLE EFFECTS OF ESTABLISHED INDUSTRIAL METHODS

So far we have been speaking of the human side of this question: the difficulty of certain groups of people controlling certain other groups against their will. But there is an underlying necessity to which both groups alike are subject, namely, the requirements of systematized and standardized machine production. All our systems of control contemplate the maintenance and even the further development of machines, system, and standardization, in the interests of productive efficiency. And any ideals inconsistent with this are doomed from the start.

The machine refuses to be displaced, and it lays down the character of man's work according to the laws of its own being, not according to his desires or the needs of his nature, physical, psychological, or biological. Even the nominal rulers of the machine, the managers and directors of industry, are free only to follow the laws of their inflexible servant. It is over sixty years since Samuel Butler sketched a picture of an imaginary country, "Erewhon," in which machines had been abolished because an early scientist had predicted that they might some day develop into a race of conscious beings and so enslave mankind. It was a prophetic insight, as we of today are in a position to realize to our cost. Not that the machines refuse to gratify men's wishes: in fact, they rule largely by bribery. They make a species of bargain with men, in which they are perfectly willing to give men anything they may think they want, always provided that it is not inconsistent with the racial needs of the machines themselves. Human beings, be it noted, make no such reservation, for the very adequate reason that they do not know what their racial needs are, and for the further reason that even if they did know them, individuals could always be found willing to barter them away. And the machines take no pains to enlighten man's ignorance in this matter, so that the ultimate consequences of the bargain come upon man as a painful surprise, after he has committed himself too deeply to draw back.

Their works include massed production and minute specialization. They have divided humanity into classes, they have increased the proportion of people who live in the cities, and they have built a whole

series of special types of community, each with its own peculiar difficulties and problems and all made in the image of the machine. Since
these groups and classes are interdependent, they must cooperate.
But since they live largely in separate districts, go to different churches
when they go at all, speak different technical jargons, and more and
more read different newspapers, it is clear that cooperation is not easy.

But to return to the more specific and tangible effects of the mechanical revolution. It has enormously increased our interdependence
and the resulting need of control, and of extending it over wider areas.
It has created the problem of business cycles and unemployment.
It has given us nation-wide trusts and the modern forms of "imperfect
competition" which must somehow be controlled.

The machines which run on rails or transmit through lines of pipes
or wires are set apart for special regulation, because here the "natural"
regulation of competition clearly fails to work its advertised results.
These industries are the recognized "public utilities." At present the
engineers are proposing to enlarge this class by adding to it nothing less
than the entire business of producing power, whether from coal or
water, generating it in huge central stations and distributing it over
the entire continent by high-voltage transmission lines. Aside from
saving some of our present waste of coal, it is hoped that this may help
to relieve some of the congestion of population which the steam factory
has brought about and may make it possible for more small plants to
survive without being fatally handicapped by high cost of power. But
the price of this easing of pressure at certain points is the addition of
another huge industry to a class we have not yet learned how to regulate effectively—the nation-wide public utilities.

Synthetic substitutes have forced another area of control on us,
wireless communication another. The machines appear to be forcing
paternalism on us, whether we want it or not, and paternalism on a
vaster, more centralized, and more impersonal scale than the world
has yet seen. And centralized paternalism is not favorable to democratic institutions as we have known them. They have been supposed
to thrive on decentralization and the exercise of rather simple and
limited powers. Yet this new enforced paternalism is expected to be
democratic—to be, in fact, the very flower and summit of democracy.
We seem to be expecting miracles!

If one contemplates the possibility of a return to something
like *laissez faire*—as some still do—the sobering fact is revealed
that this would in itself involve one of the most difficult tasks of
coercive control of any course we might try to chart. Large business
organizations would have to be broken up into small units, which might

control one another by their unregulated competition. National labor organizations would have to be similarly broken up or disarmed, with what expenditure of coercion and rousing of group hostilities one hesitates to contemplate. No, we cannot turn back: we have no choice but to go forward, into courses contrary to many of our cherished traditions.

Labor in general has been forced into collective bargaining, which many workers do not like. This means being largely dependent on the loyalty of its representatives and exposes it in practice to a considerable amount of corruption and betrayal. This is the counterpart of the small stockholder's dependence upon his board of directors, though the union leader who is loyal to his trust has heavier sacrifices to make and greater temptations to meet.

Back of this lies the effect of modern working conditions on the personality of the worker himself, which is perhaps the most important effect of all, if we only knew enough about it to diagnose and prescribe intelligently. Much has been written about it, applying modern theories of industrial psychoses; and these probably contain considerable elements of truth. Perhaps one may sum up the bearing of the discussion by saying that modern life demands the highest qualities of character, personality, and citizenship, economic and political, if it is to work successfully; but it shows no clear tendency to develop such qualities, and some tendencies in the other direction.

If, as some of these theories state, what the worker wants, consciously or unconsciously, is to exert power over the business he works in, he can secure far more spectacular results by destructive rather than constructive tactics. This appears actually to be a considerable element in the psychology of strikes and sabotage.[1] To the extent that this is true, the conflict may be said to be an end in itself— "a good war justifies any cause." Not that laborers do not want or need the increased wages and shortened hours and other things they strike for; these things are more than mere pretexts. But increased wages and shortened hours will not end strikes, as one might expect if wages and hours were the sole and fundamental causes of strikes. Strikes are rooted in the character of machine industry, in its impersonal organization and wide separation between workers, managers, and property interests. Along with this goes the fact that the individual worker's contribution is often so indistinguishably merged in the whole—*spurlos versenkt*—that no measures of it can be found which will convince, by its cogent reasonableness, all parties to the division. The professional

[1] See Carleton Parker, "Instincts in Economic Life," *Amer. Econ. Rev.*, Sup., pp. 212–231, March, 1918.

labor leader may feel that he must justify his position by delivering gains to his followers at frequent intervals, adopting the simple philosophy of "more, without limit." This difficulty also is one for which the machines are responsible.

The effects of modern life on morals and religion are clearly a part of the problem of social control. It has undermined the older and simpler sanctions of religion and has tended, for too many of us, to put an undisciplined and selfish materialism in their place. Many of our customary individualistic ways of thinking, are getting out of date, including the older forms of "economic virtues." Some of these things we can very well do without, for example, the horse-trading ethics—or lack of them—embodied in the maxim of *caveat emptor:* let the buyer beware. In this and other cases, something better may be put in the place of the older idea, as the producer's responsibility for the quality of his goods is better than the horse trader's irresponsibility. But other forms of responsibility are not faring so well.

It is impossible to tell the unemployed worker that his condition is wholly his personal responsibility or his personal fault; this is clearly not true. Some personal responsibility remains, but its nature is confused and not easily defined. Relief without stigma has become inescapable, and its relaxing effects on morale may be minimized, but not eliminated. Personal thrift as an economic virtue is subject to novel doubts, under the impact of the modern philosophy of spending. The worker's responsibility for doing a fair day's work is confused by divided loyalties and the fear of working one's self out of a job. Old moral codes need reformulation, without undermining the foundations of morality itself. This is not easy. F. W. Taylor's trained gorilla might be an efficient industrial worker, at some kinds of work,[1] but he could not build a successful system of democratic social control.

3. INHERENT DIFFICULTIES OF POLITICAL CONTROL

One disquieting symptom is the frequency with which, when a new reform is suggested, ways are sought to "keep it out of politics." Politics is the democratic way of governing; is it becoming necessary, then, to keep government itself out of politics? And if this is done, does it spell dictatorship or bureaucracy rather than democracy? This urge to keep measures out of politics means a number of things. First, it means that the administration of the measure shall be put in the hands of persons chosen for their competence, not as a reward for election services. Second, it means that the measure shall be admin-

[1] See his *Principles of Scientific Management*, pp. 26, 40.

istered with a view to the community ends which justify it, not manipulated with an eye to furnishing issues with good headline appeal. Third, it means that the administrators shall be free to follow such a course, not interfered with either by political strategists or by pressures brought to bear, via legislators or others, by particular interested groups which can command votes. All these things represent weaknesses to which our democratic political machinery is more or less unavoidably subject.

Log rolling and pressure groups have been frequently mentioned in the preceding pages, and the evils they represent sufficiently indicated.[1] Another difficulty is the well-known tendency of control to expand and to assume more and more power over more and more things. This is not merely an evidence of bureaucratic thirst for authority: it arises from the fact that the original purpose may be obstructed or evaded in unforeseen ways, so that if it is to be fully carried out, control over collateral matters becomes necessary. Another difficulty lies in the increasing number of controls, as well as the complexity of the problems they involve. Their complexity makes adequate public scrutiny difficult or impossible, while their number prevents the public from giving to any one the sustained attention necessary to educate the public mind to a point which may enable it to give such scrutiny as it may be inherently capable of. Important issues sometimes attract surprisingly little general attention.

Not only does control tend to expand, so that we commit ourselves to more than we originally contemplated; a similar result follows when measures originally thought of as temporary become permanent. The protective tariff is an outstanding example of this, though this fact is forgotten by all but students of its original history. Protective duties were originally justified on the ground that industry could fairly soon get on without them; but they resulted in building up vested interests, dependent on their indefinite continuance. A need may be perpetuated by the very measures designed to relieve it. The New Deal, as we have seen, adopted a policy of deliberate experimentation, announcing that measures which did not succeed would be abandoned. But, once adopted, these measures develop surprising powers of self-perpetuation.

Finally, there is the fact that action may be precipitated, not so much by rational anticipation of improved results to follow from the particular measures taken, as by a general feeling that existing conditions are intolerable, and that something must be done. This is not the most favorable mood for the devising of successful reforms,

[1] Cf. above, Chap. ix, Sec. 6; Chap. i, Sec. 3.

ignoring as it does the ever-present possibility that things may be made worse and not better. It is made more serious by the difficulty which even experts often find in predicting the results a given measure will have. Its immediate and obvious effects may be one thing; the indirect effects of leading people to expect it in the future may be something different and less desirable, especially if it takes the form of relieving people from the results of their own mistakes. The guarantee of bank deposits raises problems of this general character. All in all, the unavoidable difficulties of democratic control are serious enough.

4. FAKES AND PERVERSIONS IN SOCIAL CONTROL[1]

These unavoidable difficulties are made worse, however, by others which it is less easy to tolerate or to condone. Where pressure groups are active, the ostensible purposes of the measures they advocate are not to be trusted. They develop surprising fertility in finding—and perhaps in sincerely believing—other grounds for their measures than the help they will incidentally bring to the pockets of those who advocate them. The silver interests have shown especial ingenuity in this way, arguing that world trade would be expanded and the purchasing power of silver-using countries be increased if the United States Government bought large quantities of silver and raised its price. These are highly technical questions, on which even experts sometimes differ; hence arguments of this sort are not easy to refute in advance of experience. This particular experience turned out badly; China was driven off the silver standard, other silver-using countries suffered, world trade was hampered, and the total damage may prove irreparable. But the output of interested proposals shows no sign of ceasing.

Laws limiting hours of work, or having the effect of limiting output and increasing the number of jobs, are often proposed as measures to protect the public health or the public safety. Such measures need particularly searching scrutiny, as there is likely to be little relation between the active support they receive and their validity as health or safety measures. The virtual interstate tariff walls which are here and there growing up are seldom proposed as means to that end. Conservation of natural resources may be needed and may incidentally raise the present price—which feature is likely to account for the larger amount of active support? Are people's attitudes on Philippine independence free from all connection with their interests as competitors with Philippine imports?

[1] Cf. above, Chap. ix. Sec. 6.

Alongside of the interested pressure group stands the demagogue, indefatigable at throwing monkey wrenches into the delicately balanced machinery of control. Sometimes, if he has the power, he will deliberately block any reasonable settlement of a disputed question, and the fact that a settlement is reasonable may be enough to insure his opposition. For reasonable settlements do not involve sufficiently spectacular victories for the groups from which he derives his support. On a smaller scale, the most legitimate measures of control afford opportunities to the grafting official. A building code, for example, may afford the inspector a pretext for failing to approve a structure until it has been made worth his while.

Thus at many levels and in many ways the structure of legitimate control is honeycombed with irrelevancies, and its legitimate purposes perverted. And a system of control, to be reasonably successful, must not only devise wise measures but wage an endless and vigilant combat against all these forms of perversion, as well as against the more legitimate and unavoidable difficulties. We must be on our guard not only against disguised measures of self-interest, but against the tendency of the reformer to compare the imperfections of existing conditions with the anticipated results of his reform measures, conceived as working perfectly. They will not work perfectly, and this had better be expected from the start. We should learn to compare existing imperfect conditions with the other imperfections which experience teaches us are sure to result from attempts at control. .

5. AGENCIES OF CONTROL: POLITICAL AND NONPOLITICAL

All this makes the task of effective control, in the genuine interests of the community, seem like a tremendously difficult thing. It makes the political state appear a very clumsy and blundering agency, extremely likely to do more harm than good. These things are, unfortunately, quite true. Yet efforts at control will continue and must continue; they cannot be given up. But an indispensable part of the process must consist of efforts to improve the political agency.

An increase in central authority is inevitable, whether desirable or not. This means an increase in administrative bureaus and staffs, and in the scope of their power, as compared to what we were accustomed to before the New Deal. Even if some of the New Deal activities should be decreased in the future, others are likely to expand, so that it would be risky to predict any aggregate shrinkage, even from the sudden and vast expansion which the New Deal has brought about. And there will probably be a lasting increase in administrative responsibility for legislative programs. Indeed, if they are to be properly coordinated into a consistent whole, such a change will be inevitable. Some observers have long thought that our system would work better if it could be brought a little nearer the character of the responsible cabinet under the English constitutional system. Under favorable conditions, such a change might reduce somewhat the scope of log-rolling and pressure-group politics, by focusing such activities on an administration which might be harder to influence improperly than are single congressmen, and where—again under favorable conditions—the activities might be more effectively watched. The change would not be likely to do anything to reduce the real effectiveness of popular control of government. We also need, beyond question, an improved civil service.

But political government is not the only agency which can be used. "Self-government in industry" has possibilities that have not been exhausted. The NRA experiment could hardly be counted as a fair or final trial, partly because it was a first attempt, and partly because the agencies set up were so preponderantly representative of business interests alone. Probably the most important thing is that the various parties most immediately concerned, on all sides of disputed questions, should meet and try to settle their mutual questions on the footing of essential partners in an enterprise of joint concern. This is not a magic formula, but its possibilities should be given a thorough trial.

6. SUMMARY

To sum up, powerful economic interests are able to do much to obstruct and divert attempts to control them in the interest of the rest of the community, and to promote measures of control which will further their own ends instead of those of the community. The democratic political state is peculiarly subject to these pressures and obstructions, which make still more difficult a task which is in its nature difficult already. If the state is strengthened against such pressures, something of what we are accustomed to think of as democracy may be lost. Bureaucracies and centralized executive power and responsibility will grow. But there is no reason to think we must go all the way to dictatorship in order to make control reasonably effective; in fact, we may lose little that we now have of the substance of popular control over government and its activities. The chief limitations, now as always, are those of intelligence and integrity.

REFERENCES FOR FURTHER READING

ASCOLI and LEHMANN, *Political and Economic Democracy*, 1937.
BUTLER, SAMUEL, *Erewhon*.

CLARK, J. B., *The Problem of Monopoly*, pp. 21–24.

COOLEY, C. H., *Social Process*, pp. 6–26.

GRUENING, E., "Power and Propaganda," *Amer. Econ. Rev.*, Sup., p. 202, March, 1931.

HAMILTON, *Current Economic Problems* (3d ed.), Chap. iii *E*.

HUNTINGTON, ELLSWORTH, *World Power and Evolution*, Chap. i.

LIPPMANN, WALTER, *The Good Society*, pp. 106–131, 183–202.

MELDER, F. E., *State and Local Barriers to Interstate Commerce in the United States*, 1937.

MOODY, W. VAUGHN, "*The Brute*" *in Poems and Plays*, Vol. I, pp. 55–60.

MOSCA, G., *The Ruling Class* (trans. by A. Livingston), Chaps. x, xvii, 1939.

POUND, ARTHUR, *The Iron Man in Industry*.

SLICHTER, S. H., *Towards Stability*, Chap. vi, 1934.

TAYLOR, H., *Contemporary Problems in the United States*, Vol. II, Chap. viii, 1934.

VEBLEN, *The Theory of Business Enterprise*, Chap. xx.

———, *The Instinct of Workmanship*, pp. 311–327.

WALLACE, HENRY A., *New Frontiers*, Chaps. iv–vi, xx, 1934.

CHAPTER XXXI

GENERAL SYSTEMS OF CONTROL: WHERE ARE WE BOUND?

1. INTRODUCTION

The world is engaged in a war of rival social-economic systems. Communism rules a vast sector; and fascism, antithetical to communism in its class background and dominant purposes, but similar to it in renouncing the principles of democracy and liberty, rules Italy and Germany and is expanding its sphere of action ominously. The system of democratic liberalism is on the defensive and feels itself to be losing ground to a threatening extent. Not that the more important areas now occupied by opposing systems were exactly models of democratic liberalism before; but they at least embodied the principle of private business enterprise and not, as now, principles actively and militantly hostile to it.

The system of democratic liberalism is itself in a state of transition. As the realization of this fact soaks in, we can see that the process has long been going on and may be approaching a culmination of some sort. Piecemeal control has gone so far that it is high time to contemplate its total cumulative effect. We have lived through the period of special controls, either limited to incidental matters or conforming in a general way to free-market standards and leaving to private enterprise the main task of putting resources to work and determining what they should work at. This period appears to be over. The "main task" has become a matter of community concern, perhaps permanently. And this bids fair to lead us into a different economic system, with an altered keynote.

Is it possible to go on successfully without clearer ideas than we now possess as to where we are headed and what is our next definable destination? The obvious substitutes for the existing system include some form of fascism, on the one hand, and some form of socialism, on the other. Over against these stands the attempt to maintain the essential features of the existing system, while subjecting it to as much control as it will stand and still work successfully. But what are the irreducible essentials, and how much control will the system stand? If none of these programs seems promising, is it practicable to adopt the principle of evolutionary change with no known destination? Or is this simply a futile attempt to dignify with illusory words a hopeless policy of "muddling through"?

In any case, since our general system of control is changing, it appears imperative to survey the alternatives: the other general systems which appear to be possible. And here we encounter one of the greatest difficulties of the social sciences. We cannot know the real effects of the system of institutions under which we live without knowing what difference it makes whether we have this system or some other, and this means that we must know what would be the effects of some different system or systems. But absolute knowledge on this point must always remain unattainable; we must do the best we can with the aid of the scientific imagination. Even the Russian experiment in communism cannot tell us absolutely what would be the results of communism in the United States, since the conditions of that experiment could not be exactly reproduced in this country. Machine industry is the backbone of our economic system; it is indigenous rather than imported; it is supported by a tremendous and powerful business and technical class and an industrially trained population who are well aware of their complete dependence upon its continuous functioning. Whether these conditions would tend toward a more favorable outcome than in Russia, or a more disastrous one, can only be conjectured; but it is as certain as anything human can be that they would force the experiment into markedly different channels.

In the case of untried proposals of radical change, a different difficulty is encountered. Some advocates of revolution pay less attention to exact formulation of the ultimate end in view than to the means of attaining the power to bring it to pass. This was true of communism before the Russian revolution. Its advocates were correct in perceiving that the details of the system they would set up would evolve as a part of the process of attaining their main ends. Others attempt to draw up specifications which, for the reason just mentioned, are of doubtful significance as indications of what is likely actually to come to pass. If the system is to be undemocratic, the persons who draw up advance specifications are not the types likely to be found in control if the revolution succeeds. And if it is to be democratic, it is even less likely to be under the control of people of the same ideals, motives, and temperament as the small intellectual group who drafted the advance plans. They did this because they were not average persons; while if their movement succeeds, it will be because it has been taken over by the average man. And he, even if he becomes a convert to their roughly defined program, will see it through average men's eyes and give effect to it via average men's motives, incentives, and notions of the expedient and the practical. It will be changed in passing through this medium until many of its original sponsors may disown it.

This being the case, the social student seeking to know what alternatives to the present system we have open to us cannot safely take the programs of radical movements at their full face value. And in using his imagination he must take account not merely of the conscious goals set forth, but of the results which will naturally flow from the type of means used to attain these goals. Thus a party of direct action and one of political action may be advocating very similar ideals but may be actually working toward very different outcomes.

The key to an organized understanding of different industrial systems lies in the use of different organizations, agencies, and, to an extent, motives, to perform certain common underlying functions which any industrial system exists to perform or must perform to justify its existence. Functions of the first grade, those the system exists to perform, may be summed up as creating the things people need and making them accessible to those who need them. This includes (1) goods and services of the sorts we nowadays buy and sell, and (2) the accompanying conditions of work and life, as far as these are ends in themselves. Functions of the second grade, which must be performed, include the instrumental processes of organization, coordination, negotiation, discussion and decision, information and record keeping, accounting and valuation, direction and submission, as far as they represent things which must be done by some kind of agency under any scheme of industrial cooperation.

Here we strike controversial ground, for reformers are continually asserting that many of the costly operations of business are unnecessary and could be done away with, while the thoughtful conservative is likely to maintain that they represent merely the business form of services which any system must perform, in some way or other, if it is to be tolerably efficient. The business system undoubtedly does cause many people to duplicate each other's efforts and multiplies the number of points at which conflicting interests have to be adjusted, every bargain being such a point. Hence there appears to be much room for a reduction in the number of necessary processes. But when one compares alternatives, the difference is not all to the disadvantage of the business system. The elimination of bargaining does not eliminate the need of adjusting conflicting interests; it merely makes necessary different machinery, presumably of a political, diplomatic, or judicial character. Political methods are terribly crude, uncertain, and wasteful, while judicial processes are proverbially slow and costly, not excepting commerce commissions and wage boards.

Furthermore, in some cases it may be found on analysis that a single business process performs a number of distinct functions which a more utopian system would be likely to try to perform separately in order to make each one serve its ultimate purpose more perfectly. The number of functions may, at certain points, be greater and not less than the number of business processes. For instance, in the act of paying wages at least three important and distinct functions are merged. By this act (1) labor receives its claim on the necessities and comforts of life, (2) it receives its most tangible stimulus to put forth its best efforts, and (3) the labor cost of the product in question is measured, a process essential to determining intelligently what things are worth producing and what are not, and what jobs are worth the efforts of the best workers. That these are not irrevocably tied together may be seen from the fact that some communistic schemes propose to pay wages according to needs, use discipline and non-monetary prizes to stimulate industry, decide what is worth producing by a statistical canvass of needs and resources, and determine the placing of the best (and worst) workers by whatever methods administrative wisdom might devise. An interesting instance in actual practice is the family-allowance system of wages, which is being tried abroad. Even where the allowances come out of the employers' pockets, the result is that the cost of any particular laborer to his employer and the reward that laborer gets are two different sums. G. D. H. Cole has proposed a dual system of incomes, consisting of a "social dividend" regardless of work done, plus a wage based on productivity.[1] Such a system makes a fairly clear separation between the three main functions of wages and illustrates the possibility that a socialist state might have to carry out two or three calculations where private business knows but one.

Tentatively, then, we may start with the assumption that any system would have to decide what to produce and how much, to estimate demand and educate it, estimate supply and control it, place the

[1] G. D. H. Cole, *Economic Planning*, pp. 257–258, and elsewhere.

factors of production where they are most needed, and to that end have some way of reckoning what they are worth in different lines of work and what is the least valuable result that justifies using them at all. It would have to decide who is to do what or establish the system under which people will decide this for themselves, to educate and appraise the varied aptitudes of the people, and to induce them to go where they will do effective work. It must devote part of its resources to the creation and maintenance of capital equipment and must allocate these resources among rival demands of some urgency. Practically speaking, it must have a medium of exchange, a standard of value, and something of the nature of accounting if its organization is to be anything but chaos.

2. TYPES OF SYSTEMS

The lines of cleavage among the various actual and proposed systems are numerous and to some extent cross one another; and the most decisive features are not easy to select with certainty. One outstanding cleavage is that between totalitarian systems, in which the state is supreme over the individual in all phases of life, and pluralistic systems, in which there are separate spheres of state action and of individual liberty or voluntary cooperation. This is bound up with the cleavage between democratic and autocratic systems, since a democratic system must, in its essential nature, permit freedom of thought and expression in all their embodiments, including the press and publishing, education, and presumably art. Since these are economic activities, this involves some spheres of private economic enterprise; and there is some doubt whether it can maintain itself successfully in these strictly cultural spheres without having a broader base.

Another fundamental factor is the class complexion of the system. It may express mainly the ideas and aspirations of empty-handed workers or those of propertied classes, while professional and agricultural interests have to find some place, and the strictly class interests may be in varying degree modified by, or subordinated to, nationalistic and militaristic motives. Or, as in the theory of fascism, the system may purport to give equal weight to classes of unequal numbers—necessarily under the umpiring of government, which must itself have some class point of view. This, or any, system dominated frankly by minority classes must necessarily be undemocratic. A democratic system cannot be certain in advance to be dominated by any one existing class, though wage earners and farmers could dominate if they could find a common ground.

There is also the cleavage between centralized and federative or decentralized systems, democracy and decentralization having an obvious kinship. And there is the cleavage between systems to be attained by revolutionary or evolutionary means, and the cleavage between political agency and "direct action" as means of attainment. Thus the possible variety of program is fairly large, even though limited to combinations of the foregoing elements which have some inner congruity with one another.

Thus there is state socialism, which is limited in objective, nontotalitarian, nonproletarian, nonrevolutionary, and commonly centralized. There is revolutionary syndicalism, which is proletarian, decentralized, aiming at complete industrial expropriation by direct action. There is guild socialism, evolutionary, democratic, and decentralized or federative. There is social democracy, mainly political, nontotalitarian in aim, gradual in method, aiming at much greater change than is usually involved in state socialism but not necessarily at abolition of all private capital or enterprise. There is communism, proletarian, nondemocratic, revolutionary, centralized, and complete. And there is fascism, nonproletarian, nondemocratic, militaristic, retaining private capital and private income from capital, but under a degree of control which takes away much of the substance of ownership, the control being federative in form but largely centralized in fact. The German form appears to carry totalitarianism fully as far as does Russian communism. There is anarchism which, as far as it represents a definable program, is inherently decentralized and nonpolitical and depends on voluntary cooperation—and probably also on an evolution toward a simpler character of economic organization.

Communism and fascism are the two main rivals of democratic liberalism, overshadowing other programs or movements. But since these others form part of the background of fascism and of present-day communism, they may well be considered first.

3. STATE SOCIALISM

State socialism, as the term is used, means the kind of system prevailing in prewar Germany or Australasia, in which the state, without abolishing private enterprise, engages in business itself on a large scale and subjects free contract in general to large amounts of supervision, installing a system of thoroughgoing social insurance and possibly other types of control, such as the public adjustment of labor disputes. Literally speaking, these constitute, of course, only partial state socialism, and since democratic liberalism has adopted much of this program, the term has lost much of its distinctive meaning. Complete state socialism, which is the goal of the political socialists, would go further, largely abolishing private enterprise, profits, and, probably, interest and rent as private incomes. While its ultimate character can only be conjectured, we can perhaps learn something about it by study of partial state socialism as it actually exists.

While the only democratic examples are found in Australasia, the most efficient system was undoubtedly that of prewar Germany. The German system was developed by a state which was not democratic, the postwar experience with political-democratic socialism being both too brief and too abnormal to afford useful lessons. The tradition of the German monarchy, in contrast to that of other European states, was that the sovereign should not rely exclusively on taxes for his revenues but should secure a substantial part of his income from the administration of a public domain, and this tradition accounts for a large part of the difference between the German and the Anglo-Saxon methods of economic organization. It is contrary to a basic Anglo-Saxon principle of popular government, namely, parliamentary control of the purse strings. To this have been added other motives which have become more important with the passage of time: the conscious pursuit of national efficiency, economic preparedness for war, and the idea that the community has both a stake in the individual and a responsibility for him—in a word, an idea of social solidarity.

Furthermore, the foundations of success have been laid by developing public administration into a profession with a morale comparable to that of the army and navy, resulting in something which exists only spasmodically in countries like the United States—the efficient bureaucrat. Some of the conditions which have made this possible do not exist in this country, such as the possibility of a successful mayor progressing from smaller to larger towns as a regular feature of his professional advancement,[1] the security of tenure as against the prospect of displacement at any election, and the glamor of titles in a system with a crowned emperor at its head. To understand German state socialism we must always keep in mind the motive—dynastic efficiency, and the foundation—efficient bureaucracy.

Public enterprises in Germany included farms, forests, mines and potash deposits, transport—including railroads, telegraph, telephone, and express services, canals, boat lines and wharves; markets, slaughter houses, cold-storage plants, and many other things in addition to

[1] The "city-manager" system, if it comes to be more generally adopted than at present, will supply this element.

what we know as public utilities. Another large enterprise was the system of social insurance, labor exchanges, and labor placement, which was not thought of as a business enterprise, but which took the place of commercial employment agencies and, to some extent, of commercial insurance (though for the most part occupying a field which commercial insurance does not develop). The government encouraged the formation of the loose form of trusts called "cartels" and made itself a member of the most important ones, exercising an influence proportionate not to its holdings, but rather to the power of legislation which it held in reserve. It aimed at stable and prosperous industries, not attempting, as we in America do in the case of regulated monopolies, to cut earnings to the irreducible minimum in the interest of the consumers. The public industries were, almost without exception, well conducted and prosperous, up to the period of the war, and the typical German state received as much as one-third of its revenues from these sources.[1] During and following the war, as was natural, heavy deficits were incurred.

Under this system, industry expanded, export trade was promoted with notable success, the nation was able to secure efficient service at a low money cost; wages were lower than in Anglo-Saxon countries, but the worker was cared for in his various crises and saved from absolute destitution. Here were developed the principles of social insurance, which the rest of the world is gratefully adopting.

The rest of the picture is less attractive; and if America develops state socialism, it will be directed to different ends. The chief purpose will probably be to protect consumer and worker against exploitation by monopolistic business combinations, while conservation will be a secondary purpose. Hence there will be pressure on the government to lower prices and to inflate costs by raising wages and reducing hours. And there is some doubt whether a democratic government could resist this pressure sufficiently to keep the enterprises self-sustaining and prevent them from becoming a ruinous burden on the rest of the economic system. Yardstick enterprises may show losses but are unlikely to yield profits. This tendency will be strengthened if the government yields to the pressure to take over sick industries, such as railways and coal mining, which are unable to earn a profit. Largely as a safeguard against the danger of losses it has come to be accepted as essential that the business arms of the state should be as independent as possible from the political arm, so that it cannot use industrial offices to reward faithful service at the polls. The state as business man must be businesslike.

[1] See Elmer Roberts, *Monarchical Socialism in Germany*, pp. 6–7, 1913.

The success of such experiments in this country may also depend on whether, out of the engineering profession or elsewhere, we can develop a corps of capable administrators such as our political life has largely failed to furnish. It may prove desirable to set up some independent agency to regulate accounts, for government departments are prone to keep their records in ways which conceal their business standing rather than reveal it, capital and current outlays being often hopelessly merged, or overhead costs conveniently forgotten. Even the agencies of government need regulation!

State socialism of this partial sort works under rather narrow limitations, centering chiefly in the fact that it must compete with private enterprise for talent and for capital funds and must pay sufficient to attract them. Most of the capital will have to be borrowed, and the enterprises must earn enough for expenses and the charges on the borrowed capital if the system is to be adopted on any large scale. For the larger the mass of public enterprises, the more impossible it becomes for the shrunken volume of private industry to pay taxes enough to support all the costs of political government, let alone paying deficits on the public's economic enterprises. Hence it cannot at once turn over to labor the "whole product of industry," with no deduction for rent, interest, or profits. The best it can do is to set aside part of its earnings to amortize its capital. Then, if it has also made proper depreciation charges to perpetuate the physical equipment, it can own its capital free of interest charges in perhaps thirty years' time. Even allowing for the constant inflow of new investments, the state might, in a generation or two, acquire something like a "controlling interest" in its enterprises out of their own earnings—provided it ran them like private businesses in the meantime. Whether the typical American commonwealth would have this amount of patience can only be conjectured.

What are the advantages of such a system? It could take over just those industries which afford the most perplexing problems of regulation and substitute the absolute authority which goes with ownership. Budgets could be consolidated and the price would not need to be high enough to sustain an inefficient "marginal producer." Policies of conservation would not need to be forced on unwilling private companies in the face of the fact that they cost money and may make the difference between a profit and a loss. Since the "private interests" are reduced to the position of bondholders on a guaranteed income, they have no incentive to bring to bear all the pressures of massed wealth to resist the policies of government, as large private stockholders do when government regulations threaten their profits.

On the other hand, the public administration would be subject to pressures of other sorts; from customers and laborers, all armed with votes, and from the remaining private business interests in their capacity of shippers of freight, buyers of ore, etc. We should have exchanged one variety of undue pressure for another, and the new might be quite as pernicious as the old. Democratic state socialism in this country appears to have less chance of success than monarchical state socialism in prewar Germany.

4. SOCIALISM BY POLITICAL AGENCY

It is conceivable that the machinery of political government should be captured by out-and-out socialists and used as the vehicle for a socialist revolution which either might be complete or (as the more moderate political socialists think) might gain the essential ends in view while leaving some economic activities in private hands. In this country, existing constitutional protections to property would have to be removed, and the Federal Government given vastly increased powers; but granting this, the transformation would be at least thinkable. However, G. D. H. Cole has expressed doubt whether such a change could be brought about without greater security and permanence of tenure than an ordinary parliamentary government possesses. This might mean the adoption of a positively socialistic constitution, or a sort of temporary dictatorship by majority consent. In the latter case, it is not easy to imagine the dictatorship voluntarily surrendering its powers; and the struggle to regain democracy would presumably have to begin over again.

Could such a revolution be gradual? Granted security of tenure, this might be politically possible, but would it be economically practicable? If a government committed to the revolution were in firm control, it seems natural that voluntary private investment would promptly drop to the vanishing point; and since the continuance of this flow would be a necessity of successful operation, the government would be under compelling pressure to take immediate responsibility for seeing that adequate investments were made and to that extent would be forced to take an immediate hand in all those industries which were scheduled to be ultimately taken over.

What would such a system be like? What changes in the political form of government would the task of economic management make necessary, and—not less significant a question—what changes in the program of the socialists would the pressures and expediencies of actual administration bring about? Without presuming to be wiser than all the rest of mankind, it may be possible to make some very general surmises.

While our large industries are nationwide, still a dictation of all their affairs from Washington would be intolerable. Either the bureaucrat would be the slave of politics, resulting in a chaos of inefficiency, or he would be a despot. Hence there would be pressure to give more direct representation to laborers, consumers, and others directly interested. Advisory councils might be set up after the model of those which formed part of the German railway administration, representing consumers and other local interests, or these interests might be given representation on boards of directors.

As to financial mechanisms, the experience of Russian communism affords some guidance to the probable outcome. It has maintained the institutions of money, credit, wage differentials based on efficiency, some private savings as a source of capital, the distinction between services rendered free by the state and those which aim to be financially self-sustaining out of prices charged, profits, losses, and taxes. However, profits are not a source of private income, and financial losses do not necessarily veto further production. While these features of the business system would be retained, their operation would be transformed, partly through the altered distribution of incomes, and partly by the effect of a consolidated budget of incomes disbursed to individuals, prices of goods, and estimated demands at those prices. This would be on the model already discussed under the heading of socialistic planning and would be calculated to equate supply and demand at approximate capacity production, and to balance total savings (public and private) against total capital outlays.[1]

Perhaps the chief change from the present order would lie in the timing of production and the timing of the government's demand for productive goods. Here one of the dominant considerations should be the stabilizing of employment and output. At present it *appears* profitable to private industry to concentrate purchases in "prosperous" and active times, creating a rate of demand which is bound to fall flat when the special stimulus ceases. Lacking a well-balanced budget, government might make this condition worse, but any government which did not budget its activities with a view to stabilization would not be wise enough to be intrusted with the control of a socialistic state. As we have already seen,[2] a socialistic government would have the opportunity to draw up a budget providing not only for stabilized production but for production representing approximately

[1] See above, Chap. xxviii, Sec. 4.
[2] Ibid.

full use of productive resources of labor and capital. Efficiency might be reduced and wastes of new sorts substituted for the wastes of competitive business, but the form of waste represented by the present types of unemployment could, under favorable conditions, be reduced to a point at which it would not constitute a serious evil.

Apparently we should still have the familiar cleavage between the wage worker and the salaried manager with his eye on the profit-and-loss account and the balance sheet, and the conflict of interest between them would still exist in a modified form. The manager would have less to gain by exploiting the workers and might have more need to placate them. The outcome would depend on whether the constitution of the new commonwealth gave first place to the democratic pressures, thus tending to sacrifice efficiency, or to managerial efficiency, thus tending to sacrifice democracy.

To sum up, it seems that the present type of political machinery is largely inappropriate to the work it would have to do and would naturally yield its functions to other types of machinery. Congress might debate large issues of general policy, but the real legislation would be carried on within the enormously enlarged executive departments and between them. We have also seen that the logic of sub-divided production presses strongly toward retaining many features of private business, such as money and even profits. It seems probable that the mere substitution of public for private operation would not of itself produce any radical change for the better, or even any radical change at all, in the substance of economic relations. To produce the much-desired results would require a high degree of wisdom and states-manship, and the development of positive principles of economic value and economic policy to take the place of the principles of unregulated demand and supply. Some socialistic economists are now making beginnings at developing such principles, but they are still in the stage of theoretical speculation. Specific systems would wait to be hammered out under the pressures of actual administration. And then there would be mistakes and muddling, even as now.

5. SOCIALISM VIA GUILDS OR COOPERATION

The cooperative movement has sometimes been thought of as a method of transforming the whole economic society by the gradual growth of a different system. It has two forms: one starting with consumers, the other with workers. The consumers' movement started with retail stores, operated by an organization of which the consumers were the member partners, with a view to relieving them of the wastes and profit charges of business retailing. The system has grown, in

Europe, into a great network, reaching down into the manufacturing of goods. Its relation to its employees has commonly been humanized, but not revolutionized; and it has not abolished property income. It has made for itself an important place of great usefulness to workers in countries where the scale of money incomes is lower than ours, but it affords no present prospect of absorbing the whole field of private production; and if it should, it would have outgrown what might prove to have been its chief source of efficiency, namely, the necessity of competing with the regular commercial merchants. But in any realistic plan of peaceful and constructive approach to democratic socialism, the cooperatives would form one of the most indispensable elements.

In contrast to the success of consumers' cooperation, producers' or workers' cooperation has for the most part failed. Here the workers own and operate their own productive establishment or enterprise, while marketing their product on commercial principles. This movement gained a large but temporary impetus in England after the World War, under the name of the "guild movement," which was seriously considered as a way to a socialist system. The most prominent experiments were in the field of building, where conditions seemed favorable. No large fixed plant was required, and the character of the work put the ordinary factory types of discipline and incentives at a discount, while the profit-sharing incentive had a fair chance to improve efficiency. The problem of securing working capital proved not insuperable, and some of the guilds were successful for a time. But the movement failed, the most decisive weakness being apparently the incapacity of a democratic, worker-controlled organization to maintain a high enough degree of discipline.

Supposing this obstacle to be overcome, and an approach made to socialism by the guild route, it would naturally be a decentralized or federative type of system. During the transition, competition would take care of prices; but if the guilds became supreme, they would naturally become monopolistic, and some machinery would have to be set up to adjudicate the terms of exchange. The state would be the logical agency. Guild socialists would keep the state, and some of them were willing to accept it as the supreme authority, though the general spirit of the movement was that of control by economic rather than political action. What that would mean in practice is not wholly clear: whether the preservation of some kind of competition within a national guild, or deadlocks between contesting monopolies, each with the power to go on strike against the others. Mr. Cole proposed a sort of equal sovereignty between the guild and territorial organizations—something which would be difficult if not impossible to define in practice. In the experimental stage, guild socialists were willing to raise capital under existing conditions, but they looked to a time when the workers would be in a strong enough position to take the control of existing plants without paying for them, the capitalist employers relinquishing what they could no longer manage.[1]

The spirit of the movement was of the sort that expects to grapple with the difficulties of constructive organization before achieving the complete revolution, rather than committing the country to the revolution first and discovering and grappling with the difficulties of rebuilding afterward. This is the ideal method, if it works. The trouble comes when the difficulties prove too great for a transitional organization to meet. Is this to be accepted as proving that the socialistic system cannot be so efficient as private enterprise, and that therefore the attempt should be given up? It may afford *prima facie* evidence to that effect, but not proof. To a thoroughgoing advocate of socialism it will merely prove that the safer, more peaceful and constructive, step-by-step method is impossible; and that the more dangerous method of revolution is therefore necessary.

6. REVOLUTIONARY SYNDICALISM

Syndicalism is to be classed, not so much as a system of economic organization as a method of achieving revolution, with implications as to the kind of result the method is calculated to produce. In tangible ways, this result would be very similar to that contemplated by guild socialism, namely, a decentralized or federative system built on units of workers who have taken over the plants in which they work. The spirit of the movement, however, represents almost the antithesis of the guild spirit, being that of class warfare with particular emphasis on destructive tactics.

The syndicalist starts with the belief that state socialism is merely another form of capitalism, and that the ruling classes are in such complete control of the political machinery that there is no hope of a genuine workers' revolution by that route. Even more fundamental, perhaps, is the belief that the workers can never win real liberty by any plan under which they elect representatives to do their fighting for them, be they congressmen or trade-union officials. Instead, the individual workers must take some personal part in the struggle.[2]

---

[1] On this general subject, see especially G. D. H. Cole, *Self-government in Industry;* S. G. Hobson, *National Guilds;* and A. J. Penty, *Post-industrialism.*

[2] See *What Is the I.W.W.?* published by the Industrial Workers of the World, p. 15.

The syndicalists believe that a collapse of industrialism is impending; that the workers can precipitate it by their own methods of industrial warfare; and that industry should then be taken over by the workers' unions, each taking possession of the industry in which it is employed. This calls, of course, for the organization of workers by industries instead of by crafts, and this is the first step in the syndicalist program. Incidentally, it would make the workers' organization coextensive with the adversary they have to fight, so that they believe they would be able to meet an employers' organization on more nearly equal terms.

The chief methods of this movement are strikes and sabotage. Strikes are regarded as leading up to the general strike in all industries at once, by which the final revolution is to be brought about. And sabotage, or the "strike on the job,"[1] is a weapon for bringing about the collapse of industrialism, while at the same time the individual workers gain the sense of solidarity that goes with personal participation in the economic struggle. When these tactics accomplish their end, the unions would then have to transform themselves from organizations for combat into organizations for production and carry on the work of the world.

The result would naturally be a decentralized system and, as with the guilds, the separate industries would have to set up machinery to settle the terms of exchange. Since syndicalism proposes to abolish the political state, this regulatory machinery would have to be of a new sort, but of what sort we are left in uncertainty. The failure to grapple with this question is the largest gap in the syndicalist philosophy. Each union would have monopolistic control of some essential service, with the possibility of a strike to enforce its demands. That this weapon might be used is attested by the general fact that laborers' conflicts with laborers are not less bitter than those with employers; in fact, their resentment is even keener when they are exploited or their aims are opposed by those who, they feel, should be their allies. Such strikes could not be tolerated, but the syndicalist spirit is violently opposed to giving any body supreme power to prevent them by coercion, if necessary.

Furthermore, the workers would have been trained to gain their ends by destructive tactics, refusing service, spoiling work, injuring machinery, and the like, and it would be hard for them suddenly to adopt the spirit of cooperative give-and-take in adjusting vital differences. Organizations for irresponsible, warlike combat are not easily converted in a moment into organizations for peaceful cooperation.

[1] See above, Chap. vii, Sec. 2, pp. 114–115.

It is not easy to imagine a successful outcome unless, after a considerable period of chaos and suffering, a different spirit is slowly developed under the pressure of hard necessity.

Other questions which would have to be adjusted would include the right of admission to trades, the responsibility for any who might fail to gain admission, and for unemployment in case the demand for a given service falls far short of the potential supply, the support of services like the keeping of order, education, research, the provision of ports and highways, and other things which cannot easily be made self-sustaining, or not without unreasonably limiting their usefulness. Something corresponding to the political state would presumably have to be recreated to care for these things, if not to adjust the relations of union to union.

What seems more probable is that, if revolution comes, syndicalism will be found useful in bringing about a breakdown of the existing system; and after fulfilling this purpose will be promptly "liquidated" by the harder-headed exponents of centralized coercion. The latter will be thoroughly prepared for this step, realizing that a revolution so brought about must be a minority affair, unable to subsist on a democratic or a free basis.

7. ANARCHISM

Anarchism and revolutionary syndicalism are closely allied. Both would do away with the political state. In both, the industrial units would be controlled by those who worked in them. Anarchism, further, contemplates quasi-contractual arrangements. These would be enforced merely by the necessities of mutual cooperation—as many of our contractual arrangements are now, particularly in the field of labor. Such agreements would bring about organization within the industrial groups and mutual dealings between them. Some look toward a simplification of production, each area becoming more nearly self-sufficing, so that distant and complicated exchange would not be necessary on so large a scale as at present.[1]

8. REVOLUTIONARY COMMUNISM

The constructive task of revolutionary communism consists of the same elements we have been considering, in a form most nearly parallel to that resulting from political socialism, the chief differences being those resulting from the more violent method of reaching the goal, and the wiping out or revolutionizing of existing forms of political

[1] See Kropotkin, *Fields, Factories, and Workshops;* also *The Conquest of Bread.*

government. According to Marxian dogma, the state should "wither away," but in Russia this process has been indefinitely postponed. The explanation given is mainly that the rest of the world remains anticommunist. Hence armies are necessary and espionage and the whole coercive paraphernalia which the radical identifies with the state and against which he protests, when it is in "capitalistic" hands. Actually, a communistic economy in itself seems to require a directive body with some central focusing point, with a central seat of authority, and with ultimate power of coercion. This seems to be required quite apart from the existence of surrounding hostile nations. Whether ruthless coercion is inseparable from a socialist economy or not, it is a natural sequel to violent revolution. Freedom of thought and expression (even existing imperfect sorts) could not survive.

The aftermath of class struggle would hamper the work of rebuilding. While we should have in this country the engineers and other skilled managing personnel who now serve private business, the question would arise whether a revolutionary administration would dare to trust them and to use them. They might be "liquidated" as rapidly as the revolution could train others (of doubtful competency) to fill their places. In the meantime, if we may judge by the Russian experience, they might be allowed to work, under the watchful (and inexpert) scrutiny of trusted revolutionists; and under a scheme of incentives in which outright compulsion and the firing squad played a large part, as against the present system of positive rewards. The result could hardly be efficient.

The mass of rapid decisions necessary could not be made by the slow machinery of self-governing deliberation. Hence, if for no other reason, the result could hardly be democratic. Indeed, a violent revolution practically presupposes some variety of dictatorship, including presumably the repression of free thought and expression, which is perhaps the most disastrous single consequence of such a revolutionary system. In theory, suppression might apply only to dissent from the communistic system as such, leaving dissent free as to details of ways and means within the system. But this would imply freedom to criticize the administration, where the administration has unrestricted power to construe this as criticism of the system. In practice, little tolerance could be expected for dissent of any sort.

Russian communists have realized the need of replacing the morale of the class struggle with the morale of cooperative effort and have done so to a rather remarkable extent. Nevertheless, the morale of class struggle persists in the form of wholesale "purges." Where failures occur, the search for causes is biased in the direction of finding some antirevolutionary scapegoat to "liquidate." The whole resulting atmosphere is unfavorable to constructive and creative efficiency. This country is not Russia, and these tendencies might not take such a violent form here, but we could hardly escape them. They might even be strengthened here by the existence among communists of extravagant anticipations of great gains for the masses, many of which would necessarily be disappointed. The resulting discontent might require very strong measures of coercive repression.

And the power of repression at the disposal of such a government is something far outside the range of American experience. The government controls all channels of information and every access to livelihood, and is able to degrade martyrdom and rob it of news value and to set half the population spying on the rest and on one another. If its use of these appalling powers is guided solely by the revolutionist morality, which makes the interest of the revolution the supreme standard of right, undiluted by objective truth or humanitarian inhibitions, the results can better be imagined than experienced.

If our goal is democratic efficiency, revolutionary communism offers at best a starting point out of which it may be slowly evolved, after some of the necessary conditions have been either destroyed or dangerously impaired. Hence it does not seem probable that it offers as good a starting point for evolutionary development as some system which involves a less complete break with our heritage of traditions— one which would not waste the abilities of our present trained and intelligent classes, or throw overboard the invaluable social capital which we have invested in our customary ways of working together.

Communists in this country are at present adopting a policy of cooperating in organizations and measures devoted to progressive reforms in the interest of labor. From the standpoint of the evolutionary progressives to whom aid is thus given, this policy is both an advantage and a menace. It naturally lends itself to "boring from within," a phrase which indicates the dangers involved. Its ultimate effect can only be surmised. Its chief danger consists in the sabotaging of the progressive policy, by deliberately fostering the choice of unworkable measures of control, or pushing them farther and faster than business can assimilate the resulting burdens, and hastening a breakdown of the economic system which the majority do not desire. This would defeat the ends, not only of the progressives, but of the democratic socialists; since it would precipitate revolution while the revolutionists were a minority, and must inevitably set up a coercive dictatorship, "liquidating" the progressives and the social democrats in turn.

9. FASCISM: GERMAN AND ITALIAN

Fascism as it exists may be partly characterized as a regimented economic system under a personal dictator, forestalling or preventing socialism by maintaining through coercive means a balance between capital, labor, and other economic groups, and by eliminating freedom of thought and discussion, establishing the supremacy of state purposes over the individual in all departments of life and forcibly instilling an "ideology" in harmony with these ends. In Italy, it seems to have sprung largely from a reaction against economic disorders of a syndicalist complexion; while in Germany the inevitable reaction against the repressive terms of the peace of Versailles played a large part, coupled with a reaction against the postwar social-democratic government (which submitted to these terms) and affected by the older tradition of nondemocratic state socialism.

In both Germany and Italy, industry-wide economic organizations are taken into the structure of the state, under the control of the central government. In Italy the "syndicates," with equal representation of workers' and employers' associations, handle labor relations, while the more recent and less fully developed "corporations," also representing workers and employers, are supposed to establish liaison between the syndicate units, and to handle distinctly industrial problems of policy, including production and prices. The separate identity of workers' and employers' organizations is maintained. In Germany, these are apparently in effect merged in the "labor front" (in which employers are members both individually and as associations) under the control of the Minister of Economics.

Wages, and to a large extent production and prices, are controlled, and dividends are limited or any excess above 6 per cent heavily taxed. The theory of price controls is somewhat amorphous, including a general idea of covering cost plus a fair return, an idea of cheapening essential consumers' goods and so redistributing wealth, some taxes which bear heavily on the consumer, public profits made from some fiscal monopolies, and the necessity of paying world-market prices for imported goods. Large public works and armament expenditures have increased employment, while leading to large public deficits. The completeness of the general economic controls has already been indicated.[1]

The fascist systems have demonstrated that it is possible, for a time at least, to make controls so stringent as to take away most of the substance of private enterprise without abolishing the form.

[1] See above, Chap. xxviii, Sec. 5.

With this has gone a wiping-out of personal liberty which has roused the abhorrence of liberals, and a warlike psychology which has been stimulated in Germany with apparent recklessness of consequences. Modern techniques, backed by ruthless coercion, have made this possible to an extent undreamed of a generation ago, but even so its power to endure remains doubtful. Without these features, it seems probable that the economic controls could not succeed. Nor is it at all likely that these economic features of the system are capable of bringing about an efficient economic structure of the sort which uses its powers to maintain a high standard of living for the people at large.

10. SUMMARY OF SUBSTITUTES FOR THE EXISTING ORDER

These, then, are the principal possible substitutes for our present order, as far as current movements indicate them. Systems range from dictatorship to anarchism. Governing motives range from militaristic imperialism to absolute democracy in the production and distribution of goods. Methods of attainment range from armed revolt to voluntary agreement, with only such degree of virtual duress as might result from the expected breakdown of the business system itself.

All alike, except the halfway varieties of socialism, would eliminate competition as the governor of prices and rewards and the determinant of the amount of labor and capital to be devoted to each branch of production and to each local unit within each branch. For this controlling force, the centralized systems would substitute administrative rulings, which could lead to an efficient organization of productive effort only through the development of a technique of accounting which would take into consideration the productive values of different grades of labor and natural resources, and of capital as well. The decentralized systems would substitute the bargainings and compromises of autonomous monopolies, out of which no definite economic law could easily be expected to emerge. The federalized systems would substitute the rulings of some administrative body, either of the character of our Interstate Commerce Commission or of some of the various types of wage boards. Here again, it is difficult to see what economic principles, if any, would govern the body of case law which would be built up. This work of adjustment might easily consume fully as large a part of the energy of the community as now goes into the work of government, of bargaining, and of litigation, by which the present industrial order settles these conflicts.

While active competition may be superseded, the underlying forces of supply and demand are not so easily disregarded. And systems which do disregard them must be fortified with repressive controls such as we do not like to contemplate. The more thoroughgoing systems of economic control now in existence carry with them such a repression of all forms of liberty as should make us ready to try almost anything rather than subject ourselves to it, or to an economic program which might involve it as a consequence.

11. "MAINTAINING THE EXISTING SYSTEM"

To maintain the existing system, literally unchanged, is not one of the possibilities. Systems change of themselves, if they are not changed by outside forces. What this phrase really means is change within more or less fixed limits. It rests on the idea that the range of possible economic systems does not shade off from individualism to communism by continuous gradations, but that one principle or the other must be dominant, or at least that private enterprise must have some minimum adequate scope if it is to be successfully employed at all. The former statement is doubtful; the latter is probably true. And the truth underlying the program of maintaining the existing system is the need of knowing what this minimum is and making sure not to encroach upon it, unless we are ready to accept some form of collectivism.

In line with this view, there would appear to be three outstanding possibilities for this country. One is a retreat from all but the safer policies of industrial stabilization, limiting our objectives mainly to caring for the incidence of depressions, and lightening the burdens of those who suffer most heavily. It involves freeing business from burdensome restraints, and from the fear of others in the future, and hoping that depressions will in consequence be shorter and milder in the future, and chronic underemployment less likely to become serious. The second possibility is a wise and cautious advance in the direction of social-liberal planning, coupled with a readiness to stop and turn back whenever mistakes appear. This is asking a great deal of governmental self-restraint. The third possibility is an unwise advance, exceeding the limits of tolerable regulation and causing the system to collapse.

This last result must be avoided, if the basic features of our system are to be retained. If the basic premise be true, it points toward a policy of temporary and partial retreat, coupled with more serious and determined reconnaissance than we have yet made into the possibilities of planning of the social-liberal sort. Sweden, a smaller and simpler economy than ours, and probably under less serious strains, appears to have accomplished promising results in the way of industrial stabilization without complete collectivism. The possibility should not be abandoned without trial.

The weakness of a policy of retreat, without further testing the potentialities of planning, lies in the fact that it admits a major evil as inherent in the system of private business and proposes to put up with what are in their nature only palliatives. The permanence of such a policy is doubtful.

12. EVOLUTIONARY POSSIBILITIES

Is a policy of evolutionary change, without a defined goal, a safe or tenable one? We know what results we want, namely, greater economic stability, jobs for all, approximately full utilization of productive capacities to sustain a high and widely diffused standard of living, and also personal liberty (even if economic liberty has to be curtailed or given up). We know that the existing revolutionary systems for securing the economic ends involve the sacrifice of personal liberty. We do not know whether this feature is unavoidable, or how far it is necessary to go in order to secure the essential economic results desired. We cannot, then, define in advance the system of institutions which represents the best available combination of the ends in view. Should we not, then, simply go ahead step by step?

If there is no necessary sharp break in the transition between free exchange and collectivism, such a policy may be safe and rational. If collectivism were to come by such a route, each step approving itself as it was taken, there would be little or no reason to fear it. This may or may not be possible; hence the evolutionary policy involves risks. If we are to follow it, it is important to consider what methods may reduce these risks to a minimum.

We have seen that growing controls by political government do run a risk of pushing private enterprise to a breaking point, and that political government is not likely to be a safe and successful vehicle for indefinite evolutionary change. But we have also seen that there are possibilities as yet untried for developing organs of guidance and control within the economic system itself. It may be here that the greatest possibilities of genuinely evolutionary progress lie. Industry has itself gone far in developing the theory and practice of administrative organization—perhaps farther than applied politics has gone. A good modern collective bargain is more than a bargain: it is an economic constitution with governmental attributes. Industry is, in fact, to a growing extent already a form of nonpolitical government.

For the purpose in hand, the units of industrial organization which have so far been employed have been inadequate, largely because they have been industry-wide, or trade-wide, and have stopped there. This meant that their interests, like those of monopolists, lay in raising the prices of what they had to sell, at the expense of other groups and at the expense of full operation of industry as a whole. It is impracticable to expect them to sacrifice their interests voluntarily, whether through altruism or otherwise. But the interests of employers, laborers, their customers, and those who supply them with materials and equipment, taken as a whole, lie in full and stable operation of industry. If a common interest exists, there is always a chance of action to promote it, if all the parties who have this common interest can be brought together. Industry has only begun to pay serious attention to this problem. When it realizes how much depends on it, we may see its best efforts spent in this direction. And labor must cooperate in the same spirit, if the effort is not to fail. The difficulties are great, and success is doubtful. But we cannot leave the problem alone, for it will not leave us alone.

13. CONCLUSION

All of these systems call for the development of the cooperative man in place of the individualistic man. Must we develop him first before we can build the good system, or must we first create a cooperative system in order that the cooperative man may have a chance to develop? This question is at the bottom of the cleavage between the evolutionary and the revolutionary points of view. The probable answer is, as so often in human affairs, a mixture of both methods. By developing cooperative features and organizations within our system, we may develop cooperative impulses, habits, and customs, and these may enable us to develop more cooperative institutions, and so on, as far as our inherent capacities will carry us. First steps must be tried without waiting for human nature to be fully ready for them, but complete revolutions on this principle are precarious.

REFERENCES FOR FURTHER READING

ASCOLI and FEILER, *Fascism for Whom?* 1938.
BLOOMFIELD (ed.), *Selected Articles on Modern Industrial Movements.*
BRISSENDEN, *The I.W.W.*
BROOKS, JOHN GRAHAM, *American Syndicalism.*
BYE and HEWITT, *Applied Economics* (2d ed.), Chaps. xxvii–xxix, 1934.
CARR-SAUNDERS and others, *Consumers' Cooperation in Great Britain,* 1938.
CHILDS, M. W., *Sweden: The Middle Way* (rev. ed.), 1938.
COLE, G. D. H., *Self-government in Industry.*
DAVIES, *The Collectivist State in the Making.*
ELTZBACHER, *Anarchism.*
HAMILTON, W. H., *Current Economic Problems* (3d ed.), Chap. xiv.

HANSEN, A. H., *Economic Stabilization in an Unbalanced World*, Chaps. xxi–xxiv, 1932.

HEIMANN, E., "Socialism and Democracy," *Social Research*, pp. 301–318, August, 1934.

HILLQUIT and RYAN, *Socialism, Promise or Menace?*

HOBSON, S. G., *National Guilds.*

HUBBARD, L. E., *Soviet Money and Finance*, 1936.

————, *Soviet Trade and Distribution*, 1938.

INDUSTRIAL WORKERS OF THE WORLD, *What Is the I.W.W.?*

KROPOTKIN, *Anarchism: Its Philosophy and Ideal.*

————, *The Conquest of Bread.*

————, *Fields, Factories and Workshops.*

LIPPMANN, WALTER, *The Good Society*, pp. 45–90, 1937.

LOUCKS and HOOT, *Comparative Economic Systems*, Parts V–VII, 1938.

MARX, F. M., *Government in the Third Reich* (2d ed.), 1937.

MILLER, H. S., *Price Control in Fascist Italy*, 1938.

MOSCA, G., *The Ruling Class* (trans. by A. Livingston), Chap. xv, 1939.

OSTHOLD, P., "Germany: Why and How," Lloyd's Bank, Ltd., *Monthly Rev.*, pp. 674–712, December, 1937.

PATAUD and POUGET, *Syndicalism.*

PATTERSON and SCHOLZ, *Economic Problems of Modern Life*, Chaps. xxxvi–xxxviii, 1937.

PENTY, *Post-industrialism.*

PIGOU, A. C., *Socialism and Capitalism*, 1937.

PITIGLIANI, *The Italian Corporative State*, 1933.

ROBERTS, *Monarchical Socialism in Germany.*

RUSSELL, BERTRAND, *Proposed Roads to Freedom.*

SCHMIDT, C. T., *The Plough and the Sword* (agricultural programs of Fascist Italy), 1938.

SIMONS, H. C., *A Positive Program for Laissez-faire*, 1934.

SMITH, A., *I Was a Soviet Worker*, 1936.

SOREL, *Reflections on Violence.*

TAYLOR, H., *Contemporary Problems in the United States*, Vol. II, Chaps. xxvi–xxxi, 1934.

THOMAS, NORMAN, *The Choice before Us*, Chaps. iv, v, viii, ix, 1934.

TRACY, M. E., *Our Country, Our People, and Theirs* (comparative graphic statistics), 1938.

WEBB, SHAW, and others, *Socialism and Individualism.*

WEBB, SIDNEY, and BEATRICE, *A Constitution for the Co-operative Commonwealth of Great Britain.*

WELK, W. G., *Fascist Economic Policy*, 1938.

WUNDERLICH, F., "New Aspects of Unemployment in Germany," *Social Research*, pp. 97–110, February, 1934.

CHAPTER XXXII

"IF I WERE DICTATOR"

1. INTRODUCTION: A CHANGED PERSPECTIVE

When the first edition of this book was written, in 1925, the author indulged in a frankly imaginary picture of a dictator of a kind such as many like to conceive in moments of fantasy, but such as is never likely actually to gain power, or to keep it. He was devoted to the ideals of a peaceful democratic-liberal culture and accordingly exercised superhuman self-restraint in the use of his powers, aiming mainly to bring about an appreciation of our more serious problems and a constructive attitude toward them, and to carry on researches which might be a basis for later action. As an approach to some of our toughest controversial issues, he established organizations including in each case the essential interests involved in the controversy, before whom these problems might be laid with some prospect of constructive and evolutionary action on a sound and enduring basis.

During the thirteen years which have since elapsed, the world has had much experience with actual dictators, and the grim reality has robbed the benevolent fantasy of most of its appeal. Its unreal quality is more glaring and its usefulness more doubtful, even as a means of sharpening the presentation of certain ideas which a self-governing nation might well adopt, or projects which it needs to undertake. Moreover, the perspective of these problems has changed. Some have been disposed of; others have an altered setting. The problem of depression appeared in 1925 as a matter of relatively mild cyclical movements; now it is one of violent revulsions, coupled with the threat of chronic semiparalysis. It has thus become more urgent, with the result that some of the more qualitative problems of long-run goals of welfare have been relegated to a deferred position on the agenda. The dictator of 1925 could afford to be deliberate. In 1933 the demand for emergency improvisation was imperative. And in 1938 we are still under pressure, though palliatives have been provided, and the greatest need now is to search for cures. We can look toward measures which will take time to bring tangible results. We can afford to be cautious, but not to mark time or to waste it.

2. THE CENTRAL TASK

Furthermore, many of the things such a dictator might do have already been discussed in the two preceding chapters, as well as some of the things he would not do. Thus the present chapter might be reduced to a statement that the dictator should choose the most promising combination of the elements there indicated, presumably moving cautiously toward a program of social-liberal planning, in the meantime probably calling a halt on fresh measures likely to disturb business confidence, and instituting a searching and impartial critique of existing measures with a view to removing elements which may be unsound or have a tendency to retard enterprise, while keeping whatever approved itself. The chief advantage of a dictator in such a program would be that, being free from the need of seeking political issues on which to appeal to the voters, he could more easily make his survey nonpolitical and genuinely impartial.

Such a policy would help toward the outstanding immediate need: promoting a freer flow of private capital outlays, though it would not be a permanent solution. As a further immediate measure, the dictator might reform and simplify the tax system, especially taxes falling on business. He could not immediately discontinue deficit spending, but he would be in a position to announce a program for the tapering-off of such spending, though it would necessarily be an elastic affair, subject to modification by changing business conditions. He could also remove uncertainty as to the likelihood of future currency devaluation.

Meanwhile, starting with existing studies, he would (if following the policy suggested) make the best possible survey of potential demand for goods and potential productive power, of bottlenecks and the time required to enlarge them, of savings and their probable response to changed conditions, of the field for capital outlays, of means of modifying the distribution of incomes (both before and after deducting taxes), and of other matters indicated in the discussion of economic planning. These would take time, during which business could be assured that no fresh radical measures would be taken. Further assurance could be given that, even after this "breathing spell," the earnings of capital in business would not be reduced except as the cost of capital was reduced correspondingly, so that the incentive to business to make capital outlays would be preserved.

Along with the studies would go the forming of organizations in trade and industry, on the broad lines already indicated, both to take part in securing the material needed for the studies, and to consider the problems of industrial statesmanship to which the results of the studies would ultimately be applied. As an example of a problem which might be attacked at once, all the interests concerned with construction, as users and as producers, might be brought together in the way already suggested, to adopt a plan for stabilization.[1] As already noted, effective leadership might make such a plan successful. In fact, our imaginary dictator's greatest opportunity might lie in establishing economic leadership, even more than political leadership. If some features of the plan required exemption from the anti-trust laws, this could be done without making the exemption general. And a plan of this kind, making for stabilized employment rather than stabilized prices, would be worth an exemption from the anti-trust laws. But it would be only one step toward solving the problem of unused productive powers.

When the comprehensive economic survey was ready to be used, a next major step would need to be taken. By way of illustration, we might imagine its results being presented to our federated council of industry and labor in the following way. A given schedule of production, attainable in five years, would, if carried out, result in the distribution of incomes which, on the basis of normal consumer spending habits, would take the products off the market. For the first year, on account of shortages of skilled labor or essential materials, or other bottlenecks, only a given fraction of the program could be carried out. If each industry lived up to its part of the program, all could sell their goods at living prices. (Since the schedules could not be errorless, these prices could only be approximated, not guaranteed.) Each enterprise might then be invited, in secrecy if necessary, to pledge itself to undertake a given quota of the total program of increased output. And if adequate pledges were forthcoming, the initial program, or some part of it, could be inaugurated. The outcome would depend largely on the soundness of the estimates underlying the survey, and the attempt might need to be postponed until estimates were available which commanded the necessary degree of confidence.

One key to the balancing of production and demand in these estimates would be the balancing of capital outlays against the volume of savings which would be voluntarily made. For the end in view hinges on using all the purchasing power which the scheduled production would make available. What could not be taken and used for capital outlays would need to be so distributed that it would be spent for consumption and not locked up or put to uses that would do more

[1] See above, Chap. xxviii, Sec. 7.

harm than good. In the first estimates, this condition might not be met. In that case, the plan could not be put into operation until conditions had been changed so that a balance could be struck, or else failure would be certain. It might be necessary to modify further the distribution of incomes by alterations in the system of taxation, possibly supplemented by abolishing tax-exempt securities. Altering the reserve requirements of the Social Security Act would, as already indicated, be a powerful lever for securing the necessary balance. Low interest rates might be necessary but would not in themselves be sufficient. Their effect might be greatly increased by reducing the spread between high-cost and low-cost producers through a pooling of industrial knowledge, to the end that unduly high profits to some would not be necessary in order to afford any profit at all to others, and that investment in industry could be made attractive at average rates of return not too far above the basic interest rate.

Reduced rates of interest would tend to raise the prices of outstanding securities, resulting in profits not included in the industrial income account; and some of these profits would presumably be realized and spent for consumption. This factor would be hard to calculate, but it would need to be estimated and included in the tentative balance. A moderate excess of savings over investment might be offset in this way, and a wise control of credit might prevent it from being more than offset and turned into a runaway stock market and an unsound boom. This would be one of the most difficult matters to handle in the attempted industrial balance, and some mistakes would probably be inevitable.

There would be other difficulties, but perhaps enough have been mentioned. Does the task appear impossibly complex? If so, we have only to consider that it is just this complex balance that has to be struck by industry, without guidance or estimates and without even any comprehensive analysis of the bearing of all the different elements, if industry is to remain on a steady keel under existing conditions. It is no wonder if it fails. If it is ever to succeed these complexities must be brought to light in order to be dealt with. And some procedure of the general sort here presented seems to be a necessary condition.

3. OTHER PROBLEMS

In addition to this ramifying central problem, there will be many others. In the first edition of this chapter, attention was paid to the cancellation of international war debts—now in effect an accomplished fact—and to collective international security against war. Other problems there listed included industrial safety and health, representation of laborers and consumers in industry, wages and other incentives, the adjustment of labor disputes, the effects of industry on labor, efficiency and waste, conservation, the relation of industry to regional and city planning, the problems of agriculture and coal mining, and the wastes of advertising and salesmanship. Suggestions were made toward the building up, in voluntary ways, of what would today be called an "ideology," the general character of which is already sufficiently obvious.

As to problems of long-range bearing, requiring extended research, the following two paragraphs from the first edition may be indicative:

Most fundamental is the question of the needs of human beings, as workers and as consumers, in the light of their inherited biological equipment and of the social and moral requirements of living together. In particular, what are the general impulses which must find some sort of outlet or expression if the individual is to live a healthy life, and what is the range of substitute outlets which may accomplish this purpose?[1] This problem is so vast that it would be näive to expect an early and definitive answer merely from the establishment of a commission to study it; but if the researches of specialists were definitely directed toward this end, the effect of this orientation might be to bring results which would benefit future generations. The needs contemplated would include both quantitative needs for economic goods and qualitative needs for desirable conditions of life and of social and moral relations to one's fellows, which are decidedly dependent on the organization of industry.

Akin to this is the question how to determine superior or inferior biological types within the population, or whether such types exist. Along with this goes the question of means for influencing the relative increase of different types, as far as that may be found desirable, and also an intelligent control of immigration.[2] Another allied question is that of thrift, prudence, self-dependence, and the other traditional "economic virtues." To what extent are they inherently desirable and to what extent are they good only because of the requirements of particular institutions, which may be altered? How are they affected by various policies of control which free the individual from the need to looking out for himself in numerous particulars? Does adequate stimulus remain for these traditional economic virtues, as far as they are of permanent value, and are there also other economic virtues of a moral and social sort which are in equal need of cultivation?

[1] See Carleton H. Parker, *The Casual Laborer and Other Essays.*

[2] On this general group of questions, see Hamilton, *Current Economic Problems*, (3d ed.), Chap. ix. Chapter x is also pertinent to the "needs of human nature."

4. CONCLUSION

The dictator we have been considering is imaginary and must presumably remain so. But as his essential function was leadership, rather than coercive regimentation, his program, or something equally effective, might not be wholly impossible, granted the necessary leadership. The greatest difficulty would be in maintaining the necessary continuity of policy to carry out a program which would require considerably more than two presidential terms to show its real possibilities. A close second to this would be the difficulty of combining in one leader the qualities necessary to win a popular election in a country where the arts of political maneuvering are highly developed, to understand the importance of profound scientific research and to organize and apply it and, finally, to establish creative leadership over the leaders of industry in their own field. If economic stabilization has to wait until this combination of qualities is found, it may have to wait a long time.

But first steps may be made. Our machinery will be maddeningly clumsy and perverse, compared to that which a dictator could bring to bear. But the only thing that can make the task hopeless is a conviction that it is hopeless and therefore not worth the endless effort it will cost. If men keep on trying, after reasonable proposals have been wrecked by one obstacle after another, every now and then they surprise themselves by reaching a reasonable solution. And if they dislike strongly enough the alternative possibilities sketched in the preceding chapter, they will conceive a workable democratic adjustment as their main task, worth almost any material concession, and their will to keep on trying will become indomitable. In that case, it is not too late to avoid shipwreck by modernizing the constitution of industry. To quote once more from the first edition of this chapter:

The greatest legacy which such a dictator could leave would be a social and economic constitution adapted to the needs of the times, through which the interest of every group should have its most appropriate and effective channels of expression, while the symposium should be enlightened by the best results of science and social research. It should provide for as much self-government as the people can use, and as much leadership as they will accept. Its aim should be the maximum development of the individual, and this cannot be brought about unless he is not only a healthy, intelligent, and effective individual, but also a unit in a system of healthy, intelligent, and effective social organs for the adjusting of the many joint and conflicting interests in which he has a part.

INDEX